Downtown

Robert M. Fogelson

D O W N

Yale University Press

T O W N

Its Rise and Fall, 1880–1950

New Haven and London

Printed in the United States of America

Library of Congress Cataloging-in-Publication Data

Fogelson, Robert M.
Downtown : its rise and fall, 1880–1950 / Robert M.
Fogelson.
p.   cm.
Includes bibliographical references and index.
ISBN 0-300-09062-5 (alk. paper)
1. Cities and towns—United States—History.
2. Central business districts—United States—History.
I. Title.
HT123 .F64   2001
307.3′3316′0973—dc21   2001001628

A catalogue record for this book is available from the
British Library.

The paper in this book meets the guidelines for
permanence and durability of the Committee on
Production Guidelines for Book Longevity of the Council
on Library Resources.

10 9 8 7 6 5 4 3 2 1

Frontispiece: Lower Manhattan from New York harbor
(King's *Views of New York, Boston, 1915*)

To Donald and Dorothy Gonson

A man walking . . . can make the circuit [of downtown Boston] in an hour with ease. The distance is hardly three miles. Its extreme length is just over a mile, and its least width is but seven hundred feet. This little spot may well be called the heart of the city. It is so literally, as well as metaphorically. Hither, every morning, the great arterial streams of humanity are drawn, and thence every evening they are returned to the extremities of the city and its suburbs, as the blood pulses to and from the human heart, or the tides ebb and flow in the bay.

—Massachusetts Rapid Transit Commission of 1892

Contents

Downtown

Introduction

During the late 1940s and early 1950s my father practiced law in a forty-story skyscraper at the corner of Fifth Avenue and Forty-third Street, a few blocks from Grand Central Station, one of New York City's two great railroad terminals. Five or six mornings a week, he left our apartment in the west Bronx, walked a mile or so to the New York Central's Highbridge Station, rode the Harlem River line to Grand Central, and walked from the terminal to his office. Sometimes, on a Saturday or holiday, he took me and one or both of my brothers along, probably to give my mother a respite. While my father caught up on his paperwork, my brothers and I peered out the windows, banged at the typewriters, and played with the swivel chairs. Before we could do any irreparable damage, he would take us for lunch to a nearby Schrafft's, a chain of restaurants that was popular with housewives like my mother, who regularly went downtown to shop, sometimes with her reluctant sons in tow, to socialize with one or more of her many friends, or to meet my father for a play or a movie. When I went to college in 1954, I had no idea what I would do for a living. Indeed, I had only a vague idea when I graduated four years later. But I took it for granted that whatever I did, I would do downtown. And so, I later learned, did my brothers.

Things did not work out as expected, not for me and not for them. Since 1968, when I started teaching about the history of American cities at the Massachusetts Institute of Technology, I have lived in one part of Cambridge, not far from Harvard Square, and worked in another part, just across the Charles River from Boston's Back Bay. I go to downtown Boston about once a month, sometimes to shop at one of the two remaining department stores, occasionally to see the dentist, and once in a while to watch a play. I used to go to the downtown movie theaters, but over the years all of them have closed. One brother is a lawyer who went into business after two decades of law practice.

He lives in Scarsdale, a wealthy suburb roughly twenty miles north of New York, and works in an industrial park in Somerset, New Jersey, about sixty miles away. He goes downtown at most once every two months—sometimes on business, more often to have dinner with his wife (and sometimes one or both of their children). Following in the path of millions of other Americans, my other brother moved to Los Angeles thirty years ago. An oral surgeon, he lives in Hermosa Beach, a western suburb of L.A., and, with two partners, works out of offices in Culver City, Redondo Beach, and Westchester, three other western suburbs. He goes to downtown Los Angeles, a fifteen-mile trip, once every year or two—or less often than he goes on vacation to La Paz, the capital of Baja California, which is nearly a thousand miles south of L.A.

I have no way of knowing what my father would have made of this. He died before I thought of asking him. But he would have had good reason to be puzzled. Born around the turn of the century, he grew up at a time when downtown was in its heyday, a time, as historian Sam Bass Warner, Jr., has pointed out, when it was "the most powerful and widely recognized symbol of the American industrial metropolis," a "metaphor for the metropolis itself." It was a time when downtown was *the* business district, a highly compact, extremely concentrated, largely depopulated business district, and not the *central* business district, which it became in the 1920s, and not *just another* business district, which it became after World War II. By the time my father began to practice law in the mid 1920s, most Americans went downtown to work. And not only to work, but also to shop, to do business, and to amuse themselves. As Jack Thomas, a *Boston Globe* columnist, recalls, "downtown [Boston] was where you first saw Santa Claus, and where your father took you to buy the charcoal suit you were confirmed in, and where your mother helped your sister choose her wedding dress, and where you bought furniture for your first home, and later maternity clothes, and then baby clothes, and, finally, with a sense of the cycles of life, where you returned so that your own daughter could visit Santa."[1] A uniquely American phenomenon, downtown thrived everywhere in urban America, even in Los Angeles, now regarded as the archetype of the decentralized metropolis, whereas late as the mid 1920s nearly half its residents went downtown every day.

Three-quarters of a century later downtown is still very much part of the American scene. Even those who seldom go downtown, even the generation of "mall rats," are routinely reminded of it. Long before the Boston skyscrapers come into view, the signs on the Massachusetts Turnpike advise eastbound motorists that they are approaching "Downtown Boston." The signs on Interstate 95 call attention to "Downtown Providence," "Downtown New

Haven," and, as if to underscore the point that downtown was not exclusively a big-city phenomenon, "Downtown Mystic" and "Downtown Milford." Every morning newscasters tell us about traffic congestion and weather conditions downtown. And from time to time disc jockeys play Petula Clark's "Downtown," the place where "You can forget all your troubles, forget all your cares," and Billy Joel's "Uptown Girl," a girl who's "looking for a downtown man." Downtown regularly appears in movies and novels, on occasion even in the title. American reporters and other writers nowadays speak of downtown in Baghdad, Bogotá, Nairobi, Shanghai, Saigon, Madrid, and other cities, most of which do not have a downtown and most of whose residents would never use the word. (That, however, is changing. So pervasive is American culture abroad today that Madrid has a magazine called *Downtown*—a magazine devoted to "Gente" [people], "Música" [music], "Cine" [film], and "Moda" [fashion]. Paris has a restaurant named Downtown, or at least it had one the last time I was there. An ad in the Brussels airport urges travelers to stay at the Hotel Atlanta, "IN THE HEART OF DOWNTOWN." And a sign in the London Underground encourages passengers to ride "Downtown to Soho by bus and tube.")

But downtown today is not what it was seventy-five years ago, not as a word and not as a place. Having lost its original meaning in the mid nineteenth century, downtown became synonymous with the business district shortly after. By the late nineteenth century it evoked a sense of bustle, noise, and avarice, just as uptown, the fashionable residential district, evoked elegance, gentility, and sophistication. As the years passed, however, many Americans began to regard downtown as declassé, even disreputable. Witness the many New Yorkers who drew a distinction between "uptown Jews," the well-to-do German Jews who had been born in the United States and resided on the elegant Upper East Side, and "downtown Jews," the impoverished Russian Jews who had just migrated to America and lived on the squalid Lower East Side. By the late twentieth century this distinction was deeply embedded in the American mind. As Greg Hoblitt, a director of both *L.A. Law* and *Hill Street Blues,* told an interviewer, "we wanted to create something [in *L.A. Law*] as uptown as HILL STREET [was] downtown . . . as elegant and sleek and articulate and rich and beautiful as HILL STREET [was] ugly, inarticulate and bumpy and messy." At times this distinction has created more than a little confusion. In Charlotte, North Carolina, for example, a group of downtown merchants who assumed that "uptown" was more "upbeat" (or upscale) than "downtown" managed to prevail on their fellow citizens to call the central business district uptown rather than downtown. Oddly enough, downtown Charlotte is now uptown Charlotte.[2]

As much as "downtown" has changed as a word, it has changed even more as a place. Now only one of many business districts (and in some cities the central business district in name only), downtown is no longer the place where most people go every day to work, to shop, to do business, and to amuse themselves. The outlying business districts are. The downtown skyscrapers, the workplaces of millions of white-collar Americans, are as breathtaking as ever. In all but a handful of cities, however, there is more office space on the periphery than in the center. And in downtown Detroit so many old skyscrapers are now vacant, or nearly so, that a frequent visitor has proposed turning them into "a ruins park," a sort of "American Acropolis," a proposal that was not warmly received by Detroit's business leaders. In most cities the downtown movie houses, the huge picture palaces built in the 1920s, are long gone, replaced by the suburban multiplexes. Gone too are many downtown hotels. The remaining ones, some brand new and others a little threadbare, have far fewer rooms than the hotels and motels outside the central business district. Even more astonishing, there are no longer any department stores downtown in Hartford, Detroit, Denver, and Tampa. Even in Boston, Chicago, and San Francisco, there are half a dozen department stores in the outlying business districts for each one in the central business district. The decentralization of the department store is one of the main reasons that the central business district, once the mecca for shoppers, does less than 5 percent of the retail trade of the metropolitan area everywhere but in New York, New Orleans, and San Francisco.[3]

Long the subject of studies and articles, downtown's decline is now the stuff of novels as well. In *The Risk Pool,* Richard Russo writes, "Downtown Mohawk had never been much to look at and was never exactly prosperous, but it had once been whole, at least. No more." Starting with the Mohawk Grand, the town's leading hotel, one building after another had been demolished and then replaced by the parking lots and one-story garages that emphasized Main Street's "gap toothed appearance." Harry Angstrom, the aging hero of John Updike's *Rabbit at Rest,* looks at "all but abandoned downtown" Brewer and, instead of the picture palaces of his boyhood, "packed with sweet odors and dark velvet, giggles and murmurs and held hands," sees only "a patchwork of rubble and parking lots and a few new glass-skinned buildings, stabs at renewal mostly occupied by banks and government agencies." And speaking of downtown Detroit, at one time "the very center, the heart of [the city]," William J. Coughlin observes (in *Death Penalty*) that its department stores, if "still standing," are "boarded up" and its fine shops "only a distant memory." "What was once the throbbing core of the city now looks forlorn and desolate, as if an enemy army had marched through and sacked the place."[4]

As downtown has changed, so has the way Americans think about it—and about the cities of which it has long been an integral part. From the late nineteenth century through the early twentieth they assumed that downtown was inevitable, that every American city, large and small, had to have a downtown. Although a few Americans had reservations, most also believed that downtown was desirable. Employing a popular metaphor of the time, they held that a prosperous downtown was as vital to the well-being of a city as a strong heart was to the well-being of a person. Most Americans held a deep-seated belief in spatial harmony too. In their view, rivalry between cities was natural, but rivalry within cities—especially between downtown and uptown, between the center and the periphery, between the business district and the residential districts—was not. Lastly, Americans assumed that there was an equilibrium between residential dispersal and business concentration, that no matter how far away people moved, they would go downtown every day, that the more they went to the periphery to live, the more they would go to the center to work, shop, do business, and amuse themselves.

During the mid and late 1920s, however, a few Americans began to challenge these assumptions. By the late 1940s and early 1950s, by which time business in American cities had been decentralized to a degree that would have been inconceivable a generation earlier, they were very much in question. And in question they remain. Today some Americans still agree with the late Charles Abrams, a lawyer and leading authority on housing and cities, who wrote in the early 1970s that the central business district "is the city's principal magnet, its mainstay and principal taxpayer." Cities with "a pulsating CBD" prosper; cities without one stagnate. (Interestingly, this view has supporters even in the many cities where downtown is anything but "pulsating." A case in point is Tampa, whose central business district has thus far resisted every effort at revitalization. Speaking in 1992, a year after Maas Brothers, downtown Tampa's last department store, closed its doors, City Councilman Scott Paine declared, "You will not have a great city unless you have a strong, vibrant downtown.") But many Americans are skeptical. Downtown, as they see it, is neither inevitable nor desirable. Rather it is obsolete, a late-nineteenth-century creation that has no role in the late twentieth, a bad place to work, a worse place to live. In Los Angeles, one observer has written, "nobody 'loves' downtown." To the average citizen, "Downtown [L.A.] is something he and [hundreds of thousands of] other freeway drivers . . . are pleased to hurtle by every day without stopping." In Detroit, another observer has remarked, "I'd find people who had their tremendous sense of pride that they hadn't been to downtown Detroit in 15 years and don't [ever] intend to go."[5]

Lately some journalists and scholars have argued that downtown is making a comeback. "In the last decade, the downtowns have been going through their most striking revivals of this century," writes Joel Garreau in his celebration of so-called edge cities. "From coast to coast—Boston, Philadelphia, Washington, Chicago, San Francisco, Seattle—downtowns are flourishing. Downtowns that no prudent person would have bet a week's pay on twenty years ago—Los Angeles, Baltimore, even, by God, Trenton—are back."[6] But back as what? Some downtowns are doing better now than a quarter century ago, when Edward DeBartolo, then the country's largest developer of regional shopping centers, told a reporter, "I wouldn't put a penny downtown." Since then other developers, often with the strong encouragement and financial support of local governments, have invested billions of dollars in the central business district. But the results have fallen far short of expectations in most cities, among them Los Angeles, about which author Ray Bradbury said in 1993, "Downtown L.A. is nothing," and Atlanta, about which journalist Dan Shaughnessy wrote a year later, "There's not much to do [downtown]. The locals will tell you: Nobody goes downtown." Downtown is more robust in other cities, such as Boston and San Francisco. But even there, it is a far cry from what it once was. At the end of the twentieth century, after several decades of efforts to revitalize the central business district, one thing was clear. Nowhere in urban America is downtown coming back as the only business district, as it was in the late nineteenth century, or even as the paramount and virtually unrivaled business district, as it was in the early twentieth. The almighty downtown of the past is gone—and gone for good. And it has been gone much longer than most Americans realize.

Its passing has left many who grew up in the 1940s and 1950s or earlier with strong feelings of nostalgia. It pervades many of the films of Woody Allen, who, decades later, can still remember his first trip from Brooklyn to Manhattan. "I was just *stunned*," he recalls. As for Times Square—with twenty movie houses on one side of Forty-second Street and twenty on the other—"I just couldn't believe it." The sentiment is much the same in other cities. "Even in my earlier recollections, there was an aura of magic and pleasurable excitement about a trip downtown," writes a longtime Baltimore resident. "The countless downtown shopping or pleasure trips we took as adults didn't particularly seem imbued with charm and color at the time, but now, knowing they are gone, they seem infinitely endearing." "Everybody remembers the way it used to be," notes a Tampa journalist, "the halcyon days for downtown when a retailer could do no wrong and the cash registers never stopped ringing"—and when, a leading Tampa preservationist recalls, everyone used to shop at Maas Brothers, see movies at the Tampa Theater, eat lunch at Newberry's, and pay bills at the Tampa Gas Company Building. Even in Albany novelist William Kennedy can remember "the booming, bustling Downtown Age, when the crowds were six abreast on the sidewalks at high noon and all day Saturday, when all the trolley cars were crowded, and you had to stand in line to get in to the movies or to buy two pounds of ambrosia, which in those days came packaged as Martha Washington's dark-chocolate butter creams."[7]

I feel nostalgic about downtown, too—especially when I visit New York and remember going to my father's office, shopping with my mother at Barney's Boys Town, attending the New York Philharmonic's Young People's Concerts at Carnegie Hall, and delivering flowers for Wadley & Smythe on West Fifty-seventh Street, my first job. But what drove me to study downtown was not so much nostalgia as curiosity. For reasons that elude me, American historians, who have written so much about suburbs and ghettos, have written very little about downtown. So in order to satisfy my curiosity, I have written a history of downtown that begins in the late nineteenth century, at which time its dominance was well established, and ends in the mid twentieth, by which time its decline was well under way. It is about downtown, how Americans thought about downtown, and how downtown and the way Americans thought about it changed over time. The book is also about the downtown businessmen and property owners, and especially about their efforts to promote the well-being of the central business district—even, if need be, at the expense of other parts of the city. And thus it is about spatial politics, about the battles between the downtown business interests and the outlying business interests as well as about the battles among the downtown business interests.

To put it another way, the book is about how Americans shaped (or tried to shape) downtown, not about how they felt downtown. Hence it is about power, not feelings. And though it may be unfashionable nowadays, it deals mostly with those with the most power. It is about department store magnates more than about salesgirls and floorwalkers, about office building owners more than about elevator operators and dispatchers. And it is about transit planners and highway engineers (and the elected officials to whom they answered) more than about straphangers and motorists. *Downtown* is not the last word on the subject. If not the first, it is one of the first. Although it stops shortly after World War II, I hope it will be of interest not only to my fellow historians but also to the few Americans who remember when downtown was a vital part of their lives (when it was, as we used to say, "the city") and the many Americans who, in the words of one midwesterner, "don't remember when, because for them, there never was a when."[8]

I The Business District:
Downtown in the
Late Nineteenth Century

Late in 1919 A. G. Gardiner, an English journalist and former editor of the London *Daily News,* made his first trip to the United States. As his ship steamed into New York harbor, he saw through the late afternoon mist what looked like "the serrated mass of a distant range of mountains, except that the sky-line is broken with a precision that suggests the work of man rather than the careless architecture of nature." "Gradually, as you draw near," he observed, "the mountain range takes definition." It turns into "vast structures with innumerable windows," taller by far than any buildings he had ever seen.

"It is," Gardiner wrote, "'down town,'" the business district of America's largest city. Here on "the tip of this tongue of rock that lies between the Hudson River and the East River" stands "the greatest group of buildings in the world"— crowned by the Woolworth Building, fifty-three stories of offices resembling "a great street, Piccadilly or the Strand, that has been miraculously turned skyward by some violent geological 'fault.'" Here scurry the "hosts of busy people" who carry out "all the myriad functions of the great god Mammon."[1] Here, said Gardiner, was the symbol of the American metropolis and the immense country that lay behind it.

By the time Gardiner first set eyes on "downtown," the word was roughly one

hundred years old. But it meant something quite different in the early nine-teenth century. For New Yorkers like Philip Hone, a prominent businessman, one-time mayor, and indefatigable diarist of the 1830s and 1840s, downtown had a geographical meaning. When Hone spoke of downtown, he meant the southern part of Manhattan Island—just as he meant the northern part when he spoke of uptown. Here he was following the customary usage according to which south meant down and north meant up. Thus when Hone walked south from his home on Great Jones Street, then at the northern edge of the built-up district, to City Hall, he went downtown—just as George Templeton Strong, another well-known New Yorker, went uptown when he walked from his father's house on Greenwich Street, near the southernmost point of Man-hattan, to Grace Church, then under construction on what was at the time up-per Broadway.[2] (A century and a half later Americans still speak of downstate when they refer to Illinois south of Chicago and upstate when they refer to New York State north of New York City.)

Already the nation's largest city in 1830, New York grew phenomenally over the next forty years. Its population soared from under 250,000 to nearly 1.5 million, and its economy expanded at a rate that amazed contemporaries. To-gether with the huge influx of immigrants, what a special New York State Sen-ate commission called "the inexorable demands of business" transformed the structure of the city, turning lower Manhattan mainly into stores, offices, workshops, and warehouses and upper Manhattan largely into residences. As early as 1836 Hone, who then lived on lower Broadway, feared he would soon be forced to move uptown. "Almost everybody downtown is in the same predicament," he wrote, "for all the dwelling houses are to be converted into stores. We are tempted with prices so exorbitantly high that none can resist." Hone moved. So did Strong's father, whose family was no longer willing to re-main on Greenwich Street once stores, saloons, and boarding houses opened up near their elegant home in the 1840s. By the 1850s the change was strik-ing. Noting that "Calico is omnipotent," *Putnam's Monthly* remarked that the dry-goods trade has spread with "astonishing rapidity over the whole lower part of the city, prostrating and obliterating everything that is old and venera-ble, and leaving not a single landmark," not even the "dwelling houses of our ancestors." As Mr. Potiphar observed in a popular novel of the times, "When Pearl street [the center of the dry-goods trade] comes to Park Place [a fashion-

Previous page: The Woolworth Building, New York, ca. 1914 (King's Views of New York, Boston, 1915)

able residential neighborhood in lower Manhattan], Park Place must run for its life up to Thirtieth street."[3]

Although New Yorkers continued to speak of downtown and uptown when referring to the southern and northern sections of Manhattan, the words gradually took on a functional meaning that reflected the changing structure of the city. Strong, who had gone to work in his father's law firm on Wall Street in the 1840s, soon began to use "downtown" when he meant the business district and "uptown" when he meant the residential. And in the 1850s, *Harper's New Monthly Magazine* wrote of the "down-town men" who "slip uneasily through the brick and mortar labyrinths of Maiden-lane and of John-street," two of lower Manhattan's busy commercial streets. As men went downtown to work, women went downtown to shop (and also to pay bills, to deal with household matters, and, in some cases, to work). By the 1870s the functional meaning had largely superseded the geographical. As *Wood's Illustrated Hand-Book,* a guide written mainly for the British, explained, "The expressions 'down town' and 'up town' are employed to designate the business and social quarters of the city"—one devoted to "commerce, traffic, and law," the other to "private life." "If caprice takes you down town," George Makepeace Towle, U.S. consul at Bradford, informed his British readers, "you soon find yourself in the very whirl and maelstrom of commerce and trade. . . . As you proceed uptown, quiet and insouciant ease takes the place of the bustle and hurry of the down town quarters."[4]

During the mid and late nineteenth century the word "downtown" spread to many other cities, to large ones like Boston and small ones like Salem and Worcester. The word "uptown" also spread, though to far fewer cities. Outside New York both words lost their original meanings. Susan E. Parsons Brown Forbes, a Boston schoolteacher, wrote of going "down town" in the early 1860s, even though downtown Boston was north of her home on Waverly Place. After she and her husband moved to Springfield in 1866, she continued to make trips "down town," even though downtown Springfield was east of her new home on State Street. Much the same was true in Chicago, where a journalist writing just after the great fire of 1871 remarked, "As I passed up West Madison Street, I met scores of working girls on their way 'down town,' as usual, bearing their lunch-baskets as if nothing had happened." Yet the girls were walking east, not south. The words lost their original meanings because in very few cities was downtown south and uptown north as they were in New York. Downtown lay to the south in Detroit, but to the north in Cleveland, to the east in St. Louis, and to the west in Pittsburgh. In Boston, a resident pointed out in 1880, downtown was in the center of the city. Uptown was north of downtown in Cincinnati, but south of downtown in New Orleans and San Francisco. In New York, a Philadelphia real estate journal wrote in 1886, "everybody down town must go up town; here everybody down town can scatter to the four points of the compass."[5]

By the end of the century, if not earlier, downtown was synonymous with the business district virtually everywhere in urban America. When the word first appeared in dictionaries in the early 1900s—it was not included in Webster's Dictionary in 1881 or in Worcester's Dictionary in 1886—that was how it was defined. "Uptown," which had appeared in Webster's as early as 1870 and in Worcester's ten years earlier, was defined as "the upper part of a town or city." But it was commonly understood to mean the residential section, especially the affluent residential section. And it had already acquired the connotations of wealth, elegance, sophistication, and social prominence that were still strong a century later. As well as a new word, "downtown" was, as Webster's noted, an American word. It was virtually unknown in England and other Western European countries. Well into the early twentieth century English travel writers thought it necessary to explain the meaning of "down town" to their readers. And even today the English speak of the city center when they mean the urban core—just as the French use *le centre de ville,* the Spanish *el centro,* the Germans *das zentrum,* and the Italians *il centro.* American reporters and public officials routinely refer to "downtown" in cities all over the world, but the word does not have much meaning outside the United States. For downtown was not only an American word, it was also a uniquely American place.[6]

As a place, downtown was hard to define. Legally, it did not exist. Unlike the city of which it was a part—indeed, unlike every parcel of real estate in the city—downtown had no formal boundaries, no precise lines to show where it began and where it ended. Nor did downtown exist politically. For governmental purposes, every American city was divided into wards. In some cities downtown lay in one ward; in most it spread over two or more. In none—not even in Chicago, where the business district and the first ward overlapped closely—did downtown and one or more wards have the same boundaries. And in some, like Detroit, where each ward ran in a narrow strip through the whole city, downtown and the wards were completely distinct. In virtually every city downtown had some sort of physical boundaries, usually a bay, a lake, a river, or, in a few cases, a combination of them. But nowhere did these boundaries define downtown with precision—except perhaps in Pittsburgh, where downtown was hemmed in by the Allegheny and Monongahela rivers on the north, south, and west and by a steep hill known as the "Hump" on the east.[7] And nowhere did these boundaries confine downtown to its original site.

Although hard to define, downtown was easy to locate. It was the destination of the street railways, which were still pulled by horses in the 1880s, the elevated railways, which ran above the streets of New York, and the local ferries, which carried millions a year in a handful of cities. Except where the steam railroads were barred from entering it, downtown was also the site of the railroad terminals. Downtown was the home of the tall office buildings, ten to fifteen stories high by 1890. These skyscrapers, as they came to be known, were more then just very tall; they were also very convenient. In buildings like Chicago's "Rookery"—"a little city in itself," one Chicago resident called it—a businessman could "find under one roof his customers, his bankers, his principals, his restauranter [sic], his barber and his bootblack." Downtown was also the site of Macy's, Wanamaker's, Marshall Field's, and other huge department stores. Another nineteenth-century innovation, which came after the railroad station but before the skyscraper, the department store was designed to be what H. Gordon Selfridge of Marshall Field's called the "downtown home" for its customers, mostly middle- and upper-middle-class women, for whom it provided such amenities as tearooms, writing tables, and even nurseries, where they could leave their children while shopping. As late as 1890 downtown was the only part of the city wired for electricity. At night, when darkness fell over the rest of the city, what a Houston journalist described as "a perfect burst of sunlight" lit up many of downtown's streets, shops, hotels, restaurants, and theaters. Brilliantly illuminated, downtown at night was "indescribably exhilarating," wrote an English visitor at the turn of the century.[8]

Although these buildings were very large, downtown itself was very small. According to Mayor Nathan Matthews, Jr., downtown Boston had only 217 acres, just over a third of a square mile, or less than 1 percent of the entire city. Without rushing, the Massachusetts Rapid Transit Commission noted, a man could make a circuit of downtown Boston, about a three-mile walk, in one hour. Downtown Pittsburgh was even smaller. In a city of 41 square miles, it covered less than a third of a square mile. According to estimates made in the early 1890s, downtown Chicago had one-half to three-quarters of a square mile, a tiny fraction of the midwestern capital's 169 square miles. Downtown New York was somewhat larger.[9] To look at it another way, downtown Pittsburgh was only two and a half times as large as the Carnegie steel company's plant in nearby Homestead, the site of the infamous industrial dispute in

1892. Downtown Chicago was not much larger than the Union Stockyards, the slaughterhouses later immortalized by Upton Sinclair, and a little smaller than the Pullman Palace Car Company's works, located in George M. Pullman's model town a few miles south of the city. Downtown Boston was only slightly larger than Mount Auburn Cemetery, a rural cemetery on the Cambridge-Watertown line, where more than a few downtown businessmen and professionals were buried. Downtown New York was somewhat smaller than Central Park. And downtown San Francisco could have fit easily into the University of California's sprawling campus in nearby Berkeley.

In view of how small downtown was, it was striking how much business was done there. More trade was done in downtown Chicago than in the rest of the city combined, the Chicago *Real Estate and Building Journal* wrote in 1897, by which time the city had grown to 195 square miles. And trade was just part of the picture. Downtown Chicago also housed all of the city's financial institutions, most of its professional offices, and many of its light industries. "No place on earth [has] such a congregation of business interests," said Washington Hesing, a Chicago resident.[10] Downtown Chicago was by no means unique. In every big city downtown was *the* business district. The retailers and wholesalers worked there, as did the bankers, financiers, insurance, utility, and corporate executives, the lawyers, realtors, architects, engineers, and accountants, the clerks, typists, salesmen, salesgirls, and messengers, and many craftsmen and laborers. The courts, government agencies, and post and telegraph offices were located downtown, as were most hotels, restaurants, places of popular amusement, and institutions of high culture. Downtown was the site of nearly all the city's businesses except heavy industries (like steel mills), noxious activities (like slaughterhouses), and a wide range of neighborhood trades and shops, many of which catered largely to one or another of America's many ethnic groups.

Also striking was how much business downtown was done by women. Long gone was the day when respectable women were loath to venture into the business district without an escort. Except for places like Nashville's Men's Quarter, Omaha's Douglas Street, and Seattle's Yessler Way, tiny enclaves of boarding houses, saloons, pawnbrokers, cigar stores, gambling dens, and Turkish baths, no part of downtown was off-limits to women in the late nineteenth century. By then women worked there, in offices, hotels, restaurants, shops, lofts, factories, and department stores, the largest of which had well over a thousand salesgirls. Women also went downtown to dine, to watch plays, and to listen to lectures. Above all, women did their shopping downtown. They flocked to the great department stores on Market Street in Philadelphia, State Street in Chicago, Canal Street in New Orleans, and Broadway, the "Ladies Mile" of New York. Watching so many women shop on lower Fulton Street, commonly known as "the Broadway of Brooklyn," one journalist was led to imagine "what Eden might have been were Adam and his part in life dispensed with." Many women went from one store to another, sometimes buying, sometimes window-shopping. Others went to only one, shopping on one floor, lunching on another, relaxing on a third, finding everything they needed, one woman wrote, "without having been obliged to leave the store."[11]

Downtown acted on men and women alike as a small but extremely powerful magnet. In New York, a London *Times* correspondent wrote in 1887, "half a million or more rush 'down-town' every morning, and back 'up-town' at night"; hundreds of thousands more crossed the East and Hudson rivers, commuting from Brooklyn and New Jersey. Hundreds of thousands made the daily trip downtown in Boston, Chicago, and other cities. Some workers left home as early as six, and some shoppers as late as eleven; but most people went downtown between seven and nine—and returned home between five and seven. Referring to what would later become known as rush hour in New

New York's "Ladies Mile," ca. 1885 (Henry Collins Brown, ed., Valentine's Manual of Old New York, *New York, 1927)*

York, a French visitor wrote in the 1860s, "Neither the boulevards [in Paris], the Strand [in London], nor the Corso of Rome in carnival time can give an idea of this tumultuous movement." A few walked downtown. Some took ferries, in many of which, one Englishman noted, "everyone pushes up unceremoniously against his neighbour till there is scarcely anything of his neighbour left." Others journeyed by steam railroads, especially in Boston. And in New York many rode the els, which were so crowded, one writer remarked, that passengers "have literally to fight their way out of the cars [and] are often carried one or two stations beyond their destination." But most came by street railways—horse-drawn cars, cable cars, and, as a result of a technological breakthrough in the late 1880s, electric cars. The street railways carried twice as many passengers in the United States as in the rest of the world combined in 1890. And they transported far more people per capita even in ordinary American cities like Denver and Cleveland than in Berlin, Vienna, and other great European capitals.[12]

With so much business and so many people crammed into so little space, downtown was extremely congested. Besides street railways, all sorts of vehicles—some carrying people, others hauling freight—jammed the streets. On one day in the mid 1880s more than twenty-two thousand of these vehicles, or one every two seconds, passed the intersection of Broadway and Fulton Street between seven A.M. and six P.M. Even with the help of the police, traffic was regularly tied up on Broadway for ten minutes or more, one observer noted:

> For those who are not obliged to cross the choked-up thoroughfare, the scene is full of a brief amusement—hack-drivers, truckmen, omnibus drivers, swearing vehemently at each other, or interchanging all kinds of "chaff;" passengers indignantly railing at the delay, and police officers yelling and waving their clubs in their attempts to get the machinery of travel again moving smoothly. If, at such a time, a fire engine comes rattling up the street, post-haste for a scene of a fire, and attempts to enforce its right of way, the confusion becomes doubly confounded, and the scene a veritable pandemonium.[13]

The sidewalks were as congested as the streets. As *American Architect and Building News* complained in the early 1890s, downtown Boston's sidewalks were "jammed to suffocation with pedestrians," many of whom were "elbowing each other off the sidewalk into the gutter." The sidewalks were so crowded in the retail center, the *Boston Herald* noted, that now and then the women shoppers "were obliged to hold their paper boxes above their heads to keep them from being crushed."

Downtown was very busy. Except for the shoppers, many of whom went

*A traffic jam on Broadway, 1883 (*Harper's Weekly, *December 29, 1883)*

about their business in a leisurely manner, everybody was in a great hurry, rushing to and fro, trying to get as much done as possible. Downtown Chicago, one of the busiest business districts, was "like three hundred acres of the New York Stock Exchange when trading is active," wrote one journalist. Downtown was also dark, particularly in winter. The tall buildings hid the sun, as did the smoke that spewed out of the coal furnaces. Also blocking the light was what an English visitor called a "perfect maze of telephone and telegraph wires." Integral features of the city's communications system, the wires crossed and recrossed one another like "the meshes of a net." Downtown was very noisy, too. Drills whined, bells clanged, brakes screeched—a terrible din. "A few more years of the present indescribable uproar in Chicago," a St. Louis newspaper wrote, "and the people there will do nothing but make signs. As it is now, you see thousands of them walking along talking to themselves as if they had just escaped from an asylum for the insane. It is

Crowds in downtown Boston, 1889 (Courtesy of the Bostonian Society/ Old State House)

the only way they can think." It was noisy indoors as well, especially in restaurants at lunchtime. Of New York in the late 1860s, one writer observed: "From 12 o'clock to 3 of the afternoon, the down-town eating-places are in one continuous roar. The clatter of plates and knives, the slamming of doors, the talking and giving of orders by the customers, the bellowing of waiters, are mingled in a wild chaos. . . . Everybody talks at once; everybody orders at once; everybody eats at once; and everybody seems anxious to pay at once."[14]

Things slowed down at night, after the stores, offices, and other businesses closed. Downtown Philadelphia, a guidebook pointed out in the early 1870s, "though bustling and noisy enough during business hours, is a perfect desolation after six o'clock, and the thousands who throng there all day long are miles away, resting, most of them, in comfortable homes, with plenty of living-room about them." Outside its entertainment district, even downtown New York was still at night. The stillness, an observer remarked, was relieved only "by the blaze of lights in the newspaper establishments of Printing House Square and the Western Union Telegraph Building, by the occasional tramp of the policeman or reporter, or the rattling of the casual carriage over the stony pave." Downtown was quiet at night because few people lived there. Speaking of New York, one writer observed in the early 1880s, "In the strictly commercial quarters dwellings are very rare, and the population is made up almost entirely of janitors and their families, who occupy the upper floors of business houses and public buildings." Much the same was true in Cincinnati, where a visitor remarked in the late 1880s that virtually "everyone lived in the suburbs," and Chicago, where a guidebook noted in the early 1890s that residences were "entirely excluded from the business district." Only in small cities like Atlanta, Nashville, and Richmond did many people still live downtown in the 1890s.[15]

Once the most densely populated part of the city, downtown had been losing residents for a long time. The loss was most conspicuous in downtown

New York, part of which lay in ward 2, a small ward on the eastern side of lower Manhattan. Between 1850 and 1890, when New York grew from about 500,000 to more than 1.5 million people, the population of ward 2 dropped from more than 6,000 to fewer than 1,000. By 1890 ward 2 had only twelve persons per acre, far fewer than any other ward in Manhattan, far fewer even than ward 12, a sparsely settled district on the Upper West Side. Only ward 24, a huge and as yet largely undeveloped section of the North Bronx, had fewer persons per acre. The pattern was much the same in other cities. Although the population of Pittsburgh went up fivefold between 1850 and 1890, ward 3, one of four wards in downtown Pittsburgh, lost more than three-quarters of its residents. And though the population of Philadelphia nearly doubled between 1860 and 1890, the number who lived in ward 5, the core of downtown, decreased by close to one-third. As people moved out of downtown in Pittsburgh, Philadelphia, and other big cities, their homes were sometimes turned into boarding houses for single men. More often they were demolished to make room for stores and offices or converted into business quarters—the former kitchens "occupied by followers of Blackstone," wrote the *Philadelphia Real Estate Record and Builders' Guide* in the mid 1880s, and the former dining rooms "filled by insurance men, manufacturers and representatives of our industrial and commercial interests."[16]

As Philip Hone noted, some people moved out of downtown because they were offered "exorbitantly high" prices for their property. Commercial property commanded such "fabulous prices," wrote a New York real estate journal, that many homeowners looked forward to the time when their residences would be sought for business purposes. Other people moved away to escape what a Cambridge newspaper editor termed "the moral and physical miasma of the metropolis." If, as Mr. Potiphar believed, "One can't live among shops," how could one live among saloons, brothels and boarding houses, much less amid immigrants, criminals, and periodic riots? Far more appealing to the well-to-do was the new vision of what historian Robert Fishman calls the bourgeois utopia, a suburban setting at the heart of which was a single-family home on a tree-shaded lot—a setting that presumably offered the advantages of both urban and rural life (and the disadvantages of neither). To these suburban enclaves moved many downtown businessmen who no longer felt it necessary to live above their workplace or within a short walk of it. As the street railways opened up hitherto inaccessible areas, the less well-off followed. As an upper Manhattan realtor pointed out, "They find that up our way they can rent a comfortable cottage for less than they pay for a tenement or flat in the crowded down-town districts, while they get the advantage of pure country air and a little plot of green around them." Often they had no choice. At the same time that many downtown residences were being demolished to make way not only for stores and offices, but also for streets, parks, and other public improvements, the high land values made it "absolutely impossible," said one Bostonian, "to build a tenement house in the heart of the city."[17]

The emergence of downtown was a vital part of the transformation of the American metropolis, a transformation that was over in most big cities by the late nineteenth century and would be over in most small ones by the early twentieth. At its core was a strict separation of businesses and residences, a high concentration of businesses downtown, and a wide dispersal of residences elsewhere. Commenting on the change, the *Philadelphia Illustrated* wrote in 1871 that in Philadelphia, "as in every great metropolis, wealth separates the home from the workshop, and the accumulated riches are displayed and spent far from the spot where they are laboriously garnered." After observing that Boston's business "is all done on the little peninsula on which the original town was located," the *Chicago Tribune* said in 1893, "Speaking broadly, Boston works on the peninsula and sleeps on the main land." Most big cities were, as the *Globe* wrote of Boston in 1873, "two cities—the city of warehouses and the city of dwellings." The city of warehouses was dense, public, competitive, noisy, and jarring; the city of dwellings was diffuse, private, supportive, quiet, and soothing—"a place of repose" from the world of business. This dichotomy was striking in Chicago, wrote a Scot who visited the city in the early 1890s. Of the city's many contrasts, none impressed him as much as "the difference between its business and its residential quarters. In the one—height, narrowness, noise, monotony, dirt, sordid squalor, pretentiousness; in the other—light, space, moderation, homelikeness."[18]

Downtown fascinated contemporaries for many reasons, not the least of which was that they saw it as uniquely American. Nothing like downtown existed in Europe, they believed—except for the City of London, the small historic center of the giant British metropolis. In European cities, wrote *American Architect and Building News* in 1877, businesses and residences were spread over "pretty much the whole territory," not confined to separate quarters, as in American cities. They were separated, if at all, not horizontally but vertically. Speaking of Paris, *American Architect* noted in 1878, "the whole city is in layers: a layer of shops and warehouses, a layer of lesser business and domestic apartments, layers of first-class, second-class, and third-class dwellings, and layers of cheap lodgings above." Paris, said Albert Shaw, an American who knew a good deal about Europe, was an extreme case of a city without a well-defined business core. But European cities were much more like Paris than New York and Chicago, where, Shaw pointed out, "the whole tendency is to concentrate business in a compact area and then distribute residential districts over a pretty large territory."[19] Nowhere in Europe, Americans held, were businesses as concentrated (and residences as dispersed) as they were in the United States. And nowhere, except in the City of London, were the business districts so thoroughly depopulated.

Americans attributed the rise of downtown to a number of things, the most important of which was what Frederick Law Olmsted, the nation's foremost landscape architect, called in 1871 "a strong and steadily increasing tendency" toward the separation of businesses and residences. As Olmsted saw it, this tendency was a recent development. For centuries European tradesmen had lived under the roof of their shop with their wives, children, servants, and apprentices. Even well into the late eighteenth century "the largest bankers and merchants of London, Amsterdam and Paris still maintained their domestic and commercial establishments under the same roof, and the Stewarts and Tiffanies [prominent nineteenth-century New York retailers] of the day had a door opening between their show rooms and their family dining-rooms." During the early and mid nineteenth century, however, many merchants and other tradesmen moved their homes away from their workplaces. And by the late nineteenth century the separation of businesses and residences was well along, especially in American cities. This development, Olmsted wrote in 1879, pulled "most large and thriving towns in two opposite directions—one to concentration for business and social purposes, the other to dispersion for domestic purposes. The first leads toward more compact and higher buildings in business quarters, the other toward broader, lower and more open buildings in residence quarters."[20]

Olmsted traced the separation of businesses and residences to the "law of progress," "a fixed tendency among civilized men" to enhance the "cleanliness and purity" of domestic life, which could not be done amid factories, wharves, shops, and offices. Land-use segregation was as much a result of this law as sewers and waterworks. Richard M. Hurd, president of the Lawyers Mortgage Insurance Company and the nation's leading real estate economist, offered another explanation. Although he held that the separation of businesses and residences was the first step in the evolution of cities, he saw it as a "natural result" of the growing demand for commercial space, which drove residences out of the business district. Some Americans believed that the separation of businesses and residences reflected a peculiarly Anglo-American view of proper domestic life. As *American Architect and Building News* noted in

1878, "the visible juxtaposition of business and dwelling . . . offends the An-glo-Saxon sense of domesticity." Other Americans contended that the separa-tion of businesses and residences illustrated the law of development as laid out by Herbert Spencer, a British philosopher who was very popular in the United States. According to this law, wrote New York's *Real Estate Record and Builders' Guide* in 1881, all things, including cities, develop from the simple to the complex, the homogeneous to the heterogeneous.[21] But no matter how Americans explained the separation of businesses and residences, most of them believed it was a natural development.

The compactness of downtown, Americans thought, was a manifestation of the nature of business and the preferences of businessmen. "Trade tends to centralization," Representative Henry W. Muzzey of Cambridge told the Mas-sachusetts House of Representatives in the early 1880s. "Buyer and seller alike seek a common mart." *California Architect and Building News* made the point even more forcefully. "Every enterprising man seeks to get as near the center as possible," it wrote in the late 1880s, "and will put up with great lim-itations and inconvenience rather than leave the heart of trade and com-merce." Centralization was commonplace in the first-class dry-goods trade, the *Chicago Tribune* noted. "Custom and fashion have very closely restricted the localities available for such purposes. Anybody who wants to succeed must get into one of those localities." Lawyers, said a Bostonian, also prefer to work in the same district, close to one another (and presumably close to their clients, other professionals, and the courts and city halls). Even manufactur-ers, the *Philadelphia Real Estate Record and Builders' Guide* wrote in 1888, "de-sire to be as near the centre of the city as possible, within easy reach of banks, post-offices, express offices and those [merchants] who deal in the material which they use."[22]

Why did businesses, even businesses in competition with each other, tend to locate in the same small section of the city? Olmsted held that as commerce expanded businessmen had to take on more and more duties, many of which required meeting with other businessmen and professionals who worked out of separate offices. With the growing specialization of businesses and profes-sions, a transaction that formerly took one meeting now took several. For businessmen, distance was time; and as time was money, centrality was vital. Hurd argued that retailers clustered in compact sections not because they did business with one another but because they expected that the other retailers would help them attract customers. Shoppers, they believed, came to the re-tail section because they were confident they could find all they wanted there. Shoppers who went to one store would probably go to others. Most Americans, however, believed that the tendency of businesses to locate in the same small district did not need to be explained, that it was self-evident that centralization facilitated the transaction of business. As Craig McClure, a St. Louis architect, said in 1896, "The advantage of being able to do business with a dozen people in as many different lines without leaving your building or at most your block is too apparent to need argument."[23]

The depopulation of downtown, Americans believed, was a function of the basic laws of economics. As Hurd explained, urban land went to "the highest bidder"—"the highest bidder being the one who can make the land earn the largest amount." And businesses, especially retail businesses, could generate far more income from a piece of real estate than could residences. How much more was indicated by the disparities in property values. In Chicago, for instance, first-class retail space on State Street was worth three thousand dollars a front foot in 1883, which was half again as much as office space on LaSalle Street, but five times as much as "aristocratic" residential property on Michigan Avenue and ten times as much as first-class residential property on Dearborn Street. As property went to "the highest bidder," it was converted from residential to commercial use, a process that Adna F. Weber, a prominent urban demographer at the turn of the century, called "city-building." In the early history of the city, Weber argued, the original settlement becomes the business district.

> But if the city prospers, the time will come when this old center is more and more needed for strictly business purposes; houses disappear before the march of office-buildings, government buildings, banks, etc., until the only residents left are the janitors and *portiers,* the keepers of the great buildings. With continued growth, the business center extends itself and steadily pushes the dwellings toward the circumference, until at length the municipal limits are reached and passed.

This process, Weber wrote, was well along in New York and other big cities.[24]

Residents were sometimes unwilling to make way for the expansion of business. Writing about New York's lower Fifth Avenue, which was in the path of the growing retail district, the *Real Estate Record and Builders' Guide* observed in the late 1870s that it housed many old and wealthy citizens "who have stubbornly and resolutely determined not to be removed except by the undertaker." Although these people had "lifelong and priceless associations" with their homes, the journal predicted that sooner or later they would have to sell and that slowly but surely their dwellings would be converted into stores. Residents could not hold out against the pressures to make way for business, the *Real Estate Record* insisted. Nor should they, argued the *Philadelphia Real Estate Record and Builders' Guide*. Writing in the mid 1880s, it held that the "encroachments of business" upon a residential neighborhood were "a healthy innovation," a signal of growing prosperity and enhanced real estate values. These encroachments were not at all like the "inroads of vice," "a sure precursor of loss and degeneration," which drove out respectable people and drove down property values.[25]

Of the other things to which Americans attributed the rise of downtown, the development of the street, steam, and elevated railways was regarded as the most important. As early as the mid nineteenth century Americans had marveled at how the railways had opened up remote residential sections to the middle and upper middle classes. Well into the early twentieth century Americans were hopeful that the railways would enable the working classes to escape the slums—and the many medical and moral problems commonly associated with them. During the 1870s and 1880s, however, Americans came to believe that in addition to fostering the dispersion of residences the railways promoted the concentration of businesses. So long as horse-cars were the principal form of public transportation, the New York *Real Estate Record and Builders' Guide* observed, there was a fair chance that businesses would move uptown in order to be close to their customers and employees. But with the coming of steam and elevated railways, which effectively reduced the distance between the business and residential districts, merchants, bankers, and other businessmen had good reason to remain downtown. Thus, the *Real Estate Record* pointed out, the railways accelerated the centripetal tendencies of businesses as well as the centrifugal tendencies of residences.[26]

By the end of the century the *Real Estate Record*'s position was the conventional wisdom. In a report prepared for the U.S. Census Bureau, Edward Dana Durand wrote that the street railways, virtually all of which were then electrified, were "probably the most important single influence" in dispersing residences. But they also concentrated businesses, he pointed out, especially retail businesses. A spokesman for Boston's street railways agreed. "Imagine for a moment," he said, "the effect upon the business of Jordan, Marsh & Co., R. H. White & Co., and others, if they had no customers except such as could come to their shops in carriages and omnibuses, or walk." Richard Hurd took much the same position. By virtue of their high speed, he argued, "street railroads have wrought a revolution in the structure of cities, scattering population over a wide area, adding value to the circumference by rendering it accessible for residences, and to the center by concentrating traffic within it."

Elevated railways, which ran at even higher speeds, had a similar impact, Hurd added. Both forms of transportation promoted the two prevailing tendencies in American cities, "one toward greater concentration at the business centre, and the other toward greater dispersion of the residence sections."[27]

Americans viewed these tendencies as reflections of what the *Detroit Free Press* called the "universal law of change." It affected people, buildings, and, not least of all, cities. Noting that "the works of one generation are swept away by the works of the next," Henry P. Tappan, chancellor of the University of Michigan, predicted in the mid 1850s: "He who erects his magnificent palace on the Fifth Avenue to-day, has only fitted out a future boarding-house, and probably occupied the site of a future warehouse." Speaking of New York's bucolic Upper West Side, Andrew H. Green, comptroller of Central Park, contended in the mid 1860s that it "will probably be built with dwellings of a costly character, and these, after having served their day and generation, will give away, as in other localities, to the pressure of the business." Not even cemeteries were immune to change. As historian Michael Holleran has pointed out, nineteenth-century urban cemeteries were "a place for putting bodies, not for keeping them." During the nineteenth century the city of Boston sold off parts of the South Burial Ground for a street, a hotel, a factory addition, even a music hall. Referring to the Granary and King's Chapel burial grounds, Boston's Board of Health predicted in 1877 that sooner or later "the remains of those buried in these cemeteries will be removed, and the ground used for other purposes."[28]

Change left some Americans with a feeling of loss. Writing in *Harper's Magazine* in the mid 1850s, one lamented: "A man born in New York forty years ago [today] finds nothing, absolutely nothing, of the New York he knew. If he chances to stumble upon a few old houses not yet leveled, he is fortunate. But the landmarks, the objects which marked the city to him, as a city, are gone." Most Americans, however, saw change as a sign of improvement, an affirmation of their faith in material progress. In a nation where change was relentless—where, as Alexis de Tocqueville had observed in the 1830s, "a man builds a house in which to spend his old age [and] sells it just before the roof is on," "plants a garden and lets it just as the trees come into bearing"—few people developed much of an attachment to old buildings and old places. Barely a month before the great fire of 1872 destroyed most of downtown Boston, the *Globe* hailed the city's rapid growth, citing its new "palatial residences, elegant parks, [and] superb avenues," and boasted that "old landmarks and localities have almost completely disappeared." The *Philadelphia Real Estate Record and Builders' Guide* complained that the city's old landmarks—the "relics of

[William] Penn's days"—were disappearing too slowly. "The time for narrow stairways creaking with age, and low ceilings blackened with the lamp smoke of a long century, and little fort-like windows and narrow doorways, has gone," it declared in the mid 1880s. "The spirit of improvement is on us, and these old buildings, respectable with their associations, must go."[29]

Old buildings, Americans assumed, would be replaced by new buildings, short buildings by tall buildings. Residences would make way for businesses. And residents would move out of the center. Fashionable retail shops would follow in the path of affluent residential neighborhoods. Wholesale firms would move into buildings vacated by retail stores. And new banks and office buildings would be erected in old retail and wholesale districts. But no matter how much the cities changed, Americans believed that they would always have a downtown, an extremely compact, highly centralized, largely depopulated business district to which nearly all the residents, even those who lived far away, would come every day to work, to shop, to do business, and to amuse themselves. "Everything must have its nucleus," declared H. W. Kirchner, a St. Louis architect, in 1896, and every city must have its downtown.[30]

Some Americans objected to the concentration of business. Explaining his opposition to a proposed elevated railroad, Mayor Carter H. Harrison, Sr., of Chicago declared in the mid 1880s, "I don't believe in centralizing wealth by centralizing business. Business ought to be scattered instead of being centered in the heart of the city." Another critic of concentration was E. D. Lindsay, a New York architect. Admitting that he would be delighted to design a five or six hundred foot skyscraper, he nonetheless expressed the hope that "the rage for making as much money out of a given piece of land, or for crowding everything that is best into one section of the city, which amounts to the same thing, will some day come to an end." A few Americans even favored the European practice of spreading out the business sections over the American practice of "doing the greatest amount [of business] on the smallest space of ground." One of them was George A. Lespinasse, a former New York real estate broker who had lived in Paris for a while. To a reporter's remark that perhaps "business could not be so conveniently and economically carried on when distributed over a larger area," Lespinasse replied, "Why not?" Such dispersal would have been inconvenient in the past, but now, with the improved transit facilities available, it would be quite satisfactory.[31]

Other Americans objected not so much to the concentration of business as to its excessive concentration. One objection was that too much business was done in some parts of downtown as opposed to others. Boston's retail district should be compact, said Herbert L. Harding, secretary of the Citizens' Association, but it should not be confined to Washington and Tremont streets. Another objection was that too much business was done in the downtown areas as opposed to the outlying districts. Arguing that downtown Chicago, which covered half a square mile, did more trade than the rest of the city, which covered nearly two hundred square miles, the Chicago *Real Estate and Building Journal* declared, "This is congestion with a vengeance." So many people shop downtown that "none are left to patronize the midway and suburban district stores." Yet another objection was that so much business was done in such a small area that the congestion was intolerable. The streets and sidewalks were packed so tightly, Harding remarked, that a great many ladies "will not shop in the crowded section." For the good of downtown, it was essential to enlarge the business district and, in the words of the Massachusetts Rapid Transit Commission, spread out "the heaped up tide of humanity which now chokes Tremont and Washington streets."[32]

But most Americans did not object to the concentration of business. "I think that the more business is concentrated the better," said Chicago architect Henry Ives Cobb in the early 1890s. Cobb was especially impressed by the Windy City, which had a highly centralized business district even before the elevated railway loop was erected along its perimeter in the late 1890s. "There is no city in the world where it is so easy to transact business as in Chicago," he said. W. L. B. Jenney, another Chicago architect and a pioneer in the design of the steel-frame skyscraper, agreed. "Business is so concentrated that strangers claim that they can do more business in a given length of time here than in any other city," he noted. Concentration, Cobb, Jenney, and others held, greatly facilitated business. Given what the San Francisco *Evening Picayune* called "a constant and unremitted intercourse" among merchants, it was a decided advantage for them to be close to one another (and close to the bankers, lawyers, shippers, insurance agents, and other businessmen and professionals on whom they depended). Nothing brought them closer than the skyscraper. Much time was saved now that many suppliers, customers, and advisers had offices under the same roof, wrote one observer in the early 1890s, and a businessman "scarcely needs to go outside at all to transact any portion of his affairs."[33]

Downtown, most Americans believed, was supposed to be very crowded. Crowds are "just what the city of Boston wants," said Charles H. Dalton, chairman of the Boston Subway Commission, in 1894. "The larger the crowd, the better they [Bostonians] like it. It is the purpose of the city to have a great many people come here and do business with them. The more, the merrier."

Crowds were a sign of prosperity, as was congestion. If the congestion grew intolerable, the cities should devise ways to relieve it—not discourage people from doing business downtown. Noise and bustle were out of place in residential neighborhoods, Americans believed, but not in business districts. There they were signs of progress, Linus M. Child of Massachusetts told a state legislative committee in 1880. Taking issue with Bostonians who objected to a proposed elevated railroad on the grounds that it would be too noisy, he asked the chairman: "Would you like to walk down Washington Street, sir, and have it grown with grass, and not a noise to be heard, so that you could hear a pin drop, the whole length of the street? Is that what you want in Boston? Is it not desirable to have some noise, some bustle, some dust, something to show that the restless energy of man is at work there?" If anyone "is afraid of noise and bustle," Child told the committee, "he had better leave Boston and go to Salem."[34]

Some Americans were also concerned about the dispersion of residences. The growth of downtown, they pointed out, drove middle- and upper-middle-class families from the center to the periphery. Left in their wake, amid stores, lofts, warehouses, and offices, were single men, mostly lower and working class, who lived in boarding houses, cheap hotels, and tenement houses. This change created two problems, both of which seemed to grow increasingly serious in the late nineteenth century. One was fiscal. As these Americans saw it, the exodus of the well-to-do threatened to erode the tax base of the cities. In the absence of sales and income taxes, the cities relied on property taxes for the bulk of their revenue. As residential dispersal picked up, more and more property owners paid taxes not to the cities in which they worked but to the suburbs in which they lived. At a time when municipal expenditures and indebtedness were soaring—a time when, as historian Clifton K. Yearley has pointed out, the financial machinery of most big cities was breaking down— this development aroused a good deal of concern.[35]

The other problem was political. As some Americans pointed out, the exodus of the middle and upper middle classes threatened to undermine the governance of the city. Effective governance, it was widely believed, depended on these groups. As Helen Campbell, who later organized the Consumers' League of New York, put it, "The poor are too poor, the rich too rich, to be anything but indifferent as to whether the city government is administered economically or otherwise." But the middle and upper middle classes, among whose ranks were found "the best citizens," were moving to the suburbs. "If the best citizens slumber in the suburbs," warned Reverend Amory H. Bradford, "the worst will run and ruin the cities." New York's *Real Estate Record and*

Builders' Guide, which usually reflected the views of the downtown property owners, took much the same position, declaring that the governance of the city was far too important to be left in the hands of the few remaining residents. "It will never do," the journal wrote in 1879, "to commit the future control of the metropolis to the 'longshoremen, the porters, the office cleaners and the watchmen, who will be the main occupants of the few residences in the business part of Manhattan Island." Bradford and others also believed that this exodus would accelerate the polarization of urban society, its division into a plutocracy and a proletariat. At a time when many Americans feared that the nation was on the verge of class warfare this prospect aroused a good deal of concern too.[36]

But most Americans did not share these concerns. To the contrary, they regarded residential dispersal as an extremely auspicious development—"by far the most cheering movement of modern times," declared Adna Weber. They believed that the suburb was, in Olmsted's words, "the most attractive, the most refined, the most soundly wholesome" form of domestic life. For professionals and businessmen the suburbs offered a haven from the workplace, an idyllic setting in which they would do a little gardening in the morning and, after returning from a hard day downtown, dine with the family and maybe sit outdoors, reading a paper and smoking a cigar, under "their own semi-rustic 'vine and fig-tree.'" For working people, the suburbs provided an escape from the tenement houses, which were seen by many as the breeding ground of most urban problems—as, in the words of E. R. L. Gould, a leader of the model tenement movement, "standing menaces to the family, to morality, to the public health, and to civic integrity." The move to the suburbs, it was also believed, promoted the rise of home ownership, the benefits of which were spelled out by the *Detroit Free Press* in the mid 1860s. The man who owns his own home feels that he has "an interest in society," it wrote, and "becomes a better citizen and supporter of the local, State, and national governments under which he lives, [one who] sustains all regulations looking to quiet and good order."[37]

Many Americans also downplayed the fiscal impact of residential dispersal. Suppose, they reasoned, many middle- and upper-middle-class residents moved to the suburbs. They would still work, shop, do business, and seek entertainment in the cities. As a result the cities would become "more and more an exchange and mart for commerce," wrote New York's *Real Estate Record and Builders' Guide* in the late 1870s—if "less and less a place for living." So just as residential property would become more valuable in the suburbs, commercial property would become more valuable in the cities. As the cities' property values went up, so would their property taxes. By this logic, residential dispersal would ease the cities' fiscal problems, not aggravate them. Many Americans also downplayed the political impact of residential dispersal. They thought there were other ways to ensure the middle and upper middle classes more of a say in municipal government than to discourage the movement to the suburbs. One was to incorporate the suburbs into the cities, another to put the metropolitan district under a single government. Although the schemes for metropolitan government went nowhere, Philadelphia, Chicago, New York, and other cities expanded their boundaries in the mid and late nineteenth century. And despite evidence of growing opposition to annexation and consolidation in the suburbs, Americans assumed that the cities would continue to expand in the years ahead.[38]

Some Americans objected to the separation of businesses and residences. One of them was O. B. Bunce, a publisher, playwright, and novelist and editor of *Appletons' Journal*, a New York periodical, in the early 1870s. To Bunce, the separation of dwellings from shops, clubs, and cultural institutions was inimical to city life. "A man who loves the town desires to walk out his front door into all its activities," Bunce wrote in 1872. "He does not want to undertake a journey every time the opera, the theatre, the club, the art-gallery, or the library, is to be visited." Even if rapid transit one day connected the periphery with the center, the journey would need much planning and take much time. A vibrant metropolis, one that provided the "mental stimulus" of city life, is more than "a collection of villages," Bunce claimed. It thrives on compactness, not diffusion, by mixing, not segregating, activities. Cities should turn inward, not outward; they should encourage intensive development in the center, not low-density development on the periphery. With the advances in elevator technology and fireproof construction, Bunce wrote, it was now possible to build tall apartment houses in the middle of cities. Crowned with roof gardens, the apartment houses would offer residents fresh air and other suburban amenities without depriving them of "spontaneous and immediate" access to the pleasures of city life.[39]

Other Americans objected not so much to the separation of businesses and residences as to the consequences thereof. By far the most troublesome were the traffic jams that tied up the major thoroughfares, especially during rush hour. This "diurnal stampede," as one journalist called it, was exasperating. But it was inevitable—at least as long as so many Americans were obliged to travel a long way twice every day between their home and their workplace. Some Americans were so troubled by these traffic jams that they urged their countrymen to adopt the European practice of separating businesses and residences vertically rather than horizontally—a step that would have reduced commuting and thereby relieved congestion. Businesses and residences could be separated as effectively by one story as by several blocks, wrote *American Architect and Building News* in the late 1870s. The journal favored "reserving the one or two lower stories of the buildings over the greater part of the city for shops and offices, and the upper stories for dwellings which have no connection with the business premises below." As late as the early 1900s *American Architect* was still insisting that "there is no good reason why the retail-shop with apartments occupying the upper stories should not be the rule in this country as it is abroad."[40]

But most Americans did not object to the separation of businesses and residences. Far from it. The good community, they thought, was one in which the home was separate from the workplace—one in which, as Charles Mulford Robinson, a well-known city planner, wrote in the early twentieth century, people no longer live above their shops and "sleep within call of the factory whistle." A residential neighborhood had no place for stores and offices, much less for lofts and warehouses. Amid residences, Richard Hurd declared, these businesses were a "nuisance," a veritable danger to the community. Given these sentiments, it was little wonder that when business invaded a residential street or square the well-to-do "flee before it," in the words of *American Architect and Building News,* "as from a pestilence." To put it another way, most Americans did not want to live above the store. Rather than vertical separation of businesses and residences, they preferred horizontal separation—or, as *American Architect* put it, the separation "of quarters as well as premises." Horizontal separation was desirable, wrote Olmsted. "If a house to be used for many different purposes must have many rooms and passages of various dimensions and variously lighted and furnished, not less must [the] metropolis be specially adapted at different points to different ends." It was also feasible, said Weber. "All that is needed is cheap and rapid transit between the home and the workplace."[41]

Just as most Americans did not want to live above the store, neither did they want to live above one another. As one midwesterner observed in the mid 1870s, "ninety-nine Chicago families in every hundred will go an hour's ride into the country, or toward the country, rather than live under or above another family." Philadelphians felt the same way, remarked the *Philadelphia Real Estate Record and Builders' Guide.* The Parisian flat, six, seven, and eight stories high, "is with us an impossibility," wrote *Appletons' Journal.* Whereas the Parisian "*lives* out-of-doors," on the boulevards, the American "attaches more importance to the secluded comforts and pleasures of a home." As a rule he was more than ready to sacrifice easy access to shops, clubs, and cultural institutions in order to reside in a single-family house in a suburban setting. Unlike Bunce, most Americans were not favorably impressed by apartment houses—not even by the luxurious apartment houses built for the upper middle class in the late nineteenth century. Apartments, they believed, provided less space and privacy than single-family homes, not to mention fewer personal comforts and none of the moral benefits. Tainted by association with tenements, apartment houses also raised a specter of promiscuity that seemed to threaten both family and society. The apartment house is "the most dangerous enemy American domesticity has had to encounter," *Architectural Record* declared in the early twentieth century.[42]

Rivalry among cities was natural, Americans believed—as natural, wrote Richard B. Watrous, secretary of the American Civic Association, as rivalry among individuals, nations, business interests, and political parties. Also natural was rivalry among suburbs, a notable example of which was the vigorous competition of the residential communities of northern New York City, southern Westchester County, eastern Long Island, and western New Jersey. What was not natural, Americans believed, was rivalry within cities and rivalry between cities and suburbs. What was not natural was rivalry between the business district and the residential districts, between the center and the periphery, between downtown and uptown. Underlying this belief was the assumption that the metropolis was, in the words of one historian, "an interdependent system of differentiated but complementary parts," a system wherein each part operated in harmony with every other. The business district was the most important part. It was the part, wrote the *Baltimore Sun* in the aftermath of the great fire that destroyed much of downtown Baltimore in 1904, "from which the entire population must draw its sustenance, either directly or indirectly." But the residential districts were also a very important part, the part from which most Americans derived their personal well-being. A city needed both parts. And each needed the other. "Broadway and Wall Street are as necessary to the suburbs," an observer wrote in the early 1850s, "as the suburbs are to them."[43]

According to the conventional wisdom, the suburbs did not pose a threat to the cities. As New York's *Real Estate Record and Builders' Guide* wrote (with some exaggeration) in the late 1870s, the middle and working classes were moving from the city to the suburbs, leaving behind the very rich and very poor. But it was not as if New York was losing people to other cities, to such rivals as Boston, Philadelphia, and Baltimore. Indeed, the *Real Estate Record* said, "It is idle to deplore the fancied loss of our population when we can point to teeming multitudes on the surrounding hills and valleys," the outlying districts of metropolitan New York. Moreover, no matter how appealing the suburbs were as places to live, they would never be attractive as places to work. "The exchanges, the factories, the storehouses, the homes of the arts and sciences," the *Real Estate Record* declared, "will ever find their most congenial atmosphere and favorable conditions within the city proper." Thus the more people went to the suburbs to live, the more they would come to the city to work—and "to amuse themselves, to make purchases and to transact business." Or as the Chicago *Real Estate and Building Journal* put it in 1888, the growth of the "tributary districts" would increase the demand for "trading places 'down town.'"[44]

Nor, according to the conventional wisdom, did the cities pose a threat to the suburbs. Although the suburbs depended on the cities for their livelihood (and for a wide range of goods and services), the cities depended on the suburbs for their amenities. Just as the suburbs could not survive without the cities, so, Olmsted said in the late 1860s, "no great town can long exist without great suburbs." The suburbs had their boosters. But unlike city boosters, they held that the growth of their community depended, in the words of John Ford, editor of the *Cambridge Chronicle,* on "its attractions as a place of residence." The suburbs would thrive not by competing with the cities for commerce and industry but by competing with other suburbs for the middle- and upper-middle-class families that were seeking to escape the burdens of urban life—the noise, filth, and tumult, the crime, disorder, and poverty. They would prosper by offering prospective homeowners a vision of the good community, a rustic, spacious, largely homogeneous, and almost exclusively residential environment, an environment that emphasized the home, rather than the workplace, and stressed the cult of domesticity, as opposed to the cult of efficiency.[45]

The belief in spatial harmony was so deep-seated that it flourished amid the fears of social conflict that erupted in urban America in the late nineteenth century. Americans held to the belief that the parts of the city were in accord at the same time they adhered to the position that the people of the city were on the verge of class warfare. And they hailed the separation of the city into business and residential districts at the same time they deplored the polarization of society into a plutocracy and a proletariat. This deep-seated belief in spatial harmony was nicely reflected in the metaphors commonly used to describe the city. The city was like "a house of many chambers," wrote J. F. Harder, a New York architect. Writing at the end of the nineteenth century, Harder said:

"Its waterways, bridges, railroads and highways are the entrances, vestibules and exits; its public buildings are the drawing rooms, its streets the halls and corridors, the manufacturing districts the kitchens and workshops; tunnels and subways are its cellars, and its rookeries the attic; the parks and recreation places are its gardens, and its systems for communication, lighting and drainage are the furniture."[46] Americans also likened the city to a wheel, albeit a very large wheel. According to this metaphor, the business district was the hub, the major streets and street railways were the spokes, the city borders were the rim, and the residential sections were located along the spokes, between the hub and the rim.

By far the most common of these metaphors was the human body. Speaking of New York, a visitor from South Carolina remarked in the early 1850s that the city was like "a human being": "The City Hall [is] the heart, the Tombs [a downtown jail] the stomach, the Five Points [a notorious slum] the bowels, the Parks the lungs, Broadway the nose, the Piers the feet (as from these the travelling commences), Wall-street the pocket, the hotels the mouth, the theatres the eyes, the Bowery the aorta, the Avenues the veins, and Nassau and Ann streets the brains."[47] This metaphor grew more popular in the late nineteenth century, when many social scientists espoused the view that society was analogous to a human organism and that the laws of society were analogous to the laws of the organic universe. In the meantime this metaphor became more precise (if less complex), as Americans gradually reached a consensus about the relationship between specific parts of the city and specific parts of the body. By the end of the century, if not earlier, the parks were commonly regarded as the "lungs" of the city, the streets as the "arteries," the depots and wharves as the "mouth," the telegraph and telephone lines as the "nervous system," and the business district, not the city hall, as the "heart." Indeed downtown was called "the heart of the city" virtually everywhere, even in cities like Chicago (and later St. Louis and Omaha), where it was popularly known as "the Loop," a name that caught on a decade before the elevated railway loop was built.

A house, a wheel, and the human body are quite different. But as metaphors of the American city they had a few things in common. Unlike, say, a volcano, a popular metaphor of American society in the late nineteenth century, they were reassuring. They were also apolitical. The "interests" (if they can be called that) of the hub, spokes, and rim were the same. So were the "interests" of the different rooms of a house and the different organs of the body. Yet another thing these metaphors had in common was that they consisted of separate parts, all of which were vital to the well-being of the others. As a Baltimore resident put it, "Just as in the human body, the hand or the head or the heart cannot be sick by itself, but the whole body is sick; just as a fever from a wounded limb spread to every part of the frame, so with this body [the city] of ours." Applied to the city, these metaphors strengthened the idea of harmony among its parts, and especially between the center and the periphery. Just as the body could not thrive without a sound heart, so, Americans assumed, the city could not thrive without a vibrant downtown. Reflecting the prevailing view at the end of the nineteenth century, *Building Managers Magazine* pointed out a couple decades later: "The business district of a city is as important to the welfare of the whole city as the heart is to the whole body. If the heart is weak or congested, or does not function properly, the mind is sluggish; the spirit is depressed; the extremities lose strength and the whole body suffers."[48]

The belief in spatial harmony was especially deep-seated among the downtown businessmen and property owners. It was reflected not only in what they said but in what they did—and in what they did not do. A notable example was their disinclination to organize voluntary associations to promote the interests of downtown. To put their behavior in perspective, it is useful to bear in mind that during the late nineteenth century Americans formed a legion of such associations to defend the interests of other parts of the city. These associations appeared in New York in the late 1860s and surfaced later in Chicago, Baltimore, Cincinnati, and San Francisco. They proliferated everywhere in the 1880s and 1890s, by which time most cities had dozens of them. Organized along neighborhood or other territorial lines, these associations were designed to supplement the ward and other political organizations and provide property owners an additional (and presumably a highly responsive) voice in municipal affairs. Whether called improvement associations, taxpayers' associations, or property owners' associations, they all engaged in much the same types of activities. They pushed the municipal authorities to open, widen, and pave streets, to build sewers, schools, and parks, and to get rid of nuisances. They also called for street railway extensions and rapid transit lines—indeed for virtually anything that would give their part of the city a competitive edge over other parts and thereby increase its property values.[49]

By the end of the nineteenth century these associations were operating just about everywhere in the cities—everywhere, that is, except downtown. As the New York *Real Estate Record and Builders' Guide* reported in 1901, Manhattan and the Bronx were covered by these organizations; a few districts, such as the Upper West Side and Washington Heights, had as many as four or five of them. Other than a small portion of ward 21, which ran from East Twenty-

sixth to East Forty-second streets, the only district that did not have an association was lower Manhattan, the site of downtown New York. The story was
much the same in other cities. As Chicago's Subway Advisory Commission
pointed out in the mid 1920s, the downtown business interests had never
seen fit to organize an association to promote the well-being of the Loop. "[Of]
all the important districts of Chicago, the most important of all appears to be
the only district without *some* sort of district organization." Many cities had
downtown clubs of one kind or another, but they were strictly social clubs that
offered businessmen a place to dine, meet, and relax, as opposed to quasi-po-
litical bodies whose purpose was to lobby on behalf of the business district. All
cities also had chambers of commerce, merchants' associations, and boards
of trade. But as a leader of the Chicago Association of Commerce pointed out
in 1911, these citywide groups watched out for the interests of the entire city,
not just of the business district.[50]

One reason the downtown business interests were disinclined to organize
associations of their own was that they thought the citywide commercial organizations, of which they were usually the most influential members, would
suffice. Indeed, the outlying business interests would later complain that
these citywide organizations were too attentive to the welfare of the downtown business interests. The second reason was that the downtown businessmen and property owners believed that the interests of downtown and the
other parts of the city were the same. As the Chicago Subway Advisory Commission put it, the outlying districts may be rivals, but the downtown district
"is the unquestioned and intimate partner of all [of them]." The first downtown association I know of was formed in San Francisco, but not until 1906,
when in the wake of the earthquake and fire that destroyed the center of the
city some downtown retailers rented space on Van Ness Avenue, about a mile
west of the business district. Fearing a general relocation of retail trade, a
group of downtown business and real estate interests organized the Down
Town Property Owners' Association, which mounted a campaign to rebuild
the business district as quickly as possible and thereby stabilize the retail district. Although the campaign was successful, it did not inspire other cities to
follow San Francisco's lead.[51]

The deep-seated belief in spatial harmony notwithstanding, rivalry within
cities was widespread in the late nineteenth century. In New York, for example, downtown property owners saw no reason their property taxes should be
spent for the benefit of what one city official called "uptown corner lot speculators." Some New Yorkers also complained that the elevated railways enhanced the value of uptown property at the expense of downtown property, es-

pecially downtown property along which the railways ran. Many Bostonians opposed els on these grounds too. In Pittsburgh and other cities the outlying districts were resentful that the business district was normally the first to get water mains, sewer lines, and paved streets. Intra-city rivalry took another form in Black Rock, an old neighborhood two miles from downtown Buffalo, where some boosters worried that the extension of a streetcar line from downtown would "drain completely the life-blood of Black Rock." Once the line is built, one of them asked, "How long do you think the people of the Rock will continue to patronize their local merchants?" New York and Chicago real estate journals made similar points, predicting that the elevated railways would so facilitate movement between the center and the periphery that they would sap the vitality of neighborhood and suburban stores. The els would leave the midway districts "barren and desolate," warned Chicago's *Real Estate and Building Journal*.[52]

Another form of intra-city rivalry pitted one part of downtown against another or against a nearby section that aspired to become part of downtown. A striking example was the battle over the site for the new Philadelphia city hall that started in the late 1860s. On one side were businessmen and property owners from ward 5, the home of the old business district, who lobbied for Independence Square and, after it was ruled out, for Washington Square, two sites that would have stabilized downtown Philadelphia. On the other side were business interests from ward 9, the home of a new business section west of downtown, who preferred Penn Square, a site that would have accelerated the westward drift of the business district. After a long struggle, the voters selected the Penn Square site. Similar fights occurred elsewhere. In Omaha rival property owners fought to channel the growth of downtown in different directions, one to the west and another to the south. In spite of vigorous opposition from property owners in the eastern part of central Omaha, downtown moved west along Farnam Street. In San Francisco William C. Ralston, one of the wealthiest of California's mining kings, waged a long campaign to move the business district south of Market Street. Although he invested a fortune, much of it in the building of the luxurious Palace Hotel, his campaign failed.[53]

Although Americans were aware of the rivalry within cities, they tended to downplay or disregard it. One reason was that intra-city rivalry was much less pervasive and intense than inter-city rivalry. One of the most remarkable features of urban America, inter-city rivalry started in the colonial period, when coastal towns competed with each other for a share of the trade with Western Europe and the West Indies, and reached a peak in the nineteenth century, especially in the Midwest, where local boosters vied with one another to turn small towns into large cities and large cities into great metropolises.[54] Another reason was that in the face of such fierce inter-city rivalry, many businessmen and newspaper publishers believed it was vital to stress the harmony of the community. In the competition for commerce, industry, and capital, the success of a town or city might well depend on the ability of its residents to persuade outside investors that they could work together. Yet another reason was that intra-city rivalry, especially rivalry between the center and the periphery, ran counter to the belief in the interdependence of the business and residential districts and to the assumption that the interests of downtown and the other parts of the city were the same.

By the late nineteenth century Americans could no more imagine a city without a downtown than they could a skyscraper without an elevator. Although they realized that the city would change over time, they did not believe that the changes would endanger downtown. How Americans envisaged the future of downtown was revealed in a supplement about New York City that was published on December 30, 1900, by the *New York World*, the flagship of Joseph Pulitzer's newspaper empire. The highlight of the supplement, which was titled "New York as It Will Be in 1999: Pictorial Forecast of the City," were two bird's-eye views by Louis Biedermann, a veteran newspaper illustrator. One was of downtown New York and the other, a less detailed drawing, of metropolitan New York. As Biedermann depicted it, downtown New York would be a business district par excellence in 1999. It would be much larger, spreading north into upper Manhattan and east into Brooklyn, and far denser, covered by huge box-like skyscrapers, which were linked by elevated sidewalks and aerial walkways and crowned by flat roofs for airship landings. Connecting Manhattan with the outlying residential districts (and also connecting some of these districts with each other) would be more than two dozen bridges and tunnels.[55] As Biedermann and others saw it, downtown would develop into a more concentrated and less populated business district in the years ahead, one whose well-being depended on the maintenance of the equilibrium between residential dispersal and business concentration in the American metropolis.

The origins of this vision went back at least as far as the mid nineteenth century. As early as 1843, more than half a century before the *World* published its supplement, Caleb Woodhull, a New York businessman, observed that there were parts of Manhattan devoted exclusively to business, parts "in which no one dwells." In time, he predicted, "the whole island will be covered with store houses, and the residences of those doing business there will be on the opposite shores and in contiguous counties." Such predictions later became routine. Early in the 1880s A. B. Mullett, who had gone into private practice in New York after serving as supervising architect of the U.S. Treasury Department, told a journalist that henceforth "concentration will be the rule in the business part of the city"—and diffusion the rule in the residential districts. In time lower Manhattan "will be to the upper portion of the city what the city of London is to the rest of the metropolis of Great Britain." Another New Yorker who saw the future in much the same way was George E. Waring, who was famous for reforming the city's sanitation department. Manhattan will eventually be covered completely by skyscrapers, parks, and public buildings, he predicted in the late 1890s. As more and more New Yorkers move to the outer boroughs—as well as to New Jersey and Westchester County—"it is not unlikely that the whole island will be largely abandoned as a place for residences."[56]

Other cities would develop along the same lines as New York, though presumably at a less rapid pace. Writing in the late 1850s, Sidney George Fisher—a Philadelphian who was trained as a lawyer but preferred the life of a gentlemen farmer—noted that street railways were facilitating a wide dispersal of residential areas. Before long, he predicted, everyone will have a suburban villa or country home, with all the advantages of "pure air, gardens and rural pleasures," and "cities will be mere collections of shops, warehouses, factories and places of business." A decade later a journalist wrote that one day "the smoky abyss" of Pittsburgh would be occupied only by factories and other businesses, whose employees would reside elsewhere, "deny[ing] themselves the privilege of living in the smoke." Writing in the mid 1870s, a Cincinnati booster forecast that in time businesses would fully occupy the city's flatlands and residences would spread over the surrounding hills. And late in the 1880s *California Architect and Building News* predicted that while San Francisco's residents would move into the hills (and the adjacent counties) its businessmen would remain downtown, "even if they have to go twenty stories" high to do so.[57]

Some Americans thought these forecasts were exaggerated. Although they conceded that much of downtown would one day be devoted exclusively to business, they doubted that the center of the city would ever be completely depopulated. Most workingmen could not afford to move to the periphery, they pointed out: the costs of housing and commuting were too high. As an official of the U.S. Census Bureau observed at the turn of the century, "suburban life is still almost wholly confined to the well-to-do." To the dismay of tenement-

Louis Biedermann's "Pictorial Forecast" of New York City

(New York World *Supplement, December 30, 1900*)

house reformers like Robert W. De Forest, recent immigrants from Italy and Russia preferred to live near the center of the city. They were willing to put up with overcrowded and unsanitary tenements in order to be close to one another and to their common cultural and religious institutions. Some of the very rich also preferred to live near the center, usually in town houses or spacious apartments located in well-insulated enclaves not far from their offices and easily accessible to the clubs, museums, and other upper-class institutions so important to O. B. Bunce. Nor was the demand for commercial space limitless, the New York *Real Estate Record and Builders' Guide* pointed out. Although it had once predicted that businesses would one day drive residences out of Manhattan, it later changed its mind, arguing that with the coming of the skyscraper businesses would not require "a space anything as large as Manhattan" for another hundred years.[58]

Some Americans also thought these forecasts were incomplete. Most businesses would remain downtown, but as residents moved to outlying sections some businesses would follow them. One New Yorker predicted that the retail district would move north of Central Park and that the theater district would end up in Washington Heights, near the northern end of Manhattan. Another New Yorker went even further, writing that one day "our daughters will shop at the palatial dry-goods stores on Jerome avenue [in the Bronx] just as our wives now do on 6th avenue [in Manhattan]." Andrew H. Green, known as the "Father of Greater New York" for his efforts to consolidate New York with Brooklyn, Queens, and Staten Island, predicted that a subsidiary financial and business district would arise around 125th Street in upper Manhattan. And *American Architect and Building News* argued at the turn of the century that "in New York, as in London, it may, before long, be necessary to establish branches of the great banks and life-insurance offices in the different boroughs." Probably the most famous advocate of this position was the English author H. G. Wells. Widely read in the United States, Wells predicted that residential dispersal, along with advances in transportation and communication, would lead inevitably to the decentralization of business. The center would survive, but as "a bazaar, a great gallery of shops and places of concourse," not as a full-scale business district.[59]

Few Americans subscribed to Wells's position. Most believed that the dispersal of residences and the concentration of businesses would continue indefinitely. They thought that no matter where people resided, they would travel downtown every day; that the more they went to the periphery to live, the more they would come to the center to work, to shop, to do business, and to amuse themselves; that the greater the demand for residential property in the outlying districts, the greater the demand for commercial property in the business district. As one journalist put it, the exodus of residents from New York to New Jersey, Long Island, and Westchester County "does not mean that there will be fewer people coming to [do] business in Manhattan. It means that there will be more." From this it followed that the business district would become more concentrated, if less populated, in the years ahead. James B. Richardson, a Bostonian who served on the Massachusetts Rapid Transit Commission of 1892, nicely summed up the prevailing view. Referring to downtown Boston, he stated, "I cannot anticipate *any* time when this district will be less populous, less frequented, or less resorted to for the same or other kinds of business, or for pleasure, than it is now."[60] At the end of the nineteenth century few Bostonians—or, for that matter, few New Yorkers or San Franciscans—would have disagreed with him.

2 Derailing the Subways:
The Politics of
Rapid Transit

Downtown Boston, the Massachusetts Rapid Transit Commission of 1892 pointed out, was "the heart of the city," "literally, as well as metaphorically." As Mayor Nathan Matthews, Jr., chair of the commission, observed in 1894, it was there, on a "few acres between the Common and the harbor," that Greater Boston, a community of roughly one million, did its business. It was this district—a district, said Matthews, that was "smaller, more contracted, more congested than any similar part of any other large city in the world"—to which hundreds of thousands rushed in every morning and from which they rushed out every evening. Matthews and the other commissioners believed that people would routinely go downtown, provided they could get there quickly and conveniently. And if so, it followed that accessibility was the key to the well-being of downtown. It was accessibility that gave value to business property, declared Benjamin F. Butler, a former Civil War general, ex-congressman from Massachusetts, and sometime elevated railroad promoter. And it was accessibility, more than anything else, that concerned downtown businessmen and property owners. "Bring the people to our doors," J. D. Wallace urged a member of the Chicago city council, "and we will do the rest."[1]

By virtue of the separation of businesses and residences, few Americans lived within walking distance of downtown. To get there, some—5 to 10 percent in Philadelphia and 10 to 15 percent in New York—took ferries. Others—more than 20 percent in Boston and Minneapolis—came by steam railroads, most of which ran between the cities and the suburbs. But outside of New York, where many rode the elevated railroads, the great majority, perhaps as many as 80 percent in some cities, went downtown on the street railways (or streetcars). These vehicles, two-thirds of which were drawn by horses until the 1890s, when they were replaced by electricity, ran along tracks that radiated from the business district to the residential sections. Commonly likened to the arteries of the body and spokes of a wheel, the street railways made downtown accessible. By carrying tens and even hundreds of thousands of people to the center, they made possible the huge department stores, tall office buildings, and other large-scale downtown enterprises.[2] In other words, they made the separation of businesses and residences a hallmark of the American metropolis in the late nineteenth century.

The street railway first appeared in the 1830s. After a sluggish start, it caught on in the 1850s and 1860s and supplanted the omnibus, a slow, unreliable, and uncomfortable stagecoach, as the primary means of mass transit in urban America. The industry expanded at a stupendous pace during the next two decades. By 1890 close to 800 companies operated more than 32,000 streetcars along almost 6,000 miles of line and carried roughly two billion passengers, nearly four-fifths of them in the nation's twenty largest cities. In no other country were the street railways so highly developed and so heavily patronized. Philadelphia, the third largest city, had 277 miles of street railways, about average for an American city of its size, but more than three times as many miles per capita as Berlin, more than five times as many as Paris, and more than eight times as many as London (excluding the Underground). Philadelphians rode the street railways slightly less often than the residents of other American cities. Yet what transit engineers would later call the riding habit—the average number of rides per capita per year—was nearly twice as high in Philadelphia as in Berlin, more than twice as high as in London (the Underground included), and almost four times as high as in Vienna. During the 1890s, when the street railways were electrified, the riding habit soared in Philadelphia and other American cities, doubling in some, tripling in others, and reached levels unmatched anywhere else in the world.[3]

Although a great improvement over the omnibus, the street railway left much to be desired. The cars were very crowded, especially during rush hour. "People are packed into them like sardines in a box, with perspiration for oil," wrote the New York Herald in 1864. "The seats being more than filled, the passengers are placed in rows down the middle, where they hang on by the straps, like smoked hams in a corner grocery." Passengers are packed so tightly, a New Yorker remarked, "that no man can tell which legs are his own, and which his neighbor's." The cars were badly heated in winter, poorly ventilated in summer, pervaded by "the fumes of bad rum and worse tobacco," plagued by pickpockets, and prone to occasional accidents and periodic breakdowns. Worst of all, the streetcars were very slow, running only four to six miles an hour under normal conditions and one to two miles an hour in heavy traffic. They were so slow in New York that many residents spent two hours or more a day commuting to work. It was easier to cross the Great American Desert than Manhattan Island, the *Tribune* quipped. A Cambridge resident complained that it took him as long to get to downtown Boston, five miles away by streetcar, as it took his friends in Worcester, forty miles away by steam railroad. The electric railways went much faster than the horse cars in the outlying areas, but they too slowed to a crawl in the business districts. Jammed up, one on top of the other, they were "slower than a parade of cripples," said the *California Outlook* in 1911.[4]

As early as the mid 1860s some New Yorkers began to voice doubts that the street railways—or, for that matter, any form of surface transit—could be relied upon to carry people quickly and comfortably between the residential sections and the business district. During the next two or three decades these doubts grew, not only in New York, but also in Boston, Chicago, Philadelphia, and other cities. Fueling the doubts was an awareness that most of the main streets were already lined with streetcar tracks, on many of which, a Bostonian noted, "there can hardly be a place found between two cars from morning to night." The streetcar companies could have built additional tracks on the surface, but it would have been very expensive. In many cases the cost of widening the street alone would have been prohibitive. It would have been self-defeating, too. Additional tracks would have meant more streetcars; and more streetcars would have meant heavier traffic. Thus during the late nineteenth century, first in New York and later in other cities, many Americans came to the conclusion that there was only one way to transport people to and from the business district. And that was to separate the through traffic from the ordinary traffic, and especially from the carts, wagons, and carriages that clogged the main streets and blocked the major intersections. The only way to do that was to build a rapid transit system, a system that ran (on its own right of way) above or below the ground—in other words, a system of elevated railways or subways.[5]

The els came first. Built by private enterprise, they went up in New York in the 1870s and 1880s and in Brooklyn and Chicago not long after. Several companies made plans to erect els in Boston, Philadelphia, and other cities. If these plans had been carried out, most big cities would have had rapid transit by the late nineteenth and early twentieth centuries. But els aroused furious opposition, in the face of which advocates of rapid transit focused their efforts on promoting subways instead. During the late 1890s they prevailed on public authorities to build the nation's first subway in Boston and to begin building its largest in New York. Even before the New York subway was completed, Americans had come to believe that if rapid transit was to be built it should be built underground. This was a momentous turn of events, one that was not lost on downtown businessmen and property owners in cities other than Boston and New York. And starting around the turn of the century, they mounted campaigns to build subways in Philadelphia, Pittsburgh, Cleveland, Cincinnati, Detroit, Chicago, St. Louis, San Francisco, Los Angeles, Seattle, and other big cities. The downtown business interests were confident that it was only a matter of time before they succeeded. But by 1930, if not earlier, it was clear they were wrong. Their campaigns failed everywhere but in Philadelphia.[6] And they failed for a number of reasons other than the development and proliferation of private automobiles in the first third of the twentieth century.

A good place to start the story is New York in the mid 1860s, when many residents, fed up with the street railways, decided that the city badly needed some kind of rapid transit. What kind was anything but clear. Of the scores of ingenious (if not necessarily practical) plans devised between the mid 1860s and mid 1870s, some called for els, others for subways, and at least one for both. To complicate matters, some els stood on columns, others on a viaduct; some subways were covered, others open; and though most lines ran over or under the streets, some even went through buildings. Few New Yorkers knew what to make of these plans. Even the experts were divided. After reviewing dozens of plans in the mid 1860s, a special commission appointed by the New York State Senate came out in favor of subways, partly on the grounds that els were as yet untested. Less than a decade later a blue-ribbon committee of the American Society of Civil Engineers reported that subways were too expensive and recommended els instead. Some New Yorkers insisted that it did not matter whether rapid transit went above or below ground. The issue, they held, was not els versus subways—"Both are good," wrote the *Times* in 1866; either will do, said the *Real Estate Record and Builders' Guide* two years later— but rapid transit versus surface transit.[7] It might not have mattered much to them, but it mattered a great deal to others, especially the promoters of the proposed els and subways and the property owners along their routes.

For a while it seemed that New York would follow the lead of London, where private enterprise had just constructed the world's first subway. In 1864, a year after the London Underground opened, the Metropolitan Railway Company, formed by Hugh B. Willson, a Michigan railroad man, and backed by John J. Astor, Jr., and other wealthy New Yorkers, asked the state legislature for a charter to build a subway under Broadway, the city's busiest and most congested street. To the dismay of the *Times* and others who believed that a subway would have been "an immense boon to the city," the company's bill died in committee. The legislature passed a similar bill at the next session, but the governor vetoed it. And though the company kept trying, it was unable to obtain a charter. The Metropolitan's efforts were thwarted by the vigorous opposition of the powerful omnibus and streetcar companies, which feared that a subway would siphon off much of their business. No less important were the strenuous objections of the Broadway merchants and property owners, who were worried that the construction of the subway would block access to their stores and undermine the stability of their buildings. Exacerbating the Metropolitan's difficulties were the lobbying efforts of rival companies, which were seeking charters of their own to operate railways on, above, and under Broadway. If all this were not enough, some New Yorkers, including Alfred W. Craven, engineer of the Croton Aqueduct, were afraid that the excavation for the subway would disrupt the city's water supply and damage its sewer system.[8]

During the late 1860s and early 1870s other companies picked up where the Metropolitan left off. Among them were the New York City Central Underground Railroad Company, the New York City Rapid Transit Company, and the Metropolitan Transit Company, which proposed to build a combined underground, surface, and elevated railway along a private right of way through the middle of blocks. In the battle for a charter, these companies had two advantages over the old Metropolitan. They were willing to operate on streets other than Broadway, thus avoiding a major source of opposition. And they had the strong support of uptown property owners, who believed that rapid transit would enhance the value of their real estate. A few of these companies were able to obtain a charter, but none was able to raise the capital. A subway would cost a fortune, around $1–2 million per mile, or nearly twenty times as much as the most expensive streetcar line. And though the subway would be much faster than the streetcar, it would also be less pleasant and possibly more dangerous. Thus no one knew how much business a subway would do, especially if it did not run along Broadway. Indeed, no one even knew whether New Yorkers would willingly descend into what one journal called "a smoky, stinking, noisome hole in the ground." Given this uncertainty, investors were reluctant to get involved in subways, especially when the London Underground, which was very heavily patronized, paid only 4 percent a year, a small return by American standards.[9]

Short of capital, often beset by managerial problems, the companies foundered. By the early 1870s they had nothing to show for their efforts other than a short experimental tunnel built by the Beach Pneumatic Transit Company, whose chief distinction was that it planned to use compressed air rather than steam to run its trains. If prospects for a subway were dim, prospects for an el were not much brighter. The efforts to build an el, which began in the late 1860s, were opposed "at every step," wrote an official of the U.S. Census Office.

> Horse-railroad companies and property-holders brought suits and laid injunctions at every move. Charters were declared unconstitutional, and cases were carried from tribunal to tribunal. The community cried out in anguish that the noise would kill business, the unsightly objects destroy the beauty of the city, and the moving of trains in the air frighten horses and endanger human lives. Neither the Erie canal nor the Croton aqueduct encountered more fierce and determined opposition.[10]

The opposition was too much for Charles T. Harvey's West Side and Yonkers Patent Railway, the world's first elevated railroad. With the approval of the state legislature and the backing of local businessmen, Harvey built a short one-track el, driven by cables attached to stationary steam engines, along Greenwich Street in 1868. But in the attempt to extend the line along Ninth Avenue to the New York Central depot at Thirtieth Street, the railroad had trouble raising capital. It was also plagued by frequent breakdowns, occasional accidents, and a stream of lawsuits, most of them brought by rival streetcar companies and abutting property owners. Late in 1870, by which time Harvey had been forced out of the company and his cable system had been discredited, the West Side and Yonkers went out of business.

Despite this inauspicious start, efforts to build els continued. In the forefront were two companies, the New York Elevated Railroad, the successor to the defunct West Side and Yonkers, and the Gilbert Elevated Railway, which was chartered in 1872 and renamed the Metropolitan Elevated a few years later. Both companies ran into heavy resistance, especially when they proposed to operate steam-powered railroads above some of the city's major north–south thoroughfares. Much of it came from abutting property owners, who feared that the els would leave the streets dark, dirty, and noisy, doing severe damage to their residences and businesses (for which, under existing law, they were not entitled to compensation) and lowering the value of their holdings. Also active in the opposition were rival streetcar and transit companies, one of which was headed by William Marcy Tweed, the city's most powerful politician. But the New York and the Metropolitan, whose leaders included some of the city's most successful businessmen, also had plenty of political clout. They had good access to capital, too. Exploiting the growing

pressure for rapid transit in New York, hammering away that the els would reduce crowding in lower Manhattan and stimulate development in upper Manhattan, they overcame the political and legal challenges to their plans. Commenting on these developments, the *Real Estate Record and Builders' Guide,* a
strong advocate of rapid transit of whatever kind, predicted in 1876 that "the
triumph of the elevated roads is as certain as any event of the future."[11]

The prediction was on the mark—at least in the short run. During the late
1870s the New York Elevated extended the Ninth Avenue el and built the Second and Third avenue els. And the Metropolitan Elevated erected an el above
Sixth Avenue. By 1880 New York City had the nation's first rapid transit system (and the world's only elevated railway lines). From the very start, however,
the els aroused intense controversy. Critics complained that they blocked the
sunlight, creating beneath them what the *Times* called "a perpetual city of
night." Hot cinders dropped on passersby, as did oil, grease, and tobacco
juice. Coal dust coated everything, especially in summer when windows were
open. Worst of all was the noise—the rumbling of trains and screeching of
brakes—which made it hard to do business and even harder to sleep. The els
turned pleasant streets into "a howling wilderness," critics charged, driving
property values down 25 to 50 percent. All told, a New York grand jury declared, the els were "a great calamity," an "unparalleled invasion of property
rights and of public comfort, safety, and health." Supporters of the els conceded that they had injured some New Yorkers but contended that "where one
has been injured, a hundred others have been benefited." As the *Real Estate
Record* pointed out, they were "the most expeditious, cheapest and most comfortable" form of local transit in the world. They were much faster than streetcars, much more pleasant than subways. And they were extremely popular.
Ridership jumped from 2 million in 1876 to 60 million in 1880 and soared to
more than 180 million by 1890.[12] For some riders the els provided a way to
shorten the journey to work, for others a chance to live in hitherto remote and
relatively cheap sections of the city.

Inspired by the great success, not to mention the huge profits, of New
York's elevated railways, local businessmen mounted or renewed efforts to
build els in other cities. Their spokesmen, usually supported by owners of
outlying property and residents of nearby suburbs, claimed that els were desperately needed. Streetcars were too slow. And steam railways—which only
served the distant suburbs and, in the interest of public safety, were often
barred from the business district—were inconvenient. Spokesmen for the els
also claimed that they would be designed to minimize their impact on the
city's appearance, the surface traffic, and the abutting property. They would

New York's Sixth Avenue el, 1899 (© Collection of the New-York Historical Society, neg. no. 50220)

still be a little noisy, a Boston lawyer conceded, but a little noise was a normal feature of urban life, especially in a thriving business district. The els would raise property values on some streets. If they lowered them on others, the railway companies would compensate the owners—something that the courts required them to do in New York in 1882. Supporters also stressed that, by making outlying districts accessible and thus helping working people escape the overcrowded and unsanitary tenements, the els would improve public health. By enabling more and more Americans to reside on the periphery and work in the center, they would make the metropolis more pleasant for living and more efficient for doing business.[13]

The hazards of elevated railways, 1877 (© Collection of the New-York Historical Society, neg. no. 17688)

Despite these claims, the efforts to build els generated a storm of opposition, much of it from abutting property owners and local streetcar companies. Their spokesmen argued that streetcars, combined with steam railroads, were more than adequate. Worse still, another Boston lawyer declared, the streetcars would be driven out of business by the els. Els might be necessary in New York, but only because the island was so long and narrow that much of the traffic was concentrated along a few routes. And New Yorkers paid a high price for them. Drawing on statements by residents and observations by visitors, the opposition charged that els, no matter how well designed, would disfigure the city, obstruct the surface traffic, and, by leaving the streets below dark, dirty, and noisy, lower property values. They would also stunt the growth of children and cause hysteria, deafness, and paralysis in adults. If steam railroads were too dangerous to be allowed to run along the downtown streets, they were certainly too dangerous to be allowed to run above them. Some opponents also argued that by enhancing access between the periphery and the center the els would help the downtown merchants at the expense of the outlying merchants—although, interestingly, many downtown businessmen whose shops and office buildings were on the proposed routes protested that the els would drive away customers and tenants.[14]

Although well aware of the powerful opposition to els, many advocates of rapid transit believed it was only a matter of time before most big cities followed New York's lead. Some did. During the 1880s three els were built in Brooklyn, then an independent city (and the nation's third largest). And during the 1890s four were erected in Chicago, where, one alderman said, "every one is in favor of an elevated road, but . . . wants it on the other fellow's street." The companies circumvented the opposition by building the els through private property, usually in alleys, behind or between rows of houses, instead of along public streets. Sometimes they bought the property; sometimes they made deals with the owners, many of whom were willing to give their consent if the price was right. But most big cities did not follow New York's lead. In Boston the opposition blocked one plan after another in the 1880s; and in the early 1890s it prevailed on the voters to turn down a proposal to run an el along a viaduct through an alleyway in the business district. A coalition of property owners, streetcar companies, and steam railroads, which ran the commuter trains, thwarted attempts to build an el in Philadelphia. And nothing came of efforts in St. Louis.[15] Thus by the late 1890s there were only three elevated railway systems in the United States—one in New York, the largest and busiest in the world, another in Chicago, the second largest and busiest, and the other in Brooklyn, which became part of New York in 1898.

During the next three decades private companies, public agencies, and transit consultants put forward proposals to extend the existing systems in New York and Chicago and to build new systems in other cities. (More often than not they were included in comprehensive rapid transit plans—which called for the construction of subways as well as els.) Despite the dismal

Chicago's Wabash Avenue el, 1907 (Courtesy of the Library of Congress)

record of earlier efforts, there was reason to believe that these proposals might succeed. The demand for rapid transit was stronger than ever. Even if the railroad companies were obliged to compensate the property owners for damages, it was still much cheaper to build above ground than underground—except perhaps in the heart of downtown, where what one railroad executive called "the prohibitive value of abutting property" precluded the construction of els. Also, els were far less objectionable now. Having converted from steam to electricity, in Chicago and Brooklyn in the late 1890s and in New York a few years later, they no longer used steam locomotives, the source of the smoke, cinders, and dust that outraged nearby residents and businessmen. Els could be made even less objectionable in the future, less ugly by encasing the structures in concrete and less noisy by laying the rails in ballast. At a moderate increase in cost, it was possible to build els that were clean, quiet, and attractive, more like the Berlin el, widely regarded as the world's finest, than the New York el.[16]

But when Americans thought about elevated railroads, what came to mind was the New York el. And by 1900 it had a terrible reputation, the result of two decades of relentless, often virulent criticism of the railroad and its management, the Manhattan Railway Company, which had leased the New York and the Metropolitan lines in 1880 and monopolized rapid transit in the city for the next twenty years. The New York el's reputation turned Americans everywhere against elevated railroads. In Pittsburgh, for example, supporters of rapid transit told Councilman Enoch Rauh in 1919 that "we can build elevated roads cheaper [than subways]." True enough, he replied. But when he asks them, "would you like to have an elevated road running along in front of your house," they "always say no." The *Los Angeles Times* opposed els too. Spearheading a campaign in 1926 against the Pacific Electric railway's proposal to run an el into downtown Los Angeles, the *Times* attacked elevated railways with the malevolence it usually reserved for labor unions. Also opposed to els was the St. Louis Building Owners and Managers Association, a group of downtown real estate interests that believed that the disadvantages of els were so obvious that it did not spell them out. It simply cited the experience of New York and Chicago, saying, "That in itself is sufficient."[17]

In view of the deep-seated opposition to elevated railways, most Americans doubted that any more els would be built—except perhaps in sparsely settled outlying sections or along private rights of way. They had outlived their usefulness. In the words of Lawrence Veiller, secretary of the City Club of New York (and a leading tenement house reformer), they were "a thing of the past." By and large they were. During the early twentieth century a few els were built in New York, but only in Brooklyn, Queens, and the Bronx, the so-called outer boroughs. A few others, most of which started in the outlying sections and went underground when they approached the business district, were erected in Boston and Philadelphia. But no more els were constructed in Chicago. And despite strong efforts in other cities, no new els went up elsewhere. Perhaps the most compelling evidence that elevated railways were "a thing of the past" was the movement to demolish them that was launched by abutting property owners in Boston in the 1910s and in New York a decade later.[18] This movement not only underscored the precarious position of the existing els but also reflected the widespread view that henceforth rapid transit should be built underground.

To understand why, it is necessary to go back to the late 1870s, by which time the initial interest in subways had waned in New York. As the *Real Estate Record and Builders' Guide* observed in 1881, "no sane capitalist would agree to put his money into an enterprise so very costly, which would be certain to prove a failure as a competitor against the elevated roads." But as time passed, many New Yorkers grew disenchanted with els. They were not only dirty, smoky, and noisy; they were also extremely crowded. "It is not now a question as to whether there are seats enough in a car," complained one critic, "but how many people can be packed, like sheep in a pen, consistent with opening or closing the doors or gates." The els were extremely slow, too. The trains creep along, one behind the other, grumbled another critic. "Call that rapid transit?" he asked. To many New Yorkers it seemed that the els could not provide adequate transportation unless they occupied "nearly all the longitudinal streets in the lower half of the city"—and maybe not even then. As disenchantment with els grew, interest in subways revived—and not only in New York but also in Boston, Philadelphia, and Chicago.[19]

Subways, their backers had long contended, were far superior to els. They were faster and safer. They were less likely to fall off the rails; and if they did, they were less likely to injure or kill the passengers. Subways were also more reliable and comfortable than els. They were protected from snow and ice in winter, from rain and storms in summer, never too cold or too hot. If built in shallow tunnels, subways were more accessible than els, too. Subways, their supporters argued, did not mar the city's appearance or obstruct the surface traffic. Unlike els, with their large columns and wide railbeds, they were more or less invisible. No reasonable person would be offended or inconvenienced by their small, inconspicuous entrances. Perhaps most important of all, subways did not drop hot cinders, spew out dense smoke and noxious fumes, produce a nerve-wracking roar, and leave the streets in perpetual darkness. Nor did they do irreparable damage to the abutting property. If anything, subways increased values along their routes. During the late nineteenth century many Americans found these claims more and more persuasive. And by the late 1880s and early 1890s some thought it was time that American cities followed the lead of London and a few other European cities that were expanding, constructing, or considering underground rail systems.[20]

Hitherto the attempts to build subways had been stymied by political and economic constraints. The political constraints were very strong in New York, where a few more efforts were made to construct a subway beneath Broadway in the 1870s and 1880s. The Broadway merchants, among the most powerful businessmen in the city, strongly opposed these efforts, largely on the grounds that construction would block surface traffic and thus drive away customers. To block Broadway for one day would be "a great misfortune," they declared; to block it for two years, the time it would take to build a subway, would be "an irreparable calamity." The situation was much the same in Boston, where an attempt was made to construct a subway under Tremont Street in the early

1890s. Many merchants, fearful that construction would drive business to other streets, strenuously objected. "What, we ask," said one, "is to become of the business of hundreds of the merchants along the route during months if not years while the streets are impassable for travel? Are they to put up their shutters and go into the bankruptcy courts for assistance?" These businessmen were generally supported by the street and elevated railways, which saw subways as unwelcome competition. Also in the opposition were many outlying real estate owners, who believed that els still offered the best hope for rapid transit and feared that subways would impede their construction and expansion.[21]

The political constraints were powerful. But as the history of the els revealed, they could have been overcome. What could not have been overcome before the 1890s were the economic constraints. Subways were very expensive. During the late nineteenth century engineers estimated that they would cost $2–3 million a mile, depending on the location, the subsurface, and the water level—a vast sum at the time. By the early twentieth century the estimates were up to $2–4 million a mile, and even higher in and around the business district. (Disinterested experts held that subways were two to four, or even four to eight, times as expensive as els, depending on whether the els were built on the periphery or in the center, whether the railbeds were open or ballasted, and whether the property damages were low or high. Interested parties, like Cyrus W. Field, head of the New York Elevated, claimed that subways were ten to twelve times as expensive as els.) With such a tremendous capital outlay required, subways would have to generate an enormous amount of revenue to attract investors. This, well-informed financiers, like Jacob Schiff, a New York investment banker, doubted they could do.[22] For down through the 1880s it was widely believed that most Americans would not ride subways and that even if they did the number of riders would not be large enough to produce the necessary revenue.

The belief that most Americans would not ride subways had two principal sources. One was what a Chicago resident called a "horror of tunnels," a horror that grew out of the widespread association of the underground with the underworld, the world of the dead. Subways, one Bostonian said, were like "a long coffin underground." They gave him a "buried-alive feeling," wrote another. Testifying in opposition to a proposed subway, yet another Bostonian asked the members of a state legislative committee, "gentlemen, do you want to go underground [before] your time comes, [unless] it is necessary? I don't." Another source was the common perception, based in some cases on first-hand experience with the London Underground and the New York Central

Railroad tunnel under Park Avenue, that subways were invariably "dark, damp, [and] dank," "smoky and unsavory," and very noisy. The noise of the London Underground, wrote John E. Fitzgerald, a member of the Massachusetts Rapid Transit Commission of 1892, was like "the roaring of the ocean after a storm." To many Americans it seemed hard to believe that people would willingly "plunge from the [warmth] of our sunny streets in midsummer to the icy chill of these damp sub-cellars," and travel in "a place where the sun never shines," a place more suitable for the dead than the living. Especially when they could take the streetcars and, in New York, the els—which, in spite of the crowds and delays, were "a pleasure to ride," wrote one observer.[23]

During the 1890s, however, popular attitudes changed. By far the greatest impetus was the growing awareness that subways could be driven by electricity rather than steam. In 1890 a series of technological breakthroughs culminated in the opening of the world's first electric-powered underground railroad in London. The new underground had a great impact not only in Europe, where several cities soon followed London's lead, but in America as well. On the basis of several first-hand reports, most of which were highly favorable, many Americans were convinced by the mid and late 1890s that electric power was feasible, technically and financially, and that it was far superior to steam power. Speaking of a proposed electric-powered subway for New York, a subway that would be "run by electricity, lighted by electricity, ventilated by electricity," J. Hamilton Hunt, a West Side real estate agent, predicted that "it would be as different from the old, dark, smoky tunnels as daylight is from darkness." Alexander E. Orr, a prominent businessman and chairman of the New York Rapid Transit Commission of 1894, went even further, telling a British royal commission that if electric power had been available earlier subways would already have been built in New York and els would probably not have been built at all.[24]

From the perspective of riders, electricity had many advantages over steam. It was much safer—no mean thing in a society where a series of memorable disasters in Cincinnati, Hartford, and other cities in the mid nineteenth century had left people fearful of boiler explosions and terrified of the prospect of one in a tunnel. Another advantage of electricity was that it did not give off sulfuric fumes, the stench of which pervaded the old London Underground. The air would be as wholesome in electric-powered subways as in homes and schools, pointed out Professor S. Homer Woodbridge of MIT, and even more wholesome than in churches and theaters. Electric-powered subways would also be far brighter—"as light as day," said William Steinway, another member of the New York Rapid Transit Commission of 1894—and less noisy than steam-powered subways. Electricity would revolutionize rapid transit, wrote William Barclay Parsons, chief engineer of the New York Rapid Transit Commission, at the turn of the century.

> When the people realize that they secure a railway well lighted, well
> ventilated, with a temperature cool in summer and warm in winter,
> whose operations at all times will be constant and free from interfer-
> ence by fires, congestion or street traffic, fogs, snows, or the other
> causes that so frequently interfere with the surface and elevated lines;
> and to secure this in a space not now used at all, and without encroach-
> ing on the already congested street surface, or without interfering with
> light, air, and access to abutting property, a new era in urban transporta-
> tion will be begun.[25]

Indeed, "a new era in urban transportation" had already begun, at least in Boston and New York. In 1894, just a year after Bostonians had voted down the so-called alleyway el, the Massachusetts legislature authorized the Boston Transit Commission to build the nation's first subway. Roughly 1.5 miles long, the subway was designed to run under Tremont Street through the core of the retail district. Despite heavy opposition by Tremont Street merchants and the West End Street Railway Company, which monopolized the city's surface transit business, the voters endorsed the scheme by a narrow margin. Completed in 1898, the subway was leased to the West End Company, which ran its electric streetcars through it. Also in 1894, only three years after the New York Rapid Transit Commission of 1891 had failed to find anyone to bid on a franchise for a subway, the rapid transit commission of 1894 proposed that the city build a much larger subway that would run for about twenty-one miles under Broadway and up the West Side. The voters overwhelmingly approved the proposal later in the year. After a series of legal and political challenges, construction was started in 1900 and completed a few years later. From the outset both subways were very popular—the Boston subway, an integral part of the West End Company's street railway system, carrying tens of millions of riders a year, and the New York subway, an independent system operated by the Interborough Rapid Transit Company (IRT), hundreds of millions.[26]

By the early 1900s the notion that Americans would not ride subways was well on the wane. So was the belief that the number of riders would not be large enough to produce the necessary revenue. This belief had rested on two assumptions. The first was that all but a few American cities were too small, an assumption based on the rule of thumb that it took a population of at least one million to support a subway. As late as 1890 only two American cities other than New York had a million people. With the exception of Brooklyn, which was in every way except legally part of New York, no other city had 500,000 people; only three others had 400,000, and only one other 300,000. By contrast, London, at that time the only city in the world with a subway, had roughly four million people. The second assumption was that in few if any cities would residents ride the subway often enough. Although the riding habit was very high in America, in no city except perhaps New York was it high enough to support a subway as well as the streetcars.[27] Moreover, a great many potential riders—among them short-haul riders, riders who were reluctant to travel underground, riders who lived far from the subway stations, and riders who were satisfied with the streetcars—would probably not use the subways.

By virtue largely of the work of a handful of transit engineers, of whom Bion J. Arnold of Chicago was the most influential, both assumptions were largely discredited soon after the turn of the century. According to the engineers, a city's capacity to support a subway depended not only on its size but also on its rate of growth. A function of birthrates, death rates, migration flows, and industrial developments, the rate of growth was very hard to predict. But extrapolating from population trends in large American and European cities, Arnold and his colleagues came up with a set of principles according to which big cities would continue to grow, but at a steadily decreasing rate. As the data on which the trends were based were drawn largely from the nineteenth century, a century of stupendous urban growth, the projected growth rates were very high. And so were the population projections. At the turn of the century Arnold predicted that Chicago, which then had fewer than two million people, would have more than five million by 1950. Two decades later, by which time the city had grown to about three million, Charles H. Wacker, a prominent businessman, forecast that Chicago would reach eighteen million in fifty years. Other studies done in the 1910s and 1920s concluded that other American cities (or metropolitan areas) would reach one and even two million in the next two or three decades.[28] If the studies were accurate, many American cities would be large enough to support a subway in the near future.

As the engineers were well aware, a city's capacity to support a subway also depended on how often people used mass transit. And by the early 1890s, if not earlier, some Americans had observed that as rapidly as population increased, ridership increased even more rapidly, twice as rapidly, according to some, three times as rapidly, according to others. By the turn of the century the engineers developed a theory to explain the relationship between ridership and population. According to this theory, ridership increased as the square of population growth—at least until the riding habit reached a "saturation point," after which ridership increased at the same rate as population growth. In other words, if the population of a city doubled, ridership would quadruple. If a city of 200,000 had 20 million riders a year, by the time it reached 400,000 it would have 80 million. Applying this theory, the engineers predicted that the riding habit would rise sharply in most cities over the next few decades. According to one study, it would go up in Chicago from 243 rides per capita annually in 1910 to 299 in 1920, 348 in 1930, and 406 in 1940. Other studies estimated that it would climb to more than 350 in Cleveland, nearly 400 in Detroit, and more than 450 in New York.[29] If these studies were reliable, not only would cities have more people in the future, but people would use mass transit more often.

As contemporaries saw it, the riding habit increased much faster than the population for two main reasons. As the cities grew, more people moved to outlying residential districts, far from their workplaces, far from their stores, theaters, and restaurants, and even far from their friends, many of whom lived in other outlying districts. For them mass transit was essential. Also, as mass transit improved, people rode it more often. "Where transportation is slow and infrequent," *American Architect and Building News* wrote, "people stay at home; where it is rapid and convenient, they find a multiplicity of errands which never occurred to them before." As New York City comptroller Theodore Myers put it, rapid transit creates "its own traffic." More important than the reasons were the consequences. Assuming a sizable growth in population and therefore a sharp increase in ridership, the inevitable result would be a tremendous rise in transit revenue. "Within reasonable limits," B. J. Arnold wrote in 1910, "the *annual transportation income of any large center of population increases approximately as the square of the population.*" If a city of one million generated $10 million in fares, it would generate $40 million when it reached two million. And, as the New York Public Service Commission pointed out, the additional revenue would go largely to rapid transit lines—as long as "they are provided as the need arises."[30] If so, many Americans came to believe, subways would produce more than enough revenue to offset the high cost of construction.

By the early twentieth century most Americans were convinced that no form of surface transit could carry people quickly and comfortably between the residential sections and the business districts. They were also convinced that underground railroads were far superior to elevated ones. It had long

The Boston subway, ca. 1926 (E. R. Kinsey and C. S. Smith, Rapid Transit for St. Louis, *St. Louis, 1926)*

been evident that subways were technologically feasible. As a result of the work of Arnold and other transit engineers, it now seemed clear that they were economically feasible as well. Reinforcing the view that subways were the wave of the future was the recent surge in underground construction both at home and abroad. The Boston subway was finished in 1898; a second tunnel was built to East Boston in 1904, a third under Washington Street four years later. An even more impressive achievement, the New York subway opened in 1904, prompting Mayor George B. McClellan to predict that it would be "the first of many more" and leading residents of other cities to claim, "If New York can have a subway, so can we." During the late nineteenth century a few lines were added to the London Underground, by far the world's largest subway. Construction began on the Budapest subway in the early 1890s and, after a long battle, on the Paris subway a few years later. A subway opened in Glasgow in the mid 1890s and in Berlin in the early 1900s. During the 1910s work got under way on subways in Hamburg and Madrid (as well as in Buenos Aires, the first in South America).[31]

But Americans were well aware that to build subways would take a strong and sustained effort. Starting around the turn of the century and continuing until the onset of the Great Depression, advocates of rapid transit mounted campaigns to build subways in more than a dozen cities besides Boston and New York. These campaigns took place not only in most big cities but also in some medium-sized ones. A case in point that highlights the tremendous enthusiasm for subways in the first third of the twentieth century is Providence, Rhode Island, a city of only 225,000 in 1910. Responding to growing demands for rapid transit, the Providence city council hired B. J. Arnold in 1911 to make a study of the city's transportation problems. Arnold reported that a subway was not warranted then or in the foreseeable future. The Providence Board of Trade and other commercial and civic organizations disagreed. Impressed by the success of the Boston subway, confident that Providence's population would double and its ridership quadruple in the next two decades, they launched a campaign for a subway in 1913. A year later, on the basis of a favorable report by William W. Lewis, a civil engineer from Boston, the city council endorsed a proposed six-mile, $13.6 million subway, whose four lines all converged on downtown Providence.[32]

In the forefront of these campaigns were the downtown business interests, the most important of which were the department stores (and other retailers), the banks, utilities, and insurance companies, the major newspapers, the property owners (and managers), and the commercial realtors. Sometimes they acted on their own, more often through trade associations, like the Detroit Real Estate Board, commercial organizations, like the Chicago Association of Commerce, and civic groups, like the Los Angeles Traffic Commission. These business interests had a tremendous stake in the growth of downtown's trade and the rise of its property values. They firmly believed in the conventional wisdom that the well-being of downtown depended on its accessibility. Thus if a subway was needed to move people in and out of the business district, it should be built. Moreover, by the mid 1920s, at which time the

first signs of commercial decentralization appeared, many downtown businessmen and property owners were becoming extremely concerned. Watching the sharp increase in traffic congestion in and around downtown, an increase due largely to the proliferation of private automobiles, they began to
fear that some downtown stores would move to other parts of the city. To prevent this, one businessman declared, it was vital to maintain "unimpaired access" to the existing business districts—or, in other words, to build subways.[33]

The downtown business interests were a formidable bunch. They had lots
of money and plenty of clout, and they were willing to spend the one and use
the other. In one city after another they pressed the municipal authorities to
appropriate funds to retain Arnold or one of his colleagues to study the local
transportation problem and draft a rapid transit plan. In some cities, including Cincinnati and Seattle, they supplied the money themselves. The downtown business interests also worked hard to persuade local officials (and, in
some cases, state officials) to approve transit plans, to incorporate them into
bond issues, and to place these issues on the ballot. Through trade and civic
associations—as well as nonpartisan and purportedly nonpolitical groups
like the All Chicago Council and the Detroit Citizens' Better Transportation
Committee—they underwrote (and on occasion managed) the campaigns for
the bond issues. Now and then downtown business interests opposed a subway proposal. The Cleveland Association of Building Owners and Managers
came out against a $15 million bond issue for a subway in 1920. And seven
years later downtown property owners in St. Louis refused to support state
legislation that would have enabled city officials to assess their holdings for
the cost of a subway.[34] But now that subway construction was less disruptive
than it had been in the late nineteenth century, such opposition was rare even
among abutting property owners.

Although the downtown business interests led the campaigns for subways,
their efforts were usually supported by other groups. Among them were
many outlying real estate interests, which backed rapid transit in the hope
that it would stimulate the development of their remote (and otherwise inaccessible) property. Some large industrial firms, including the Ford Motor Company and other Detroit automakers, also endorsed subways on the grounds
that they were the only way to reduce the commute of their employees, many
of whom were spending an hour and a half getting to work. More often than
not, organized labor supported subways—not so much to improve local
transportation as to create jobs for union members. Also in favor of subways
were streetcar riders and streetcar companies, two groups often at logger-

heads with each other. Many riders were fed up with the frequent delays, recurrent accidents, and chronic overcrowding on the surface lines. Convinced that the companies cared more about stockholders than passengers, the straphangers thought an independent subway system would bring them better service. Some streetcar companies also supported subways—but only if they were designed to be used by the existing surface lines, not by an independent transit system. These companies assumed that the streetcars would run more rapidly (and hence more efficiently and more profitably) if they went underground as they approached the business district.[35]

As a rule the downtown business interests could also count on the support of a small but influential group of transit engineers that included B. J. Arnold, William Barclay Parsons, Charles De Leuw, R. F. Kelker, Jr., Henry M. Brinckerhoff, Daniel L. Turner, and John A. Beeler. Leaders in their field, these men were retained in one city after another to make a study of its transportation problems (and sometimes to serve as consultants to local transit commissions and other public agencies as well). With a few exceptions, of which Arnold's report to the Providence city council was one, these studies all came to the same conclusion—that what was needed to solve the problem was a rapid transit system, all or part of which should run underground. Although the engineers saw themselves as professionals whose judgment would not be influenced by political considerations, they were private consultants, well aware that their clients were very much in favor of subways. They were as deeply committed to railways as a later generation of highway engineers would be to automobiles. Most important of all, these engineers strongly believed that American cities had what Arnold called a "natural tendency" to develop around a highly concentrated business district and widely dispersed residential sections. From this belief it was only a short step to the conclusion that once a city reached a certain size, a population of a million or a radius of ten miles, it would be impossible for people to travel between their homes and workplaces in a reasonable time without a subway system (or a system of subways and els).[36]

In their efforts to mobilize support, downtown businessmen, transit engineers, and other advocates stressed that subways were badly needed to relieve traffic congestion. It was already a serious problem in the late nineteenth century. Indeed it was so bad in Boston that the city built the nation's first subway largely in the hope that by removing the streetcars from Tremont Street it would facilitate the flow of traffic downtown. But traffic congestion grew even worse in the early twentieth century, especially in the 1920s, when more and more Americans opted to drive downtown. The flood of streetcars, automobiles, and other vehicles left many major thoroughfares impassable, threatening the well-being of the business district, the viability of street railways, and the usefulness of private automobiles. Subways, their advocates contended, would resolve these problems. By providing unobstructed passage into the business district, subways would make it more accessible. By giving streetcars (and interurban railroads) their own rights of way, subways would improve their service, reduce their operating expenses, and increase their net earnings. (Some Americans even argued that without rapid transit many street railway companies, which were in desperate financial straits at the end of World War I, would go bankrupt.) By removing street and interurban railways from the surface, by putting mass transit underground and reserving the streets for what Daniel L. Turner called "individual transit on wheels"—by, in effect, enlarging the capacity of the streets—subways would also expedite the movement of automobiles and other motor vehicles.[37]

Subways were much more expensive than other forms of urban transportation, their advocates acknowledged, but they were also much more efficient. In the same (or even less) space, they carried far more passengers than other vehicles. According to the American Electric Railway Association, the industry's leading trade group, subways had a carrying capacity at least four and a half times as large as streetcars, eight times as large as motor buses, and fourteen times as large as private autos. Subways also ran much faster than other vehicles, especially during rush hour. Operating on a separate grade and an exclusive right of way, they sped along, unobstructed by pedestrians, other vehicles, cross traffic, and traffic signals, all of which slowed down surface traffic. If subways were not built, their supporters argued, cities would have no alternative but to widen the streets. But street widening, which involved not only grading and paving the roadway but also condemning the abutting property, was very expensive. It was prohibitively so in and around downtown. It was there, where traffic congestion was heaviest, that property values were highest. Although cities spent a great deal of money on street widening, tens of millions in the late nineteenth century and hundreds of millions in the early twentieth, traffic congestion got worse. As a St. Louis electric railway executive pointed out, wider streets attracted heavier traffic, which produced greater congestion. Subway advocates claimed that opening new streets and double-decking old ones would be no less expensive and no more effective.[38]

Subways, their advocates also contended, were badly needed to promote residential dispersal, a process that would reduce overcrowding, especially in working-class quarters. Overcrowding had emerged as a serious problem in New York and other big cities in the mid and late nineteenth century. Along with inadequate sanitary facilities, it was widely regarded as one of the main reasons for the wretched conditions in the tenement houses—which, according to many upper-middle- and upper-class Americans who did not live in them, were the principal source of poverty, crime, vice, disease, and disorder. Tenement-house reformers believed that the enactment of restrictive legislation and the erection of model tenements would do much to alleviate overcrowding. But to eradicate it required the dispersal of the working classes, their movement from the center to the periphery, where, the Philadelphia *North American* wrote, "the hard-toiling mechanic" and his family could enjoy "the advantages of pure air, open grounds, and the quiet comforts of rural retirement." To make it possible for working people to live in outlying sections and still get to the business district in a reasonable time, quick and cheap mass transit was imperative. For several decades many Americans thought the streetcar—"the poor man's friend," as one contemporary called it—was the answer. And to some extent it was. Writing at the start of the twentieth century, a U.S. Census Bureau official remarked that the street railway had done much to foster residential dispersal and promote the practice, "so characteristically American, of living in independent houses instead of in tenements."[39]

But by the late nineteenth century (and in some cities even earlier), many Americans realized that once a city reached a certain size the streetcars could not solve this problem. To do that, it was necessary to make remote outlying sections accessible to working people. But as demographers and transit engineers pointed out, accessibility was a function of speed. Applying laws of geometry, they calculated that as the speed doubled, the accessible area quadrupled. Hence the need for rapid transit, which was twice as fast as surface transit and thus four times as effective in reducing overcrowding. During the late nineteenth century promoters of elevated railways repeatedly exploited the widespread concern about overcrowding in working-class quarters. The els, promised Cyrus Field, president of the New York Elevated, "will take [the] working class out of the tenement houses, the breeding-places of cholera, where they sicken and die, and give them neat little homes, where they can have pure air, and a bit of green grass before the door." Advocates of subways hammered away at the same point in the early twentieth century. Voicing the conventional wisdom, Fielder Sanders, a Cleveland Street Railway commissioner, declared in 1920 that a subway was imperative if Cleveland was to remain a "city of homes and not of tenements."[40]

Subways, their advocates also argued, gave the city an edge in its rivalry with other cities. Big cities are competitors, remarked Mayor E. V. Babcock of

Pittsburgh, a strong supporter of a proposed subway, "and we must be alive and ready to act to see that no other city gets more for her people than Pittsburgh gets for hers." "If we want to stay in the big league while other cities are forging to the front," he warned, "we must play big league ball." In the late nineteenth century playing "big league ball" meant building an elevated railway. In the early twentieth century it meant constructing a subway. Hence the *Pittsburgh Post* backed a proposed subway in 1919 in order "to keep Pittsburgh from falling behind other cities." After visiting several eastern and midwestern cities, most of which had already built a rapid transit system or were planning to build one, a committee of the St. Louis board of aldermen reported in 1925 that unless St. Louis provided rapid transit in the near future, "it will be outclassed by other cities of about the same population and size." And the Detroit Rapid Transit Commission, which led the campaign for a subway in the "Motor City," declared in 1926 that rapid transit was essential if Detroit was "to become one of the world's greatest cities."[41]

Subways, most Americans believed, not only should be built; they would be built. The need was too pressing, the logic too compelling. It was only a matter of time before other big cities followed the lead of Boston and New York—and, as one engineer put it, "The ground beneath the city will be honeycombed with subways, one, two, three tiers deep." Commenting on a proposed subway for downtown Baltimore, which had been recommended by city electrical engineer Charles Phelps in 1905, John Gill, president of the Mercantile Trust and Deposit Company, said, "Ten years from now it will not only be an accomplished fact, but the citizens will derive so much comfort and satisfaction from its operation that they will wonder why it was not done sooner." Mayor P. H. McCarthy of San Francisco forecast in 1911, "The subway in this, as in other great cities, is inevitable." A subway would be expensive, Seattle mayor C. B. Fitzgerald said several years later, "but just as we would have to have water if it cost a dollar a gallon, so will we have to have a subway some day." And in 1925, by which time there was ample reason to think otherwise, a group of traffic experts insisted that underground railroads were destined to form "the backbone of the collective transportation of our great cities."[42]

At the outset, in New York in the 1860s and in other cities a decade or two later, it had been taken for granted that rapid transit would be built by private enterprise. After all, private enterprise had built the surface transit lines, all of which operated under a franchise, a contract by which the city granted a company permission to lay tracks and run cars along the streets provided it complied with terms that specified the schedule, fare, and level of service. And private enterprise was now willing, indeed eager, to build the rapid transit lines. In New York alone scores of companies were organized to construct and operate els, subways, and depressed railroads (and to do so, their promoters stressed, without a subsidy from the local authorities). Private enterprise had also built the London Underground, and at the end of the century it would build subways in other European cities. By the mid 1870s some New Yorkers, frustrated by the lack of progress, recommended that the city build a rapid transit system. But most New Yorkers (and, for that matter, most Americans) disagreed. As the blue-ribbon committee of the American Society of Civil Engineers pointed out in 1874, municipal enterprise (or, as it would soon be called, municipal ownership) "is so foreign to American ideas, so fraught with political dangers, that it is looked upon by taxpayers . . . with great suspicion."[43]

By the 1890s it was clear that private enterprise could build els. It had already built several in New York and Brooklyn (and, in an attempt to stop construction of a subway, was now offering to extend its lines into upper Manhattan and the Bronx). Before the decade was over, private enterprise would also build several els (and an elevated loop) in Chicago. Private capital was willing to finance els because they seemed to be good investments. The els had done well in New York, where the Manhattan Elevated Railway paid better than 6 percent on heavily watered stock. And according to the Massachusetts Rapid Transit Commission, they would have done well in Boston—well enough to retire the debt and still pay a dividend of 8 percent. Private enterprise constructed very few els after 1900, among them the Philadelphia Rapid Transit Company's Market Street line and the Boston Elevated Railway Company's line to Charlestown and Everett. But this was because of the deep-seated opposition to els, not because of a lack of capital. If not for this opposition, private enterprise could probably have found the capital to build els in a number of big cities until the outbreak of World War I, when a great surge of inflation exacerbated a host of long-term problems that drove the electric railway industry to the brink of bankruptcy.[44]

But it was not clear that private enterprise could build subways, even in New York. Although promoters had formed one company after another, capitalists had been extremely reluctant to invest. Indeed, some well-informed New Yorkers predicted that private enterprise would never be able to raise the capital to build a subway. The issue came to a head in 1891, when the city's rapid transit commission asked for bids for a franchise to build an electric-powered subway that would run from the Battery, along Broadway, up the

West Side, and through the Bronx to Yonkers. To the commission's dismay, no bids were submitted. Whatever the reasons—whether the huge capital outlay required, the competition of the elevated railroads, the $3 million security bond, the fixed five-cent fare, or the five-year completion deadline—private capital found the proposed subway too risky. After the commission's failure, many New Yorkers lost hope that private enterprise could build a subway. Referring to what had long been the prevailing view, the *Real Estate Record and Builder's Guide* declared in 1893, "Greater nonsense never got into the heads of people out of a lunatic asylum. The fact is, private capital *cannot* give New York the transit service it needs and is looking for." One year later the rapid transit commission told Mayor Thomas Gilroy that an underground railroad was unlikely to be built in New York in the near future "by private capital alone."[45]

By the early twentieth century few Americans believed that private enterprise could build subways anywhere. They had turned out to be very poor investments in Western Europe, wrote one transit expert in 1907, and there was no reason to think they would do better in the United States. If Arnold and his colleagues were right, subways would in time attract enough riders to justify their tremendous costs. But it would take too long, observed Philadelphia's transit commissioner in 1913, to interest private capital. Calling subways a luxury, even in New York, the *Electric Railway Journal* contended in 1914 that "as a purely commercial enterprise [a subway] is financially impracticable"— precisely the words used to describe it by the Massachusetts Rapid Transit Commission of 1892. If the prospects were bleak before World War I, they were hopeless afterward. As the costs of material and labor soared, Pittsburgh transit commissioner E. K. Morse declared, "there is not a single rapid transit system that can be laid out—long, short, elevated or subway, or both combined—that will to-day pay fixed expenses and a reasonable return on the investment." Frank O. Wetmore, president of the First National Bank of Chicago, agreed, as did the Cleveland Association of Building Owners and Managers and the Los Angeles City Club. R. F. Kelker, Jr., made the point even more bluntly. "There is not a subway anywhere that pays its own way," he told the Industrial Club of St. Louis in the late 1920s. If a subway was built in St. Louis, the fixed charges alone "would exceed the gross annual receipts of the surface street railway system."[46]

Despite the growing evidence that subways did not pay, promoters kept trying to obtain franchises to build them. In some cases they had no intention of building anything. In Seattle, for example, two shady characters, one of whom had been arrested a couple of times for financial chicanery, asked the city council for a franchise to construct a $25 million subway in 1908. Given that the city had fewer than a quarter million people, far too few to support a subway, some councilmen speculated that the promoters saw the franchise as a gimmick by which "neatly engraved [but worthless] shares of stock could be sold to New England school teachers." In other cases the promoters hoped that the city officials would grant a franchise for a subway for such a long period or on such favorable terms that private capital might invest in it. The Pacific Electric railway said it could raise the money to build a subway if given a forty-year franchise. A Cleveland businessman made the same claim, provided that the city council earmarked one cent of every streetcar fare to pay the interest and principal on the subway's debt. But under pressure from riders and reformers, many of whom were extremely hostile to the street railway companies, the local politicians were seldom willing to oblige the promoters. After visiting several cities that were planning to build or expand rapid transit facilities, a St. Louis aldermanic committee found that by the mid 1920s nowhere was anyone even suggesting that private capital provide the funds.[47]

Realizing that private enterprise could not build subways, Americans turned to municipal ownership. Although Boston had made the decision to build subways with some misgivings, its success had demonstrated that this approach was feasible. For financial reasons it was also highly advantageous. As a result of their good credit ratings and the tax-exempt status of their bonds, cities could borrow money at very low rates. During the early 1890s municipal bonds could be sold at interest rates ranging from 2.5 to 3 percent, or roughly one-third to three-fifths the rates of corporate securities. The cities' ability to obtain capital at low rates was especially important because a subway's fixed costs were so high—and because under even the most optimistic projections it would be a long time before a subway would earn enough to cover these costs.[48] Whether the cities would operate the subways or, like Boston and New York, lease them to private companies was not yet resolved by the early twentieth century. Nor was it resolved whether the cities would rely entirely on general obligation bonds or also resort to revenue bonds and special assessments. But the issue was no longer whether subways would be built by corporations or cities but whether they would be built by cities or built at all.

For advocates of rapid transit, this was a mixed blessing. Its financial advantages notwithstanding, municipal ownership had serious drawbacks. One was political. During the late nineteenth century many Americans looked upon municipal ownership with dismay, believing, in the words of the Massachusetts Rapid Transit Commission of 1892, "that it is better to submit to almost any inconvenience and discomfort rather than to entrust to public servants work which they do so badly." A few years later a special committee of the New York State Assembly, which held hearings on municipal ownership of mass transit, reported that most witnesses, even William Steinway, a member of the commission that had designed the New York City subway, opposed it. So did the committee. The controversy over municipal ownership intensified in the early twentieth century, when many civic reformers, labor unions, and socialist organizations (and even some business groups) called upon the cities to take over the gas, telephone, electric power, and street railway companies. The private utilities, most of which commanded huge resources, wielded great clout, and as a rule could count on the support of local commercial associations, fought back—none harder than the street railways. The result was that in the early twentieth century, at just about the same time that the downtown business interests and their allies launched their campaigns to build subways, municipal ownership developed into one of the most contentious issues in urban America.[49]

Americans objected to municipal ownership on political, economic, and ideological grounds. Pointing to previous examples of municipal enterprise, like the Tweed Ring's exorbitant New York County Courthouse, they declared that every public work was a chance for graft, every public agency a source of patronage. As Steinway told the special committee of the New York State Assembly, a municipal transit system would inevitably be turned into "a huge political machine, a refuge for old political hacks." At a time when reformers everywhere were working hard to reduce the influence of the political machines, it made no sense to provide them with what one New Yorker called another "splendid big plum." Public officials were not just corrupt, opponents of municipal ownership contended; they were also incompetent. "The city government hasn't enough executive ability at present to run an inkstand," claimed a Chicago merchant in 1905. In the absence of personal interest, which was so essential for efficient management, municipal ownership led to waste, extravagance, delay, and ultimately poor service and high rates. By any measure, an opponent of public power argued in the 1920s, private enterprise was far superior to municipal ownership: "One is responsible and can be held to the performance of duty; the other cannot. One must keep its engagements, fulfill its promises, or lose money, while the other has no money to lose, no investment to safeguard, and can, therefore, promise anything under the dome of heaven, trusting that the people may forget, and if they don't, that they will have to pay anyhow."[50]

Municipal ownership, its opponents insisted, was also "inconsistent with our form of government." It was un-American, a forerunner of socialism and

Bolshevism. The system of municipal ownership "cannot continue in a democracy," contended the president of the Southern California Edison Company in the mid 1920s. "Either the democracy or the system must go." The Committee on Municipal Ownership of the American Street and Interurban Railway Association, the predecessor of the American Electric Railway Association, agreed. In a democracy, it argued, the function of government, "so far as the industrial well being of the governed is concerned," was to prevent fraud, enforce contracts, and safeguard individual freedom. It was not to engage in business, a practice that would sap individual initiative, undermine personal responsibility, and "impede industrial growth." Putting it bluntly, the special committee of the New York State Assembly declared, "no government, either national, state or municipal, should embark in a business that can be as well conducted by private enterprise." There might be exceptions to this rule, but urban transit was not one. Private enterprise had created the world's most highly developed local and interurban railway system, a system that operated under strict regulation by public authorities—and also provided very good service at very low fares. It now stood ready to make the system even better.[51]

Advocates of municipal ownership denied these charges. Many politicians were corrupt, they conceded, but it was the street railways and public utilities that corrupted them. With so much at stake, these companies were willing to go to almost any lengths to influence the public officials who regulated their activities. The tighter the regulation, the worse the corruption—and the greater the demoralization of local government. As Eugene N. Foss, former governor of Massachusetts, told the Federal Electric Railways Commission in 1919, municipal ownership would take utility companies out of politics. And in conjunction with civil service, nonpartisanship, and other Progressive reforms, it would keep politics out of public utilities. Municipal ownership was just as efficient as private enterprise, its advocates insisted. The construction of the Croton Aqueduct and the Brooklyn Bridge showed that cities were capable of building large-scale public works without undue delay or excessive cost. The operation of municipal waterworks in the United States and municipal gas plants in Western Europe proved that cities could provide essential services at reasonable prices. What held for water and gas also held for transit, wrote Professor Frank Parsons of Boston University in the mid 1890s. Guided by the well-being of the community, as opposed to the balance sheet of a corporation, municipal ownership of mass transit would not only bring about lower fares and safer (and more convenient) travel. It would also help to reduce the hostility between private and public interests in urban America.[52]

Nor was municipal ownership un-American, its advocates declared. It "is not a step towards socialism," wrote New York's *Real Estate Record and Builders' Guide* in 1892; "it is not a blow at democracy; it is nothing more than a measure of economy." (To claims that if the city built a subway it might as well sell meat, the *Real Estate Record* replied, "Talk of this sort is theoretical chatter. Private enterprise to-day amply meets all our demands for butchers' meat; private enterprise to-day does not and . . . cannot supply us with Rapid Transit.") To socialists and capitalists, municipal ownership might well be an ideological issue, the Municipal League of Los Angeles pointed out in 1907. But to other citizens, it was a practical one. If asked if they believed in municipal ownership, most of them would probably answer, "Yes, at some times, in some places, of some things." One of these things was mass transit. Other than water, no public utility was so vital to daily life as mass transit—not gas, not electricity, and not telephone. As Mayor James Couzens of Detroit said in 1919, mass transit affected people in a much more personal way than other public services such as sanitation, sewerage, and waterworks. Cities were already responsible for highways; and as the Massachusetts Rapid Transit Commission of 1892 put it, a railway was "nothing but a special use of a highway." If cities build roads, why shouldn't they build railbeds—and if on the streets, why not below them? It would be very expensive, but the costs would be offset by a rise in property values and an increase in tax revenues.[53]

The opposition to municipal ownership could be overcome—provided the backers of rapid transit took certain steps. One was to make a compelling case that the city desperately needed a subway and that it would either be built by the public or not be built at all. Another step was to downplay the ideological significance of municipal ownership, to stress, as the *Real Estate Record* did, that whether the subway was built by a corporation or by the city was wholly a question of expediency. Yet another step was to ensure that after the city built the subway it would lease it to private enterprise, a step that would reduce the subway's value to the political machine as a source of graft and patronage. By taking these steps, the backers of rapid transit were able to persuade many Americans like B. F. Romaine, Jr., a New York lawyer and property owner who believed that municipal ownership "does some violence to our traditions," to support subways.[54] But other Americans remained opposed to municipal subways not so much because they objected to subways as because they objected to municipal ownership. If the controversy over municipal ownership did not make it impossible for cities to build a subway, it did make it harder.

Municipal ownership had two other serious drawbacks. By the turn of the century most American cities had the authority to grant franchises to private companies to build and operate mass transit. But few had the authority to do so themselves. To get it, a city needed a state law (or, in some cases, a charter amendment). Even if the state legislature passed the law, the city officials still had to approve a plan and submit a bond issue to the voters. It required a simple majority in some cities, two-thirds in others. If all went smoothly, which was exceedingly unlikely, it would take at least four years before construction began; and construction would take at least three or four more years. If time was one problem, priorities were another. To build a subway, a company had to be convinced it was a good idea. For a city, however, a subway had to be not only a good idea, but a better idea than others. For cities had limited resources, not to mention constitutionally imposed debt limits, and almost limitless needs, many of them for streets, parks, sewers, and other things that could not be provided by private enterprise. To gain approval for a subway, its backers had to persuade politicians and voters that it could be built without diverting resources from more pressing projects.[55] To appreciate the impact of these drawbacks, it is helpful to look at two abortive efforts to build subways in the early twentieth century, one in Pittsburgh and the other in Cleveland.

The efforts to build a subway in Pittsburgh began in earnest in 1910, when the city retained B. J. Arnold to make a study of the local transportation problem. To the more than half million residents of Pittsburgh, then the nation's eighth largest city, the problem was simple. The local streetcar service, provided by the Pittsburgh Railways Company, was awful. And each year it got worse. The service was especially bad in and around downtown Pittsburgh, an extremely compact business district that was hemmed in on all sides by rivers and hills. Between 1905 and 1910 local engineers and other citizens had discussed this problem. By the time Arnold arrived, there was a consensus that Pittsburgh had to do something to relieve traffic congestion downtown—but that under no circumstances should it permit els to run along the streets. In what was by far the most comprehensive such report in the city's history, Arnold concluded that the problem could be solved by improving the surface transit lines and building a downtown subway system that would cover roughly four square miles. Modeled on the Boston subway, it would give the existing street and interurban railways easy access to downtown Pittsburgh. Arnold did not design the subway or estimate its cost, but he forecast that though it would lose money during the first years of operation it would pay "eventually." It would make sense for a company to build the subway, he wrote, but only if it could obtain capital at 5 percent or less. If not, the city should build it.[56]

For a while it seemed that private enterprise might seize the opportunity.

Four years before Arnold submitted his report, the Pittsburgh Subway Company, a local firm backed by New York investors, had asked the city council for a franchise. During the next seven years the council received nearly a dozen other requests, some of which were supported by the Pittsburgh Chamber of Commerce and other groups. The promoters claimed that with a reasonable franchise they could raise the capital. But what was reasonable to the promoters was not necessarily reasonable to city officials. The two groups were sharply divided over fares and other issues. Attempts to reach a compromise were stymied by Mayor William A. Magee, a strong supporter of municipal ownership, who vetoed an ordinance granting a franchise to Pittsburgh Subway on the grounds that it did not give the city adequate control over the system. In the face of this impasse, the city asked the state legislature for permission to build a subway of its own. Despite opposition by the chamber of commerce, the legislature gave its approval in 1915. Two years later, seven years after Arnold's report, E. K. Morse, the city's newly appointed transit commissioner, proposed that the city build a subway from downtown Pittsburgh to the East End (and later a subway to the north side and elevated lines to the outlying districts). The initial line would cost $7 million, the entire system $35 million. If possible, the subway would be leased to Pittsburgh Railways; if not, it would be operated by the city.[57]

The campaign for a subway resumed shortly after World War I. But to the surprise of many, Pittsburgh's new mayor, E. V. Babcock, rejected Morse's plan in March 1919 and endorsed instead a far less ambitious one prepared by the city's Department of Public Works. This plan called for a downtown subway (consisting of a loop, about half a mile long, and a few portals) that would funnel the local streetcars in and out of the business district. The subway, which would be leased to Pittsburgh Railways, was estimated to cost $6 million. To pay for it, Babcock asked the city council to put a $6 million bond issue on the ballot in July. Morse and others sharply criticized Babcock's proposal, stressing that the DPW's plan would not provide Pittsburgh with rapid transit and that the city had no assurances that Pittsburgh Railways, then in receivership, would lease the subway. The $6 million bond issue would greatly reduce the city's bonding capacity, and in the end the subway would probably cost more like $12–18 million. The mayor responded not only that the subway was badly needed to relieve traffic congestion in downtown Pittsburgh but also that it could serve as the nucleus of a rapid transit system, if and when the city decided to build one. Caught between the mayor and the transit commissioner, between those who saw the subway as a way to relieve traffic congestion and those who saw it as a way to promote residential dispersal, the city council vacillated. But Babcock lobbied hard. And in late May, after a heated debate that foreshadowed the fierce battle to come, the council, which had approved several other bond issues unanimously, voted seven to three to put the $6 million subway on the ballot.[58]

The chamber of commerce supported the bond issue, but the Real Estate Board opposed it, as did the Allied Boards of Trade. The *Post* and the *Telegraph-Sun* endorsed it, but the *Dispatch* denounced it. Some city councillors sided with the mayor, others with the transit commissioner. Supporters of the bond issue argued that the subway would relieve traffic congestion in downtown Pittsburgh and that if it was not built the city might have to erect elevated railways. All big cities had to build subways sooner or later, supporters said, and after a decade of talk it was time for action. Babcock, to whom competition among cities was as natural as competition among companies, pointed out that Cleveland, Cincinnati, and other cities were planning to build subways and warned that if Pittsburgh did not do so it would fall behind. Opponents of the bond issue contended that it made no sense to spend $6 million (and perhaps two or three times as much) without getting rapid transit. Morse also dismissed the notion that the downtown subway loop could serve as the nucleus of a rapid transit system. Pittsburgh should either build rapid transit or save its money, he declared. Some opponents held that traffic congestion could be relieved by street widening, a bond issue for which was also on the ballot. Others objected to the subway on the grounds that the principal beneficiaries would be Pittsburgh Railways and a small group of downtown property owners. In the end, the voters approved the subway bond issue, though by a much narrower margin than the others on the ballot. A majority of the wards voted against it, but their opposition was offset by strong support in about half a dozen wards, most of which were in or adjacent to downtown Pittsburgh.[59]

Immediately after the election Mayor Babcock announced that the city would soon solicit bids from contractors. The *Electric Railway Journal* reported, "Construction is expected to start within sixty days." But to the dismay of its advocates, the subway ran into one obstacle after another. Opponents demanded a recount, which confirmed that the bond issue had passed, though by a very small margin. Also, the local officials and Pittsburgh Railways, to which the city intended to lease the subway, could not agree on terms. Worst of all, the Pennsylvania Supreme Court ruled that if the city could not complete the subway with the funds available it could not go ahead. And by virtue of the soaring inflation during and after World War I, the proposed subway could no longer be built for $6 million. During the next five or six years, citizens' groups, transit engineers, and downtown business interests came up with several plans to resolve the dilemma, but nothing came of them. In the meantime Pittsburgh's street railways deteriorated; its residents relied increasingly on automobiles; and the value of the $6 million steadily eroded. By the late 1920s, the *Electric Railway Journal* wrote, it was clear that given the costs of a subway "$6,000,000 would not even pay for a good beginning." During the early 1930s the chamber of commerce, once a strong supporter of the bond issue, conceded, "What appeared advisable in 1919 is today of questionable wisdom."[60] And in 1934, twenty-four years after Arnold submitted his report and fifteen years after the voters approved the $6 million, the city council vacated the bond issue and gave up the attempt to build a subway in Pittsburgh.

The efforts to build a subway in Cleveland got under way in 1917, a little over a decade after a chamber of commerce committee had reported that it was "only a question of time when a complete system of subways will be required in Cleveland." Cleveland was then the nation's fifth largest city, a rapidly growing metropolis of about 800,000 people, many of whom were dissatisfied with the surface transit system, owned and operated by the Cleveland Railway Company. Although there was widespread sentiment that the city sorely needed a rapid transit system, there was no consensus about what kind to build or how much to spend. With the mayor, city council, and Cleveland Plan Commission unable to reach agreement, the city in 1918 retained Barclay Parsons & Klapp, a prominent transit engineering firm, to look into the issue. Barclay Parsons & Klapp reported that Cleveland's huge population and high riding habit made rapid transit imperative and recommended that it be built in two stages. The first stage called for a downtown subway consisting of short loops, a terminal, and feeder lines, all radiating from Public Square. Estimated to cost about $15 million, the subway, which would be leased to the Cleveland Railway Company, was designed to relieve traffic congestion downtown by removing the streetcars from the streets. The second stage called for a system of rapid transit lines running either above ground, in open cuts, or on private rights-of-way to the outlying sections.[61] At the urging of the Cleveland Rapid Transit Commission, which had been established a couple of years earlier, the city council voted in early 1920 to put a $15 million bond issue for a downtown subway on the April ballot.

The bond issue provoked a fierce struggle, which in some ways resembled the battle in Pittsburgh a year earlier. Supporters, among them the chamber of commerce, the builders' exchange, and the federation of labor, made the same claims that the subway would relieve traffic congestion downtown and could later become the nucleus of a rapid transit system. They said that the surface transit system was "breaking down" and that it was impossible for the streetcars to provide quick and comfortable service as long as they had to fight for space with private autos and trucks. Supporters also argued that the proposed subway would reduce traffic accidents, save commuting time, facilitate vehicular traffic, and, in the words of street-railway commissioner Fielder Sanders, raise property values in Cleveland "by an amount which will make the bond issue look small." Opponents, among them the Civic League, the real estate board, and the *Press* and *Plain Dealer,* countered that the subway would not provide Cleveland with rapid transit and that traffic congestion downtown could be relieved by tightening traffic regulations, rerouting streetcar lines, and adopting other less expensive measures. The proposed subway was very costly, they stressed; and even if the ultimate costs did not exceed $15 million, which was highly unlikely, they would drive property taxes up. The Civic League was particularly incensed that the suburbs, by far the fastest growing part of metropolitan Cleveland, were not required to pay a fair share of the subway's costs.[62]

Opponents of the bond issue also raised the issue of priorities, which had not been raised in Pittsburgh. As the *Cleveland Plain Dealer* pointed out, the city already had the second largest per capita debt in the nation; and it was "going into debt faster than any other large city." Moreover the proposed subway had to be considered "in connection with other urgent or prospective needs of the city." Among the most pressing of these needs were hospitals, jails, schools, and, above all, homes. "Which does Cleveland need most," the *Plain Dealer* asked, "homes and schools or a subway terminal?" All other considerations aside, can the city "afford to divert from the building of homes and schools the labor and material required for carrying out the recommendation of the rapid transit commission?" The *Cleveland Press* also hammered away at the issue of priorities. "What shall it be," it asked—"more homes and lower rents, or relief of downtown traffic conditions?" Even if the city could afford it, there were not enough workers and supplies to do both. Whereas homes were essential to life and health, even to "the future of the race," subways were not. Urging the citizens to "vote for homes and lower rents!" the *Press* argued shortly before the election that "a vote AGAINST the subway is a vote FOR more homes."[63]

Supporters of the bond issue did what they could to rebut these arguments. Cleveland could afford to build a subway; indeed, in the interest of its long-range prosperity, it could not afford not to. The city had a housing shortage, Charles A. Otis, head of the rapid transit commission, conceded. But construction of the subway would not block the building of homes. If anything, it

Opposition to the proposed Cleveland subway, 1920
(Cleveland Press, April 26, 1920)

would stimulate home building by opening up remote districts for residential development. Finally, construction of the subway would not start for six to eight months, "by which time the home-building program [which was then under way in the city] would have been completed." But these arguments did not carry much weight. Cleveland was caught up in a nationwide housing crisis. At the heart of it was the virtual standstill in construction during and immediately after World War I, a result first of a serious shortage of manpower and material and later of a sharp rise in their costs. The consequences were alarming. Rents climbed, in some cases by 100 percent a year, and evictions soared. "Women and babies have been driven into the streets," wrote the *Press,* "and their household effects thrown after them." At a time when a grand jury was probing the high costs of building, when the state legislature was considering laws to slow down evictions, and when the commercial and civic groups were mounting a campaign to build a thousand homes a year, Otis and his associates were hard pressed to generate popular support for the bond issue.[64]

The election, which was held in late April, went much worse than the subway's supporters expected. By a more than two-to-one majority, the voters turned down the $15 million bond issue. (A $2 million bond issue for jails also failed, though a $3.5 million bond issue for hospitals passed.) According to the *Cleveland Press,* the vote was a clear mandate to "build homes first." The voters had decided that the city should undertake virtually no public works that would divert labor and materials from home building and also that it should adopt stricter traffic regulations and other relatively inexpensive measures to relieve traffic congestion downtown. The *Cleveland Plain Dealer,* which had held that the city "will probably need subways one day," but that the day had not yet arrived, called the vote "a triumph for common sense." It also predicted that the subway "is not dead. It is merely postponed until some more favorable day." On that point, the paper was wrong. The subway was dead. Although a few private companies made efforts to obtain a franchise to build a subway in the late 1920s, nothing came of them—other than a rapid transit line that was built by the Van Sweringen brothers, Oris P. and Mantis J., and ran on a private right-of-way between their residential development in suburban Shaker Heights and their railroad terminal in downtown Cleveland.[65] The city would try again in the 1930s and 1940s, but it would never come as close to building a subway as it did in 1920.

Other cities that attempted to build a subway ran into many of the same problems as Pittsburgh and Cleveland. A case in point is Cincinnati, where in 1912 B. J. Arnold proposed that the city build a subway along an abandoned canal bed, a subway whose main purpose was to provide the interurban railways access to downtown. After a vigorous campaign, which was backed by nearly all the city's commercial and civic associations, the voters approved a $6 million bond issue for the subway in 1917. But construction, which was delayed by legal problems and wartime restrictions, did not get under way until 1919. By then inflation had so driven up costs that only part of the subway could be built. Moreover, by 1923, when this part was finished, Cincinnati's interurban railways were bankrupt. For years local officials debated whether to complete the subway, which would have cost at least another $10 million. But in time they gave up on the project (and later paved over the $6 million tunnel). Detroit is another case in point. The city began to think about building a subway a few years before the United States entered World War I, and by the time the war was over Barclay Parsons & Klapp had designed a $68 million rapid transit system. But the proposed system was shelved because the city was deeply involved in the last stage of a long-drawn-out struggle to take over the local streetcar lines, which were owned and operated by the Detroit

United Railway Company. Given its debt limit, not to mention its political divisions, Detroit could not have bought the street railways and constructed a rapid transit system at the same time. And Mayor James Couzens firmly believed that municipal ownership of the streetcar system took priority.[66] Not until after 1922, when Detroit finally acquired the street railways, did the city mount an all-out campaign to build a subway.

The campaigns to build subways ran into other formidable (and, to some extent, unanticipated) obstacles that made the job of mobilizing support for rapid transit even harder. Americans who were in favor of subways in general were often at odds over subways in particular. Assuming that the cities would build the subway, should they run it, too? Or should they lease it to private companies? If so, on what terms? Should the subway be integrated with the surface transit lines, as in Boston? Or should it be operated as an independent transit system, as in New York? Also, where should the subway run—along which streets, in which neighborhoods, and, in the case of Pittsburgh, along which side of the river? Where should the terminal be located—in the core of downtown, on the edge, or, in the case of Cincinnati, in a nearby business district adjacent to the old canal bed? Should there even be a downtown terminal? Some subway advocates called for a downtown loop instead; others claimed that through service was preferable. A few even argued that some subway lines should bypass the business district entirely. Lastly, how many stops should the subway make? And how far apart should they be? What came first—convenience, which meant many stops, or speed, which meant few stops?[67]

Although these issues were highly divisive, they were only moderately important. They often slowed down the campaigns to build subways but seldom brought them to a standstill. There were, however, more momentous issues that sharply divided subway advocates and did irreparable damage to their efforts. First, what was the primary purpose of the subways? Was it to relieve traffic congestion in the center or to promote residential dispersal on the periphery? If a city had to make a choice, should it build a downtown subway to remove the streetcars from the streets or a rapid transit system to connect the residential and business districts? Second, how should the subways be built? Should subways be constructed in a comprehensive manner, all the lines more or less at the same time, or in a piecemeal way, one or two lines at a time—first the lines with the greatest demand, and then, as resources became available, the less pressing ones?[68] Third, how should the subways be financed? If the taxpayers would have to bear part of the costs (which was generally taken for granted after World War I), how much should come from direct taxes on all property in the city and how much, if any, from special assessments on the properties that derived the largest benefit?

A look at the efforts to build a subway in Chicago in the early and mid 1910s helps to illuminate the first issue. The commercial, financial, and industrial capital of the Midwest, Chicago was then the country's second largest city, a huge and sprawling metropolis of more than two million people, many of whom were dissatisfied with the local transportation system. Consisting of one of the nation's most extensive street railway networks and an elevated railway network second only to New York's, the system had recently been renovated, the result of the "Settlement Ordinance," which embodied an agreement reached by the city and the railway companies in 1907. But it was still prone to chronic delays and severe overcrowding, particularly in and around the Loop. With the streetcars operating at full capacity (and with no space available downtown for additional tracks), many residents came to the conclusion that some sort of rapid transit was imperative. Given the antipathy to the els, a subway was the only alternative. A good deal of planning had already gone into a Chicago subway. B. J. Arnold alone had written three reports about the subject, one in 1902, another in 1906, and still another in 1911. Some of the plans called for a small downtown subway to ease traffic congestion, others for a large rapid transit system to link the residential and business districts. But nothing came of these efforts until July 1912, when the city council instructed the Harbor and Subway Commission, a municipal agency that had been set up by Mayor Carter H. Harrison, Jr., in 1911, to prepare a plan for a citywide subway system.[69]

The commission's plan, submitted a few months later, was very ambitious. It called for a huge subway system, 56 miles long (with 131 miles of track), that was estimated to cost $130 million ($95 million for construction and $35 million for equipment). The system, which was completely independent of the existing street and elevated railways, would radiate from the Loop to the outlying sections. It was so designed that roughly three-fourths of the population would live within half a mile of one of the lines and that anyone who lived within ten to twelve miles of the Loop could commute to and fro in less than an hour and a half. The system would not only provide rapid transit, said the commission; it would also relieve traffic congestion, speed up the surface railways, raise their revenues, and lower their expenses. To finance the subway, the city would issue bonds, which would be secured by the system's properties and revenues. Given the projected increases in the city's population and its riding habit, the subway would generate enough income to pay off the bonds without imposing additional burdens on the taxpayers. In preparing the report, the commissioners had visited Boston, New York, and Philadelphia—the three American cities with rapid transit. But it was the New York system, the only independent rapid transit subway, that most impressed them. As John Ericson, city engineer and chairman of the Harbor and Subway Commission, pointed out, they were confident that if New York could build a first-rate subway, so could Chicago.[70]

From the very start, however, the commission's plan ran into strenuous opposition. Some of it came from groups that were against the building of any kind of subway anywhere in the city. But some came from groups that were in favor of subways in general but against the proposed subway in particular. The opposition claimed that there was no need to construct so expensive a subway. Chicago could obtain rapid transit and relieve traffic congestion by extending and improving the street and elevated railways and constructing a small downtown subway, which could be leased to the existing transit companies. The opposition also contended that the number of riders was not large enough to support both an independent subway system and the existing transit companies, and that the operation of yet another transit system would exacerbate the traffic problem in the Loop. The commission rebutted these claims. But a year later, at the behest of opponents of the commission and political rivals of the mayor, who supported the plan, the Board of Supervising Engineers, the overseer of the surface railway companies, made another study. It recommended the construction of a downtown subway, as opposed to an independent citywide rapid transit system, a subway that was designed primarily to relieve traffic congestion in the Loop. Estimated to cost about $18 million, most of which was already available in the traction fund, another product of the Settlement Ordinance, the subway would be built by the city and leased to the street railway companies.[71]

Shortly before the board of engineers issued its report, Harrison attempted to resolve the conflict by asking the city council to place two ordinances on the April 1914 ballot and leave the choice up to the voters. The first ordinance, a revised version of the commission's plan, called for a citywide rapid transit system, to be built and operated by private enterprise under terms that would guarantee municipal ownership in thirty years. The second, which embodied the recommendations of the report by the board of engineers, called for a downtown subway, to be built by the city and leased to the surface railway companies. Early in 1914, however, negotiations between the city and the companies broke down over the rent for the downtown subway, and the second ordinance was taken off the ballot. Supporters of the downtown subway thereupon launched a vigorous attack on the first ordinance. They made the same objections that critics of the commission's original plan had. They also raised new ones. They said that it would be impossible for the city to attract private capital on terms guaranteeing municipal ownership and that under state law Chicago could not grant a franchise for a subway for thirty years. An independent subway would also undermine the ongoing campaign for a uniform fare and jeopardize the solvency of the existing transit companies. Whereas a downtown subway could be built right away—the money was in hand and the legislation in place—an independent citywide rapid transit system would be so hamstrung by financial, political, and legal problems that it would not be built for years and perhaps could not be built at all.[72]

Supporters of the ordinance, notably the Harrison administration, the Cook County Democratic machine, and the *Chicago Examiner,* responded that Chicago could not obtain rapid transit simply by running the streetcars through what the mayor derided as "the dinky [downtown] subway." They argued that an independent citywide subway would pay for itself and that a thirty-year franchise would induce private capital to build it, even on terms that would eventually lead to municipal ownership. Supporters also denied that the subway would intensify traffic congestion in the Loop and claimed that by promoting competition in the transit business it would hold down fares and improve service. They pointed out that many of the criticisms of the proposed Chicago subway had been made earlier about the New York subway, which had succeeded beyond expectations. These responses were not convincing, however. Not to the Cook County Real Estate Board and a host of outlying business associations and neighborhood improvement organizations, which represented non-Loop interests and opposed subways in general. Not to the street and elevated railways, which feared competition from an independent transit system. Not to most of the major newspapers, which favored the downtown subway. And not even to the Chicago Association of Commerce, whose members included the leading downtown business interests, most of which supported not only the downtown subway but subways in general. With subway advocates divided between some who wanted to relieve traffic congestion in the Loop and others who sought to provide rapid transit between the residential and business districts, the outcome was predictable. In April the voters rejected the ordinance by a majority of more than two to one.[73]

A look at the efforts to build a subway in Detroit in the mid and late 1920s illuminates the issue of how subways should be built. These efforts got under way late in 1922, shortly after the city took over the local street railways, when

Mayor James Couzens created the Detroit Rapid Transit Commission. The chairman (and driving force) of the commission, whose other members were three prominent businessmen and a former city engineer, was Sidney D. Waldon, a former vice president at both Packard and Cadillac. A millionaire, he had retired at forty-three and subsequently devoted himself to solving the city's transportation problem. To Waldon (and the other commissioners), the nub of the problem was that Detroit's facilities were lagging far behind its growth. Between 1900 and 1920 the city's railways and highways had grown very little, even though its population, stimulated by the tremendous expansion of the auto industry, had soared from less than 300,000 to nearly a million, making Detroit the fourth largest city in the country and, after Los Angeles, the fastest growing. To transport a population that had already passed one million and would probably reach two million in a decade or two, the commission concluded that the city needed both a system of superhighways (about which more later) and a rapid transit system. Besides designing a master plan of superhighways, the commission spent much of its first year developing a financial plan for a rapid transit system, a plan that relied heavily on special assessments. Late in 1924 the voters endorsed this plan in principle.[74] With the help of transit engineers Daniel L. Turner and John P. Hallihan, the commission then turned its attention to the job of designing a comprehensive system of subways for Detroit.

About the superiority of comprehensive, as opposed to piecemeal, construction, the commission had no doubt. Comprehensive construction was more equitable. It would spread the benefits of rapid transit over the entire city, treating all sections alike and ensuring that no section would derive much of an advantage over another. Comprehensive construction was also less disruptive. Under piecemeal construction, the first line would act as "a magnet" to population and business. It would soon be saturated with traffic, leading to demands for additional lines along the route even before the other lines were built. Comprehensive construction was politically advantageous too. As Mayor Couzens observed, people were not likely to vote for a subway unless it served their neighborhoods. "Find a plan to serve the whole city," he recommended, "and then build it as a continuous project. That will win votes." Although a few groups, among them the Michigan Manufacturers' Association, which was dominated by the auto companies, had voiced concerns about the costs of a comprehensive system, the commission was not deterred. In August 1926 it unveiled a plan for a citywide subway completely independent of the street railways, a four-line, forty-seven mile system that was estimated to cost a whopping $280 million. With an unusual combination of radial and crosstown lines, the subway was designed to connect the residential sections not only with the business district, but also with Ford's Highland Park plant and other major auto factories.[75]

The subway, declared the commission, was vital to Detroit's development as "one of the world's greatest cities." Designed to transport more than 90 percent of the work force to within half a mile of their jobs, the subway would reduce the journey to work and thereby increase Detroit's efficiency as an industrial metropolis. The subway was expensive, the commission conceded, but by virtue of the financial plan it would not raise property taxes or increase the city's debt; and the sooner the project was begun, the less expensive it would be. Detroit had delayed long enough. Other cities were even smaller when they started to build rapid transit; by the time the subway was finished, Detroit would have more than two million people. The Ford Motor Company was persuaded. So were the downtown business interests, which feared that without improved access to the business district stores and offices would move elsewhere, perhaps to General Motors' "New Center," a rival business district three miles from downtown Detroit. Other groups, however, were skeptical. The Michigan Manufacturers' Association, whose general manager lamented that "it takes an hour and a half for the average worker to get to his place of employment," agreed that Detroit needed a subway, but it did not believe that the city could afford to build one all at once. Other commercial associations took much the same position, as did many civic groups and local newspapers. Also opposed was Detroit's Street Railways Department, which was worried about the subway's impact on the city's surface transit system. In the face of widespread opposition, the commission was unable to prevail upon the city council to submit its plan to the voters at the November election.[76]

Hitherto the commission had withstood pressure to scale down the project. As late as November one member wrote that he "would rather see the whole thing go down to defeat than to [compromise on this issue]." But early in 1927 the commission gave in. Adopting the piecemeal approach, it drafted a modest plan for a two-line, twenty-two mile subway, which was estimated to cost $135 million. By then, however, the local economy was in trouble. Auto sales were down, unemployment was up, and property values were falling. Some residents held that even a $135 million subway was too expensive. Others believed that Detroit should not spend any money on a subway unless the suburbs, which would share in the benefits, agreed to pay part of the costs. Still others were critical of the commission's choice of routes and concerned about the subway's impact on the streetcar system. Not long after the mayor's finance committee voted against including the subway in Detroit's long-term capital plan, Mayor John W. Smith shelved the proposal. The commission bided its time. When the economy picked up early in 1929, it submitted an even more modest plan, which called for one subway (and elevated) line, 13.3 miles long, and, as a concession to Detroit's Street Railways Department, two downtown streetcar tunnels, 2.5 miles long. The cost came to $91 million. The plan won the support not only of the downtown business interests but also of virtually all the city's newspapers, auto companies, and commercial and civic organizations. To finance the initial construction, the city council voted to put a $55 million bond issue on the April ballot. To lead the campaign for the bonds, senior executives at Ford, Packard, and other automakers formed the Citizens' Better Transportation Committee.[77]

What little organized opposition there was came mainly from the Committee of Fifty-One, a loose coalition of neighborhood improvement associations and outlying business interests that were opposed to rapid transit of any kind. Responding to the by then familiar arguments of the rapid transit commission and the Citizens' Better Transportation Committee, it charged that the subway would not pay and thus would impose additional burdens on the already hard-strapped taxpayers. The city should look for less expensive solutions to the traffic problem. Although it appeared that the opposition was fighting an uphill battle, the voters rejected the bond issue by a margin of more than two and a half to one, thereby putting an end to the campaign to build a subway in Detroit. Some voters, it turned out, were skeptical of municipal ownership and worried about higher property taxes. Others believed that the plan relied too heavily on special assessments, that the subway would benefit downtown Detroit at the expense of the outlying districts, and that mass transit was no longer the most effective way to solve the city's transportation problems. As Couzens had warned, still others, particularly residents of the north side, saw no reason to support a one-line subway that ran nowhere near their neighborhood.[78] How many of these residents would have voted for the commission's original plan is impossible to tell. But it is safe to say that the political drawbacks of the piecemeal approach did as much damage to the subway's prospects as the financial drawbacks of comprehensive construction.

Of the three momentous issues that sharply divided the advocates of rapid transit, by far the most nettlesome was how to pay for it. Given the tremendous costs of construction, the cities could not raise the money out of general funds. Hence they had only two choices. They could issue bonds of their own, as Boston did. Or in some states they could guarantee bonds issued by a company that would construct and operate the subway for the city, as New York did. In either case the cities had to find a way to pay off the bonds. One option was to draw on fares, placing the burden entirely on the passengers, an approach adopted by Boston, which leased the subway to a company for a sum that covered interest, amortization, and maintenance. Another option was to draw on fares and, if need be, taxes, placing the burden partly on passengers and partly on property owners, an approach adopted by New York. It too leased the subway to a company, but in the event that the rent did not cover the costs the city would defray the deficit out of general funds. Yet another option was for the cities to pay for the bonds, in whole or in part, by assessing the property adjacent to the subway, which would presumably rise in value by virtue of its enhanced accessibility. Based on the principle that property owners who benefited from public improvements ought to pay for them, special assessments had long been used in American cities to finance streets, sewers, and parks.[79]

In practice, however, cities operated under strong constraints. Special assessments had never been used to finance rapid transit. Even those who favored using them conceded that it would be "a radical innovation"—one whose legality was very much in doubt. Moreover, most people believed that mass transit, subways and els included, should be self-supporting. Hence most cities were under considerable pressure to follow Boston's lead and rely exclusively on fares to pay off the bonds. This approach made good sense, provided that the subways were self-supporting. Initially, most Americans assumed they would be, that as the population grew and the riding habit rose, subways would generate more than enough income to cover the costs of construction. But this assumption was undermined before World War I and completely discredited soon after. Revenues did not increase as fast as expected, and expenses increased much faster. The Boston rapid transit system suffered such a grave fiscal crisis that in 1918 the Massachusetts legislature put it in the hands of a board of trustees, which raised the fare from five to ten cents. And in New York, when the companies that operated the city's second subway system, the so-called Dual System, were unable to pay the rent, local officials had to shell out $80 million to cover the interest and amortization charges on the bonds.[80] Even before the war was over, it was evident that no subway would generate enough income to pay the costs of construction, at least not on the basis of the traditional nickel fare.

One way to resolve the problem was to charge a higher fare. After all, the subways provided much better service than the streetcars. They were faster and more reliable, less prone to delays and breakdowns. They saved riders a good deal of time and enabled many of them to live in outlying residential sections. If a streetcar ride was worth five cents, surely a subway ride was worth more. But as even subway advocates realized, this scheme had serious drawbacks. Except in cities where riders thought that it was already too high, the nickel fare was sacrosanct in the early twentieth century. Given the widespread view that the transit companies were extorting money from the public in order to pay high dividends on watered stock, an attempt to charge a higher fare would run into strenuous opposition. A higher fare might also be self-defeating, especially if many passengers opted to ride the streetcars or use their automobiles instead. Worst of all, a higher fare might well undermine the efforts to build subways. These efforts were justified in large part on the grounds that subways would enable the working class to escape the over-crowded inner-city slums. If the fare was high enough to cover the costs, it would be too high for most working people. For those who believed that rapid transit was more than "a purely business proposition" and that fares should be kept as low as possible, a subway of so little social value was hardly worth fighting for.[81]

Another way to resolve the problem was to subsidize the subway, to use general funds (or, in effect, property taxes) to make up the deficit between the income from fares and the costs of construction. This scheme had much to commend it. A subway benefited everyone, not just the riders. It relieved traffic congestion and reduced the need for street widening. It promoted residential development on the periphery and reduced severe overcrowding in the center. It raised property values and thus increased tax receipts. But this scheme had serious drawbacks too. A proposal to subsidize a subway normally required a bond issue, which would have to be approved by either a simple or two-thirds majority of the voters, no mean task. Most cities operated under various types of debt limits, as a rule constitutional provisions that restricted their capacity to issue general obligation bonds. Some cities were approaching these limits. Those that were not were under strong pressure to build other public facilities, which usually could not be financed except by general obligation bonds and were often viewed as more urgent than subways. As the abortive attempt to build a subway in Chicago in 1918 revealed, it was very hard to win popular approval for a rapid transit system. It was even harder when the proposed system depended on a subsidy from the taxpayers. At that point even many citizens who were otherwise inclined to support rapid transit drew the line.[82]

In the search for other ways to help finance rapid transit, some subway advocates decided that special assessments were worth another look. Instrumental in this decision was a report prepared by the City Club of New York, a prominent civic group, and submitted in 1908 to the city Board of Estimate and Apportionment and the state Public Service Commission. Based on the first systematic investigation into the relationship between rapid transit and real estate values, the study found a sharp rise in values in upper Manhattan and the Bronx after the construction of the subway. It calculated that the subway had boosted values north of 135th Street by more than $80 million, nearly twice as much as the cost of the entire line (and roughly six times as much as the cost of the line from 135th Street to the Bronx). In other words, the rise in real estate values in just one part of the city would have covered the whole cost of subway construction and generated a sizable surplus. Given these findings, the City Club asked, "would it not be reasonable to require property benefited in outlying districts to pay for the cost of a rapid transit line built to serve it?" The report's findings were confirmed five years later by A. Merritt Taylor, transit commissioner of Philadelphia, whose less systematic analysis revealed that real estate values had risen far more sharply than would otherwise have been expected along both the city's underground and elevated lines and in both the outlying sections and the business district. Here too the rise in values far exceeded the cost of construction. Subsequent studies came up with similar findings and thereby strengthened the case for special assessments.[83]

The first attempt to use them was made in New York. The results were not encouraging. Three years after the City Club submitted its report, the state legislature gave the city permission to assess property for rapid transit. In 1915 a proposal was made to use special assessments to finance construction of a subway along Utica Avenue in Brooklyn. A year later the Board of Estimate instructed its chief engineer to work out a plan and in particular to define the boundaries of the assessment district and develop a formula for apportioning costs. Although the Public Service Commission approved the plan, it was shelved. So were other proposals in the mid 1920s to use special assessments to construct other lines. These proposals went nowhere largely because of objections from property owners, who denounced special assessments as inequitable. They were already paying taxes to support the existing subways, they pointed out. There was no reason why they should be assessed to build the new subways when other property owners had not been assessed to build the old ones. New York's failure did not discourage supporters of special assessments in other cities. Only New Yorkers could reasonably object that special assessments were inequitable, because only New York had already built a vast subway system that was heavily subsidized by the taxpayers. Supporters of special assessments drew a lesson from New York's experience. But it was not that cities should not use special assessments to build rapid transit. It was that they should not build so much as "one foot of rapid transit" without using special assessments lest they "be precluded from [resorting to] this important method of financing for all time to come."[84]

Although the idea of using special assessments for rapid transit was endorsed by a few influential groups in the 1910s and early 1920s, it did not take hold until the mid 1920s. The breakthrough occurred in November 1923, when the Detroit Rapid Transit Commission released its financial plan, the keystone of its proposed transit system. The commission took it for granted that in view of the current costs of labor and material a rapid transit system could not be built on the basis of a five-cent fare. It also took it for granted that under Detroit's debt limit the city could not build a rapid transit system by issuing general obligation bonds. Thus the commission reasoned that the only way to build a rapid transit system was to divide the costs equitably among the beneficiaries—namely the riders, the city, and the nearby property owners. Intent on keeping the fare as low as possible, it proposed that the riders pay only for equipment, cars, storage yards, and the like, which came to 32 percent of the cost. For what the commission referred to as the "permanent way," the structure, stations, and tracks, the city should pay one-fourth (or 17 percent of the total cost), which would come from property taxes, and the property owners three-fourths (or 51 percent of the total), which would come from special assessments. The assessments would be imposed on all real estate (except buildings) within half a mile of the tracks, with the rates governed by proximity to the stations and ranging from one to seven cents per square foot a year for seven years.[85]

Other transit planners soon followed the Detroit commission's lead. In 1925 Kelker, De Leuw, one of the nation's leading transit engineering firms, prepared a comprehensive rapid transit plan for Los Angeles. It recommended that three-fourths of the costs of the structure, a combination of subways and els, be paid for by special assessments, imposed, as in Detroit, on all land within half a mile of the tracks. A year later the St. Louis Board of Public Service, relying heavily on the work of consulting engineer C. E. Smith, submitted an ambitious rapid transit plan to the city's Board of Aldermen. Under the plan the operating company would pay for the equipment, and the city and nearby property owners would share the costs of the structure; one-quarter would be covered by public utility bonds and three-quarters by special assessments. The Greater Cleveland Transportation Committee came out in support of special assessments for rapid transit in 1925, as did the Pittsburgh Transit Commission a year later. Also in 1926, the Chicago Subway Advisory Commission, an organization of downtown business interests, said that Chicago should use special assessments and declared that its members would be more than willing to pay their share. Toward the end of the decade, by which time most transit planners had come around, the Beeler Organization, another prominent engineering firm, recommended that Cincinnati consider using special assessments to finish its small subway. And the Seattle Traffic Commission, which was sponsored by the downtown business interests, proposed that special assessments be used to finance rapid transit.[86]

To many advocates of rapid transit, the case for special assessments was overwhelming. Given the support for low fares and the opposition to subsidies, special assessments were the only substantial source of funds available. Just how substantial was revealed by the enormous increase in property values along and near the subway lines in New York. What happened in New York, the Detroit Rapid Transit Commission contended, was "a fair indication of what will happen [in Detroit and other cities]." The use of special assessments, their supporters held, was not only a sound way to raise money, a way that would not increase the city's debt and impair its credit, but also an equitable way. It honored the principle that general benefits should be financed by general funds and local benefits by local funds. To tax all property owners for rapid transit, yet allow some property owners to retain the "unearned increments," was unfair, claimed the St. Louis Board of Public Service. "It favors the minority who are benefited and penalizes the majority who are not." The use of special assessments for rapid transit was not "a new principle," argued the Federal Electric Railways Commission, but "merely the application of an old principle." Special assessments had long been used to provide other public improvements in the United States, even, on two occasions (once in San Francisco and once in Denver), to build railroad tunnels. Their use for rapid transit did not differ in principle from their use for other public facilities.[87]

But to many Americans, including many who otherwise supported rapid transit, the case for special assessments was less compelling. The use of special assessments for rapid transit was a "radical departure," wrote the Seattle Municipal League, an "experiment" that had not yet been tried anywhere in the country. It was unjustified, said Greely Kolts, president of the Northwest Civic League, one of the many neighborhood improvement associations in Los Angeles. Mass transit was a business, and should be treated accordingly. There was no more reason for property owners to help pay to construct a subway for a railway company than to help pay to erect "a building for a department store." The use of special assessments for rapid transit was neither sound nor equitable, opponents charged. It was very hard to foresee with accuracy the impact of rapid transit on property values. Some properties might be helped, others might be harmed. Even if property values increased, the increases were illusory, declared Howard A. Starret, one of the leaders of Detroit's Committee of Fifty-One. Property owners received no benefits at all until they sold their land. For investors and speculators, who were ready to sell at any time, this was not a problem. But for ordinary homeowners, who had no intention of selling, it was a very serious problem. Not only would they have to pay the assessments, but as their property was appraised at a higher value, they would also have to pay higher taxes. For small property owners the use of special assessments for rapid transit was "absolutely confiscatory," said a Detroit city councillor.[88]

In the end the proposals to use special assessments fared as poorly in other cities as they did in New York. During the late 1920s Pittsburgh and Allegheny County representatives asked the Pennsylvania legislature to submit to the voters a constitutional amendment allowing cities to assess property for rapid transit. Swayed by opposition from other parts of the state, the legislature refused. At around the same time a bill was introduced in the Missouri legislature permitting St. Louis to assess property for rapid transit, but the bill was shelved when transit advocates could not agree on how much of the costs should be paid for by special assessments. Nothing came of the proposals to resort to special assessments in Los Angeles, Chicago, and other cities either. Indeed, only in Detroit did a proposal that provided for special assessments even reach the voters. And as Sidney Waldon and other advocates of the rapid transit commission's 1929 plan conceded, the opposition to special assessments was a major reason for the failure of the bond issue.[89] Several months after the voters rejected the commission's plan, the Great Depression struck—leaving in its wake a wave of defaults among property owners all over urban America that buried the idea of using special assessments for rapid transit.

A year or so after taking over as the first chairman of the New York City Board of Transportation, an agency that had been created by the state legislature in 1924 and empowered to build new rapid transit lines, John H. Delaney spelled out the financial problems facing the board. "Apparently, everybody wants more subways," he wrote; "everybody wants to preserve a uniform five-cent fare and everybody wants to have the new subways financed in the same way as the existing lines were financed, and nobody wants to pay any of the cost of building the new line by taxation or assessment upon property." This, Delaney pointed out, "is impossible."[90] A strong supporter of special assessments, Delaney may have exaggerated, but not by much. Most riders favored maintaining the five-cent fare; most taxpayers opposed additional taxes; and most property owners objected to special assessments. About the only thing these groups agreed on was that one or both of the others should pay all or most of the cost of rapid transit. Despite these problems, New York managed to embark on the construction of the Independent Subway System (IND) in the mid 1920s, the last major expansion of the city's subway system. But in the absence of a consensus about how to pay for subways, other cities were severely hampered in their attempts to build them. As the Detroit Rapid Transit Commission found out, it was one thing to make the case that the costs of rapid transit should be distributed equitably among the beneficiaries. It was quite another to prevail on the beneficiaries to go along.

On one point, however, Delaney was wrong. By the mid 1920s, if not earlier, not everyone in New York wanted more subways. Indeed, some New Yorkers believed that the city had already built too many. In other cities a small but growing number of residents did not want a subway at all. These Americans were opposed to subways in general, as opposed to specific subway proposals. They held that cities should not build subways, even if they could find ways to resolve the many issues that sharply divided advocates of rapid transit. Some were opposed to subways on the grounds that they would impose too heavy a burden on the city and its hard-strapped taxpayers. Often they suspected that by the time the subway was finished it would cost much more than estimated.[91] Others objected to subways because they were opposed to municipal ownership, suspicious of local officials, doubtful that they could run anything, much less a complicated rapid transit system—still others because they were opposed to private operation of mass transit. Others, notably the streetcar companies and elevated railways, were opposed to subways for fear that they would siphon off much of their business. Still other opponents held that subways would not relieve traffic congestion in the center or promote residential dispersal on the periphery, the two principal rationales for rapid transit since the late 1860s.

Although much of the opposition was expected—for example, there was no reason to expect that els would be less hostile to subways than street railways had been to els and omnibuses had been to street railways—some of it was not. A case in point is the opposition to subways on the grounds that they were a ploy to build up downtown at the expense of the outlying sections, and especially of the outlying business districts. The principal spokesmen for this position were neighborhood improvement associations and outlying businessmen's organizations. This opposition was unexpected because it ran counter to the widespread belief in spatial harmony, the belief that intra-city rivalry was unnatural, that the fortunes of the center and periphery were inseparable. The opposition was also unexpected because the outlying real estate interests had long been strong supporters of rapid transit. Indeed, other Americans had complained that they would do anything to raise the value of their property, even campaign for elevated railways, not caring if they did irreparable damage to residences and businesses along their routes and elsewhere in the city.[92]

Although this opposition was unexpected, the idea underlying it—that rapid transit might serve to build up one part of the city at the expense of another—was not new. It had surfaced in the late 1870s and 1880s, when some New Yorkers predicted that the elevated railways would not only foster residential dispersal but also promote commercial concentration. Downtown would prosper, but the outlying business districts would decline. Once residents could travel quickly and comfortably between their homes on the periphery and what the *Real Estate Record* called "the great depots of trade" in the center, neighborhood stores would founder. So would suburban stores. The idea spread to Chicago in the late 1880s and 1890s. Observers there forecast that the elevated railways would encourage residents to move to outlying sections—leaving the close-in residential neighborhoods with higher vacancy rates and lower property values—and also to shop in the Loop. By enabling people, as one businessman put it, to "fly over the midway districts from the suburbs to the [Loop] and back again," the els would sap much of the vitality out of the outlying business districts.[93] This idea began to catch on in the early twentieth century, a time when the outlying business districts were rapidly growing in number, size, and importance—a time also when small homeowners were replacing large subdividers and speculators in the outlying residential sections.

The idea did not catch on everywhere. During the mid 1910s property owners in upper Manhattan called on the city to extend the subway into their territory; so did real estate interests in the outer boroughs. Some New Yorkers even thought subways would stimulate commercial development outside Manhattan, especially in the vicinity of the stations. At about the same time a host of commercial organizations, civic groups, and improvement associations from all over Philadelphia endorsed a $6 million bond issue to build a subway and el in the business district. And a decade later property owners in the San Fernando Valley, an as yet largely undeveloped part of Los Angeles, backed rapid transit as the only way to open their remote holdings for residential development. But the idea did take hold elsewhere. In Detroit the Committee of Fifty-One, which spoke for outlying real estate and business interests, attacked the rapid transit commission's 1929 plan as a ploy to enrich the downtown merchants at the expense of the rest of the city. Many residents agreed. "Home owners would have to pay the bulk of the [subway's] cost as usual," one wrote, "while the downtown business people will be the chief beneficiaries." The same was true in Los Angeles, where many outlying business interests viewed rapid transit as a ploy by the downtown business interests to strengthen their weakening hold over the commercial life of the metropolis (and to pass the costs on to property owners elsewhere in the city).[94]

Nowhere did the outlying business interests oppose subways more vigorously, implacably, and effectively than in Chicago. By the early twentieth century downtown Chicago was one of the nation's marvels, an extremely compact, highly concentrated business district widely known for its palatial department stores, towering office buildings, and imposing elevated railway loop. The commercial hub of the Midwest, it did more trade than any business district except downtown New York. But even if most of Chicago's trade was done in the Loop, a good deal was done in dozens of outlying business districts all over the city, most of them located along transit lines and major thoroughfares. By the 1910s and 1920s the small ones consisted of a few groceries, drug stores, bakeries, hardware stores, and taverns that served nearby residents. The large ones—the ones, for example, at Milwaukee and Logan Square, Halsted and Sixty-third, and Madison and Crawford—drew customers from a wider area and also included branch banks, movie houses, professional offices, furniture stores, and real estate firms.[95] These outlying business interests were organized into a host of often overlapping street, neighborhood, district, and even citywide associations. Among them were two of the strongest opponents of subways, the Northwest Side Commercial Association, which was led by Tomaz F. Deuther, and the Cook County Real Estate Board, most of whose members dealt in real estate outside the Loop.

For the outlying business interests, the issue first came to a head in early 1909, when the Chicago Subway Bureau recommended the construction of a $100 million subway that radiated from the Loop into the north, south, and west sides. Even before the bureau made its report public, west-side merchants mounted a campaign against the plan. It soon spread to other parts of the city. The campaign was then taken over by the Chicago Retail Merchants' Association "Outside the Loop," an organization of about five thousand outlying merchants that had just been formed to lobby against an eight-hour-day bill supported by Loop merchants. The association contended that the proposed subway was designed to increase trade and raise property values in the Loop at the expense of the outlying business districts. As Robert W. Schoenfeld, who owned a department store at Halsted and Sixty-third, declared, "Every merchant outside the loop knows that if a subway were built it would practically mean his end so far as business is concerned. It would take most of the trade to the loop and leave us nothing." A small downtown subway might be acceptable, said R. J. Carroll, a Milwaukee Avenue merchant and president of the association. "But the minute it is proposed to extend it outside the loop we are against it. It would tend to take most of our business away, and in a short time we would all be going into bankruptcy." Far better, the association argued, to spend the money on new streets and other much needed improvements. Although Mayor Fred A. Busse, Alderman Milton J. Foreman, chairman of the city council's Local Transportation Committee, and the *Chicago Tribune* called on the outlying merchants to abandon this shortsighted opposition, they refused to back down. The Subway Bureau's plan was subsequently shelved, at least in part because of their efforts.[96]

This campaign was only the first of many. With the Northwest Side Commercial Association and the Cook County Real Estate Board spearheading the efforts, the outlying business interests joined the opposition to the Chicago Harbor and Subway Commission's rapid transit plan of 1912. With funds provided by a dozen or so outlying businessmen's associations (and a couple of neighborhood improvement and taxpayers' organizations), they mounted a campaign that helped persuade the voters to reject the proposed subway in 1914. Two years later Deuther and W. D. Kerr, a spokesman for the Cook County Real Estate Board, spelled out their objections to subways at a hearing of the Chicago Traction and Subway Commission. This commission, which consisted of Parsons, Arnold, and Robert Ridgway, then prepared another transit plan that made several significant concessions to the outlying sections. But when a revised version of this plan, which was strongly supported by the Chicago Association of Commerce and other downtown business interests, was put on the ballot in 1918, the outlying business districts fought against it, too—again with success. Things changed somewhat in the early and mid 1920s, when the Association of Commerce, still strongly committed to a subway, made an effort to coopt the outlying business districts, inviting them to join the All Chicago Council, a citywide group whose goal was to develop a rapid transit plan acceptable to both Loop and non-Loop interests. Some outlying districts favored its plan, which called for streetcars and els as well as subways and provided additional service to the periphery. Others opposed it. A revised version of this plan was submitted to the voters in 1925. Although the Association of Commerce and Mayor William E. Dever lobbied hard for it, the plan was rejected—even losing heavily in many of the outlying sections that were supposed to be the chief beneficiaries.[97]

To the advocates of rapid transit, the outlying business interests were at once selfish and wrongheaded. Selfish, said John Ericson, chairman of the Harbor and Subway Commission, because they were willing to "sacrifice the welfare of the entire community rather than see any action taken whereby some section of the city would profit more than the one in which they live and own property." Wrongheaded, insisted Walter L. Fisher, one of the architects of the 1918 ordinance, because they were wedded to the preposterous notion that "they are somehow going to build up the business of the outlying districts by making it difficult for the people who live in those districts to come downtown." Subways, their advocates contended, were not designed to build up the Loop at the expense of the outlying business districts; they were designed to benefit the entire city. Once the subway was built, the outlying business districts would lose some customers but gain others. In general their business would increase, as would their property values. The streetcars and els had stimulated development in the outlying districts. So would the subways. Drawing on the traditional notion of spatial harmony, the advocates of rapid transit dismissed the idea that there was a conflict of interest between the center and the periphery. Speaking at a conference of Loop and non-Loop interests, a leader of the Chicago Association of Commerce declared in 1911, "our interests are yours and your interests are ours." The Chicago Subway Advisory Commission made the same point a decade and a half later.[98]

The well-being of the Loop depended on the growth and prosperity of the outlying districts, the subway advisory commission conceded. But by the same token the growth and prosperity of the outlying districts depended on the well-being of the Loop. Calling it "a great economic fact," the *Chicago Tribune* wrote in 1915 that "the Chicago loop is the most efficient natural organization to do business possessed by any city in the world. It is, indeed, to the city of Chicago what the city is to the surrounding territory. It is centralization within centralization." It was reasonable for the outlying business interests to try to increase their trade and raise their property values. But it was not reasonable for them to think they could do so "by killing the business center," said Mayor Carter H. Harrison, Jr. "You cannot wipe out this great center," a leader of the Chicago Association of Commerce advised representatives of several outlying businessmen's associations in 1911; "you cannot eliminate it, it is here to stay." In the interest of the entire city, it was incumbent upon the outlying business districts to acknowledge the importance of the Loop and to lend their support to the efforts to enhance its accessibility. As the subway advisory commission put it:

> There would seem to be little question as to the interest of the outside districts of Chicago in a downtown district from which a half a million of their residents derive their livelihood. There would seem to be no doubt of the intimate dependence, in considerable part, of every outside district upon that downtown district from which they so extensively draw. There would seem to be no proper improvement in the downtown district, no just encouragement of its growth, no reasonable measure to increase its prosperity, in which the outside districts may not well cooperate. To their own and distinct advantage.[99]

To Deuther and other spokesmen for the outlying business districts, these arguments were disingenuous at best and self-serving at worst. Subways, they contended, would build up the Loop at the expense of the outlying business districts. Everyone knew it, even the downtown business interests, which were the major force behind what the Cook County Real Estate Board's transportation committee labeled in 1912 "the past eight years of subway agitation." Contrary to their rhetoric, the downtown business interests were well aware that they were locked in competition with the outlying business districts, the outcome of which would have profound impact on profits and property values. Deuther and his associates argued that the downtown business interests were not concerned about improving transportation for the entire city. That could be done more effectively and less expensively by upgrading and extending the streetcar lines and by rerouting them so that it was no longer necessary for residents to travel through the Loop to get from one part of the city to another. Nor were the downtown business interests concerned about relieving congestion. To the contrary, wrote Benjamin Levering, a local lawyer on whom Deuther relied heavily, the Loop merchants and property owners "want to intensify and perpetuate it, for the congestion means good business to them and increase in values of real estate." They want to perpetuate "our present policy of development," said Deuther, a policy of "centralization within a small and limited area" that well serves the Loop, but not the rest of the city.[100]

As spokesmen for the outlying business interests saw it, the Loop was anything but a natural development, much less a beneficial one. It was, wrote Levering, "a vast monopoly of mercantile business and unearned increment of land values" which should be spread over the whole city, a monopoly that thrives "at the expense of the outside sections" and that "works great hardship and injustice to the millions who are not interested in loop real estate or in loop stores and shops." The Loop was the product not of geography but of transit policy, a policy whereby nearly all streetcars and els converged on the same small spot. Now that traffic was growing worse in the Loop, shoppers were finding it harder to get to State Street, and trade was on the verge of expanding to the outlying sections, the Loop merchants and property owners were demanding a subway. But a subway—in Levering's words, the "greatest instrumentality which has ever been devised for shoveling business and people into [the Loop]"—was exactly what Chicago did not need. It would lead to more concentration, more traffic, more congestion, and eventually to demands for more subways—until a point was reached at which the congestion would grow so intolerable that, in Deuther's words, "strangulation might set in," bringing about a much needed dispersal of business, doing "a job which our mayors and alderman[,] either through ignorance or through fear, [have] failed to do."[101]

Late in 1926 the subway advisory commission finally conceded that subways would benefit the Loop more than other parts of the city. In yet another proposal for a rapid transit system, the commission therefore recommended

Opposition to the Loop and a Chicago subway, 1910s (Tomaz F. Deuther, Local Transportation, *Chicago, 1924)*

that the city pay for it largely by special assessments, a fair share of which would have fallen on downtown real estate. Like the previous proposals, this one went nowhere. By the late 1920s Chicago had little to show for the many attempts to build a subway other than a shelf full of reports and studies. There were several reasons that the city was unable to build a subway, some of which have already been mentioned. But according to two Chicago aldermen who were involved in the struggle, the opposition of the outlying business interests was the most important. It is not clear that a subway would have built up the Loop at the expense of the outlying business districts, although according to Homer Hoyt, the leading authority on land values in Chicago, the construction of the els in the 1890s did slow the development of some of these districts.[102] But many of the outlying business interests believed that it would—and that belief fueled the opposition to subways at what was perhaps the one time in Chicago's history that the city could have built them.

Also fueling much of the opposition to subways was a small but influential group of social reformers, city planners, and transit engineers who had gradually come to believe that subways would neither relieve traffic congestion nor promote residential dispersal.[103] Their opposition was as unexpected as the opposition of the outlying business interests. Down through the late nineteenth century it had been taken for granted that subways, no matter how expensive and unpleasant, would relieve traffic congestion by removing streetcars from the streets and diverting passengers from surface transit to underground transit—by, in other words, increasing the capacity of the streets without increasing their load. It had also been taken for granted that subways would promote residential dispersal by opening up remote and relatively cheap sections for development, thereby enabling workingmen and their families to move from tenement houses to single-family homes.

By the early 1910s, however, some Americans began to have second thoughts about these notions. One was Charles K. Mohler, consulting engineer to the Chicago City Club, who could not understand how the proposed subways would relieve congestion if they were designed to carry even more people into the city's small and already overcrowded business district. Another was Ernest P. Goodrich, a New York city planner, whose doubts were inspired largely by the experience of New York's first subway. From the start the IRT had attracted far more riders than anticipated; within a decade it poured a million or so people a day into the already packed streets and sidewalks of lower and midtown Manhattan. By the 1920s many other Americans believed that subways intensified traffic congestion. They too pointed to New York

City, where after nearly three decades of subway construction congestion was worse than ever. "Despite every scheme of traffic control so far devised," the *New Republic* wrote in 1928, "New York ties itself up in a knot twice a day from Thirty-fourth to Fifty-ninth Street and almost from river to river." It was even worse in lower Manhattan, others pointed out, especially in the financial district. On the basis largely of New York's experience, a blue-ribbon group of municipal officials, traffic engineers, and city planners, some of whom had once been strong advocates of subways, concluded in 1927 that "congestion in the business centers of our great cities is a malady which cannot be cured by providing facilities for greater congestion." The Regional Plan Association of New York took the same position, as did the National Municipal Review and the American Institute of Architects.[104]

At the core of this position was the theory of what Daniel Turner, consulting engineer to the New York Transit Commission, called "a vicious circle of transit development and city congestion." Subways, Turner wrote, did more than just remove traffic from the surface. They also created additional traffic. And they drove up the value of real estate along the lines, which encouraged property owners to replace small office building and retail shops with giant skyscrapers. These generated even more traffic—transit, vehicular, and pedestrian—and even more congestion. The downtown businessmen and property owners then demanded new subways to relieve the increasing congestion. "In this way," argued Turner, "the problem has gone around and around in a circle, from congestion to new subways—and then again to congestion." No city could possibly build enough subways to keep up with the demand, wrote Henry H. Curran, a former New York City alderman and later counsel to the New York City Club, not even New York. The city had already spent $700 million on subways without solving the traffic problem and now found itself with "a coagulated bunch of skyscrapers" and no money to spare for bridges, schools, parks, and playgrounds. New York was an object lesson for Chicago, Detroit, and other cities thinking of building a subway, Curran warned. It was an object lesson of what "not to do."[105]

During the 1910s and 1920s many Americans were also having second thoughts about the notion that subways would promote residential dispersal. These were an outgrowth of one of the principal paradoxes of rapid transit. Rapid transit, its supporters had long believed, was needed to open outlying sections for residential development, to enable the middle and working classes to live in single-family homes in sparsely settled neighborhoods. But as even B. J. Arnold and other experts who were favorably disposed toward rapid transit pointed out, subways were very expensive. Whether built by private enterprise or public authority, they were invariably saddled with heavy fixed charges. To meet these charges, subways had to carry many passengers. But many passengers meant "dense traffic," argued planner Milo R. Maltbie in 1913; and dense traffic meant "congestion of population." A district of single-family houses, "each with its own grass plot and garden," could not support a subway at anything like what Americans considered a reasonable fare. (Indeed, such a district could not even support a combined elevated and subway line, claimed Henry C. Wright, deputy commissioner of the New York City Department of Charities.) Unless cities can find ways to defray part of the cost of construction, Maltbie said, "it is impossible for [them] to have subways unless at the same time they are content to have congestion—tenement houses, solidly built blocks[,] and not separate dwellings."[106]

But most Americans were not content to have tenement houses. As Wright put it, "the apartment or tenement house . . . tends to destroy the sense of individual responsibility and loyalty to the community." Others viewed the tenements as a threat to public health, personal morality, family stability, political integrity, and public order. It was hard for them to see why they should campaign hard for subways if the result would be to replace tenement or apartment houses near the center with tenement or apartment houses on the periphery. This paradox also raised knotty questions. Take the case of St. Louis, one of many American cities that were already built up mainly of one- and two-family houses. According to Kelker, De Leuw, a subway there could only cover its costs if much of the city "changed from a residence to an apartment district." (To many Americans, an apartment did not qualify as a residence.) But if the population of St. Louis was already widely dispersed, what sense did it make to build a subway to promote residential dispersal?[107] A subway might have done better in New York and Boston, two of the nation's most densely populated cities. But if it succeeded in promoting residential dispersal, if it managed to reduce population density, the subway would not attract enough passengers to cover its fixed charges and operating expenses. If the subway could not meet its obligations, who would put up the money to ensure that the residents who had moved to the periphery would be able to travel to and from the business district?

Most Americans who doubted that subways would relieve traffic congestion and promote residential dispersal fell into one of two groups. One believed that subways were not the only cause of overcrowding. Subways could relieve congestion and promote dispersal, provided that they were designed to serve the outlying residential sections, to connect these sections with the outlying business districts, and to bypass the downtown business district—provided, in other words, that they were designed to distribute residences and businesses, not to concentrate them. And provided also that they were built according to a comprehensive land-use plan that included measures to prevent the erection of giant skyscrapers and thereby break the "vicious circle of transit development and city congestion." The other group believed that subways, no matter how designed, would only make things worse, that the solution to overcrowding would be found not in rapid transit but in other policies. Chief among them were the proposals to impose height restrictions on office buildings, a measure that would spread out commercial activities; to promote the deconcentration of industry, a step that would allow people to live in suburbs not far from their workplaces; and, not least of all, to encourage the shift from streetcars to automobiles, a move that would further stimulate the decentralization of the American metropolis.[108]

By the mid and late 1920s a good many Americans viewed subways as a problem rather than a solution. Nowhere was this view held more strongly than in Los Angeles. The story began in 1906, when E. H. Harriman, a national railroad magnate whose company owned a local interurban railway, announced a plan to build a four-mile subway running west from downtown Los Angeles. Nothing came of the plan, which was abandoned because of the panic of 1907. Nor did anything come of a more ambitious plan prepared by B. J. Arnold a few years later. As late as the mid 1910s, by which time Los Angeles was well established as the metropolis of southern California, most residents believed that the city was too small (and too widely dispersed) to support a rapid transit system. During the 1910s, however, the population soared from 319,000 to 576,000, making Los Angeles the largest city west of Chicago and the tenth largest (and fastest growing) in the nation. In the meantime, traffic congestion in and around downtown Los Angeles, which had been bad enough in 1910, grew much worse. With the Los Angeles Railway streetcars, the Pacific Electric trains, and a rapidly growing number of autos and trucks pouring into the business district, the streets were close to impassable during rush hour. The downtown business interests, afraid that their stores and offices would soon become inaccessible to the outlying residential sections, began to call for rapid transit. Joining them were some outlying real estate interests, which were dissatisfied with the surface transit systems, and the local railway companies, particularly the Pacific Electric, which regarded rapid transit as the only way to relieve traffic congestion and thereby reduce its expenses, improve its service, and eliminate its chronic deficits.[109]

The issue came to a head in the mid 1920s, when the Los Angeles Traffic Commission, a recently formed but very influential advisory group on which the downtown business interests were well represented, called on the city and county governments to underwrite a study of the transit problem. At the urging of the Los Angeles Board of Public Utilities, a municipal agency whose chief engineer had recently come out in favor of a subway system for central Los Angeles, the city council appropriated $20,000 for the study, a sum that was matched by the county board of supervisors. On the advice of the Board of Public Utilities, the council retained Kelker, De Leuw, whose principals took it for granted that rapid transit was essential for the continued growth and prosperity of Los Angeles. The firm began work in May 1924 and submitted a report about a year later. It recommended a vast rapid transit system, coordinated with the existing surface lines, operated and managed by one agency, and constructed in two stages, the first of which would cost an estimated $130 million, the second an additional $190 million. Two features of the Kelker, De Leuw plan were especially noteworthy—and extremely controversial. In an attempt to design a comprehensive system at a reasonable cost, a difficult task in such a dispersed metropolis, Kelker, De Leuw favored els, which were much cheaper than subways, on most of the lines outside downtown Los Angeles. For each mile of subways, it proposed more than three miles of els in the first stage and about ten miles of els in the second. In an attempt to keep fares as low as possible and to rely as little as possible on property taxes, Kelker, De Leuw also recommended financing the system largely by special assessments—which would have covered 51 percent of the total cost (and 75 percent of the cost of construction).[110]

The report sparked a heated debate that raged for several years. In favor of the plan were the downtown business interests, some outlying real estate interests, and the surface transit companies. Allied with them were the Los Angeles Traffic Commission and the Board of Public Utilities (as well as Mayor George E. Cryer). Spokesmen for these groups defended the plan on the grounds that Los Angeles sorely needed a rapid transit system not only to relieve traffic congestion and stimulate residential development but also to affirm its standing as a great metropolis. They also said that Los Angeles should follow the lead of New York, Boston, and Chicago, all of which had begun to build a rapid transit system at about the time their population reached a million. Opposed to the plan were a good many small residential property owners, not all of whom objected to rapid transit per se. Some of them were opposed—"unalterably opposed," wrote the head of the Taxpayers' Anti-Elevated League—to the construction of elevated railways, which were an integral part of the plan. They rejected Kelker, De Leuw's position, one held by many transit engineers in the mid 1920s, that els could be built in a way that would not darken the street, disfigure the city, or lower the value of the abutting property. Others were opposed to the imposition of special assessments. How, their spokesmen asked, could the authorities even think about imposing so heavy a burden on property owners in order to build a transit facility that would reduce the value of their holdings?[111]

Also opposed to the plan were two groups that objected to rapid transit per se—whether built above ground or below ground and whether financed by special assessments or property taxes. Many outlying businessmen regarded rapid transit as a ploy to build up downtown Los Angeles at their expense. And many other residents feared that rapid transit would do there what it had done in other cities, namely "increase congestion and the evils which flow from it." In this group were the members of a special committee of the Los Angeles City Club that urged the city to reject the Kelker, De Leuw plan. Applying Turner's theory of the "vicious circle," it pointed out that subways and els would drive up downtown property values, triggering skyscraper construction and thereby exacerbating traffic congestion. The problem would be solved by enabling residents to work and shop on the periphery, not by building new facilities to carry them into the center. The committee also held that rapid transit was not needed to promote residential dispersal. A city mainly of single-family houses, Los Angeles was already extremely dispersed. Given the incipient movement toward the decentralization of commerce and industry, plus the growing reliance on automobiles and telephones, it was likely to become even more dispersed in the future—even without rapid transit. "Considering the results obtained in cities like New York, Boston, and Philadelphia," the committee declared, "we may well ask whether Los Angeles is justified in beginning the endless chain program of expenditures in subway and elevated structures which inevitably have tended to increase the congestion in those centers of population."[112]

C. A. Dykstra, a well-known city planner who opposed the Kelker, De Leuw plan, made the same point. Writing in the *National Municipal Review* in 1926, he pointed out that rapid transit would funnel more and more people into downtown Los Angeles, thereby creating a more centralized business district. But, he asked, is that what Los Angeles needs or wants? "Is it inevitable or basically sound or desirable that larger and larger crowds be brought into the city's center; do we want to stimulate housing congestion along subway lines and develop an intensive rather than an extensive city; . . . is it ultimately desirable to have an area of abnormally high land values with its consequent demand for the removal of all building height restrictions; must all large business, professional and financial operations be conducted in a restricted area[?]"

Dykstra held that the answer was no. So did most residents of Los Angeles, who no longer believed that an extremely compact, highly concentrated business district was either inevitable or desirable. Far more attractive to them was a more decentralized metropolis in which the populace, in Dykstra's words, "for the most part lives near its work, has its individual lawns and gardens, [and] finds its market and commercialized recreational facilities right around the corner." Dykstra and many others envisioned the future Los Angeles as a huge metropolis of small but largely self-contained communities, each of which revolved around its own business center, one that would have little need for rapid transit because it would have little traffic congestion in the center and little long-distance commuting on the periphery.[113]

The debate over rapid transit dragged on into the early 1930s. But by then the Kelker, De Leuw plan was dead, as were the prospects for rapid transit in Los Angeles. As even its supporters conceded, rapid transit could not be built by private enterprise, certainly not by the Los Angeles Railway or the Pacific Electric, both of which were in serious financial trouble. Nor was public authority a viable alternative. Given the fiscal constraints, it could not build a comprehensive rapid transit system; but given the political constraints, it could not build anything else. The downtown business interests still supported rapid transit, but this was offset to a considerable extent by the opposition of the outlying business districts. A few large landowners in the San Fernando Valley and other remote sections also favored rapid transit, but they were outnumbered by the many small property owners elsewhere in greater Los Angeles. As C. J. S. Williamson, a member of the Santa Monica Planning Commission, explained, many of these people were already relying heavily on their automobiles. They were unlikely to use rapid transit and unwilling to help pay for it, especially when they were already supporting a local highway system that served them pretty well. They were interested in keeping their property taxes and special assessments as low as possible, not in seeing remote sections opened for residential development—and not in helping out the local transit companies. And for the most part they subscribed to the emerging conventional wisdom that rapid transit would slow down the movement toward a decentralized metropolis, which was viewed as the ultimate solution to the local transportation problem.[114]

By the late 1920s America's cities had built about 350 miles of rapid transit lines, of which a little more than one-third ran below ground, a little less than two-thirds above. That may seem like a lot, but in a country with almost 41,000 miles of street railways, it was not. Moreover, about two-thirds of the rapid transit lines—close to three-fifths of the els and roughly five-sixths of the subways—were located in New York. Most of the other elevated lines were in Chicago, and most of the other subway lines were in Boston. To put it another way, by the late 1920s, after more than two decades of vigorous efforts, after the preparation of scores of studies and reports, after the expenditure of millions of dollars, and after a host of predictions that most big cities would soon build a rapid transit system, nearly 90 percent of the els, close to half of which had gone up before the turn of the century, were in New York and Chicago. And more than 90 percent of the subways were in New York and Boston, both of which had begun to build their first underground lines before 1900.[115]

The campaign for rapid transit made some progress in Philadelphia, where the city and the Philadelphia Rapid Transit Company joined forces to build roughly forty miles of els and subways by the late 1920s (and about thirty additional miles of subways by the early 1930s). But it went nowhere in the dozen or so other cities that attempted to follow in the steps of New York and Boston.[116] Pittsburgh approved a bond issue for a subway, but as a result of wartime inflation did not build it. By the early 1930s even former supporters were no longer certain that a subway was the solution to the city's traffic problem. With money from a bond issue, Cincinnati constructed a large part of a small subway. But it did not finish it, partly because the city officials were reluctant to submit another bond issue to the voters and partly because the local transit company was unwilling to lease the subway without a guarantee against any losses. Cleveland turned down a bond issue for a rapid transit system, as did Detroit. Chicago rejected several different transit proposals. The Kelker, De Leuw plan never even made it to the ballot; neither did an ambitious plan prepared by the St. Louis Board of Public Service. Nothing came of several much less ambitious (though probably even less promising) schemes submitted in Baltimore, Milwaukee, and San Francisco. Despite Mayor C. B. Fitzgerald's remarks that Seattle needed a subway as much as it needed water, nothing came of the proposals to build one there either.

Several transit plans were still under consideration in the late 1920s. But even before the depression hit, leaving most big cities in no position to build much of anything, there was little chance that these plans would be adopted. The downtown business interests backed rapid transit as strongly as ever. But they faced heavy opposition, and they could no longer count on much support from their traditional allies. Most outlying real estate interests, now made up of small homeowners as opposed to large subdividers, were more concerned about holding down property taxes than opening up remote sections for residential development. Many outlying residents were by now firmly wedded to the automobile. Many transit engineers, including some who had designed major rapid transit plans in the early and mid 1920s, now held that subways and els should not be built anywhere except in a few very large and extremely dense cities. According to Kelker, De Leuw, even St. Louis, the nation's seventh largest city in 1930, was too small and too diffuse for rapid transit. Moreover, the Boston and New York rapid transit systems, long the models for other cities, were in trouble. The Boston system was so plagued by financial problems that the state legislature put it in the hands of a board of public trustees, which raised the fare and then assessed the deficit against the cities and towns served by the system. Some Bostonians held that the els should be demolished, and others believed that their grandchildren would live to see the subways "converted into catacombs." The New York transit system was running a huge deficit too. It was draining the city of much-needed funds, critics charged, and filling it with little-needed skyscrapers. Its service was deplorable, wrote the City Club of New York, which strongly objected to the "uncomfortable, unsanitary, indecent, offensive and dangerous crowding and packing and crushing of people" on the trains.[117]

The long and unsuccessful campaign for rapid transit had far-reaching consequences, some of which were noticeable as early as the late 1920s. The failure to build rapid transit had a profound impact on the many Americans who went downtown regularly to work, to shop, to do business, and to amuse themselves, the many Americans whose trade was crucial to the well-being of the business district. A few could walk downtown or commute by steam railroad, but in the absence of rapid transit, most had to rely on the streetcars, which were getting slower and less comfortable. And the streetcar companies, most of which were in financial trouble, could not raise the capital to upgrade equipment or otherwise improve service. Some Americans continued to use mass transit anyway. (By the late 1920s, though, they were much more likely to do so in the few cities that had built rapid transit than in the many cities that had not. Indeed, in the cities without rapid transit the riding habit, which had risen steadily in the 1900s and 1910s, fell sharply in the 1920s, in some cases dropping below prewar levels.)[118] But others, fed up with paying higher fares for poorer service, stopped riding the streetcars, a development the full impact of which would not be felt until the 1930s. Some went downtown by auto. And others went downtown less often, doing more of their shopping and business in outlying districts.

The failure to build rapid transit had a profound impact on the downtown business interests too. It made them aware of the limits of their power. It showed that despite their great wealth and political influence—despite the support of other business interests and most transit engineers, despite the widespread enthusiasm for traffic relief and residential dispersal, and despite the undeniable advantages of rapid transit—they could not always get what they wanted. The long struggle over rapid transit also led many downtown businessmen and property owners to the conclusion that they could no longer depend exclusively on citywide organizations to promote their interests—that much like the outlying business districts, they would have to form associations of their own.[119] Assuming that accessibility was the key to their well-being, as most of them still did, they were left with three options, all of which would be exercised in the 1930s and 1940s. One was to continue to press for rapid transit—and in particular to look for other ways to underwrite the tremendous costs of construction, which were widely viewed as the principal obstacle. Another option, the repercussions of which were not foreseen, was to push instead for highways and parking lots to make it easier for residents to drive downtown. Still another option, which would have been unthinkable a generation earlier, was to move their offices and stores to the outlying business districts, an option that was extremely unnerving to the downtown property owners.

The campaign for rapid transit also forced many Americans to question the underlying assumptions about downtown and the structure of the American metropolis that had emerged in the late nineteenth century. Most Americans still believed that downtown was inevitable and desirable—that the cities would always revolve around an extremely compact, highly concentrated, and largely depopulated business district to which most people would go every day. But the struggles over rapid transit prompted some Americans to begin to ask whether it might be possible and even preferable for the metropolis to be organized around a host of business districts, of which downtown would be only one. Many Americans still held that rivalry between the business districts and residential sections was unnatural. But in light of the battles over rapid transit, in light especially of the deep hostility toward downtown in the outlying business districts, some Americans began to lose faith in the concept of spatial harmony, to wonder whether rivalry within cities might well be as natural as rivalry among cities. And some Americans also started to have second thoughts about the conventional wisdom that the equilibrium between residential dispersal and business concentration would hold indefinitely.

3

The Sacred Skyline:

The Battle over

Height Limits

Architect A. B. Mullett was extremely optimistic about New York City's prospects. It will soon be "the metropolis of the world," he told the *Real Estate Record and Builders' Guide* in 1881, "as populous as London, as luxurious as Paris." Downtown will thrive, he predicted. It will also change. It will be rebuilt with "immense structures, ten, twelve, and even fourteen stories high." As well as more concentrated, it will become more specialized. One part "will be given over to dry goods, another to wholesale clothing, a third to insurance companies. Real estate brokers will cluster in one quarter and mining brokers in another."[1] During the next thirty years downtown New York changed even more than Mullett anticipated. It continued to expand northward—a seemingly inexorable movement that vexed occasional visitors, who discovered that the same restaurant or hotel that was uptown one decade was downtown the next. The financial district, which stayed on or near Wall Street, was largely rebuilt, first with ten- to fifteen-story buildings and later with twenty-, thirty-, and even forty-story ones. The fashionable retail district, which had long been located on Broadway, unexpectedly moved to (and then up) Fifth Avenue, which emerged as a mecca for shoppers. These changes confirmed what Americans had long believed—that downtown was not only inevitable and desirable, it was also highly unstable.

Downtown was highly unstable because it was constantly on the move, its boundaries changing all the time. Downtown New York spread north. So did downtown Seattle, the core of which shifted from Cherry Street to Union Street, about seven blocks, between 1895 and 1915. Downtown Portland also moved north, away from its original site near the Willamette River, as did downtown Tampa, which expanded, slowly but steadily, up Franklin Street. Downtown Cleveland drifted southeast, toward Public Square, up to 1890, when it turned east and advanced along Euclid Avenue. Downtown Philadelphia moved west. As one observer noted in the early 1870s, "The advancing tide of commerce and trade, ever surging westward from the Delaware [River], has already swept over Broad Street in the centre of the city, driving the dwellings of the people before it." Downtown St. Louis also moved west, leaving the East End virtually deserted. So did downtown Omaha, which spread along Douglas, Farnum, and Harvey streets from Tenth to Sixteenth street. Downtown San Francisco headed south from its original location near Portsmouth Plaza and then, as it approached Market Street, turned west. Downtown Los Angeles also drifted south, away from the site of the original pueblo.[2] Americans were baffled. They were sure that there would always be a downtown, but not where it would be located. They knew that downtown would move over time, but not how far, how fast, or even in which direction.

Nor was that all. Downtown, Americans assumed, would remain highly compact and extremely concentrated, but how compact and how concentrated was hard to say. As the demand for office space increased, the business district could grow either horizontally or vertically. Builders could put up new structures on the fringe or, taking advantage of changes in building technology, replace existing structures in the center with much taller ones. The great department stores would locate close to each other. But whether they would cluster on one or two blocks, as they did in Boston, or spread over several, as they did in New York, was not clear. Downtown, Americans assumed, would become more specialized; but which streets would attract which types of enterprises was also hard to say. During the late 1860s and early 1870s there was a good deal of uncertainty in San Francisco about whether the leading retail stores would continue to move south, below Market Street, or turn west. Things were much the same in Chicago, especially in the wake of the great fire that destroyed much of the city in 1871. Some people were not rebuilding, one observer wrote, because they had no idea where and what to build. "There is great uncertainty as to where business centres are to be, as to which streets will be plebeian and which aristocratic [and as to] which streets should be given up to saloons, which to boarding houses, which to wholesale and which to retail trade."[3]

Instability was not an academic matter. Huge stakes were involved. Vast sums could be made or lost when downtown moved. Potter Palmer, a Chicago capitalist who made one fortune speculating in cotton during the Civil War, made another when many of the leading retail stores and financial institutions moved from Lake Street to State Street in the late 1860s. Less fortunate was William C. Ralston, the San Francisco mining king, who spent a fortune in an unsuccessful effort to drive the city's business district south of Market

Street to New Montgomery Street in the early 1870s. Property values soared on New York's Fifth Avenue when many department stores moved there in the early 1900s, but they dropped in St. Louis's East End when merchants and other businessmen moved west in the 1870s and 1880s. Even minor moves could mean major windfalls or wipeouts because of the tremendous disparities in real estate values in and near the business district. "I know real estate values," said a Chicago alderman in 1910, "and I can point out a piece of property in the loop worth $6,000 a foot and only four blocks away another piece that the owner couldn't sell for more than $500 a foot." Downtown's instability also forced many merchants to relocate periodically, sometimes for better, sometimes for worse. And by the early twentieth century it was a source of concern for the insurance companies and other financial institutions that held tens of millions of dollars of mortgages on downtown real estate.[4]

Downtown was highly unstable for a number of reasons, but by the late nineteenth century none seemed more important than the coming of the skyscraper. For property owners, skyscrapers offered a splendid opportunity to increase rental income and raise real estate values. But they also posed serious problems. Given their capacity to house thousands of tenants, they centralized office work, thereby reducing property values on the fringe of the business district. They also displaced tenants from older and less up-to-date buildings, thereby reducing the rental income of the structures, but not necessarily the assessed value of the land. And they lowered the value of adjacent buildings by depriving them of light and air.[5] The skyscraper owners might well earn a substantial return on their investments. But they would always have to worry that a developer might one day put up an even taller building on an adjacent lot and do to them what they had done to others. Some downtown business interests thought the costs of skyscrapers outweighed the benefits and urged that something be done to prevent the erection of taller and taller buildings. Others disagreed. And they soon found themselves on opposing sides in the movement to impose height limits on tall buildings.

The movement started in New York in the 1880s, spread to other big cities in the 1890s and 1900s, and then became enmeshed in the battle over zoning in the 1910s and early 1920s. Although many Americans thought zoning would resolve the issue, the debate over skyscrapers revived in the mid and late 1920s (and did not subside until the early 1930s, when the depression brought construction to a standstill). At the heart of the battle over height limits was a deep ambivalence about skyscrapers and a strong disagreement about the structure of the business district.[6] Joined in this battle were a wide range of groups. Besides downtown businessmen and property owners, they included architects, engineers, and planners, doctors, lawyers, and fire chiefs, novelists, academics, and intellectuals, and specialists in public finance and public health. Even more than the fight over rapid transit, the battle about height limits was a struggle among the upper and upper middle classes in which the lower and lower middle classes took virtually no part.

By the early twentieth century skyscrapers were the most striking feature of the business district. These tall buildings—which is what they were called before the word skyscraper became popular—dominated the skyline, towering over the city much like a mountain range, to which they were often likened. And much like a mountain range, the skyscrapers were so awesome that it was sometimes easy for contemporaries to forget that they were a new building type, barely a generation old. As Montgomery Schuyler, the dean of American architectural critics, pointed out in 1903, "No such innovation in the art of building has been so swiftly accomplished since the development and expression of groined vaulting in masonry in the twelfth and thirteenth centuries, and that took two generations." As late as 1870, when railroad terminals, street railways, and department stores were fixtures downtown, there were no skyscrapers. There were many office buildings, some solid, ornate, and even monumental. But they were no taller than other buildings, few of which were more than four and five stories. Everywhere the skyline was still dominated by church steeples, some of which soared two hundred feet high. In New York it was not until the early 1890s, when the Pulitzer Building went up on Park Row, the home of the city's principal newspapers, that an office building rose above the steeple of Trinity Church.[7]

Prior to the erection in 1869 of New York's Equitable Building, the first office building to employ passenger elevators, there had been a de facto height limit in New York and other cities. It was based on the widely held assumption that people would not climb more than four flights of stairs to get to an office. As Schuyler explained, "Five stories had been found to be the maximum beyond which no tenant would pay rent, and to which no 'paying guest' would ascend without grumblings." Passenger elevators, the earliest of which had been installed in hotels and stores in New York in the late 1850s, abolished this limit. They were soon installed in office buildings all over the country. By the end of the century there were thousands of them. Manhattan alone had about three thousand, which transported 1.5 million passengers every day— and in the case of first-class elevators, the type normally found in office buildings, traveled on average the equivalent of thirty miles a day. Often referred to as "our perpendicular railway," elevators were among the wonders of the time.

Broadway before the skyscraper, ca. 1880 (Henry Collins Brown, ed., Valentine's Manual of Old New York, *New York, 1920)*

Although they were little more than "frail-looking baskets of steel netting," one journalist wrote, they "fly up through the towers like glass balls from a trap at a shooting contest." They were safe, fast, and—except for the occasional jolt, "which makes the passenger seem to feel his stomach pass into his shoes"—comfortable.[8] The elevator enabled the builders to go well above the fifth floor and, by making the upper floors as valuable as the lower ones, gave them an incentive to do so.

By itself the elevator would have had a strong impact on the business district. In conjunction with the growth of the service sector, which created a tremendous demand for office space, and the expansion of the street railways and commuter trains, which funneled millions of managers, professionals, clerks, and secretaries downtown every day, it transformed the skyline. Office buildings now expanded vertically. New York took the lead when several large corporations erected the first generation of skyscrapers in the 1870s. In the vanguard were the life insurance and newspaper companies, many of which saw tall office buildings not only as a sound investment but also as a source of prestige and a form of advertising. Even taller buildings—ten, twelve, and fifteen stories high—went up in the 1880s, first in New York and then in Chicago. In the Windy City, one observer said in the early 1890s, "high is now merely a comparative term, since high ten years ago is now low." "The demands for large return on investments has [sic] now reached such a point," he added, "that no one would contemplate a down-town improvement of less than ten to twelve stories, while sixteen, eighteen and twenty stories are now as glibly talked about as seven, eight and nine were but a few years ago."[9] The skyscrapers came even to staid Boston. There too the insurance companies led the way, putting up a few tall office buildings in the mid 1870s. Others followed in the late 1880s, erecting three skyscrapers on State Street, the ten-story Fiske Building, the fourteen-story Ames Building, and the eleven-story Exchange Building—each of which stood more than 160 feet tall.

For a while, from around the mid 1880s to the early 1890s, it seemed that the skyscraper had gone about as high as it would go. A product of masonry construction, whose structure was supported by the exterior walls, it was held down by the rule that the taller the structure, the thicker the walls. Beyond about sixteen stories—the height of Chicago's Monadnock Building, one of the tallest masonry structures ever built—the walls would have to be so thick that they would take up most of the first floor, the most valuable floor in the building, and much of the next few floors. What little space was left would be needed for the elevator shafts. Starting in Chicago in the mid 1880s and in New York a few years later, however, architects developed an alternative to masonry construction. In what soon became known as steel-frame (or steel-skeleton) construction, the building was supported not by the walls but by a steel frame, which was encased, wrote Schuyler, in "a mere envelope of stone or clay." Steel-frame construction was widely adopted in Chicago and New York in the 1890s and soon spread to other cities—though in Boston it was rejected as "too visionary." By abolishing the thick masonry walls, steel-frame construction allowed builders to erect extraordinarily tall office buildings. It also enabled them to build very rapidly, an important consideration for property owners who were reluctant to tear down an old building and put up a new one if it meant forgoing the rent for the better part of two or more years.[10]

And build they did. By the turn of the century downtown New York had more than a dozen buildings over 250 feet, the tallest of which, the thirty-story Aetna Building, stood 455 feet high. "When I was here in 1877," wrote William Archer, a British visitor, in 1900, "I remember looking with wonder at the [New York] Tribune building . . . which was then considered a marvel of

The Chicago Loop, State and Madison Streets, ca. 1910 (Courtesy of the Chicago Historical Society, CHi-04787)

architectural daring. Now it is dwarfed into absolute insignificance by a dozen Cyclopean structures on every hand." The Aetna Building was soon sur-passed by the Singer Building, the Metropolitan Life Building, and the Wool-worth Building—a fifty-three-story structure built by the retailing magnate (and the tallest building in the world until the late 1920s). Dozens of sky-scrapers went up in downtown Chicago, too—"gigantic buildings" of fifteen and twenty stories, wrote a French visitor in 1895, amid which six- and seven-story buildings "seem to be the merest cottages." These buildings were soon dwarfed by many others, the tallest of which, the Montgomery Ward Building, stood nearly 400 feet high. Skyscrapers were built not only in New York and Chicago but in "every large American city from Seattle to Bangor, from Los Angeles to Galveston," wrote architectural critic A. D. F. Hamlin in the mid 1910s. Indeed, one of the tallest buildings in the country, the forty-two-story Smith Tower, was erected in downtown Seattle in 1914. Some builders hoped to capitalize on the seemingly insatiable demand for office space. Others, no-tably insurance companies and other large corporations, saw skyscrapers as a source of prestige and publicity. Still others built skyscrapers in order to pay rising real estate taxes and to deter tenants from moving to more up-to-date office buildings. By so doing, Archer wrote, "the Americans have practically added a new dimension to space."[11]

As the skyscrapers grew taller and taller, Americans began to wonder whether there were any limits to how high they could go. As early as 1890 Chicago residents, caught up in the enthusiasm for the upcoming World's Fair, had fantasized about one building fifty stories tall and another, in the form of an eagle, one thousand feet high. By the mid 1890s such buildings were no longer fantasies. With the development of steel-frame construction (and the perfection of high-speed elevators), *Engineering Record* declared that "there is no structural difficulty attached to the safe and efficient design of buildings of essentially unlimited height." Architect George B. Post agreed, as did New York's *Real Estate Record and Builders' Guide* and Boston's *American Architect and Building News*, a strong advocate of height limits. As early as 1896 Harding & Gooch, a New York architectural firm, drew plans for a two-hundred-story building, three times as high as the Eiffel Tower, that would hold 100,000 offices and accommodate 400,000 people. A decade later Theodore Starrett, a New York builder, proposed a one-hundred-story build-ing—with a swimming pool and roof garden on top. At the request of Ernest Flagg, a New York architect and another strong advocate of height limits, O. F. Semsch, a civil engineer, calculated in 1908 that a two-thousand-foot building was feasible. Another New York architect remarked a few years later that he would be willing "to go up 2,000 feet," provided he had a base two hundred feet square. Shortly after the completion of the Woolworth Building in 1913, Montgomery Schuyler concluded that if there was a limit to the height of buildings, it was "commercial, not technical."[12]

The skyscrapers were "a purely American product," wrote Barr Ferree, an architecture critic, in 1896. They are found "in no other country," said New York's *Real Estate Record and Builders' Guide* (and "at no other period"). European visitors, many of whom were appalled by the skyscraper, agreed. These buildings "are unlike anything else on earth," wrote one Englishman in 1904. American hotels were so tall, another Englishman pointed out, that "if you could slice off the stories above the thirteenth, as you slice off the top of an egg, and plant them down in Europe, they would of themselves make a biggish hotel according to our standards."[13] European visitors were well prepared for the railroad station and the department store, two other downtown building types, both of which had their origins in Western Europe. They were even prepared for the electric railways (and, less so, for the els). But nothing in their experience had prepared them for the skyscrapers. European office buildings were often monumental, but they were seldom tall. Well into the early twentieth century even the tallest of them rarely rose above five or six stories or reached more than seventy or eighty feet. Nowhere in Europe, not in Paris, Berlin, and even London, by far the largest city in the world, was there a building that by any stretch of the imagination could be called a skyscraper.

This, a large number of Americans believed, was just as well. As early as the 1880s, some of them started looking for ways to stop the construction of ever taller buildings. Two approaches had worked well in Europe. One drew upon the doctrine of "ancient lights," a doctrine derived from English common law that prevented a property owner from depriving adjacent property owners of the light and air to which they were accustomed. But for the most part American courts had rejected this doctrine, taking the position that it could not be applied in the nation's rapidly growing cities "without working the most mischievous injustice." The other approach seemed more promising. Starting in the eighteenth century, the authorities had imposed height limits on buildings in Paris and a few other cities. By the late nineteenth century these limits had spread all over Europe. Paris had a height limit of sixty-five feet in the 1870s (and a lower one on streets less than twenty meters wide). The limit was seventy-eight feet in Berlin in the 1880s and seventy-two in Brussels in the 1890s. As late as 1913—by which time buildings of two hundred feet and higher were common in American cities—virtually all European cities imposed stringent height limits, ranging from forty-three feet in Zurich to

"A 2,000-Foot Building," 1908 (Scientific American, *July 25, 1908)*

eighty-two in Vienna. More often than not, the limits were even lower on all but the widest streets.[14]

The first serious attempt to impose height limits in the United States was aimed not at office buildings but at apartment houses. It was launched in New York in the mid 1880s, when builders were erecting nine- and ten-story apartment houses (and even planning a fourteen-story one). Troubled by these tall buildings (and ambivalent about apartment houses in general), some New Yorkers urged the state legislature to impose a height limit. They argued that these buildings would leave the streets below "in an almost perpetual shadow" and deprive the nearby buildings of sunlight, "the most potent of sanitary agents." In the event of fire, they would be death traps for residents of the upper floors. Opponents responded that tall apartment houses were inevitable in New York. To deal with potential problems, the authorities should require that buildings be fireproof and allow them to cover only part of the lots—not limit their height. Despite these objections, the legislature imposed a limit of seventy feet on streets sixty feet wide or less and eighty feet on streets wider than sixty feet. Although some condemned the law as "a veritable curse," claiming that it "stops building, reduces assessments, ruins values," others complained that it had little impact. Lacking provisions for enforcement and penalties for violations, the law was "a dead letter," wrote *American Architect and Building News*. But if the law had little impact, it nonetheless set a precedent, one that led many to conclude that if the authorities could impose height limits on residential buildings they could also impose them on commercial ones. Indeed, for some of its advocates the law was "the entering wedge" in the campaign to curb the skyscraper.[15]

From the start it was clear that it would be an uphill struggle—that it was one thing to lobby for a height limit on apartment houses and quite another to lobby for one on office buildings. Even advocates of height limits acknowledged that tall buildings were more disruptive and dangerous in the residential sections than in the business district. As one put it, "contagious diseases do not occur in office-buildings." A proposed height limit on apartment houses would generate a controversy in New York and possibly one or two other cities. A proposed height limit on office buildings would arouse a storm of opposition virtually everywhere. Moreover, it would be led by wealthy and powerful business interests with a huge stake in the outcome. They would be joined by other Americans who believed that individuals had the right to do whatever they wanted with their land and that government should not infringe upon this right except to protect life and property. And they took a very narrow view of the circumstances under which life and property needed protection. Other Americans, especially midwesterners and westerners, strongly objected to any governmental action that might deter eastern capital from investing in their cities. They feared that every dollar not invested in their city would be invested in one of its rivals.[16] Still other Americans were in favor of skyscrapers or, at the least, skeptical of the complaints about them.

The campaign to impose height limits was also an uphill struggle because even after the development of steel-frame construction many Americans who opposed skyscrapers believed that what *American Architect and Building News* described in 1897 as "the craze for building [them] anywhere and everywhere" was "beginning to die out." One reason was that above a height that skyscrapers were fast approaching a building needed so many elevators that gains from rentable space on the upper floors were offset by losses of rentable space on the lower ones. As R. H. Robertson, a New York architect (and an opponent of tall buildings), pointed out in 1894, there was a limit to how much floor space could be devoted to elevator shafts if a building was to pay. In other words, skyscrapers could not go much higher and still make money. The other reason was that given the demands of commercial tenants for adequate light and air the city had only a limited number of sites that were favorable for skyscrapers, the majority of which had already been built on. With few sites available, journalist Burton J. Hendrick argued, few skyscrapers would be erected. As the New York *Real Estate Record and Builders' Guide* later pointed out, Hendrick was wrong; so was Robertson. More and more skyscrapers went up—and went up higher and higher—in the 1900s and 1910s. But so long as many Americans held that the problem would "cure itself," they saw no reason to impose height limits on commercial buildings.[17]

Still, a good many Americans joined the campaign to impose height limits. They were driven by a deep-seated conviction that the skyscraper posed a grave problem and that in view of the advances in building technology and the dynamics of the commercial real estate market the problem would not solve itself. They strongly believed that nothing short of restrictive legislation—in the form of either a flat height limit or one based on the width of the street on which the building stood—could curb the skyscraper.[18] The advocates of height limits had a few things going for them. Drawn mainly from the upper middle and upper classes—indeed from the same classes as their opponents—composed largely of professionals, businessmen, and public officials, they had considerable economic and political resources of their own. They could also count on the support of many Americans who had come to believe that government had a responsibility to regulate the built environment in the public interest. Perhaps most important of all, many Americans shared their belief that the skyscrapers were causing (or, at any rate, compounding) some of urban America's most pressing problems—that they were endangering public safety and public health, exacerbating traffic congestion, undermining property values, and marring the city skyline. From the mid 1880s through the mid 1910s the advocates of height limits hammered away at these points and incorporated them into a wide-ranging indictment of the tall buildings (and, to some extent, the business districts of which they were the most powerful symbol).

At the core of this indictment was the charge that skyscrapers posed a grave threat to public safety. In the event of a serious fire—not to mention a conflagration of the sort that destroyed much of Chicago and Boston in the early 1870s and much of Baltimore and San Francisco a generation later— these buildings were death traps. They might be "fireproof," but they were not incombustible. They might be safer than stores and factories, which were usually full of highly flammable material, but as a St. Louis businessman pointed out, "in case of a general conflagration no building is safe." If a serious fire broke out downtown, it would take the fire department a long time to get to the skyscrapers, many of which were located on very narrow, highly congested streets. Once they arrived, what could they do? As most fire chiefs conceded, they could throw "an effective stream of water" no higher than 85 feet. In New York, where some buildings stood two hundred feet high, Chief Hugh Bonner warned in 1894, "We have nothing up to date that will aid us in extinguishing fires" above 125 feet. Nor had the fire departments anything to help evacuate the hapless people trapped by flames and smoke on the upper floors. "The only thing we could do," Chief D. J. Swenie of Chicago said in 1891, "would be to shoot up a rope from one of our guns and let them take their chances in climbing down." In the interest of public safety, many architects, fire chiefs, insurance underwriters, and building inspectors called for height limits on office buildings. Early in the 1890s the Chicago Fire Underwriters' Association even threatened to stop writing policies on buildings more than 120 feet high.[19]

Fire was not the only danger. As the skyscrapers rose higher and higher, it was not clear that they could withstand an earthquake or other natural cataclysm. Nor, as builders shifted from masonry to steel, was it clear that the skyscrapers would hold up over time even under ordinary conditions. As *American Architect and Building News* observed in the mid 1890s, "No one knows exactly how the metal in these structures is going to behave, for the reason that such combinations [of steel and other material] have never before been exposed in the same manner to the action of the elements." The uncertainty gave rise to a good deal of anxiety. According to engineers, there was evidence that electricity was escaping from the railway tracks, seeping into the ground, and eroding the water and gas pipes. There was reason to believe that electricity was starting to erode the foundations of the skyscrapers, too. Unless a solution was found to what a former Chicago city engineer called "the engineering problem of the age," the *Chicago Tribune* predicted that the skyscrapers would suffer "a gradual settling or an unforeseen crash." Also, according to engineers, moisture and damp air would slowly percolate into the steel frame, which would begin to rust, a process that would corrode the columns and thereby undermine the structure. Since the steel frame was encased in other material and thus completely invisible, there was no easy way to know whether it was deteriorating. And therefore, said Ernest Flagg, a New York architect who later designed the Singer Building, "it is impossible to tell whether they [the skyscrapers] are safe or not."[20]

Skyscrapers were also a serious menace to public health, advocates of height limits charged. As early as the mid 1880s, they said that tall office buildings were turning the streets below into dark, damp, and gloomy canyons. During the winter they blocked the sun, leaving the cold streets even colder. During the summer, wrote *American Architect and Building News*, they acted as "storehouses of heat," driving up the temperature after sunset, making the once cool and refreshing nights unbearable. The skyscrapers also shrouded the nearby buildings in darkness, forcing the office workers to rely on artificial light—which, it was believed, put a strain on the eyes. Worst of all, the skyscrapers deprived both the streets below and the adjacent buildings of fresh air and sunlight. To Americans who still held that disease was a product of the "miasma," the noxious vapors that permeated the cities, the lack of fresh air was bad enough. To Americans who believed in the new germ theory of disease, the lack of sunlight was even worse. For it was sunlight, described by doctors as "the best disinfectant," "the best bacteriacide," and "our greatest sterilizer," that killed the microbes that caused disease. Sunlight and wind were as vital to public health as pure water, argued a representative of the Chicago Medical Society in 1891; without them "life would be almost impossible in crowded communities."[21]

From a sanitary viewpoint, skyscrapers were "an outrage," declared George B. Post, a prominent New York architect. By creating the conditions "in which bacteria and microbes flourish best," skyscrapers turned the streets into what a Chicago doctor called "the breeding ground for germs." "To shut off the sunbeams from the earth," a Chicago businessman added, "is to encourage the bacteria, to breed fevers, to sap vitality, to make men and women pale cellar plants." A few skyscrapers here and there would not pose much of a problem, critics conceded. But "if the down-town area were covered with twenty-story buildings," the Chicago doctor claimed, "there would hardly be enough sunlight and air to support life." There would be a sharp rise in the incidence of bronchitis, pneumonia, and consumption (or tuberculosis), the so-called white plague. The business district would become as unhealthy as the tenement districts, a grim prospect indeed. Writing at the turn of the century, another opponent of the skyscraper pointed out that some New Yorkers were planning to build a hospital for consumptives at the same time that others were planning to build a thirty-story skyscraper. This made no sense, he declared. "We build hospitals for the poor consumptive, and then we turn around and erect skyscraping structures where consumption may breed." "We shall not lack for patients," he said.[22]

Also central to the indictment of skyscrapers was the charge that they exacerbated the traffic problem. Designed for cities of five- and six-story buildings, the streets were much too narrow to handle the traffic generated by buildings two or three times as high. They were already very congested, one Chicago real estate dealer noted in 1891. If they were "lined with sixteen and eighteen story buildings," he said, "it would be an utter impossibility to get along them." With the opening of the World's Fair in 1893, another predicted, the traffic will make it so hard to do business downtown that "Chicago might as well take a long holiday." Things were pretty bad in other cities too, especially "in the vicinity of the sky-scrapers at noon and in the evening," a St. Louis real estate dealer observed in 1895. Traffic congestion grew worse after the turn of the century. Before long many Americans were convinced that it was one of the cities' most pressing problems and that the skyscrapers were its "principal source." The sidewalks were very crowded too, especially during rush hour and lunch hour, when thousands of office workers poured in and out of the skyscrapers. It was already "impossible to walk [downtown] without jostling some one," a Chicago engineer noted; imagine what it would be like with even more skyscrapers and two or three times as many pedestrians. The congestion "would be terrible to contemplate." Also very crowded were the streetcars, els, and subways. No matter how rapidly these transit facilities were expanded, architect William O. Ludlow contended, they could not possibly keep up with the heavy traffic generated by tall office buildings.[23]

To opponents of the skyscraper, the traffic problem was a sign that downtown was too compact and too concentrated—that too much business was being done in too small a space. The cities were outgrowing their business districts. It was time to ask, said a Chicago real estate dealer, "Is it wise to concentrate all business in a few blocks in the heart of the city?" Few Americans would have taken this question seriously in the 1870s or 1880s. But by the early 1890s, by which time the invention of steel-frame construction made possible an unheard-of degree of concentration, a good many did. For more than a few, the answer was no. August Gatzert, chairman of the Chicago Association of Commerce's Committee on Downtown Streets (and a staunch supporter of height limits), nicely summed up this position in the mid 1910s. "It is better that there should be miles of commodious, well-lighted and well-

HOW IT MIGHT BE IF THE 6,000 PEOPLE IN THE MONADNOCK SHOULD LEAVE AT ONE TIME.

Tall buildings and pedestrian congestion in Chicago, 1896 (Chicago Tribune, February 24, 1896)

ventilated six, eight and ten-story buildings, than a congested group of twenty-two story structures," he wrote. By imposing stringent height limits (by, in effect, preventing the construction of skyscrapers), European cities had scattered business "over a wide area," *American Architect and Building News* pointed out in 1896.[24] It was time for American cities to follow their lead.

Advocates of height limits also charged that skyscrapers had a baneful impact on property values in and near the business district. They drove up values on a few sites, usually large corner lots that had plenty of light and air. But they drove down values on many sites that were not suitable for tall buildings. By concentrating office work in a very small space, the Minneapolis Civic and Commerce Association's committee on height limits argued, they held down property values "just outside or within a few blocks [of the] business districts." Even within the core, or what one architectural critic called "the charmed circle," the skyscrapers generated a high degree of instability. They attracted tenants from nearby buildings—partly by depriving these buildings of light and air and partly by offering their tenants a higher level of amenities. Sometimes the owners of these buildings managed to retain their tenants by reducing rents. But their income still fell, and so did the value of their buildings. Imposing height limits—or, in the words of one of their advocates, New York architect John M. Carrère, "scattering the tenants horizontally instead of piling them up vertically"—would reduce values on a few downtown sites that were already wildly overpriced. But it would stabilize values inside "the charmed circle" and raise them outside it. Height limits, claimed the *Chicago Chronicle,* would "equalize real estate values by stimulating higher prices in localities a few blocks away [from the Loop] and [even] more remote."[25] In the long run all but a handful of property owners stood to gain from the imposition of height limits.

And virtually no one stood to lose—not even the skyscraper owners. For according to advocates of height limits, skyscrapers were poor investments. Most earned only a modest return, some much less. The notion that skyscrapers were not profitable surfaced in the early and mid 1890s, and by the turn of the century even some of their supporters conceded that they might not make sense financially. By the early 1910s some experts were convinced that above a certain height—twelve to fifteen stories, according to some, even lower, according to others—an office building reached what was called "the point of diminishing returns." A building's income did not rise in proportion to its height. The taller the building, the higher the cost of construction per cubic foot and the lower the percentage of rentable space per floor. "In other words," reported A. H. Albertson, a Seattle architect (and secretary of the Seattle Building Code Commission), "a high building costs more and produces less space than a low building." Although skyscrapers did not pay, Ernest Flagg pointed out, property owners erected them anyway, afraid that if they did not, nearby property owners would. A skyscraper, a leading financial adviser wrote, was a good idea as a monument for an insurance company or as an advertisement for a business corporation, "but not as a big revenue producer." The head of a large Chicago real estate firm made the point more bluntly. Noting that even in the Loop a three-to-five-story building paid better than a twenty-story one, he declared: "The skyscraper in Chicago is an economic and financial blunder."[26]

According to advocates of height limits, the skyscrapers were an eyesore too. Individually, they were very ugly, at best "unsightly," at worst, in the words of Councilman Halsey C. Ives of St. Louis, an "abomination." Even many of the architects who had designed skyscrapers were highly critical of them. They "are really engineering feats," wrote one, of "little or no architectural value." The facade might be attractive, said another, "but the plain brick masonry on ends and rear will always be a hideous mass." Montgomery Schuyler was even more critical. Writing about the typical skyscraper in 1899, he pointed out that its front was nothing but "an obviously irrelevant compilation of historical architecture, while its equally conspicuous sides and rear make no pretensions to architecture at all." To architects, the skyscraper posed a perplexing problem. Nothing in their repertoire seemed appropriate for this unprecedented building type—a building type characterized by what one architectural periodical called an "almost invariable disproportion of breadth to height." Given the absence of an appropriate style—and pressures from clients to maximize rental space and minimize construction costs—tall buildings "cannot possibly be satisfactory in an artistic sense," wrote one New York architect. Indeed, from "a purely artistic point of view," another held, it was impossible "to build over ten or twelve stories high."[27]

Collectively, skyscrapers were even uglier, critics charged. Erected to various heights and in various shapes and, as one journalist put it, "piled together without any comprehensive plan," they turned the New York skyline into what Schuyler described as "a horribly jagged sierra." (It resembled "nothing so much as a horse's jaw-bone, with the teeth broken or dislodged at intervals," wrote William Dean Howells in his utopian novel, *Letters of an Altrurian Traveller*, in 1893.) These buildings gave New York "a ragged, wild Western appearance," said Flagg, "more suitable to a half-civilized community than to a city which claims rank with the other great capitals of the world." The skyscrapers deeply offended Schuyler and Flagg because they were committed to the ideal of what historian Michael Holleran calls "an orderly city of horizontal monumentality," an ideal epitomized by the squares of London and boulevards of Paris, by Boston's Back Bay and Chicago's White City. Central to this ideal was the notion of the "sacred skyline," a skyline characterized by an even cornice line broken only by the spires and towers of churches, monuments, and important public buildings. It was the sacred skyline, many Americans believed, that made European cities so dignified, restrained, and beautiful. To preserve it required more than good design; it required height limits. As Schuyler pointed out:

> If every architect employed to erect a skyscraper should do his very utmost to produce a logical, sincere, and beautiful expression of what he was doing, their united efforts would leave the city of skyscrapers little less appreciably ugly than before. How can it be otherwise when each owner's view of his own interest is the only rule he is bound to follow, and when this view leads one owner to build ten stories, a second twenty, and a third thirty? Like Frankenstein, we stand appalled before the monster of our own creation, literally.[28]

The "sacred skyline": Boston's Commonwealth Avenue, ca. 1889 (King's Handbook of Boston, Boston, 1889)

To advocates of height limits, skyscrapers were also symbols of some of the worst features of American life. They were "the outward expression of the freest, fiercest individualism," of "almost savage, unregulated strength," wrote a British journalist at the end of the century. Schuyler agreed with him, as did William O. Ludlow, a New York architect who pointed out that "the character of a people can be easily read from the character of their buildings." To Schuyler, skyscrapers were also a symbol of unbridled materialism, an obsession with money-making, an indifference to spiritual and aesthetic matters— "an arraignment of our pretensions to civilization, a grievous and a just arraignment." To Ludlow, they were a sign of "ostentation" and a passion for size as opposed to grace. These gargantuan structures dwarfed the people beneath them, protested Henry James, turning them into "a welter of objects in which relief, detachment, dignity, [and] meaning, perished utterly." Maxim Gorky, the Russian writer who visited the United States early in the twentieth century, was even more critical. He likened "these dull, heavy piles" to prisons. Their "monstrous height" did not impress him. "In great houses dwell small people," he wrote.[29]

Skyscrapers, critics charged, were also symbols of a callous attitude toward the country's architectural and historical landmarks. Some, including Richard Morris Hunt's Lenox Library, had been demolished to make way for skyscrapers. Others had been "smothered quite out of existence" by the "skyscraping monsters," wrote William Merritt Chase, a New York artist. Trinity Church was a case in point. Once "the pride of the town," the splendid building was now dwarfed by skyscrapers, Henry James lamented. Its "charming elements are still there," but "they have been mercilessly deprived of their visibility." New Yorkers "now look down on it as on a poor ineffectual thing." Another case in point was Boston's Athenaeum. A "library, gallery, temple of culture," wrote James, it was once to Boston what Boston was to New England. Now surrounded by tall office buildings, it "looked only rueful and snubbed, hopelessly down in the world." His instinct was to pass by "on the other side" to avoid its humiliation. Towering above everything, "these houses of business reduce to insignificance the houses of worship," a British visitor pointed out. Beside them once-beautiful public buildings "are made to appear ridiculous," Flagg protested, and "structures of faultless design and beautiful proportion [are] dwarfed into insignificance," declared the *Philadelphia Public Ledger*.[30]

To the skyscraper's supporters, this indictment was untenable, these charges unfounded. Skyscrapers, they argued, were not a threat to public safety. Of all the buildings in the city, they were among the least vulnerable to fire. It was extremely unlikely that a fire would ever start in one. Even if it did, most skyscrapers were so thoroughly fireproof—constructed almost entirely of incombustible materials—that it was extremely unlikely the flames would spread from one floor to another (or even from one room to the next). By virtue of the development of the standpipe and high-pressure hose, big-city fire departments were now capable of fighting fires on the upper stories of even the tallest buildings. If any doubts remained about the effectiveness of fireproof construction in skyscrapers, their defenders claimed, they were dispelled by the conflagration that destroyed much of downtown Baltimore in 1904. As one of them wrote: "Never before in the history of fires have the theories of fireproof construction received so severe a test, and that those dozens of skyscrapers that were in the burned district are still standing, and that their structural members that were properly protected are intact, is all the vindication the most enthusiastic supporters of fireproof theories could hope for."[31] Indeed, in the wake of serious fires in Baltimore and other cities, some Americans concluded that skyscrapers served as a bulwark against the spread of fires that started in other buildings. American cities were full of firetraps. But as *American Architect and Building News,* no friend of the tall office building, conceded, the firetraps were not the new skyscrapers. Rather, they were the old, relatively low buildings, such as Chicago's seven-story Ayers Building, in which thirty people died in a fire in 1898.

Skyscrapers were also very sturdy, their defenders claimed. And not without reason. During a storm in which the winds reached eighty miles an hour, engineers estimated that Chicago's Monadnock Building swayed less than a two-story house. Observers reported that New York's Flatiron Building, an extremely thin skyscraper, withstood violent winds with "great steadiness" and little vibration. San Fran-

*The Union League amid Philadelphia's skyscrapers (*Joseph Pennell's Pictures of Philadelphia, *Philadelphia, 1914)*

cisco's skyscrapers were unscathed by a mild earthquake in 1898. And though badly damaged by the great quake of 1906, they fared better than many buildings half as tall. Many architects and engineers also dismissed predictions that in time the skyscrapers would collapse. Steel was completely reliable, they contended, provided it was properly encased. Daniel H. Burnham, a Chicago architect, declared in 1904 that the Rookery, a steel-frame building he had designed fifteen years earlier, showed no signs of corrosion whatever. To Burnham and other architects, the success of the Rookery and even taller skyscrapers proved that steel-frame buildings would hold up at least as well as masonry ones. (Minneapolis architect L. F. Buffington wondered what all the fuss was about. Suppose, he said, that someone fell from a proposed twenty-eight-story building for which he had been severely criticized. "I do not think that [he] would very much care whether he fell from the twenty-eighth or the eighth story, and, in case he did, we probably should not know it unless by spiritualistic media.")[32]

Nor were the skyscrapers a menace to public health, their defenders argued. As a Chicago builder (and former judge) put it in 1891, the new high structures "are better lighted, better drained, better ventilated, better heated, better arranged in every way than the old low buildings which are to be found here." Their tenants, especially the ones above the fifth floor, work in "light, airy" rooms, wrote another Chicago resident, which were comfortable in all seasons and free from "the din of the streets" below. The tall buildings blocked the sunlight, a St. Louis architect conceded. But the shade was welcome during the long, sweltering summer. Whether a lack of fresh air contributed to disease was "only a matter of opinion," an architecture critic pointed out. And besides "the wind never blows so swiftly and so strongly as around high buildings." After voicing his reluctance to take issue with the medical community, a Chicago alderman declared that "cholera and smallpox spread where filth invited it and without regard to density of population or sunlight." Height limits might be needed to assure light and air in European cities, where the streets were very narrow, wrote *California Architect and Building News,* but not in San Francisco, where many were 60, 80, and even 100 feet wide. An influential New Yorker raised a different objection. Solid lines of 90-foot buildings would darken the streets as much as long rows of buildings 125, 150, or even 300 feet tall. And no one in New York was seriously proposing a height limit of less than 90 feet. If architects were so worried about the lack of sunlight, another New Yorker argued, they would be better advised to remove the cornices on office buildings, which "tend needlessly to obstruct light and air," than to press for height limits.[33]

As the skyscraper's defenders saw it, advocates of height limits were miss-ing a crucial point. A building's safety was a function of its quality, not its height. Safety, argued Chicago architect W. L. B. Jenney, "is not measured by feet but by the skill of the architect, the engineer, and the builders." His col-league Dankmar Adler agreed. The danger, he wrote, lies not in height but in incompetence and greed, and above all in builders who cut costs with no re-gard for the risks involved. From the standpoint of public safety and public health, height limits were extremely ill-advised. They would prevent the erec-tion of the safest and healthiest buildings in the city, those, wrote an architec-ture critic, that were constructed with the greatest care and the most "thought-ful regard for the convenience and safety of the people who pass their working days within them." Moreover, height limits would discourage property own-ers from replacing old worn-out structures. It would make no sense for them to demolish one building in order to erect another with only two or three ad-ditional floors. As Jenney noted, property owners, "who otherwise would have put up buildings that would be an improvement to the city, will be tempted to repaint and redecorate their old structures."[34] In other words, height limits would add years to the life of the "ill-ventilated, ill-smelling, insanitary" old rookeries that were a grave threat to public safety and public health.

Opponents of height limits also denied that skyscrapers exacerbated the traffic problem. As a prominent Chicago property owner pointed out, it was not office buildings but department stores that were mainly responsible for traffic congestion. They generated the bulk of the thousands of carriages, teams, and streetcars that jammed the Loop. Another Chicago resident made a similar point. He observed that the portion of La Salle Street adjacent to the Rookery, a section surrounded by very tall buildings, "is the least crowded por-tion of that street." The reason was that the businessmen who worked there were able to meet with their customers and bankers—and even to eat their lunch or have their hair cut and shoes shined—without ever leaving their building. The authorities should not impose height limits—which had not solved the traffic problem in Europe and might well make it worse in Amer-ica—but improve transportation facilities and regulate streets and sidewalks more strictly. On the principle that the streets should be adjusted to the build-ings, not the other way around, opponents of height limits favored proposals to provide additional facilities above and below the streets, ranging from ele-vated sidewalks to underground railways. They also urged the authorities to clear the streets and sidewalks of the many obstacles to vehicular and pedes-trian traffic (and, in particular, to stop the practice of making "a public livery stable of curbstones, where horses and buggies are kept all day long").[35]

To opponents of height limits, a certain amount of congestion was a reasonable price to pay for a high level of concentration. And a high level of concentration was "in every respect a decided advantage," claimed St. Louis architect Craig McClure. It was far more convenient to transact business when so many businessmen (and those on whom they relied) worked in the same very small area—often even in the same large building. It saved time (and therefore money), Richard M. Hurd pointed out. And nothing so concentrated business like the skyscraper. To attempt to spread out the business district by imposing height limits was at once misguided and pointless. It was misguided because, as a Chicago architect put it, "the more business is concentrated the better." And it was pointless, *California Architect and Building News* wrote, because businessmen "will put up with great limitations and inconvenience rather than leave the heart of trade and commerce." Some opponents of height limits went even further, contending that congested streets were a sign of a prosperous city. "Crowds are what make up a big city," declared McClure, "and all I can say is that we need more of them."[36]

Opponents also denied that skyscrapers had a baneful impact on property values in and near the business district. By virtue of tall buildings, downtown real estate values had risen steadily and sharply, wrote C. H. Blackall, a Boston architect, in 1896. The skyscraper "has so enormously increased the earning capacity [of the land] that property which would hardly carry itself in former times on a valuation of one hundred dollars per foot, can now be made to yield a handsome surplus on a valuation of three hundred dollars [a foot]." Height limits would do more than just reduce property values. They would also ruin many investors who had bought property on the assumption that they could erect a sixteen-, eighteen-, or twenty-story building. For a nine- or ten-story building, the tallest possible under a height limit of, say, 125 feet, would never cover expenses, pay taxes, and still earn a reasonable return. Opponents of height limits acknowledged that downtown real estate was sometimes unstable, that some property owners lived in fear that others would construct a taller building next door. But instead of asking the authorities to impose a height limit, they would be better off buying the adjacent buildings or reaching some sort of understanding with their owners.[37]

Opponents of height limits were extremely skeptical of the argument that skyscrapers were not good investments, an argument that underlay the position that very few property owners would be hurt by these restrictions. Most tall buildings were fully rented, some well in advance of completion. Despite dire predictions to the contrary, they paid far better than most low buildings. By the late 1890s *American Architect and Building News*, which had only recently argued that ten- and fifteen-story buildings earned a higher return than taller ones, noted that under normal conditions a New York skyscraper "is as desirable an investment as can be found." And New York's *Real Estate Record,* which had voiced doubts about the profitability of the skyscraper in the late 1890s, changed its mind in the early 1900s. At a time when a record number of skyscrapers was under construction, it wrote: "Somehow it seems useless to prove a particular enterprise is not worth while, when [so] many people are ready to undertake [it]." By the late 1900s the issue was settled, the journal declared: "The twenty-story buildings, which formerly were considered to be the limit of desirable height, have been succeeded by buildings which have run from twenty-two up to over forty stories, and buildings of this kind have been erected not only by institutions as an advertisement, but by speculative building companies exclusively as a profitable investment."[38] If height limits were a bad idea if skyscrapers were profitable, they were an even worse idea if skyscrapers were unprofitable: in that case, no one would build them. Since "the matter will adjust itself satisfactorily in [the] course of time," it made no sense to impose height limits.

Nor were skyscrapers an eyesore, their defenders argued. The early ones left much to be desired architecturally, they conceded. They were "damned without stint," wrote New York's *Real Estate Record and Builders' Guide;* and they probably deserved it. But that was to be expected, a New York architect pointed out. A new building type, the skyscraper posed difficult problems, which could only be solved after "long and hard study." But the problems were not insuperable, another New York architect argued; some of the world's tallest buildings were among its most beautiful. For a gifted architect, the skyscraper offered an unparalleled opportunity. And in Ernest Flagg, Louis Sullivan, Bruce Price, and Cass Gilbert, America had many gifted architects. By the turn of the century, some Americans noticed a striking improvement in the appearance of the skyscrapers. Many were beautiful, endowed with what C. H. Blackall called "intrinsic nobility." They were also "a distinctively American product," their supporters noted, "the first absolutely genuine expression of an original American architecture." By 1908 *American Architect,* a longtime critic of the skyscraper on aesthetic grounds, acknowledged that it had "a certain architectural grandeur not to be found in many of the justly celebrated and universally admired architectural monuments of the old world." In 1913, the year the Woolworth Building—hailed by Schuyler as "the culminating triumph of commercial architecture"—was finished, the journal remarked that some might still have doubts about the skyscraper on sanitary and other grounds. But that "a satisfactory solution to the architectural difficulties of the tall building" has been found, "there can be no further doubt [at all]."[39]

To many Americans, even to some who still doubted that a satisfactory solution had been found, these buildings were collectively "one of the marvels of the world." As the artist Childe Hassam said, "It is when taken in groups with their zigzag outlines towering against the sky and melting tenderly in the distance that the skyscrapers are truly beautiful." The skyline was especially lovely at sunset, one journalist said, when "the towering cornices take a radiance scarcely less beautiful in itself than the glow that suffuses a snow-capped Alp," and at night, another observer noted, when "the streets run molten gold and the sky is decked with millions of jewels." How beautiful was "the high ridge of skyscrapers," wrote John C. Van Dyke, a lecturer and critic, when "shrouded in that silver-gray mist, their tops half disappearing in the upper blend of rain and clouds." What had changed was not merely the skyline, but the response it evoked. To more than a few well-known architects and city planners, the "sacred skyline" of the late nineteenth century, the skyline of Paris and other European cities with its even cornice line, its air of restraint and dignity, now seemed monotonous, boring, even, wrote one Bostonian who had once supported a uniform eighty-foot height limit, insipid.[40] Far more attractive to them was the jagged skyline of lower Manhattan, a veritable hodgepodge of short, tall, and very tall buildings, a picturesque assortment of slender towers and solid blocks, a skyline that conveyed an aura of extravagance and excitement and a sense of limitless progress.

Nor were skyscrapers a symbol of the worst features of American life. Rather than a reflection of "unbridled materialism," they were a symbol of what C. H. Bebb, a former president of the Washington chapter of the American Institute of Architects, called the "New Industrial age," of the amazing progress of American business, of "the colossal energy and aspiring enterprise of American life." Instead of an expression of the "freest, fiercest individualism," they were a symbol of "Yankee ingenuity," of outstanding advances in science and technology, of an extraordinary degree of collaboration and coordination in the construction industry. To some, the skyscrapers were a symbol, in the words of architecture critic Claude Bragdon, of "our need and our power to build,—to build on a gigantic scale, and in an unprecedented manner." To others, they were a symbol of "the growth and commercial importance of great American cities." To yet others, skyscrapers were a symbol of America itself, of its disdain for tradition, its willingness to experiment, and what an English visitor called its "heaven-storming audacity," a symbol of a young and assertive nation with its best years still ahead. To make way for them, old landmarks would have to be demolished. But the skyscrapers that replaced them would be America's new landmarks.[41]

Even if tall buildings were offensive aesthetically and symbolically, the authorities would not be justified in imposing height limits, their opponents argued. Although a property owner's rights were not "absolute and unlimited," the state should not interfere with them save under exceptional circumstances. The fewer the restrictions the better, said architect Dankmar Adler. The state, declared the chairman of a commission that drafted New York State's proposed building laws, could act only on grounds of public safety and public health. With aesthetic issues, it has "nothing whatever to do." Chicago's corporation counsel advised the city council that it might consider the impact on traffic congestion and property values as well. But "unless the fact that high buildings are dangerous or otherwise injurious is pretty clearly established," Chicago's *Real Estate and Building Journal* wrote, "the benefit of the doubt should be given to the owner of the building."[42] According to opponents of height limits, it was far from "pretty clearly established" that skyscrapers endangered public safety and public health, much less exacerbated traffic congestion and impaired property values.

At the heart of the struggle over height limits was the question of the future of the business district, a question that was sometimes obscured by the debates over public safety and other issues. It was not whether downtown would grow—that was taken for granted—but whether it would grow vertically or horizontally, whether it would become more or less compact. As the Chicago *Real Estate and Building Journal* pointed out, few people cared—most of them upper-class and upper-middle-class property owners in and just outside the business district.[43] But they cared very much—largely because of the tremendous disparity in values between property inside downtown and property just beyond it and even among properties in different parts of downtown, on different streets, and even on the same streets. To these Americans the battle over height limits was above all an issue of spatial politics, an issue that is nicely illustrated by the stories of Boston and Chicago, two of the first American cities to impose height limits.

By the late nineteenth century Boston was a city whose best years were behind it. The third largest city in the nation in 1790, a serious rival to New York and Philadelphia, it had grown steadily but slowly in the next hundred years. By 1890 it was the fifth largest, by 1930 the ninth. The city's real estate market was stable but far from booming, and the demand for office space was nowhere as strong as in New York and Chicago. Boston's elites regarded their city as the country's cultural and intellectual capital. And more than other Americans, they looked for inspiration to Europe, from which they derived the concept of the sacred skyline. In their attitude toward the built environment, Bostonians were quite conservative—so much so that many still considered steel-frame construction "experimental" after the turn of the century.* Thus it is not surprising that Bostonians moved to impose height limits so early. Responding to a resolution from a Boston state representative, a legislative committee recommended in 1891 a height limit of 140 feet for all Massachusetts cities. Towers, steeples, and cupolas erected for strictly ornamental purposes were exempted. At the urging of a large minority of the committee, the legislature lowered the limit to 125 feet and then approved it almost unanimously. A year later, again at the city's request, the legislature adopted a new building code for Boston that retained the 125-foot limit and, following the prevailing practice in European cities, further limited the height of any building to no more than two and a half times the width of the widest street (or square) on which it stood.[44]

What is surprising is that height limits aroused virtually no opposition. Other than the lack of demand for skyscrapers and the belief that the "congested district" was already too congested, the reasons were twofold. One was that many Bostonians who owned property on the edge of downtown or just beyond it assumed that if tall buildings were outlawed the business district would expand and their holdings would appreciate. The other, and more important, reason was that most downtown property, probably as much as three-quarters, was owned by large family trusts, which had been created out of old Boston fortunes made in trade and manufacturing. The trustees tended to be highly conservative. They invested in commercial real estate in the hope of obtaining a modest but reliable income. They were not inclined to take risks. And abiding by the old rule of thumb that it was too risky to put up a building

---

* Walking across the Boston Common in 1891, C. H. Blackall ran into Walter Winslow, one of the city's leading architects. Blackall, he said, "'I understand that you are about to erect a building at the corner of Washington and Water Streets and in that you are about to use that abominable steel skeleton construction which has come to us from the wild and woolly west. Don't do it; you are sure to have trouble.' 'Well' I said, 'what would be the trouble?' 'Why', he said, 'we know that steel expands with heat and contracts with the cold, that a column 125 feet high will expand during the middle of the day at least 1 [inch] over its length at night, consequently there will be a movement up and down, and it is only a question of time when the inside plaster will be cracked at every ceiling line and the outside brickwork will be shaken loose and fall to the ground.' I said, 'Well, I am sorry, but the frame is all ordered and I am afraid it is too late.'" (C. H. Blackall, "Looking Back on Fifty Years of Architecture," *American Architect*, March 1930, page 88.)

that was worth much more than the land on which it stood, they had little interest in putting up skyscrapers. What they had much interest in was in preventing others from putting up skyscrapers, which would tower over their buildings, depriving them of light and air and competing with them for tenants. Hence for Boston's trusts—and for their wealthy beneficiaries—height limits were tailor-made.[45]

During the 1890s and early 1900s the consensus in favor of height limits grew even stronger. With few exceptions—one of whom was C. H. Blackall, who designed and built Boston's first steel-frame structure—Bostonians had little enthusiasm for skyscrapers. They might be appropriate in New York, but not in Boston. Nor did height limits bother builders. Some built as high as 125 feet. Others stopped one or more stories below the limit. If there was any pressure, it was to make the limit even lower. William Minot, Boston's largest landowner and a member of the commission that revised the city's building code in 1891, preferred a height limit of 100 feet. In response perhaps to the erection in 1894 of Haddon Hall, an eleven-story apartment house on Commonwealth Avenue, *American Architect and Building News* called for an 80-foot limit for residential structures. Edward T. Atkinson, a fire insurance company executive and prominent Boston reformer, came out in favor of an 80-foot limit for commercial buildings as well, a limit, he wrote, that was needed to prevent the "skyscraper folly" from gaining a foothold in Boston. In response to these views, the state legislature imposed even tougher height limits in other parts of Boston in the mid and late 1890s—first along the edges of parks and parkways, then along the four streets that bordered Copley Square, and later in the vicinity of the State House.[46]

The movement for height limits culminated in 1904, when the state legislature enacted a law retaining the 125-foot limit in the business district, the "A" district, and imposed an 80-foot limit in the rest of the city, the "B" district. (Mayor Patrick A. Collins then appointed a special commission that set the boundaries of these districts, which would remain in effect for fifteen years—although, under pressure from property owners, the commission later raised the height limit in the "B" district to 100 feet on streets at least 80 feet wide.) There was a sharp disagreement about the objectives of the law. According to some, it was designed to divide Boston into residential and business districts—and, above all, in the words of *American Architect and Building News*, "to prevent the intrusion of sky-scrapers into the residential districts." From that perspective, the law was mainly about land use and only incidentally about building heights. But according to former mayor Nathan Matthews, Jr., a member of the special commission, this view was "without one tittle of foundation." The act was primarily about building heights, he said. The commission was so strongly opposed to tall buildings that it very much wanted to recommend an 80-foot limit for the entire city. But so many buildings 100 to 125 feet tall had already been erected downtown that it felt obliged to retain the current limit there. Anything less, Matthews testified a decade later, would have been "an act of gross injustice" to the many downtown property owners who had not built as high as 125 feet.[47]

The consensus in favor of height limits remained intact down through the mid 1910s, at which time the state legislature set up a special commission to review the boundaries of the "A" and "B" districts. Its hearings, held in the spring of 1916, revealed that most Bostonians who cared fell into one of three groups. One favored retaining the existing boundaries. Its chief spokesman was Matthews, a passionate opponent of tall buildings, who represented the Boston Real Estate Exchange, an organization that consisted largely of downtown property owners, some of whom feared that an expansion of the "A" district might draw business away from the center. A second group called for an expansion of the "A" district or, better still, the imposition of a uniform height limit for the entire city. This group was made up mainly of property owners from business districts other than downtown Boston who objected not so much to height limits, or even to a 125-foot limit, as to different limits for different parts of the city. A third group favored raising the limit to 150 feet. Its spokesmen argued that an additional two or three stories would increase the rate of return on office buildings in Boston from a meager 2 to 4 percent to a substantial 6 (or so) percent. In the end the commission recommended a slight expansion of the "A" district westward along Boylston Street into Back Bay, where a thriving business district had already been established not far from downtown.[48] Otherwise it left the boundaries (and the system) unchanged.

Whereas Boston was the nation's oldest city, Chicago was one of its youngest. Settled in the 1830s, by which time Boston was over two hundred years old, it started out as one of many small midwestern towns that hoped to become a great city. Most were disappointed—but not Chicago. Between 1840 and 1890 it grew into a huge metropolis, the second largest city in the country. More than a few Chicagoans believed it was only a matter of time before it overtook New York. To its boosters, Chicago was above all a great workshop and a giant storehouse—a city, wrote the Chicago Real Estate Board's Committee on Industrial Location at the turn of the century, whose "keystone was materialism."[49] Although they took issue with critics who branded Chicago "a city of the 'almighty dollar,'" they took pride in the fact that it was a good place to make money—in trade, in manufacturing, and, not least of all, in real estate, in residential subdivisions on the periphery and in office buildings in the center, the booming, bustling Loop. Chicago was also more open to innovation than most other cities, less resistant to such technological advances as steel-frame construction and more responsive to the view that the fewer the regulations the better. Hence it came as no surprise that when the movement to impose height limits was launched in Chicago in the late 1880s and early 1890s, it triggered a vigorous, protracted, and extremely divisive struggle, one that would have been inconceivable in Boston.

On one side were Mayor Hempstead Washburne (plus his fire chief, building commissioner, and corporation counsel) and many prominent Chicagoans who charged that tall buildings had a baneful impact on public safety, public health, traffic congestion, and property values. Allied with them were the Chicago Fire Underwriters' Association, Chicago Medical Society, Chicago Builders' and Traders' Exchange, Chicago Real Estate Board, and the Illinois chapter of the American Institute of Architects. Also in favor of height limits, though for different reasons, were property owners on the edge of the Loop or just outside it. They feared that skyscrapers would concentrate business within the core of the Loop and thus hold down the value of their real estate. (More than a few west-side property owners backed height limits in the hope that they would drive businesses out of the south side, in which the Loop was located.) A few downtown property owners also supported height limits. Some had already put up tall buildings and, in an attempt to preserve their dominant position, opposed the erection of taller ones. Others owned lots on which it was not feasible to build a skyscraper. Still others who were unable or unwilling to build a skyscraper, but whose property was assessed on the basis of its value as the site for one, viewed a height limit as a way to lower its assessed value and reduce their property taxes.[50]

On the other side were many other prominent Chicagoans who believed that the charges against tall buildings were groundless and the imposition of height limits unwarranted. Although the local chapter of the AIA held that its members overwhelmingly supported limits, many of Chicago's foremost architects spoke out against them. *Inland Architect and News Record,* the city's leading architectural journal, argued that they were "ridiculous from every standpoint." And though the Chicago Real Estate Board's Public Service Committee recommended a 135-foot limit, many of its members preferred a higher one—or none at all. Also opposed to height limits were downtown property owners who intended, sooner or later, to build a skyscraper. But for opponents of height limits, it was an uphill battle. As one of them pointed out, a great many Chicagoans were genuinely concerned about the impact of tall buildings. For every property owner who favored vertical expansion of the business district, there were several who favored lateral expansion. Furthermore, the downtown property owners who intended to build a skyscraper some day—and who had the largest stake in the battle—could always apply for a building permit before a height limit was imposed (and thereby protect themselves against what the Chicago *Real Estate and Building Journal* called "legislation adverse to high buildings"). Hence early in 1893—after a long struggle in which several different proposals were made and many lengthy hearings held, an ordinance was passed and then vetoed, and a blue-ribbon committee was appointed to study the city's building laws—Chicago adopted a height limit of 130 feet.[51]

But as Chicagoans soon found out, it was one thing to adopt a height limit and another to implement it. One problem was that several tall buildings for which permits had been obtained in 1891 and 1892, when Chicago had no limit, were erected in 1892 and 1893. Construction fell off in the mid 1890s, but the decline was probably due less to the height limit than to a glut in the commercial real estate market and the nationwide recession that started in 1893. Another problem was that early in 1896 several architects and property owners called on the city council to raise the height limit to 160 feet. They argued that given the high cost of land in the Loop it was impossible to earn a reasonable return on a 130-foot building. Instead of putting up new fireproof buildings, owners were remodeling old unsafe structures, W. L. B. Jenney and William A. Holabird pointed out. The council responded by lifting the ceiling—though only to 155 feet. Two years later a terrible fire broke out in the Ayers Building downtown, leaving nearly thirty dead and many injured. Over the objections of Jenney and others, the council reimposed a 130-foot limit. Once again many downtown property owners rushed to apply for building permits before the law went into effect. Yet another problem was that under all the ordinances, the city council was empowered to waive the height limit for individual buildings. And the council, which was infamous for its willingness to oblige well-connected and well-heeled Chicagoans, issued so many waivers that some observers regarded the height limit as a "farce."[52]

From the viewpoint of advocates of height limits, things went from bad to worse around the turn of the century. As the market for office space grew tighter, prompting the Chicago First National Bank and other large companies to move ahead with plans to build skyscrapers in the Loop, the downtown interests brought pressure on the city council to raise the height limit to 175 feet or higher. Even the Chicago Fire Underwriters' Association, long a staunch supporter of stringent limits, backed the change. High buildings, it now held, were no more dangerous than low buildings. Early in 1902 the city council, which had shown no enthusiasm for enforcing the 130-foot limit, approved a limit of 260 feet, probably the highest in the world. A good many tall buildings went up during the next several years, and at the end of the decade yet another campaign got under way to lower the height limit. Predictably, the campaign triggered a flurry of new construction in 1910 and 1911. At the urging of outlying property interests, the council reduced the limit to 200 feet in 1910. But as the ordinance, which did not go into effect until 1911, included a provision that anyone who obtained a permit before then could build up to 260 feet through 1914, the construction boom continued for three more years. An effort to raise the limit back to 260 feet failed in 1913, but with so much new office space on the market, it probably made little difference.[53]

By the mid 1910s height limits were just over twenty years old in both Boston and Chicago, but they had had a much greater impact in the former than in the latter. In Boston, where the authorities had maintained a stringent 125-foot limit and enforced it very strictly, buildings of nine, ten, and eleven stories lined the downtown streets. The skyline was dominated by the Ames, Fiske, and Exchange buildings, all of which had been erected before the restrictions were imposed and stood between 160 and 190 feet tall, and the Custom House tower. A thirty-story, 495-foot obelisk, the tower had recently been built atop the U.S. Custom House, which was not subject to local ordinances (and in any event was viewed more as a civic monument than as an office building). In Chicago, where the authorities had raised and lowered the height limit almost half a dozen times and enforced it very loosely if at all, forty-five buildings of twenty or more stories towered over the Loop. Several stood more than 200 feet tall. But it is not right to say, as one advocate of height limits did, that Chicago was "in the same position" as New York, which had no height limit at all. For whereas Chicago had nearly as many tall buildings as New York, it had no buildings anywhere as tall as the Woolworth, Singer, and Bankers Trust buildings, which ranged from almost forty to more than fifty stories high.[54] And for this the height limits were partly responsible.

The efforts to impose height limits went fairly smoothly in a few cities other than Boston. In February 1904 much of downtown Baltimore was destroyed by a fire, probably the worst in the United States since the great Boston fire of 1872. Although some experts later argued that tall fireproof buildings had withstood the blaze better than other structures, the devastation was so extensive that many residents concluded that "fireproofing" was

The Boston skyline in the late 1920s (Courtesy of the Bostonian Society/Old State House)

"a delusion" and skyscrapers a menace. To advise the city about rebuilding, Mayor Robert McLane appointed a Citizens' Emergency Committee, which consisted of business and professional leaders, half of whom belonged to the Municipal Art Society, a civic group that was engaged in an attempt to limit building heights on Mount Vernon Place, a fashionable residential enclave. The Citizens' Committee formed several subcommittees, one of which dealt with building heights and building laws. Chaired by John E. Semmes, a lawyer who held that ten stories was high enough for any building, the sub-committee recommended a limit of 175 feet (and in the case of non-fireproof buildings, 85 feet). The Citizens' Committee endorsed the recommendation and incorporated it into an ordinance that was introduced in Baltimore's city council at the end of February. The proposed ordinance was hotly debated, but only because some councilmen wanted a stricter limit of 150 or even 125 feet (and for non-fireproof buildings 75 feet). Approved in March, the ordinance followed the Citizens' Committee recommendations.[55]

The Chicago skyline in the late 1920s (Chicago Commerce, *December 7, 1929)*

In other cities, however, the efforts to impose height limits aroused widespread opposition. In St. Louis, for example, City Councilman Halsey C. Ives introduced a bill in December 1895 that was closely modeled on Boston's law. Besides requiring that all new buildings more than 70 feet tall had to be fireproof, a relatively noncontroversial issue, it provided that no new structures (other than church spires) could be more than two and a half times as high as the width of the street on which they stood—and in no case higher than 125 feet. Ives and his supporters defended the proposal largely on the grounds that tall buildings were not only "an unsightly abomination" but also a threat to public safety. "A general conflagration would wither and snap the steel framework like glass," he declared. Much as the *St. Louis Post-Dispatch* predicted, the proposal generated "a storm of protest." Leading it were the *Post-Dispatch* and a host of architects and property owners who denied that tall buildings were a fire hazard and argued that if properly designed they could be just as beautiful as short buildings. Pointing out that a 125-foot office building would not pay in downtown St. Louis, the opposition claimed that the proposed height limit would reduce property values there 50 percent. It also stressed that a height limit would discourage "foreign [presumably New York or Boston] capitalists" from investing in St. Louis. Capitalists expect to get "a certain income from a certain number of stories," a real estate man explained.

"If they are not permitted to build the required number of stories they will stay out."[56]

On one point both sides agreed. If a height limit as low as 125 feet was imposed, the business district would spread out. So much the better, argued some. In the interest of increasing property values, a St. Louis real estate agent claimed, "It is better to have lower buildings scattered over fifteen or twenty blocks than to have a few big buildings in half a dozen blocks." Not so, responded others. If downtown St. Louis was spread over a wider territory, it would make it harder to do business in the city. The more compact the business district, the better. For several weeks spokesmen for both sides spelled out their views at meetings of the St. Louis chapter of the AIA and the St. Louis Real Estate Board as well as at hearings before the city council's Committee on Legislation. Gradually a consensus emerged that St. Louis should not impose a height limit as stringent as 125 feet—at least not until it had as many tall buildings as Chicago and other big cities.[57]

Late in January 1896 the St. Louis chapter of the AIA, many of whose members opposed Councilman Ives's bill, proposed what it thought was a reasonable compromise. Under its proposal, any building could henceforth be erected as high as two and a quarter times the width of the street on which it stood. On a 60-foot-wide street, a building could be 135 feet tall; on a 100-foot-wide street, 225 feet; and on a 150-foot-wide street (the widest in the city), 337½ feet. A building could go up even higher, but only if the owner was willing to set back the upper stories. Although the restrictions were far from stringent, the opponents of height limits were not satisfied. Neither were the advocates. The setback arrangement was roundly criticized, too. By February the bill was pretty much dead, but the issue was very much alive. Later in the year a committee consisting of members of the AIA, the Master Builders' Association, and the St. Louis Board of Public Improvements made another effort to resolve it. After making a study of building ordinances in the principal cities of Europe and the United States, it drafted one that was adopted by the city council in April 1897. No building could thereafter be erected higher than two and a half times the width of the street—and in no event higher than 150 feet—and all buildings taller than 100 feet (as well as all buildings used for public purposes) had to be fireproof.[58]

In still other cities it turned out to be at least as hard to maintain a height limit as to establish one. A case in point is Denver, which had adopted a height limit of nine stories or 125 feet in 1905. In December 1908 a firm called Puget Sound Realty Associates asked the board of aldermen, the lower house of the city council, for permission to erect a twelve-story office building several blocks southeast of the core of downtown Denver. The request ran into stiff opposition. Much of it came from owners of two- and three-story office buildings in the core, who their critics referred to as "the rent trust." These property owners were worried that the proposed skyscraper would draw the business district away from its present location—away, in other words, from their holdings. As an alderman who represented that district put it, "The lower part of the city would be permanently injured if high buildings were constructed uptown." Also opposed to Puget Sound's request was Mayor Robert Speer, a Democrat who had a good deal of influence over the mainly Democratic board of aldermen and who objected to tall buildings in general. The *Denver Post,* which claimed that tall buildings were appropriate now that Denver had grown from "a struggling town" into "a real metropolis," strongly supported Puget Sound. But at the urging of the mayor, a sharply divided board of aldermen turned down the firm's request—though as a concession to the minority it voted to raise the height limit from 125 to 135 feet.[59]

The concession satisfied neither Puget Sound nor the *Post* and other champions of tall buildings. To increase the pressure on the board of aldermen, Puget Sound announced that it would submit its petition to the board of supervisors—the upper house of the city council, which was controlled by Republicans and supportive of tall buildings. A couple days later the company asked the supervisors to raise the limit for everyone, a step that was designed to gain the support of other property owners who wanted to build skyscrapers. Puget Sound threatened to challenge the constitutionality of the height limit. And several members of the Denver Real Estate Exchange indicated that they were ready to try to amend the charter to allow the erection of fourteen-story buildings. Meanwhile, the *Post* demanded that the board of aldermen "abolish the limit." It argued that the height limit would drive outside capital away from Denver—and expressed amazement that anyone would stand in the way of reputable businessmen who wanted to invest $800,000 in the city. The paper lambasted the eleven aldermen who had voted against Puget Sound's request, prominently displaying their names on top of its blistering editorials. It also pointed out that many other western cities, including Seattle, Portland, San Francisco, and Salt Lake City, had already erected steel-frame skyscrapers. In the name of progress, the *Post* urged Mayor Speer to persuade the board of aldermen to reverse its position and called on the board of supervisors to raise the height limit.[60]

The *Post* voiced especially strong objections to the argument that a height limit was necessary to prevent new buildings from undermining the profitability of old ones and to deter the business district from moving from one

Opposition to height limits in Denver, 1908 (Denver
Post, *December 14, 1908)*

location to another. That was "Municipal Socialism," it declared. The city had no more business regulating development than running a department store. Municipal authority was already encroaching on private enterprise in too many ways. "And if it be permitted to limit the economic development of the city it might as well buy the city outright and conduct it as a Socialist Elysium." In the face of this barrage, the board of supervisors raised the height limit to fourteen stories. Under tremendous pressure from property owners, build-ers, and labor unions and afraid that his backing of the current height limit might cost him support for a proposed civic center, Mayor Speer gave in. The board of aldermen, after defeating one motion to raise the limit to fourteen stories, unanimously passed another lifting it to twelve, a compromise that was promptly adopted by the board of supervisors. Puget Sound, fully satis-fied, announced that it would start construction at once. Much as its oppo-nents feared, this decision helped spur the movement of downtown Denver to the southeast. Less satisfied, the *Post* insisted that the city would be better off without a height limit of any sort.[61]

Another case in point is Seattle, which had imposed a height limit of 200 feet or sixteen stories, a limit recommended by the National Association of Building Inspectors early in the twentieth century. In 1910 a few downtown property owners asked the Seattle city council for permission to build above the limit. One of them, L. C. Smith, a typewriter magnate from Syracuse, New York, wanted to put up a twenty-six-story office building (which would have been the tallest such building west of Chicago). According to historian J. M. Neil, the proposed skyscrapers were an integral part of an ongoing effort by a group of property owners in the south end, the site of downtown Seattle, to prevent the business district from moving north. These property owners— dubbed by their critics "the southend interests"—had become concerned in the mid 1900s, when federal officials erected the new Federal Building ten blocks north of Yesler Way, the core of the south end, and local officials built the Seattle Public Library six blocks north of Yesler. This concern grew a few years later, when the city finished leveling Denny Hill, which had hitherto obstructed the business district's northward movement. With Denny Hill out of the way, it was possible that downtown Seattle could extend all the way to Lake Union, roughly two miles north of the south end, a grim prospect for downtown property owners. To prevent this, they adopted a strategy of building skyscrapers in the south end—a strategy that was designed to anchor the business district and to create a highly compact downtown Seattle along the lines of downtown New York.[62]

Opposed to the planned skyscrapers were property owners who favored the northward movement of the business district. Along with Seattle city engineer R. H. Thomson, they believed that the Lake Union section was destined to become "a great business center within a reasonable period of time." Also opposed were some people who strongly objected to skyscrapers, no matter where they were located. The principal spokesman for this position was the Washington chapter of the AIA—although, as an indication of how divisive the issue was, a former president, C. H. Bebb, was one of the strongest advocates of tall buildings in Seattle. The chapter passed a resolution urging the city council to retain the existing height limit, arguing that if buildings of twenty or more stories were put up, it would be necessary to "dig subways, erect two, three or five elevated street levels, [and] disregard all consideration of health and comfort." Also opposed to the skyscrapers were those who hoped that downtown Seattle would expand horizontally rather than vertically. As the *Seattle Post-Intelligencer* wrote, shortly before abruptly changing its position, the city should "build out, not up." Pointing to downtown New York and the Chicago Loop, it warned that "what would happen in case of a panic, due to fire, or some more extraordinary occurrence in these overcrowded skyscraper districts would stagger and sicken the imagination." Paris had not built skyscrapers. Neither should Seattle.[63]

The battle over the height limit dragged on for more than two years, largely because Seattle was caught up in two other closely related and even more ferocious struggles, one over the development of a civic center a mile or two north of downtown and the other over the construction of a county courthouse in the south end. At issue in both struggles was the future location of the business district. Although the Washington chapter of the AIA continued to hammer away at the point that tall buildings posed a host of serious problems, it was fighting a losing battle. Just as the south-end interests prevailed in the struggles over the civic center and the county courthouse, they also prevailed in the battle over the height limit. In September 1912 the city council voted not to raise the 200-foot limit but to eliminate it. In its place the legislators passed an ordinance regulating the volume of buildings, an ordinance that closely resembled the proposal put forth by the St. Louis chapter of the AIA nearly twenty years earlier. Under it, a building could be erected to any height—provided the upper floors were set back from the street line. Two years later the voters rejected a proposal to restore the 200-foot limit. In the meantime L. C. Smith built his tower, which ended up forty-two rather than twenty-six stories high, making it the tallest office building in the country outside New York City. Much as opponents of height limits hoped, the erection of the Smith Tower (and other south-end skyscrapers) helped stop the northward movement of the business district.[64]

Because some cities that adopted height limits later abolished them, and others that raised them later lowered them, it is hard to tell how common these limits were at a particular moment in time. But it is safe to say that by the mid 1910s, roughly twenty-five years after the movement to curb tall buildings got under way, they were in place in most of the nation's largest cities and many of its medium-sized

Seattle's L. C. Smith Building, ca. 1914 (Special Collections Division, University of Washington Libraries, photograph by A. Curtis, neg. no. 26390)

ones. Besides Boston, Chicago, Baltimore, and St. Louis, Cleveland, Buffalo, Milwaukee, New Orleans, Los Angeles, and Washington, D.C., had height limits. So did Rochester, Indianapolis, Denver, Portland, and San Diego. Among the most conspicuous holdouts were New York, Philadelphia, Detroit, Pittsburgh, and Minneapolis. Most of the cities imposed flat height limits, which ranged from a low of 125 feet in Boston to a high of 250 feet in St. Paul. Others based the limit on the width of the street on which the building stood. In Buffalo the limit was four times the street width, in Youngstown, Ohio, two and a half. A few, notably Boston and Charleston, employed both strategies, imposing a flat, relatively low limit on all buildings and an even lower limit on buildings located on all but the widest streets.[65]

That so many cities adopted height limits in so few years was remarkable, especially in light of the widespread view that the fewer the restrictions on the use of private property the better. By this measure, the movement to curb the skyscraper was a striking success. By other standards, however, the results were something of a disappointment. As the story of Chicago shows, some cities enforced the height limits very loosely or not at all. And as the stories of Denver and Seattle reveal, other cities sometimes bowed to pressure from property owners to raise or even abolish them. From the perspective of European cities, the American height limits were very high. None of them had a height limit anywhere as high as Boston, which had the lowest in the United States. Indeed, no European city had a height limit even two-thirds as high as Boston—though Vienna (at 82 feet) and London (at 80 feet) came close. Moreover, most European cities also imposed even more stringent limits on all but the widest streets. As New York City's Heights of Buildings Commission observed in 1913, the height limits in most American cities had no effect on most buildings, even on most office buildings in the business district. All they did was prevent "the erection of a few exceptionally high buildings."[66] And sometimes they did not do even that.

Opponents of tall buildings took pride that they were able to prevail upon so many cities to adopt height limits. But they felt their efforts could not be judged a success until a limit was imposed in New York City. And as late as the early 1910s, more than two decades after Boston and Chicago had adopted height limits, New York imposed no limits whatever on buildings (other than tenement houses), provided they were fireproof. New York was crucial to the campaign for height limits because it had far more tall buildings (and far more of the tallest buildings) than any city in the world. As of January 1913, when the Woolworth Building was completed, it had sixty-two buildings of twenty or more stories, all but ten of which were office buildings, and more than a thousand of ten or more stories. It looked, wrote a German who made a visit in 1913, like a city that had been built by giants "for giants." No other city had more than a handful of skyscrapers except Chicago, which had forty-five buildings of twenty or more stories. But Chicago had nothing like New York's nine office buildings that soared from thirty-two to fifty-five stories. Its skyline was very impressive, but not nearly as "spectacular and striking," in the *Chicago Tribune*'s words, as New York's. If the Chicago skyline reminded European visitors of the Alps, the New York skyline—which H. G. Wells described as "the strangest crown that ever a city wore"—made them think of the Himalayas.[67]

To opponents of skyscrapers, the New York skyline was a symbol of failure—though not lack of effort. As early as the mid 1880s a few New Yorkers had argued that something had to be done to curb tall buildings. Not long after, an attempt was made to limit the height of apartment houses. But it was not till the mid 1890s, after the development of steel-frame construction had demonstrated that structures of virtually any height could be erected, that New Yorkers made their first serious effort to impose height limits on office buildings. In the lead was the Architectural League of New York, which called a meeting in March 1894 to discuss what if anything to do about the proliferation of tall buildings in lower Manhattan. Most of the speakers, including several prominent architects and doctors, condemned these buildings on aesthetic and hygienic grounds. But some were not sure that legislative action was necessary or what form it should take. And a few were doubtful that the architects had enough clout to do anything about the problem. "It is one thing to talk about limiting the height of buildings and another thing to do it," remarked William J. Fryer—who, as chairman of the commission that had drafted the building law then pending in the state legislature, was well informed about New York politics and the formidable power of the real estate interests. "The Architectural League," he added, "being without legislative experience or political influence, and probably unwilling to provide the capital that might be required in order to obtain a recognition of the overwhelming merits of [height limits], would meet with ignominious defeat in a legislative contest with those who think otherwise. If the League only wants to talk about the desirability of a limitation of height no one can object. If it proposes to try and get legislation to that end my advice would be . . . don't."[68]

Ignoring Fryer's advice, the Architectural League launched a campaign to curb the skyscraper. It made little headway until early 1896, when two much more powerful organizations came out in favor of height limits. One was the

New York Chamber of Commerce, the city's foremost commercial association, which, after a spirited debate, took the position that henceforth the
height of all buildings should be restricted according to the width of the street
on which they stood—and that no building more than 80 feet tall should occupy more than 80 percent of its lot. The other was the City Club of New York,
perhaps the city's leading civic group, which decided to sponsor a height-limit
bill in the state legislature, a bill that was introduced in February by Senator
Frank D. Pavey and commonly known as the Pavey bill. Under this bill—the
original version of which was drafted by architect George B. Post, a leader of
the Architectural League and a strong critic of the skyscraper—no building
could be erected higher than fifteen times the width of the square root of the
street on which it stood—and in all but a few cases no higher than 150 feet. If
the owner set back a portion of the building from the street line, he could
build the upper floor of that portion to an additional height of twice the size of
the setback. The bill, Post explained, was designed to solve the problems
posed by the skyscraper by limiting buildings to the height they had reached
prior to the introduction of steel-frame construction—and to do so without
limiting all buildings to the same height and preventing the ornamental and
artistic treatment of the upper story and roof. If the bill passed, its backers
stressed, the business district would spread out, raising property values in all
but a few parts of lower Manhattan.[69]

Although the Pavey bill was endorsed by a host of architects, firefighters,
newspapers, and civic and professional groups, it ran into a great deal of opposition from downtown property owners and real estate and building interests in general. The opposition argued that the objections to tall buildings
were unfounded—that in terms of public safety and public health the new
steel-frame buildings were far superior to the old masonry buildings. It also
pointed out that the Pavey bill would give owners of the existing tall buildings
a monopoly of the commercial real estate market. Some of these owners had
done nothing to ensure adequate light and air for their buildings in the event
that others erected a tall (or even taller) building alongside. But their "lack of
foresight" was no reason for legislative action. Opponents insisted that the
Pavey bill would benefit some property owners at the expense of others. Indeed, it would do irreparable damage to the many property owners on narrow
streets in lower Manhattan who wanted nothing more than the opportunity to
build to the same heights as the many tall buildings nearby. The Pavey bill was
un-American too, opponents charged. Describing it as "extremely arbitrary
and unjust, subversive of property rights, and in many cases impracticable," a

downtown real estate man claimed that the bill "savors strongly of paternalism in its worst type, and is obnoxious to the sense of a free people."[70]

Although the Pavey bill was endorsed by the New York chapter of the AIA, it was opposed by some local architects. George E. Harding, a well-known New York architect (and a member of a group of architects, builders, and property owners who went to Albany to testify against the bill), declared that such limits would destroy "the incentive to make buildings fireproof, durable, and sound from a hygienic standpoint." Hugh Lamb, a principal in Lamb & Rich, a firm best known for its "Collegiate" architecture, agreed—though Lamb's partner, Charles Alonzo Rich, believed that the Pavey bill "did not go far enough." Others—like F. H. Kimball, an architect who held that tall buildings were "an absolute necessity" in the business district and later designed several of Manhattan's well known ones—favored some sort of height limit, but opposed the Pavey bill. Also in this group was Ernest W. Cordes, who took the position that centralization was required by the city's commercial and financial interests, several of which were (or would later be) clients of his firm, DeLemos & Cordes. Cordes approved of height limits in principle but insisted that the Pavey bill was "too sweeping," that it gave "undue advantages" to the owners of existing buildings and worked "great injustice" on the owners of "unimproved property." He proposed that some sections of lower Manhattan should be exempted from the bill, a proposal made a few months earlier by New York's *Real Estate Record and Builders' Guide,* which favored confining the proposed height limit to Manhattan north of City Hall Park, where very few tall buildings had as yet been erected.[71]

Although some observers held that the Pavey bill never had a chance, it stayed alive until December 1896, when, in the words of the *Real Estate Record and Builders' Guide,* it "died a natural death." A few other attempts were made to impose a height limit in New York in the late 1890s, but they too went nowhere. By the end of the decade, the movement had lost much of its drive. The failure of the Pavey bill was due mainly to the vigorous opposition of the downtown property owners and other real estate interests, about whose power William Fryer had warned the Architectural League. And the sharp divisions among the city's architects made a tough campaign even tougher. But the bill also labored under two other handicaps. One was that many New Yorkers thought it was inequitable. How, they wondered, could the authorities impose a height limit of 150 feet (or, on streets less than a hundred feet wide, even lower) when so many buildings in lower Manhattan already exceeded that limit? As the *Real Estate Record* pointed out, "The high-building move-

ment has, unfortunately, now gone too far to be stopped by a peremptory enactment without doing gross [in]justice to very many people." The other
handicap was that many New Yorkers believed that the tall buildings were
rapidly approaching their economic height, that they would soon reach a
point at which the additional cost of the extra stories would offset the additional income from the extra space. If the problem would soon solve itself,
why bother to impose a height limit?[72]

In the absence of height limits, a record number of skyscrapers were
erected in lower Manhattan in the early 1900s—and not only on lower Broadway and in the financial district. As the *Real Estate Record and Builders' Guide*
wrote in 1902, these buildings "have become so numerous and widespread
that they are continually in men's eyes and minds." Taking issue with Burton
Hendrick and others who predicted that the age of the skyscraper was coming
to a close, it declared: "The end, and the beginning of the end[,] is not yet in
sight." Another surge in construction took place in the mid 1900s, when the
City Investing Company, the United States Express Company, and the Singer
family erected skyscrapers on the west side of lower Broadway, dwarfing Trinity Church and hemming in its venerable graveyard. "Never before in the history of the world has so much steel, brick, stone, mortar, and terra cotta been
piled up in such a small space," wrote a *New York Times* reporter in 1907. The
Singer Building attracted the most attention. Standing just over 600 feet, it
was the tallest building in the world—although much of it consisted of an elegant tower that covered only one-sixth of the site. It was designed by Ernest
Flagg, one of the most articulate critics of run-of-the-mill tall buildings. To
many, the erection of the Singer Building seemed to confirm the belief that
the time was fast approaching "when Manhattan would be given over exclusively to business and transient trade." By the time the Singer Building was
finished, moreover, work was well under way on the Metropolitan Life
Tower—"a larger, higher, and in some ways an even more remarkable building," wrote a *Times* reporter, that would rise to more than 650 feet.[73]

The proliferation of skyscrapers troubled many New Yorkers, one of whom
wrote in 1903 that it "seems a pity that the colonists did not fetch over among
their legal baggage some allegiance to the English doctrine of 'Ancient
Lights.'" But as late as 1906 the *Real Estate Record* pointed out that "there is
practically no influential demand from any quarter that the height of hotels
and business buildings in Manhattan should be restricted." A year later, however, the skyscrapers were under attack again. Appalled by the prospect of
forty- or even eighty-story buildings, architect William O. Ludlow declared
that "Paris, London, Boston, and a dozen other cities, including even trade-

wild Chicago, recognize the gross injustice of excessively high buildings and impose restraint accordingly. When will New York wake up?" The problem would not solve itself, Flagg argued. Or by the time it did New York would be a city whose streets were "little better than deep can[y]ons" and whose employees were dependent on "artificial light all day long." "It is now high time to call a halt" to these "monuments to greed." Also seriously concerned was George W. Babb, president of the New York Board of Fire Underwriters, who warned that the business district was on the verge of a conflagration so awful that the city's insurance companies "would not be able to pay more than twenty or twenty-five cents on the dollar." Although the *Real Estate Record* held that nothing would come of these protests, the issue attracted a lot of attention in 1907. And it came to a head a year later, soon after the Building Committee of the board of aldermen appointed another in a long line of commissions to revise the city's building code, one that included architects, engineers, builders, the borough presidents, and the fire chief.[74]

One of the Building Code Revision Commission's first steps was to form a Committee on Limits of Height and Area. The committee held hearings, on and off, for about six months. Although some New Yorkers opposed restrictions on tall buildings, taking the position that the problem was not all that serious or, even if it was, that private enterprise would come up with a solution, most of the witnesses supported some sort of regulation. Some, like Babb and Ludlow, called for stringent limits, either a uniform height, imposed over the whole city or in one or more zones, or an uneven limit, varying according to the width of the street. Others wanted to regulate the volume of buildings, to allow them to rise to almost any height as long as they were erected on only a portion of the lot, were set back from the street line, or both. Probably the chief spokesman for this approach was Flagg, who had employed it in his plans for the Singer Building. Still others, the best known of whom was New York architect John M. Carrère, suggested that the authorities regulate buildings not by imposing height or volume limits but by taxing them according to size. A tax based on cubic footage would encourage property owners to erect lower buildings and provide more open space, he argued.[75] Although some New Yorkers were willing to back any of these proposals in order to curb the skyscraper, most were reluctant to support any proposal other than their own.

The hearings did little to resolve the Building Code Revision Commission's dilemma—which, wrote the *Real Estate Record,* was to curb the skyscraper in a way that would solve "the three-fold problem of congestion, ventilation and light" and at the same time "conserve the great real estate values which are at stake," without completely depriving some property owners of the opportuni-

ties that had long been available to others. But at a time when forty-story buildings had already been erected, when sixty-story buildings were expected to be
put up in the near future, and when rumors were circulating that Ernest Flagg
was working on a 1,000-foot (or roughly eighty-story) building, the commission was under great pressure to do something. Consequently, it attempted to
accommodate what *American Architect* called the many "widely differing
views" by backing a height limit and then setting it much higher than any
other in the world. As spelled out in the commission's final report, which was
submitted to the board of aldermen in October 1908, office buildings (as well
as hotels, churches, and apartment houses) could henceforth be erected as
high as three times the width of the street on which they stood, but no higher
than 300 feet—unless they faced a park, square, or other public place, in
which case they could go as high as 350 feet. (There were two principal exceptions. Lofts, warehouses, and other commercial buildings were limited to 150
feet. And on streets less than forty-five feet wide, of which there were many in
lower Manhattan, buildings could be erected no higher than 135 feet.)[76] Although the proposed limit was very high, it was not nearly as high as the
Singer Building, the Metropolitan Life Tower, and several other buildings already erected or under construction.

The commission's report was discussed at length for more than a month,
both in trade journals and at public hearings held in November by the Building Committee of the board of aldermen. With a few exceptions, one of whom
would only say that the report was "a step in the right direction," the speakers
were extremely critical, especially of the 300-foot (and the 350-foot) limit. One
or two protested that it "would work great injustice," both on owners, whose
property values would go down, and on tenants, whose rents would go up
(and who might have to rent offices farther from the business center). A large
group complained that the proposed limits were so high "that scarcely any
one would care to build higher." In this group were spokesmen for the Board
of Fire Underwriters, which wanted a 150-foot limit, but was willing to go as
high as 200 to 225 feet. Another large group, which included Flagg and a
spokesman for the New York chapter of the AIA, objected to the report not so
much because the limit was too high as because it was based on height rather
than on volume. One critic, architect Grosvenor Atterbury, who testified on
behalf of the Committee on Congestion of Population in New York City, insisted that the commission's recommendations were irrelevant—that they
would do nothing to solve New York's most pressing problem, the excessive
concentration of people, a problem of which the construction of skyscrapers
was but a small part.[77]

Despite such widespread opposition, the board of aldermen adopted the commission's recommendations and referred them to the board of estimate, the city's highest-ranking body, which consisted of the mayor, other officials, and the borough presidents. Shortly after. however, the board rejected them, thereby bringing to an end another attempt to curb the skyscraper in New York. This attempt failed because the architects, builders, insurance under-writers, and others who wanted to regulate tall buildings could not agree how to do so. It also failed for another, more baffling reason. As the *Real Estate Record* pointed out, a height limit would have spread the business district "over a much larger area," and thus would have raised property values every-where in Manhattan except on or near lower Broadway and Fifth Avenue, where most of the skyscrapers were erected. "But," the journal wrote, "the owners of less advantageously situated property, who are, of course, in the majority, have never appreciated that their interests would have been fur-thered by a limitation on the height of buildings, and they have never taken any step or made any move in the matter."[78] Why they did not—why, for ex-ample, they did not follow the lead of Chicago property owners outside the Loop, who strongly supported height limits—is hard to tell. But operating, as many New York real estate owners did, on the assumption that Manhattan would in time be devoted entirely to business, they may have been reluctant to support a height limit for fear that it might one day prevent them from build-ing skyscrapers of their own (or selling their property, at a great profit, to someone who would). After all, more than one fortune had been made that way.

By the early 1910s, if not earlier, many New Yorkers believed that nothing short of legislative restrictions could prevent the erection of taller and taller buildings. Many also believed it was high time New York joined the long list of American and European cities that had adopted a height limit of one sort or another. The outlook, however, was far from promising. Many of the objec-tions to tall buildings were less compelling now than they had been a decade or two earlier. Despite the charges that skyscrapers were a menace to public safety, none had collapsed. By virtue of improvements in fireproofing, the new tall buildings were less likely to catch fire than the older and shorter ones; and if they did, the fire departments were better equipped to handle the blaze. As a New York fire chief said in the mid 1910s, "no matter how high a building is the department has facilities to force water to its top." Although the tall buildings deprived the streets and adjacent structures of light and air, the evi-dence that they were a threat to public health was far from compelling. More-over, some of the skyscrapers' strongest critics conceded that not all were eyesores. It is clear, wrote *American Architect* in 1913, "that the much maligned American skyscraper is not of necessity ugly; that if these structures have not always been pleasing to the eye, it is not altogether the type, but the handling of it to which many of the artistic shortcomings of tall buildings are properly chargeable." If some of New York's skyscrapers were stunning by themselves, together they were spectacular, creating a skyline that was admired even by some Bostonians.[79] Given that New Yorkers had not imposed a height limit before, when the case against tall buildings was at its strongest, there was little reason to think they would do so now.

But they did, and in a way that had a profound impact not only on New York but on American cities in general. Unlike Boston, Chicago, and other cities, New York did not just adopt a height limit. It adopted the nation's first comprehensive zoning ordinance. Under this ordinance, which was passed by the board of estimate in July 1916 by a vote of fifteen to one, the local authorities were empowered to regulate the use, height, and bulk of all new buildings. All private property was placed into one of four use districts, which restricted what could be done with the property; one of five height districts, which limited how high the buildings could rise; and one of five area districts, which mandated minimal sizes for yards, courts, and other open spaces. Henceforth no building could be put up unless it conformed to the regulations in each of its three districts. Some American cities had previously imposed one or another of these regulations, though usually only in certain sections. New York was the first to incorporate them all into one law and to extend the law throughout the whole city. The 1916 ordinance was widely praised. *American Architect* called it "the most important step in the development of New York City taken since the construction of the subways" and wrote that it marked "a new epoch in the physical development of American cities." George McAneny, the borough president of Manhattan without whose support the ordinance would not have passed, hailed it as "the greatest single achievement in city planning in America." Going even further, *World's Work* claimed that New York's zoning law opened "a new era in urban civilization."[80]

The history of the New York zoning ordinance has been told many times, but in order to understand why New York adopted height limits, a short summary may be helpful. The campaign that culminated in the 1916 zoning ordinance started in 1912. In the vanguard were two groups. One was made up of prominent Fifth Avenue businessmen and property owners, led by Robert Grier Cooke, president of the Fifth Avenue Association, who were troubled by the encroachment of the garment industry on their elegant retail district. The other group consisted of civic reformers, the most important of whom was Edward M. Bassett, a lawyer, planner, and vigorous advocate of zoning, who were concerned about the proliferation of skyscrapers in lower Manhattan. Together, these groups prevailed upon McAneny and his colleagues on the board of estimate to appoint a committee to look into the advisability of regulating "the height, size, and arrangement" of new buildings in New York. The committee delegated the task to a blue-ribbon commission, chaired by Bassett and known as the Heights of Buildings Commission, which held hearings, made studies, and in late 1913 issued a report in favor of dividing New York into use, height, and area districts. A year later the state legislature passed an act that enabled the city to carry out the commission's proposals. At McAneny's request, the board of estimate set up another blue-ribbon commission, also chaired by Bassett, the Commission on Building Districts and Restrictions. After consulting with property owners and other real estate interests as well as with commercial, civic, and neighborhood associations, it issued a report, the core of which was a set of recommendations defining the use, height, and area districts and drawing their boundaries. It was these recommendations that were enacted, more or less intact, in the 1916 zoning ordinance.[81]

If the ordinance had been proposed "only a few years ago," the board of estimate wrote in 1916, the protests "would doubtless have been legion." In the face of these protests, yet another attempt to impose height limits in New York would probably have been stymied. But as the board pointed out, the ordinance generated little opposition. (It is worth noting, however, that what little opposition there was revolved around the issue of height limits. On one side were the City Club of New York, which held that the proposed limits were too lenient, especially in the outer boroughs, and a few architects and engineers, who favored more stringent limits in Manhattan. On the other side were several property owners, who feared that the proposed height limits would do serious damage to real estate values in lower Manhattan, especially below Chambers Street.) Nearly all the commercial and civic associations supported the proposed zoning regulations, as did almost all the neighborhood improvement, taxpayers', and property owners' groups. Indeed, remarked the board of estimate, "Not a single organization of any kind has opposed the general plan." Much more important, virtually all the city's powerful real estate interests, the owners, managers, brokers, and builders, as well as the banks, insurance companies, and other financial institutions, supported it.[82] Without their support there would have been no zoning ordinance, and without the zoning ordinance no height limits.

Why did New York's real estate interests support a zoning ordinance of which height limits, a regulation many of them had opposed for more than twenty years, were an integral part? The answer is that by the mid 1910s most of the city's real estate interests had come to believe that height limits (and land-use restrictions in general) would serve to protect (and perhaps even to enhance) property values. To understand why, it is important to bear in mind that the New York real estate market was in a profound slump in the early and mid 1910s. It "is about as dull as it can be," a well-informed observer noted in 1914. Although New York's population was growing and its economy recovering from a recent downturn, the real estate industry was stuck in a "depression," wrote the *Real Estate Record and Builders' Guide*. Property values were off. (After soaring by close to 50 percent from 1906 to 1911, they remained more or less stationary for the next five years.) Building was slow, and speculation was "at a standstill." It was also very hard to sell property "except in a few favored locations or at a sacrifice," the *Real Estate Record* noted. Laboring under what the journal called "heavy tax burdens and inquisitorial impositions," the one a function of wasteful expenditures by the city and the other a product of heavy-handed regulations by the state, real estate was unable to earn an adequate return.[83] Small wonder it had lost much of its appeal to investors.

As well as extremely sluggish, the New York real estate market was highly unstable. Many properties, among them some lots and buildings that had long been regarded as gilt-edged investments, lost as much as one-half to two-thirds of their value in the early and mid 1910s. According to Lawson Purdy, president of the New York Department of Taxes and Assessments since 1906, the depreciation was so widespread that each year eight to ten thousand property owners applied for a reduction in the assessed value of their holdings. Purdy, a strong advocate of height limits and vice chairman of both the 1913 and 1916 commissions, estimated that hundreds of millions of dollars of real estate values had been lost in New York in the previous decade. Lost, he declared, "because we have disregarded the old principle that a man may not use his land so as to invade the rights of others." This instability did great damage to property owners. By discouraging investment and reducing turnover, it also worked a severe hardship on builders and brokers. No less important, it posed a serious problem for the city's banks and insurance companies that held mortgages on local real estate. The Metropolitan Life Insurance Company alone had more than $200 million tied up in New York real estate. It was "as largely interested in real estate in the city as any corporation and more than any individual," said Walter Stabler, the comptroller of the company and a member of the 1916 commission.[84] For financial institutions like Metropolitan Life, few things were more unsettling than a highly unstable real estate market.

To a large and growing number of members of the real estate industry, it now seemed time to rethink their opposition to height limits (and, as it turned out, to restrictions on use as well). Tall buildings might not be a menace to public safety and public health. They might not be an eyesore either. But if the unstable and sluggish real estate market was any indication, they might well have a baneful impact on property values in and around the business district, an argument that had been made by advocates of height limits for more than twenty years. In the absence of limits, it now seemed that many property owners were putting up taller and taller buildings, even though there was little demand for them, creating what one prominent real estate man called "ruinous competition" and thereby driving down rental income and property values. Many of these buildings also deprived the adjacent structures of light and air, making them less appealing to tenants and thus less attractive to investors. A notorious case in point was the new Equitable Building, which replaced the old Equitable Building, a nine-story office building that burned down in 1912. On a large site in lower Manhattan purchased from the insurance company by Thomas Coleman duPont, this massive structure rose straight up for forty stories, casting a dark shadow over the nearby buildings (and adding 1.2 million square feet of office space to the market). Their values fell 30 percent or more.[85]

Convinced that skyscrapers like the Equitable Building had a baneful impact on

The Equitable Building, New York, ca. 1914 (King's Views of New York, Boston, 1915)

property values, many real estate men, most of whom had hitherto opposed any form of land-use regulation, now endorsed height limits. A good example was George T. Mortimer, vice president of the United States Realty and Improvement Company, a member of both the 1913 and 1916 commissions, and a strong defender of the New York City zoning ordinance. As someone who had built many tall buildings, he had once believed that "the sky was the limit," Mortimer told the annual convention of the National Association of Building Owners and Managers in 1915. But in response to the excessive competition and extreme instability of the commercial real estate market, he had changed his mind. An "ardent advocate for stringent regulation," he now held that reasonable restrictions would "work to the mutual advantage of all [property] owners." Sharing Mortimer's view were Clarence M. Kelsey, president of Title Guarantee and Trust Company, and Frank M. Lord, vice president of Cross & Brown, both of whom believed that height limits (as well as use and area restrictions) would, in Lord's words, "conserve values and stabilize districts." To the leaders of New York's real estate industry, the timing was highly propitious. Height limits and other land-use restrictions would probably do some good and, as business was so sluggish and values so low, could not possibly do much harm. Lord, who had spent more than forty years in the real estate business, remarked in 1916 that he could not remember "a time since 1875 [when the nation was in a depression] when the plan of restricting heights and limiting areas would have caused less disturbance to real estate values than now."[86]

The 1916 zoning ordinance passed not only because so many real estate men supported it, but also because so few opposed it. For this McAneny, Bassett, and the other leaders of the campaign deserve much of the credit. From the outset they made a strong effort to coopt the city's real estate industry. They made sure that its leaders were well represented on both the 1913 and 1916 commissions. Indeed, roughly half of the fourteen members of the 1916 commission, including Mortimer, Stabler, and Alfred Marling, head of a prominent real estate firm and director or trustee of a handful of local banks and insurance companies, were involved in New York real estate. If a hardheaded and successful businessman like Mortimer, a man who could be trusted to put property values ahead of aesthetic concerns, spoke out in favor of height limits and other restrictions, it was hard for other real estate men to take a stand against them. Both commissions also invited members of the real estate industry to testify at public hearings; and the 1916 commission gave them an opportunity to comment on the general principles and specific details of the proposed ordinance (and, to some extent, revised it to meet their objections). To further undermine the potential opposition of real estate interests, Bassett, Purdy, and their associates hammered away at the point that their principal objective was to conserve real estate values. Time and again they assured the real estate industry that whatever regulations were adopted would, as the 1913 commission put it, "be carefully devised so as not to interfere unduly with existing property values."[87]

There were two other reasons so few real estate men opposed the zoning ordinance. One was that the proposed height limits, which were its most controversial feature, were much more liberal than the ones in force in other cities. Well aware of the fate of previous efforts, Bassett and his associates adopted a different approach than the sponsors of the Pavey bill and the members of the Building Code Revision Commission. Instead of a uniform height limit, they proposed five different height districts, each with its own limits—a proposal that had been floating around for a decade or more. Instead of a flat height limit, they recommended an uneven one. Depending on the district, a building could rise anywhere from one to two and a half times the width of the street on which it stood. Perhaps inspired by a recent Seattle ordinance, Bassett and his associates also proposed that if a landowner was willing to set back his building from the street line he could go even higher, as much as five feet up for each foot in. If the building (or any part thereof) covered 25 percent of the lot or less, he could erect it (or that part) to any height at all. As the construction of the Chrysler and Empire State buildings later showed, these height limits were so lenient that given a wide enough street and a large enough lot a building could rise well above even the Woolworth Building. As a further concession to the real estate industry, the zoning ordinance provided that owners of undeveloped (or relatively underdeveloped) property in the financial district, much of which stood on very narrow streets, could build as high as the average height of the buildings adjoining their property on either side or across the street.[88]

Another reason that so few real estate men opposed the zoning ordinance was that many who stood to lose by its passage also stood to gain. Take the case of the owners of small and medium-sized lots located on narrow streets in the financial district, the site of most of the city's skyscrapers. Under the proposed height limits, they could not build as high as they wanted (and, even worse, not nearly as high as the owners of larger lots located on wider streets a block or two away). But under the proposed use restrictions—which were designed, as the 1916 commission put it, "to strengthen and supplement the natural trend toward [the strict] segregation [of land uses]"—industry would henceforth be prohibited in the financial district. And the landowners there would presumably be insulated from the sorts of problems that had plagued the Fifth Avenue merchants. The ordinance also gave the financial district an edge over other business districts. Under the proposed height limits, it was the only part of the city in which a building could rise as high as two and a half times the width of the street on which it stood. Even in midtown Manhattan, which was emerging as a rival to the financial district, the maximum height was only twice the width of the street. The ordinance also provided that only in the financial district could a building go up an additional five feet for each foot it was set back from the street line. Elsewhere it could rise only an additional two to four feet. Other things being equal, a property owner could build higher in the financial district than in any other part of the city.[89] Thus for many lower Manhattan property owners who were concerned not only about the instability of the market but also about the encroachment of industry and competition from other sections, the zoning ordinance had much to recommend it.

To many observers, the New York zoning ordinance was an inspired solution to a seemingly insoluble problem. That problem, wrote the editors of *American Architect* in May 1916, was to formulate a policy about tall buildings that safeguarded the interests of both the landowners and the public. Thus far most American cities had followed the lead of either New York, where a building could be erected "to a height limited only by the desires and financial resources of the owner, and the ingenuity and skill of the architect and his consulting engineers," or Boston, where the authorities had long imposed a height limit so stringent that capital had left the Hub for other cities where "it can be made to return a much larger rate of interest from similar ventures." Neither approach was satisfactory, insisted the editors. What was needed was a "happy mean," a "reasonable restriction" on the height of the buildings that "lies somewhere between the absolute liberty amounting to license obtaining in New York, with its long array of ghastly mistakes resulting in grossly congested areas with insufficient light, air and utilities to serve the population, and the other extreme, represented perhaps imperfectly in Boston, which leads to inadequate development of property."[90] The zoning ordinance of 1916, with its innovative combination of height, use, and area regulations, seemed to embody that highly elusive "reasonable restriction."

The passage of the New York zoning ordinance marked a watershed in the movement for height limits in the United States. Hitherto advocates of height limits had lobbied for the passage of laws dealing exclusively with building heights. After 1916, the proposed height limits were usually incorporated into comprehensive zoning ordinances that dealt with use and area restrictions as well. Started over a decade earlier, mainly in an attempt to keep commerce and industry out of residential neighborhoods, zoning had made little progress before 1916. But as word of the New York ordinance spread, many cities sent delegations to look into its pioneering efforts; and several appointed commissions to consider the advisability of following New York's lead. All over the country public officials and civic leaders studied the reports of the 1913 and 1916 commissions. And in a barrage of articles and speeches, veterans of the New York campaign carried the gospel of zoning to other cities, where it was warmly embraced by city planners. Zoning, its supporters claimed, would reinforce the natural trend toward strict segregation of land uses, thus ensuring that everything would be in its place and that there would be a place for everything. By so doing, it would protect residential neighborhoods, stabilize property values, reduce population density, relieve traffic congestion, and improve public health and public safety.[91] Promoted as a panacea for a wide range of urban problems, zoning moved to the top of the public agenda in the late 1910s and early 1920s.

The campaign for height limits underwent one other striking change after the passage of the New York ordinance. Prior to 1916 advocates of height limits had usually called for the imposition of a uniform height, a flat limit above which no building could be erected anywhere in the city. Afterward, they generally called for the creation of several height districts, each of which would have a limit of its own—a flat limit, a limit based on the width of the street, or both. These limits varied from one district to another, though the highest were invariably reserved for downtown and its immediate surroundings. More often than not, the builders were allowed to exceed the height limits, but only if the building (or part of it) was set back from the street line or occupied only a small portion of the lot. Implicit in the post-1916 height limits was the assumption that the problem was not tall buildings, but tall buildings that blocked light and air and produced excessive congestion, and that the solution was to regulate, not ban them. Also implicit was the belief that the skyscraper was a permanent part of American life—that, as *American Architect* wrote in late 1913, it "is as peculiar to our country as the chateau is to France, the cathedral to England, or the temple to Greece."[92]

In many cities the efforts to impose (or to lower) height limits through zoning made a good deal of headway after the passage of the New York ordinance. In St. Louis, where the height limit had been raised from 200 to 250 feet in 1913, the city plan commission started work on a comprehensive zoning ordinance in 1917. Drafted by Harland Bartholomew, the ordinance, which was modeled on New York's, established five height districts, with limits of 35 feet in residential neighborhoods and 150 feet in the business district (and even higher if the builder was willing to go along with the setback and lot coverage provisions). The board of aldermen passed the ordinance in 1918, although five years later the Missouri Supreme Court found it unconstitutional. Another example was Baltimore, which had imposed a height limit of 175 feet in 1904. In 1921 the city set up a zoning commission, which drafted an ordinance that established five height districts, in all but one of which the limit was based on the width of the streets. It also retained the 175-foot limit, even in downtown Baltimore, where buildings could otherwise go as high as two and a half times the width of the streets on which they stood. Backed by Bassett, Purdy, and, with some reluctance, the Baltimore Real Estate Board, the ordinance was adopted in 1923. Similar ordinances were passed in other cities in the late 1910s and early 1920s. Indeed, by the mid 1920s more than two-thirds of the nation's largest cities were zoned in one way or another.[93]

Even Boston, the first American city to impose a height limit, followed New York's lead, though not for the same reason as other cities. During the early 1920s some downtown property owners began to bring pressure on the authorities to revise the long-standing limit of 125 feet. Boston needed more office buildings, they argued, but New York's financial institutions would not underwrite them as long as the current limit was in force. From the perspective of these institutions, a flat 125-foot limit was anachronistic. Despite the pressure, the state legislature shelved a petition to abolish the height limit in 1922. But over the objections of the owners of many of downtown Boston's ten- and eleven-story office buildings, it raised the limit to 155 feet a year later. The opposition was not satisfied. In 1927, by which time Boston had adopted a zoning ordinance, it mounted a campaign to replace the flat height limit with a volume limit, the sort popularized by the New York zoning ordinance. Under this proposal, a building could rise to any height—provided it was set back one foot from the street line for every two and a half feet it went above 125 feet. At the urging of real estate developers and city officials, the state legislature approved the change in 1928, thereby ending close to forty years of flat height limits in Boston.[94] Only three skyscrapers were erected under the new limits before the Great Depression brought construction to a halt, but along with the Custom House Tower they dominated the Boston skyline for the next thirty years.

In some cities, however, the efforts to impose height limits through zoning ran into strong resistance. Sometimes the resistance was fueled by the opposition to zoning, which, it was charged, was "unfair, undemocratic and un-

American." It was unfair because it discriminated among property owners. As Horace Groskin, director of the Philadelphia Real Estate Board, declared: "By what right has a zoning commission to set itself up as the judge and distributer [sic] of property values? To take the value away from one property owner and give it to another, or not to give it to anyone but to destroy it entirely for the imaginary benefit of the community, strikes me as coming mighty close to Socialism." Zoning was undemocratic because it placed too much power in the hands of appointed commissions and other bureaucratic agencies over which citizens had no control. And it was un-American, William P. Gest, a Philadelphia banker, claimed, because it "takes private property for public use without compensation" and for reasons other than public health and public safety. Thus it was a patent abuse of the "police power." According to its opponents, zoning (and in particular use and area restrictions) would block home ownership, inject politics into development, drive business out of the city, lower property values, and reduce municipal revenues. It would also prevent the conversion of real estate from residential to commercial and industrial use. Americans, opponents of zoning argued, would be well advised to leave the operations of the real estate market to the natural laws of economics—constrained, when need be, by existing nuisance laws and private deed restrictions.[95]

More often, however, it was the hostility to height limits that fueled the opposition to zoning. In Milwaukee, for example, the Board of Public Land Commissioners prepared a comprehensive zoning ordinance four years after the New York ordinance was passed. The proposed use and area restrictions aroused little opposition, the board reported. But to the proposal to lower the height limit, then 225 feet, to 125 feet, "considerable objection was taken." The response was much the same in Washington, D.C., and Akron, and not that different in San Francisco and Pittsburgh. In San Francisco the Real Estate Board, a trade group dominated by large brokers who specialized in downtown property, favored zoning in principle, but opposed a zoning ordinance that limited building heights. And in Pittsburgh the chamber of commerce voiced support for use restrictions, but expressed reservations about height limits, which were strongly opposed by the Real Estate Board and the Board of Trade. Reviewing the history of zoning in the 1920s, two experts found that height limits had been "the sticking point" in a good many cities.[96] The strategy of linking height limits and use restrictions, which had worked well in New York, backfired in these cities. Instead of strengthening the case for height limits, it weakened the case for comprehensive zoning.

A case in point is Philadelphia, the nation's third largest city. In June 1920,

Mayor J. Hampton Moore appointed a zoning commission, consisting of several high-ranking public officials and representatives of the city's architects, engineers, builders, realtors, commercial organizations, and labor unions, to prepare a comprehensive zoning ordinance. Drawing heavily on the work of a prior zoning commission—which had been created in July 1916, the same month in which the New York zoning ordinance was adopted—the commission drafted an ordinance in roughly six months. Closely modeled on New York's, it provided for four use districts, five area districts, and five height districts, in each of which both a flat limit and a limit based on the width of the street were imposed. Depending on the district, a building could go as high as one to three times the width of the street, to a maximum height ranging from 40 feet in the "one times" district to 150 feet in the "three times" district, downtown Philadelphia and the area adjacent to it. An owner could build to any height—provided that the part of the structure that exceeded the height limit was set back from the street line. For every foot it was set back, a building could rise an additional one to three feet, depending on the district. The setback allowance notwithstanding, this was a fairly stringent restriction in a city that had no height limits at all and already had one building more than 300 feet tall, ten others 200 feet and higher, and another six 150 feet or more.[97]

Introduced in the city council in late 1921 (and referred to its Committee on City Planning and Zoning soon after), the zoning ordinance aroused a great deal of opposition, especially among downtown real estate and financial interests. Most of it was aimed at the proposed height limits and had a familiar ring. Tall buildings, it was claimed, were much the safest, healthiest, most economical, and most attractive commercial structures in America's cities. To impose so stringent a height limit would bring their construction to a halt. It would increase the already serious shortage of office space in the city. And it would lower real estate values in the business districts, thereby reducing assessed values and municipal revenues. The opposition also attacked the reasoning of advocates of height limits, who argued both that skyscrapers did not pay and that unless height limits were imposed they would be erected all over the business district. "Now both of these propositions cannot be true," wrote Horace Groskin. "One of them must be wrong. If property owners no longer find high buildings profitable, why try to frighten us about solid blocks of skyscrapers in the future? Why then is there need for the Height limit? Will not the natural economic law automatically take care of the situation?"[98]

But some of the objections had seldom been raised before. One was that Philadelphia would be mistaken to follow the lead of New York, which, by virtue of its unusual topography and extreme congestion, was not a model for other American cities. Besides, as George H. Earle, Jr., a Philadelphia financier, pointed out, even New York had not adopted a height limit—and a fairly lenient height limit at that—until it had far more tall (and very tall) buildings than any other city in the world. Another objection, one that would be raised more often and spelled out in more detail in the mid and late 1920s, was that the tall buildings were not the principal cause of the traffic problem. Much of the traffic on Broad and Market streets consisted of shoppers, Groskin said. And traffic was very heavy on streets on which there were no office buildings at all. Still another objection was that Philadelphia had long been assessing much downtown real estate on the basis of its value as the site for a skyscraper, one that many property owners hoped to build some day. "Is it just," asked Gest, "when the City has been taxing the property according to the taxpayer's hopes, and has received a vast amount of income therefrom, suddenly to destroy those hopes without compensation or redress of any kind, under the guise of the exercise of the 'police power'?"[99]

Despite these objections, the zoning ordinance was endorsed by the Philadelphia Chamber of Commerce, the Philadelphia chapter of the American Institute of Architects, and some of Philadelphia's leading civic groups. Edward Bassett, who testified before the Committee on City Planning and Zoning, lent his support, as did Lawson Purdy, who spoke at a joint meeting of Philadelphia's engineering societies. But the ordinance was opposed by many of Philadelphia's banks, trust companies, and large downtown real estate interests—at least one of which, the Stephen Girard Estate, was planning to erect a 320-foot skyscraper that would have been the tallest building in Philadelphia. Some of them made it clear that they preferred no zoning ordinance at all than one with a 150-foot height limit. In the face of this opposition, the council committee eliminated downtown Philadelphia and environs—the area bounded by Vine and South streets and by the Schuylkill and Delaware rivers—from the ordinance and referred it back to the zoning commission for reconsideration. As William Gest observed, this action "practically killed the Ordinance," because a zoning ordinance that covered some parts of the city but not others would have been struck down by the courts. If any doubts remained about its fate, the city council dispelled them in February 1922, when it refused to appropriate additional funds for the zoning commission.[100]

Opposition to height limits was largely responsible for the defeat of comprehensive zoning ordinances in Detroit and Cleveland, too. And it was a major stumbling block in San Francisco, where the newly created city planning commission began work on a zoning ordinance in 1918. The main opposition came from the San Francisco Real Estate Board, many of whose members feared that height limits would deter development downtown. Allied with the board were the Downtown Association and the local branch of the National Association of Building Owners and Managers. Together these groups put so much pressure on the San Francisco Board of Supervisors that it removed the height limits from the zoning ordinance before adopting it in 1921. Opposition to height limits was also a major stumbling block in Chicago, where the zoning commission drafted a comprehensive zoning ordinance in the early 1920s, only a couple of years after the city council raised the height limit from 200 to 260 feet. The ordinance was supported in most parts of the city—but not in the Loop, where many property owners (as well as some architects and businessmen) took strong exception to the proposal to lower the height limit. After a long controversy, during which the Chicago Real Estate Board made the most extensive study of height limits since the New York City commissions of 1913 and 1916, the city council adopted the zoning ordinance, but only after exempting the Loop from the height limits at the last minute.[101]

Overall, however, the passage of the New York zoning ordinance gave a big boost to the movement for height limits. By the mid 1920s most cities had adopted a comprehensive zoning ordinance that either lowered the existing limit or imposed a limit for the first time. Following New York's lead, most of them rejected a uniform limit. Instead they established several height districts, each of which had its own limits, usually a flat limit—which ranged from 110 feet in Portland, Oregon, to 265 feet in Pittsburgh—and sometimes a limit based on the width of the street. Also following New York's lead, most cities allowed owners to build above the height limit provided the building (or a part of it) was set back from the street line or covered only a portion of the lot. Despite these gains, the issue was far from settled. Philadelphia, Detroit, and Cleveland still had no height limits. And outside of Los Angeles, where the limit was incorporated into the city charter, most height limits were based on municipal ordinances, which could be changed at any time.[102] Just how precarious these limits were was revealed in the mid and late 1920s, when a movement was launched in many cities to raise or, if possible, abolish them.

Leading this movement were the local chapters of the National Association of Building Owners and Managers. Active in most big cities, these trade groups represented the major downtown real estate interests—the large brokers, builders, investors, and property owners. About zoning, and especially about use restrictions, BOMA leaders had mixed feelings. But about height limits, which some regarded as a "separate and distinct" issue, they had strong reservations. Starting in the early 1920s, local BOMAs and their allies worked hard in several cities to prevent the enactment of zoning ordinances that included height limits. Afraid that a limit would make it impossible to capitalize on the booming real estate market, they intensified their efforts in the mid and late 1920s. During the mid 1920s the national association also got involved in the battle. In 1925 it formed a Committee on Height Limitation, which issued a series of annual reports attacking height limits and defending tall buildings. A year later the association's leaders passed a resolution denying that tall buildings were a danger to public health and public safety and a major cause of traffic congestion, claiming that height limits were a grave threat to property values, and declaring that they were "unalterably opposed to any unreasonable limitation of the Height of Buildings." By this they meant any limitation that reduced the earning power of real estate or inhibited the economic development of American cities.[103]

The movement against height limits had mixed results. It stymied the efforts to enact comprehensive zoning in Detroit, Philadelphia, and Cleveland, where an ordinance was passed in 1928 but repealed soon after. During the late 1920s downtown real estate interests also blocked an attempt, by Lawson Purdy and others who had grown increasingly troubled by the proliferation of immense skyscrapers in Manhattan, to revise the 1916 zoning ordinance and lower the height limits. Under pressure from developers, Boston raised its height limit in the 1920s. So did Seattle, St. Paul, and Atlanta, where

The skyscrapers of lower Manhattan, 1929 (New York Times, March 4, 1929)

the limit was virtually nullified in 1929 by a law that raised it from 150 feet to 325 feet, with no setbacks required. In most cities, however, the movement had little success in abolishing or even raising the limits. (In some cities, developers were able to prevail on local authorities to allow a building to rise well above the height limit. But in other cities they were not. In Chicago, for example, developers prevailed on the city council to amend the zoning ordinance in 1929, raising the height limit from 264 feet to 440 feet, and then to grant a permit for a 440-foot building with a 217-foot tower on top. But in the face of opposition from the Illinois chapter of the AIA and other groups, the council revoked the permit and repealed the amendment.)[104]

At the heart of this struggle was a deep ambivalence about tall buildings, one that was as pronounced in the mid and late 1920s as it had been in the early and mid 1890s. Nowhere was it reflected more clearly than in the nationwide debate over skyscrapers that raged in the second half of the 1920s, a full decade after the New York zoning ordinance had seemingly resolved the issue. Although many Americans participated in the debate, probably the most active were two New Yorkers: Henry H. Curran, counsel to the City Club of New York (and former Manhattan borough president), who detested tall buildings, and Harvey Wiley Corbett, an architect (and, in Curran's words, "a delightful gentleman," of whom he was "very fond"), who admired them. Curran and Corbett debated the skyscraper in the *New York Times Magazine* in late 1926 and in the *National Municipal Review* in early 1927. Later that year they took opposite sides in a debate sponsored by the Civic Development Department of the U.S. Chamber of Commerce. Among the other Americans who joined the debate were Frederic A. Delano, president of the American Civic Association, whose critique of the skyscraper published in *American City* in January 1926 was promptly rebutted by the editors of *Buildings and Building Management,* a leading trade publication.[105]

Although the debate raised few new issues, its focus changed. Both sides still argued about whether tall buildings were a menace to public health and safety. Opponents charged that they were a barrier to sunlight and fresh air and, in the event of fire, a death trap. Defenders responded that they were the healthiest and safest commercial structures in urban America. The two sides still disagreed about the aesthetics of the skyscraper. Critics lamented the loss of the "uniform cornice line." Viewed broadside, one complained, the New York skyline "looks like a baggage room after Labor Day, full of trunks and boxes up on end." Admirers claimed that the skyscraper was uniquely American, "the most important contribution we have made to the building arts." A well-designed skyscraper could hold its own against the great cathedrals of the old world. Both sides still debated the economics of the skyscraper too. Opponents argued that the notion that tall buildings were profitable was, as Lawson Purdy put it, "a delusion." Defenders replied that the price of down-town property was so high that in order to earn a reasonable return owners had no choice but to put up skyscrapers. They conceded that above a certain height a building reached a point of diminishing returns. But drawing on a se-ries of studies by local BOMAs, they pointed out that the "economic height" of office buildings was much higher than the advocates of height limits realized. Indeed, a study commissioned by the American Institute of Steel Construc-tion, which had an obvious stake in the results, found that on a prime mid-town Manhattan site a building would not reach the point of diminishing re-turns until it went above sixty-three stories.[106]

But for all the talk about public health, public safety, aesthetics, and eco-nomics, it was traffic congestion, hitherto only one of several issues (and by no means the most important), that emerged as the overriding one in the mid and late 1920s. According to Curran, tall buildings were the principal cause of downtown's traffic problem. "Wherever a skyscraper rises congestion fol-lows," he said. With hundreds of thousands of office workers fighting their way in and out of the business district, the streets and sidewalks, which had not been designed to handle the traffic generated by the skyscrapers, were jammed. Traffic came to a standstill. It was so heavy in Manhattan, wrote Cur-ran, that the only way an automobile can go from midtown to the financial dis-trict "is to take wings at 42nd Street, go high in the air, then fly downtown, and alight in Wall Street—or else try to swim there, under the rivers." A stringent height limit, no higher than eight stories, would relieve congestion, argued ar-chitect Thomas Hastings. It would also render unnecessary the current pro-posals to double-deck the streets, build elevated sidewalks, and undertake other prohibitively expensive public works to solve the traffic problem.[107]

Even a subway could not handle the immense traffic generated by the sky-scrapers, at least not "with any degree of comfort." Whenever a city built a subway, it drove up the value of the abutting property, prompting the owners to erect skyscrapers along the line. A subway took much more time to build than a skyscraper. And as Curran wrote about New York's new Eighth Avenue subway, "By the time that the subway reaches completion the thoroughfare will be lined upon both sides with massive buildings. And the subway no sooner will go into service than the skyscraper population will fill it to suffoca-tion." The subway will do nothing to relieve congestion. Despite an expendi-ture of hundreds of millions of dollars, which were desperately needed for schools, parks, and playgrounds, the traffic problem will be as bad as ever.

Americans were approaching the problem from "the wrong end," Curran argued. Instead of building subways, they should stop building skyscrapers—or at least stop building so many of them. Other Americans took a similar position, claiming that a subway would exacerbate the traffic problem unless it was accompanied by legislation limiting the height (or bulk) of office buildings. Otherwise a subway would only contribute to the "vicious circle of transit development and city congestion." If a subway were to be built at all, Daniel Turner contended, it should be designed to promote development in the outlying business districts rather than to increase congestion in the central business district.[108]

Traffic congestion was a serious problem, Corbett and others agreed. But tall buildings were not its principal cause. Citing statistics compiled by local BOMAs, they pointed out that department stores generated far more traffic than office buildings, a point also made by Miller McClintock, the nation's leading authority on traffic congestion. In Detroit, they noted, a major department store attracted more than ten times as many people a day as the tallest office building. In St. Louis eleven big retail stores generated more than three times as much traffic as twenty-seven tall office buildings. Everywhere the traffic was at its worst not on streets lined with office buildings but on those lined with department stores—on Chicago's State Street, San Francisco's Market Street, and Pittsburgh's Fifth Avenue. Compounding the problems caused by department stores (and, to a lesser extent, theaters and restaurants) was the proliferation of automobiles, which, Corbett stressed, took up roughly forty times as much space as pedestrians. The skyscraper's defenders also pointed out that downtown Boston—with a stringent height limit (as well as a subway that removed the streetcars from the busiest streets)—was more congested than downtown San Francisco. New York, the skyscraper capital of the world, had a terrible traffic problem; but so did London, which, by virtue of its 80-foot height limit, had no skyscrapers at all. And the London Underground was just as crowded as the New York subway, Corbett wrote, the passengers "as badly squeezed and shoved" in one as in the other.[109]

Far from exacerbating the traffic problem, the skyscrapers alleviated it, Corbett argued. They concentrated so many businesses in one building and so many buildings in one district that businessmen were able to transact their affairs without doing much traveling. ("In downtown New York," Corbett wrote, "a business man consults his broker, eats his lunch, sees his lawyer, buys his wife a box of candy, gets a shave, all in the same building. At most he walks a few blocks.") Working in skyscrapers, they moved vertically rather than horizontally, transported by high-speed elevators instead of slow-moving streetcars and autos. Imagine what would happen if stringent height limits were imposed and many low buildings replaced a few high ones. Businessmen would have to travel longer distances from one appointment to another, crowding the streets (and street railways), raising the already high levels of traffic congestion. "Remove the skyscraper," wrote Corbett, "and this congestion would long since have reached the saturation point." The traffic problem could be solved not by abolishing skyscrapers, but by enforcing traffic regulations, increasing street capacity, and redesigning rapid transit.[110]

Both sides agreed that skyscrapers—some of which, said Thomas A. Edison, house as many people "as we used to have in a small city"—made the already highly concentrated business districts even more so. But they sharply disagreed about the effects of concentration. To Curran, excessive concentration made it very hard to move from one part of the city to another. Responding to Corbett's claim that tall buildings relieved traffic congestion, Curran asked, "how do the skyscraper people get there in the morning? Do they live on the 20th floor and take the elevator down to the 15th floor to go to work? Do they go back home from the 12th to the 14th floor?" Excessive concentration also imposed a heavy burden on the city's infrastructure. It levied what Lewis Mumford, a fierce critic of the skyscraper, called an "economic tax" on the whole community for the benefit of a few property owners. Excessive concentration generated a huge disparity in property values within the business district too. It was vital to curb the skyscrapers, "not merely to provide the adequate light and air for workers in those buildings," city planner Harland Bartholomew wrote in the early 1920s, but also to "distribute the [business] district over a greater area" and thus reduce the extreme concentration in a few small parts of it.[111]

To Corbett this argument was preposterous. Concentration facilitated business, he claimed. In addition to relieving congestion, it saved time, lowered overhead, increased efficiency, and encouraged the close contact among businessmen that was so crucial to modern enterprise. Indeed "it is only through the concentration in comparatively small areas of large numbers of business people that we can conduct our affairs at all." Corbett's view was shared by most downtown businessmen, said Louis E. Honig, a St. Louis real estate man and the chair of the BOMA Committee on Height Limitation in 1927. From their perspective, the skyscraper was a reflection of "the demands of American business," in the words of Honig's successor, W. E. Malm of Cleveland. For business purposes, it was "the most efficient building known to Man," wrote Charles F. Abbott, executive director of the American Institute of Steel Construction. To ban the skyscraper and thereby disperse the business district would reduce the efficiency of American business, Corbett contended. As proof, he pointed to London, which had neither skyscrapers nor a concentrated business district and where, he wrote, "if you attempt to make three business appointments in a day, you will do very well, because they will be scattered over every portion of the city."[112]

By the end of the decade the two sides were as far apart as ever. As W. C. Clark, a New York real estate agent who held that the economic height of a modern office building was sixty-three stories, pointed out:

> At the one extreme we have a group of critics, chiefly city planners of the more doctrinaire type, who are bitter and extravagant in their criticism of the skyscraper, who find in it the source of most of the evils in our city life and who advocate a definite restriction of building height to a maximum of eight or ten stories. At the other extreme is a school of protagonists who are enthusiastic and even lyrical in their praise of the skyscraper, who see in it both a necessary result of American conditions and a characteristic product of American genius and who protest against any attempt to restrict or regulate its development.[113]

Some believed there was a middle ground. Thomas Adams, a consultant to the Regional Plan of New York, wrote that the skyscraper itself was desirable, "wherever it is useful and economically sound." What was undesirable was the erection of skyscrapers next to one another. If the skyscrapers were built on large lots, with plenty of open space around them, they would not pose a problem. In an otherwise highly critical article published in the *New Republic,* R. L. Duffus took much the same position. If we plan wisely, he wrote, the skyscraper of the future "will be a lone giant, higher, perhaps, than any we now possess, but sufficiently separated from its fellows to keep the *average height* of buildings in its area down to a reasonable level." Despite the efforts to find a middle ground, the debate showed no signs of waning.

With hindsight, it seems naive, even anachronistic. For at the same time that Curran, Corbett, and others were arguing about the skyscraper, the United States was heading toward the Great Depression, which struck in late 1929 and soon brought construction to a standstill. It took the nation a decade to recover; and by then the outbreak of World War II deterred construction for almost another decade. But at the time the debate was widely regarded as crucial and timely. To Curran and other Americans who were dismayed by the proliferation of thirty- and forty-story buildings, not to mention the proposals for an 870-foot building in Detroit and a 1,200-foot building in New York, now might be the last chance to stop the madness. It might also be the last chance to shape the future of downtown, to force it to expand outward rather than upward, to put an end to the process by which more and more business was done in less and less space. To Corbett and others who were exhilarated by the power to build to almost any height, now was the time to put up more skyscrapers, the taller the better, and to rebuild the business districts around them. It might even be time to erect what we call mixed-use skyscrapers— with stores, shops, and theaters on the lower floors, offices above them, then clubs, hotels, and restaurants, and, on the upper floors, apartments. Ironically, one of these buildings was proposed, though not designed, by Raymond M. Hood, president of the New York Architectural League, the organization that had led the first campaign for height limits in New York a generation earlier.[114]

The onset of the Great Depression is as good a time as any to look at the effects of the campaign for height limits. As even Edward Bassett conceded, it had much less of an impact than its advocates had hoped. It did not stop the construction of tall buildings. Despite forty years of strong opposition, the United States was the skyscraper capital of the world. By 1929 it had about five thousand buildings ten stories or taller, of which nearly four hundred were more than twenty stories. Almost half of them were located in New York, where, as a result of a spectacular surge of construction, the number of skyscrapers had more than doubled after the passage of the zoning ordinance of 1916. Chicago had well over four hundred skyscrapers, and Los Angeles, Detroit, Philadelphia, and Boston more than one hundred. Even much smaller cities had them. Beaumont, Texas, population 58,000, had six buildings ten stories or taller, which is more than London, Paris, or Berlin had. And Allentown, Pennsylvania, population 93,000, had a twenty-two-story skyscraper, erected in the 1920s by the Pennsylvania Power and Light Company. Nor did the campaign for height limits stop the construction of extraordinarily tall buildings. By 1929 ten skyscrapers over 500 feet had been erected in the United States; five others were under construction, among them the Chrysler Building and the Bank of Manhattan Building, both of which would rise above 800 feet. And work was about to begin on the Empire State Building, which proved that it was possible to build higher than 1,000 feet (and over one hundred stories) under the zoning ordinance of 1916. Finished two years later, it remained the tallest building in the world for several decades. By the early 1930s some observers were starting to wonder not whether American cities would follow the lead of European cities and stop building skyscrapers, a common belief a few decades earlier, but whether European cities would follow the lead of American cities and start building them.[115]

But it is not fair to say, as some Americans did, that the campaign for height limits had no impact. It all depended on the city. The campaign had a great impact in Boston and Los Angeles, where the authorities imposed stringent limits and strictly enforced them. In the absence of height limits, it is inconceivable that on the eve of the depression Boston would have had more than a hundred buildings ten stories or taller but only two buildings taller than twenty stories—or that Los Angeles would have had more than 130 buildings ten or more stories but only one building more than twenty stories. The campaign had much less of an effect in Philadelphia and Detroit, where the authorities refused to establish a height limit and where, as a result, a large proportion of the tall buildings—far larger than in Boston and Los Angeles and larger even than in New York and Chicago—stood more than twenty stories high. The campaign had a moderate impact in Chicago and New York. Chicago's height limit probably prevented the construction of a few very tall buildings. Although New York's zoning ordinance did not, it did force the builders to erect them on large lots and to set them back from the street line. It also inspired architects to design them in a novel way.[116] To put it another way, the zoning ordinance allowed the erection of the 102-story Empire State Building, but it blocked the erection of another 40-story Equitable Building.

Although the campaign for height limits did something to curb the construction of skyscrapers, it did little or nothing to reduce the instability of the business district, which had been one of the principal reasons for launching it in the first place. Indeed, downtown's instability was at least as much a source of concern to real estate interests in the mid and late 1920s as it had been at the end of the nineteenth century. No matter how the battles over height limits turned out, the business districts continued to move. Although a few real estate men saw this as normal (and even beneficial), most viewed it as a serious problem. Wherever the business district moved, it left in its wake real estate whose earnings fell and whose values dropped. Property owners lost huge sums, as did lending institutions. This instability discouraged investment in real estate, not only downtown but in other parts of the city. As David Whitcomb of Seattle told the annual convention of the National Association of Building Owners and Managers in 1928, "if there is no stability in the value of the most improved properties in the heart of the city, there can be no assurance as to values in other portions." The association was so concerned about the constant movement of downtown that in the mid 1920s it established a Committee on Stabilization of Business Districts, which urged the local BOMAs to study the problem and use their influence to solve it.[117]

By the 1920s, however, it was clear that the skyscraper was not the only reason for downtown's instability. Nor was it the most important. According to well-informed real estate men, the constant shifts in the business districts were a function of a great many things. Some were viewed as natural, even inevitable. Among them were the growth of population, the expansion of commerce and industry, and the tendency of fashionable retail stores to move in the direction of affluent residential sections. Others were seen as the result of public action—and, in some cases, public inaction. Among them were the development of transportation facilities, especially rapid transit lines and inter-city railroad terminals, and the increase of traffic congestion. Still others were viewed as the product of private decisions. Among them was the reluctance of some downtown property owners to upgrade their buildings in order to hold on to their tenants.[118] Thus even if the campaign for height limits had been more successful, even if it had more or less blocked the skyscraper, it would not necessarily have prevented shifts in the business district. Indeed, to the extent that these limits led to the construction of relatively low office buildings on the fringe of the business district, they might have increased downtown's instability.

Although the campaign for height limits had some impact on the size and design of skyscrapers, it had very little on the structure of the business district. For things turned out to be far more complicated than expected. Their imposition did not mean that the business district would necessarily spread out over a much larger area. Nor did their absence mean that the business district would inevitably be concentrated in an ever smaller area. Business was more centralized in downtown Boston, which had a stringent limit, than in downtown Detroit, which had no limit at all (and where several huge skyscrapers were erected in General Motors's "New Center," three miles north of it). Despite a height limit, albeit a loosely enforced one, the Chicago Loop remained one of the most compact business districts in the United States. It was not until after 1920, when the height limit was raised from 200 to 260 feet, that the Chicago Tribune Building and a few other giant skyscrapers went up outside the Loop, mainly across the river on Michigan Avenue. And although the New York zoning ordinance of 1916 imposed the least stringent height restrictions in the financial district, the great surge of skyscraper construction in the 1920s took place not around Wall Street but in midtown Manhattan. By the end of the decade half the city's skyscrapers were located there.[119]

Nor did the campaign for height limits have much of an impact on the assumptions about downtown (and the structure of the American metropolis) that had emerged in the late nineteenth century. With a few exceptions, the advocates of height limits believed that a compact and concentrated business district was desirable and inevitable. So did the opponents. What they disagreed about was how compact and how concentrated it should be—whether economic activity should be spread over the entire business district or confined to a small part of it. In other words, they disagreed about the structure of the center, not about its relation to the periphery. The campaign for height limits raised some doubts about the notion of spatial harmony. But unlike the fights over rapid transit, the battles over tall buildings revolved around the conflicts within the business district, between the old core and its emerging (or potential) rivals, not around conflicts between the business district and the outlying business centers. If the politics of rapid transit gave Americans reason to think that intra-city rivalry might well be as natural as inter-city rivalry, the politics of height limits gave them reason to think that rivalry within the business district might well be natural too.

4 The Central Business
District: Downtown
in the 1920s

Late in 1923 Professor Ernest W. Burgess, a University of Chicago sociologist and one of the founders of the Chicago School of Sociology, delivered a paper on the growth of the American city at the annual meetings of the American Sociological Society. In this brief but extremely influential essay, Burgess presented for the first time his "concentric zonal" theory, the theory, as one geographer has summarized it, "that as a city grows it expands radially from the center to form a series of concentric zones." As Burgess spelled it out a few years later, the innermost zone was the "Loop," or downtown, "the focus of [the city's] commercial, social, and civic life." Encircling downtown was the "Zone in Transition," which consisted of factories, deteriorating neighborhoods, and disreputable activities. Farther out were a "Zone of Workingmen's (or Independent Workingmen's) Homes," a "Residential Zone" (or "Zone of Better Residences"), and, on the periphery, a "Commuters' Zone," a zone of suburban communities and "satellite cities."[1] Burgess's paper was noteworthy for a number of reasons, one of which has been overlooked by scholars. In it Burgess referred to downtown, the innermost zone, not as the "business district," which is how Americans had referred to it in the late nineteenth and early twentieth centuries, but as the "central business district," a term that would become virtually synonymous with downtown in the 1930s and 1940s.

By the time Burgess wrote of "the central business district," the term was about two decades old.[*] It had been used, though very rarely, as early as 1904. Writing one day after the great Baltimore fire, the *Baltimore Sun* reported that the fire "devastated practically the entire central business district." "To all appearances," it wrote, "Baltimore's business section is doomed." The term was

---

[*] Even older was "central business section," which was used in the *New York Mail and Express* as early as 1897. (See *Architecture and Building,* October 23, 1897, page 145.)

The Chicago Loop, ca. 1930 (Pictorial History of Chicago, *1930*)

also used, though not much more often, in the next decade. At the request of the Newark City Plan Commission, an architectural firm called Bigelow & Tuttle drafted a plan of proposed improvements for the "Central Business District" in 1913. And three years later the Chicago Traction and Subway Commission, appointed by the city council to study local transportation in the Windy City, referred to the Loop as the "central business district." The term finally caught on in the 1920s. Kelker, De Leuw, a transit engineering firm, used it, as did McClellan & Junkersfeld, one of Kelker, De Leuw's competitors. Traffic consultants also spoke of the "central business district." So did downtown businessmen, city planners, and real estate economists, even when talking about cities as different as Boston and Los Angeles.[2]

Down through the 1910s the "central business district" had two different, though not necessarily incompatible, meanings. One was geographical. Central meant in, at, or near the center. Bion J. Arnold, the nation's leading authority on rapid transit, used the term in this way when he pointed out in 1910 that Pittsburgh had once been "a one sided city like San Francisco," but that now that it had expanded, across the Allegheny and Monongahela rivers, it was a city with "a centrally located business district." So did Harland

Bartholomew, a fledgling city planner working for the St. Louis City Plan Commission, who noted in 1918 that although the St. Louis business district was not in "the physical center of the city," it was in the center of the "metropolitan district," another recent addition to the vocabulary of urban America. The other meaning was functional. Central meant most important. It was with this meaning in mind that the *Electric Railway Journal* described the Chicago Loop as the "main business center" and McClellan & Junkersfeld referred to downtown Milwaukee as the "central business district."[3] By the time Burgess delivered his paper, the functional meaning had superseded the geographical.

The central business district had much in common with downtown. It was a uniquely American term, one that would not be used elsewhere until well after World War II. It was also a uniquely American place. And as a place, it, too, was hard to define. Legally, the central business district did not exist. Nor did it exist politically, at least not in a formal sense. It was, as Bartholomew remarked in the early 1930s, "somewhat of a vague area with no definite boundaries." Transit engineers and traffic consultants made an effort to trace these boundaries in the mid and late 1920s, an effort that would be continued by urban geographers in the 1950s. But the efforts to define (or, in the geographers' words, to delimit) the central business district faced serious handicaps. One was that the central business district could be defined by one or more of several features, among which the most important were retail sales, daytime population, and property values. Another handicap was that its boundaries were constantly changing. As one real estate economist pointed out in the mid 1920s, a time when downtown New York was spreading into mid Manhattan and downtown Chicago was expanding across the Chicago River and up Michigan Avenue, "No part of the man-made landscape of our country changes so rapidly as does the central portion of the growing American city."[4]

If the central business district was so imprecise a term, why was it used so commonly in the mid and late 1920s? To put it another way, why did so many Americans now refer to downtown not as *the* business district, but as the *central* business district? The answer is that down through the late nineteenth and very early twentieth centuries downtown was the only business district. It was the place, wrote Stone & Webster, the engineering firm, of downtown Pittsburgh in 1909, where "all of the business of the city except manufacturing" was carried out. It was the "common center," said the Massachusetts Rapid Transit Commission of 1892 of downtown Boston, into which most people poured every day to work, shop, do business, and amuse themselves. During the first third of the twentieth century, however, a great many outlying

Chicago's Uptown Center, 1926 (Courtesy of the Chicago Historical Society, ICHi-04122)

business districts emerged in all the big cities. Some were located in old and well established neighborhoods, like Boston's Back Bay and Chicago's Uptown, but others, like Los Angeles' Wilshire Boulevard, were found in places "which a few short years ago were barley fields," a Los Angeles real estate man observed. Given the growth of outlying business districts—or what Burgess, from his perspective in Chicago, called "satellite loops"—Americans realized that downtown was no longer the only business district. But it was still far and away the most important—the one, wrote Burgess, that "visibly or invisibly" dominated all the others.[5] It was the central business district.

With hindsight, it is clear that this change reflected changes in the structure of the American metropolis in the first third of the twentieth century, of which the growth of the outlying business districts was by far the most momentous. These changes in turn reflected other changes in urban America at the time, among them the increasing dispersal of residences, the growing decentralization of industry, the decline of mass transit, and the proliferation of private automobiles. All this had a strong impact not only on downtown as a place but on the assumptions about downtown that had emerged in the late nineteenth century. Although Americans still thought that downtown was inevitable and desirable—that, as Burgess put it, "Quite naturally, almost inevitably, the economic, cultural, and political life centers there"—some were no longer sure.[6] Americans still believed in spatial harmony, but many were now aware of the deep conflicts between the periphery and the center (as well as within the center). And by the late 1920s some Americans were even beginning to wonder whether the equilibrium between the dispersal of residences and the concentration of business would last much longer.

Although no longer the only business district, downtown was in many ways much the same. Despite the hopes and expectations of many Americans, it was still highly compact. According to Homer Hoyt, downtown Chicago cov-

Hollywood Boulevard, Los Angeles, 1927 (Courtesy of the University of Southern California, on behalf of the USC Library Department of Special Collections)

ered roughly one square mile in the early 1930s—only a little more space than it had in the early 1880s, when the city had fewer than one-sixth as many people. It covered about one-half of 1 percent of the city and about one-tenth of 1 percent of the metropolitan district. According to studies made in the late 1920s and early 1930s, when most big cities were spread over scores and even hundreds of square miles (and some metropolitan districts over a thousand square miles), things were much the same elsewhere. Downtown was less than a square mile in St. Louis, Los Angeles, Boston, and Detroit and less than half a square mile in Baltimore, Kansas City, and Pittsburgh. Downtown Philadelphia was a little more than two square miles, and downtown New York, which included a small financial district in lower Manhattan and a large retail and office district in midtown, was even bigger. But nowhere, not even in New York, did downtown cover more than 1 or 2 percent of the city—or more than a fraction of a percent of the metropolitan district.[7]

   Why was downtown still so compact? Why had it not grown to meet the growing demands for commercial space? Why had it not spread out as the rest of the city had? The answer was that downtown had expanded vertically, not horizontally. "Instead of going outward it went upward," said Miller Mc-Clintock, an expert on street traffic control. Office buildings soared to unprecedented heights in the first third of the twentieth century. So did hotels—some of which were taller than all but the tallest office buildings. Department stores also climbed to extraordinary heights. Newark's Bamberger's rose more than fifteen stories; Detroit's J. L. Hudson's, the tallest department store in the world when it opened in 1927, stood more than twenty. Public buildings soared as well. Forty stories tall, New York's Municipal Building dwarfed the old City Hall. And the Los Angeles City Hall, a twenty-eight-story building that had been approved by the voters even though it far exceeded the city's height limit, towered over downtown L.A. This upward movement checked "the normal tendency toward [the] horizontal growth [of the business district]," wrote Thomas Adams, a well-known city planner, in 1928.[8]

Downtown was still extremely concentrated, even more so in the 1920s than in the 1890s. It was the destination of nearly all the street railways and commuter trains (as well as the main highways). Even the rapid transit lines were designed not so much to move people around the city, as they were in London and Paris, as to carry them to and from downtown. Downtown was the site of the tall office buildings, which housed the white-collar workers, the managers, professionals, clerks, and secretaries who ran the rapidly growing service sector. It was the site of many workshops, lofts, and small factories too. Downtown was home to the huge department stores, whose salesgirls offered a cornucopia of goods and a wide range of services to their largely middle- and upper-middle-class customers. It was also home to a rapidly growing number of immense, often quite luxurious, hotels, which historian William Leach has described as "multistory monoliths run like factories and staffed by thousands of workers toiling from dawn to dusk." And it was home to theaters, movie houses, restaurants, beer gardens, political and social clubs, post offices, courts, government agencies, some cultural institutions, and many highly specialized retail stores. Downtown was "the city's vortex," wrote Harvey Warren Zorbaugh, another member of the Chicago School of Sociology, the place into which most Americans were drawn every day.[9]

Precisely how many is hard to say. But according to cordon counts, a by-product of the early efforts to measure traffic flows in American cities, the numbers were enormous. On a typical weekday in 1927 about 825,000 people entered downtown Boston, which was more than the entire population of the city and more than one-third of the population of the metropolitan district. The situation was much the same in other big cities. During the mid 1920s roughly 270,000 people poured into downtown St. Louis every day,

355,000 into downtown Pittsburgh, and 375,000 into downtown Baltimore. More than half a million people a day went downtown in Los Angeles and San Francisco, more than three-quarters of a million in Chicago and Philadelphia, and close to three million in New York—where downtown was defined as Manhattan south of Fifty-ninth Street. These cordon counts left more to be desired than just their arbitrary boundaries. On the one hand, they excluded people who walked downtown, as many as 160,000 a day in San Francisco, and people who lived there, a sizable number in New York because of the way downtown was defined. On the other hand, they included people who traveled downtown only because the transit systems were so designed that often the easiest, if not the only, way to get from one part of the city to another was to go downtown first. These qualifications notwithstanding, it is safe to say that most people who lived in big cities—as many as one-half to two-thirds, according to one transit engineer—went downtown every day in the mid and late 1920s. And so did as many as one out of three who lived in large metropolitan areas, another transit engineer estimated.[10]

Downtown was still largely depopulated. It had long been losing residents in big cities—among them Pittsburgh, where, an engineer observed in 1910, everyone lived "entirely outside the down-town business section," and Baltimore, where, an economist remarked two decades later, the central business

Crowds in downtown Los Angeles, 1924 (Courtesy of the University of Southern California, on behalf of the USC Library Department of Special Collections)

district "had practically no residential population." During the first third of the twentieth century, downtown also lost residents in medium-sized cities, like Atlanta, Nashville, and Richmond, where a local historian wrote, "Almost overnight Grace [Street] changed from a street lined with houses to one lined with stores." Many lived on the fringe of downtown. Some dwelled in working-class neighborhoods (the most famous of which was New York's Lower East Side), where first- and second-generation European immigrants rented small apartments in tenement houses and what had once been single-family homes. Others lived in what we think of today as "skid row," small, run-down places like New York's Bowery, Chicago's West Madison Street, and San Francisco's South of Market district, where single men rented rooms in cheap lodging houses. Still others resided in hotels, apartment hotels, and, in New York and a handful of other cities, small upper- and upper-middle-class residential enclaves. But in the "heart" of the city, Mark Jefferson, an urban geographer, wrote in 1913, "nobody lives but janitors and caretakers of store[s] and office buildings."[11]

Residents moved out of downtown in the early twentieth century for the same reasons they had moved out in the late nineteenth. Some were forced out when their homes were purchased by businessmen and demolished to make way for stores and offices. Also, property values rose so much downtown that it no longer made sense to build homes (or even apartment houses) there. And in any case, the well-to-do were reluctant to raise their families amid stores and offices. Other residents were driven out when their houses were knocked down to make way for public improvements, a practice that started in the mid nineteenth century (and continued well into the mid twentieth). To give one example, roughly 16,500 New Yorkers were displaced by the new Pennsylvania Railroad Station in the early 1900s. The depopulation of downtown was also an outgrowth of what H. L. Mencken called "a centrifugal movement," a movement from the center to the periphery, from the cities to the suburbs. A product of the prevailing vision of the good community and the improved technology of the street railway, this movement had gotten under way in the mid and late nineteenth century. But spurred by the proliferation of automobiles and the dispersal of industry, it made much greater headway in the early twentieth. And by the late 1920s it had transformed the landscape of urban America.[12]

There were a few other noteworthy ways in which downtown was much the same. It was still very busy. "Chicago is in perpetual motion," wrote an Italian visitor. People rush along the streets without greeting one another, without exchanging "a word of welcome or of affection." To an English visitor, it seemed as if each person on State Street was holding "a stop watch in his hands, ever listening to its remorseless tick."

> Looking neither to the right nor left each one hurries forwards intent but on one purpose, and that, to "hustle" as much work as possible out of the succeeding hours. An earthquake in the next street would scarcely stop his progress, a street accident would not stay him for an instant . . . ; ahead of him lies some work into which the whole of his nervous energy is to be thrown, and he will go through it at a rush whether it be the mere sacking of an office boy or the formation of a new Trust.

Downtown was still very noisy, too. The streetcars and els made a terrible din. "How," asked a French visitor, "can any human beings endure the sudden shocks of sound and the aggressive noisiness of all the vehicles fretting and fuming and flashing, stopping and starting again and coming and going in every direction and without a moment's interval[?]" Just as bad was the noise of the incessant construction. "Whenever I think of New York," wrote an Irish visitor who had watched a tall building going up on Broadway near Thirty-fifth Street, "I shall remember the shrill scream of the steam drill which made holes in the steel girders." The steel "suffers and shrieks through a long chromatic scale of agony." New York, he said, "drills a hole, pauses to readjust its terrible force, and then drills again."[13]

Downtown was less hectic in the early evening, by which time most people had gone home. (The financial district would be more or less deserted until the next morning. So would the retail district, though starting around 1930 Macy's and other department stores in New York and Chicago inaugurated what soon became the customary practice of staying open until nine on Thursday and Saturday.) But later in the evening things began to pick up. Restaurants opened for business, as did theaters, vaudeville houses, movie houses, cabarets, dance halls, and nightclubs. The "Great White Ways" started "to roar and flare," wrote Rupert Brooke, the English poet. And they roared and flared long past midnight, especially on the weekends. The "Great White Ways," of which Times Square was much the most celebrated, were incandescent. Their electric (and later neon) signs blazed from movie marquees, hotel roofs, and huge billboards. These "skysigns," as an English visitor called them, ran "across the facades of lofty buildings," advertising everything from motor cars to men's underwear. Using 17,500 lights, one depicted an army of elves whose spears pointed to "Wrigley Spearmint Gum." Another portrayed a giant Moses, tablet in hand, calling attention to Cecil B. DeMille's new movie, *The Ten Commandments.* From another loomed a colossal woman's head, a "beautiful, passionless, [and regal]" head, said Brooke, "whose ostensible message, burning in the firmament beside her, is that we should buy pepsin chewing-gum." "Pity the sky with nothing but stars," wrote a French visitor.[14]

Downtown was still the site of the worst traffic jams. Not for nothing was it commonly referred to as "the congested district" in Boston and Detroit. With tens, even hundreds of thousands of streetcars, automobiles, trucks, taxis, and buses filling the streets, traffic downtown was often brought to a standstill, especially during rush hour. At times it was faster to walk than to ride. Sometimes the streetcars were so crowded that the passengers had to fight their way on board—and then, wrote the Los Angeles Record, "to stand for miles at a stretch, often herded together like cattle or sheep in a stock car" (and at times "hanging all over the steps and outside of [the] cars"). The subways were much faster, but no less packed, again especially during rush hour. The New York subway was so crowded that at some of the busiest stations it was often impossible to board the train. With nearly 200 passengers packed into cars designed to hold at most 125, the subway was so jammed, a British visitor noted, "that if a person had his hands above his shoulders or at his waist he could not hope either to lower them or raise them until the journey was ended." The sidewalks were packed too, especially in the vicinity of the department stores. Between 8:30 A.M. and 6:30 P.M. one day in November 1915, 146,000 pedestrians, more than the entire population of Worcester, Massachusetts, passed Fifth Avenue and Thirty-fourth Street. It was "impossible" to walk there, said the Fifth Avenue Association's attorney, "unless one is prepared to shove and fight one's way through [the] crowds." It was even more crowded at the intersection of Chicago's State and Madison streets.[15]

Traffic downtown was a mess because so many people poured into the same small area each day and nearly all of them used one form of mechanical transportation or another. Making matters worse was that outside of New York, the only American city with an extensive rapid transit system, most people traveled on the surface. And most of them made the trip in the same direction, to downtown in the morning and from downtown in the evening, and at the same time, between seven and nine in the morning and five and seven in the evening. If all this were not enough, a large and rapidly growing number of people now went downtown in automobiles rather than streetcars. To give one example, between 1916 and 1930 the number of people who rode streetcars to downtown St. Louis fell from 180,000 to 150,000, while the number who came by automobiles rose from 30,000 to 103,000, an increase of more than 300 percent. Some Americans initially believed that the automobile would relieve traffic congestion downtown by replacing the many slow (and extremely cumbersome) horse-drawn vehicles. But after a while they realized that the downtown streets, which were hard pressed to handle a few thousand streetcars a day, were woefully incapable of coping with tens and even hundreds of thousands of autos.[16]

Downtown still had the highest property values as well. The Chicago Loop is a case in point. "If land values in Chicago were shown in the form of a relief map, in which the elevation represented high land value," the Loop would be "the Himalayan Mountain peaks," wrote Homer Hoyt. From these "peaks," Broadway and Wall Street in New York, State and Madison streets in Chicago, and Washington and Winter streets in Boston, property values dropped precipitously. In general, they were 50 to 90 percent lower at a half-mile radius and 90 to 99 percent lower at a one-mile radius, city planner J. Rowland Bibbins estimated in 1927. The disparities were so great in Chicago that in 1926 the central business district, which covered less than 1 percent of the city, had one-fifth of its land values, about as much as it had in 1892, though only half as much as it had in 1910. Things were much the same in St. Louis, where downtown had more than one-fifth of the city's assessed value in the mid 1920s, and in Los Angeles, where it had one-sixth of the assessed value in the early 1930s. As a result downtown paid a large share of the city's property taxes, as much as one-half in Cincinnati, a group of downtown businessmen claimed in 1919. As George F. Washburn, president of the Massachusetts Real Estate Exchange, complained in 1916, Boston's tax structure resembled "an inverted pyramid with the small end of it resting for its support on [a] very small congested area," the downtown retail district.[17]

To contemporaries, it was no mystery why downtown was the site of the highest property values. (If there was a mystery, it was why downtown lots varied so much in value—why lots on State and Madison streets in Chicago were worth nearly ten times as much as lots on Madison and Market, only six blocks away—and why some downtown lots rose so much and others did not—why between 1907 and 1926, a time of tremendous growth in Los Angeles, property at Seventh and Olive went up 800 percent, while property at Third and Main barely went up at all.) It was no mystery because according to the conventional wisdom the value of a piece of commercial property depended on its accessibility—or, as the New York *Real Estate Record* put it, on "the number and the character of the people that habitually pass it." The rule was simple, wrote Paul H. Nystrom, an economist who specialized in retail trade, in 1915. "The greater the number of people, other things being equal, who live near, who come to, or who pass by a certain location, the more valuable that location is." And given what Ernest W. Burgess called "the natural tendency" for local and regional transportation "to converge in the central business district," that was where property values would always be highest.[18]

Although downtown was much the same in many ways, there were some in which it was different. For one thing, downtown was less important as an industrial district in the 1920s than in the 1890s. Much heavy industry had moved to the periphery in the late nineteenth century—to such places as Pullman, Illinois, site of the Pullman railroad works, and Homestead, Pennsylvania, site of the Carnegie steel mill. But downtown was still the principal industrial district in 1900. Indeed, as late as 1906 more than half of New York's manufacturing was carried out in the 1 percent of the city located in Manhattan south of Fourteenth Street. But as geographer Allan Pred has written, the pace of decentralization picked up after 1900. Old firms left downtown— Philadelphia's Baldwin Locomotive for suburban Eddystone, Cincinnati's United States Playing Card for suburban Norwood, and Doubleday, Page & Company, a New York publishing house, for nearby Garden City. New firms went to the periphery too. Following Ford's move to nearby Highland Park in 1910, General Motors, Chrysler, and Detroit's other automakers built plants in the outlying sections, many of them along the Detroit Terminal Railway, six miles from downtown. Some firms were attracted to large, self-contained industrial districts, of which the North Kansas City, Missouri, Industrial District, a three-thousand-acre site developed by Armour, Swift, and the Burlington Railroad, was typical. Other firms were drawn to nearby industrial towns, among the most noteworthy of which were East St. Louis, Missouri, Flint, Michigan, and Gary, Indiana, the home of U.S. Steel. As a result, the industrial workforce grew much more slowly in the center than in the periphery after 1900. In lower Manhattan it actually shrank after 1917.[19]

Industrial enterprises moved away from downtown mainly because land was very expensive, often prohibitively so. For the automakers and other manufacturers whose assembly lines required enormous single-story structures, it was impossible to find a large enough site downtown at any price. A striking illustration is Ford's River Rouge plant, the largest factory in the world, which stood on a site in Dearborn that was more than twice the size of downtown Detroit. Property taxes downtown were very high too. So were insurance premiums. And the chronic traffic jams raised the costs of doing business. As a New York banker remarked in 1911, all but the lightest manufacturing could be carried out "more economically" in the outer boroughs than in Manhattan. After the passage of the 1916 zoning ordinance, manufacturing could not be carried out at all in many parts of Manhattan. The periphery also had advantages over the center other than "cheap land, low taxes and elbow room"—to quote one observer. It had waterways, highways, and belt-line railways, which linked manufacturers there with suppliers and customers elsewhere. With the recent improvements in telephone service, it was easy for these manufacturers to stay in close touch with their bankers, lawyers, and accountants in the center. On the periphery firms could also avoid what they regarded as onerous smoke and noise regulations and frivolous complaints by nearby property owners. Provided the site was not too far from the city, firms could still draw upon the abundant supply of local labor. Some industrialists felt that once their employees moved away from the city, once they left what a Chicago industrialist called the "hotbed of trades unionism," they would be more productive, more content, and more tractable.[20]

The dispersal of industry did not come as much of a shock. As early as 1883 the *Real Estate Record* predicted that the high price of Manhattan real estate would in time drive some manufacturing to Brooklyn. And in 1907 it forecast that much of it would gradually "be transferred to other boroughs." The situation was the same in other cities. As a Chicago engineer wrote in 1912, "there are many industries located in the congested districts which could just as well, if not better, carry on their business operations in the outlying districts." Nor was the dispersal of industry a cause of concern. Many industries were located downtown that "do not properly belong there," planner Robert Whitten pointed out in 1920. If they moved to the periphery, their employees would follow. Cities would become less crowded, and traffic less congested. Manufacturing was no longer essential to the well-being of downtown, *Architectural Forum* declared in 1920. Praising the work of the "Save New York Committee," a group of Fifth Avenue merchants and property owners that had forced the garment industry to move from Fifth to Seventh Avenue, the journal wrote that it would have been better if the committee had "removed the industry from the heart of the city entirely." Downtown would be better off without manufacturing, the *Real Estate Record* wrote in 1907. "If Manhattan loses as a manufacturing center, it is destined to gain enormously as a center of retail and wholesale trade," as "a place of amusement," and, the journal might well have added, as a center of offices, hotels, and corporate headquarters.[21]

For another thing, downtown was less important as a cultural center in the 1920s than in the 1890s. Many cultural institutions had left downtown even before 1900. New York's Metropolitan Museum of Art moved to a site in Central Park on upper Fifth Avenue. And the New-York Historical Society built a new home on Eighth Avenue between Seventy-sixth and Seventy-seventh streets, next to the American Museum of Natural History. Boston's Museum of Fine Arts moved to Copley Square, a mile or so west of downtown, as did the Boston Public Library. Even farther west stood the new homes of the Boston Symphony Orchestra and the Massachusetts Historical Society. More cultural institutions left downtown after 1900—more often than not for affluent residential neighborhoods. The Museum of the City of New York moved to Fifth Avenue and 103d Street. The Cleveland Museum of Art left for University Circle, the site of Western Reserve University. And the Baltimore Museum of Art moved to Homewood, next to Johns Hopkins University, which gave the city the site for the museum. The Detroit Institute of Art and the Detroit Public Library built new homes on opposite sides of Woodward Avenue, two miles from downtown. And most of Pittsburgh's cultural institutions gradually assembled in the Schenley Farms district, about three miles east of downtown. There were exceptions. Boston's Athenaeum remained downtown. And the Chicago Art Institute, Public Library, and Orchestra Hall, home of the Chicago Symphony, were all within a few blocks of the Loop. But as the trustees of the art institute pointed out, the trend in most American cities was for art (and culture generally) to "set itself apart," to move away from "the heart of the city."²²

Sometimes cultural institutions moved because they could not afford to stay. The Museum of the City of New York accepted the city's offer of an uptown site after it decided that a downtown site was too expensive. The Baltimore Museum of Art left for Homewood after concluding that it would be too costly to expand at its present site. Some cultural institutions would have been hard pressed to find a large enough site downtown at almost any price. One example is the Detroit Art Institute, which stood on more than eight acres, another the Boston Museum of Fine Arts, which left Copley Square for a thirteen-acre site on the Fenway. More often, however, cultural institutions moved because they did not want to stay. As their benefactors saw it, these institutions were not just supposed to house works of art; they were supposed to be works of art—beautiful, dignified, monumental public buildings. Located downtown on small lots and narrow streets, amid smoke, noise, bustle, and what Charles Mulford Robinson called "a wilderness of commercial structures," the buildings would lose much of their artistic value. "To expend large sums in the construction of noble architecture," wrote another planner, "only to have it almost effaced in a crowded business street, is the height of folly and extravagance." The coming of the skyscrapers made matters worse. "American cities," said the *Philadelphia Public Ledger*, "are already too familiar with instances of structures of faultless design and beautiful proportion dwarfed into insignificance by some towering commercial building, which has nothing to commend it but its impressive height." If cultural institutions were to ennoble and elevate American society, they needed large sites in a stable, affluent residential neighborhood, preferably in a park or on a square. Or so their benefactors thought.[23]

Some Americans were troubled by this exodus. The trustees of the Chicago Art Institute, for example, thought that a downtown location would not only make these institutions more accessible to the public, but would also enable them to act as what historian Helen L. Horowitz calls "countervailing spiritual forces" to the city's pervasive materialism. (It may be worth noting that, by virtue of the Loop's proximity to Lake Michigan, Chicago was one of the few American cities where a cultural institution could have both a downtown location and a spectacular site.) But few Americans shared this concern. Even fewer viewed the exodus as a threat to the welfare of downtown. It did not have much impact on the number of people who went downtown to work, shop, do business, and amuse themselves. Nor did it have much impact on downtown real estate values. Indeed, for the downtown business interests, it was more satisfactory for the cultural institutions to leave than for them to compete for space, campaign for land-use restrictions, and otherwise try to change the business district to suit their needs. By moving away, historian Daniel M. Bluestone has observed, these institutions "conceded to commerce not only the skyline but also the central position in the city."[24]

Downtown changed in yet another way, a profound though largely unexpected way, after 1900, and even more so after 1920. It became less important, relatively if not absolutely, as a business district. A good many stores, offices, and places of amusement moved away, stimulating what W. G. Strait, a New York railway executive, described in 1926 as "an amazing growth of shopping and amusement centers in residential sections." Here was the beginning of what Miller McClintock called in 1927 "a phenomenal tendency toward the decentralization of business activities," one that was manifested in "the development of rapidly growing secondary business districts." Downtown businesses had always moved around. But hitherto they had gone from one part of the business district to another, from the center to the fringe, from old sections to new ones. After 1920 many moved from the central business district to the outlying business districts, most of which were on the periphery of the city, some in the surrounding suburbs. The outlying business districts had been in place well before 1900. But they had so few shops (and so few types of shops) that as late as 1920 few Americans viewed them as a challenge to what two St. Louis transit experts referred to as the "dominance" of downtown. By the late 1920s, however, many outlying business districts had been transformed. As a U.S. Department of Commerce economist wrote in 1926: "The subcenter shopping district no longer consists of only the corner grocery, a drug store, and a delicatessen. It includes stores representing all kinds of merchandise and usually a bank. In our largest cities, the subcenter is a complete shopping district differing from the down-town district only in size and magnitude of establishments."[25] In some cases, observed the *Atlanta Constitution* in 1929, the outlying business district was "a complete city within itself."

Downtown was a very important business district in the 1920s. But as McClintock and others pointed out, it was losing ground. The investment banks and stock and commodity exchanges were still clustered in the central business district. So were the head offices of almost all the commercial banks, public utilities, and giant industrial corporations—as well as most insurance companies, law firms, advertising agencies, and accounting firms. (Interestingly, in an attempt to reduce their rent, several of these firms were already moving some of what would later be called their "back-office" personnel to outlying sections.) But many professionals no longer worked downtown. In Los Angeles, for example, more than two-fifths of the architects had offices elsewhere in 1931; so did about a third of the engineers, more than half the dentists, and roughly two-thirds of the doctors. A small but rapidly growing number of lawyers practiced in the outlying districts, too. Although the pace of decentralization was very rapid in L.A., the trend was much the same in other cities. Banking was also highly decentralized. As a result of the tremendous growth of branch banking, a practice that had been outlawed in many states in the nineteenth century, only 15 percent of Los Angeles banks were located downtown in 1931, down from about 55 percent in 1920. Even in New York, where the pace of decentralization was fairly slow, only half of the branches of commercial banks and trust companies were found downtown in 1926. And in Chicago the outlying banks grew so much faster than the Loop banks that they held nearly 60 percent of the total deposits in 1929, up from only 15 percent in 1909.[26]

With a few exceptions, all the department stores were clustered in the central business district—and in most cities clustered very tightly in its core. Also located downtown were many retail stores, which were much smaller and more highly specialized. Offering a wide variety of goods and a great deal of choice, the downtown stores attracted so many customers that even in cities like Los Angeles much more retail trade was done in the central business district than in even the largest outlying business districts. By the 1920s, however, retail trade was growing faster in the periphery than in the center; and as a group the outlying business districts were outselling the central business district. Contributing to this development was the phenomenal growth of chain stores, the number of which skyrocketed from two chains with five stores in the mid 1880s to nearly 1,500 chains with about 70,000 stores in the late 1920s. The chains, among the best known of which were J. C. Penney, Walgreen, W. T. Grant, Kresge, Fanny Farmer, and F. W. Woolworth, preferred to rent space in the outlying districts, where their customers lived and where, as Homer Hoyt pointed out, forty stores "could be rented at the same cost as one store on State Street." The chain stores brought large-scale retailing to the outlying residential sections, selling mainly standardized items at low prices. As a result, wrote a demographer in 1930, many who lived in these sections were "finding less and less need for downtown stores in their every day life."[27]

Prompted in part by competition from the chain stores, a few department stores (and specialty shops) took a step that also contributed to the decentralization of retail trade. They established branches in the suburbs. Such a step would have been inconceivable in the early 1900s—as inconceivable as the erection of a skyscraper anywhere but downtown. According to the conventional wisdom, a convenience store could be profitable in the suburbs, but not a department store, for which a central location was indispensable. By the mid 1920s, however, department stores were facing stiff competition from outlying stores. Sales were growing slowly. Costs were rising rapidly. And profits were falling. Despite a strong preference to keep its business "as much as possible under one roof," E. P. Slattery of Boston, an upscale women's clothing store, decided in 1923 to open a branch in Wellesley, to take "the store to the people," as its president put it. Four years later it opened another branch in Brookline, which convinced Slattery that branch stores could be successful, provided they were well located and properly managed. During the late 1920s several department stores followed suit. Chicago's Marshall Field established branches in the suburbs—in Evanston, Lake Forest, and Oak Park; so did New York's Best & Company, Philadelphia's Strawbridge and Clothier, and Cleveland's Halle Brothers. B. H. Dyas took the lead in Los Angeles, opening a branch in Hollywood in 1928, followed by Bullock's, which opened a branch on Wilshire Boulevard a year later. As a well-informed observer pointed out in 1928, department stores were far less decentralized than banks and chain stores. But they were heading in the same direction. As Joseph Appel, president of Wanamaker's, wrote in 1928, it was time for the store to go to its customers rather than to try "to force them to come to us."[28]

Most theaters were still clustered in the central business district—though only in New York were there enough of them to form a full-fledged theater district. So were most dance halls, night clubs, and, while they lasted, vaudeville houses. The nickelodeons, however, were found all over the city, especially in lower- and middle-class neighborhoods. They were soon displaced by the movie houses, which rapidly emerged as by far the most popular amusement places in the 1910s and 1920s. At first their owners looked for sites downtown, which became the home of many large and spectacular movie houses. A striking example is New York's Roxy Theater. Located on Seventh Avenue between Fiftieth and Fifty-first streets, it had an auditorium that held 6,200 people—as well as a four-hundred-foot-long marquee, a five-story rotunda, a broadcasting studio, a music library, and a pit large enough to hold a symphony orchestra. But before long several chains, including Loew's in New York, the Stanley Company in Philadelphia, and Balaban & Katz in Chicago, began building movie houses in the outlying districts. Indeed, Balaban & Katz built three movie theaters in the outlying districts before it built one in the Loop. Theater owners in Detroit, St. Louis, and Milwaukee soon followed Balaban & Katz's lead. By the late 1920s there were far more movie houses in the periphery than in the center. For every downtown movie house, there were five outlying movie houses in Los Angeles, six in San Francisco, seven in Detroit, and nine in Milwaukee. Although most were small and unpretentious, some were as large and spectacular as all but the very largest and most spectacular of the downtown picture palaces.[29]

At a quick glance, downtown seemed to be thriving in the mid and late 1920s. And to some extent it was. Fueled by almost a decade of tremendous, if uneven, economic growth, downtown business interests built more and bigger skyscrapers, hotels, and department stores in these years than at any other time in American history. But a closer look reveals that downtown was beginning to feel the impact of decentralization. Although the daytime population of downtown was going up, there is evidence that it was not keeping up with the growth of the city. In Los Angeles, for instance, downtown's daytime population went up only 15 percent between 1923 and 1931, a time when the city's population nearly doubled. How much of the relative decline of the daytime population was due to the growth of the outlying business districts and how much to the impact of the Great Depression is hard to say. Although property values were rising rapidly in the central business district (and in fact reached their highest levels on the eve of the depression), there is evidence that they were rising even more rapidly in the outlying business districts. In Chicago, for example, the average value of outlying business corner lots doubled between 1910 and 1915 and then tripled between 1921 and 1927. The sharp rise was a major reason that the value of commercial property outside the Loop went up from $200 million to $1.3 billion between 1910 and 1928, or more than eight times as much as the value of commercial property inside the Loop, which went up from $600 million to $1 billion. It was also a major reason that the Loop's share of the city's land values, which had risen from 23 percent in 1892 to 40 percent in 1910, fell to 20 percent in 1926.[30]

Americans disagreed about the causes of the incipient decentralization of commerce. Some viewed it as a "natural tendency," to quote a group of prominent city planners, a normal response to the growth of the city. As they saw it, outlying business districts emerged to meet the increasing demand for goods and services that could not be met by the central business district and to house many of the businesses squeezed out by the high cost of real estate. Other Americans attributed decentralization to recent advances in technology. The telephone enabled businessmen to communicate with one another as easily from two or three miles as from two or three blocks. And the automobile allowed shoppers to get to outlying business districts more quickly than to the central business district. Still other Americans held that decentralization was due to the sharp rise in streetcar fares, one of many steps taken to deal with the fiscal crisis of the electric railway industry in the wake of World War I. Rather than spend the extra money to go downtown, many people opted to drive to the outlying business districts. But many Americans did not believe that these explanations were sufficient to account for the "phenomenal" pace of decentralization, for what Miller McClintock called "premature" (or "abnormal") decentralization. That, they held, was due mainly to traffic congestion downtown.[31]

As much as Americans disagreed about the causes of decentralization, they disagreed even more about its impact. And the ensuing debate raised doubts regarding the assumptions about downtown that had emerged in the late nineteenth century—doubts that had not been raised by the dispersal of manufacturing firms and the exodus of cultural institutions. Assuming, as most Americans did, that the outlying business districts would continue to grow, some observers thought they would have a considerable impact on the central business district. One group, which included McClintock, held that decentralization would not destroy downtown, but would slow its growth, leaving its businesses less profitable and its real estate less valuable. Also in this group was Gordon Whitnall, a Los Angeles planner and a strong advocate of decentralization, who wrote that downtown would remain the "Sun" in "our

Metropolitan Solar System"; although it might not grow any "dimmer," "there may be reason to question whether it can become much more brilliant." The other group, which included Clarence Stein, a champion of new towns, held that as a result of decentralization downtown would in time lose most everything other than the offices of the large corporations to outlying districts. In this group was a prominent merchant from a large eastern city who warned that if nothing was done to relieve traffic congestion "within 15 years there will be no down-town shopping districts of any importance."[32] And what would downtown be without a shopping district? In other words, to some Americans it no longer seemed that downtown was inevitable.

To some it also seemed that downtown was no longer desirable. As they saw it, a very small, highly congested, and basically unrivaled business district served the interests of a few downtown businessmen and property owners, but no one else. Not the outlying residents, many of whom found it so hard to get downtown that they went to other business districts; not the outlying property owners, many of whom hoped that the decentralization of commerce would raise the value of their holdings; and not the local taxpayers, to whom the municipal authorities turned each time they made an attempt to do something about the traffic congestion downtown. Rather than one business district, surrounded by many residential sections, American cities would be better off organized around a group of "well-balanced, self-contained community sub-centers," wrote Whitnall, who accurately reflected the views of most planners. To this end, the cities, which had earlier encouraged the dispersal of industry, should now promote the decentralization of commerce. Decentralization, its sponsors claimed, would improve urban life. It might injure the few downtown business interests for which congestion meant larger sales and higher values. And if done haphazardly, it might leave in its wake reduced values and blighted areas. But if decentralization was carried out in an orderly way, virtually everyone would be better off.[33]

A few Americans went even further. Downtown, they claimed, was unnatural, the artificial creation of a coalition of retail merchants, property owners, and transit officials, all of whom had a great stake in congestion. With the help of local politicians, they had built up the center at the expense of the periphery. Probably the most forceful spokesman for this position was Tomaz F. Deuther, secretary of the North West Side Commercial Association of Chicago, a group of outlying business interests. Deuther took strong exception to a *Chicago Tribune* editorial that said the Loop was "the most efficient natural [place]" in the world to do business. There was nothing natural about the Loop, he wrote. It owed its dominant position not to its intrinsic efficiency but to the machinations of the department store magnates and downtown property owners who used their influence to make sure that the streetcars and els all converged on the Loop. The elected officials helped maintain the Loop's dominance by rejecting proposals that would have made it possible to go from one outlying district to another without first going into the Loop. Now that the Loop had become too congested, business was beginning to move away, Deuther wrote. But without the interference of the downtown interests and the connivance of the elected officials, it would have spread over the entire city long ago.[34]

Other Americans were skeptical. "We hear much of the word 'decentralization,'" wrote E. J. McIlraith, a Chicago transit engineer, "and we talk glibly as though the cities were going to become scattered villages." But the term is highly misleading and its influence greatly exaggerated. Miller McClintock had his doubts too. A good many people believe that the "central business districts have no logic, have no utility," he noted, that "the ideal city" is a decentralized city. "Such an attitude, I believe, is wrong." Most skeptics were aware that decentralization was well under way in American cities, that the outlying business districts were growing rapidly and that as the population continued to grow they would continue to grow, perhaps even more rapidly than the central business districts. They were also fully aware that downtown had drawbacks. Even so, the skeptics argued, downtown was holding its own; its businesses were prospering, its property values soaring. The outlying business districts, they predicted, would not have much of an impact on the central business district. As the *Kansas City Star* said in 1926, it was still difficult to conceive of a highly compact and extremely concentrated business district "as anything but natural, economic, and perhaps inevitable."[35]

Downtown was natural, wrote Russell Tyson, a Chicago real estate man (and member of the Chicago Real Estate Board's zoning committee). "It was not brought about by a wicked conspiracy of selfish property owners," as Deuther and others argued, but "by the natural desire of the people to do all their varied business . . . at the greatest possible convenience," which meant "within the smallest possible area." Downtown was not "an artificial creation," said John G. Bullock, who, ironically, was one of the first department store owners in Los Angeles to open a branch in an outlying district. Nor was it the result of "mere chance," in McIlraith's words, or "some vague gregarious urge," as McClintock put it. Rather downtown was a manifestation of what he called "a stern economic law," "the law of accessibility," according to which businesses would always flow to the most accessible point in the city. And that point, wrote a Los Angeles realtor, "is always the central business district." "Central business districts exist," McClintock pointed out, "because they have an economic utility, to be found in the efficiency of doing business in a compact, well-balanced, highly unified business district." That utility, that efficiency, was lost in "smaller decentralized [business] districts." Going even further, Harvey Wiley Corbett, one of the leading defenders of tall buildings, argued that "it is only through the concentration in comparatively small areas of large numbers of business people that we can conduct our affairs at all."[36]

Not all economic activities need be carried on downtown, McIlraith pointed out. There was no reason to manufacture steel or to sell groceries "in the heart of the city." These activities should be decentralized, not only for their own sake, but also for the sake of other economic activities that, as a group of planners put it, "have a better right to a central location." But much business had to be done downtown, argued G. A. Richardson, a Chicago street railway executive. Even with the telephone and telegraph, "people still do business most quickly and satisfactorily when they meet face to face." Or as Corbett said, "every business transaction is settled by personal contact." ("You finally have to get the man into your office, have him take out his fountain pen and sign on the dotted line.") By facilitating personal contact among businessmen (and between businessmen and their advisers) downtown saved time, money, and physical effort. Much shopping had to be done downtown, too. As Tyson said, the downtown department stores enabled customers to shop "with the least possible loss of time." Downtown was also the only place that offered such a wide range of goods that shoppers could compare them for price and quality. And despite the growth of outlying business districts, downtown was the only place where shoppers could find luxury goods and other merchandise for which there was a limited market.[37]

Downtown was not only inevitable, its supporters claimed. It was also desirable. "When business is concentrated," said Stanley Clarke, president of the St. Louis Public Service Company, "the cost of doing business is lessened and the product reaches the consumer at a lower rate." As the price of goods and services goes down, the standard of living goes up. Concentration brought congestion. But "the greater the congestion, the greater the city," declared a New York real estate man—one of the few well-to-do New Yorkers who did not subscribe to the conventional wisdom that congestion in residential sections, even in such highly congested residential sections as the Lower East Side, was necessarily a bad thing. A Chicago real estate man agreed. "We should not make too great a bugbear of [congestion]," he said. "To a large extent crowds are a good thing for the city and result in much greater dispatch of business and are a positive convenience and even enjoyment to many of the citizens." Downtown had a traffic problem, its supporters conceded. But the problem would have been even worse if businesses were scattered all over the city, argued Corbett and others who believed that tall buildings reduced traffic congestion. And whether by street improvements, parking regulations, or rapid transit, the traffic problem would be solved in time.[38]

From the assumption that downtown was inevitable and desirable, Americans drew two somewhat different conclusions. One was that it would remain more or less the same. As Richardson noted, there was no reason "to think that traffic troubles need to, or will cause a change in the manner of development of the city center." The central business district, argued McIlraith in 1930, "is used much more today than ten years ago, or twenty years ago, and each year that use is more intensive than the preceding—and it will continue to be so." Mason Case, a Los Angeles commercial realtor who was well aware that the outlying business districts were growing very rapidly, made the same point. "A downtown business district will always exist [in Los Angeles]," he said. Office buildings will always be there. So will public buildings, financial institutions, and department stores. And real estate values will always be highest there, even though they may at times rise faster elsewhere. As one of Case's fellow realtors said, "A well located piece of central business property is like a gold mine, with this difference. The more the owner takes out in rent dividends, the more there is left remaining for him."[39]

The other conclusion was that downtown would change. According to planners Frederick Law Olmsted, Jr., Harland Bartholomew, and Charles H. Cheney, it would not only continue to grow, but as a result of the growth of the outlying business districts it would also become more specialized. Just as it no longer housed many residents and much manufacturing, so it soon would no longer house a good many retail shops, amusement places, and other enterprises that could be carried on more profitably in outlying business districts. Downtown would be devoted increasingly to offices, theaters, hotels, department stores, and specialty shops—to businesses that, as Olmsted and his associates said, "must have a central location if they are to do business at all." As Robert Murray Haig, a Columbia University economist, put it, downtown would henceforth be the site of only those types of businesses that have the greatest ability "to make profitable use (all costs considered) of the accessibility of central sites." By virtue of specialization, downtown would thrive; so would the rest of the city. This enthusiasm for what one sociologist called a "territorial differentiation of specialized functions" was in part a response to the growth of the outlying business districts. But it was also in part a reflection of a deep-seated preference for land-use segregation that had been part of the conventional wisdom of the planning profession even before the rapid growth of the outlying business districts.[40]

From the assumption that downtown was inevitable and desirable, it was only a short step to the conviction that there was no inherent conflict between the central business district and the outlying business districts. The growth of the outlying business districts "does not diminish the importance of the Downtown business district," declared John G. Bullock, one year after he opened his branch on Wilshire Boulevard. "In fact, as these other parts of the community grow and prosper, the Downtown district must also grow to serve them and to keep pace with their growth." The Loop and the outlying business districts were interdependent, a leader of the Chicago Association of Commerce claimed at a meeting with representatives of outlying businessmen's organizations. Pointing out that in many cases it was Loop businessmen who had built up the outlying business districts (and Loop banks that had financed them), he argued that there was no cause for animosity between these districts and the Loop. Even J. C. Nichols, the developer of Kansas City's Country Club Plaza, the nation's most famous shopping center prior to 1930, believed that the central business district was "vitally important to every city." Notwithstanding the trend toward decentralization, "every effort should be made to conserve the values of downtown business property, to stabilize its location, and to increase its efficiency and service to the community."[41]

It is hard to tell where most Americans stood in this debate. But a few things are clear. On one hand, most city planners no longer believed that a highly compact and extremely concentrated business district was inevitable and desirable.[42] Many traffic experts thought that business districts would and should spread out. So did most spokesmen for the outlying business districts. On the other hand, most downtown business interests, and especially most downtown property owners—who, unlike the downtown department store magnates, did not have the option of setting up stores in the outlying business districts—still held that a city had to have a downtown. So did many commercial real estate brokers and street railway executives, two groups whose fortunes were closely linked to the fate of the central business district. But where most Americans stood on this debate is not crucial. What is crucial is that there was a debate at all. For it would have been inconceivable in the late nineteenth century, a time when downtown was the business district, not the central business district, a time when its inevitability and desirability were taken for granted. That this was no longer so was not the least of the consequences of the growth of the outlying business districts.

Another consequence was that the belief in spatial harmony, the belief that rivalry between the center and the periphery was unnatural, lost some of its strength. With the conspicuous exception of Tomaz Deuther and other spokesmen for the outlying business districts, Americans still employed the rhetoric of spatial harmony. Chicago mayor Carter H. Harrison, Jr., put it bluntly when he said that "the outlying centers cannot be built up by killing the business center." The Chicago Subway Advisory Commission, a group of downtown businessmen and property owners, made the same point. The Loop was "the unquestioned and intimate partner of all [the outlying districts]." The Loop businessmen, many of whom had their plants in the periphery and their headquarters in the center, "well knew that their business is intimately dependent upon the prosperity and growth" of the outlying districts. And the outlying districts, half a million of whose residents earned their living in the Loop, had a great stake in its well-being. What applied to the center and the periphery also applied to the city and the suburbs. Without the city, there would not be any suburbs, a Seattle engineer pointed out. "Build one," he declared, "and you build the other."[43]

Americans still used the metaphors of spatial harmony too. The city was much like a house, said some; the parts of the former had to be laid out with as much care as the rooms of the latter. To others, the city was more like a wheel, "an immense wheel," wrote one planner. People work in the hub and live along the spokes and on the rim, noted another. To still others, indeed to most Americans, the city was much like the human body. Downtown was the heart, "the great heart," said a Chicago architect, "the huge throbbing heart," wrote a transit engineer, who described each resident as "an additional drop of blood flowing to and ebbing from the heart of the city." According to this metaphor, congested streets were much the same as clogged arteries, the one as dangerous to the city as the other was to the individual. To these old metaphors, Americans added a couple of new ones after 1900. Gordon Whitnall likened the metropolis to the solar system; downtown was the sun, and Hollywood, Pasadena, and the other outlying communities were the "satellites," each with its own orbit. And Herbert B. Dorau and Albert G. Hinman, two urban economists, described the city as a manufacturing plant, pointing out that each was "made up of a number of elements which must be properly fitted together."[44] Much like the old metaphors, the new ones depicted the city as a host of separate but interdependent parts, each of which was vital to the well-being of the others.

Although Americans talked as if they believed in spatial harmony, they did not act that way. Before 1900 downtown businessmen and property owners had been so wedded to the notion that they had seen no need to organize voluntary associations to promote the interests of the business district. By the 1920s, however, they had changed their minds. The Down Town Association of San Francisco, which had been formed to prevent the relocation of the retail district after the earthquake and fire of 1906, was still going strong. But it was no longer unique. Buffalo's Main Street Association, founded in 1921, looked out for the interests of downtown Buffalo. Los Angeles' Central Business District Association, organized in 1924, did the same for downtown L.A. Other downtown associations operated in Detroit and Cleveland. Although the Chicago Subway Advisory Commission complained that the Loop was the only part of Chicago "without some sort of district organization," the president of the Chicago Association of Commerce acknowledged that "we seem to be the self-constituted guardians [of the Loop]."[45] In addition to these organizations, downtown businessmen and property owners formed a host of other, more specialized associations. Some were organized by street, among them New York's Fifth Avenue Association, Chicago's State Street Association, and Baltimore's Howard Street Association. Others were organized by trade, including Seattle's Retail Merchants Association and Cleveland's Association of Building Owners and Managers, a branch of the nationwide trade group.

These associations campaigned for better lighting, cleaner streets, more effective drainage, and other improvements that would make downtown a more attractive place to work and shop. They also urged the local authorities to build downtown auditoriums and convention halls and to lower the assessed values of downtown buildings. They led the campaigns for rapid transit and worked to find ways to relieve traffic congestion. Downtown businessmen and property owners insisted that their efforts were designed to benefit not just the central business district but the entire city. As August Gatzert, chair of the Chicago Association of Commerce's Committee on Model Downtown Streets, said, "We must improve our city from the heart outward," first downtown, then the immediate environs, and finally the outlying areas. How, he asked, can "we expect to enlist the aid of the citizen in plans for [the] betterment [of] the entire city when he sees, every day and all the time, needless dirt, disorder, and darkness in the heart of our city?"[46] Gatzert may well have been sincere. But there is little doubt that most of what he and other downtown businessmen and property owners did was designed primarily to serve the interests of the central business district, even at times at the expense of the outlying business districts. Nor is there much doubt that many outlying business interests saw these efforts that way.

The belief in spatial harmony lost much of its strength largely because rivalry between the central and outlying business districts became common and extremely intense after 1900. The efforts to build subways often pitted the downtown business interests against the outlying business interests. This conflict was fierce in Chicago, where nothing that the Loop interests said or did could persuade Deuther and his allies that a subway was anything but a device to promote downtown Chicago at the expense of the outlying business districts. It was also sharp in Detroit and Los Angeles—though less so in Philadelphia, where many outlying businessmen's associations endorsed the proposed Broad Street subway. The efforts to impose height limits sometimes pitted the downtown business interests against the outlying business interests too. In Boston, for example, many property owners protested against what they viewed as an invidious distinction between the "A" district (downtown Boston), which had a height limit of 125 feet, and the "B" district (the rest of the city), where the limit was only 100 feet. They wanted a uniform height limit throughout the city. As George F. Washburn of the Massachusetts Real Estate Exchange declared, "We must give South Boston, East Boston, Charlestown and Dorchester the same opportunity to prosper [as downtown Boston]."[47]

A revealing example of rivalry between the center and the periphery took place in Los Angeles in the early and mid 1920s. As historian Marc A. Weiss has written, it started shortly after the end of World War I, when the Los Angeles Realty Board mounted a campaign to replace the city's pioneering but rudimentary zoning law with a comprehensive zoning ordinance. One of the primary objectives of the board, which was dominated by downtown real estate interests, was to stem the tide of commercial decentralization and thus bolster the position of the central business district. To this end the board asked the city council to adopt a law that would restrict virtually the entire west side, including Wilshire Boulevard, to single-family houses, thereby forcing the residents to work and shop downtown. As the struggle over the future of the west side heated up, the board requested an emergency ordinance that would block the erection of stores and apartment houses there until a new zoning law was adopted. By then, however, many west-side realtors and property owners had broken ranks with the realty board. Forming the Wilshire Improvement Association, they attacked the proposed ordinance on the grounds that it would stop the natural movement of commerce to the west side and give an artificial monopoly to the downtown business interests. With many of its members up in arms, the realty board withdrew its request for an emergency ordinance. The city council then instructed Gordon Whitnall, secretary of the city planning commission, to begin work on a new zoning law. Adopted in 1921, the law met some of the realty board's other objectives, but it did nothing to slow down commercial decentralization. Indeed, by zoning most of the frontage of the major streets for commercial (or "C") use, the law may well have accelerated it.[48]

The future of Wilshire Boulevard was far from settled, however. Assuming the authorities intended one day to turn it into a wide and well-landscaped parkway running from downtown Los Angeles to Santa Monica, the planners had zoned virtually all of Wilshire for multifamily residences, designated as "B" use. Less than two years later a group of Wilshire property owners asked the city council to rezone the eastern portion of the boulevard, from Westlake to Western avenues, for commercial use. They argued that high land values and heavy traffic flows made their property much more suitable for businesses than for residences, even multifamily residences. The city planning commission urged the council to deny the request, saying that the owners knew of the restrictions on commercial development when they bought the property and that the city already had much too much commercial frontage. The change would jeopardize the well-being of downtown Los Angeles and undermine the prospects of the proposed parkway. The council sided with the Wilshire property owners. The planning commission then sponsored a referendum, which left the final decision up to the voters. Leading the campaign for "B" use was the Community Development Association, a group of prominent downtown businessmen and property owners, the realty board, and the local Association of Building Owners and Managers. These groups were driven less by concern for the proposed parkway than by fears of what one real estate man called "the wholesale decentralization of the downtown shopping district." Leading the struggle for "C" use was the Wilshire Boulevard Association, whose spokesmen made the same arguments to the voters that they had made to the council (and added that if the property was zoned for business, its owners would spend millions to widen and beautify the boulevard). To the dismay of the downtown business interests (and local planners), the voters upheld the council's action in late 1924.[49]

Inspired by the outcome of the referendum, another group of Wilshire property owners asked the authorities to rezone the western portion of the boulevard for commercial use. The city planning commission refused. But over the objections of the Municipal League of Los Angeles, which argued that another reversal of the commission would subvert the zoning process, the city council rezoned Wilshire from Western to Rimpau and from Detroit to Curson. The stage was thereby set for another referendum. Leading the campaign to nullify the council's action was the newly formed Central Business

District Association. Its spokesmen argued that Los Angeles had no need for so much additional commercial frontage and that if the council's action was upheld Wilshire Boulevard would be turned into an "eyesore," full of tacky shops and stores. Now that east Wilshire was zoned for business, west Wilshire should be reserved for high-class apartments, hotels, churches, and educational institutions, all of which were allowed under "B" zoning. Leading the campaign to uphold the council's decision was the West Wilshire Development Association, whose members argued that they had always intended to use their land for business and that it was already being taxed as business property. A rezoning would generate millions of dollars of new construction and turn Wilshire Boulevard into "the Fifth Avenue of the West." This time the voters reversed the council's action. But if the downtown business interests won the battle, they lost the war. One by one the west Wilshire property owners asked the city council for a variance, which was invariably given. Before long much of Wilshire Boulevard was zoned for commercial use.[50]

Rivalry within the center—between one part of downtown and another or between downtown and a nearby district that aspired to be part of downtown—also became common and extremely intense after 1900. The efforts to impose height limits on tall buildings often pitted the core of the business district against the fringe (or against a section just beyond it). The conflict was intense in Chicago, where it was widely assumed that a height limit would encourage the lateral expansion of the Loop and, as one real estate dealer said, "give a healthy impetus to real-estate a little distance away from the business center." The issue also divided the south-end interests and Lake Union interests in Seattle, and the downtown and uptown interests in Denver. The attempts to build a civic center frequently pitted one part of downtown against another too. One such fight broke out in Los Angeles in the late 1910s, when the local officials decided it was time to build a civic center. The decision set off a long struggle over its location among several groups of downtown businessmen and property owners, some from the northern part and others from the southern, all of whom hoped that the civic center would help to stabilize their part of the business district. The struggle dragged on until 1923, when the voters approved a $7.5 million bond issue for a new city hall and chose a northern site on which to build it.[51]

A revealing instance of rivalry within the center took place in Cincinnati in 1919. It started in early February, when Mayor John Galvin disclosed that as a result of inflation the city's proposed subway would cost far more than the $6 million approved by the voters in 1917. As the Cincinnati Rapid Transit Commission looked for ways to solve the problem, a group of businessmen suggested that as much as a million dollars could be saved if the main terminal were built not under Fountain Square, the core of downtown Cincinnati, but on Canal Street, next to the abandoned canal bed along which the subway would run. Not coincidentally, the canal site was located in a business district about half a mile north-northwest of Fountain Square. And it was its businessmen and property owners who led the campaign for the change. Their spokesmen contended that the canal site not only would cost less but would also provide better access to City Hall, Music Hall, and other public buildings and cultural institutions. A terminal at Canal Street would enhance property values and increase tax revenues. A terminal at Fountain Square, where property values were as high as they could be, would only intensify the congestion in a district that was already much too congested. Pointing out that Cincinnati should not tie itself to "a single hitching post," spokesmen for the canal site also stressed that a subway terminal there would spread out the business district. Driven less by these arguments than by its financial problem, the rapid transit commission announced in mid March that it would build the main terminal on the banks of the canal and run a spur line from the terminal to a station under Fountain Square.[52]

The announcement infuriated the Fountain Square interests, who promptly launched a campaign to persuade the commission to reverse its decision. Leading the campaign was the Downtown Terminal Committee, whose spokesmen contended that the original subway plan, on the basis of which the voters had approved the $6 million bond issue, had called for a terminal at Fountain Square. Moreover, as one downtown retailer put it, Fountain Square was "the heart of the city," the site of its most important hotels, banks, theaters, office buildings, and retail stores, the destination of the great majority of people who would use the subway. It was also the site of the most valuable real estate in the city and thus the source of a lion's share of its property taxes. To build the terminal at any site other than Fountain Square would be unfair to the voters and inconvenient for the riders, almost all of whom would be required to transfer to get where they wanted. A terminal at the canal site would also reduce retail sales and property values downtown. It might give a boost to "uptown" business interests. But the rapid transit commission had no mandate to divert trade from one district to another, let alone to move the center of the business district from one location to the next. If it cost more to build a terminal at Fountain Square, its businessmen and property owners would pay the difference, said George Golde, chairman of the Downtown Terminal Committee.[53]

The debate was acrimonious. Supporters of the Canal Street site argued

Cincinnati's Fountain Square, ca. 1927 (Beeler Organization, Report to the City of Cincinnati on a Rapid Transit Railway, *New York, 1927)*

that the "downtown" interests were trying to confine the city's businesses to just a few blocks. "It is time," said one, "to remove the Chinese wall from around Fifth street [the major street on Fountain Square] and let the city grow." Supporters of the Fountain Square site claimed that the "uptown" interests were trying to "'scrap' the downtown business section in order to further their own ends." If they had their way, downtown Cincinnati would be nothing but "a way station" on the subway system. The issue polarized the city. In favor of the Canal Street site were a host of "uptown" businessmen's organizations, the Central Labor Council, and the Federated Improvement Association, an organization of neighborhood improvement groups. In favor of the Fountain Square site were the "downtown" business interests, which included the businessmen and property owners on Government Square, a block east of Fountain Square, and the Cincinnati Chamber of Commerce. Caught in the crossfire was the rapid transit commission, which stressed that it was not trying to promote one part of the city at the expense of another, only to provide the best possible service at the lowest possible cost. In late March it finally came up with a compromise that satisfied both sides. The terminal (and storage yards) would be built on Canal Street, but the main station, into which the trains would run directly, would be located under Government Square, one block from Fountain Square.[54]

What will Baltimore be like in 1950? a *Baltimore Sun* reporter asked a few well-informed residents in 1925. The answers were instructive. "The beautiful countryside surrounding Baltimore by that time will be almost filled with individual homes," predicted W. W. Emmart of the city planning commission. But "no matter how attractive life out in the farther suburbs may become, the tendency will remain unchecked, so far as we can see now, to crowd into town for the transaction of business." C. D. Emmons, president of the United Railways, the local streetcar company, agreed. People will continue to move to the outlying areas, and the electric railways will follow them. But "nearly everybody who will use these lines will use them to come down town," forcing Baltimore to build els or subways sooner or later. "Even if the business men live twenty or forty miles away they will come to the city by some means or other during the day," he pointed out. "Our suburban steam lines may have passed by 1950, but something will be in existence to bring these citizens to the heart of their city."[55] These predictions reveal that by the mid and late 1920s, by which time the incipient decentralization of commerce was well under way, many Americans still believed that the dispersal of residences was compatible with the concentration of business.

Nowhere was this belief articulated more forcefully than in New York's *Real Estate Record and Builders' Guide,* the city's leading real estate journal. Manhattan, it pointed out, would continue to lose population to the outer boroughs as well as to Westchester County, Long Island, and New Jersey. Indeed, the time would soon come when few if any New Yorkers would live in lower Manhattan. But as New Yorkers moved to the outlying districts, they would continue to come to Manhattan, where businesses "will be centralized as they have never been centralized before in the history of the city." The residents of Queens, to which a subway had just been built, "will be as closely tied to Manhattan as are the inhabitants of Harlem," the journal wrote in 1915. "They will not merely work in Manhattan but they will patronize Manhattan stores, restaurants and places of amusement." Referring to Long Island and Westchester County, it wrote two years later: "Their growth does not mean New York's decline or its loss of prestige. If anything, it accentuates New York's supremacy over the numerous competing cities aspiring to the title of America's greatest municipality." Whatever benefits the periphery benefits the center, "from which," said one article, "the life of the whole city radiates." Commenting on the findings of the 1920 census, the journal held that, although the population was growing faster in the outer boroughs than in Manhattan, "its importance as the keystone of the city's arch must inevitably increase with the passing years. No one need worry about Manhattan's future, even if it some

A vision of downtown Baltimore in 1950 (Baltimore Sun, *June 14, 1925*)

day reaches the point where no one can claim it as a place of residence."[56]

Other Americans took much the same position. Robert E. Simon, a vice president of a New York real estate firm (and a man who was not above mixing his metaphors), said that the growth of the suburbs would strengthen the position of Manhattan. For "as we know," he wrote, "the larger the circumference of the wheel the stronger . . . the hub [and] the greater the area made accessible to the heart of the city the greater [the] volume of business done there." Ernest W. Burgess did not see a conflict between the dispersal of residences and the concentration of business. Neither did George A. Damon, a Los Angeles planner. "It is not hard to draw the conclusion," he wrote in 1924, "that, at any one time, a district will reflect an exact balance between the forces of expansion and the forces of contraction." The centrifugal forces will always equal the centripetal forces. The larger the outlying residential sections, the stronger the central business district. "The more low-value land we open up and use," he said, "the higher will become the land values in our central congested areas." According to historian Blaine A. Brownell, many southerners also believed in the equilibrium between the outlying residential sections and the central business district.[57]

By the mid and late 1920s, however, some Americans had come to the conclusion that the centrifugal forces were beginning to overpower the centripetal forces—or, in other words, that the dispersal of residences might well lead in time to the decentralization of business. At the same time that Raymond Hood, Hugh Ferris, and other architects were envisioning a city of multipurpose skyscrapers, in which, writes historian Carol Willis, "residents, perched like Olympian gods, inhabited the upper floors and rooftop terraces," they saw instead a metropolis of sprawling residential suburbs, outlying business districts, and even self-contained garden cities.[58] If, they asked, suburbanites could patronize the outlying business districts—if they could do their business at branch banks, if they could watch movies at neighborhood theaters, if they could shop at chain stores, which offered many of the same goods at much the same prices as downtown department stores—why should they go to the central business district as often? Indeed, now that the street railways were providing poorer service (and charging higher fares), now that the downtown streets (and the streets leading to them) were becoming more congested, and now that parking places were getting harder to find, why should suburbanites go to the central business district at all?

A few Americans had also come to the conclusion that it would be just as well if the dispersal of residences led to the decentralization of business. As they saw it, the growth of the outlying business districts was not a problem, but a solution, a solution to many of the worst problems of American cities. It would ease traffic congestion, thereby making it unnecessary to build subways, widen streets, and undertake other costly public works projects that the cities could ill afford. It would also diffuse (and even increase) real estate values, which were currently concentrated to an unhealthy degree in a very small part of the city. And it would discourage the erection of more skyscrapers, for which the cities had no need. To these Americans, residential dispersal and business decentralization were integral features of the future metropolis, one organized around small, largely self-sufficient communities in which people lived, worked, shopped, and amused themselves, all without going downtown. Here was an alternative to what Lewis Mumford called "the titanic city of the present" and the skyscraper city of the future, a city whose gods were commerce and traffic and whose saints were Astor, Wanamaker, and the other "martyrs and pious folk, who translated the ancient words, Hope, Faith, and Charity, into Boost, Credit, and Six Percent [and] whose miracles in making a million dollars exist where one had been before, outdo the ancient stories of the fish and the loaves of bread."[59]

But many Americans were skeptical. As W. W. Emmart said, "The dream of a diffused population living in a garden, with nodules of stores and offices here and there, is, I fear, only a dream, unless more radical changes occur than any that are now foreseen." Watching residential suburbs spread over the periphery, and huge hotels, department stores, and office buildings go up in the center, these Americans saw no reason to question what one observer called the "universal tendency" toward residential dispersal and business concentration. Much like their fathers or grandfathers, they found it hard to imagine a metropolis without a highly compact, extremely concentrated business district. Lower Manhattan, wrote a New York civil engineer in 1930, was destined to remain "the hub" of metropolitan New York, the center of its "commercial and social activities." The Loop, declared the *Chicago Tribune* in 1920, would always be "the towering central range of our business structure." Even in Los Angeles, where the outlying business districts were growing very rapidly, downtown was the magnet drawing the region's business, said an executive of the Southern California Edison Company. Watching the delivery trucks heading from the center to the periphery, "filled to the brim, but returning empty," he did not think that downtown Los Angeles would be any less powerful a magnet in the foreseeable future.[60]

5 The Specter of Decentralization: Downtown During the Great Depression and World War II

By the mid 1930s the owners of Detroit's Temple Theater, a nine-story office building that had once been the home of the city's most successful vaudeville house, had had enough. In a city reeling from the Great Depression, the vacancy rate for office buildings was running between 35 and 40 percent. With tenants hard to find—and rents, which had been falling steadily, hard to collect—the Temple Theater no longer paid. In an attempt to lower property taxes and operating expenses, its owners did what other downtown property owners in Detroit and other cities had done. They demolished the building and turned the site into a parking lot. The demolition of office buildings, even nine-story ones, was nothing new, though never before had so many of them been demolished in so short a time. But hitherto these buildings had been torn down to make room for taller, more up-to-date buildings, which, it was assumed, would make more money. Now, in the depths of the worst depression in the nation's history, the owners were facing a unique situation, in which, said one real estate appraiser in 1934, "there is no demand for tall buildings representing the theoretical highest and best use of the site." It was "only natural," he added, that they should look for ways to reduce costs and "cast about for some means of securing the maximum income from a modest improvement until the lot is ripe for maximum development." Hence the demolition of buildings like the Temple Theater and their replacement by parking lots or one- and two-story garages, which were commonly referred to as "taxpayers."[1] The "taxpayers" were as much a legacy of the depression as the "Hoovervilles," bread lines, soup kitchens, and dance marathons. They symbolized downtown in the 1930s as much as skyscrapers, department stores, and high-rise hotels had in the 1920s.

As the proliferation of "taxpayers" revealed, the depression left downtown devastated. As economic conditions went from bad to worse, forcing some businesses to close their doors and others to reduce their workforce, the demand for office space decreased sharply. Coming after almost a decade of record construction, the consequences were catastrophic. Starting in 1930, rents fell—by as much as 30 percent in some cities. And arrears rose. By 1931 construction came to a standstill. More buildings were being torn down than put up, and still the vacancy rate soared. In an industry that considered 10 percent normal, it climbed from about 8 percent in 1926 to nearly 12 percent in 1929 and then jumped to almost 20 percent in 1932 and a whopping 28 percent two years later. Saddled with heavy debts and other fixed charges, many owners were hard pressed to hold on to their properties. By the mid 1930s many were in default. Driven mainly by the depreciation of office buildings, downtown real estate lost much of its value. Between 1928 and 1931 land values in the Chicago Loop fell 25 to 50 percent on some streets and even more on others. On a few streets land values were lower in 1931 than in 1910; and on one street they were lower in 1931 than in 1894. The total value of land in the Loop, which had gone up from $600 million in 1910 to $1 billion in 1928, dropped to $500 million in 1933.[2]

Department stores were also hit hard. With unemployment rising and wages falling, sales declined about 40 percent between 1929 and 1932. In Chicago, Detroit, and Pittsburgh they were down nearly 50 percent. In the meantime costs soared to what Malcolm P. McNair, director of Harvard University's Bureau of Business Research, called "a new all-time peak," climbing from 28 percent of net sales in the early 1920s to 40 percent in the early 1930s. As expenses "went through the roof," profits "went out the window." Although most department stores stayed in business, few made money. As a group they reported a net loss of 6.4 percent in 1932, down from a net profit of 3.1 percent in 1926. Hotels were hit even harder. Extremely labor intensive, they required a high occupancy rate to break even under ordinary circumstances. And by virtue of a great surge in hotel construction in the late 1920s, which culminated in the erection of the new forty-seven-story Waldorf-Astoria in midtown Manhattan, circumstances were far from ordinary after 1930. With far more rooms available than ever and far fewer businessmen on the road, the occupancy rate fell from nearly 70 percent in 1929 to roughly 50 percent in 1933. With room rates falling too, revenues dropped by about half. Unable to reduce operating expenses to a point where they could meet fixed charges, many hotels went under. By 1934, 80 percent of them were in the hands of creditors.[3]

Few Americans thought the depression would have a lasting impact on downtown. Late in 1931, by which time the vacancy rate in office buildings had reached 18 percent and showed no sign of leveling off, a journalist asked Raymond M. Hood, Ralph Walker, and other prominent architects their opinion about the future of the skyscraper—and, by implication, of the central business district of which it was the centerpiece. All were optimistic, confident, as Walker said, that when "people learn at last—as they must some day—how to use land," the skyscraper "would truly come into its own." None so much as mentioned the depression, much less attempted to estimate its long-term impact.[4] As most Americans saw it, downtown would return to normal as soon as the recovery got started—as soon, in other words, as the depression, the inevitable downside of the periodic business cycle, ran its course. As business improved, generating jobs and increasing purchasing power, vacancy rates would fall, retail sales would rise, and hotel rooms would fill up. Construction would resume, and property values would climb. Downtown would regain its prosperity—though for some businessmen and property owners it would be too late.

One reason few Americans thought the depression would have a lasting impact on downtown was that it was a national crisis, as devastating to the countryside as to the cities. And in the cities it hit the periphery as well as the center, the residential districts as well as the business districts, the outlying business districts as well as the central business districts. Consider Chicago. Between 1928 and 1933 land values dropped by 50 percent in the Loop, but by 60 percent in the city as a whole and by more than 75 percent in the outlying business districts. Very few office buildings were constructed, but even fewer residential subdivisions were recorded. Rents fell all over the city—by as much as 80 to 90 percent in some outlying business districts. Foreclosures reached record levels everywhere. Loop banks struggled, though with the help of the federal government most stayed open and even reported slightly higher deposits. Non-Loop banks, whose fortunes were closely tied to the outlying real estate market, fared much worse. More than 160 closed; and total deposits, which had soared from $50 million in 1910 to $800 million in 1928, dropped to $100 million by 1933.[5] Hence it is understandable that most Americans saw the plight of the downtown business and property interests not as a product of specific problems of the central business district but as the result of general problems of the American economic system, which would presumably be solved in the near future.

Another reason few Americans thought the depression would have a lasting impact on downtown was that it struck at the end of the biggest boom in American history, a boom that had produced a great deal of excess commercial space and left downtown extremely vulnerable to a downturn in the economy. Between 1925 and 1931, by which time there were eighty-nine buildings thirty stories or taller in Manhattan, the amount of office space nearly doubled in New York. It went up by almost three-quarters in Chicago, nearly two-thirds in Philadelphia, and more than one-half in Denver and New Orleans. At the peak of the boom new construction approached $500 million per year. The department stores also expanded in the 1920s—none more so than Macy's, whose store on New York's Herald Square was the largest in the world. So did the hotel industry, especially in New York. During the 1920s half a million new hotel rooms, many of them in the vicinity of Grand Central and Penn stations, were added to the existing stock. Between 1927 and 1933 eighty-four large hotels (including the famous triumvirate, the Savoy-Plaza, the Sherry-Netherland, and the Pierre, at the southeast corner of Central Park) were built, increasing the available space by two-thirds.[6] Americans thus had reason to believe that once the recovery got started the excess space would be absorbed and things would return to normal downtown.

By the mid 1930s there were signs that the recovery—slow and far from robust, but a recovery nonetheless—was under way. The gross national product, which had hit bottom in 1933, began to rise. So did industrial output and personal income. And unemployment, which had risen to nearly 25 percent in 1933, started to fall, dropping to 14 percent by 1937. The recovery slowed down in the late 1930s, but it picked up after the outbreak of World War II. And during the early 1940s the nation finally came out of the depression. There were also signs that the excess commercial space was being absorbed. Vacancy rates in office buildings dropped from 28 percent in 1934 to 20 percent in 1936, hovered at about 18 percent in the late 1930s, and then dropped sharply in the early 1940s, falling to less than 4 percent by 1945, an all-time low. In Atlanta, Hartford, and Dallas there was no vacant space at all. Department store sales, which had fallen to $2.5 billion by 1933, went up slowly in the mid and late 1930s, reaching almost $4 billion by 1939, roughly 10 percent less than in 1929, and then climbed sharply in the early 1940s. By 1945 they exceeded $7 billion. Occupancy rates in hotels followed the same pattern. From a low of 51 percent in 1933, they rose to 66 percent by 1938, fell a bit in the next couple of years, and then soared in the early 1940s, reaching 90 percent, an all-time high, in 1944. Revenues also soared, if not quite as sharply. An industry that had lost money in the early 1930s and barely broke even later in the decade now earned a substantial profit.[7]

But despite the recovery, things were not returning to normal downtown. Outside of New York (and perhaps one or two other big cities), downtown's daytime population, which had gone down during the worst years of the depression, was not going up much if at all afterward. As a Detroit traffic engineer observed in 1941, its growth had come to "a practical standstill" in most cities. A case in point is Chicago. From a peak of over 925,000 in 1929, the Loop's daytime population fell to under 760,000 in 1935 and then rose, slowly and sporadically, in the late 1930s and early 1940s. Not until World War II was over did it reach 925,000 again. Between 1929 and 1949, a time during which the population of the city went up 7 percent and the population of the metropolitan area twice as much, the daytime population of downtown Chicago went up one-third of 1 percent. By 1949 fewer than one-quarter of the residents of the metropolitan area went downtown each day. The pattern was much the same elsewhere. So were the consequences. According to cordon counts in eleven of the nation's twenty largest cities in the late 1930s and early (and, in one case, mid) 1940s, only in Boston, Milwaukee, and San Francisco did more than one-half of the residents of the city go downtown each day. Only in Milwaukee did more than one-third of the residents of the metropolitan area do so, and in six of the other metropolitan areas—Pittsburgh, Detroit, Los Angeles, Cincinnati, and Cleveland, as well as Chicago—fewer than one-quarter did.[8]

The growth of downtown's daytime population came to a standstill because most cities grew very slowly in the 1930s, far more slowly than at any other time in modern American history, and only a little faster in the 1940s. A few even lost population. The metropolitan areas grew somewhat faster, especially in the 1940s, though not nearly as fast as they had before 1930. But even in the few cities that grew rapidly after 1930, downtown's daytime population lagged far behind. Los Angeles is a good example. Between 1931 and 1947, during which time the population of the metropolitan area nearly doubled, the daytime population of the central business district dropped by almost two thousand. Per each one thousand residents of Los Angeles County, nearly all of whom lived in metropolitan L.A., downtown's daytime population fell from 307 to 192—and showed no sign of leveling off.[9] Downtown's daytime population also came to a standstill for two other reasons. One was that many Americans now worked, shopped, did business, and amused themselves in the outlying business districts. Some stopped going downtown, and others went much less often. The other reason was that more Americans now used automobiles rather than streetcars. Since the highways did not converge on the central business district to the same degree that the railways did, fewer Americans had to go downtown in order to get from one part of the city to another.

Another sign that things were not returning to normal downtown was that even after the recovery got under way retail trade grew much more slowly in the central business district than in the outlying business districts. A striking example is Los Angeles, where retail sales had dropped 46 percent downtown and 19 percent in the rest of the county during the worst years of the depression. Between 1935 and 1939, a time when retail sales rose almost 50 percent in the outlying business districts, they went up less than 10 percent in the central business district. From 1939 to 1948, retail sales more than doubled downtown, but nearly quadrupled in the rest of the county. The result was that downtown's share of the county's retail trade fell from about 30 percent in 1929 to 22 percent in 1935, 17 percent in 1939, and a minuscule 11 percent in 1948. It is true that retail trade had been more widely decentralized in Los Angeles than in other big cities since the late 1920s, that in few if any other cities did downtown decline so rapidly as a retail center in the 1930s and 1940s, and that in none of them was so small a share of retail trade carried on downtown in the immediate postwar years. But it is also true that what happened in Los Angeles occurred to one degree or another in other big cities, that throughout the United States retail sales not only went down much more sharply in the central business district than in the outlying business districts during the depression, but also went up much more slowly afterward.[10]

The decentralization of retail trade extended to a wide range of merchandise—to items that had once been sold mainly in the central business district as well as to goods that had long been sold mainly in the outlying business districts. Fueling the decentralization of retail trade was the continued growth of the chains, most of whose stores were located on the periphery. The chains had fared relatively well during the depression, when their sales declined by less than one-third as much as the sales of the department stores; and they prospered afterward. As an expert on retail trade wrote, much of their success came "at the expense of department stores," which were far more likely to be located in the center. Also fueling the decentralization of retail trade was the growth of outlying department stores, all (or almost all) of which were branches of downtown department stores. The development of branch stores, which had started in the mid and late 1920s, slowed down in the early 1930s, resumed later in the decade, slowed again during World War II, and, led by Macy's and other major retailers, surged after the war. The result was that downtown's share of department store sales dropped steadily, falling in the Loop, for example, from virtually 100 percent in the early 1920s to just over 60 percent in the mid 1930s.[11]

Yet another sign that things were not returning to normal downtown was that the "taxpayers"—which, it had been assumed, would disappear once the recovery got under way—were becoming a fixture in the central business district. Between 1932 and 1940 about 92 million cubic feet of commercial space, close to 10 percent of the total, was demolished in the Chicago Loop, most of it replaced by parking lots and one- or two-story garages. (Among the many substantial structures demolished was the Masonic Temple, an office building erected on State and Randolph streets in the early 1890s. Designed by Daniel H. Burnham and John W. Root, it had been the first twenty-story skyscraper in Chicago and for a short time the tallest building in the world.) By the early 1940s more than 18 percent of the Loop was either vacant or used for parking. The number of "taxpayers" also went up in downtown Detroit, where nearly one hundred buildings were torn down between 1936 and 1939. (Speaking of the many old and obsolete buildings still standing, one observer wrote in 1940 that "odds are high that many of these will be torn down in the near future.") In a business district where "almost every square inch of land [once] had a building on it," more than three-quarters of the blocks now had one or more vacant parcels. Things were much the same in downtown Los Angeles, where so many buildings were torn down and replaced by parking lots or "taxpayers" in the 1930s that by the early 1940s roughly 25 percent of

the buildable land was used to store autos. In a business district of less than one square mile there were now more than nine hundred parking lots and garages, with space for more than sixty-five thousand cars.[12]

The proliferation of "taxpayers," which were found not only on inexpensive sites on the fringe but also on expensive ones at the core, ran counter to the conventional wisdom, which held that downtown property would be de-

veloped more intensively over time. But for the many property owners who were losing money, the theory was irrelevant. They were stuck with old

Chicago's Masonic Temple, 1916 (Architectural Record, July 1916)

Downtown Detroit, ca. 1940 (Architectural Forum, January 1940)

and obsolete buildings, "too far gone," wrote one observer, "for moderniza-
tion." By virtue of the depression and competition from outlying business districts, the demand for commercial space downtown had not reached the point
where it made sense to erect new buildings. Making matters worse, many institutional investors had "blacked out" (or, as we now say, redlined) chunks of
the central business district, refusing to make loans there because of what
Business Week called "progressively declining values."[13] By tearing down the
buildings, the owners could lower their tax bills and reduce their operating expenses. By replacing them with parking lots or one- and two-story garages,

they could capitalize on the growing demand for parking space and generate enough income to hold on to their property until the vacancy rate dropped to a point where new construction was warranted. By the time it did, however, the country was in the middle of World War II, and the government had imposed tight restrictions on all nonessential construction.

Perhaps the most striking sign that things were not returning to normal downtown was that even after the recovery began property values in the central business district did not rise much if at all. They did not go up nearly as much as property values elsewhere. Downtown Seattle is a case in point. From a peak of almost $68 million in 1929, the assessed value of the central business district dropped to about $51 million in 1935. It fell to about $46 million by 1940, hovered at around $45 million in the mid 1940s, and barely reached $48 million by the end of the decade. As property values elsewhere in Seattle fell less in the 1930s and rose more in the 1940s, downtown's share of the city's assessed value dropped from nearly 30 percent in 1929 to 27 percent in 1935, 24 percent in 1940, 22 percent in 1945, and just under 18 percent in 1949. The pattern was much the same in other big cities, among them Baltimore, St. Louis, and Los Angeles (where the assessed value of the central business district plummeted 60 percent in the 1930s). What Los Angeles city planner Gordon Whitnall called "the spectacular shrinkage of values in the commercial centers of American cities" would probably have been even worse were it not for a provision of the U.S. tax code that permitted new owners of old buildings, even buildings that were fully depreciated, to depreciate them anew on the basis of their purchase price—a provision that generated tax-free income and thus increased property values.[14]

Downtown values had fallen before. During the panic of 1873, for example, they dropped sharply all over downtown Chicago—by 50 percent on State Street, between Washington and Madison, at the center of the Loop, and by 33 percent on Franklin Street, between Wacker and Lake, on the fringe. But hitherto they had rebounded, often much more sharply. After falling from $1,000 a front foot in 1873 to $500 a front foot in 1877, property on State Street climbed to $14,000 a front foot in 1894. In the meantime property on Franklin Street, which had dropped from $300 to $200 a front foot, soared to $2,500 a front foot. By virtue of the shifts in the business district, property values had fallen for good in parts of downtown. But hitherto losses in some had always been offset by gains in others. When Manhattan's leading department stores moved north in the early twentieth century, a move driven by what their owners regarded as the encroachment of the garment industry, property values went way down near Union Square and Madison Square, but they went up even more near Herald Square and on Fifth Avenue above Thirty-fourth Street.[15] Never before had values downtown fallen so sharply and so widely for so long. Never before had values downtown fallen so much more than values elsewhere in the city. To make matters worse, the current decline in downtown property values could not be attributed to either a downturn in the business cycle or a shift within the business district.

By the late 1930s and early 1940s it was clear downtown was in trouble. In most cities its daytime population was still below pre-depression levels. So were its retail sales. Large hotels and office buildings were being demolished. With no new construction going on, buildings were getting older—and, in some cases, seedier. Once-valuable parcels were vacant or occupied by "taxpayers." Nowhere, wrote a journalist who visited Chicago, St. Louis, and a score of other cities in the winter of 1939–40, "is there any downtown activity to speak of after dark," not even in the entertainment districts. Theaters were boarded up; movie houses were "more than half empty," restaurants even emptier, and streets "woefully deserted."[16] By the late 1930s and early 1940s Americans were starting to realize that these problems were the product not so much of the collapse of the national economy as the decentralization of the urban economy. They were beginning to believe that downtown was in trouble not so much because the country was mired in the depression as because a large and growing number of people were going to the outlying business districts rather than to the central business district—that they were shopping in chain stores, doing business with branch banks, and patronizing neighborhood movies and roadside restaurants.

Decentralization had aroused only mild concern among downtown businessmen and property owners when they first became aware of it in the mid and late 1920s. As a Los Angeles realtor remarked in 1930, decentralization was a relatively new phenomenon, one whose long-term impact was hard to gauge.[17] Moreover, at the same time that downtown business interests were first becoming aware of decentralization, the central business district was undergoing the greatest boom in history. Retail sales were at record levels. So was new construction. Property values were at an all-time high. And downtown's daytime population was larger than ever—at least in absolute terms. Downtown had serious problems. But as its businessmen and property owners saw it, they were the result of too many, not too few, people coming downtown, and too much, not too little, business being done there. What concerned them was less the impact incipient decentralization of business might have one day than the impact full-blown centralization of business was having already. On their minds was less how to compete with outlying business districts than how to funnel hundreds of thousands of people a day into the central business district, how to relieve traffic congestion and provide adequate parking, and how to stabilize property values in a place that was constantly on the move.

All this changed after 1930. Decentralization was now at least a decade old. According to one real estate man, it had gotten started long before anybody had noticed. The boom of the 1920s was over. Gone were the soaring retail sales and rising property values, which had hidden the fact that the outlying business districts had already made sizable inroads on the central business district. As one journalist noted, the outlying business districts were also recovering from the depression at a much faster pace than the central business district. Unless something was done to stop (or at any rate to slow down) the decentralization, there was good reason to believe that before long downtown would be "a mere ghost of its former self," wrote John A. Miller, a transportation consultant.[18] To put it another way, there was good reason to believe that what had once been the business district and was now the central business district might end up one day as just another business district, and not necessarily the most important.

Downtown businessmen and property owners began to voice strong concern about what was called "the spectre of decentralization" in 1936. Among the first to sound the alarm was R. F. Hewitt of Seattle's United Pacific Realty and Investment Corporation. Speaking at the annual convention of the National Association of Building Owners and Managers (BOMA), Hewitt declared that decentralization was a "disease" afflicting the central business district of all American cities. Hewitt and John R. Fugard, a Chicago architect and building manager, warned about decentralization at BOMA's annual convention in 1938. And three years later the association held a session at its annual convention at which several prominent Americans, among them Leo J. Sheridan, president of the Chicago BOMA, and Philip W. Kniskern, president of the National Association of Real Estate Boards, talked about decentralization and the future of the central business district. The session was "without precedent," Sheridan said. It was the first time in history that BOMA had held a business meeting in the evening, a time its members had invariably set aside for socializing. Indicative of the concern about decentralization, the session was extremely well attended, and not only by members of BOMA, but also by many of Chicago's business and civic leaders.[19]

Downtown business interests voiced their concern about decentralization in a number of ways other than by talks at the annual convention of the National Association of Building Owners and Managers. They wrote articles for *Buildings and Building Management, Skyscraper Management, National Real Estate Journal,* and other trade publications. In 1940, for example, the *National Real Estate Journal* published a symposium in which Newton C. Farr, president of the National Association of Real Estate Boards (NAREB), Walter S. Schmidt, chairman of the association's committee on commercial districts, and other NAREB leaders discussed the problem of decentralization and what the association was doing to solve it. Downtown spokesmen also warned about the dangers of decentralization at meetings of professional and civic groups. By virtue of these efforts, decentralization emerged as a major public issue in the late 1930s and early 1940s—and remained an issue of interest during World War II. The National Conference on City Planning discussed the problem; so did the Western Society of Engineers. The American Institute of Appraisers even decided in 1941 to add a series of lectures on "the disintegration and decentralization of urban communities" to its regular summer - courses at Columbia University in New York and Southern Methodist University in Dallas.[20]

Decentralization, Hewitt pointed out, was not "a movement of the retail district from one part of the [central] business district to another." Rather it was a process by which the outlying business districts grew "at the expense of the central [business] districts," said A. A. Oles, secretary of the Seattle BOMA. Every dollar spent in the outlying business districts was a dollar lost to the central business district, he wrote. And for every dollar lost, there is "a direct reduction in rental income and a consequent loss in capital value." As Hewitt noted, decentralization was more acute in some cities than in others. And as the editors of *Buildings and Building Management* said in 1940, it was more serious for some businesses than others. Of "all the interests now located in central business districts," they pointed out, "building owners and managers are almost the only ones who cannot escape the effects of decentralization by moving elsewhere." But as Leo J. Sheridan noted, decentralization was a serious problem for the department stores and other retailers. It was also a serious problem for the banks and insurance companies that held mortgages on downtown property and notes from downtown businesses.[21]

A "virulent" disease, in Hewitt's words, decentralization had a host of striking symptoms. Chief among them were the sharp decline in downtown retail sales and property values, which were "shrinking almost beyond recognition" in the Loop, said George Richardson, trustee of the estate of Marshall Field, the Chicago department store (and real estate) magnate. Another symptom was the proliferation of "taxpayers," which were springing up "like mushrooms," observed Graham Aldis, a Chicago real estate man, in 1938. It was shocking, if no longer surprising, that high-priced downtown real estate "cannot be put to more profitable use than storing itinerant cars." Other symptoms included record levels of bankruptcies, foreclosures, and tax delinquencies. Since the depression, Sheridan pointed out in 1938, more than one of every four of the Loop's 2,400 parcels of real estate had been delinquent for a year or more, and nearly one of every ten had been delinquent for at least five years. Still another symptom was what Fugard called the "no-man's land" (or "blighted areas") that "rings the [central] business district and forms a cancer which is slowly but surely gnawing away at the vitals of centralized business."[22] A few observers argued that some of these symptoms were the result of the overbuilding of the 1920s and the depression of the 1930s. But as the years went by, this argument was less and less compelling.

How did downtown businessmen and property owners explain decentralization? To a small degree, they blamed themselves. Downtown was losing its competitive edge partly because some property owners were neglecting their holdings. The result, wrote Kniskern, was that much of downtown was "dingy, noisy, dirty, and unattractive," not the sort of place likely to appeal to shoppers or others with money to spend. Other property owners were demanding unreasonable rents, forcing some businessmen to move to the outlying business districts. Still others were asking exorbitant prices—in the hope, wrote Aldis, that someday someone would decide to build a skyscraper on the site—and thereby preventing other businessmen from developing the property. As a group, wrote *Buildings and Building Management,* downtown businessmen and property owners were inclined to persist in "the wishful thinking that an improvement in general business conditions will solve all of their problems." To make matters worse, many of them were so preoccupied by the problems of a particular building or particular street that they were hesitant to join forces to defend the central business district as a whole against what Hewitt called "a common enemy."[23]

Downtown business interests also attributed decentralization in part to the misguided policies of local officials. As the history of Wilshire Boulevard revealed, these officials tended to bow to pressure to zone undeveloped land for commercial use. As a result, most cities had far more potential commercial space than they would ever need. Rather than exclude business from the outlying residential districts and thereby strengthen the position of the central business district, zoning spurred the development of the outlying business districts. According to downtown business interests, local officials also took other measures that gave the outlying business districts a competitive edge.

They imposed more stringent fire, sanitary, and building regulations in the central business district, a step that drove up the costs of doing business downtown. Even worse, they assessed central business property at a much higher rate, a practice that drove costs up even more. As a result, wrote Oles in 1935, a downtown Seattle lot that rented for five dollars per square foot a month was paying ten times as much in property taxes as a suburban Seattle lot that produced the same income. Local officials, downtown business interests complained, were assessing property not on a basis of its "revenue producing power," but on the basis of "a theoretical ad valorem figure"—a figure that was based on its potential, though highly unlikely, use as the site for a tall office building.[24]

Above all downtown businessmen and property owners attributed decentralization to two other phenomena, both of which had their origins in the late nineteenth century. One was traffic congestion. Americans had long assumed that traffic congestion was one of the principal threats to downtown's accessibility. A grave problem in the late nineteenth century, it grew even worse in the early twentieth, especially after World War I. Thus it is not surprising that when decentralization gained momentum in the mid and late 1920s Miller McClintock, Harland Bartholomew, and other experts blamed it on traffic congestion. Their view was supported by a study of traffic congestion and retail trade done by the U.S. Bureau of Foreign and Domestic Commerce in 1926. Downtown business interests promptly embraced this position, which was firmly established as the conventional wisdom by the late 1930s.[25] At its heart was the belief that most Americans still wanted to work, shop, do business, and amuse themselves in the central business district, but that they were finding it too hard to get there.

The other phenomenon to which downtown businessmen and property owners attributed decentralization was residential dispersal. Americans had long assumed that people would move from the center of the city to the periphery and from the city to the suburbs. And they had done so at a pace unmatched anywhere else in the world. Americans had also long assumed that the dispersal of population would be beneficial for the downtown business interests. By the late 1930s and early 1940s, however, it was clear that this internal movement was not only heavier than expected; it was also highly "selective," as sociologist R. D. McKenzie put it. The middle and upper middle classes were leaving the center. But the lower class, made up in large part of ethnic and racial minorities, was staying behind. As one member of BOMA said in 1937, the metropolis was caught in "a vicious circle," "growing out on the edge and dying in the middle." The results were disastrous. The central business district was losing many of its best customers, keeping many of its worst, and ending up surrounded by blighted areas, which were viewed as a cause as well as a symptom of decentralization. The belief in residential dispersal was so deeply ingrained that most downtown businessmen and property owners were reluctant to speak out against it. But as the central business district lost more and more trade to the outlying business districts, they were forced to acknowledge that residential dispersal might well be incompatible with business concentration. John A. Miller spoke for many when he wrote in 1941: "The basic question [a question that no one would have asked a generation ago] is whether we can retain the city as a central market place, and at the same time decentralize residences to the extent that everyone lives out in the suburbs or country."[26]

A few downtown businessmen and property owners held that the concern about decentralization was unwarranted (or at least exaggerated). One of them was Joseph Laronge, a Cleveland real estate man. Writing in *Buildings and Building Management* in 1938, he took the position that decentralization was a "natural" development, the product of the growth of the urban population and the emergence of outlying residential sections. "As long as I can remember," he said, Americans have always shopped at outlying business districts, patronizing neighborhood grocers, bakers, butchers, tailors, and druggists. These outlying business districts are growing, but they "only serve the residents who surround them." They "do not draw to any appreciable extent from downtown stores," even those with branches elsewhere. Contrary to the cries of the "alarmist[s]," downtown still had much going for it, Laronge argued. A "truly American institution," it had the huge department stores, where most people preferred to shop for everything but food and convenience items. It also had an enormous built-in market in the thousands of people who worked in its office buildings, passed through its railroad and bus terminals, and attended the conventions, expositions, and cultural and sports events that took place nearby. Other than to curtail its growth, decentralization would not have much of an impact on the central business district, he concluded.[27]

Among the other skeptics were Alan F. Schnell, secretary of BOMA of Buffalo, and George J. Eberle, a Los Angeles economist. According to Schnell, decentralization was "a threat more than an actuality." The outlying business districts had thus far had little impact on the downtown retail district, even less on the downtown office and financial districts. Downtown had its problems, Schnell admitted, especially high vacancy rates, low rental income, and obsolete office buildings. But these problems were not due to decentralization. According to Eberle, the concern was overstated even in Los Angeles, the nation's most highly decentralized metropolis. The outlying business districts posed a threat to the central business district, he remarked in 1941. But "there appears to be nothing [now going on] which would lead one to believe that the downtown area in the future will not uphold its dominant position." Downtown will change. Some activities will be "thrown out," others "drawn in or retained." But decentralization notwithstanding, it will remain the "governmental, social, and business center [of the metropolis], a heart, a core, a hub from which all or most major functions are directed."[28]

But most downtown businessmen and property owners were not so optimistic. Decentralization had already done serious damage, and in time it might destroy the central business district. To prevent this, the central business district had to be made cleaner, brighter, quieter, and more attractive, "so attractive," wrote Schnell, "that the woman who wanted to shop, unless she just wanted to buy a spool of thread, would come downtown for the fun of coming down and looking around." Even more important, the central business district had to be relieved of its heavy tax burden, which put it at a serious competitive disadvantage. Commercial property should be assessed on the same basis in the central and outlying business districts. Most important of all, the central business district should be made more accessible—which meant that a solution had to be found to the problem of traffic congestion. "If we are to encourage people to come downtown to shop," Richardson declared, "we must make it easy for them to do so." Lastly, the blighted areas surrounding the central business district should be eradicated and replaced by middle- and upper-middle-class neighborhoods, a step that would create a vast new market for downtown goods and services. As Miles Colean, an expert on housing, put it, residential dispersal, one of the oldest and strongest movements in American history, would have to be reversed to some extent.[29]

The downtown business interests were aware that these steps would not eliminate the outlying business districts. They were too well established. They had powerful economic and political backers. And they provided a valuable service to outlying residents, many of whom had no desire to go downtown each time they wanted to buy a shirt, see a movie, or deposit a check. Carlton Schultz, a Cleveland real estate man, spoke for many when he responded to an editorial in *Buildings and Building Management* urging downtown property owners to take the problem of decentralization more seriously. "I do not believe that the larger cities can successfully stop decentralization any more than you can keep a child from growing up," he wrote. But the downtown businessmen and property owners were confident that these steps could create a balance between the outlying business districts and the central business district—that they could save, in Schultz's words, "what we have left of the central business district." These steps, their backers believed, could boost retail sales, stabilize property values, protect the billions invested in real estate, and safeguard the mortgages and other loans for which this property served as collateral. There might not be a "cure" for decentralization, Schultz wrote, but there were "remedies," which would "alleviate the pain."[30]

To preserve downtown as, in Eberle's words, the heart, the core, and the hub of the metropolis, Schultz and his associates believed that the central business districts would have to be at least as well organized as the outlying business districts. To put it another way, the downtown business interests would have to form organizations devoted exclusively to the well-being of the central business districts, organizations of the sort that had already been formed in San Francisco and Los Angeles. The logic of this position was nicely spelled out by the *Downtown Merchantman,* a publication of the Downtown Association of Milwaukee. Downtown Milwaukee needed an organization of its own, it declared, because it could not rely on others. Not the Milwaukee Association of Commerce, an organization made up of business interests from all over Milwaukee that "can be expected only to sponsor such projects and proposals as will affect the entire city." Not the Milwaukee Real Estate Board, another citywide organization that "cannot throw its influence behind proposed legislation looking toward the advancement of a single area." Not the Milwaukee newspapers, which were unlikely to "take up the cudgel for downtown interests as against the interests of neighborhood business districts." And not the outlying businessmen's associations, who sought "the advancement of [the] neighborhood [business] districts."[31]

Driven by their concern about decentralization, downtown businessmen and property owners formed organizations of their own in one city after another in the 1930s. One of the best known was the Downtown Property Owners Association of Oakland, which served as a model for a number of other cities. The association was set up in 1931 in an effort to stop the movement of retail trade to uptown Oakland, a rival business district about half a mile north. Downtown Milwaukee's business interests formed the Downtown Association in 1935. And three years later Chicago's BOMA, whose members were troubled by the decline of retail sales and property values in the Loop, launched a campaign to create a separate organization for downtown Chicago, the absence of which had long been bemoaned by Loop businessmen and property owners. Within less than a year the Downtown Council of

Chicago was established, with George Richardson as chairman and roughly two hundred prominent businessmen and property owners as members. By the late 1930s the Detroit Business Property Owners' Association was at work too.[32] So were several older organizations, among the most noteworthy of which were the Down Town Association of San Francisco, the Central Business District Association of Los Angeles, and the Main Street Association of Buffalo, whose membership represented business interests in downtown Buffalo.

Downtown business interests followed suit in other cities in the early and mid 1940s. In Baltimore they formed the Downtown Committee in 1941. Organized to combat the decentralization of retail trade, the committee "will work for the downtown business section," said one of its members, "in precisely the same way that neighborhood improvement associations do [for] residential areas." Later that year a group of downtown Atlanta businessmen and property owners led by Robert Maddux, a banker, property owner, and former mayor, set up the Atlanta Central Improvement Association. Its goal, wrote *Skyscraper Management,* was "to swing back the trend of decentralization and build up the heart of Atlanta's business district." Downtown business interests took somewhat different approaches in St. Paul and Pittsburgh. In St. Paul they prevailed on the Minnesota legislature to authorize big cities to establish central business district authorities, quasi-governmental bodies empowered to condemn property, issue bonds, and take other measures to revitalize downtown. In Pittsburgh, Richard King Mellon and other leaders of the city's corporate elite created the Allegheny Conference on Community Development, a broad-based civic group whose principal objective was the redevelopment of the "Golden Triangle."[33] So successful were these organizing efforts that by the end of World War II most big cities had an association of one sort or another devoted exclusively to promoting the interests of the central business district.

The proliferation of these organizations reflected more than just the concern about decentralization and anxiety about the future of downtown. It also reflected a widespread loss of faith in the notion of spatial harmony. As downtown businessmen and property owners now saw it, the central business district was locked in a fierce struggle with the outlying business districts. Commenting on a proposal to remove buses from Wisconsin Avenue, one of downtown Milwaukee's most important streets, the *Downtown Merchantman* declared in 1943: "Strong forces are at work within the city to emasculate . . . the downtown business section." "Sectionalism" was getting worse and worse, turning the city into "a series of villages each fighting the other at every turn."[34] This proliferation also reflected the new belief that in order to curb decentralization the downtown interests had to work together. Businessmen had to join forces with property owners, retail merchants with building managers. The various parts of the central business district had to work together too. No longer could downtown Chicago leave its fate in the hands of the State Street Council, Michigan Avenue Association, and other groups that represented only parts of the Loop. Decentralization posed a threat to the downtown business interests as a group. And it was up to them to respond to it as a group.

How they responded varied from one city to another, even from one decade to the next. But in general the efforts to slow decentralization and shore up the central business district fell into two categories. In the first were promotional activities designed to entice people to go downtown. To give a few examples, the Downtown Association of Milwaukee sponsored a "Downtown Day" on June 17, 1944. By way of a vigorous advertising campaign, the association urged residents to spend the day downtown. "Shop where you can supply all your needs!" said the ads. "Visit banks and attend to other downtown business. Highlight the day by dining in downtown restaurants. . . . Plan, too, to attend a downtown movie or stage show." One year later the association launched "the most extensive promotional campaign of its history," a year-long effort in which it spread the slogan "Downtown Milwaukee Has Everything" on billboards and streetcars and in newspapers and on radio. "Through repetition of the slogan and of the idea," the *Downtown Merchantman* wrote, "[many] thousands of potential customers and clients will become downtown-conscious." Oakland's Downtown Property Owners Association also sponsored a Downtown Day, and Baltimore's Downtown Council a Downtown Week, which was highlighted by parades, fashion shows, and tours of historic sites. Closely related to these promotional activities were efforts to prevail on downtown business interests to give their buildings facelifts, install display windows, suspend flower baskets from light poles, and otherwise modernize and beautify the central business district.[35]

In the second category were what might be called political activities. These required action by municipal (and, in some cases, state and federal) authorities. They affected not only the central business district but also other parts of the metropolis; they tended to be very expensive or highly controversial or both; and they often aroused a good deal of opposition. Included in this category were efforts to help downtown property owners appeal to local boards to reassess the value of their land and buildings and thereby reduce their property taxes. Although Buffalo's Main Street Association, Oakland's Downtown

Property Owners Association, and a few other organizations had some success, these efforts had little impact on decentralization.[36] Also included in
this category were efforts to persuade the authorities to build rapid transit, improve local highways, provide parking facilities, and thus increase downtown's accessibility. Included, too, were efforts to convince the authorities to
eradicate the blighted areas surrounding the central business district, replace
them with middle- and upper-middle-class neighborhoods, and thereby create a vast new market for downtown goods and services.

By the late 1930s the downtown business interests had also come to believe
that decentralization was a national problem and that some sort of national
organization was needed to deal with it. Their chief spokesman was Walter S.
Schmidt, a Cincinnati real estate man who had large holdings in both the center and the periphery and was a past president of the National Association of
Real Estate Boards, which represented all types of brokers, residential, commercial, and industrial. At the behest of Schmidt and his backers, NAREB set
up a committee on commercial districts in 1938 and named him chairman. In
a report issued a year later, the committee warned that decentralization had
already done serious damage to the central business districts and, if left
unchecked, would eventually do serious damage to the outlying business districts. It urged the downtown business interests to join forces to combat decentralization—to figure out its causes, to find short-term remedies, and, in
conjunction with local officials and planning agencies, to develop long-range
solutions. The committee also called on NAREB to create a central agency,
"independent and free of control by any body politic," to gather information
about decentralization and serve as a clearinghouse for it. This task should be
entrusted to the National Real Estate Foundation, which NAREB had established in 1936, and, in particular, to its newly formed "research arm," the Urban Land Institute (ULI).[37]

With NAREB's blessings, the ULI took on the task of helping cities reduce
the impact of decentralization. Schmidt was president of the institute and one
of its twenty trustees. George Richardson was also a trustee. So was Philip W.
Kniskern, president of the First Mortgage Corporation of Philadelphia, and
George McAneny, chairman of the board of Title Guarantee and Trust Company of New York (the same McAneny who as borough president of Manhattan had been instrumental in the passage of the city's 1916 zoning ordinance).
Other trustees included R. R. Deupree, president of Procter and Gamble,
which was located in Cincinnati (Schmidt's hometown), and Harry Chandler,
publisher of the *Los Angeles Times* and one of the largest landowners in southern California. With the exception of Walter B. McCornack, dean of the MIT

School of Architecture, all the trustees were prominent merchants, bankers, insurance executives, or property owners who had a large stake in the well-being of the central business district. As consultants to ULI, the trustees retained Harland Bartholomew, the city planner from St. Louis and past president of the American City Planning Institute, Miller McClintock, the traffic consultant and head of Yale University's Bureau for Street Traffic Control, and, among others, E. P. Griffenhagen of Chicago, an expert on municipal government and public finance.[38]

The ULI got off to a fast start. In April 1940 it published a report titled *Decentralization: What Is It Doing to Our Cities?* Based on a survey of more than five hundred real estate appraisers and brokers from over two hundred cities, the report spelled out the many "adverse results of decentralization," especially, though not exclusively, in the central business district. It also compiled a long but "far from complete" list of the causes of decentralization, which ranged from traffic congestion in the center to premature subdivision on the periphery and poor planning and zoning just about everywhere. "We cannot afford to let our cities destroy themselves through uncontrolled decentralization," said the report. At stake were not just the huge investments downtown and the fiscal solvency of the cities, but also "much of what we now prize as civilization." Later that year ULI published an essay by Harland Bartholomew titled *The Present and Ultimate Effect of Decentralization Upon American Cities.* What he described as "an almost subconscious desire to escape the city" was leaving in its wake large blighted areas, which threatened the economic well-being not only of the central business district but of the entire central city. To curb decentralization, Bartholomew recommended that local, state, and even federal authorities take steps to slow down residential dispersal on the periphery, rehabilitate blighted areas in the center, and help begin the process of rebuilding America's cities.[39]

With grants from NAREB and Marshall Field III, the grandson of the late Chicago magnate, ULI sponsored a series of studies of the central business district in thirteen large American cities. Some of the studies, which dealt with Boston, Cincinnati, Detroit, Louisville, Milwaukee, New York, and Philadelphia, were published between January 1941 and August 1942. Nothing came of the others, which dealt with Chicago, Cleveland, Des Moines, Los Angeles, Richmond, and St. Louis and may have been minor casualties of World War II. With the exception of the New York study, a long and scholarly monograph by Robert H. Armstrong and Homer Hoyt, the studies were much the same. Each was done by a local appraiser or other businessmen who had a "wide knowledge [of] and experience in downtown real estate" and who shared ULI's views about decentralization. Following guidelines laid down by ULI and working under the supervision of a committee of trustees consisting of Schmidt, Richardson, and E. L. Ostendorf of Cleveland, the authors collected statistics and interviewed local businessmen and property owners. The authors then spelled out the causes of decentralization and recommended ways to deal with it—all in fewer than a hundred pages.[40]

A reflection of the conventional wisdom of the downtown business interests, these studies provided no new or striking insights. Nor were they expected to. As ULI's historian pointed out, the institute did not want "research-for-research-sake." It wanted research that would call attention to the perils of decentralization and the plight of the central business district, research that would lead to action, research that would prompt the cities "to do something about the problems they already knew they had." By these criteria, the studies were successful. Accompanied by press releases and sometimes highlighted at public conferences, they provoked a good deal of discussion about decentralization. (William H. Ballard's report on Boston generated a furor because of his recommendation that the state put the city into receivership for ten years in order to allow a reorganization of its finances, a recommendation that was denounced by the Boston Real Estate Board and the *Boston Herald*.)[41] Through these studies (and through the many articles about them in newspapers and journals), ULI heightened the awareness of decentralization, raised the level of concern about the central business district, and turned what had been thought of as a local problem into a national one.

Of the many causes and consequences of decentralization, none worried ULI more than the blighted areas that surrounded the central business district. What to do about them was the principal issue at a three-day conference of businessmen, public officials, planners, and civic leaders sponsored by the institute and held at MIT in October 1941. It was also the subject of two pamphlets published by ULI in 1942, a ULI board meeting in January that year, and a legislative program put forward by the institute in June. The ULI and other proposals for what became known as urban redevelopment were the focus of another conference held at the Cranbrook Academy of Art in Bloomfield Hills, Michigan, in September 1942. From that point on ULI played a very active role in the struggle for urban redevelopment (or, as it was later called, urban renewal). As soon as the war ended the institute also established a Central Business District Council, an organization chaired by A. J. Stewart, who had done the ULI study of downtown Louisville. Its mission was to help cities combat decentralization in the postwar period. At a series of clinics and panel sessions held in Louisville, San Francisco, and other cities, the

Central Business District Council offered advice to downtown businessmen and property owners about traffic, parking, and other problems, the solutions to which were regarded as crucial to the long-term survival of downtown.[42]

In their efforts to slow decentralization and shore up the central business district, the downtown business interests could ordinarily count on the support of two other groups. Local officials were one. Perhaps the best known was David L. Lawrence, mayor of Pittsburgh and head of the local Democratic machine, whose "working relationships" with Richard King Mellon, leader of the city's business community, were vital to the effectiveness of the Allegheny Conference on Community Development. Many local officials, especially big-city mayors, supported the efforts of the downtown business interests for several reasons. For one, they wanted to stay on good terms with a group whose help might well be crucial in electoral campaigns in the city and legislative battles in the state. For another, they still viewed downtown as the "mainspring" of the city's economy—to quote a division of the Western Society of Engineers—and an invaluable asset in its rivalry with other cities.[43] Above all, local officials supported the efforts of the downtown business interests because a thriving central business district was essential to the fiscal well-being of America's cities.

To understand why, it is necessary to bear in mind that down through World War II cities derived the bulk of their revenue from property taxes, of which the central business districts paid a share out of all proportion to their size. They paid a very large share because their assessed values, on which their property taxes were based, were very high—20 percent of the city's assessed value in Chicago, 27 percent in Milwaukee, and nearly 30 percent in Seattle in the late 1920s, by which time the incipient decentralization of commerce was well under way. Their assessed values were high partly because their property was the most valuable in the city and partly because, in the view of two experts from Milwaukee, it was "greatly over assessed." The ratio of assessed value to actual value was much higher in the central business district than in other parts of the city, sometimes twice or even three times as high. This disparity was especially striking on the edge of downtown. As William H. Ballard explained, property there was normally assessed not on the basis of its actual value—the capitalized value of its current earnings—but on the basis of its speculative value—the value if someone wanted to develop it as a site for an office building, department store, or luxury hotel. This property was so assessed (and thus so "excessively and unequally taxed"), observed Cuthbert E. Reeves, a Los Angeles real estate economist, even if there was "not a chance in the world to finance or find tenants for such [a] development."[44]

Downtown was hit so hard in the 1930s and 1940s, first by the Great Depression and then by decentralization, that some property owners demolished their buildings and either replaced them with "taxpayers" or left the site vacant. Others persuaded the local officials to lower the assessed value, no easy task. Still others refused to pay their taxes, a practice that drove the number and value of delinquent properties up to record levels. Despite these maneuvers, the central business district still paid a large share of the property taxes in most cities in the 1930s and 1940s, if not as large a share as it had in the 1920s. According to several studies, moreover, downtown produced much more in property taxes than it consumed in public services—two and a half times as much in St. Louis and even more in Boston, where the central business district generated enough revenue not only to meet its own expenses, but also to make up most of the deficit attributed to the blighted areas. Small wonder that Graham Aldis of Chicago, where about one-third of 1 percent of the city paid over 17 percent of its taxes, called the central business district "a milch-cow for the tax collector." And that Albert D. Hutzler, owner of Hutzler Brothers, Baltimore's largest department store, referred to downtown's tax base as "the lifeblood of the city."[45]

A thriving downtown, one with high (and steadily rising) property values that generated more than its fair share of municipal revenue, was vital to more than the city's ability to meet its day-to-day expenses. It was vital to its ability to undertake long-term capital projects as well. As a rule the cities financed these projects by issuing general obligation bonds, which were backed by their "full faith and credit" and formed part of their bonded debt. The cities, however, were subject to debt limits, most of which had been incorporated into state constitutions in the second half of the nineteenth century. In general, a city's debt limit was pegged to its assessed value. Hence a sharp decline in the assessed value of the central business district could impair a city's capacity to issue new bonds, especially if it was at or near its debt limit. As a result of an enormous increase in bonded debt in the 1920s and a substantial decrease in assessed values in the 1930s, many cities were in that unenviable position. According to a 1941 study, New York was able to stay under its debt limit only by assessing Manhattan real estate on the basis of "fictitious" (that is, highly inflated) values. If the city had assessed property on the basis of earnings, a policy that had recently been adopted in Seattle, its bonded debt would have exceeded its debt limit, and New York would have been "legally bankrupt."[46]

From the perspective of local officials, the wave of decentralization that swept over urban America in the 1930s and 1940s could not have come at a worse time. During the 1920s, a decade of prodigious growth, most cities had not only launched a wide range of very expensive public works, of which New York's new subway system was the most expensive, but also greatly increased the size of their workforce. Municipal debt skyrocketed, and municipal expenditures soared. All this was predicated on what one scholar has called "an ever rising curve of taxable property," a curve based largely on the rising property values and amazing building boom in the central business districts. After the depression struck, assessed values fell, tax delinquencies rose, and, as a result, revenue from property taxes declined. So did other sources of revenue. Most cities tried hard to cut costs (or, as it was then called, "to retrench"). But under enormous pressure to provide emergency assistance to unemployed workers and their families and temporary relief to hard-strapped taxpayers, many cities were hard pressed to pay the interest on their debt. Detroit and a few small cities defaulted. New York City barely avoided bankruptcy. Even after the nation began to recover from the depression, many cities remained stuck in a fiscal bind that some thought would in time lead to widespread "municipal bankruptcy."[47]

Local officials could deal with this crisis in a number of ways, none of which looked too promising. They could try to raise the property tax. But this might provoke a taxpayers' revolt of the sort that had recently prompted several states to pass laws and adopt constitutional amendments that imposed limits on tax rates in the cities. They could also seek additional sources of revenue, notably income taxes and sales taxes. But such taxes normally required permission from the state legislature. And in the unlikely event that the legislature gave its permission, these taxes might drive businesses and residents to the suburbs. Local officials could attempt to cut costs too, mainly by trimming the municipal workforces and cutting wages and benefits—a move that would arouse strong opposition from well-organized public employees. They could also appeal to the state for aid and ask the suburbs to help pay for local airports, convention centers, and other municipal facilities that served the metropolitan area. But thus far neither the states nor the suburbs had shown much sympathy for the cities' fiscal problems.[48] Another strategy was for local officials to work with downtown businessmen and property owners to raise values in the central business district. It was by no means clear that this strategy would work. But it was much less controversial than the others, all of which were adopted to one degree or another. And as far as most local officials were concerned, it was worth trying.

City planners were the other group on whose support the downtown business interests could ordinarily count. This was an unexpected turn of events. Through the 1920s, at which time most city planners were architects, engineers, lawyers, and others with little or no formal education in planning, most had strongly backed decentralization. They had favored the growth of outlying residential sections as a way to reduce congestion in the inner city and solve the many problems attributed to it. They had also favored the growth of outlying business districts as a way to reduce concentration and thus relieve traffic congestion and diffuse property values. And they had favored the growth of a more specialized central business district, one that would be occupied exclusively by department stores and other enterprises that could not do business successfully elsewhere. Most planners had even come to believe, as a small group of their leaders put it in 1927, that "in the public interest, every city must consider a policy for deliberate decentralization." This enthusiasm for decentralization was inspired largely by a vision of a metropolis of garden suburbs, if not garden cities, a metropolis of socially and racially homogeneous communities a short drive from an outlying business district yet still accessible to the central business district.49

A few city planners had voiced doubts about decentralization in the 1920s, but it was not until after 1930 that a large and growing number began to have second thoughts. In the forefront was Harland Bartholomew. A native of New England who had studied civil engineering at Rutgers, Bartholomew made his reputation as a planner in St. Louis, where he joined the staff of the City Plan Commission in the mid 1910s and formed his own consulting firm, Harland Bartholomew and Associates, several years later. As well as running the firm, working for St. Louis, and developing plans for scores of other cities, he served as president of the two leading professional organizations—the American City Planning Institute and the National Conference on City Planning (NCCP). A strong advocate of residential and commercial decentralization in the 1920s, Bartholomew changed his position soon after the depression. Delivering the presidential address at the annual meeting of the NCCP in 1931, he advised his fellow planners "not to be deluded by the false prophets of decentralization," whose "presumed advantages," he argued, were "largely mythical." During the next two decades Bartholomew attacked decentralization in articles for professional journals, plans for American cities, and talks to planners, merchants, and mortgage bankers. He also served as a consultant to ULI, under whose auspices he wrote a pamphlet in 1941 warning that decentralization "has now reached the point where the main central city, at least, is in great jeopardy."50

Among the many other planners who had second thoughts about decentralization were C. A. Dykstra and Gordon Whitnall. An executive at the Los Angeles Department of Water and Power (and professor of municipal administration at UCLA), Dykstra had been a strong supporter of decentralization in the mid 1920s—and a strong opponent of rapid transit for Los Angeles. But by the mid 1930s, by which time he had been named city manager of Cincinnati (and was widely regarded as one of the nation's foremost experts on urban America), Dykstra concluded that decentralization would not solve the nation's urban problems and might even exacerbate them. Whitnall, director of the Los Angeles City Planning Department from 1920 to 1930, when he went into the consulting business, had been the principal spokesman for decentralization in Los Angeles, a powerful advocate of the view that L.A. could avoid the mistakes of New York and other large eastern cities by building horizontally rather than vertically. But by the early 1940s, at which time he was working as a consultant to ULI as well as lecturing on "the disintegration and decentralization of urban communities" for the American Institute of Real Estate Appraisers, Whitnall acknowledged that decentralization was a mixed blessing.[51]

Bartholomew and other planners objected to decentralization on several grounds. Americans were moving from the center to the periphery in record numbers, a move that planners had long hoped for. But few were moving to well-located, well-planned, well-designed, and well-managed communities. These were so rare that Bartholomew called them "small islands in the vast area of urbanization." Most were moving to fringe areas that had little or no subdivision regulation and few if any building codes. They were the blighted areas of the future. Many of these areas also lacked schools, parks, police, and other essential services, the costs of which would in no way be offset by additional property taxes. As Americans moved from the center to the periphery, the planners also pointed out, they left in their wake large vacant areas, as much as 35–40 percent of what had once been the outlying sections of the city (and even more of the close-in suburban areas). Worse still, they left behind the blighted areas surrounding the central business district, old, run-down residential neighborhoods that consumed much more in public services than they produced in property taxes. It was the growth of these blighted areas that drove Dykstra to say in 1934, "We have come to the time when old values are being destroyed faster than new ones are being created.[52]

Decentralization was also doing more damage to the central business district than anticipated, Bartholomew and other planners pointed out. Indeed, down through the 1920s most planners had not worried much about downtown. They had assumed that even if it lost some trade to the outlying business districts it would continue to grow—that its properties would be converted to higher and better uses and that its businesses would absorb the adjacent working-class housing. "Under this beneficent process," wrote Homer Hoyt, "there was a constant expectation that a succession of higher land uses moving from the center in the form of concentric circles would take up any slack and prevent any decay in the urban structure."[53] But as decentralization gathered momentum, the slack was not taken up. Nor was the decay prevented. To the dismay of many planners, it seemed that the central business district was rapidly becoming "just another" business district, as a Los Angeles traffic engineer put it in the early 1940s. America's cities, these planners believed, needed the central business district for many reasons, not least of which was that it was a tremendous source of revenue. Now that the municipal tax structure was reaching "the breaking point," Bartholomew wrote in the early 1940s, the cities needed the central business district more than ever.

A "decentralized city" is "a beautiful ideal," Bartholomew said at the annual meeting of the American Institute of Planners in 1939. But like most ideals, it is "largely if not wholly impractical and unsound." No one had yet figured out how everybody can live "on the edge of the city" or how the city can survive without the central business district. Nor had anyone yet figured out the economic consequences of abandoning the central city and writing off the huge investments there in real estate, buildings, businesses, and infrastructure. If cities continued to decentralize, where would it end, planners wondered. As Whitnall wrote in 1941, some of the problems that had plagued the central business district for decades, including traffic congestion and inadequate parking, were already beginning to plague many of the older outlying business districts, too. In parts of Los Angeles, Henry Babcock, a local engineer, observed in 1937, "each of the *outlying* [business] centers, whether large or small, also had its little ring of blight or potential blight"—an ominous development.[54] Something had to be done to prevent the progressive disintegration of the American metropolis, Bartholomew and his colleagues believed. It was their job to help figure out what to do and how to do it.

At a quick glance, the downtown business interests, local officials, and city planners were a formidable coalition, a strong combination of money, power, and technical expertise that boded well for the efforts to curb decentralization and prop up the central business district. But on a close look, this coalition was much less formidable. There were sharp divisions among the three groups. The downtown businessmen and property owners had one overriding concern—namely, the well-being of the central business district, to which their fortunes were very closely linked. They favored rehabilitation of the blighted areas not so much in the hope that it would improve day-to-day life for their residents as in the hope that it would create an affluent market for downtown goods and services. For local officials, and particularly for big-city mayors, the central business district was only one of many problems—and not necessarily the most pressing—and the downtown business interests only one of many constituencies. Most voters lived in the outlying sections and were extremely sensitive to any sign that the authorities were favoring downtown at the expense of the neighborhoods. For city planners, decentralization was a citywide (or even a metropolitan-wide) problem. In the pamphlet that he wrote for ULI, for example, Bartholomew voiced concern about the impact of decentralization on the nearby suburbs as well as on the central business district. What most concerned him was its impact on the blighted areas in between.[55]

There were also sharp divisions within these groups. The downtown business interests were divided between businessmen, many of whom had the option of moving to the outlying business districts, and property owners, most of whom did not. The businessmen were also divided between department store owners, who catered to a mass market that depended heavily on streetcars, els, and subways, and small, often highly specialized merchants who catered to the carriage trade, which relied largely on private automobiles. As the struggles over height limits revealed, there were sharp divisions among downtown property owners as well. The local officials were divided too. Mayors tended to be highly responsive to the downtown businessmen and property owners, whose taxes provided a major source of the city's revenue (and whose contributions may well have provided a lion's share of their campaign funds). City councillors tended to be more responsive to the residents and businessmen in the outlying sections. Also divided were the city planners, some of whom held that nothing could or should be done to stop decentralization. Among them was Harry D. Freeman of Portland, Oregon, who insisted that "the decentralization of central business districts was inevitable" and that, as far as real estate values and property taxes were concerned, any losses in the center would be offset by gains in the periphery.[56]

Another obstacle facing the downtown business interests and their allies was the strong opposition of other groups. Much of it came from outlying business interests, which felt they were locked in fierce competition with downtown business interests—and believed, as Herbert Klee, president of one of Chicago's outlying businessmen's associations, put it, that "too much time, effort and money are being spent to serve the downtown district." Opposition also came from homeowners, who were generally unwilling to support measures to help the central business district that were likely to raise property taxes. It came from realtors too. From their standpoint, wrote Charles L. Kendrick of Detroit, "it really makes little difference whether all of the business of the city is concentrated in the downtown district or whether it is spread about over 50 or more outlying business centers in addition to the downtown section."[57] As the battles over the efforts to build rapid transit in Chicago revealed, the outlying businessmen and property owners were already a force to be reckoned with in the 1910s and 1920s. As decentralization gathered momentum in the 1930s and 1940s, as more residents and businesses moved from the center to the periphery, these interests grew even more powerful.

Opposition also came from groups with no financial stake in the matter. A good many upper-middle-class intellectuals and professionals held that decentralization had rendered the central business district obsolete. Downtown had outlived its usefulness. So had the big cities of which it was a vital part— the "crowded cities," wrote geographer Ellsworth Huntington, "with [their] towering skyscrapers, mammoth apartment houses, deep tunnels, roaring elevated railways, dusty, smoky air, and hurrying pushing crowds." "There is no valid reason for the concentration of a large portion of the economic functions now focused at the center of urban areas," economist Ernest M. Fisher argued. "They can be as easily and as profitably performed if spread over a wide area as if concentrated at or near the center of the community." E. E. East, chief engineer of the Automobile Club of Southern California, agreed. Taking issue with critics of decentralization, he insisted that it was no longer true that "every city must have one large central business district" or that "a business center must be closely built up to attract business." The transition from a centralized city to a decentralized city would reduce property values in the central business district, conceded Carol Aronovici, a planner and writer. But "the heavier the losses in urban values, the greater the awakening to its [the centralized city's] inefficiency, the sooner will we shift to a form of urban reconstruction that will meet human needs. Let the cities perish so that we may have great and beautiful cities."[58]

Thus even with the support of many local officials and city planners—and even with the backing of organizations like NAREB and ULI—downtown business interests were fighting an uphill battle. Although decentralization was a relatively new development, the forces driving it—the decline of mass transit, the proliferation of private automobiles, and, among others, the standardization of retail trade—were extremely powerful. And to the extent that decentralization was a product of residential dispersal, whose roots were planted in the nineteenth century and well nourished by local, state, and federal policies in the twentieth, it probably could not be slowed down, much less reversed. The timing made a very hard task even harder. During the 1930s the Great Depression brought private construction to a standstill and left many cities in no position to help the downtown business interests. And during the first half of the 1940s World War II precluded most domestic initiatives and spurred a nationwide decentralization of industry and people.

A final point. From the start the downtown business interests took it as given that private enterprise, to which they were strongly committed, could not by itself curb decentralization. And with hindsight, there is no reason to think otherwise. Decentralization was largely, though not exclusively, the result of market forces. It was these forces that drove many retailers and theater owners to move to outlying business districts and prompted many banks and department stores to open branches there. If left unchecked, these forces would no doubt have led to even greater decentralization. Much as it may well have pained the downtown business interests to acknowledge it, the revitalization of the central business district required action by local, state, and even federal authorities. Whether they could prevail on the authorities to act—especially whether they could prevail on them to take the necessary measures to relieve traffic congestion and rehabilitate blighted areas—remained to be seen. It also remained to be seen whether these measures would make much of a difference—whether, in other words, the downtown business interests and their allies knew what they were doing. Lastly, it remained to be seen whether these measures would have unintended consequences, the results of which might be to hasten decentralization and undermine the central business district.

6
Wishful Thinking:

Downtown and the

Automotive Revolution

In May 1941 the newly formed Downtown Committee, an organization of about thirty of downtown Baltimore's largest property owners, sent G. Harvey Porter, director of the committee's Downtown Study, on a trip to find out what other cities were doing about decentralization. Porter visited Oakland, Los Angeles, Kansas City, and St. Louis, "each of which," said the *Baltimore Sun*, "has taken more or less elaborate steps to combat the process." On his return he made several recommendations, most of which were later adopted by the committee. Porter's trip was enlightening. But it was also superfluous. On the basis of studies in other cities and reports by the Urban Land Institute, Porter and his associates had already made up their minds about how to curb (and, if possible, to reverse) decentralization. "The principal objective," Porter said shortly before leaving, "is to get persons in and out of the downtown area as quickly and easily as possible, by whatever means." Once downtown was made more accessible, business would pick up, values would rise, capital would flow in, and decentralization would slow down (or even stop).[1] Underlying this belief was the assumption that people were not going downtown because they were unable to—that, as a leading Los Angeles reformer (and sometime real estate speculator) pointed out when decentralization first appeared there two decades earlier, "They wanted to[,] but they couldn't."

The belief that accessibility was the key to the well-being of downtown had emerged in the second half of the nineteenth century and became part of the conventional wisdom in the first half of the twentieth. But between 1915 and 1925 the meaning of accessibility changed. Before then it had been synonymous with mass transit. For down through the 1910s most people used it to go downtown, the large majority traveling on streetcars (and, in a few cities, els and subways) and a small minority on ferries and commuter trains. The rest came by automobiles, trucks, taxis, bicycles, and horse-drawn vehicles (or on foot). None of these vehicles, not even the automobile, carried nearly as many people as the streetcar. According to early cordon counts, straphangers outnumbered motorists by close to five to one in San Francisco (1912), more than six to one in Denver (1914), and roughly four to one in Chicago (1921)—and almost twice again as much if the els and commuter trains are counted. That an effective system of mass transit was vital to the well-being of a highly compact and extremely concentrated business district was taken for granted before 1920, especially by the downtown businessmen and property owners. Witness their support for the attempts to build subways. Witness too their backing of the street railways in their efforts to drive the jitney out of business. A commercial motor vehicle that was faster than a streetcar and cheaper than a taxi, the jitney "stole" so many riders from the street railways that the railway companies saw them as a threat to their long-term solvency.[2]

Starting around 1920, however, many Americans stopped using mass transit to go downtown—some because they stopped going downtown, opting to patronize outlying business districts instead, and others because they stopped using mass transit. The growth of these business districts took Americans by surprise. So did the decline of the riding habit. According to the conventional wisdom about the relation between transit patronage and population growth, the riding habit should have gone way up in the 1920s, a decade during which big cities grew even bigger. But in every city except New York, where it went up about 15 percent, or around two-thirds as much as the population, the riding habit went down. Between 1920 and 1930 it fell 10 to 20 percent in Boston, Philadelphia, Chicago (the only cities other than New York with a rapid transit system), and San Francisco, whose riding habit was the highest in the country until 1927, when it dropped below New York's. Elsewhere the riding habit fell more sharply—20 to 30 percent in Pittsburgh and Milwaukee, 30 to 40 percent in Baltimore, Cincinnati, and St. Louis, and 40 to 50 percent in Buffalo, Cleveland, and Los Angeles. In general it fell even more sharply in small and medium-sized cities. During the 1930s, a terrible time for the transit industry, the riding habit dropped still further. By the end of the decade it was lower than it had been at any time since the turn of the century. As a result of gas rationing and other fallout from World War II, the transit industry regained some of its riders in the early and mid 1940s. But shortly after the war ended, it resumed its long and irreversible decline.[3]

Of the many Americans who stopped using mass transit but kept going downtown, most traveled by private automobiles (as opposed to taxis or other commercial vehicles). What might be called the driving habit soared in the late 1910s and 1920s, more than doubling in some cities, more than tripling in others. By 1930, 50,000 to 100,000 autos poured into downtown Boston, downtown Philadelphia, and downtown Detroit on a typical weekday. More than 100,000 poured into downtown Chicago, more than 250,000 into downtown Los Angeles. (Autos carried over three-fifths of the daytime population of downtown L.A. in 1931, up from under two-fifths in 1924, a period during which the number of people who went downtown by mass transit declined by nearly one-third.) The driving habit rose more slowly in the 1930s, partly because of the Great Depression and partly because of decentralization. Even so, by early 1941, a few months before Baltimore's Downtown Committee was organized, 30 to 40 percent of those who went downtown traveled by auto in Boston, Philadelphia, and Chicago, 40 to 50 percent in Pittsburgh, Detroit, and San Francisco, and more than 50 percent in St. Louis and Los Angeles. Only in New York did less than 20 percent travel downtown by automobile. A larger proportion, from two-thirds to as high as nine-tenths, drove downtown in small and medium-sized cities. In only four cities other than New York did as many as one-half of downtown's daytime population still ride the streetcars, els, subways, and motorbuses, which had replaced many of the streetcars in the 1920s and 1930s.[4]

To understand why a large and growing number of Americans opted to drive downtown after 1920, it is important to bear in mind that many of them had long been dissatisfied with mass transit. The streetcars were extremely crowded, especially during rush hour, when it was very hard to find a place, much less a seat. They were uncomfortable and unreliable, especially in inclement weather. And once they reached the central business district, they moved "at a snail's pace," wrote the *Los Angeles Times*. The els and subways were faster and more reliable, but more crowded and less comfortable. The service, bad before World War I, deteriorated afterward. In an effort to deal with the fiscal crisis triggered by the phenomenal wartime inflation, the railway companies kept antiquated equipment in service, deferred much-needed repairs and maintenance, and abandoned miles of unprofitable lines. They raised fares too. Exacerbating the industry's problems, driving its revenues down and its expenses up, was the proliferation of private automobiles, the number of which soared from 8,000 in 1900 to 500,000 in 1910, 8 million in 1920, and 23 million in 1930. By then, there was one automobile for every five people—and as many as one for every four in Detroit, the home of the auto industry, more than one for every three in Baltimore, and nearly one for every two in Los Angeles.[5] The bane of the transit industry, the automobile was a boon for many Americans, especially once the automakers began to build better and less expensive cars and the authorities began to construct more and better roads. Despite the traffic jams and parking problems, it was not long before many decided that as a way of getting downtown the automobile was preferable to the streetcar and other forms of mass transit.

This decision had a number of momentous consequences, not least of which was that it changed the meaning of accessibility. By the late 1920s, about the time that many downtown business interests first became concerned about decentralization, accessibility was no longer synonymous with mass transit. Instead, it was synonymous with private as well as public transit, with automobiles as well as streetcars, with highways as well as railbeds. Thus when G. Harvey Porter said in 1941 that it was imperative to get people "in and out of the downtown area as quickly and easily as possible, by whatever means," he meant that the central business district had to be made more accessible to both electric railways and motor vehicles, and above all to private automobiles.[6] The change was reflected not only in what the downtown business interests said, but also in what they did. Starting in the mid and late 1920s, they intensified their efforts to persuade the authorities to take whatever steps were necessary to enable motorists to drive "quickly and easily" to the central business district and to find a place to park when they arrived. During the 1930s and 1940s they also continued their efforts to persuade the authorities to build rapid transit systems, insisting that in view of the heavy traffic in and around the central business district rapid transit was the only viable form of mass transit. By virtue of these efforts, the downtown businessmen and property owners were drawn into several major controversies, the resolutions of which would have a great impact, not only on downtown, but on other parts of the metropolis as well. And the most momentous was over traffic congestion.

Traffic congestion had long been a serious problem in American cities. As early as the 1870s New York's *Real Estate Record and Builders' Guide* wrote that the narrow downtown streets could no longer handle the growing traffic. "The universal cry down town is for 'more elbow room,'" it said.* A product of the tremendous growth of commercial activity, the extreme concentration of the business district, and the growing separation of the business and residential sections, traffic congestion grew much worse in the 1880s and 1890s. And not just in New York. In downtown Boston, *American Architect and Build-*

---

* Broadway was "almost impassable" at some times of the day, wrote one observer in 1870. It reminded him "of the story of the Scottish pedestrian who, when offered a seat in the toiling old 'day-coach,' declined the accommodation on the ground that he was in a hurry and must get on." ("The Future of New York," *Galaxy,* April 1870, page 548.)

ing News observed, the sidewalks were "jammed to suffocation" with pedestrians, while the streets, as narrow and crooked as any in the United States, were packed with streetcars, wagons, carts, and other horse-drawn vehicles. To make things worse, some of the streets were lined on one side by "a long string of [stationary] carriages" and on the other by "a similar string of miscellaneous vehicles, the horses attached to which munch their oats peacefully" while the traffic inches past them. Despite the electrification of the street railways and, in New York, Brooklyn, and Chicago, the construction of the elevated lines, the traffic problem was as serious as ever at the turn of the century. In 1903 *Scientific American* warned that

Traffic congestion on Chicago's State Street, 1880s (Courtesy of the Rotch Library Visual Collections, MIT)

"unless some heroic measures are taken, we are bound to witness within a few years in the busiest hours of the day a positive deadlock [in lower Manhattan]." In 1909, when only one of every two hundred Americans owned an automobile, the *Los Angeles Times* pointed out that traffic congestion downtown "has become so great that the police and the officials of the street railway companies are at their wits' end to find a solution."[7]

Some Americans believed that the automobile (and truck) would help solve the traffic problem by displacing slower and more cumbersome horse-drawn vehicles. One of them was Thomas Edison. If all of New York's horse-drawn vehicles "could be transformed into motor cars overnight," he remarked in 1908, it would "so relieve traffic [congestion] as to make Manhattan Island resemble 'The Deserted Village'." Other Americans were less sanguine. By the late 1910s it was clear they were right. Motorcars did displace most horse-drawn vehicles, but as more people drove, they flooded the downtown streets, especially during rush hour. Visiting Los Angeles in 1919, a Cleveland doctor commented that at six in the evening it seems that "every automobile owner in the city suddenly decides to motor through the business section." With thousands of cars, trucks, streetcars, and the remaining horse-drawn vehicles fighting for space downtown, traffic often slowed down to a crawl—sometimes to a standstill. Traffic congestion in New York "is growing worse every day," the *Real Estate Record and Builders' Guide* said in 1917. It "[has] become well-nigh unbearable" in Atlanta, a special committee of the chamber of commerce reported three years later. In Chicago traffic congestion "is so great that matters have almost reached a deadlock," observed British city planner Raymond Unwin in 1923. In the business district of many American cities, he pointed out, it was no faster to drive than to walk.[8] The result was that by the early 1920s there was a widespread consensus that the traffic problem was in large part the product of the phenomenal proliferation of private automobiles.

Some engineers, city planners, public officials, and street railway executives held that the only way to solve the problem was to ban private automobiles (or at least "pleasure" vehicles) from the central business district. If a ban was imposed, its sponsors pointed out, motorists could drive downtown, park at the fringe, where garages and lots would be located, and take

"Creeping Sickness" (American City, April 1929)

mass transit to the center. At the heart of this position was the belief that automobiles were a very inefficient means of urban transportation—that they took up more space than streetcars and carried fewer passengers. It was impossible to provide enough space downtown to accommodate the growing number of motor vehicles, a New York street railway executive declared in 1926. To open new streets and widen existing ones would only bring more motor vehicles into the business district, which would increase congestion and thereby encourage decentralization. Even if the city did not impose a ban on motorcars, said Boston mayor Malcolm E. Nichols in the mid 1920s, traffic congestion would force many motorists to use mass transit to get downtown. It was highly unlikely that private automobiles would continue to enjoy "unlimited access" to the central business district much longer, he predicted.[9]

But most Americans—most motorists, automakers, traffic experts, and above all most downtown businessmen and property owners—were opposed to a ban on private automobiles downtown. (A ban on "pleasure" vehicles only was impractical, argued one expert, for the simple reason that "no one but the motorist himself could tell whether the trip was for business or pleasure.") These Americans were well aware that the traffic problem was very serious and that the growing number of motorcars was largely responsible for it. By the mid and late 1920s they were also aware that traffic congestion was widely regarded as the main reason for the decentralization of business. But they were convinced, as the Building Owners and Managers Association of St. Louis put it in 1925, that "the so-called pleasure car is a business necessity." It made downtown more accessible, especially for well-to-do motorists, who were highly prized customers and tenants. The private automobile was "here to stay," most Americans assumed. And as the editors of *Engineering Magazine* put it, any attempt to limit its usefulness would be "altogether undesirable, ill-advised, and futile." "Some means simply will have to be found to make room for necessary auto traffic," said W. W. Emmart, a member of the Baltimore City Planning Commission, in 1925. Surely, most Americans believed, the authorities could do something less draconian to unclog "the arteries of the city" than impose a ban on private automobiles in the central business district.[10]

But what could they do? To find the answer, engineers, planners, and other experts made hundreds of studies of traffic congestion in the early twentieth century. Out of these studies, most of which were commissioned by downtown businessmen or, at their behest, by local officials, emerged a diagnosis, according to which traffic jams downtown were largely a product of four things other than the centralization of business and the proliferation of private automobiles. One was that the streets were too few and too narrow—and, in many instances, poorly paved and badly designed. How, asked a New York City architect, could a street system that was developed when two- and three-story buildings were the rule possibly handle the traffic generated by sixteen- and twenty-story buildings? Another was that there were few traffic regulations—and few police officers to enforce them. And "without proper regulation[s]," a street railway executive warned, the motorcars will "congest new arteries as fast as they can be opened." Yet another was what experts viewed as nonessential traffic. Many motorists drive downtown not because they have "a desire to go there," a New Jersey engineer observed, but because they do not know "how to get through the city any other way." "They go through the Triangle," wrote a director of the Pittsburgh Chamber of Commerce, "because there is no other convenient way to [get from one part of the city to another]." The fourth was what planners termed "the promiscuous mixing of different types of traffic." By this they meant that all the surface traffic—rail and motor, commercial and pleasure, local and through—ran on the same streets, one type of vehicle blocking the other and the slowest holding down the speed of the fastest.[11]

From this diagnosis, it followed that the authorities could do several things to relieve traffic congestion short of imposing a ban on private automobiles. Perhaps most important, they could open new streets and widen existing ones. The streets should be widened, declared the Cleveland Building Owners and Managers Association, "wherever possible and as rapidly as finances will permit." Almost as important, the authorities could adopt and enforce tough traffic regulations to maintain a steady flow of vehicles. The authorities could also build crosstown highways (and inner and outer belts) to divert nonessential traffic from the business district. "What a rejuvenation downtown business organizations could experience through the removal of [the estimated] 40 to 50 percent of non-business-producing traffic and its replacement by an equal volume of business producing traffic!" proclaimed Pittsburgh's Better Traffic Committee. Last of all, the authorities could segregate the different types of traffic, forcing them to run along separate streets (or possibly on separate grades)—and perhaps even segregate vehicular and pedestrian traffic. Such a move, it was widely held, would not only relieve traffic congestion but also improve traffic safety—a subject of growing concern during the 1920s.[12]

Many Americans opposed these measures, some because they were skeptical of the diagnosis of the traffic problem and others because they were afraid that the solutions might be worse than the problem. Street opening and widening, they argued, was very disruptive, especially to abutting businesses. It was also very expensive. It was prohibitively so in the central business district—where the streets that had the heaviest traffic also had the most valuable real estate, a point that even some advocates of street improvements conceded. It was self-defeating too, opponents contended. No sooner was a street opened or widened than traffic increased and congestion worsened. In the face of such opposition, some proposals were shelved—among them a plan by New York mayor William J. Gaynor to relieve traffic congestion on Fifth Avenue by opening a new avenue that would run between Fifth and Sixth avenues from Washington Square to Fifty-ninth Street. But with the support of downtown businessmen, outlying real estate interests, motorists' associations, and auto manufacturers and distributors, many other schemes were carried out. At a cost of tens and even hundreds of millions of dollars, most of which came from bond issues, special assessments, and motor vehicle taxes, the authorities opened new streets in one city after another. Often laid out according to comprehensive plans prepared by Miller McClintock, Harland Bartholomew, and other experts, most of them were wide, direct, well designed, and well-paved roads that radiated from the central business district to the outlying residential sections. At the same time the authorities widened existing streets in city after city, sometimes by condemning the abutting property and sometimes by narrowing the adjacent sidewalks. By virtue of these measures, the street systems were able to handle far more motor vehicles in the late 1920s than in the early 1900s.[13]

The early attempts to regulate traffic ran into opposition too. It came from merchants who feared that one-way streets would render their stores less accessible and engineers who believed that traffic signals would slow down traffic. It also came from teamsters, taxi drivers, and ordinary motorists— many of whom, historian Clay McShane has written, regarded traffic regulations as "unwarranted intrusions on personal freedom." As a Baltimore reporter later observed, "It was not always easy to persuade citizens to break the habits of a lifetime and to prevent them from cutting corners, parking at random and driving both ways on a one-way street." But as traffic congestion and traffic safety grew worse, traffic experts, auto industry leaders, and downtown business interests forged a consensus that the authorities had to do something to regulate motor vehicles and their drivers. Beginning in the early twentieth century, they adopted a host of regulations, many of which were designed by William Phelps Eno, a well-to-do New Yorker who spent his life working for effective traffic control. All vehicles had to be registered, all drivers licensed. Drivers also had to stay to the right, signal before turning, abide by posted speed limits, and use lights after dark. To facilitate the flow of traffic, the authorities also created one-way streets, first in Philadelphia (1908) and then in Boston (1909), and installed stop signs, which first appeared in Detroit (1915), and traffic signals, at first manual semaphores with "go" and "stop" signs and later on electric lights with their familiar green, yellow, and red glow. To enforce these regulations, most cities formed a special traffic squad, a branch of the police department, and a special traffic court, which removed routine traffic violations from the criminal justice system.[14] Taken together, these measures revolutionized traffic control in America's cities in a short period and at little cost.

The authorities also took steps to divert nonessential traffic from the central business district. To enable motorists to go from one part of the city to another without going downtown first, they built a few crosstown highways, most of which were laid out according to the traditional gridiron plan. By the late 1920s some cities also began to build an outer-belt (or circumferential) highway system. To encourage motorists to drive around the central business district rather than through it, the authorities built a few inner belts, the best known of which was the quadrangle of streets—Roosevelt Road on the south, Michigan Avenue on the east, Canal Street on the west, and South Water Street on the north—that encircled the Chicago Loop. An integral feature of Daniel H. Burnham's famous plan for Chicago, this inner belt was strongly supported by the Chicago Plan Commission, on which the Loop's interests were well represented. Started in the early 1910s, it was completed in the late 1920s. But these crosstown highways and inner and outer belts made up only a small fraction of the major thoroughfares, most of which still converged on the central business district, funneling in tens of thousands of automobiles en route elsewhere.[15] Why were so few of them constructed before 1930? The answer is that the authorities could not build all the proposed bypasses and radial highways without raising property taxes to unacceptable levels. Given the choice, most downtown businessmen favored radial highways over bypasses. So did the many motorists who worked and shopped downtown. And though many planners and engineers thought bypasses were the most economical way to relieve traffic congestion, they also believed radial highways were necessary to make the central business district "directly accessible" to all the other parts.

The authorities took steps to segregate different types of traffic, too. They eliminated grade crossings, the points at which the railroads and highways intersected and the sites of many of the worst traffic jams and traffic accidents. In Atlanta, for example, they persuaded the voters to approve two bond issues, one in 1921 and the other in 1926, to help pay for three north–south viaducts that carried motor vehicles over the railroad tracks that bisected the central business district. Other cities also built viaducts to separate motor traffic at busy intersections. Following the completion of the Bronx River Parkway in 1923, the authorities also created parkways in a handful of cities and suburbs. Most of them not only excluded cross traffic but also banned commercial vehicles. (After a highly promising start in the late nineteenth century, due in large part to the pioneering efforts of Frederick Law Olmsted, the parkway movement had fallen into disfavor in the early twentieth. And its revival in the late 1920s would be short-lived.) But these measures did little to segregate different types of vehicular traffic, much less to separate vehicular and pedestrian traffic. Most vehicles still ran on the same streets and on the same grade. These efforts were stymied by both financial and political constraints. Building separate street systems would have been prohibitively expensive, especially in or near the central business district. And banning private automobiles from commercial thoroughfares would have been very unpopular—and probably unenforceable. In a country that had already segregated land uses through zoning, and racial and economic groups through deed restrictions, the segregation of traffic may have seemed "inevitable," as the Cleveland Building Owners and Managers Association wrote in 1924.[16] If so, its time had not yet come.

By the late 1920s more automobiles were pouring into the central business district than ever, far more than would have been possible if the authorities had not opened new streets and widened existing ones. And as a result of the new regulations, traffic was more orderly than ever. American motorists are so well disciplined, observed a German visitor, that traffic "regulates itself to a large extent." In New York the policeman does not have "to wave his arms about like a windmill" to direct traffic; "A gesture of the hand and a tweet [of the whistle] are enough." But even though some motorists no longer went downtown to get from one part of the city to another and others no longer went downtown at all, traffic congestion was as bad as ever. "Despite every scheme of traffic control so far devised," midtown Manhattan still "ties itself up in a knot twice a day," wrote the *New Republic* in 1928. Broadway had traffic jams seventy-five years ago. "It has them still." Although Baltimore spent millions of dollars on street widening after the great fire of 1904, traffic conditions downtown were just as bad twenty years later, a special committee informed the mayor. Despite the efforts of Harland Bartholomew, chief planner for St. Louis, traffic downtown "moves slowly and irregularly," wrote the president of the St. Louis street railway system in 1926. "Conditions are bad in the middle of the day, and in the morning rush, but are well nigh intolerable in the evening rush." Conditions were very bad in downtown Los Angeles too, the city's traffic commission acknowledged in 1930, a decade after it had been formed by downtown business interests and civic and commercial groups to solve the city's traffic problem.[17]

Despite a good deal of evidence to the contrary, some Americans remained convinced that the cities could solve the traffic problem by building more and wider streets and imposing more and tougher regulations. But others were beginning to have second thoughts. As they saw it, the cities were caught in "a vicious circle." To relieve traffic congestion, the authorities opened and widened streets; but the new streets attracted more traffic, the additional traffic generated more congestion, and eventually every street system reached what a Minneapolis engineer called "a saturation point," a state of "almost but not quite intolerable congestion," to quote Frederick Law Olmsted, Jr., and two of his associates. Another planner, George A. Damon of Los Angeles, went even further. "Every possible cure [for the traffic problem] seems to be worse than the original disease," he wrote. From this pessimistic prognosis, Americans drew one of two very different conclusions. The first was that the traffic problem could be solved only if the cities reduced the number of motor vehicles that entered the central business district. Banning autos downtown would help. So would imposing height limits, improving mass transit, and encouraging decentralization. The second conclusion, the one favored by most downtown businessmen and property owners, was that the problem could be solved only if the cities took what William J. Wilgus, a New York engineer, called "radical measures" to facilitate the flow of traffic—more expensive, more disruptive, and more far-reaching measures than any taken thus far.[18]

That "radical measures" were needed to solve the traffic problem was not a new idea. It had been around as early as the late 1860s, when New York built a short-lived pedestrian overpass across Broadway, the most congested street in the city. During the next three or four decades Americans came up with a host of other ingenious schemes. Elevated sidewalks were one. A combined sidewalk and overpass, they were designed to expedite vehicular traffic by removing pedestrians from the streets. Pedestrian "walks," bridges that ran over the streets from rooftop to rooftop, were another. Although this scheme "is hardly practicable yet," New York's *Real Estate Record and Builders' Guide* wrote in 1882, "it may be worth thinking about seriously a few years from now."* Even more important were a couple of other schemes, both of which were inspired by the plans to build rapid transit lines. One called for subsurface streets, which would carry commercial traffic. The other called for double-decked streets. Speaking of one such scheme to extend the floor system of the elevated railways to the building lines and then create a roadway and sidewalk on each side of the tracks, *Scientific American* wrote in 1903 that it "may sound radical, and even chimerical; but not so much so, surely, as did the first

---

* A closely related scheme was the street-level arcade built inside the property line. Designed to replace the existing sidewalk, which would be incorporated into the street system, it was viewed as a relatively inexpensive means of street widening, the cost of which was soaring in the later nineteenth and early twentieth centuries.

suggestion to build an underground city railroad."[19] (It is perhaps worth noting that these schemes—and others even more outlandish, like rooftop landing fields for dirigibles—were staples of the futuristic visions of the late nineteenth and early twentieth centuries.)

These schemes were "chimerical"—so much so that none of them made it off the drawing boards. But they were not frivolous. For if nothing else they at least tried to come to grips with the fact that most of the worst traffic jams occurred at the busiest intersections, almost all of which were located in or near the central business district. The points at which thousands of automobiles, streetcars, and pedestrians crossed, these intersections generated the excessive friction that prevented "a continuous flow [of traffic]," wrote *Cassier's Magazine* in 1907. During the next two decades many traffic experts came to believe that the intersections, especially the downtown intersections, were a major cause of traffic congestion and a major reason the efforts to solve the traffic problem had thus far been ineffective. Wide streets were a good idea. But no matter how wide the streets, they still had to cross other streets. At these points motorists had to slow down, stop, wait for the signals to change (and often for other drivers to turn and for pedestrians to cross), and then start up again—only to repeat the process a few blocks later. According to experts, the intersections reduced the capacity of even the widest streets by more than half. Traffic regulations were a good idea, too. But no matter how tough the regulations, motorists still had to stand in long lines at the intersections, especially during rush hour. In some cases, Raymond Unwin observed, the lines were so long that the cars "may have to wait through two, or even three, halts before their turn comes to cross one of the streets."[20]

There were several things that could be done to alleviate the problem, according to traffic experts. Most of them fell into one of two categories. In the first were measures to reduce the congestion produced by cross traffic when it ran into through streets. Among the most important were measures giving through traffic right of way over cross traffic; erecting stop signs on cross streets, especially at busy intersections; and programming traffic signals in ways that would give through traffic precedence over cross traffic. (One method would give through traffic a longer green light than cross traffic; another, the "synchronized" system, would allow through traffic to go for a fixed period before it was forced to stop for cross traffic; and yet another, the "progressive" system, would enable through traffic to move more or less continuously at a moderate speed.) In the second category were measures to reduce the congestion produced by through traffic when it turned onto cross streets. Among the most important were measures allowing right turns from the right lane only and setting back the building line far enough to create a lane in which drivers could wait to turn without blocking traffic. A much tougher measure, one in place in Los Angeles by the mid 1920s, banned left turns in the central business district. Yet another measure regulated the movement of pedestrians, requiring them to obey traffic signals, to wait on the sidewalk for the light to change, and to stop "jaywalking," the practice of crossing streets in places other than intersections and crossing intersections at other than right angles.[21] Many of these measures were adopted to one degree or another in most cities.

But to solve the problem, traffic experts concluded, some of them reluctantly, there was only one thing that could be done. And that was to apply the principles of rapid transit to vehicular traffic—to separate through traffic and cross traffic and, less important, to separate vehicular traffic and pedestrian traffic. To this end engineers and planners devised a host of "radical," sometimes quite ingenious, schemes after 1900. To separate through traffic from cross traffic, they recommended the building of viaducts, one of the best known of which was Kansas City's Twelfth Street Trafficway. A device that was often used at railroad grade crossings, the viaduct was considered especially appropriate where the topography created a natural grade separation. A similar scheme was the overpass (or underpass), which was designed as a way to keep traffic apart at busy downtown intersections. To separate vehicular traffic from pedestrian traffic, the experts proposed elevating and double-decking the sidewalks, raising them to the second floor of abutting buildings, and linking them to pedestrian overpasses at the intersections. To lessen the inconvenience to pedestrians, who would have to climb a long flight of stairs, sidewalks and abutting buildings could be designed to provide direct access to stores and offices at the second floor.[22]

Much more radical were the schemes calling for elevated highways, also known as double-decked streets, and superhighways, also known as expressways (and later as freeways). A steel or reinforced concrete structure, the elevated highway was a multilane artery that ran above the surface streets, to which it was connected by ramps spaced a half mile or more apart. It was designed to handle vehicular traffic only and expected to attract mostly through traffic. Free of streetcars, pedestrians, and cross traffic, the elevated highway was capable of carrying far more vehicles than even the widest surface streets—and carrying them at a much higher speed. According to the Merchants' Association of New York, a group of downtown businessmen, it was the most effective way to relieve traffic congestion in the city and enhance access to the business district. A visionary notion at the turn of the century, it was an idea whose time had come by the 1920s. Early in the decade, at which time some New Yorkers were talking about building an elevated highway along the Hudson River, Charles W. Leavitt, a civil engineer, proposed the construction of more than half a dozen elevated highways running between and parallel to most of Manhattan's north–south arteries. Later in the decade, by which time Chicago had just finished Wacker Drive, its first elevated highway, the city council began hearings on a proposal to double deck at least three major streets that radiated from the Loop. Before the decade was over, similar proposals had been made in Boston, St. Louis, and Detroit, where elevated highways were suggested as an alternative to the rapid transit commission's ill-fated subway.[23]

A superhighway could be an elevated highway—and vice versa. But it need not: it could also be a surface artery. If so, it had two features that set it apart. First, a superhighway was very wide, in some cases two hundred feet, wider by far than the widest surface streets. (It was not, however, as wide as the widest parkways; nor did it ban commercial traffic, as parkways did.) Second, a superhighway was free of grade crossings, which was not true of New York's Grand Concourse and Philadelphia's Roosevelt Boulevard, two of the widest streets in the country. Cross traffic ran over or under it. As a result, a superhighway was capable of handling a huge amount of vehicular traffic—about three and a half times as much as an ordinary street of the same width, according to one estimate, and seven to ten times as much as New York's Fifth Avenue and Detroit's Woodward Avenue. The traffic would also flow "continuously," as fast as the law permitted. Thanks in large part to the work of Detroit Rapid Transit Commission (and its chairman, Sidney D. Waldon), the superhighway struck many Americans as another idea whose time had come by the 1920s. At the same time that the commission started its campaign for a rapid transit system, it proposed the construction of twenty superhighways, most of them radiating more or less from the city limits to the outlying residential districts in Wayne, Oakland, and McComb counties. Many of the proposed superhighways were two hundred feet wide—with lanes for through traffic, local traffic, and even rapid transit lines. By the end of the decade superhighways were under consideration in other cities too, among them Chicago, which was looking into a system of elevated roads running from the periphery to the inner quadrangle surrounding the Loop.[24]

More radical still were the schemes calling for multilevel streets—two-, three-, five- and even six-level streets. Once a vision of novelists and other allegedly impractical types, the multilevel street was now viewed as a natural development, as natural as the multistory building. Plans for such streets were drawn by many prominent figures, including Harvey Wiley Corbett, the architect and defender of the skyscraper, Henry Harrison Suplee, an engineer and co-editor of the *Engineering Index,* and Dr. John A. Harriss, former special deputy police commissioner for traffic in New York City. It was Harriss who in 1927 designed a six-level street to solve Manhattan's traffic problem for the next hundred years. Local or mixed traffic would run on the bottom level, motor trucks on the next, one-way buses on the third and fourth levels, passenger cars on the fifth, and high-speed automobiles on the top level. Motorists would move from one level to another on ramps, pedestrians on moving stairways. Harriss's plan may well have been impractical. But it was no more far-fetched than Angus Hibbard's proposal to fill in the Chicago River and convert it to a highway; architect Ernest Flagg's proposal to sell off much of Central Park and, with the proceeds, buy the land between Sixth and Seventh avenues from Lower Manhattan to the Harlem River and turn it into a parkway; and New York City police commissioner Richard E. Enright's proposal to build elevated highways through existing buildings in the middle of blocks, a sort of second-story tunnel, wide enough for express and local traffic, both of which would run on ramps to the streets below.[25]

By 1930 only a handful of "radical measures" had been adopted. And apart from a few of the more notable viaducts and overpasses, only three of them, Chicago's Wacker Drive, New York's West Side Elevated Highway, and Detroit's superhighways, had much of an impact on the flow of vehicular traffic. Named for Charles H. Wacker, first chairman of the Chicago Plan Commission, Wacker Drive, formerly South Water Street, was a one-mile double-decked street, part of the inner quadrangle that surrounded the Loop. The upper level, 110 feet wide, was for general traffic, the lower level, 135 feet wide, for heavy commercial traffic. Supported by Loop business interests and financed by general obligation bonds, it was started in 1919 and finished seven years later. The West Side Elevated Highway—brainchild of Julius Miller, borough president of Manhattan—was a 65-foot-wide expressway that ran from Canal Street in lower Manhattan to Riverside Drive, four miles north. Seven ramps, located about half a mile apart, linked the highway to the streets below. Backed by the Broadway Association and other downtown businessmen's organizations, it was authorized by the state legislature in 1926; financed largely by special assessments on abutting property, it was completed in the early 1930s. The Detroit superhighways, designed by the rapid transit commission in 1924, ran into little opposition—much less than the commission's proposed subway system. The city council approved the master plan early in 1925, and voters endorsed the financial plan later in the year. After the state

*"Double-Deck Streets—A Relief for Traffic Congestion" (*Scientific American, *June 22, 1907)*

legislature passed an enabling act, Wayne, McComb, and Oakland counties gave their approval, too. By the end of the decade the city and the county superhighway commissions had purchased over one-third of the necessary rights-of-way.[26]

There were several reasons so few radical measures were adopted before 1930. Many Americans, downtown businessmen and property owners among them, believed they were too expensive. According to one estimate, a

"A Five-Storied Street" (Cassier's Monthly, *June 1913)*

single overpass cost roughly $130,000, a single underpass more than twice as much, and an elevated highway about $1.7 million a mile. The West Side Elevated Highway cost much more. So did Wacker Drive. One engineer estimated that Charles W. Leavitt's elevated highway plan for Manhattan would cost $1.4 to $1.8 billion, a huge sum even for the country's wealthiest city. Superhighways were very expensive, too, especially in and near the central business district. And multilevel streets were so costly, wrote three planners, that "no solution can be found in this direction." Separating through traffic and cross traffic is the most effective way to increase street capacity, noted Daniel L. Turner and John P. Hallihan, the Detroit Rapid Transit Commission's principal advisers, "but it is a costly procedure and should only be resorted to when other means are exhausted." The editors of *American City* took the same position. Such "surgical remedies" as double-decked streets were so expensive that they should be employed "only when surgery is the only remedy for strangulation, and with due precaution lest the operation send the patient from the hospital to the poorhouse." Nor was it clear where the money would come from. Special as-

New York's West Side Elevated Highway (New York City Bureau of Borough Works, reproduced in Norman Bel Geddes, Magic Motorways, *New York, 1940)*

sessments were one source. But most property owners were aware that elevated highways and superhighways would probably not raise property values. Traffic generated business only if it stopped, and these highways were designed to keep it moving. Property taxes were the other source. But many taxpayers, some of the largest of whom were downtown businessmen, objected to tax hikes even more than to traffic jams—and believed there were other, less expensive ways to solve the traffic problem than by building elevated highways and superhighways.[27]

Many Americans also believed that radical measures were futile. Even if the money could be found, they pointed out, elevated highways and superhighways would generate even more traffic; and as one group of planners wrote, "the new thoroughfares thus created would soon be crowded to capacity." Given that traffic increased at a faster rate than population—twice as fast, according to some, and even faster, according to others—there was no way cities could provide enough space for all the motorcars. As a New York street railway executive put it, "the supply of street space will never catch up with the demand." To the extent that the elevated highways and superhighways converged on the central business district, where the thoroughfares were "already overtaxed," they would make matters even worse. "While ways in are multiplied the capacity at the center remains constant," said a Philadelphia planning engineer, who argued that elevated highways and superhighways would have the same baneful impact on the central business district as subways. They would promote excessive centralization and intolerable congestion. If most Americans drove downtown, the results would be catastrophic, wrote one transit engineer. So much of the central business district would have to be devoted to highways that in time there would be nothing left but skyscrapers and parking lots. To many Americans it was clear that the solution to the traffic problem lay not, as a Los Angeles planner put it, in piling streets "on

Proposed Detroit superhighway (Detroit Rapid Transit Commission, Proposed Superhighway Plan for Greater Detroit, *Detroit, 1924)*

top of one another," but in reducing the demand for space (and in using the existing space as efficiently as possible).[28]

Many Americans felt that radical measures were unnecessary, too. The traffic problem, they believed, would solve itself. The cities were approaching what was known as the "saturation point," the point at which it would take so long and cost so much to drive downtown that many motorists would leave their cars at home and use mass transit instead. The "saturation point" had almost been reached in Los Angeles, wrote three engineers in 1926:

> With the [traffic] congestion in the inner city steadily increasing; with police regulations affecting the automobile growing stricter; with free parking space in city streets becoming more and more restricted; with the danger and the inconvenience of driving in and out of, or through[,] the congested district during almost any hour of the business day becoming greater, a steadily increasing number of automobile users [have] returned to the use of the street car as the better means of getting in and out of the business district and to and from their homes.[29]

If cities would soon reach the saturation point, it made little sense to spend huge sums on elevated highways, superhighways, and multilevel streets. Some took this position a step further. Pointing out that the streetcar was a much more efficient means of transportation than the automobile, that one lane of streetcars could carry more than three times as many people as three lanes of automobiles (and one lane of subways or els nearly fifteen times as many), they argued that the cities would be better advised to improve mass transit systems than to build limited-access highways.

As many Americans saw it, the traffic problem was a function of the centralization of business—of, in other words, a highly compact and extremely concentrated central business district. Too many people poured in and out of too small a space; and too many of them came and left at the same time. Elevated highways and superhighways would do nothing to solve this problem—and might even exacerbate it. Rather than build highways to funnel more people into the same cramped space, the cities should impose height limits and take other steps to enlarge the central business district. If they did, they would have no need for multilevel streets and elevated sidewalks, wrote Harland Bartholomew in 1920. Besides enlarging the business district, the cities should also encourage the decentralization of industry and the growth of outlying business districts. If most people no longer had to make the long trip downtown, there would be no need for superhighways and elevated highways. According to McClintock and others, it would also help if the cities took steps to reduce traffic during daytime, especially during rush hour. They should urge, perhaps even require, truckers to deliver merchandise and collect trash at night. And they should encourage stores to stagger their business hours, to open and close a little later than offices.[30]

The downtown business interests had long been concerned about the traffic problem (and, through groups like the Chicago Association of Commerce and Los Angeles Traffic Commission, had made efforts to solve it). But their concern grew much stronger in the late 1920s and stronger still in the 1930s and 1940s. Fueling the growing concern was the decentralization of business. Most downtown businessmen and property owners had long assumed that unimpaired access was the key to the well-being of the central business district. They had also come to believe that the chronic traffic jams were spurring the growth of the outlying business districts. McClintock and others had warned that unless the cities took steps to relieve traffic congestion, decentralization would accelerate, leading to a decline in downtown business activity and a fall in downtown property values. By the mid 1930s this warning was hard to ignore. Also hard to ignore was the advice that the cities would have to adjust to what the Milwaukee Board of Public Land Commissioners called the "Automotive Revolution" in order to curb decentralization.[31] At stake was nothing less than the survival of the central business district.

But as the downtown business interests were well aware, the conventional remedies had not worked. The cities had opened many streets and widened others. But the costs were staggering—roughly a million dollars a mile in medium-sized cities and more in big cities, especially in and near the central business district, where real estate values made street widening "practically impossible," wrote one city planner. ("Most cities could soon exhaust their bonding power paying for street opening and widening projects," Bartholomew noted in 1929.) And no sooner was a street widened than it was filled to capacity, Los Angeles city engineer Lloyd Aldrich told a congressional committee in 1944. "There is absolutely no relief whatever." The cities had also imposed many traffic regulations. "We have been regulating traffic for nearly twenty years," wrote Commissioner Enright in 1923. "Year after year we have drawn up additional and more elaborate regulations." "Indeed," he added, "there is hardly anything along the line of traffic regulations that we have not adopted." Yet traffic was as congested as ever. Regulations were not the answer, he argued. Aldrich agreed. Traffic signals, he testified, do not move traffic. Others held that they benefited no one but their manufacturers.[32] If wider streets and tougher regulations were not the answer, neither, it seemed, were crosstown highways, inner and outer belts, and other conventional remedies.

Hence many downtown businessmen and property owners concluded that it would take drastic measures to relieve traffic congestion. Other groups reached the same conclusion. By far the most important were the country's automakers (and their trade associations), which had gradually come to believe that the demand for automobiles was limited less by the purchasing power of consumers than by the capacity of the streets. They feared that if traffic got much worse, Americans would stop buying cars. Closely allied with the automakers were their distributors and suppliers, the steel and rubber manufacturers among them; the petroleum industry; the local, state, and national motorists' associations; the contractors who built the roads and the unions that represented their employees. They formed the core of the formidable highway lobby. Also in favor of taking more drastic measures to solve the traffic problem were planners and engineers, who designed highways (and often made the studies that justified them); mayors and other local officials, who supported highways, especially if the state or federal government paid for them, as a way to revitalize downtown; and national officials, who viewed highway building as a way to create jobs during the Great Depression and to help stabilize the economy after World War II.[33]

By the 1930s, moreover, there was growing support for the view that drastic measures were needed to relieve traffic congestion. True, they were very expensive. But street widening, the principal alternative, was very expensive too, perhaps even more so in and near the central business district. And according to experts, the costs of even the most expensive highways were dwarfed by the costs of traffic congestion, traffic accidents, and premature decentralization. Drastic measures might not eliminate traffic congestion. Probably nothing would. Still, if such measures facilitated the flow of traffic and enhanced the accessibility of the central business district, they would be worthwhile. By the late 1920s and early 1930s, by which time many cities should have reached the saturation point, it was evident that the traffic problem was not solving itself. Driving downtown was becoming more time-consuming and costly. But instead of riding streetcars to the central business district, many Americans were driving to the outlying business districts. Rather than stop driving, they stopped going downtown.[34]

In response to mounting pressure for drastic measures, the cities commissioned a slew of studies in the 1930s. In some cases the downtown business interests paid (or helped pay) for them. A good example is Los Angeles, where the Central Business District Association persuaded the U.S. Works Progress

Administration (WPA), a New Deal agency set up in 1935, to give the city $90,000 for a traffic study. When the L.A. city council refused to contribute the required $20,000 in matching funds, downtown businessmen, led by the president of Bullock's Department Store, raised the money. Done in the late 1930s by an ad hoc group headed by city engineer Aldrich, the study laid out the framework for the Los Angeles freeway system. Many of these studies were done by the Bureau for Street Traffic Research, which was directed by McClintock, the country's foremost authority in traffic control. With money from Studebaker, a leading automaker, the bureau started out at UCLA in 1925, moved to Harvard, where it was named after Albert Russel Erskine, president of Studebaker, a year later, and left for Yale in 1938. Among the bureau's most influential studies was the one done for the Chicago city council in the early 1930s, in which McClintock proposed a set of what he called limited ways for greater Chicago.[35]

Most of the studies came to the same conclusion. The way to solve the traffic problem was to build a new type of highway, a highway known as a freeway, a term coined by Edward M. Bassett, a leader of the zoning movement, and also as a limited way, expressway, and motorway. An offshoot of the superhighway, the freeway was a very wide roadway, with three or four lanes of traffic running in each direction and often a median or barrier separating them. It could be elevated, depressed, or on the surface. But in any case it was free of traffic lights and cross traffic, which ran above or below it; and it was linked to the ordinary streets by ramps—and sometimes by elaborate cloverleafs. An offshoot of the parkway, too, the freeway was a limited-access roadway that allowed motorists to enter and exit only at specific points and denied access even to abutters, a right they had long enjoyed under common law. By limiting access, the freeway's designers hoped to prevent gas stations, foodstands, and the like from springing up along the roadway—the so-called ribbon development that exacerbated the problems of traffic congestion and traffic safety. Freeways, McClintock and others believed, would eliminate the friction that generated traffic jams and traffic accidents, especially at the intersections, in the middle, and along the edges of the roadways. They would ensure "a free flow of vehicular traffic," wrote Bassett. And they would "make automobile collisions impossible," said Norman Bel Geddes, an industrial designer who did much to popularize the idea of an interstate highway system. Implicit in the concept of the freeway was the novel idea, as a Chicago real estate broker put it in 1940, that "there should be no more reason for a motorist who is passing through a city to slow down than there is for an airplane which is passing over it."[36]

According to experts, the freeways should be built from the outlying residential sections "directly to the heart of the community," "as near the [central business] district as may be possible," wrote McClintock. Here was a revolutionary idea. Hitherto experts had believed it was too expensive and too disruptive to run highways through the central business district. Few would have imagined extending them beyond an inner loop. After 1930, however, they grew increasingly concerned about the accessibility of the central business district. What good would it do, experts asked, to provide motorists with high-speed freeways that stopped short of the central business district and left them stuck in "a traffic jam which takes up much of the time saved en route?" "The day has gone," declared a spokesman for the American Association of State Highway Officials in 1944, when it was enough to build "broad highways up to the city gates"—and end them there. Geddes disagreed. "A great motorway has no business cutting a wide swath right through a town or city," he said. So did Joseph Barnett, chief of the urban roads division of the U.S. Public Roads Administration. "To dump [the freeway] traffic on to downtown surface streets already overcrowded," he wrote, "would defeat a prime purpose of free-flowing facilities—the relief of traffic congestion in the area of greatest congestion."[37] But Geddes and Barnett were in a minority, at odds not only with most traffic experts but also with most downtown businessmen and most local, state, and federal officials.

The freeways, the experts claimed, would stimulate residential dispersal, allowing even Americans of modest means to live in the suburbs. But they would also encourage the centralization of business. By providing uninterrupted movement from the periphery to the center, by relieving traffic congestion and thereby enhancing downtown's accessibility, they would anchor the central business district. Or as Fred Grumm, a California highway engineer, said in 1944, the freeways would enable the cities "to remedy, or possibly to halt, the decentralization [of business] and the deterioration of [downtown] property values." Most downtown businessmen and property owners agreed. Thus far the automobile had fostered decentralization, wrote Joseph Laronge, a Cleveland real estate broker, in 1938. But it could foster centralization too—especially, wrote the Cleveland Regional Plan Commission, if downtown was the hub of the freeway system. It could stimulate downtown business activities and stabilize downtown property values. Were the downtown businessmen and property owners indulging in wishful thinking? A. E. Nemetz, general manager of the Building Owners and Managers Association of Los Angeles, thought not. Writing in 1940 about a proposed freeway system that made provision for rapid transit bus lines, he said: "It is not wishful thinking to assume that [this] system will go a long way in solving the traffic problems and consequently make the trip to downtown Los Angeles pleasant for customers and productive for downtown merchants and office tenants alike, and thereby recentralize businesses and offices in a compact area that will at once prove desirable and profitable."[38]

Some Americans, the most conspicuous of whom were planners, engineers, and spokesmen for the transit industry, had strong reservations about freeways. They were prohibitively expensive, wrote John A. Miller, editor of *Transit Journal*, in 1941. To handle the traffic in, say, Houston, Kansas City, or Indianapolis, each of which had about 400,000 people, would require at least twenty four-lane freeways, he estimated. Making the conservative assumptions that each freeway would be ten miles long and could be built for roughly $3 million a mile, he calculated that the system would cost $600 million. This came to $1,500 a person, or more than the per capita value of all the real estate in each of the cities. Where would cities find the money, skeptics asked? And suppose they found it. What would happen, a St. Paul planner wondered, to the thousands of residents who lived in the path of the freeways, most of which would be two or three hundred feet wide? They would have to leave their homes and neighborhoods. Thousands of other residents would be forced to live next to what one journalist called a "roaring river of steel and rubber," a "river" that would leave miles of blighted property in its path in the outlying residential districts. Freeways would have a baneful impact on the central business district as well, critics argued. They might make it easier for motorists to drive downtown. But if it is made easier and easier, a Maryland civil engineer pointed out, "eventually the central zones will be so filled with automobiles there will be no room left for people—or for business."[39]

Some critics raised other, more pointed objections. Freeways, they argued, would not solve the traffic problem. They would "only perpetuate it." The problem, one critic explained, was that "there are always more cars waiting to fill the newly available space than it will hold," a point that had been made earlier by opponents of street-widening projects. Hence the freeways will be "loaded beyond capacity almost as quickly as they are completed," said Charles Gordon, managing director of the American Transit Association, the industry's leading trade organization. Freeways would also undermine mass transit, which, in the view of many critics, was the only permanent solution to the traffic problem. Nor would freeways slow down decentralization, critics argued. They might make the drive downtown "a few minutes faster," one engineer conceded. But by rendering outlying residential districts more accessible (and inner-city residential districts less livable), they would foster decentralization. Too much was made of the freeway's ability to move people from the periphery to the center, remarked Walter H. Blucher, executive director of the American Society of Planning Officials. "If you say that it is easy for people to get into the city [on freeways]," he told the Institute of Traffic Engineers in 1943, "I say it is just as easy for them to move out. If you make it too easy for them to drive in they certainly will move out." And if they move out, they might not drive in at all.[40]

The highway lobby was not swayed by these arguments. Neither were the nation's motorists, most of whom were enthralled by the vision that one day they would be able to drive from their homes to their offices and stores along high-speed highways free of congestion. The downtown business interests were not swayed by these arguments either. Indeed, by the late 1930s and early 1940s they were prepared to go to almost any lengths to curb decentralization, even if it meant supporting schemes to run massive freeways through residential neighborhoods. With so strong a consensus, one city after another hired Miller McClintock and other experts to design freeways and freeway plans, the most extensive of which called for hundreds of miles of highways costing hundreds of millions of dollars. Most of the proposed freeways ran on the surface, but some went above or below ground. In deference to the wishes of the downtown business interests, most of them converged on the central business district; they were designed, one expert said, to carry traffic "to, or through, the heart of the city." One example was Boston's Central Artery. An elevated highway that was supposed to curb decentralization in the Hub, it was built through downtown Boston in the 1950s. Another example was a set of elevated highways proposed by Robert Moses, the czar of highway planning in New York City, but never built. In line with his new view that such highways should be built "right through town," Moses planned an Upper Manhattan Expressway that would cross the island at about 125th Street, connecting the Triborough Bridge with a new Hudson River bridge; a Lower Manhattan Expressway that would link the Holland Tunnel with the Manhattan and Williamsburg bridges; and, by far the most spectacular, a Mid Manhattan Expressway that would run, in Robert A. Caro's words, "through a forest of skyscrapers" from the Queens–Midtown Tunnel to the Lincoln Tunnel.[41]

A few freeways were built in the late 1930s and early 1940s. And several others were started shortly after World War II. But by the late 1940s most of the freeways, including a good many that had already been approved by the local authorities, were still on the drawing boards. The problem was that urban freeways were extremely expensive. The cities did not have the money. Nor could they raise it. They could not increase property taxes without run-

ning the risks of triggering a taxpayers' revolt and driving residents and businesses to the suburbs (or even to other cities). Nor could they impose special
assessments, the traditional way of paying for minor street improvements.
The costs to abutting property owners would have been too high and the benefits, if any, too low. By the late 1940s, however, the solution was on the hori-
zon. Under pressure from the highway lobby, city officials, and downtown
business interests, both the states and the federal government reluctantly
abandoned their long-held position that urban highways were a local responsibility. The states began to designate urban freeways as state highways and to
earmark funds, mostly from gasoline taxes, to build them. The federal government, which had long provided funds for rural roads, started to subsidize
urban highways, first as part of the New Deal programs and later as part of the
national defense efforts. And Congress was holding hearings on legislation
that would eventually lead to the creation of the National Interstate and Defense Highway System, which would include most of the nation's as yet un-
built urban freeways.[42]

Aside from the multilevel interchanges, of which the four-level inter-
change at the intersection of the Hollywood and Arroyo Seco freeways at the
edge of downtown Los Angeles was probably the most spectacular, the most
striking features of the freeway systems were the elevated highways. There
had been much talk about double-decked streets and elevated highways in the
early twentieth century. But little had come of it until the early 1930s, when
McClintock, Moses, and other experts, inspired in part by the initial success of
Chicago's Wacker Drive and New York City's West Side Elevated Highway,
recommended the construction of elevated highways in many big cities. By
the late 1930s at least one thousand miles of them were on the drawing
boards. Not all were built. In the face of vigorous opposition, New York City
officials eventually shelved Moses' proposed cross-Manhattan expressways.
After much discussion, Detroit officials decided that the downtown segment
of the John C. Lodge Expressway, which was named after the former mayor
who had supported the ill-fated subway plan in the late 1920s, should not run
above ground, as originally designed, but below. But with New York in the lead
and other cities not far behind, the authorities erected many of these huge
concrete structures, most of them a hundred feet wide (and even wider), high
above the surface streets, along riverfronts (and lakefronts), through outlying
residential communities, and even in the central business district.[43] A few
went up in the 1930s, even more in the 1940s, and more still in the 1950s, including two of the most notorious—Oakland's Chester W. Nimitz Freeway,

which was destroyed by an earthquake in 1989, and Boston's Central Artery, which, thanks to the largesse of the federal government, is now being demolished and rebuilt underground.

In view of the longstanding and deep-seated opposition to elevated railways, the construction of elevated highways is more than a little puzzling. This opposition had grown so vociferous that by the 1920s most Americans had come to believe that elevated railways should never have been built in the first place. Despite assurances by several leading engineers that it was possible to build els that were quiet, clean, and attractive (and would not reduce property values), they remained convinced that under no circumstances should any more be constructed.[44]

The cities should not only stop building elevated railways, many Americans insisted; they should start demolishing them. This idea, which had surfaced in the first two decades of the century, caught on in the 1920s, especially in New York and Boston. In favor of it were abutting businessmen and property owners, who believed that the removal of the els would improve trade and raise values. Allied with them were public officials (among them Julius Miller, borough president of Manhattan and chief advocate of the West Side Elevated Highway), who thought the demolition of the els would foster economic development; traffic experts (including New York City Police Commissioner Enright, another advocate of elevated highways), who assumed that the removal of the elevated structures would facilitate the flow of vehicular traffic; and others who felt that the els were unsightly, unnerving, and anachronistic, a once valuable form of urban transportation that had long outlived its usefulness. By the mid and late 1920s—or even earlier, according to the *New York Times*— most Americans were convinced that it was only a matter of time before the elevated railways were removed from the city streets. Noting that the Sixth Avenue el "ought to have been taken down years ago," New York mayor John F. Hylan predicted in 1924 that there would soon be no elevated structures left in Manhattan. Two years later the Massachusetts Division of Metropolitan Planning reported that popular sentiment would eventually force the demolition of at least some of Boston's elevated railways. The els "are doomed," wrote architect Ernest Flagg in 1927, "and the sooner they go the better."[45]

And they went, though not as soon as expected. At the behest of the Forty-second Street Property Owners and Merchants Association and other midtown business interests, the New York state legislature approved the demolition of a short elevated line on East Forty-second Street in 1923. Two other spur lines were torn down later, one in 1924 and the other in 1930. During the late 1930s New York City also demolished the Sixth Avenue el, whose owner, the

Interborough Rapid Transit Company, had gone into receivership several years earlier. (Sixth Avenue property owners had urged the city to tear down the el and replace it with a subway in 1923. They had even offered to pay the cost. But the project had gotten bogged down because many New Yorkers felt the el should not be demolished until the Sixth Avenue subway was finished.) Shortly after, the city also tore down the Second and Ninth avenue els in Manhattan and a few lines (or parts thereof) in Brooklyn, the remains of the defunct Brooklyn–Manhattan Transit Company. A decade later the city tore down the Third Avenue el, the oldest in New York, a "relic," wrote the general manager of the New York City Transit Authority, of a "bygone era." After its demolition, there were no els left in lower and mid Manhattan, only in upper Manhattan and some of the outer boroughs. Change came more slowly in Chicago, Philadelphia, and Boston, where the authorities were reluctant to tear down the els, no matter how "undesirable" they were, until they could be replaced with subways. But after World War II Boston began to demolish them too.[46]

John A. Miller was one of the few Americans who was puzzled by the construction of elevated highways. "Elevated railways with a capacity of 40,000 persons per hour in one direction are [being] torn down," he wrote in amazement in 1935, "while elevated highways with a capacity of 6,000 persons per hour are being erected." If Americans believed that elevated railways were so offensive—that they should not have been built in the first place, should not be built anymore, and should be demolished as soon as possible—why were they building elevated highways? Why were people like Borough President Miller and Police Commissioner Enright, who were so eager to tear down elevated railways, so eager to put up elevated highways? Why, asked the *Transit Journal,* is it that "one elevated structure [New York's Second Avenue elevated railway] should be considered a 'blight' while another [New York's West Side Elevated Highway] is considered a civic improvement"? The construction of the Gowanus Parkway highlights the puzzle. New York City had long planned to demolish the old BMT el on Third Avenue in Sunset Park, a quiet, pleasant working-class neighborhood in Brooklyn, as soon as it opened a parallel subway on Fourth Avenue. But instead of just tearing it down, the city adopted a proposal by Robert Moses to replace it with an elevated highway, a four-lane highway that was more than twice as wide as the elevated railway (and would later be widened to six lanes). To build the highway and its ramps and to turn the street below into a ten-lane roadway to be used mainly by commercial vehicles, one hundred stores had to be demolished and thirteen hundred families evicted. According to Robert Caro, the Gowanus Parkway set in motion the "vicious gyre of urban decay" from which the community never recovered.[47]

Moreover, a good many Americans were opposed to elevated highways. Writing in 1925, several years before he became a strong advocate of them, Miller McClintock insisted that they should not be employed "until other remedies have been exhausted." A few years later the *New Republic* wrote that elevated highways were "a monstrosity which should be contemplated only under the most desperate necessity." What one engineering journal called a "general public antipathy to elevated construction" persisted into the 1930s and 1940s. According to critics, elevated highways were objectionable for the same reasons elevated railways were. They blocked the sunlight. (Indeed, it was darker under the elevated highways than the elevated railways, partly because the elevated highways were much wider and partly because the elevated railways allowed light to seep through the gaps between the ties.) They also generated a lot of noise. (According to one contemporary, the incessant hum of the autos and trucks was even more nerve-wracking than the occasional roar of the trains.) Elevated highways obstructed surface traffic too, especially around the ramps connecting them to the streets below. And they lowered the value of the abutting property, leaving what one observer called "ribbons of blight" in their path. Many Americans were opposed to elevated highways, wrote one of their defenders, because of their "unhappy experience" with the dark, dirty, noisy, and unsightly elevated railways in New York and other cities.[48] But that did not mean their opposition was any less strongly held.

Why did a society that favored the demolition of elevated railways support the construction of elevated highways? To put it another way, how did advocates of elevated highways overcome the widespread antipathy to elevated structures? Part of the answer is that the first elevated highways were built on sites where their objectionable features would not arouse much opposition. New York's West Side Elevated Highway ran along the waterfront, through a run-down commercial and industrial district that had few shops and offices and even fewer residences. In the hope that the highway would spur development, the abutting property owners even offered to pay for it with a special assessment. Chicago's Wacker Drive ran above South Water Street, a busy commercial artery and site of the city's produce market. To soften the opposition, the city appropriated $10 million for a new market. Another elevated highway that was located so as to minimize opposition was the Pulaski Skyway, which soared above the empty New Jersey meadowlands, linking northern New Jersey with New York City. Advocates cited these projects as proof that elevated highways posed no problems if they were properly located. And many who held that elevated highways were inappropriate in residential communities and the central business district conceded that they might well be appropriate on commercial waterfronts, in industrial districts, and at other places where they would not damage abutting property—especially if they were built along wide streets. From there it was only a small step to the position that elevated highways might also be appropriate in slums and other run-down neighborhoods, which was the position Robert Moses took when residents of Sunset Park criticized the proposed Gowanus Parkway.[49]

Advocates of elevated highways also made a vigorous effort to undermine the widespread prejudice against elevated structures, a prejudice they attributed to the "evils" of the old elevated railways. Leading the way were the American Institute of Steel Construction (AISC), whose members were driven by the depression to look for new markets, and the American Road Builders' Association (ARBA), whose members had a huge stake in highway construction. With the support of auto, trucking, and petroleum interests, the AISC sponsored a competition in 1937 for what Clyde G. Conley, president of the association, called "a more economical, a more efficient, a more aesthetic design of an elevated highway." Attracted by a first prize of $5,000, a substantial sum at the time, nearly three hundred architects and engineers entered. The institute put the prize winners on display in New York and half a dozen other cities. A year later the ARBA formed a committee on elevated highways, which was chaired by V. G. Iden, secretary of the AISC, and included McClintock and several prominent engineers. During the late 1930s and early 1940s the committee issued a series of reports that celebrated the progress of elevated highways, highlighting their benefits and downplaying their drawbacks.[50] Joining in the effort were many architects, engineers, and traffic experts, who made the case for elevated highways at meetings, in journals, and in a barrage of studies and reports.

Aside from arguing that elevated highways were not very expensive, even that they were often less expensive than street widening, their advocates made several points, all of which were meant to distinguish elevated highways from elevated railways. Provided that elevated highways were properly designed, they would be "almost noiseless," a Chicago engineer declared. A San Francisco engineer pointed out that the noise from the elevated highways carrying traffic onto the new Bay Bridge would not "disturb a fever-struck patient in a hospital." If elevated highways were properly designed and located on wide streets, they would not deprive people of light and air, Moses claimed. They would also be free of the dirt and dust that made elevated railways so offensive. Nor need elevated highways be eyesores. Given a sleek, streamlined look, they could even be "beautiful," wrote a Detroit engineer. A "correctly designed elevated Limited Way would actually add to the total architectural value of the area traversed," said McClintock. Elevated highways would not impede surface traffic either, especially if erected on a single row of columns, with the roadway cantilevered above. Most important of all, they would not reduce the value of abutting property. Indeed, the ARBA's committee on elevated highways pointed out, they would enhance it, in part because they would make the abutting property more accessible and in part because they would be more attractive than "the outmoded elevated railways."[51] Although these arguments did not move the residents of Sunset Park and other communities through which elevated highways were routed, they did undermine the widespread prejudice against elevated structures.

Besides stressing that elevated highways would be free of the objectionable features of elevated railways, their advocates hammered away at the point that they would relieve traffic congestion. Unobstructed by cross traffic and traffic signals, automobiles and trucks would move swiftly and smoothly on elevated highways—so swiftly and smoothly, a Detroit engineer pointed out, that not too many of them would have to be built, and none more than six lanes wide. Police Commissioner Enright predicted that elevated highways would allow a motorist to drive "from Harlem to Wall Street in fifteen minutes," a variation of the slogan around which backers of New York City's first subway had rallied in the 1890s. For a while it seemed that they might live up to expectations. As John S. Crandall, a civil engineer and professor of highway engineering at the University of Illinois, reported in 1937:

> Several years ago my office was located in New York City at the lowest tip of Manhattan Island. Occasionally I would ride uptown to 42nd Street with a colleague who frequently drove to and from the office. The time required never was less than 45 minutes, and often was over an hour, yet the distance is less than four miles. Since those days the elevated express highway has been built along West Street. Last year I traversed the same distance, at the same hour of the day, in nine minutes. Furthermore, I was not a nervous wreck when I reached 42nd Street, as I had invariably been on previous occasions.[52]

In hindsight, Crandall might have been well advised to enjoy the trip while he could.

Advocates of elevated highways also hammered away at the point that the cities were running out of alternatives. Street widening, on which tens and even hundreds of millions of dollars had been spent, was not the answer; nor was traffic regulation. This left only two options. The cities would have to "go up or down," as a St. Louis traffic expert put it—to build elevated highways or depressed highways. And depressed highways had more drawbacks. They would require overpasses at every major intersection, which would be impractical, and street crossings at every minor intersection, which would be inconvenient. Fenced in for public safety, they would also form a "Chinese Wall" between one part of the community and another. Above all, depressed highways were extremely expensive, roughly twice as expensive as elevated highways, according to McClintock, and prohibitively so in the center of the city. In the minds of the advocates of elevated highways, indeed in the minds of most Americans, this drawback more than offset the advantages of depressed highways. As one traffic expert pointed out, the issue was not whether to build elevated highways or depressed highways. It was how to build limited access highways at the lowest possible cost.[53]

Some Americans were unmoved by these arguments. They remained skeptical that elevated highways were less objectionable than elevated railways, that they were the answer to the traffic problem, and that they were preferable to depressed highways. But most found them persuasive. And many of them supported elevated highways. Their support reflected a curious blend of optimism and desperation. The optimism was revealed in a vision of elevated highways soaring above the city streets, beautiful, streamlined, and virtually noiseless elevated highways, wrote one engineer, which stood on "well-shaped columns" surrounded by "playgrounds, parks and wooded areas." A vision of highways on which motorists sped along at more than fifty-five miles an hour, without having to stop (or even slow down) for cross traffic and traffic lights, without having to put up with long and dangerous traffic jams. (Many early photos show the elevated highways with so few cars moving along them that it is hard to see why they were needed at all.) The desperation was revealed in the refusal to heed the warnings that elevated highways would not work—that they would encourage more motorists to use cars and thereby bring more cars downtown than the streets could handle and that they would wreak havoc wherever they ran, in the central business district as well as in the outlying residential sections.[54] At the core of this desperation was the deep-seated belief that drastic measures had to be taken, no matter what the cost, to make the central business district more accessible.

By the 1920s Americans had come to believe that accessibility meant not only that motorists had to be able to drive to the central business district, but also that they had to be able to find a place to park there. As Miller McClintock told the National Association of Building Owners and Managers in 1926, "It would not profit a business district greatly to have the most convenient arteries of travel in the world if the district were so restricted that there were no place to put the [cars] once they arrived." Adequate parking facilities were essential, argued John Ihlder, manager of the civic development department of the U.S. Chamber of Commerce. Otherwise "there is no purpose in [driving]." During the late 1910s and early and mid 1920s, however, it became harder and harder to find a parking place in most cities. In downtown Los Angeles, wrote the *Times*, "There are times when it is absolutely impossible to obtain parking accommodations for a distance of several blocks from where one desires to make a purchase." In downtown Memphis, an observer noted, "Finding an unoccupied space large enough to park a car . . . is like sighting an oasis in the desert." The lack of adequate parking "has paralyzed business downtown," declared a Philadelphia councilman. It has driven customers to patronize suburban stores, a Nashville business journal pointed out. And it has stimulated the growth of outlying business districts, wrote J. Borton Weeks, president of the Keystone Automobile Club.[55] To many Americans, and to most downtown businessmen and property owners, inadequate parking was second in importance only to traffic congestion as a cause of decentralization.

According to traffic experts, inadequate parking was part of an even more serious problem, a problem that arose not so much because motorists had trouble finding a parking space as because most of them eventually found one. This was the problem of the parked car, which was distinct from what was later referred to as the parking problem. What made this problem so serious was that it exacerbated the traffic problem. According to a survey of municipal engineers made in the mid 1920s, parked cars and narrow roadways were the leading causes of traffic congestion. Writing in *Nation's Traffic* in the late 1920s, W. W. Arnheim went even further, declaring that "the parked car is the principal problem in present-day street congestion"—a view, he said, that was held by public officials, civic leaders, and downtown businessmen as well as traffic experts. Indeed, wrote the *National Municipal Review*, the parked car is an even greater obstacle to the flow of traffic than the moving car. The crux of the problem was that the streets were unable both to move motor vehicles and to store them. This was especially true in the central business district, which had the heaviest traffic and thus the greatest demand for parking space.[56] Hence the downtown business interests were in a bind. If motorists could not park at their destination, the central business district would lose trade; but since parked cars increased traffic congestion, it would lose trade even if they could.

Although McClintock thought otherwise, the problem of the parked car, broadly defined, was nothing new. Long before the coming of the automobile, private carriages had lined the streets of the business district, standing in front of stores and offices, the coachmen, wrote an observer, "sit[ting] quietly in their boxes for hours, if necessary, until their master [or perhaps their mistress] chooses to appear." Peddlers left their wagons at the curb or even on the sidewalk, often forcing pedestrians into the street. Even worse were the many carts, wagons, and other horse-drawn vehicles that made deliveries to downtown businesses. The drivers stop wherever they want, and traffic comes to a halt, wrote one observer, until all the "bales of cotton or wool, or bundles of hides, or casks of beer, have been carefully unloaded, deposited on a neighboring elevator and stored neatly in their places." By reducing the capacity of the downtown streets, these carriages, wagons, and carts slowed down other horse-drawn vehicles; and by forcing many of them onto the tracks in the middle of the street, they blocked the streetcars. The situation was completely out of hand in Boston, wrote *American Architect and Building News* in the 1890s. The city had already spent tens of millions of dollars to widen the streets and was now thinking of spending millions more to make them even wider. All this would do would be "to perpetuate that amazing system under which the roadway is devoted to the rest and refreshment of horses and tired teamsters [and] to the traffic in 'Moxie' [a soft drink], peanuts, 'ice cream candy,' buttons, toys, and other articles."[57]

With the coming of the automobile, the problem grew much worse. Tens and even hundreds of thousands of motorists drove into the central business district each day; and most of them had to leave their cars, some for an hour or two, others all day. Some used private garages or other off-street facilities. But most parked on the streets, thereby reducing their capacity by as much as onethird to one-half. Finding all the curbside spaces occupied, other motorists resorted to what became known as double-parking. According to historian Paul Barrett, even triple-parking was not unheard of. With automobiles, trucks, and streetcars left with only one or two lanes in each direction, even some of the widest streets were "almost impassable," observed Atlanta mayor James G. Woodward as early as 1913. To make matters worse, many motorists had to drive around the central business district for ten or fifteen minutes to find a parking place, making the streets even more congested. And when they found an empty space, they ordinarily had to back in, bringing the cars behind them to a standstill.[58]

As the traffic problem got worse, as the downtown streets became so congested that it was often faster to walk than to ride, traffic experts concluded that parking would have to be restricted in one way or another, especially in the central business district and on the major streets leading into it. Also in favor of parking restrictions were the street railways (as well as the public agencies that regulated them). Their spokesmen believed that as long as motorists were allowed to park wherever and whenever they liked the industry would not be able to provide adequate service or control operating costs. The parked car was the streetcar's biggest problem, declared the head of the American Electric Railway Association. Public safety officials endorsed parking restrictions too. Parked cars, they held, endangered pedestrians, blocking their vision when they crossed the streets. Even worse, they posed a fire hazard, making it harder for firemen to get to a blaze and into position to extinguish it. With cars parked everywhere in the Loop, even in front of emergency exits at theaters, a catastrophe was inevitable, warned Chicago fire chief J. C. McDonnell.

The parking problem in the late 1920s (Survey, *October 1, 1929)*

Also supportive of parking restrictions were some downtown businessmen and property owners, who feared that traffic congestion, for which they thought the parked car was largely to blame, raised the cost of doing business and reduced the volume of business done.[59]

The street, advocates of parking restrictions argued, is not a garage, much less a storage yard. "It is a public highway," wrote Hugh E. Young, an engineer with the Chicago Plan Commission—and a strong supporter of elevated highways in the late 1920s and early 1930s. And on a public highway, which should be devoted to the greatest good for the greatest number, "there can be no denial that the right of moving traffic over standing traffic is paramount." This principle had originally been spelled out in the early nineteenth century, when Lord Ellenborough, chief justice of England, held, in *Rex v. Cross*, that coaches could not remain on a public street for an unreasonable time. "The king's highway is not to be used as a stable-yard," he ruled—a ruling that was probably cited more often in the United States than in England. From this principle, which was later adopted by American courts, it followed that people had a right to move, but not to park. Or to put it another way, parking was at best a privilege, one that should be honored only when it did not obstruct traffic. At worst, said McClintock, it was "an abatable nuisance." Summing up the conventional wisdom, Young argued that "the parking or storage of motor vehicles on any street in which they interfere with moving traffic should not be tolerated."[60] By the late 1910s and early 1920s many streets in the central business district (and more than a few outside it) fit into that category.

Cities not only had the right to impose parking restrictions, their advocates claimed; they had a duty. Parking cost millions of dollars a year, $60 million a year in Chicago alone, Young estimated—an estimate that was based largely on the time lost making deliveries and otherwise doing business in the Loop. To allow motorists to park wherever and whenever they want makes no sense, said Robert B. Brooks, director of streets and sewers in St. Louis. Why, he asked, should the city let motorists park on Olive Street near Seventh, the heart of downtown St. Louis, where the "cost" per car came to at least $480 a year? Of the American practice of storing cars on the street, Sir Henry P. Maybury, director-general of the roads department of the British Ministry of Transport, observed, "A more expensive garage cannot be conceived." Why, advocates of parking restrictions also asked, should cities widen streets, at tremendous cost to taxpayers (and narrow sidewalks, at terrible inconvenience to pedestrians), and then permit one-third to one-half of the space to be filled by parked cars? Why should the cities allow unlimited parking in the central business district when the result was to increase traffic congestion to the point that motorists were hard pressed to get there?[61]

Not everyone found these arguments convincing. J. P. Snow, a Boston civil engineer, contended that parking restrictions would not relieve traffic congestion because the worst congestion occurred at intersections, "where there is no parking"—a position that had a certain logic to it. Other experts pointed out that parked cars were only one of many reasons for traffic congestion, and not necessarily the most important, and that parking restrictions were only one of many ways to relieve it, and not necessarily the most effective. Also skeptical of parking restrictions were motorists, who wondered, as a New York contractor put it, "What is the use of an automobile, if a person is not to be allowed to go anywhere with it within the business zone?" To motorists, parking was an essential use of the streets, which their taxes had helped build. It might be a privilege, as advocates of parking restrictions claimed, but it was not one they would give up without a fight. Many downtown businessmen and property owners had reservations as well. Parking restrictions might facilitate traffic, they conceded, but they would also drive away customers. Reasonable parking restrictions might be worth a try—but only after an efficient, up-to-date rapid transit system was in place and adequate parking garages and other off-street facilities were available.[62]

Despite opposition from motorists and merchants, advocates of parking restrictions made a good deal of headway in the 1910s and 1920s. The restrictions on where motorists could park, which were justified in terms of public safety, were relatively noncontroversial. To protect pedestrians, to provide them an unobstructed view of the oncoming traffic, cities banned parking at intersections and in crosswalks. To safeguard streetcar passengers, most of whom entered and exited in the middle of the streets, cities prohibited parking between "safety zones" and curbs. Cities also forbade parking next to fire hydrants, in front of firehouses and police stations, and at entrances to theaters, hotels, and hospitals. And they designated loading zones, at which parking was banned, in front of business establishments—though this was as much for the convenience of businessmen as for the protection of pedestrians. By the late 1920s these restrictions had been adopted in most cities—and also incorporated into model municipal traffic ordinances drafted by the National Conference on Street and Highway Safety and the National Highway Traffic Association.[63]

More controversial were the restrictions on when motorists could park, which were justified in terms of traffic relief. Most of these restrictions fell into one of two categories. In the first were parking bans, which were imposed on the downtown streets (and on the main streets leading into them) during rush hour—roughly from seven to nine in the morning and from five to seven in the evening. With support from the Chicago Association of Commerce, Chicago Building Owners and Managers Association, and Chicago Real Estate Board, Chicago adopted a rush hour ban in 1917. Believing that such a ban would relieve traffic congestion without disrupting business, many other cities followed Chicago's lead—so many that by the late 1920s most motorists took these bans for granted. In the second category were parking limits, which allowed motorists to park downtown at times other than rush hour, but only for a limited time, at the most two hours, at the least a half hour, and ordinarily somewhere in between. The earliest limits aroused so much opposition that they were soon rescinded. But eventually many downtown businessmen and property owners came to believe that they might be the only way to relieve traffic congestion and still allow motorists to shop and do business downtown. They might also be the only way to prevent the all-day parker, the notorious "parking hog," from monopolizing much of the available parking space. Hence one city after another adopted parking limits.[64]

These restrictions cut down all-day parking, but as McClintock and other experts pointed out they did nothing to relieve traffic congestion. Parking limits, it turned out, had severe drawbacks. Unlike rush hour parking bans, they were unenforceable. The police did not have the manpower. Chicago, for example, assigned two officers to do a job that required dozens. (It involved marking each parked car with chalk, returning half an hour later and, if it was still there, issuing a citation and then appearing in court another day.) Moreover, the prosecutors did not give parking violations high priority. Nor did the judges. Neither was enthusiastic about using the criminal sanction against well-to-do and otherwise law-abiding citizens. In Buffalo, a consulting engineer conceded, "we put up the signs and then trust to the Lord that the people generally will observe them." Faith, however, was not enough. Motorists regularly exceeded the parking limits, sometimes by as much as two or three hours; if cited, they often failed to appear in court. In Milwaukee, one resident pointed out, so many motorists ignored the half-hour parking limit that the city concluded that "it was as bad as all day parking." Many cities had imposed parking limits, said George W. Elliott, Philadelphia's public safety director, but none had been able to enforce them.[65]

Even if the cities had been able to enforce them, it would not have helped to facilitate the flow of traffic. Unlike rush hour parking bans, parking limits did not remove cars from the streets. As W. W. Arnheim remarked, they "merely shuffle[d] them around." It did not matter whether one car was parked for eight hours or eight cars for one hour. In either case, there was one lane less to handle traffic. A spokesman for the Atlanta Motor Club made the point nicely in the early 1920s. Criticizing a proposed one-hour parking limit for the central business district, he argued that even if it could be enforced, which he doubted, "there would be no relief noticeable—simply because limited parking periods are equivalent to permanent parking in so far as the movement of traffic is concerned." McClintock even warned that parking limits, if strictly enforced, might obstruct the flow of traffic by increasing the turnover at the curbs. Motorists would park for an hour, then pull out, drive around, look for another spot, and back in, only to repeat the process an hour later. From the perspective of the traffic engineer, if not the downtown merchant, all-day parking was bad, but a 100 percent turnover every hour was even worse.[66]

If parking limits could not relieve traffic congestion, many experts concluded that the only alternative was a parking ban, a complete ban on daytime parking in the central business district. The idea had been around since the mid 1910s, and by the early and mid 1920s many big cities were seriously considering it. McClintock and other experts assumed that it was only a matter of time before such a ban was widely adopted. As one of them wrote, "we are rapidly approaching the point where we will not allow any parking on our congested streets," which would be restricted to the loading and unloading of passengers and merchandise. But to their dismay, the proposed parking bans aroused a furor. "I know of no phase in the treatment of traffic congestion that appears to bring so much opposition as the prohibition of parking," said Leslie J. Sorenson, a Chicago traffic engineer. Journalist Raymond S. Tompkins agreed. "The parking controversy is one of the hottest things to handle in the whole traffic tangle."[67]

Nowhere was the controversy more heated than in Philadelphia. It started in late December 1926, when Mayor W. Freeland Kendrick submitted an ordinance to the city council that banned all parking in downtown Philadelphia from 6:30 A.M. to 7:00 P.M. Its architect and leading advocate was public safety director Elliott, who had become convinced that nothing short of a complete parking ban would solve the traffic problem. Supporting Elliott were the mayor and the police chief, William B. Mills, the Philadelphia Rapid Transit Company and the Philadelphia Chamber of Commerce, and some downtown businessmen who believed that curbside parking was disrupting commercial activity. "Trucks can't unload before [my stores]," complained a Chestnut Street merchant. "Customers can not stop in front of them." The opposition, which was led by other downtown businessmen, notably Market and Arch street retailers, lost no time in making its views known. A parking ban would stifle business and reduce property values, it argued. The city could solve the traffic problem by enforcing existing parking restrictions and eliminating unnecessary cruising by taxis (as well as by increasing the capacity of the streets). There was no need for more draconian steps. Also opposed to the parking ban was the Keystone Automobile Club, which claimed that it favored streetcars over motor vehicles. To assuage the opposition, Elliott made two concessions. The city would try the ban for thirty days, after which it would be evaluated; and the police would give motorists a week to get used to it and allow a reasonable time for loading and unloading. Under these conditions, the opposition reluctantly went along. And in mid January the city council unanimously adopted the parking ban.[68]

No sooner did the ban go into effect than its opponents decided they had had enough. In mid February they prevailed on Councilman Morris Apt to introduce an ordinance repealing the ban and replacing it with a half-hour parking limit. Other councilmen proposed a one-hour limit. At private meetings with Elliott and rancorous hearings of the council's Committee on Public Safety, many downtown retailers testified that business had fallen off since the ban was imposed. Downtown Philadelphia was like "a dead city," said one. Some motorists no longer shopped downtown, while others rushed out of the store each time they saw a policeman. Meanwhile, the outlying business districts were thriving. A few downtown businesses were thinking about moving. And it would not be long before property values fell in the central business district. Elliott defended the ban, stressing that very few shoppers drove downtown, and even fewer parked on the street. City council president Charles B. Hall backed him. So did a spokesman for the chamber of commerce who argued that whatever business was lost by banning parking would be more than offset by reducing traffic congestion. Also in favor of the ban were other downtown businessmen, including manufacturers and wholesalers who were impressed by how much more smoothly traffic flowed since the ban was imposed. Elliott pleaded with the opponents to wait the thirty days before reaching a verdict. But they refused. When even dispassionate observers began to ask why Philadelphia banned parking when most other big cities did not, its fate was sealed. In mid March a sharply divided council passed an ordinance that banned parking on some downtown streets, ordered one-hour parking on others, including Market and Arch, and allowed unlimited parking on the rest.[69]

The outcome was much the same in other cities, among them Los Angeles and Atlanta. In Los Angeles the issue came to a head in November 1919. According to historian Scott Bottles, the Los Angeles Railway and two regulatory agencies—the California Railroad Commission and the L.A. Board of Public Utilities—led the movement for a parking ban. They believed that only by completely eliminating parking downtown would it be possible to reduce traffic congestion to a point at which the streetcars could provide adequate service. Joining the movement were the Merchants' and Manufacturers' Association, the Wholesale Dry Goods Association, the Business Men's Co-operative Association, a group that represented many large downtown businesses, and, for a time, the Automobile Club of Southern California—all of which were deeply troubled by the traffic problem. Over the opposition of the Motor Car Dealers' Association and many downtown merchants, who feared that a parking ban would drive customers to outlying business districts, the city council adopted a revised version of the railroad commission's original proposal in early February. The ban went into effect two months later. Much as the experts had predicted, it reduced traffic congestion. But according to downtown merchants, it devastated retail trade. With many customers driving to outlying business districts, downtown was "like a graveyard," said H. W. Frank, a former president of the Downtown Business Men's Association. Barely a week later the Business Men's Co-operative Association denounced the parking ban. So did the three leading newspapers, among them the *Los Angeles Times*, which had opposed the ban from the outset. The protest soon gained widespread support from merchants and motorists. Over the objections of the railroad commission and the board of public utilities, which argued that the opposition had not given the parking ban a fair trial, the city council replaced it with a forty-five-minute parking limit, which went into effect at the end of April.[70]

In Atlanta, according to historian Howard L. Preston, the city had been reluctant to restrict parking down through the early 1920s. But by November 1922 traffic congestion was so bad that a group of merchants and automobile dealers called for a one-hour parking limit in the central business district. The Atlanta Motor Club objected, arguing that parking limits were unenforceable and ineffective, and proposed instead a parking ban on some downtown streets. Despite opposition from a few merchants, the city council passed an ordinance in December that banned parking on the two major retail streets, Peachtree and Whitehall. But before Mayor James L. Key signed it, scores of downtown merchants and hundreds of women shoppers protested. And the council, with only one dissenting vote, reversed itself. The council made two other halfhearted attempts to curb parking downtown. In 1923 it banned parking on a few streets, none of which handled especially heavy traffic; and three years later it adopted a measure that banned parking on one side of the downtown streets, a measure backed by the local engineering societies. Even these attempts were opposed by many retail merchants, one of whom filed a suit against the city. And they were enforced loosely, if at all. The issue came up again in 1929, when Mayor Isaac N. Ragsdale appointed a special commission to look into the traffic problem. But the commission was unable to reach a consensus, and nothing came of its efforts.[71]

The one exception—the only city, wrote McClintock, that "has ever succeeded in maintaining blanket parking restrictions in the central business district"—was Chicago. Its parking ban, which was adopted by the city council in January 1928, was largely the work of the Chicago Association of Commerce, the city's leading business organization. It retained McClintock to make a study of Chicago's traffic problem, which recommended a total parking ban in the Loop, and persuaded the Building Owners and Managers Association and other downtown business interests to support it. The proposed ban provoked vigorous opposition, mainly from Loop merchants, who had blocked earlier efforts. But the council voted to give it a ninety-day trial. What was unusual was not that Chicago adopted a parking ban, but that in spite of vigorous opposition, in spite of a barrage of protests, threats, and lawsuits, it retained it. The reasons are murky. It may be that some aldermen were impressed by McClintock's findings that less than 10 percent of the Loop customers came by car and less than 2 percent parked on the street. And it may be that some aldermen favored the ban as a way to promote the development of the outlying business districts. It may also be, as Paul Barrett has suggested, that Chicago had a good many off-street parking spaces, several thousand in Grant Park and under Wacker Drive and thousands more in private lots and garages. It may even be that the ban owed its success to its timing. For the Chicago parking ban was imposed at the peak of the boom of the 1920s. In the year or so afterward not only did more motorists drive downtown and not only did traffic flow more easily in the Loop, but, even more important, many Loop businessmen, including some who had originally opposed the ban, reported strong, even record sales.[72] Thus for the time being it was very hard for the opposition to make a compelling case that the parking ban had adversely affected business.

The controversy over parking bans raises several intriguing questions. If the great majority of Americans came downtown by streetcar, if (as Elliott claimed and McClintock showed) only a very small minority used autos to get downtown and an even smaller minority, so small as to be negligible, parked on the streets, and if under even the shortest possible time limits the curbs could not accommodate more than a small fraction of the autos entering the central business district, why did parking bans arouse such strong opposition? Also, if the streetcar companies, most traffic engineers, some auto clubs, and many downtown businessmen, among them manufacturers, wholesalers, and truckers, supported parking bans as a way to reduce traffic congestion—and many banks and other financial institutions did not feel strongly about the matter one way or another—why was the opposition able to stave them off in every city except Chicago?

According to advocates of parking bans, the opposition was at best short-sighted, unaware that the long-term well-being of the central business district depended more on reducing traffic congestion than on preserving curbside parking, and at worst selfish, prone, said a spokesman for the Philadelphia Chamber of Commerce, to put "their own interests before the greater interests of the large majority." One engineer claimed that the opposition was just plain stubborn, against change, "no matter what it may be." The issue, how-

Downtown Chicago, before (top) *and after the parking ban (*Electric Railway Journal, *February 23, 1929)*

ever, was not that simple. Aside from motorists, many of whom believed that they had a right to park downtown, if not wherever and whenever they wanted, at least on some streets for a hour or so in the middle of the day, the opposition to parking bans came mainly from merchants. Many of them were small, highly specialized retailers who catered to the "carriage trade." A substantial number of their customers came downtown by automobile and preferred to park on the street. Contrary to what McClintock and others said, it was not only a matter of numbers; it was also a matter of purchasing power.

Motorists tended to be well-to-do; they had money to spend, and they spent it. According to two surveys made by Los Angeles firms in the mid 1920s, the average motorist spent more than five times as much downtown as the average straphanger.[73]

A parking ban would cost these merchants a lot of money. "If we lose only five customers a day who come to us in motor cars, and we have lost fully that many," said the manager of a Philadelphia shoe store after the parking ban was imposed, "we would feel the financial loss." Even a 1 percent loss would hurt, declared a spokesman for the Market Street Merchants' Association. And in Los Angeles some merchants reported losses of 25 to 35 percent and even as high as 50 percent. A parking ban would also send the wrong message, downtown merchants told the manager of the Kansas City Safety Council. "We don't care whether there are facilities to park or not so long as the prospective customer feels that he can still park downtown. If he thinks he can not park, he will go to some suburban center where parking is permitted." Many Los Angeles merchants also feared that a parking ban would drive customers to outlying business districts. So did many Philadelphia merchants, especially after they heard that at the same time that business was falling off downtown it was picking up in West Philadelphia, Germantown, and Norristown. By the late 1920s, at which time the incipient decentralization of commerce was well under way, downtown merchants had good cause to be afraid. And nothing reassured them less than the statements of the defenders of parking bans, one of whom, a Chicago alderman, said that even if trade left the Loop because of the ban it would not go to Gary or Milwaukee, but to Wilson Avenue, Howard Street, and Chicago's other outlying business districts.[74]

According to advocates of parking bans, they themselves were partly to blame for the outcome. Before starting their efforts, they should have mounted educational campaigns to persuade merchants and motorists that a parking ban was in their best interest. Also partly to blame were the elected officials, who shelved the parking bans in some cities and rescinded them before they had a fair trial in others. Once again there was more to it than that. The elected officials were under enormous pressure from the downtown retailers. None of the other business interests, not the manufacturers, wholesalers, and truckers, and certainly not the banks and other financial institutions, felt so deeply about the matter. None of them defended the parking bans as strongly as the retailers attacked them. As one Philadelphia councilman acknowledged, the downtown merchants made a compelling case that the parking ban had done such severe damage to their businesses that it should be repealed as soon as possible. It is not surprising that many elected officials were swayed more by the protests of downtown merchants that parking bans were driving away customers today than by the promises of traffic engineers that they would stimulate business tomorrow.[75]

Besides charging that a parking ban would encourage decentralization, the opposition made several other points that may have influenced the elected officials. One was that a parking ban was extremely heavy-handed. As the Boston Chamber of Commerce remarked, not all downtown streets were alike. Some were wider than others, some were busier than others, and some, not others, were lined with railway tracks. Why, asked the chamber, should the city treat them all the same? Another point was that a parking ban was inequitable. In the name of traffic relief, it placed a heavy burden on motorists, as opposed to streetcar riders and taxi drivers, whose cruising greatly contributed to traffic congestion downtown. It also placed this burden on ordinary motorists, but not on very wealthy motorists, who could afford to hire a chauffeur. Probably the most important point was that a parking ban was anachronistic. It reflected the thinking of a time when the automobile was strictly a "pleasure car," a time that "is long since past," declared a spokesman for the Los Angeles Car Dealers' Association in 1920. The motorcar, he argued, is now "just as much a necessity to business as the street car." If anything good came out of the Los Angeles parking ban, it was that it demonstrated "the extent to which the automobile has become a part of our everyday life."[76] American cities should not do anything to discourage its use, least of all impose a parking ban downtown.

On the eve of the Great Depression Chicago was the only American city that banned parking downtown all day. All the others imposed parking limits—except during rush hour, when many of them banned parking too. Parking limits were what most downtown merchants wanted; and parking limits were what they got. But these restrictions did little to solve the traffic problem. Nor did they do much to solve the parking problem. For as McClintock and others pointed out, it was very hard, if not impossible, to enforce them. And even if they could be enforced, there was not enough space along the curbs to accommodate more than a small fraction of the cars that poured into the central business district every day. Thus by the late 1920s both advocates and opponents of parking bans came to the conclusion that parking lots, garages, and other off-street facilities were the only solution to the parking problem.[77] And this conclusion became the conventional wisdom in the 1930s and 1940s.

Although the parking problem grew steadily worse in the 1920s, some Americans thought a solution was in sight. As a Rochester engineer wrote in

March 1929, automobile ownership was rapidly approaching the saturation point; and when it reached that point, parking would no longer be a problem. After the onset of the Great Depression, it seemed they might be right, though for the wrong reasons. For one thing, the demand for parking space was falling—or, if not falling, leveling off. The reason was that the number of motorists who drove downtown was holding constant or even declining. In Detroit, for example, the number of automobiles entering the central business district on a typical weekday climbed more than 25 percent between 1924 and 1930 and then dropped nearly 15 percent during the next four years.[78] Some motorists stopped driving downtown because they preferred to go to the outlying business districts. Others stopped because they had no jobs to go to downtown and no money to spend there, or because they could no longer afford to own and operate an automobile.

For another thing, the supply of parking spaces was growing. It had started in the mid and late 1920s, when for the first time the increase in off-street parking more than offset the decrease in curbside parking. Off-street parking came in many forms. At one extreme were huge garages, as many as eight or ten stories high, which could accommodate thousands of autos. Also known as "automobile hotels," some of them offered a wide variety of services to motorists in addition to parking. At the other extreme were small lots, at most a few thousand square feet of empty space, with room for a few dozen autos. In between were what were called "integral garages," located in the basements or subbasements of high-class office buildings. Public authority supplied some of these facilities, setting aside unused space in parks, above markets, and along riverfronts and lakefronts. For example, Chicago provided parking space for 5,200 cars in Grant Park and 1,700 under Wacker Drive. But most were supplied by private enterprise. Some were built by hotels and department stores for the convenience of their guests and customers. Others were put up by large corporations, like Chicago's Motoramp Garages, Inc., which hoped to capitalize on the growing demand for parking space. Still others were established by property owners who had not yet found a more profitable use for their land. So many garages and lots popped up in and near the central business districts in the mid and late 1920s that by the end of the decade there were more than 15,000 off-street parking spaces in Boston, Chicago, and Kansas City, more than 20,000 in Philadelphia and Detroit, and more than 55,000 in Los Angeles.[79]

Although it had been widely expected that many of these off-street parking facilities would soon be turned into stores and office buildings, the supply of parking space continued to grow in the early and mid 1930s. It doubled in

Dallas and Cincinnati. And in Philadelphia the number of parking lots soared from one hundred in 1931 to eight hundred in 1938. By the late 1930s about 90 percent of the many vacant lots in downtown Milwaukee were used for parking. And by the early 1940s roughly one-fourth of downtown Los Angeles was occupied by parking lots and garages. The continued growth of off-street parking was a result of the Great Depression. As vacancy rates climbed and rents dropped, many property owners demolished their buildings and turned them into parking lots and "taxpayers." As one planner wrote, they hope to get "some income (if not enough to pay all, then at least part, of the taxes) awaiting the day when through some heaven-sent action they can improve their property to the point where it will show a return on the fictitious values." Sometimes the cities encouraged the property owners to tear down their buildings. On occasion the federal government helped out. The government was "plowing under" cotton, not to mention killing hogs and paying farmers not to plant, said Byron T. Shutz, president of the Kansas City Real Estate Board, in 1934. "Why not 'plow under' obsolete buildings [too]?"[80]

Other Americans, many downtown businessmen and property owners among them, doubted that a solution to the parking problem was in sight. The decline in the demand for parking space was temporary, they believed. As soon as the depression was over, automobile use would grow, and motorists would pour into the central business districts in record numbers. By the mid 1930s traffic was on the increase in Cleveland, reported traffic commissioner Edward J. Donahue. And in Chicago about 25 percent more automobiles entered the Loop on a typical weekday in the late 1930s than in the late 1920s. The driving habit fell sharply in the early 1940s, a result mainly of gas rationing. But by virtue largely of the steady decline of mass transit, it rose just as sharply after the war. During the late 1930s and early and mid 1940s many Americans also pointed out that the cities were plan-

A technological fix to the parking problem (Illustrated London News, *July 9, 1932*)

ning to build huge high-speed, limited-access highways to link the central business district with the outlying residential sections. They noted that it was only a matter of time before Congress agreed to underwrite them. It made no sense to build major highways through the city without providing adequate terminal facilities downtown. In the absence of cheap and convenient parking, motorists would steer clear of these highways. And, said a Southern California businessman, rather than drive downtown, they would head for the outlying business districts.[81]

The growth in the supply of parking space was also temporary, many Americans believed. Property owners had converted their land into parking lots only because they had not yet found a more profitable use for it. They had conceived of "taxpayers" as a short-term solution to a financial problem, not as a long-term commitment to the parking business. (According to experts, these off-street parking facilities had other shortcomings. More often than not, they were inconvenient, located on the edge of the central business district, a long walk, or a short streetcar ride, from the destination of most motorists. They were also unsightly, declared Thomas H. MacDonald, commissioner of the U.S. Public Roads Administration. "Over-crowded, over-priced and ill-designed, these unattractive properties resemble more closely the scars of mass bombings than utilities performing a public service.") As soon as the economy recovered, the demand for commercial space would increase, driving vacancy rates down and rents up. Before long property owners would replace parking lots and "taxpayers," especially centrally located ones, with stores, hotels, and office buildings. Whereupon the number of off-street parking spaces would fall—as it did in downtown Chicago, which lost 3,200 of them, nearly one of every five, between 1939 and 1946.[82]

It was also highly unlikely that the decline in curbside parking space would be reversed, especially because the elected officials were under pressure to ban parking in the central business district. Much as it had in Los Angeles and Philadelphia a decade earlier, the pressure came from traffic experts, local officials, street railway managers, and some downtown businessmen—all of whom thought a parking ban would help relieve traffic congestion. In some cities it also came from downtown parking lot and garage owners, who emerged as a powerful interest group in the 1930s and argued that they could not make a profit as long as motorists were permitted to use the streets as garages. As expected, most downtown retailers opposed the proposed bans on the grounds that they would drive shoppers away from the central business district. In most cities—in Cleveland in the early 1930s and in San Francisco in the late 1930s—they were successful. But if elected officials were reluctant to impose a parking ban downtown, they were willing to restrict parking in other ways, even to ban it on selected streets. New York adopted this approach, prohibiting parking on many major east–west streets in the late 1930s. So did San Francisco, where, as a result of piecemeal restrictions, the central business district lost more than one-quarter of its curbside parking space between 1937 and 1944. Some San Franciscans believed that it would eventually lose the rest too.[83]

As engineers, planners, and local officials wrestled with the parking problem, a former Oklahoma newspaperman named Carl C. Magee invented an ingenious device that led some Americans to believe that the solution was "nearer than ever before." The device was the parking meter—or, as it was originally called, the "Park-O-Meter." Designed to regulate curbside parking, it was little more than a timepiece mounted on a post—with a slot into which a motorist could insert a nickel and park for a short time, usually an hour or less. Lining the streets of the central business district, one every twenty feet or so, the first parking meters were installed in Oklahoma City in 1935. Wrote one observer, they "spread like wildfire throughout the Southwest," first to Dallas and El Paso, then to Houston and Fort Worth. Despite political and legal challenges, they soon caught on in Miami, Passaic, Toledo, and other medium-sized cities elsewhere in the country. By 1937 roughly 20,000 parking meters were in use in 35 cities; three years later there were 70,000 of them in 160 cities. Most retail merchants favored them. So did many downtown property owners, street railway executives, and city officials. "In our opinion," the U.S. Conference of Mayors said in late 1936, "the parking meter is the most noteworthy development in traffic control since the advent of the now universally used traffic light."[84]

How would parking meters help solve the parking problem? How, in the words of the *Passaic News-Herald,* could they "guarantee to any and every motorist who drives downtown on business the certain and full enjoyment of the privilege he now has in theory only—that of parking undisturbed for one hour, or any part thereof"? And for only five cents? According to advocates of parking meters, the answer was simple. Parking meters would make the curbside space at which parking was allowed available to more motorists. This they would do by making long-term parking so expensive and inconvenient that all-day parkers would be driven out of the central business district and ordinary motorists would be encouraged to park for at most an hour or two. When parking meters were installed in downtown Toledo, a traffic engineer pointed out, the turnover rate among parkers nearly doubled. Parking meters, it was argued, had great advantages over other forms of parking limits, which were almost impossible to enforce. Very few police officers would be needed to monitor them—perhaps, another traffic engineer estimated, only one for every five hundred meters. At a time when most cities were under pressure to reduce their payroll, this was not to be sneezed at. Also, if the meter showed that time had expired, few motorists would dispute it. How, asked another traffic engineer, could a motorist hope to win an argument with a parking meter?[85]

According to their advocates, parking meters would also help solve the traffic problem. By discouraging all-day parkers from driving into the central business district, they would reduce the amount of traffic. They would also expedite its flow. Once they were installed, motorists would not have to double-park. Nor would they have to spend so much time looking for a parking space. Parking meters would make it easier to enforce traffic laws, too. Cities would be able to shift policeman from parking duty to traffic duty. With the revenue from parking meters, they would also be able to hire additional officers. Spokesmen for the American Automobile Association protested that it was unfair to tax the motorist to use the streets, and especially to make him put money into "a device the primary purpose of which is to make it easier to apprehend and fine him for parking violations." Advocates of parking meters answered that if a nickel was a tax, it was "a fair one." Why should motorists pay nothing to use the streets, they asked? Why should the costs of building and maintaining streets, not to mention the costs of providing traffic signals, traffic officers, and traffic courts, all be charged to taxpayers?[86]

Although many Americans were favorably impressed by parking meters, others had strong reservations. Hence the proposals to install them ran into resistance—especially, though not exclusively, in the big eastern and midwestern cities. A case in point was Baltimore. The issue surfaced in what was then the country's seventh largest city in July 1937, when the Baltimore Traffic Commission, a citizens' advisory group that had been created in the mid 1920s, recommended that the city install a thousand parking meters in the central business district. The commission was not unanimous. But most of its members believed that parking meters were worth a try because even if they did not solve the parking and traffic problems they would at least put an end to illegal parking, which was rampant in downtown Baltimore. The retail merchants' association endorsed the commission's recommendation. So did the Association of Commerce and the Howard Street and Charles Street associations, the leading downtown businessmen's groups. But the Baltimore Police Department, notably Chief William P. Lawson and traffic engineer Wallace L. Braun, opposed it. So did the Automobile Club of Maryland, whose spokesman was its counsel, Palmer R. Nickerson. Also opposed were the downtown garage owners, who complained that it was unfair for the city to tax their business and then compete with it.[87]

Parking meters, the opposition argued, would not help motorists or merchants. They would not relieve traffic congestion. To do this, the city should prohibit parking in the central business district, not promote it, said Nickerson. Parking meters would make matters even worse, Chief Lawson pointed out. "Our idea is eventually to clear all the downtown streets of parked cars," he declared, "and parking meters would delay our obtaining this objective for many years." Nor would meters eliminate long-term parking. A motorist could still park as long as he wanted to, Nickerson pointed out. "All he had to do is to send somebody to put another nickel [into] the meter." Also, how would parking meters be monitored? The Baltimore Police Department had not been able to enforce parking limits in the past. Why did anyone think that it would be able to enforce them in the future just "because a little flag pops up on those slot machines?" The opposition acknowledged that some people would support parking meters because they might raise revenue (and possibly lower taxes). But "if it is revenue alone that is sought," Nickerson argued, "why not have our sidewalks lined with candy slot machines every twenty feet, or weighing machines"? Indeed the city might as well "line them with gambling machines."[88]

The issue came to a head in June 1938, when at the request of the traffic commission the city council opened hearings on an ordinance that authorized the installation of 856 parking meters on twelve downtown streets. The ordinance polarized the community. On one side was Chief Lawson, who argued that the only way to relieve traffic congestion in the central business district was to ban parking. Joining him were garage owners and trucking companies, the Junior Association of Commerce, whose spokesman insisted that "if we want traffic to move, we must get parked cars off the streets," and the Automobile Club of Maryland, whose spokesman pointed out that many cities that had installed parking meters had subsequently removed them. On the other side was Joel G. D. Hutzler, vice president of Hutzler Brothers and president of the retail merchants' association, many of whose members feared that a parking ban would drive trade to the outlying business districts. "Eliminate parking," Hutzler declared, "and you will destroy the central business section." Install parking meters with reasonable time limits, and downtown will thrive. Also in favor of parking meters were the businessmen's associations of Charles and Howard streets, and the Baltimore Real Estate Board. The city council, it turned out, was as divided as its constituents. Unable to reach a consensus, it shelved the ordinance.[89] (Baltimore eventually installed parking meters, but not until the 1950s.)

During the late 1930s and early 1940s the downtown business interests grew more concerned about the parking problem. And by the end of World War II, inadequate parking was at the top of the "worry list" of the Urban Land Institute, the closest thing to a national organization of downtown businessmen and property owners. It "is the most important single problem facing the central business districts of large cities today," declared the ULI's Central Business District Council in 1946. A solution of the problem "is essential to the preservation of an adequate central business section," insisted the institute's board of trustees. Fueling the concern, a concern shared by many planners, engineers, motorists, and public officials, was the awareness that parking space in the central business district was extremely scarce. In downtown Philadelphia, one expert reported, it was very hard to find a space off the street and even harder to find one along the curb. When the freeways were built, it would get even harder. Also fueling the concern was the belief that inadequate parking was now at least as much a cause of decentralization as traffic con-

Parking meters in downtown Baltimore, 1958 (Baltimore Sun, December 28, 1958)

gestion. Unless the problem was solved, downtown business interests feared that motorists would abandon the central business district for the outlying business districts, most of which had plenty of free parking.[90]

The downtown business interests were also disenchanted with the conventional solutions. Although parking limits were a good idea—and, in the view of downtown retailers, much better than parking bans—they were not the answer. Nor were parking meters. They made things easier for the police departments and harder for the all-day parkers. But they did not provide adequate parking. As one expert put it, parking meters were "a helpful palliative," not "a permanent solution." From this position it was but a short step to the conclusion that the answer to the parking problem was not more (and tougher) parking regulations but more (and better) parking lots and garages, especially in the core of the central business district. This idea had surfaced in the late 1920s, a time when the parking problem was rapidly getting worse. It appealed both to advocates of parking bans, who saw off-street parking as an alternative to curbside parking, and to opponents of parking bans, who saw it as a supplement to curbside parking. The idea lost some of its appeal during the depression, but more than regained it in the late 1930s and early 1940s. By the mid 1940s the downtown businessmen and property owners were convinced that the only way to solve the parking problem—and to solve it without exacerbating the traffic problem—was to provide more off-street parking.[91]

The number of off-street parking facilities had risen steadily (and, in some places, sharply) in the late 1920s and early and mid 1930s. By the late 1930s most big cities and more than a few medium-sized ones had hundreds of parking lots and garages, which could accommodate thousands and even tens of thousands of automobiles at a time. Setting the pace was Los Angeles, which had more than 900 off-street parking facilities with room for 65,000 cars in 1938—up from 50, with a capacity of 4,000, in 1922—of which 432, with a capacity for 56,000, were located in the central business district. With a few exceptions, of which the municipal parking lot in Chicago's Grant Park was by far the largest, the vast majority of parking lots and garages were private. Most were "taxpayers" or ordinary commercial enterprises. Some were adjuncts of large department stores and office buildings. And a few were cooperative ventures, undertaken by one or another group of downtown businessmen. Perhaps the most successful of these groups was Oakland's Downtown Merchants Association, which in the late 1930s owned and operated about half a dozen fair-sized parking lots with a capacity of almost a thousand autos. More than a million motorists a year parked in these lots; and if their tickets were validated by a member store, they parked for free.[92]

But private enterprise had not provided enough spaces to keep pace with the growing demand, experts pointed out. And there was no reason to believe that it would do better in the future. Most private parking lots and garages were "makeshift" arrangements, wrote city planner Gordon Whitnall. Sooner or later they would go the way of "the 'jitney' of yesteryear." Ironically, said Commissioner Thomas H. MacDonald, their success would be their undoing. If private parking facilities made the central business district more accessible, they would so increase the demand for commercial space that they would soon be replaced by stores, hotels, office buildings, and other potentially more profitable enterprises. Off-street parking was far too important to be subject to the speculative drives of property owners and the temporary availability of vacant land, experts argued.[93] In order to ensure enough permanent, convenient, and reasonably priced off-street parking, cities would have to do more than encourage private enterprise to step up its efforts. In one way or another, on their own or through some sort of public authority, they would have to go into the parking business.

That cities should provide off-street parking was not a new idea. It had been floating around since at least the late 1920s. But with some exceptions, Americans had long believed, as one Bostonian put it in 1930s, that parking "is distinctly a field for private capital rather than municipal enterprise." Harland Bartholomew made the point even more strongly. In light of the high price of real estate in the central business district, he remarked in the early 1920s, the attempt to provide off-street parking at public expense would drive cities into bankruptcy. In the face of the widespread preference for private parking, public parking made little headway down through the late 1930s. According to a survey of nearly 150 cities, fewer than a quarter had any off-street public parking. Of the few that did, most were small cities. Only in Chicago and Memphis could public parking facilities accommodate as many as three thousand autos, and only in Quincy, Massachusetts, and Clintonville, Wisconsin, as many as one thousand. If the survey was reliable, the number of private parking spaces in Los Angeles exceeded the number of public parking spaces in the entire country. Usually located on land that had long been owned by the city or had recently been taken for nonpayment of taxes, most of these public facilities were run like anything but a business. Only in Chicago and Ithaca, New York, did they even charge for parking.[94]

But as the survey also found, many cities were already under pressure to go into the parking business—and to do so on a larger scale and in a more businesslike way. As the pressure built, it generated a controversy that swept through urban America in the postwar years. On one side were parking lot and garage owners, conservative businessmen and public officials, and spokesmen for the transit industry—all of whom argued that the cities should not go into the parking business. Public parking was un-American, they declared. It was a step toward municipal socialism and "price control." It was also unfair to private enterprise, which had provided a good deal of off-street parking and was ready to provide a good deal more. Public parking is justified as a way to stop decentralization, said Marston Campbell, Jr., who owned and operated a parking facility in San Francisco. But decentralization, he argued, "is a red herring fished out by the downtown interests who look for charity from industry, from the wage earner, from the home owner—the very patrons of their stores." The downtown interests cry, "Private enterprise had failed." Nonsense, he wrote. "If downtown parking area is inadequate, it is the same downtown property owner[s] and merchant[s] . . . who have failed to provide adequate parking to protect their own investment who now say to the city-wide taxpayer, 'Buy a garage for us, and we will save you from decentralization.' These champions of private enterprise propose socialization of the property of others, but not their own."[95]

Public parking was also impractical, its opponents claimed. Baltimore did not have the money to enter "the highly speculative garage business," argued Frederick Philip Stieff, a downtown merchant (and strong supporter of parking meters), in the late 1930s. Given its limited resources, New York could not even "make a dent in the [parking] problem," wrote Robert Moses, chairman of the Triborough Bridge and Tunnel Authority, several years later. "There is no reason why the city, with its many more urgent post-war commitments involving traffic relief, should enter the garage business." (Moses later changed his mind, saying that the authority's proposed multistory garages—"two, three, four stories or whatever height they have to be"—would help solve the parking problem.) Rather than alleviate the parking problem, public parking would exacerbate it, the opposition charged. In the face of competition from public authority, private capital would be reluctant to invest in off-street parking. Public parking would also undermine the cities' precarious fiscal condition, said B. N. Stanton, president of the National Parking Association, owner of a small chain of parking lots in Norfolk, Virginia, and leader of a successful effort to keep Norfolk out of the parking business. There was no way that the cities could develop off-street parking in the central business district without providing large subsidies—and also without removing valuable property from the tax rolls.[96]

Some Americans opposed public parking for another reason, one that applied to private parking too. As John A. Miller pointed out, it took as much space to store a motorcar as to house an office worker. Hence "if everyone working in a 20-story office building came to work by private auto, a 20-story garage would be needed to accommodate the vehicles during the hours the workers were at work." In which case "half the buildings in the business section of the city would have to be garages, or we would have to build a second business district of equal size composed wholly of garages." And just imagine, said Miller, if motorists parked in lots! According to Miller and others, it was physically and economically impossible to provide convenient and inexpensive parking for everyone who wanted to drive downtown. Private enterprise could not do it. Neither could public authority. (As David D. Bohannon, a San Francisco realtor and developer, put it, "you would have to demolish approximately half of downtown San Francisco to come close to providing adequate parking.") The only way to solve the parking problem was to improve mass transit and encourage Americans to use it. A lack of adequate parking, especially centrally located and reasonably priced parking, is often cited as the reason for the decline of downtown, observed H. H. Allen, a consulting engineer, in the mid 1940s. "If that reason is valid," he warned, "the present [central] business districts in most of our large cities are doomed."[97]

On the other side of the controversy were downtown businessmen, city planners, and traffic experts, who argued that these charges were groundless. Public parking was not un-American. It was no more socialistic for cities to provide parking than to build highways (or, for that matter, to provide schools, parks, and playgrounds). It was as important to provide off-street parking in the central business district as to build high-speed freeways to it. "What good is more street capacity," asked one expert, "if there is no place to put your car when you get downtown?" Nor was it any more un-American for taxpayers to subsidize off-street parking than to support other essential public services. Many advocates of public parking, especially many downtown businessmen, believed that private enterprise was preferable to municipal ownership (and that the cities should do their utmost to encourage private capital to enter the parking business). But as Jay D. Runkle, general manager of Crowley, Milner and Company, a Detroit department store, and chairman of the board of the National Retail Dry Goods Association, pointed out, private capital was reluctant to invest in off-street parking.[98] This reluctance was understandable. But at a time when decentralization was threatening the well-being of downtown and the solvency of urban America, it left cities with no choice but to go into the parking business.

Nor was public parking impractical, its advocates argued. The cities might not have the money to go into the parking business, but they could borrow it at relatively low interest rates. For a while cities might have to subsidize off-street parking. But in time it would become self-supporting, provided that the cities made effective use of their competitive advantages, especially their access to capital markets, power of eminent domain, and tax-exempt status. A public agency could charge much less for parking than a private company and still break even, contended advocates of public parking—who also pointed out that municipal garages and parking lots would raise the value of adjacent property by more than enough to offset the revenue lost when the real estate on which they stood was removed from the tax rolls. Public parking, its supporters conceded, would not solve the parking problem, especially in the core of the central business district in the middle of the day. But it would alleviate it. Some advocates of public parking acknowledged that improved mass transit might be the long-term solution to the parking problem. But as a special committee of the Chicago Association of Commerce reported, many Americans would still prefer to drive.[99] And whether they drove downtown depended largely on whether they could park there.

The battle over public parking, a battle that raged in city halls and state capitols as well as at the polls and in the courts, dragged on into the early 1950s. But by the late 1940s the outcome was no longer in doubt. The parking industry and its allies could block some cities from going into the parking business, if not permanently, at least for the time being. Failing that, they could stop or at least delay the proposed public lots and garages. In the state of Washington they twice defeated legislation that would have enabled Seattle and other cities to set up a public parking authority. Similar legislation was turned down in Texas. In Jackson, Mississippi, where the voters had approved a $400,000 bond issue for off-street parking, the courts blocked the city's attempt to acquire a downtown lot by condemnation. The courts were also reviewing a proposal to build a public garage under the Boston Common. But in most cities the parking lot and garage owners were no match for the other downtown businessmen—and the powerful organizations that looked after their interests. At their urging, one state after another authorized the cities to go into the parking business. Many of them did, sometimes on their own, often through a public parking authority.[100] Before long they were busy trying to acquire sites, raise capital, choose contractors, and remove the host of legal and other obstacles that stood in their way.

More often than not, they were successful. By the end of the decade San Francisco had authorized $5 million for off-street parking facilities, including an underground garage that could accommodate 900 cars—about half as many as the Union Square garage, a huge underground garage built by a private firm in the mid 1940s on land leased to it by the city. Perhaps inspired by San Francisco's efforts, Los Angeles was asking for bids on an even larger garage, a four-level one under Pershing Square, the capital for which would come from the Downtown Parking Association, an offshoot of the Downtown Businessmen's Association, the chief advocate of off-street parking in the central business district. In the meantime New York's Triborough Bridge and Tunnel Authority was building a 1,050-car garage in lower Manhattan. And Detroit, whose proposed garage under Washington Boulevard was stalled by construction problems, was moving ahead with a large above-ground garage. Boston, whose proposed garage under the Common was tied up in the courts, acquired half a dozen other sites, razed the buildings, and leased the properties as parking lots until construction got under way. Denver approved a $4.5 million bond issue for off-street parking. Baltimore authorized a $5 million loan to its Off-Street Parking Commission. And Pittsburgh's Parking Authority drafted a $36 million plan to build 25,000 off-street parking spaces. With the support of the Mellon interests and the Allegheny Conference on Community Development, many of them were built in the early and mid 1950s.[101]

Although the downtown business interests worked hard to make the central business district more accessible to motorists, they were well aware that many people still relied on mass transit. They also knew that it would be impossible for everyone to drive downtown, much less park there. Hence the downtown business interests tried hard to make the central business district more accessible to straphangers too. At the same time they pushed for high-speed, limited-access highways and conveniently located, reasonably priced off-street parking, they pushed for improved mass transit. And that, it was widely assumed, meant rapid transit. Rapid transit was not as high on the agenda of the downtown business interests in the 1930s and 1940s as it had been in the 1910s and 1920s. But it was still fairly high, at least in some big cities. (In others, even in some whose residents had long assumed they would have a subway sooner or later, it was no longer on the agenda at all. By the late 1920s and early 1930s many Americans had come to the conclusion that subways were feasible only in the nation's largest cities.) It was in these cities, among them Chicago, Detroit, San Francisco, and Los Angeles, that the downtown business interests continued to fight for rapid transit in the 1930s and 1940s.[102]

It was, to say the least, an uphill battle, one that may well have been doomed from the start. To understand why, it is important to remember that the downtown business interests had made virtually no headway in their efforts to per-

suade the authorities to build subways in the 1910s and 1920s, when most big
cities had plenty of money to spend on public improvements and the vast majority of Americans relied on streetcars to get downtown. If the campaign for
rapid transit had fared so poorly in the 1910s and 1920s, there was little
chance that it would fare any better in the 1930s and 1940s, when conditions
were much less favorable. The depression left most big cities in dire financial
straits, hard pressed to meet existing obligations, let alone to take on additional ones, especially expensive ones. And subways were very expensive,
roughly $3–5 million a mile during the depression, $6–18 million a mile after the war, and far more for a four-track system that provided express and local service. Moreover, a large and growing number of Americans were now
driving downtown. The riding habit was plummeting. The transit industry,
which, in hindsight, was doomed by the late 1920s, was collapsing. And in
city after city the authorities were forced to take over the transit systems,
which were kept afloat only by subsidies from taxpayers.[103] In an age of low-
cost automobiles and high-speed highways, many Americans believed that
intra-urban rail transportation was obsolete. To make matters worse, the
downtown business interests could count on the support of few groups other
than the American Transit Association (ATA) and the manufacturers of transit equipment. They could also expect opposition from the outlying business
interests, who were more powerful than ever, from planners and engineers,
many of whom were closely allied with the highway lobby, and from residential property owners, who were not inclined to use rapid transit and not willing to pay for it.

Hence the downtown business interests were in a bind. They were aware
that rapid transit was by far the most efficient form of transportation in big
cities. According to a study by the American Electric Railway Association, the
forerunner of the ATA, a four-track subway could carry 100,000 to 120,000
people an hour, about twenty-five to thirty times as many as a one hundred-
foot roadway devoted exclusively to automobiles and six to eight times as
many as a one hundred-foot roadway used by both automobiles and streetcars.
Limited-access highways were far more efficient than ordinary highways, the
ATA conceded. But it would still take roughly twenty four-lane elevated highways to move as many people as one two-track subway. And suppose these
highways could funnel the motorists into the central business district. Where
would they park? But the downtown business interests were also aware that
the cities could not afford to build subways—not during the depression and
not after the war. Take the case of Detroit. According to an estimate made in
1947, it would cost the city $554 million to build a citywide subway that could

have been built for $280 million in 1926, and $65 million to build a downtown subway that could have been built for $33 million in 1929. Even the Detroit Rapid Transit Commission, which had led the fight for a subway in the mid and late 1920s, was discouraged. Pointing to New York, where the transit system's chronic deficits had undermined the city's solvency, it declared in the late 1940s that the construction of a subway system "would plunge the City of Detroit into a sea of debt."[104]

By the early 1930s it was clear that the cities could not build subways without help from the states or the federal government. Hitherto this would have been out of the question. Down through the 1920s Americans regarded mass transit as a local responsibility—and, until one transit company after another went bankrupt after World War I, as the exclusive province of private enterprise. During the 1930s and 1940s, however, two unexpected developments gave the downtown business interests reason to think that there might be hope for rapid transit. At the behest of President Franklin D. Roosevelt, Congress created a host of federal agencies to deal with the devastating impact of the Great Depression. Among the most important was the Public Works Administration (PWA), which was set up in 1933 and headed by Harold L. Ickes, Roosevelt's secretary of commerce. It was empowered to promote the construction of large-scale public works—which, it was hoped, would stimulate the lagging economy, generate much-needed employment, and upgrade the nation's infrastructure. This it did largely by providing grants and loans to federal agencies, states, and other public bodies. With this money, which ran into the billions, they built highways, dams, bridges, sewers, airports, and public buildings.[105] Perhaps, the downtown business interests thought, the PWA might be willing to spend some of it on subways too.

Hence the advocates of rapid transit renewed their efforts in a handful of cities in the mid and late 1930s. As a rule they hired experts to design a subway system and then urged the local officials to apply to the PWA for funds to build it. A subway, they argued, would not only relieve traffic congestion. It would also create many sorely needed jobs and reduce the rapidly growing relief rolls. In no city was this argument made more forcefully than in Detroit, where at the depths of the depression the rapid transit commission proposed a two-line, twenty-mile subway (and elevated) system that would have cost $88 million and taken four years to build. "Think of $22,000,000 a year spent for wages and materials, most of it right here in Detroit!" said the *Detroit News*, a strong supporter of the plan. According to the commission, the transit system would be financed by a $26 million grant from the PWA and a $62 million loan from the National Recovery Administration, a loan secured

by the system's revenues and properties. The subway would cost the taxpayers nothing, argued its backers, who added, "If Detroit refuses this gift of
$26,000,000, it will go to some other city or state," a rationale that would
later be used to justify the construction of interstate highways in many cities.
A subway would have to built sooner or later, its advocates claimed. If built
now, when the cost of labor and materials was unnaturally low, it would be
relatively cheap, and the federal government would help pay for it. If built
later, it would be much more expensive. And the entire burden would fall on
the people of Detroit.[106]

More often than not, these efforts ran into fierce resistance. Some Americans feared that a subway would promote the development of the central business district at the expense of the outlying business interests. Others worried
that a subway would do serious, perhaps irreparable, damage to the streetcar
systems, which were in precarious financial condition. Still others were concerned that the construction of a subway would disrupt traffic and reduce
trade for so long that some downtown merchants would be driven out of business before they could benefit from it. Some Americans also objected on the
grounds that the federal government would provide only part of the money
needed to build the subways and none of the money needed to run them.
Where, they asked, would the rest come from? To make things worse, the
PWA was not eager to provide funds for subways. Unlike highways, which enjoyed strong support in the countryside as well as the cities, subways had a
constituency of fewer than a dozen large cities, not all of which had much
clout with the Roosevelt administration. Under its mandate, moreover, the
PWA was supposed to provide funds only for facilities that would pay for
themselves—as, for example, highways did, through user fees and gas taxes.
Although some supporters of rapid transit, among them Sidney Waldon, head
of the Detroit Rapid Transit Commission, argued otherwise, most Americans
doubted that a rapid transit system could support itself.[107]

Thus of the billions spent on public works by the federal government in the
1930s, very little went to rapid transit. And what little that did went mainly to
the three cities that already had subways. With the help of the PWA, New York
completed the Eighth Avenue subway, and Philadelphia constructed the
South Broad Street and Ridge Avenue Connector subways. And with the help
of another federal agency, the WPA, Boston built a subway under Huntington
Avenue, part of what is now known as the Green Line. But rapid transit made
little progress elsewhere. In Cleveland a proposed Euclid Avenue subway
went nowhere. In San Francisco a proposed Market Street subway was rejected by the voters. The PWA refused to provide funds for a Los Angeles sub-

way sponsored by the Central Business District Association and a Detroit sub-way endorsed by the voters. Detroit's application was "technically deficient," said the agency's State Advisory Board; and its project, which included an el as well as a subway, was "socially undesirable." Of all the cities without a subway, only Chicago managed to obtain federal funds to start one. With the help of the PWA, it built a two-line system that ran north and northwest from the Loop in the late 1930s and early 1940s.[108]

The other development that gave downtown business interests reason to think there might be hope for rapid transit was the highway program. During the 1930s and 1940s city and state officials began planning (and, in some cases, building) high-speed, limited-access highways, most of which required extremely wide rights-of-way. If the authorities had to acquire a two- or three-hundred-foot right-of-way for motor vehicles, experts reasoned, would it not make sense for them to acquire a slightly wider right-of-way and reserve a strip, either in the middle or along the sides, for electric railways? A rapid transit system could be built on these strips at a small fraction of what it would cost to build a citywide subway system. As early as 1923 Daniel L. Turner, a New York transit engineer, had proposed the construction of a superhighway in Queens that would accommodate railways as well as automobiles. A year later the Detroit Rapid Transit Commission, for which Turner was a consult-ing engineer, included in its proposed 204-foot-wide superhighways an 84-foot-wide right-of-way for four rapid transit lines. But it was not until the 1930s and 1940s, by which time it was clear that rapid transit could not be financed in the conventional ways, that the idea caught on. In one big city af-ter another engineers, planners, transit executives, and downtown business-men urged the authorities to reserve space for railways on the freeways. It was, they believed, the best, possibly the only, hope for rapid transit in the foreseeable future.[109]

Advocates of rapid transit stressed several points. It would not cost much more to acquire a right-of-way for electric railways and motor vehicles than for motor vehicles only—as much as one-sixth more, according to one estimate, and as little as one-tenth more, according to another. An additional 10 or 20 percent was not much to spend on a project that would increase the carrying capacity of the freeways at least threefold—and, if the rapid transit lines pro-vided express and local service, more than tenfold. It was indefensible to spend so much on highways designed exclusively for motor vehicles—and which by themselves would not solve the traffic problem. The freeway pro-gram offered the cities a golden opportunity, wrote Arthur F. Ager, an engi-neer with the California Public Utilities Commission, in 1947. If space is set

Freeways and rapid transit (American Institute of Planners, Committee on Urban Transportation, Urban Freeways, *New York, ca. 1947)*

aside for electric railways, "Los Angeles can today obtain a rapid transit system for a fractional part of what one will cost the City in the future." But "unless provision is made for rail rapid transit in these freeways where they are needed today," he warned, "Los Angeles will in all probability never have a rapid transit system."[110]

To incorporate rapid transit into the freeway system was easier said than done, however. Even if the extra space would add only 10 to 20 percent to the cost of the right-of-way, a great deal of money would be needed to acquire it. A great deal more would be needed to lay the tracks, build the stations, and run the trains. Where would the money come from? Private enterprise would not provide it. Nor would the state highway departments and the U.S. Public Roads Administration, which had no authority to fund mass transit. Short of changing state and federal laws, which was out of the question at the time, the advocates of rapid transit had no alternative but to turn to the cities and the metropolitan areas. But as historian Sy Adler has pointed out, there was strong opposition to rapid transit in the outlying districts. They did not need it; they did not want it; and above all they did not want to pay for it. As the *Santa Monica Outlook,* a suburban Los Angeles newspaper that opposed the attempt to incorporate rail lines into the freeway system, put it, rapid transit was a gimmick "to save the downtown shopping district of Los Angeles at the expense of other [business] districts and at terrific costs to all taxpayers." Given time, advocates of rapid transit might have overcome this opposition, though the odds were against them. But none of the members of the highway lobby—least of all the highway engineers, who, as Detroit city engineer George R. Thompson said, were "not overly enthusiastic about mass transit"—were inclined to defer construction of the freeway system until funds for rapid transit became available.[111]

It was "unthinkable" that the cities should build freeways without setting aside space for rapid transit, wrote Charles D. Forsythe, chief engineer of the Chicago Transit Authority, in the early 1950s. It might have been unthinkable in Chicago, which had already incorporated railway lines into the Congress Street Expressway and would later incorporate them into the Ryan and Kennedy expressways. But it was not unthinkable in Detroit. No provision was made for rapid transit on the John C. Lodge Expressway—"a costly error in judgment," said the Detroit Rapid Transit Commission. And though the commission urged the authorities to incorporate rapid transit into Detroit's freeway system, no provision was made for it on the other freeways either. Nor was it unthinkable in Los Angeles. Despite pressure from the downtown business interests, the Los Angeles County delegation to the state legislature voted against a proposed metropolitan transit district that would have had the authority to levy taxes for rapid transit. The L.A. council voted against it too. As a result there would be no rapid transit on what would become the country's largest freeway system. The story was much the same elsewhere. Indeed, nowhere but in Chicago was rapid transit incorporated into the freeway system. By the late 1950s it was clear that a golden opportunity was gone. And gone for good.[112]

By the late 1940s and early 1950s the central business districts were more accessible than ever to motorists, if not to straphangers. Thanks in large part to the efforts of the downtown business interests, many high-speed, limited-access highways now linked the outlying residential sections with the central business district. Many more were on the drawing boards. Also thanks in large part to the efforts of the downtown business interests, thousands of off-street parking spaces were now available in the central business district. Thousands more were in the works. But neither the construction of new freeways nor the provision of additional off-street parking did much to curb decentralization. Here then was a paradox. At the same time that the central business district was becoming more accessible, it was becoming less important. Nowhere was this more striking than in Los Angeles, then the nation's fourth largest city. No city had adopted as comprehensive a freeway system as L.A., and no city had provided as much off-street parking. Yet no city was so decentralized. Of the eighteen American cities with more than half a million people, Los Angeles was the only one in which the central business district did less than 10 percent of the retail trade of the metropolitan area in 1948. In only one other did it do less than 15 percent.[113]

How did Americans account for this paradox? One school of thought—the one to which most downtown businessmen subscribed—held that though the central business district was becoming more accessible it was still not accessible enough. Despite the new freeways, downtown traffic still moved at a snail's pace. Despite the new garages and lots, parking spaces were still hard to find. And despite repeated efforts, very little had been done to improve the existing mass transit facilities. From this position it followed that in order to curb decentralization the authorities would have to build more freeways, provide more off-street parking, and upgrade mass transit. Underlying this position was the longstanding assumption that Americans were not going downtown because they were unable to—not because they did not want to.

According to the other school of thought—to which only a few planners, engineers, and other experts subscribed—the authorities were making matters worse by building new freeways (and, to a lesser degree, providing additional off-street parking). Far from curbing decentralization, the freeways promoted it. They made it easier for people to get into the center, wrote Charles M. Nelson, editor of *Better Roads*, but they also made it easier for them to move out of it. And once they moved out they stayed out. Underlying this position was the assumption that Americans were not going downtown because they did not want to—not because they were unable to. If so, it was pointless to build new freeways and additional off-street parking. Given that the central business district was losing ground to the outlying business districts even in New York, Boston, Philadelphia, and Chicago, the few American cities with a rapid transit system, it might also be fruitless to build subways or els.[114]

With hindsight, it is clear that the critics were correct. The freeways did more to spur decentralization than to curb it. They also had a baneful impact on the central business district. They eviscerated it. In one city after another, they displaced many of the stores, offices, and other enterprises that were its lifeblood. They accelerated the process by which more and more of the central business district was devoted to traffic and parking and less and less to trade. Designed to save downtown, the freeways would kill it, a few experts predicted. If we continue "to invite more cars into congested areas and [to] destroy more buildings to provide parking when they arrive," a Detroit realtor warned in 1939, "we will in time destroy the incentive to assemble there."[115]

It is also clear that the freeways had a baneful impact on many outlying residential sections. As Robert Moses, who probably built more of them than anyone else, wrote in the mid 1940s, "These are prodigious undertakings, the full extent and nature of which the average city dweller does not yet grasp." The noise, dust, detours, and traffic tie-ups, the inevitable by-products of highway construction, were bad enough. Much worse were the demolition of buildings along the rights-of-way, the eviction of residents, and the displacement of shopkeepers. It was very disagreeable to remove these people, acknowledged V. E. Gunlock, Chicago's commissioner of subways and superhighways, in the early 1950s. But the highway engineers (and the state and local officials to whom they answered) were up to it. During the postwar years they hacked their way through the cities—"with a meat ax," in Moses' words—on a scale that would have been unimaginable a generation or two before. More often than not, freeways had a devastating impact, not only along the rights-of-way, but also in the surrounding neighborhoods, especially in the low-income neighborhoods of the inner city. As Lewis Mumford, one of their most outspoken critics, put it, "our modern highway systems are repeating most of the mistakes that were made by the railway—piling into the heart of the city, smashing through houses and buildings, . . . recklessly tearing up space."[116]

The problem, as Mumford saw it, was that "instead of planning motor cars and motorways to fit our life, we are rapidly planning our life to fit the motor car"—which, he added, revealed "that we have no life that is worth living." He was only partly right. During the first half of the twentieth century Americans made a vigorous effort to adjust their cities to the automobile. But the freeways and parking lots and garages, the most conspicuous products of this effort, reflected several things more tangible (and less subjective) than a life that was not worth living. Chief among them were the pressures of the highway lobby, the desires of ordinary motorists, and, not least of all, the desperation of the downtown business interests. They had long assumed that the well-being of downtown depended on its accessibility. And they now had reason to doubt that they could prevail on the authorities to upgrade street railway lines, much less to build rapid transit systems. In order to curb decentralization, they therefore saw no alternative but to support new freeways and additional off-street parking. The downtown business interests did not know how much damage the freeways would do. But had they known, they would have supported them anyway. If they had second thoughts about the efforts to make the central business district more accessible to motorists, they kept them well hidden.

7

Inventing Blight: Downtown

and the Origins of Urban

Redevelopment

Early in 1944, by which time the outcome of World War II was no longer in doubt, the U.S. House Committee on Roads held hearings on federal aid for postwar highway construction. Among the witnesses was Mayor Edward J. Jeffries of Detroit. Reading from a prepared statement, Jeffries said that in order to solve the city's traffic problem Detroit was planning to build 168 miles of limited-access highways after the war. We need these highways, he declared. "And we need Federal funds to help finance them." When he finished, Representative Angier L. Goodwin of Massachusetts, a junior member of the committee, asked, do you really think we should encourage Americans to use automobiles in cities? Departing from his prepared statement, Jeffries gave an uncommonly candid and extremely revealing reply. "I am not sure," he said. "I am not sure whether bringing people [into the heart of the city] more expeditiously and quicker than they have ever been able to get in before will not be the ultimate ruination of Detroit." By this Jeffries meant that the proposed highways, which were designed to make the center more accessible to the periphery, would also make the periphery more accessible to the center. As a result, more people would move farther away until "there is nothing left [in Detroit] but industry"—a development that would bankrupt the city (and devastate its central business district).[1]

Jeffries's remarks reflected a radical change in the way many Americans, especially local officials, city planners, and downtown businessmen, thought about residential dispersal. Hitherto they had assumed that it was a natural and highly beneficial process that the authorities should do all they could to encourage. As they saw it, most people—first the well-to-do, then the middle class, eventually even the wage earners—would move from the center to the periphery and from the city to the suburbs. This outward movement aroused little concern because it was also assumed that no matter where people lived, no matter how far from the center, most of them would go downtown every day. Thus the periphery would prosper as a residential section, and the center would thrive as a business district. And as the business district thrived, it would expand into the adjacent residential sections, where old houses would be replaced by new hotels, office buildings, department stores, and other commercial structures. Few Americans questioned these assumptions in the early twentieth century—not in the 1920s, a time of great prosperity, when the outlying sections of the metropolitan areas grew more than twice as fast as the central cities, and not even in the early and mid 1930s, a time of severe depression, when the outlying sections grew roughly three times as fast as the central cities, some of which actually lost population.[2]

During the late 1930s and early 1940s, however, many Americans began to have second thoughts about residential dispersal. In their efforts to account for the sorry state of the central business district, they were struck by two unexpected (and extremely ominous) developments. One was that a large and growing number of people who had moved to the periphery were no longer going downtown—or were going downtown less often. Instead they were patronizing the outlying business districts, shopping at chain stores, doing business at branch banks, and relaxing at neighborhood restaurants and movie theaters. The other development was that the movement outward was highly selective. The upper and middle classes were moving to the periphery and the suburbs. But the lower class, many of whose members belonged to one or another of the nation's ethnic and racial minorities, were staying put—some because they did not want to move, others because they could not afford to. More often than not, these people lived within a long walk or short ride of the central business district. But they had little money to spend in downtown stores and specialty shops, little reason to retain downtown lawyers and accountants, and little cause to deal with downtown banks and insurance companies.[3]

In view of these developments, many Americans concluded that it would not be possible to stop or even slow down decentralization just by increasing the accessibility of the central business district. It would also be necessary to check residential dispersal and, above all, to attract the well-to-do back to the center. As T. T. McCrosky, executive director of the Chicago Plan Commission, said, it would be necessary to encourage "a recentralization of residential population near to the main business district." Underlying this position was an assumption that, in the words of a leading consulting firm, "if we can again make the city an attractive place in which to live we can lure back many of the higher-income families from the suburbs." These families would fill what economist Ernest M. Fisher called "an economic void at or near the center." They would "breathe life into the [central] commercial areas," argued Milwaukee city attorney Walter J. Mattison. "Just think of what would happen to our downtown business district, with all the surplus buying power within walking distance of the center of the community," he wrote in 1944. "Just think how it would build up the assessed values in the land down there, possibly even to the point where it would sustain the value that existed there in 1930."[4]

To attract the well-to-do back to the center, much less to entice them to live within walking distance of downtown, was easier said than done. As Jerrold Loebl, a Chicago architect and developer, pointed out in the mid 1940s, conditions in the central city were pretty bad. And nowhere in the central city were they worse than in the old residential neighborhoods surrounding the central business district. Here were the slums and "blighted areas." These "urban deserts," to quote Arthur W. Binns, chairman of Philadelphia's Committee on Housing and Blighted Areas, were filled with dilapidated dwellings, often mixed with run-down warehouses and factories. Home to the poor (and transient), these neighborhoods were unsafe and unhealthy, lacking open spaces, fresh air, and the other features most Americans looked for in a good community. Indeed it was the conditions in these inner-city neighborhoods that had driven many Americans to move to the periphery in the first place. Why would the well-to-do return to a city that was "rotting at the core," asked one observer? Why would they choose to live in what Charles T. Stewart, director of the Urban Land Institute, called "the dismal areas that form the dirty collar around [the] central business [districts]?" Why would they move from their suburban enclaves to what John R. Fugard, a Chicago architect and building manager, spoke of as "the 'no man's land' which rings the business district and forms a cancer which is slowly but surely gnawing away at the vitals of centralized business?"[5]

To the downtown business interests and their allies, the answer was clear. Well-to-do Americans would return to the center only if the slums and blighted areas were eliminated and replaced by safe, healthy, and attractive middle- and upper-middle-class neighborhoods. In other words, it would be necessary to raze and rebuild much of the central city (or, in Mattison's words, to create a suburban setting "right in the center of the city"). This was a huge undertaking. To carry it out, the downtown business interests and their allies would have to join the slum clearance movement, which had emerged in the late 1920s and early 1930s as an alternative to tenement house reform. They would then have to transform it from a movement that was designed mainly to provide decent housing and pleasant neighborhoods for working people to one that was designed mainly to curb decentralization and shore up the central business district. To put it another way, the downtown business interests and their allies would have to turn slum clearance into urban redevelopment (and later urban renewal), one of the most controversial policies of the postwar years. This they did with such success that by the early 1960s Catherine Bauer, Charles Abrams, and other champions of slum clearance were mourning that a movement begun as an effort to provide good housing for low-income groups ended up as "a program to rebuild the downtown."[6]

To understand how this happened, it is necessary to go back to the mid and late nineteenth century. It was then that Americans discovered the slums of New York, Boston, Chicago, and other big cities. To their dismay, they found once-fashionable inner-city neighborhoods now occupied by the poor, the great majority of whom were first- and second-generation European immigrants who lived in squalid and cramped tenement houses of one kind or another. As Roy Lubove and other scholars have shown, the tenement houses aroused a good deal of concern among the many upper-middle- and upper-class Americans who were troubled by the growing polarization of American society and fearful that the country was on the verge of class warfare. Convinced, as the *New York Times* wrote in 1880, that "the condition of our tenement-house population is the source of the worst evils, physical and moral, in [the] City," they made a vigorous effort to expose the worst features of the tenement houses, an effort that they hoped would eventually bring about the abolition of the slums.[7]

Out of this effort, which spawned a host of reports, articles, and books, the most influential of which was *How the Other Half Lives* by Jacob A. Riis, came a scathing indictment of the tenement house and its surroundings. By far its "greatest evil," argued E. R. L. Gould, one of the leaders of the model tenement movement (about which more later), was overcrowding. Apartments in the tenement houses were very small, usually only two or three rooms—at most four or five—few of which were larger than ten by ten feet, some as tiny as eight by six. In these tiny apartments lived entire families, sometimes more than one. (In Chicago thousands of former single-family houses and cottages "are now packed with a family in each room," E. E. Genung, a Chicago tenement house inspector, wrote in the early 1880s. In one Italian neighborhood "several families [huddle] together in one large room, with mere boards and curtains for partitions between their scanty household goods.") There they cooked, ate, slept, often a few to a bed, and worked, rolling cigars, sewing

Mulberry Street, New York's Lower East Side, ca. 1870 (© Collection of the New-York Historical Society, neg. no. 33544)

dresses, and washing other people's laundry. If this was not enough to make ends meet, they took in lodgers and boarders. To make matters worse, the tenement houses stood several stories high, often cheek by jowl, and covered most, if not all, of their narrow lots. The density was mind-boggling, especially on New York's Lower East Side. At a time when New York had seventy-six persons per acre, the Lower East Side had from three hundred to seven hundred an acre. In one neighborhood the density approached a thousand persons per acre, which was more crowded than the most crowded parts of London, Paris, and even Bombay.[8]

The tenement houses were highly unsanitary too, the reformers charged. The apartments were dark and poorly ventilated. The basements and cellars, into which the overflow from the privies often seeped, were dank. The houses were cold in winter, hot in summer, and vulnerable at all times to fire, from which the wooden ladders that served as fire escapes offered little or no protection. Many were infested with insects and vermin. Few apartments had hot water—hence the term "cold-water flat." Fewer had a water closet—just a privy, one or at most two to a building, located in the hall or the yard. In neighborhoods full of saloons, brothels, stables, junkyards, and even slaughter-houses, there were no bathtubs. "If in all the health-destroying, vermin-breeding places along these streets there is one bath tub," another Chicago building inspector wrote, "I have never seen it nor been able by inquiry to locate it." The sanitary conditions were appalling, reported a New York state legislative committee in the late 1850s. Witness, it said, the "hideous squalor and deadly effluvia; the dim, undrained courts oozing with pollution; the dark, narrow stairways, decayed with age, reeking with filth, overrun with vermin; the rotted floors, ceilings begrimed, and often too low to permit you to stand upright." The tenement houses were "unfit for habitation by civilized people," wrote Genung. Indeed, added B. O. Flower, editor of the *Arena,* a crusading New York periodical, they were "totally unfit to be shelter for the lower animals."9

What troubled the reformers was not so much the belief that these "sordid quarters" took a heavy toll on their tenants as the fear that they would degrade the working class and destroy the whole society. This fear grew out of the widespread belief in environmental determinism, the notion, as one architecture critic put it, that man "is molded by his environments." ("Be the man what he may," he said, "be his aspirations of the highest, the good that is in him will be stifled if his house be bad and his surroundings worse.") "Strong-willed, intelligent people may create or modify environment," wrote Gould; "the weaker-willed, the poor, the careless and the unreflective become subject to it." Into which category the tenement-house dwellers fit he had no doubt. "Populous masses, crowded together one thousand to the acre, as they are in some parts of New York, are absolutely unable to resist the influences by which they are surrounded." From this perspective, the residents of the

Rear of a tenement house on Plymouth Court, an Italian neighborhood in Chicago's First Ward (American Journal of Sociology, *January 1913*)

slums were not so much wicked as weak, not so much villains as victims, "creatures of adverse circumstances," said a Boston minister, with no control over their fate—honest and kind people, wrote a Chicago reformer, who could not escape from "their material surroundings," at least not "by their own initiative." It was this belief in environmental determinism that led Gould and others to conclude: "As they now exist, the tenements are standing menaces to the family, to morality, to the public health, and to civic integrity." And "it is to be hoped," Gould said, "that it will not require some public calamity to arouse the people to their danger or their duty."[10]

Gould and other reformers hammered away at this point in articles, books, lectures, and interviews. The tenement house weakened the family. Demoralized by the overcrowded and unsanitary conditions, deprived of the independence and privacy vital to its well-being, the family disintegrates. Fathers, their prospects poor and hopes fading, turn to alcohol, abandoning their homes for the nearby saloons, where they find temporary solace. Mothers, worn out by the strain of running households in so hostile an environment, give up. Instead of delighting in their children, they are, said Gould, "soured into ill-feeling or brutalized into a state of callous indifference." Just as the adult "goes to the saloon," wrote William Howe Tolman, secretary of the City Vigilance League of New York, so the child "goes on the street"—where, in the absence of parks and playgrounds, "boys, while yet of tender age, are introduced to viciousness and petty crime," Gould pointed out. And "young girls from their earliest teens engage in an almost hopeless struggle for moral preservation." The tenement house blocks the "development of true domestic life," Gould insisted; "every member of the family from earliest childhood becomes prey to those forces which drag down, a stranger to those which uplift." The *New York Times* concurred. What, it asked, "can be hoped from the influence of schools, churches, civilization, and religion in laborers' families, who live twenty to a room, of all ages and both sexes, and thus pass a great part of their lives?"[11]

The tenement house also fostered immorality. It was "the most fruitful breeding ground for vice," wrote Gould, and "the cradle, nursery, kindergarten, school, [and] university . . . of the dependents, defectives, and delinquents," said Tolman. It produced "these noxious and unhappy elements of society as surely as the harvest follows the sowing," claimed Alfred T. White, a Brooklyn businessman and philanthropist who built some of the earliest model tenements. If "it be hard for a dyspeptic millionaire, surrounded by the delights of affluence, to be a good Christian," remarked Gould, "how much more difficult is it for a poor man, living in squalor and filth." The crux of the problem, said the *Times*, was that the tenement house "saps self-respect, weakens the resistance to temptation, aggravates the evil passions, and breeds the habit of unmanly and unwomanly conduct." Nothing, not intemperance and not even crime, so upset the reformers as "unwomanly conduct." With so many people, adults and children, male and female, sharing the same room and even sleeping in the same bed, the tenement-house dwellers had no privacy, no sense of modesty, the reformers pointed out. Hence women yielded to temptation, and girls were taken advantage of. More often than not, the lodgers and boarders were responsible. In a pamphlet widely distributed in the slums, the New York Tenement House Department and the Tenement House Committee of the Charity Organization Society warned: "Lodgers often cause trouble in the family and sometimes break up the home. Lodgers have even been known to betray little girls—the daughters of the family they live with."[12]

The tenement house endangered the public health, too, the reformers argued. Inspired by what Lubove calls the "bacteriological revolution" of the late nineteenth century—the discovery that "specific micro-organisms were responsible for specific diseases"—they charged that the dark, damp, and badly ventilated apartments provided fertile grounds for the germs that carried typhoid, diphtheria, tuberculosis, and other infectious diseases. "No one will deny that sickness bears a close relation to bad housing," Gould argued, or that the high incidence of mortality in the slums was a result of the physical conditions of the tenement houses. Nor was the danger confined to the slums, the reformers pointed out. In many cities the slums stood "perilously close" to solid middle- and upper-middle-class neighborhoods. Their residents rode on streetcars, worked in stores, and went to schools. How could anyone be confident that they were not inadvertently infecting other people? Even worse, many tenement-house dwellers took in "homework" or "piecework"; they made clothes (and boxes and paper flowers) and rolled cigars, most of which were sold in other parts of the city (and even in other parts of the country). If these goods were made by ill men and women, perhaps in the same room that housed a sickly child or a dying grandparent, how could anyone be confident that they were not contaminated?[13]

Not least of all, the tenement house undermined civic integrity. It was, wrote Tolman, *"a menace to a republican form of government."* It was a leading source of municipal corruption and a serious threat to private property, said another reformer. It was "an evil which is gnawing at the vitals of the country," argued Henry Morgenthau, a New York real estate magnate; and unless it was wiped out, "our great body politic will be weakened." According to the tenement-house reformers, life in the tenements weakened the resistance to the unscrupulous tactics of the ward bosses, the leaders of the political machines that were widely blamed for the rampant corruption and incompetence of local government. It also increased the susceptibility to socialism, communism, and anarchism. As Gould observed at the turn of the century, "The genesis of 'isms most often takes place in the miserable tenements of a great modern city." This warning struck a responsive chord in a society that had been racked by fears of class warfare since the late 1870s, a society, as Chauncey M. Depew, a prominent lawyer and businessman, told New York's Charity Organization Society, that had "enough human dynamite [in it] to overturn any government in Europe."[14]

The problem was serious, the reformers insisted, but it could be solved. (Or as Riis put it, "The poor we shall have always with us, but the slum we need not have.") Hence they mounted a vigorous campaign to upgrade the quality of working-class housing that started in New York and Boston in the 1850s and 1860s and spread to Chicago and other cities in the late nineteenth and early twentieth centuries. At its core were three distinct, but more or less complementary, objectives. By far the most important was to prevent builders from putting up new tenement houses that were as bad as the old ones. To this end the reformers urged the authorities to impose a wide range of regulations on future construction. Despite strong opposition from builders, these regulations were adopted, to one degree or another, in most big cities. Often modeled on New York's Tenement House Law of 1901 or the model tenement house law drafted by Lawrence Veiller, the principal architect of the 1901 law, the regulations were intended mainly to reduce overcrowding and improve sanitary conditions. As a rule they limited building heights and lot coverage, banned rear tenements, and mandated larger rooms, higher ceilings, bigger windows, metal fire escapes, and a sink and separate water closet in each apartment.[15] The new tenements, it was believed, would be much less of a menace not only to their tenants but to other Americans as well.

Another objective of the reformers was to demonstrate that it was possible to build decent tenements, charge a reasonable rent, and still make a modest profit—or, in Gould's words, to show that "the proper housing of the great masses of working people can be furnished on a satisfactory commercial basis." Hence the model tenement movement, a movement that spread from England to America in the second half of the nineteenth century. In the vanguard was a small group of wealthy New Yorkers and Bostonians who believed that "investment philanthropy," an approach, said Gould, that occupied "a middle ground between pure philanthropy and pure business," offered a solution to the housing problem. Underlying this approach was the assumption that the wealthy—or, in Gould's phrase, "the large-hearted rich"—would be willing to underwrite the construction of model tenements that yielded a moderate (or lower-than-average) rate of return. Operating on this assumption, the reformers set up several model tenement companies, of which Brooklyn's Improved Dwellings, formed by Alfred T. White, was the best, and New York's City and Suburban Homes Company, headed by E. R. L. Gould, the largest. These companies built tenements with more space, better sanitary facilities, and more stringent regulations that ordinary tenements. It was hoped that the model tenements would provide decent housing for some working people and inspire commercial builders to provide decent housing for others.[16]

Yet another objective of the reformers was to expedite the movement of the working class from tenement houses in the center to single-family homes on the periphery, a movement, it was believed, that would in time drain the slums. Tenement reform was essential, the reformers believed; so were model tenements. But no matter how well built, a tenement house was inferior to a single-family home, a tenant inferior to a homeowner. How much can be expected of a workingman, asked Veiller, whose "home is but three or four rooms in some huge building in which dwell from twenty to thirty other families [and] whose home is his only from month to month." "Democracy was not predicated on a country made up of tenement dwellers," he argued, "nor can it so survive." Robert Treat Paine, one of the pioneers of the model tenement movement in Boston, agreed. So did Gould. Speaking of home ownership, he declared, "Every man undertaking it is distinctly helped to a far greater degree than he could be in the best class of model tenements. He becomes reflective, careful, prudent, wedded to order and rational conservatism, and usually turns a deaf ear to specious 'isms." To encourage workingmen and their families to leave the tenements, some reformers built low-cost cottages in suburban districts. And virtually all of them campaigned for rapid transit. Following the conventional wisdom, they assumed that by making undeveloped and relatively inexpensive land accessible, rapid transit would enable working people to live in modest versions of middle- and upper-middle-class "bourgeois utopias."[17]

By the early twentieth century tenement house reform was on a roll, model tenements were under construction, and rapid transit was in place in some cities and under consideration in others. But whether these efforts would succeed was far from clear. Although most Americans were optimistic, a few were skeptical. Some held that these measures were unlikely to do much good because the slums were a product of the inferiority of the slum dwellers, not of the inadequacy of the housing stock. As one skeptic put it, Americans—as opposed to immigrants—"would simply refuse to be overcrowded; refuse to live in vile, unsanitary quarters; refuse to accept starvation wages; refuse to be terrorized by ward bosses and cunning padrones and penurious landlords." Others held that these measures were unlikely to do much good because the slums were not so much a housing problem as an economic problem, a problem of irregular employment and inadequate wages—of, in a word, poverty. The solution would require a great many changes more radical than tenement house reform. What the tenement-house residents thought of the reform effort is hard to say. Their voices were rarely heard; and when they were, it was usually when the reformers asked for their opinions on matters about which they had already made up their minds. It is worth noting that when the tenement-house residents spoke out, as they did during the great rent strikes on New York's Lower East Side early in the twentieth century, it was to protest rent hikes, not housing conditions.[18]

The reform movement did much to improve working-class housing. The new-law tenements, a New York term that was widely used to refer to tenement houses erected under the 1901 law, were far superior to the old-law tenements—though they were far from "the best type of multiple family houses . . . in the world," as a committee of high-level New York officials boasted in 1924. The model tenements, which housed thousands of working-class families at reasonable rents, were also an improvement over the old-law tenements—though they were only marginally better than the new-law tenements. Had they been much better, Gould and others feared, they would have attracted not the "worthy poor," for whom they would have been too expensive, but well-to-do wage earners, who were, it was commonly believed, better off in the suburbs. Another sign of progress was that tens of thousands of old-law tenements were demolished, most because the owners found more profitable use for the land, some because the authorities deemed them unfit for habitation. Tens of thousands more were upgraded. Hot water was provided, windows were installed in interior rooms, and the notorious "school sinks" and privy vaults were replaced by water closets. The tenement houses were not only more sanitary; they were also less crowded. The new laws helped. But they were probably less important than the rise in real wages (and advances in mass transit) that enabled many second-generation immigrants to move from tenement houses in the center to one- and two-family homes on the periphery—from the Lower East Side to the Bronx, Brooklyn, and

Queens, for example. And there were few newcomers to replace them after Congress ended unrestricted immigration in the early 1920s.[19]

But the reform movement made little progress in wiping out the slums. Writing in 1921, Veiller pointed out that they were still "spreading and extending . . . over the face of the land." (A decade later he claimed that "the United States has probably the worst slums in the world.") Ralph Adams Cram, a Boston architect and chairman of the city's planning board, agreed. "It is still possible to-day," he declared in 1918, "to find in any industrial city slums that in their ugliness and their disease-breeding and vice-breeding conditions [are] as bad as any recorded in history." Well after the reform movement got started, Boston still had a good many unsanitary and overcrowded tenement houses, Chicago had more than ten thousand dilapidated rear tenements, and New York, which had about 640,000 old-law tenements in 1909, had roughly 525,000 in 1932—most of which, wrote one reformer, were "without heat, without baths and affording little more accommodation than shelter from rain and snow." These tenements were being demolished so slowly, reported the housing committee of the New York State Reconstruction Commission, that it would take one hundred years to get rid of them, a hundred years in which they would continue to breed poverty, crime, disease, and degeneracy. (The New York Mayor's Committee on Housing agreed, but added that "in the scheme of the universe," a century was not all that long.) The old-law tenements survived in some cases because they were highly profitable and in others because there was little or no demand for the land on which they stood.[20]

Thus by the late 1920s, if not earlier, many reformers were forced to acknowledge that the conventional approaches had serious limitations. The tenement house laws were routinely challenged by landlords and other real estate interests, sometimes in the legislatures, sometimes in the courts, and sometimes, as in Wisconsin, with success. Even when the laws withstood the challenges, they were very hard to enforce. The cities had far too few inspectors—fewer than one for every five hundred tenement houses in New York in 1916. Most were overworked and underpaid, often willing to overlook minor violations (and, for a price, even major ones). "For a God-fearing man, the job of inspector was a nightmare of temptation," writes historian Thomas Lee Philpott. "For anybody else it was a dream." Even when the inspectors issued citations, it sometimes took years for the courts to process them. More often than not, the penalties were trivial. The enforcement process had so broken down, wrote the New York State Board of Housing, that it was more serious to deface park property "than to maintain a tenement house in such condition as to continually menace the health and safety of its occupants." Even worse, the tenement house laws applied only to new buildings. They also raised the cost of construction, by as much as 10 to 15 percent in Boston, so that far from stimulating the production of much-needed new housing, they deterred it. Edith Elmer Wood, one of the leaders of a new generation of housing reformers, nicely summarized the growing disenchantment with tenement house reform in 1919: "The best restrictive legislation is only negative. It will prevent the bad. It will not produce the good. Especially it will not produce it at a given [meaning reasonable] rental."[21]

If model tenement laws were a disappointment, the model tenement movement was a fiasco. After a promising start in Brooklyn, the movement was stymied in Chicago. It also got bogged down in Boston. Even in New York, where it was supported by many of the country's wealthiest and most prominent citizens, it produced very little housing. For every model tenement that was put up by the city's semi-philanthropic housing companies between 1902 and 1916, the heyday of the movement, more than three hundred ordinary tenements were put up by the city's commercial builders. Of the roughly 2.9 million New Yorkers who lived in tenements in 1917 and paid $25 a month or less in rent, these companies housed only two-thirds of one percent. Moreover, the model tenement movement lost what little momentum it had after World War I. By virtue of wartime inflation, it became impossible to build decent low-income housing. It also became very hard to persuade "the large-hearted rich" to invest in model tenements. Some were reluctant to settle for a lower than ordinary return on capital. Others were put off by the stigma attached to the tenement house business. Still others thought that it was unnecessary, impractical, and even immoral to resort to philanthropy to solve the housing problem. August Heckscher and a few other wealthy New Yorkers made a last-ditch effort to revive the model tenement movement in the mid 1920s. But nothing came of it.[22] By the end of the decade it was clear that the movement had done very little to house the working class, even less to inspire the commercial builders, and virtually nothing to abolish the slums.

By the late 1920s it was also clear that the attempt to drain the slums was at best a qualified success. Although some working people moved from the center to the periphery, others did not. Some stayed in the slums because they had no choice. Holding menial, often highly insecure and poorly paying jobs, they could not afford to rent an apartment in a new-law or model tenement, much less to buy a home of their own, especially if it was not within walking

distance of their workplace. Others stayed put even though they had a choice.*
Some placed a much lower value on the importance of housing than the reformers did. A close family, loving and hard-working parents and happy and
well-behaved children, counted for more than a nice apartment. As Sam Lev-
enson, a Jewish comedian who grew up in a squalid tenement, later wrote,
"My environment was miserable: I was not." Others wanted to spend as little
as possible on rent, especially if the money saved might be enough to bring a
wife, parent, or sibling from Europe to America, to enable the father to open
his own business, or to allow the children to stay in school longer (and perhaps take advantage of opportunities closed to their parents). Still others preferred to stay close to relatives and friends who spoke the same language, wor-
shipped at the same churches, and supported the institutions that kept their
culture alive. For many first- and second-generation immigrants it made little
or no sense to move to better housing on the periphery if it forced them to
sever the ties that gave meaning to their lives.[23]

In view of the serious limitations of tenement house reform and other conventional approaches, some reformers came to the conclusion that more
drastic measures were needed. By far the most drastic was what was known as
slum clearance, a process by which the municipal authorities condemned the
tenement houses, tore them down, and then reused the land for working-
class housing. As a form of social policy, as opposed to, say, a by-product of
street widening or other public improvements, slum clearance had its origins
in England in the mid and late nineteenth century, when Parliament passed a
series of laws that culminated in the Housing of the Working Classes Act of
1890. Several European nations followed England's lead. And the movement
gathered momentum shortly after World War I. Slum clearance made some
headway, notably in England, where the local authorities tore down some
parts of the worst slums of London and other cities and put up decent working-class housing in their place. But even in England, Edith Elmer Wood
pointed out in the mid 1930s, roughly three-quarters of a century after the

---

* Some observers had predicted as much. Late in the 1870s, a real estate expert wrote
that even "if any number of attractive cottages were constructed on this island [of Man-
hattan], and offered at the same rents now asked for tenement suites, it would be impossible to dislodge a large proportion of present tenants." (New York *Real Estate Record and
Builders' Guide*, September 22, 1877, page 729.) Roughly two decades later a New York reformer noted, with regret, that a large majority of the tenement-house dwellers, even
many who worked outside the city, were reluctant to move from the Lower East Side. (See
Royal Commission on London Traffic, *Appendices to the Report of the Royal Commission on
London Traffic with Index* [London, 1906], page 74.)

movement was launched, "Slum clearance, though much talked about, has been practiced very little."[24]

It was talked about in America too—though not as much as in Europe. As early as 1884 Felix Adler, a leader of New York's Charity Organization Society, contended that the government must reduce overcrowding, must improve the tenements, and "where that is no longer possible, must dismantle the houses and remove them from existence." Gould took a similar position, arguing that there is no "satisfactory way of dealing with irremediable insanitary premises than to tear them down." (Noting that "such property cannot in morals have any rentable value," Gould added that the owners should be compensated only "for the value of the materials as salvage.") If the government could throw out decayed meat and spill diseased milk, surely it could demolish pernicious tenements. Jacob Riis and architect I. N. Phelps Stokes agreed. So did Robert W. De Forest, chairman of New York's Tenement House Commission of 1900 and first commissioner of the city's tenement house department. Speaking of one of the worst blocks on the Lower East Side, a block known as the "lung block" because it was "permanently infected with the germs of tubercular disease," De Forest argued at the turn of the century that "every consideration of public health, morals and decency require[s] that the buildings of this block be destroyed at an early date."[25]

But down through the 1920s slum clearance was, in the words of historian Max Page, "a stock rhetorical device rather than a tool of public policy." Aside from demolishing a small number of dilapidated buildings that were deemed "unfit for habitation"—or defined, legally, as a "nuisance"—only a few American cities cleared any slums. Even they cleared very few. Under the state's Small Parks Law of 1887, New York razed Mulberry Bend, a 2.7-acre parcel, and a couple of other notorious slums—which, said Riis, were "not fit for Christian men and women, let alone innocent children to live in"—and replaced them with small parks, "breathing-spaces" that served as the "lungs of the poor." ("I have seen an armful of daisies keep the peace of a block better than a policeman and his club," Riis observed.) Under pressure from tenement-reform groups and settlement houses, Chicago demolished hundreds of tenements and evicted thousands of tenants to make way for dozens of small parks and playgrounds. (Astonished by the intense grief of the uprooted residents, a leading reformer wrote, "It was strange to find people so attached to homes that were so lacking in all the attributes of comfort and decency.") Boston also engaged in slum clearance, notably in the North End, but on a much smaller scale than New York and Chicago. These "few casual, non-related efforts" aside, it was fair to say, wrote Veiller, "that the people of the United States have done little or nothing in the way of slum clearance"—and even less, said the Boston City Planning Board, in the way of "erecting new homes upon the sites thus cleared."[26]

Slum clearance made so little headway in the United States before 1930 for several reasons. More often than not, the landlords strongly opposed attempts to tear down their buildings, especially if the authorities took the position that they were a "nuisance," a danger to public health or public safety, and thus could be condemned without compensation. Even if the authorities were willing to offer compensation, the landlords usually objected, particularly if they thought the offer was below fair market value. As a result of political opposition, official inertia, and public indifference, it took more than a decade to turn Mulberry Bend into a city park. And in the face of vigorous objections from landlords and developers, New York's Tenement House Department abandoned its efforts to raze the city's infamous rear tenements. If need be, the landlords could also appeal to the courts, which, in their zeal to protect private property, interpreted the police power so narrowly that the authorities could demolish only those buildings that were a "nuisance," a very small fraction of the many wretched tenements. Even when some states empowered the cities to demolish buildings that were not a "nuisance," provided they compensated the owners, the courts held that demolition was permissible only as a last resort. Under these legal constraints, New York's Tenement House Department concluded in 1902 that tenements could be "vacated," or temporarily closed, but rarely demolished.[27]

Moreover, the costs of slum clearance were staggering. Unlike British cities, which could acquire unsanitary buildings for very little, American cities were obliged to pay fair market value—which, Veiller and others complained, was often two to three times what the property was worth. Hence it would have cost at least a million dollars to "take" an ordinary city block on the Lower East Side in the 1920s. Even in the 1930s, the secretary of the Lower East Side Chamber of Commerce estimated, it would have cost at least half a billion dollars to completely rehabilitate the whole district—a vast sum in those days. Down through the 1920s it was inconceivable that the federal government would provide funds for slum clearance, which was what the national government did in Britain. It was also unlikely that the states would help out. Hence the cost would fall entirely on the cities, which were in no position to meet it. As a committee of high-level New York City officials put it in 1924: "The cost of the wholesale demolition which would be necessary to materially improve the conditions in this city [would] be prohibitive. To confiscate the property to be condemned, to pay the property owners therefor and subsequently to demolish the buildings and erect new houses in their stead would obviously be a burden upon the City of New York amounting to hundreds of millions of dollars."[28] Although the numbers would have been lower, what was true for New York was true for other big cities.

Lastly, slum clearance did nothing to solve the housing problem. It created much-needed "breathing spaces" for the poor, but at the expense of thousands of tenants who were forced to move from one unsanitary and overcrowded tenement to another. It might have made more headway had there been cause to think that someone would build improved housing on the sites to accommodate the displaced residents. But there was not. Private enterprise had no intention of doing so. Neither had public authority. For with a few exceptions, Americans opposed public housing. Even the leading tenement-house reformers took exception to it. Committed, in Page's words, to "the inviolability of private property and limited government action," they contended that it would drive private enterprise out of the housing business and create additional opportunities for official skulduggery. "There is nothing in foreign experience with municipal housing of working people to render its repetition with us either desirable or attractive," declared Gould. To tax one class for the benefit of another "is bad principle and worse policy." "Municipal regulation, not municipal ownership, is the best watchword for American policy." De Forest agreed. So did Veiller, who argued, "It is foreign to our principles of government, foreign to the accepted views of American people, to have the government compete with private enterprise by providing houses." In the face of opposition from reformers like Gould, De Forest, and Veiller, it was unlikely that the cities would try to raze the slums and build working-class housing in their place. Even if they did, it was unlikely that their efforts would survive a legal challenge.[29]

Under the circumstances it is small wonder that even the most dedicated tenement-house reformers were skeptical about slum clearance down through the early twentieth century. Deeply scarred by the long and extremely frustrating battle to turn Mulberry Bend into a city park, Jacob Riis pointed out in 1890, "The drastic [slum clearance] measures adopted in Paris, in Glasgow, and in London are not practicable here on anything like as large a scale." ("Doubtless the best [thing] would be to get rid of it [the tenement] altogether," he added; "but as we cannot, all argument on that score may at this time be dismissed as idle.") This skepticism persisted into the 1920s. "When one considers the vast number of tenements that are below the minimum standard of our present tenement law," a New York State housing committee reported, "it seems impractical to attempt slum clearance on the vast scale that is necessary." (And where, a New York City housing committee asked, would

the tenants live while their apartments were being town down?) Some reformers derived consolation from the belief that the slums would eventually
disappear, a belief that would be sorely tested during the Great Depression. Either the tenants would get fed up and move away, or business would find a
more profitable use for the land. Indeed, wrote Riis in 1890: "Business has
done more than all other agencies together to wipe out the worst tenements.
It has been New York's real Napoleon III" (the French emperor who presided
over the reconstruction of Paris in the 1860s).[30]

Although Riis did not live to see it, the political constraints on slum clearance began to wane after World War I—slowly in the 1920s, more rapidly
in the early and mid 1930s. As tenement-house reformers had long hoped,
many workingmen and their families moved from the center to the periphery
in the mid and late 1920s, thereby "siphoning off" the population of some of
the worst slums and sharply reducing the demand for housing there.
Nowhere was this process more striking than on New York's Lower East Side,
which lost close to half of its residents in the 1920s. In the wake of the depression many of the remaining tenants could no longer pay their rent. Vacancy rates soared, rent rolls plummeted. Some landlords were inclined to
hold on—"awaiting the time," wrote the New York State Board of Housing in
1930, "when some change, the causes of which they cannot foresee, may restore values sufficiently to permit them to recover their investment and possibly to make a small profit." But many others, having lost all hope that downtown business interests would soon find more profitable uses for their
property, were eager to unload. If the city was willing to buy their buildings,
even if only to demolish them, they were happy to sell. Having long opposed
slum clearance, they now welcomed it. This turnabout offended several housing reformers, who held that the acquisition of these buildings would be a
huge windfall for the property owners "who have [long] been exploiting the
slums as a matter of sound business practice."[31]

The fiscal constraints on slum clearance also began to wane in the postwar
years. Slum clearance was still much too expensive for the cities and the
states. But it was not too expensive for the federal government. As Thomas
Adams, a Canadian planner who later worked on the regional plan for New
York City, pointed out in 1918, the war revealed that "there was absolutely no
limit to the amount of money we could raise [if we had to]." (Just how much
money the federal government could raise would be underscored a decade
and a half later, when the Roosevelt administration, in an effort to create jobs
and stimulate the economy, poured billions of dollars into highways, airports,

sewers, and other public works.) Not long after the war, moreover, some housing reformers started to stress that while it was very expensive to clear the
slums, it was even more expensive to maintain the "hospitals, prisons, refor-
matories, police and all the intricate mechanism of modern government,
much of which is necessitated by the very slum that we hesitate to destroy."[32]
According to this argument—which was documented in a host of studies in
the 1930s, when it emerged as the conventional wisdom—slum clearance
would in the long run save a great deal of money.

The ideological constraints on slum clearance began to lose much of their
force in the postwar years, too. Led by Edith Elmer Wood and Catherine
Bauer, a new generation of reformers took issue with the prevailing view that
public housing was un-American. Pointing to the federal programs to build
housing for defense workers during World War I and the state programs to
subsidize housing for veterans during the 1920s, they argued that government could provide low-income housing without driving private enterprise
out of business and without creating opportunities for official skulduggery.
And not only could but should. As Bauer declared, private enterprise was no
longer capable of building adequate housing at prices low-income Americans
could afford. Under these circumstances, insisted Nathan Straus, who would
later serve as the first head of the U.S. Housing Authority, it was "not only the
right but the solemn duty" of the government "to step in." The government,
Straus and others claimed, had as much a responsibility to provide housing as
to provide water, roads, and schools, one that every "civilized country" except
the United States had already accepted.[33] By stressing that public authorities
could provide adequate low-income housing at a reasonable price, the reformers undermined the argument that slum clearance could do nothing to
solve the housing problem—that it would only drive tenants from one unsanitary and overcrowded tenement to another.

At the same time that these political, fiscal, and ideological constraints were
losing much of their force, other developments were taking place that did
much to strengthen the case for slum clearance. The most important was the
postwar housing crisis. During the war (and for a few years thereafter) the
construction of new housing came to a standstill, a result of the inflationary
spiral that sent the costs of capital, labor, and materials skyrocketing. In New
York City, for example, fewer than one hundred new-law tenements were
erected in 1919, down from more than thirteen hundred in 1915. By the early
1920s most cities had an acute housing shortage. Vacancy rates plunged, to
less than one percent in New York's tenements. Rents soared, so much so that
for the first time in American history the authorities imposed rent control in

some cities. Dilapidated houses, once regarded as uninhabitable, were now occupied.[34] The situation improved in the mid and late 1920s. But by then many reformers (and, for that matter, many other Americans) realized that the housing problem was more serious than ever and that it affected not only the lower class but even, to a lesser degree, the lower middle class. As they saw it, the problem was a product not so much of the greed of individual landlords as of a shortage of adequate housing. The solution lay not in imposing tougher restrictions on tenements, but in stimulating the construction of additional housing—and, above all, in lowering the cost of new construction so the lower and lower middle classes could afford it.

But as architects and other experts pointed out, it would be impossible to lower the cost of new construction to this point without a revolution in the housing industry. As A. C. Shire put it:

> [Housing,] the second largest industry in the country, operating as a large number of picayune businesses, is overloaded with a whole series of overheads and profits, bogged down by waste and inefficiency, unable to benefit by advancing productive techniques developed in other fields, and tied down to an obsolete and expensive system of land utilization. In an age and in a country of big money, power, and mass production, we have the anachronism that the production of one of the three essentials of life has been allowed to remain a matter for small capital, individual action, and handicraft.[35]

To reduce the obsolete practices that put adequate housing beyond the reach of so many Americans, Shire and others held that the housing industry had to adopt the principles that had proved successful in other industries, namely, mass production, standardization, scientific management, and large-scale operation. Their adoption would revolutionize the housing industry, but only if the industry embraced large-scale development—only if it focused its efforts not on buildings or even blocks but on neighborhoods and whole communities. Formulated by architects Ernest Flagg and Grosvenor Atterbury in the early twentieth century, the concept of large-scale development was promoted by the Regional Planning Association of America in the 1920s and endorsed by the President's Conference on Home Building and Home Ownership in the early 1930s. It was the inspiration for several new residential communities, among the most famous of which were Forest Hills Gardens, New York, and Radburn, New Jersey.

According to its backers, large-scale development was the only way to improve the quality of housing in the slums. As Henry Wright and the other members of the new generation of housing reformers saw it, a piecemeal approach would not work. No matter how well designed and no matter how well constructed, "a single good building in a slum area is foredoomed to failure," argued Edith Elmer Wood. By itself, it would inevitably succumb to the blight that surrounds it. "The development of a whole block is only slightly better," she contended. At best these blocks would form "little islands of good housing in a sea of slum," in the words of Langdon Post, chairman of the New York City Housing Authority. At worst these islands would in time be inundated. "A complete neighborhood unit, large enough to create and preserve its own atmosphere, should be the minimum size of a development [in a slum]," Wood insisted. But the slums had few if any sites suitable for large-scale development. Thus the cities would first have to clear them—buy out the many small property owners, tear down the existing structures, and then assemble large parcels on which private enterprise or public authority would build decent low-income housing.[36] To put it another way, slum clearance was a prerequisite for large-scale development in much of the inner city.

Spurred by these developments, a couple of states decided to give slum clearance a try in the late 1920s. One was New York. After a long battle that pitted some of the city's most powerful real estate interests against some of the nation's leading housing reformers, the state legislature enacted a law in 1926 that authorized private companies to engage in slum clearance and provide low-income housing. The companies were given the power of eminent domain and a partial exemption from state and, if the cities approved, local taxes, in return for which they had to accept limits on rents and dividends and strict supervision by the newly formed state board of housing. New Jersey followed New York's lead in 1929, when the legislature passed a bill that permitted insurance companies to undertake slum clearance and low-income housing and authorized the cities to acquire the land for them by eminent domain. Under these laws only two projects were built in New Jersey, and fewer than a dozen in New York. (About half were in Manhattan, the rest in the outer boroughs. Some, though not all, went up in the slums. The best known was the Amalgamated Dwellings, a cooperative housing project that was sponsored by the Amalgamated Clothing Workers of America and erected on the site of an old printing press on the Lower East Side. The largest was Knickerbocker Village. Located on the Lower East Side's notorious "lung block," it was built by Fred F. French, a prominent New York realtor, and housed nearly sixteen hundred families.)[37]

But if these laws did not stimulate the construction of much low-income housing, they did indicate that the resistance to slum clearance had been severely weakened since World War I. Just how much was revealed in the 1930s, when in the wake of the Great Depression an uneasy alliance of architects, social workers, housing reformers, labor unions, and construction companies launched a campaign to persuade the federal government to provide funds for slum clearance and low-income housing. Their spokesmen argued that the United States lagged way behind England and other European countries, which had demonstrated that public authority could provide decent housing at reasonable rents for low-income tenants. "America," wrote Langdon Post, "is the most backward civilized country in the world as far as housing is concerned." The slums had long been a national disgrace. Now that residential construction had come to a standstill, exacerbating the shortage of low- and middle-income housing, the situation was getting worse. But to rebuild the slums would cost more that the cities or the states could afford. If the job was to be done, the federal government would have to do it. By providing funds to demolish the slums and construct low-cost housing, the government would also create much-needed jobs in the moribund building trades. As Wood put it, a large-scale effort to clear the slums and replace them with good low-income housing would help not only to solve the housing problem but also to deal with "another even more urgent national emergency."[38]

As expected, the campaign ran into a good deal of opposition. Much of it came from conservative business and real estate interests, which held that it would be un-American for the federal government to underwrite slum clearance, much less public housing. It would be socialistic, said Jacob O. Pedersen, president of the Bronx Borough Taxpayers' League, who pointed out that if the government provided housing it might as well provide food and clothing too. Housing should be left to private enterprise, which would be driven out of business by government competition. Low-income housing should be left to private philanthropy. If the government wanted to help alleviate the housing problem, it would be better advised to offer insurance for residential mortgages and to encourage the cities to reduce property taxes and modernize building codes. Also in opposition was a group of housing reformers, among them Henry Wright, Lewis Mumford, and Carol Aronovici, who contended that slum clearance would do little but bail out the slumlords. To provide decent housing for working people, the authorities should not build on high-priced sites in the center of the city, but rather on cheap land on the periphery that was suitable for large-scale development. By building decent low-cost housing there, the authorities would induce people to leave the tenements, thereby draining the slums and driving down property values to the point at which slum clearance might make economic sense. In the absence of a huge public housing program on the periphery, Mumford wrote, slum clearance "will only create grislier and greater slums."[39]

Under ordinary circumstances, the campaign would probably not have gotten very far. But circumstances were far from ordinary. The nation was paralyzed by the worst depression in its history. Many Americans were convinced that in order to revive the economy the federal government would have to take a number of unprecedented steps, among the most important of which was to mount a massive public works program that would create hundreds of thousands of jobs in the construction industry. Here was a splendid opportunity for advocates of slum clearance, who pointed out that demolishing slums and building homes was at least as good a way to generate employment as constructing roads. In 1932, the same year Franklin D. Roosevelt was elected president, Mary Simkhovitch, Edith Elmer Wood, and other housing reformers called on New York senator Robert F. Wagner to sponsor legislation to allow the Reconstruction Finance Corporation, a federal agency that had been set up to lend money for self-liquidating public works projects, to make loans for public housing. Reluctant to endorse so radical a proposal, Wagner instead inserted into the Emergency Relief and Reconstruction Bill a provision authorizing the RFC to lend money to limited-dividend companies for the purposes of clearing slums and building low-income housing, a provision that was approved by Congress. Although a major breakthrough, it had little immediate impact. Aside from lending Fred French $8 million for Knickerbocker Village, the RFC approved very few of the hundreds of applications for funds for slum clearance before the program was transferred to the housing division of the Public Works Administration in 1933.[40]

According to Harold L. Ickes, head of the PWA, the housing division's objective was, first, to create jobs, especially in the building trades and heavy industry, and, second, to demolish slums and construct low-cost housing. But it could not do the first without doing the second. Thus under the leadership of Robert Kohn, a housing reformer and president of the American Institute of Architects, the division initially followed the RFC's approach and offered loans to limited-dividend companies. The results were disappointing. (In the end only seven housing projects, with roughly three thousand units, were erected, about three-quarters of them in the outer boroughs of New York City.) The division subsequently abandoned this approach and decided to go directly into the housing business—in conjunction with local housing authorities, if possible, on its own, if need be. But beset by political, fiscal, bureaucratic, and legal problems, the agency managed to demolish only about ten thousand substandard housing units, out of an estimated six million nationwide, and to build only about twenty-two thousand low-cost housing units, some of which were located on vacant land on the periphery, as opposed to cleared slums in the center.[41]

If the housing division did little to clear slums and build low-income housing, it did much to pave the way for the Housing Act of 1937, also known, after its sponsors, Senator Robert F. Wagner and Representative Henry B. Steagall, as the Wagner-Steagall Act. The culmination of a long and fierce struggle, the act was one of the legislative landmarks of the 1930s. Although conceived as a way to reduce unemployment, it was more than just another short-term relief program. It was also a long-term housing program, a program that was designed to alleviate both "the unsafe and insanitary housing conditions" in the nation and "the acute shortage of decent, safe, and sanitary dwellings" for low-income families. The act established the U.S. Housing Authority and empowered it to make loans and grants to local housing authorities for the purpose of clearing slums and building low-cost housing. To underscore the commitment to slum clearance, the law required that at least one substandard dwelling had to be eliminated for each new dwelling constructed in every project. The passage of the act did not end the opposition to slum clearance, much less to public housing, which was far more controversial. And it raised almost as many issues as it settled. But with its passage, slum clearance became national policy. In the wake of the act, one state after another passed legislation to permit the cities to create local housing authorities, without which they could not take advantage of the federal program. And by the end of the decade most big cities had done so.[42]

The downtown businessmen and property owners were not involved in the battle over slum clearance. If they stood anywhere on the issue, it was on the sidelines. Slum clearance was not on the agenda of the local downtown businessmen's associations or the National Association of Building Owners and Managers. Nor was low-income housing. During the 1920s these organizations were mainly concerned about the accessibility and stability of the central business district. They devoted most of their energies to such issues as rapid transit, traffic congestion, parking bans, and height limits. During the early 1930s they focused on tax relief and other measures designed to help the central business district cope with the devastating consequences of the depression. Like other Americans, many downtown businessmen and property owners were distressed by the deterioration of the inner-city slums and the shortage of low-income housing. (And some belonged to civic groups that were trying to solve these problems.) But as owners and managers of enterprises whose customers, clients, and tenants came for the most part from the upper, upper middle, and middle classes, they saw no reason to believe that the well-being of the central business district was related to the deterioration of the inner-city slums, no matter how advanced, or the shortage of low-income housing, no matter how acute.

During the 1930s a few downtown businessmen and property owners began to realize that slum clearance could be used in ways that might well serve their own interests. Consider what happened in Miami. According to historian Raymond A. Mohl, most of the city's 25,000 blacks lived just northwest of downtown Miami in a 350-acre district known then as "Colored Town" (and now as Overtown), a district filled with small, dilapidated, and unsanitary shacks—a "deplorable slum district" that was the "plague spot" of the city, declared the *Miami Herald*. Under the leadership of John C. Gramling, a well-connected lawyer and civic booster, the city's elites organized a campaign to persuade the housing division of the PWA to provide funds to raze Colored Town and build public housing for blacks in Liberty Square, five or six miles from downtown Miami. What makes the campaign so interesting is that it was backed not only by white and black leaders, who saw it as a way to remove one of Miami's worst eyesores and improve the quality of housing for its black residents, but also by downtown businessmen and property owners, who saw it, in Mohl's words, as a way "to eliminate the downtown black community entirely to make way for further expansion of the [central] business district." That further expansion would be necessary, the downtown business interests had no doubt. With the help of the PWA's housing division, Miami proceeded to demolish Colored Town, displace its black residents, and erect the nucleus of what later became known as Liberty City, the site of major race riots several decades later.[43]

Some downtown businessmen and property owners also believed that slum clearance might well serve their interests in other ways. In this group were several Brooklyn merchants. As historian Joel Schwartz has observed, interest in slum clearance picked up momentum in New York in 1934, when Robert Kohn announced that the PWA's housing division would spend $25 million in the city—about enough to rebuild twenty square blocks. Where the money should be spent would be decided by Langdon Post, who had just been named head of the city's tenement house department by Mayor Fiorello H. La Guardia, and the Slum Clearance Committee, a blue-ribbon citizens group. As Schwartz points out, Post and the SCC "were deluged with offers" from groups that wanted the authorities to clear the slums in their neighborhoods. One of these groups was the Sands Street Board of Trade, a merchants association from downtown Brooklyn, a once-thriving business district that had fallen on hard times. Slum clearance, the Sands Street merchants believed, would attract to the residential sections surrounding downtown Brooklyn a new type of tenant, "a better type" who would pay his rent and patronize downtown businesses. The Brownsville Board of Trade and Pitkin Avenue Merchants Association, which spoke for other Brooklyn businessmen, also favored slum clearance and even pledged to get property owners to support the program.[44]

But these Miami and Brooklyn businessmen were the exceptions. Through the mid 1930s most downtown businessmen and property owners did little or nothing to mobilize support for slum clearance. Some were indifferent to the idea. Downtown had problems, they acknowledged. But the solution lay in enhancing its accessibility, not in clearing slums. Other downtown businessmen and property owners were hostile to the idea. Dyed-in-the-wool conservatives, who strongly believed that the government should interfere as little as possible in the market, they opposed slum clearance on fiscal and ideological grounds. One of their spokesmen was Walter S. Schmidt, the Cincinnati real estate man, president of the National Association of Real Estate Boards, and founder and first president of the Urban Land Institute. Testifying before a Senate committee in 1936, Schmidt argued that if the federal government undertook a full-scale slum clearance and low-cost housing program it would cost $50 to $60 billion, which was much more than the country could afford. If it mounted a more modest effort, if it tore down some old tenements and put up new buildings on the same sites, it would unwittingly create the slums of the future. The reason, he told the committee, was that "it is people who make slums, and not houses," a position that was completely at odds with the conventional wisdom of housing reform.[45]

Starting in the late 1930s, however, the downtown business interests began to change their minds about slum clearance (if not about low-income housing). What brought about this change was not the Housing Act of 1937, for whose passage they had done virtually nothing, but the growing concern over decentralization. By then they realized that the central business district's worst problems, especially its declining property values, slumping retail sales, and high vacancy rates, were mainly the product of decentralization, not of the depression. Contrary to expectations, they discovered that many well-to-do Americans who had moved to the periphery were no longer coming to the center, that they were patronizing the outlying business districts rather than the central business district. Many downtown businessmen and property owners also realized that in order to curb decentralization and revitalize the central business district it would be necessary to do more than just increase downtown's accessibility. It would also be necessary to induce the well-to-do to move back to the residential neighborhoods surrounding the central business district—a step, it was assumed, that would greatly enlarge the market for downtown goods and services.

But these neighborhoods—many of which stood in the shadows of downtown skyscrapers, "right up against the highest cost real estate in the city," said New York congressman Ralph A. Gamble—had fallen on hard times. The houses were old and dilapidated, high in tax delinquencies and code violations, at best unsanitary and at worst uninhabitable. Many of the streets were dirty and dangerous. The few parks and other open spaces provided little relief from what Harland Bartholomew called "a nightmare of ugliness and blandness." The well-to-do had long fled from these neighborhoods, leaving in their wake the poor and the transient, two groups that were highly susceptible to delinquency, crime, disease, and dependency. If conditions were bad now, they would soon be worse. As R. F. Hewitt, a Seattle real estate man, pointed out, these neighborhoods were "no loan" territories. They were "blacked out," or redlined, by the banks and insurance companies. Thus, said Hewitt, the neighborhoods "most in need of improvements will have to do without any improvement at all, with nothing in sight for the property that is there but to keep on going down hill." It would not be long, warned A. J. Stewart, a Louisville banker, before many of the buildings in these neighborhoods would deteriorate "to the point where [no one would] live in them," and "we would probably have a desert around our [central] business section."[46]

Before the late 1930s such a warning would not have alarmed the downtown business interests. They did not think these run-down areas would remain residential neighborhoods indefinitely. They assumed that in time they would be needed for more intensive uses. As two experts explained, the conventional wisdom was "that the belt of land encircling the central business district would [eventually] be used for the expansion of department stores, wholesale houses, warehouses, and factories" as well as office buildings. By the late 1930s, however, this assumption was open to question. During the mid and late 1920s office buildings were expanding vertically rather than horizontally. And during the early and mid 1930s they were not expanding at all. As a result of the collapse of the economy and competition from outlying business districts, neither were department stores. Warehousing and wholesale trade were declining too, a result in part of direct buying from factories. And factories were moving farther and farther away from the center. Well aware of these trends, Charles T. Stewart, director of the Urban Land Institute, declared in 1941, "There is nothing to lead us to believe that we shall need [the run-down inner-city neighborhoods] for commercial or industrial purposes."[47]

Once the downtown business interests realized that the run-down inner-city neighborhoods were unsuitable for middle- and upper-middle-class residences and unnecessary for commercial and industrial purposes, they viewed them with growing alarm. So did other Americans. To some, these run-down areas were "urban deserts," to others a "housing swamp," and to yet others "the collar of slums which is threatening to strangle [the] downtown business section." "Here and there a central [business] section has maintained itself in the face of blight all about like New York's Wall Street or Chicago's 'Loop,'" one observer pointed out. But they were the exceptions. In most cities it was not clear that the central business district would survive "surrounded by an ever increasing zone of slum property," wrote another observer. Given these dire prospects, most downtown businessmen and property owners came to the conclusion that it was imperative to do something about the run-down inner-city neighborhoods, to rehabilitate the buildings if possible and to demolish them if they were structurally unsound or had outlived their usefulness. Private enterprise should take the initiative, but if necessary, public authority, local, state, and even federal governments, should help out.[48] In other words, downtown business interests were now ready to support slum clearance to shore up the central business district.

But slum clearance had not been designed to shore up the central business district—or, for that matter, as a way to create jobs in the building trades and give a boost to the American economy. Rather it had been designed with two other objectives in mind. The first was to wipe out the "lung blocks," "Bed-bug Rows," "Whiskey Islands," and, in the words of Merlo J. Pusey, other "such symbols of human degradation"—and to wipe out the worst of them, not necessarily the ones adjacent to the central business district. By cleaning out what Pusey called "the Augean stables of our cities," by demolishing the unsanitary and overcrowded tenements and shacks infesting them, the advocates of slum clearance hoped to abolish (or at the very least reduce) the crime, immorality, disease, and disorder that had long plagued urban America. It was not just rhetoric. More often than not, slum clearance was not carried out in the run-down neighborhoods adjacent to the central business district. With the help of the PWA and the U.S. Housing Authority, New York undertook just over a dozen slum clearance projects between 1935 and 1942, more than any other American city. But as a result of the high cost of land on the Lower East Side, only two, First Houses and Vladeck Houses, were in lower Manhattan, not far from Wall Street and the financial district. Two were in upper Manhattan, one in Harlem, and one in East Harlem. The rest were in the outer boroughs, half of them in Brooklyn.[49]

The second objective was to build decent housing for low-income Americans—not for all of them, said Senator Wagner, only for those who lived in "conditions which are detrimental to morals, to health, and also to safety." (And not for the unemployed or the poorest of the poor, noted the U.S. Housing Authority, but for working-class families that could not find decent housing at reasonable rents.) Since private enterprise could not afford to put up decent low-cost housing, the job fell to public authority—to local housing authorities, which would build it, and the federal government, which would subsidize it. Once identified with parks and playgrounds, slum clearance was now synonymous with public housing. Public housing follows slum clearance just "as night [follows] day," Henry J. Linton, a member of the Columbus, Ohio, Metropolitan Housing Authority, told a joint congressional committee on housing. Build better houses for slum dwellers and you "do away with the slums," Helen Alfred, secretary of the National Public Housing Conference, advised the Senate Committee on Education and Labor. Again, it was not just rhetoric. Through the late 1930s most of the slums cleared in Atlanta, New York, and other cities were reused for low-income housing. Most of it was put up by local housing authorities, some by limited-dividend companies. The new houses were better than the tenements and shacks they replaced, more sanitary, less crowded, and more attractive. But though the rents were low, they were usually too high for the tenants whose homes had been demolished in the name of slum clearance.[50]

From the perspective of the downtown business interests, slum clearance left much to be desired. What good would it do if local authorities wiped out slums in Harlem and East Harlem or Williamsburg, in Brooklyn, and Queensbridge, in Queens, while leaving in place "the dirty collar" of run-down neighborhoods around the central business district? What good would it do if they cleared the Lower East Side, but built public housing on the sites, thereby providing decent housing at reasonable rents, yet leaving the central business district surrounded by low-income groups?[51] In other words, what would slum clearance do to increase the demand for downtown goods and services? The answer was, not much. What the downtown business interests needed was therefore a form of slum clearance that would wipe out not the worst slums, but rather the run-down neighborhoods adjacent to the central business district, some of which, strictly speaking, might not even be slums. A form of slum clearance in which the slums would be used not for public hous-

ing for the poor, but for private housing for the well-to-do, high-quality housing that would attract the upper middle and middle classes from the periphery
to the center, where their great purchasing power would help revitalize the
central business district. What the downtown business interests needed was
not so much slum clearance as what would be called urban redevelopment
(and later urban renewal).

Although the most powerful, downtown business interests were only one
of several groups in favor of urban redevelopment. Among the others were local officials, who believed that run-down inner-city neighborhoods were a
heavy burden on the cities' fiscal system. Replacing them with stable upper-
middle- and middle-class residential communities would not only reduce the
cities' soaring expenditures but also enlarge their shrinking tax bases. Also in
this category were city planners, many of whom, observed Catherine Bauer,
"saw redevelopment as the means toward more rational and efficient organization of central areas," a way to remove "wasteful or inappropriate land uses"
from the inner city. For some it may have been a source of power and prestige,
too. Many real estate interests also supported urban redevelopment. Some believed that it would stimulate residential construction and boost property values in the inner city, while others hoped that it would head off the growing
demands for subsidized housing in urban America. Ironically, some advocates of public housing also favored urban redevelopment, especially after
World War II. They assumed, mistakenly it turned out, that urban redevelopment would displace so many inner-city residents that the authorities would
have no alternative but to build public housing to relocate them.[52]

Although these groups formed a powerful, if unstable coalition, they had
their work cut out for them. Politically and legally, it was not hard to make a
strong case that the cities should demolish buildings that were a nuisance, a
threat to public health and public safety and a menace to the general welfare
of the community.[53] That was surely a legitimate use of the police power. Nor
was it hard to make almost as strong a case that the cities should tear down dilapidated buildings, provided they paid the owners fair market value. But it
was very hard to make a case that the cities should raze the run-down residential neighborhoods adjacent to the central business district when many were
not the worst slums and some were not slums at all. Moreover, property in
these neighborhoods was as a rule far more expensive than property in other
run-down sections that were much farther from the central business district
but in even worse condition. How could the municipal authorities justify
razing the close-in run-down neighborhoods when they could rebuild even

worse slums in other parts of the city at even less expense? The answer, said the downtown business interests and their allies, was that the cities should wipe them out because they were blighted areas (or blighted districts). To put it another way, the cities should use urban redevelopment to get rid of blight.

Americans had used the term "blight" to describe slums at least as early as the turn of the century. But it was not until the early 1910s that they began to speak of "blighted areas" or "blighted districts" as a distinct part of the urban environment. Speaking at the Fourth National Conference on City Planning in 1912, J. Randolph Coolidge, a Boston architect, pointed out that Boston, New York, Philadelphia, and other cities all had "blighted districts," which he defined as areas "in which land values after a period of increase are stationary or falling." Blight, he went on, was an economic, as opposed to a social, problem. Its causes were well known to city planners, but its remedies were "more easily suggested than applied." Coolidge's talk, which greatly impressed Lawson Purdy, one of the architects of New York City's pioneering zoning ordinance, sparked a lengthy discussion. Dana W. Bartlett observed that Los Angeles had a "blighted neighborhood" just north of the central business district, on the site of the proposed new civic center and Union Station. Walter B. Stevens added that St. Louis had blighted districts, which were a concern of the newly appointed city planning commission. And Frank B. Williams, a lawyer and another leader in the campaign for zoning in New York, said that "where the blight goes far enough in time it may even tend to become a slum district." He saw no reason why blighted districts should not be condemned, replanned, sold off, and redeveloped.[54]

During the next quarter of a century Americans grew more concerned about blight. But they had an even harder time defining a blighted district than they had defining a slum, about the definition of which, Lawrence Veiller once wrote, "no two people agree." To some, a blighted area was one in which property values increased less rapidly than they did in other parts of the city— or in which they actually decreased. To others, it was an area in which "buildings have become more or less obsolete," an area characterized by "building vacancies, a general appearance of decay and dejection, and no prospect of a renewed market for its original use or for other purposes." To still others, it was "any area in which the large majority of buildings, whether commercial, industrial, or residential, are old, and in which fundamental repairs are not being made." According to the Committee on Blighted Areas and Slums of the President's Conference on Home Building and Home Ownership, a blighted area was "an economic liability to the community"—as opposed to a slum, which was "a social liability." Following a similar line of reasoning, others defined it as "any area in which economic development has been substantially retarded," "one in which a normal development has been frustrated," and "one in which the taxes do not pay for public service." As if to underscore how vague the concept was, William A. Stanton, secretary of the Comprehensive Plans Committee of Philadelphia, wrote that broadly speaking a blighted area "is a district which is not what it should be."[55]

But if it was hard to define blighted districts, it was easy to find them. By the late 1930s and early 1940s they were visible everywhere in America, in cities big and small, filling the space, wrote Harland Bartholomew, between the close-in slums surrounding the central business district and the outlying residential sections that housed the well-to-do. In Chicago, for example, the blighted districts, which more or less encircled the Loop, covered fully 51 square miles, about one-quarter of the entire city (and twice the size of Manhattan Island), and housed around 1.3 million people, two-fifths of the city's population. Chicago was by no means unique. Based on the 1930 census, one study found 54,000 blocks in 93 cities with more than 100,000 people that were in "an advanced state of blight and obsolescence." A decade later another study reported that 173 square miles of 117 large cities were "so blighted as to require complete rebuilding." According to other estimates, anywhere from one-fifth to one-half of the cities' residential, commercial, and industrial districts were blighted. And in 1944 W. E. Reynolds, commissioner of the Public Buildings Administration of the U.S. Federal Works Agency, told the House Committee on Public Buildings and Grounds that "urban blight and slums, next to the war, constitute the greatest threat which confronts the American people."[56]

Reynolds's statement is more than a little puzzling. To argue that slums were one of the greatest threats facing the American people was one thing.[57] But to couple urban blight with slums—and to argue that blighted districts were also one of the greatest threats—was quite another. It was regrettable that property values rose less rapidly in some areas than in others (and even that they fell in still others). But values could not always go up, much less go up at the same rate everywhere. It was also regrettable that some buildings grew old and obsolete, that some landlords did not make needed repairs, and that some neighborhoods went into decline. But that was to be expected. And it was regrettable that property taxes did not cover the costs of public services in some districts, that some of these districts were "an economic liability" and that others were not what they "should be." But that too was to be expected. Even assuming that the municipal authorities should clear the slums, why should they also raze the blighted districts, many of which, even their critics conceded, were not slums?

Blighted districts should be razed, the downtown business interests and their allies responded, because they were incipient slums, a point made as early as 1912 by Frank B. Williams. "Every blighted district is a potential slum," wrote Bartholomew in the early 1930s. ("Reconstruction of slums will be an endless process," he insisted, "unless we stem the[ir] chief source—the blighted district.") Henry Wright, a landscape architect, housing reformer, and leader of the Regional Planning Association of America, made a similar point. The slum, he contended, "represents an advanced case of 'blight.'" As incipient slums, blighted districts were as much a social as an economic liability, the breeding grounds of the crime and other pathologies that, said Milwaukee city attorney Walter J. Mattison, had "disastrous effects [on the] health, safety, morals and welfare of the community." In blighted districts as well as slums, observed Edward S. Burrell, a midwestern sociologist, one found "blighted lives, stunted, dwarfed, twisted lives . . . acts of violence and immorality, [and an environment] where pauperism and alcoholism come to be regarded as natural and normal."[58]

Blighted districts should also be razed because they were "civic cancers." Americans had begun to employ cancer as a metaphor for social problems in the late nineteenth century. And before long it was routinely applied to the slums. "There is no cure for cancer but the knife," E. R. L. Gould pointed out in 1900, "and so the slum can be eradicated in no other way than by uprooting it, stock and branch." Lawrence Veiller agreed. "The slum," he declared in 1920, "is exactly like a cancer on the body social and body politic." The only remedy for it is "the surgeon's knife," he added, "and the sooner it is out, the less serious the operation." Edith Elmer Wood, who disagreed with Veiller on other issues, took the same position. By the mid 1920s Americans began to liken blight to cancer, too. Over the next two decades the metaphor became commonplace. Thomas C. Desmond, a New York state senator, referred to "the cancerous disease of blight" (as well as to "the fatal plague of blight"). And Homer Hoyt, probably the country's foremost real estate economist, argued: "Like a cancer, blight spread[s] through all the tissues of the urban body and the urban organism [is] unable to cure itself except by a major surgical operation."[59]

This view led inescapably to the conclusion that blighted districts were "infectious," in the words of the Boston City Planning Board—a "contagion," in the words of A. R. Clas, director of the housing division of the Public Works

Administration. Blight "engulf[s] ever larger sections of the city," a Temple University political scientist warned. It "spreads in an inward direction toward the central business district," wrote Charles T. Stewart, "and in an outward direction toward the substantial residential areas." It was therefore "a menace" to "the entire community," Stewart declared. Inner-city residents could try to escape blight by moving to the outlying residential districts, but eventually it would catch up with them. And these districts too would be blighted. Surgery was the only remedy. "If the cities are to live," said Joseph L. Kun, a Philadelphia judge, "they must remove the blighted areas, which like a cancerous growth would eventually destroy them." Remove and then rehabilitate them, wrote the Boston City Planning Board, before they "sapped the vitality of the city's existence."[60]

According to the downtown business interests and their allies, blighted districts and slums were a threat not only to the city's social well-being but also to its fiscal solvency. As Clas put it, they were an "economic drain" on the community. By this Clas meant that blighted districts and slums consumed much more in public services than they produced in property taxes—three times as much, estimated Ernest J. Bohn, president of the National Association of Housing Officials, five times as much, calculated Nathan Straus, then head of the Hillside Housing Corporation of New York. This was a novel idea. For decades Americans had been deeply concerned about the social costs of the slums, about the impact of overcrowded and unsanitary housing on public health, public safety, personal morality, and public order. But through the 1920s they had not made a connection between the rising levels of crime, delinquency, immorality, and poverty, and the growing fiscal problems of the city. With the coming of the Great Depression, however, property values fell and municipal revenues plummeted. Stuck with a heavy bonded debt and soaring relief payments, most cities were hard put to reduce expenditures. As many cities found themselves in dire financial straits, even on the brink of bankruptcy, many Americans began to make the connection between social and fiscal problems. Once it was made, blighted areas came under sharp attack on the ground that they did not pay what Edith Elmer Wood called their "[fair] share of the economic burden."[61]

In defense of this position, Wood, Clas, and others pointed to several studies made in the early and mid 1930s. One, which was done in Indianapolis by Indiana University's Bureau of Social Research, found that the city spent $4 per capita on public services in most neighborhoods, but $27 per capita in one blighted district. To put it another way, Indianapolis spent 26 percent of its taxes for police, fire, health, and sanitary services on only 10 percent of its population. A more elaborate study was done in Cleveland in 1934 for the Metropolitan Housing Authority. It found that one small, largely black run-down district that had 2.5 percent of the city's population produced $225,000 in property taxes, but consumed $2 million in public services. Studies in Boston, Birmingham, and Chicago came up with similar findings. And in 1939 the Public Buildings Administration of the Federal Works Agency reported that the cities' slums and blighted districts, which made up about one-fifth of the residential areas, generated only 6 percent of the property taxes yet absorbed fully 45 percent of the public services. During the 1940s similar studies revealed that slums and blighted districts were a fiscal drain in Atlanta and Los Angeles too.[62]

These studies left a lot to be desired. When they estimated how much different parts of the city paid in property taxes, they were highly accurate. But when it came to apportioning the costs of public services by neighborhood, they were much less reliable. To make things more complicated, it was very hard to draw the boundaries of blighted districts and slums, to figure out where they stopped and normal neighborhoods started. Nor was that all, wrote Mabel L. Walker, an expert on both blighted districts and tax policy. Given the great differences in income levels and property values in the city, it was not "surprising or even distressing" to find that some sections "pay more in taxes than they receive in services, just as other sections receive more than they pay." Moreover, it was very hard to tell whether the disparities were a function of blight or poverty. Since the blighted districts were ordinarily the most congested districts, it was also very hard to tell whether the disparities were a function of blight or density.[63]

Despite their shortcomings, these studies were widely cited as proof that blighted districts were a fiscal drain on the community, one that would grow larger over time. As blight spread, many residents would try to escape it by moving to what Commissioner W. E. Reynolds called "the far-flung fringe of cities." But blight would follow them. To provide public services to the growing blighted areas—and also to maintain the old infrastructure in the center and build a new infrastructure on the periphery—would force the local authorities to raise property taxes. This would drive businesses and residents out of the city and push tax rates even higher. The result, Wood wrote, was that the cities, already "facing death from dry rot at the center," would be forced into bankruptcy. It would cost lots of money to raze and rebuild the blighted districts, Reynolds conceded. But as James Sweinhart, a *Detroit News* reporter, pointed out, the cities were already spending a fortune to subsidize the slums and blighted districts, as much as $30 million a year or $1 billion in a generation, which was more than enough to cover the costs.[64]

By the late 1930s it was not hard to make a strong case that the cities should build spacious and sanitary dwellings on the sites of the cleared slums and blighted areas and, even if it took a small subsidy, set their rents within the reach of the working class. Given the acute shortage of adequate low-cost housing and the deep-seated belief that poor housing was the main source of the cities' worst social problems, it was not hard to make almost as strong a case that the federal government should help out. Even Senator Robert A. Taft, the nation's leading conservative, conceded as much.[65] But it was very hard to make a case that the cities should demolish lower- and working-class homes and replace them with middle- and upper-middle-class housing that the former residents could not possibly afford. At a time when housing was in short supply, it was even harder to make a case that the cities should not use the cleared sites for housing at all, but instead for commerce and industry (or even parks and playgrounds). In other words, why should the cities build anything but low-income housing on the sites of the slums and blighted areas adjacent to the central business district? Why should they reuse them in a way that would reduce the supply of housing for the very groups most in need of it?

According to the downtown business interests and their allies, there were several reasons. One was that property there was much too expensive for low-cost housing. With prices running as high as $6 to $20 a square foot, far more than the $1.50 a square foot that the Federal Housing Authority was willing to pay for slum clearance, it was impossible to build good low-income housing on these sites without charging rents well beyond the reach of working-class families. It would have been possible to hold down rents by redefining good low-cost housing—by, for example, lowering the sanitary standards, eliminating the courtyards and other open spaces, and abandoning the goal of reducing population density. But the reformers would have strongly objected to these measures. It would also have been possible to hold down rents by providing what the New York Times called "back-breaking subsidies," local, state, or federal. But such subsidies would have been unacceptable to officials like Harold Ickes, who held that "[public] housing must be able to pay its own way," and to reformers like Wood, who conceded, albeit reluctantly, that slum clearance should "at least approximately pay its own way."[66]

At a time when cities were reeling from the Great Depression—and the center was losing population to the periphery—why did property values remain so high in many of the worst slums and blighted areas? According to contemporaries, the reasons were twofold. In some places, the landlords could squeeze so many families into so little space that the buildings were very profitable. In others—even in places where the depression and residential dispersal had driven rents down and vacancies up—the owners believed their property would in time be needed for the expansion of downtown stores, offices, and hotels. They behaved in an "ostrich-like" manner, wrote Henry Wright, ignoring the facts and "cling[ing] to values that never existed or that have long since disappeared." Helping to maintain what Wright called "fictitious" values were the banks, which were unwilling to write off, or even write down, their mortgages and thus lower the book value of their assets, and the cities, which were reluctant to lower assessed values and thereby reduce revenue from property taxes. As Earl Bryan Schwulst, executive vice president of New York's Bowery Savings Bank, told a congressional committee, the cities "have got to keep the assessed value up in order to collect sufficient taxes to keep going."[67]

Sooner or later, Wright and others argued, property values would fall in the slums and blighted areas, even in those adjacent to the central business district. Sooner or later they would reach a point where, in the words of Homer Hoyt, they would reflect the property's "net present income" rather than the owner's "false hopes for the future." But until then the local authorities should build low-income housing on low-cost sites on vacant (or largely undeveloped) land on the periphery. Only on these sites would it be possible to provide high-quality low-income housing. Not only should the lower and working classes be encouraged to move to the periphery, a recommendation made by the Regional Plan of New York as early as the late 1920s, but the middle and upper middle classes should be encouraged to live in the center. As planner Carol Aronovici said, "we should quit trying to rehabilitate lower Manhattan for the poor and give it back to the well-to-do by building expensive, luxurious and well planned apartment houses in which they could live close to the financial district." Walter Mattison agreed. Move the population out of the blighted areas, he told a congressional committee. Construct large housing projects for them on the outskirts of the city. Encourage private enterprise to build high- and middle-income housing near the central business district "for people who could afford to pay for it."[68]

According to the downtown business interests and their allies, there were also fiscal reasons why the cities should not build low-income housing in the slums and blighted areas adjacent to the central business district. Most cities were in dire financial straits, plagued by increasing costs and decreasing revenue, caught between the growing demand for services and a shrinking tax base. The construction of low-income housing in the center would only make matters worse. It would not increase revenue. To the contrary, it would surround the central business district with poor people, few of whom could afford to shop in downtown stores and hire downtown professionals. It would therefore do little to revitalize the central business district and raise property values there. This was a grim prospect because the central business district produced a large share of the city's property taxes and consumed a small share of its public services. As late as 1930, a few years before the full impact of the depression had been felt, downtown Milwaukee accounted for fully 25 percent of the city's revenues and barely 5 percent of its expenses. And in the mid 1930s downtown Boston generated more than twice as much in income as it absorbed in services.[69] If property values continued to decline in the central business district, the local authorities would be forced to raise taxes in the residential sections, a step that would drive more well-to-do residents to the suburbs and further undermine the cities' fiscal position.

The construction of low-income housing in the center would not reduce expenses either. For low-income and, to some degree, middle-income neighborhoods were a fiscal drain on the cities. Take the case of Boston. According to a survey by the city planning board, a congested part of South Boston consumed more than $5.7 million in services, but produced less than $500,000 in income. A residential neighborhood of triple-deckers, the typical housing type in many of Boston's working-class communities, absorbed more than twice as much in services as it generated in taxes. Even a residential neighborhood in suburban Roslindale produced slightly less in revenue than it consumed in services. Only a high-rent residential neighborhood in the Back Bay and what the planning board called a miscellaneous residential neighborhood in the Fenway generated more than enough in taxes to offset their costs. Summing up, the board wrote, "About 88½% of the population, using about 90% of the gross area, fail to pay taxes enough to cover the services rendered their residential areas." Roughly three-quarters of the deficit was made up by the central business district—the remainder by the high-rent and miscellaneous residential areas.[70] Unless Boston was highly idiosyncratic, it was hard to escape the conclusion that the construction of low-income housing in the center would not help solve the cities' fiscal problems.

What would help was the construction of high- and middle-income housing in the center, especially on the sites of the slums and blighted areas adjacent to the central business district. If public authority was able to clear the sites and private enterprise was willing to build the housing—and if, as a result, the well-to-do moved back from the periphery to the center—the fiscal benefits would be substantial. As brand new apartment houses replaced run-down tenements, property values would rise—not only in the inner city, but also in the central business district. Municipal revenues would go up. And as the well-to-do displaced the poor, who relied much more heavily on public services, municipal expenditures would go down. Also, if the construction of attractive high- and middle-income housing in the center slowed down residential dispersal, the cities would not have to build as many schools, highways, and other facilities on the periphery—another fiscal benefit. The center, Mattison pointed out, already had the necessary infrastructure. "We have all the facilities in the center of the city that we want. We want . . . people to come back, and take advantage of those facilities. And if [they do], I am satisfied that the present tax rate, which is on a [downward] spiral, and has been for years, will be arrested, and actually recede." If the slums and blighted areas could be cleared and redeveloped for the well-to-do, "we will be able to restore the economic stability of the cities themselves."[71]

Another reason the cities should not build low-income housing in the slums and blighted areas adjacent to the central business district was that it was not necessarily "the best and highest use" of the land. By this standard, one area might be best used for commerce or industry. Another might be more appropriate for parks and playgrounds. Still another might be best used as a parking lot or a garage—especially if automobile parking was what "the community most needs at that spot," remarked John Ihlder, former head of the community development department of the U.S. Chamber of Commerce. In some places "the best and highest" use might be housing, conceded Walter H. Blucher of the American Society of Planning Officials (ASPO). But it might not be low-income housing. As one observer wrote, it might be high-, medium-, or low-income housing or some combination of the three. To assume every blighted area should be reused for housing and every housing project should be built for low-income groups would be a terrible mistake, argued Alfred Bettman, chair of the Cincinnati Planning Commission, first president of the American Society of Planning Officials, and chair of ASPO's Committee on Urban Redevelopment.[72]

How could the cities get "the best and highest use" out of a slum or blighted area? Given that inappropriate land use was considered one of the principal causes of blight, what could they do to make sure that the cleared sites were not reused in inappropriate ways? What could they do to prevent redevelopment from giving rise to the conditions that had made slum clearance necessary in the first place? The answer, many Americans believed, was that the cities would have to plan—and to plan well. As the ASPO Committee on Urban Redevelopment said, "With the exception of small neighborhoods which are simply ailing a little, the problem of the redevelopment of a blighted area is a city planning problem, par excellence." New York mayor Fiorello La Guardia, a strong supporter of public housing, agreed. Although slum clearance was designed "to provide decent homes in decent neighborhoods for American families," the process "will frequently leave land that should be used for a variety of purposes, rather than housing alone, and we should turn to good city planning for a guide to what these uses should be, as well as for the general physical pattern according to which redevelopment should take place."[73] Here was a splendid opportunity for many city planners who were looking for new tools to shape the physical development of the city, and especially to attract more of the well-to-do from the periphery to the center and thereby slow down the dispersal of population and the decentralization of business.

Bettman told a congressional committee how the planners would figure out "the best and highest use." Consider a typical blighted area of small-scale industries and run-down residences. To determine whether it should be redeveloped for industry or housing, the planners would have to pose a set of questions. For what types of industry was the area an appropriate place? Within the area, what was the best location for which industries? Also, for what types of housing was the area an appropriate place? And where should the housing be located? To answer these questions, Bettman pointed out, the planners would have to develop "a general plan for the whole urban unit," a plan that would spell out "the future land uses of the whole city," not only the workplaces and residences, but also the street systems, recreational spaces, public schools, and parking facilities. Then they would have to see how the blighted area in question fit into the plan. "A general, comprehensive or master plan—giving it one or the other of those names—is an absolute essential for [an effective] redevelopment of any portions of the urban territory." In this process of "planning for the future," Bettman said elsewhere, the planners "should not be weighted down at the very start with devotion to the past."[74]

Not everyone found these reasons convincing. Despite the high cost of land, many champions of public housing argued that it was possible for the cities to clear the slums and blighted areas and, with a small subsidy, build good and cheap houses for low-income groups. If it could be done in Europe, it could be done in America. And if it could be done, it should be done—and in such a way that the rent was within the reach of the lower- and working-class residents whose homes would be torn down in the name of slum clearance. If the cities did not build housing for these people, clearance would do little but move the slums from one part of the city to another. Other Americans took issue with the arguments that the construction of low-income housing in the slums and blighted areas adjacent to the central business district would exacerbate the cities' fiscal problems and preclude using the land in the most appropriate way. One of the most outspoken critics of the effort to divorce slum clearance from low-income housing was Elizabeth Wood, executive secretary of the Chicago Housing Authority. Taking it as given that the objective of slum clearance was not just to wipe out bad housing but also to build good low-income housing, she lashed out against urban redevelopment. Cities, she said, should not rebuild blighted areas *"for the purpose of* restoring purchasing power to the central business districts," *"for the purpose of* restoring municipal income," or *"for the purpose of* giving private enterprise new areas in which to operate its business."[75]

Many housing reformers shared Wood's position. But they were a very small group. By the 1940s a large and growing number of Americans were more than willing to divorce slum clearance from low-income housing. Inclined to blur the line between slums and blighted areas, Americans were also inclined to sharpen the line between urban redevelopment and housing and even between urban redevelopment and slums. As the ASPO Committee on Urban Redevelopment wrote, "it is of the utmost importance to realize that urban redevelopment is not to be restricted to slum areas or to housing [and] that urban redevelopment legislation, though important for housing, is not housing legislation." Ulysses S. Grant III, head of the National Capital Park and Planning Commission (and grandson of the Civil War general and U.S. president), agreed. "Urban redevelopment is not merely an effort to provide decent homes for the poor," he remarked. "Slum clearance will necessarily be included as an important element, but only one element of the redevelopment [process]."[76] The ASPO Committee on Urban Redevelopment stressed the importance of building housing for the residents who were displaced by urban redevelopment. But it was moved not so much by the prospect that these residents would be uprooted as by the fear that the problem of relocating them might stall the attempt to rebuild the slums and blighted areas for the well-to-do.

By the early 1940s the downtown business interests and their allies had laid the ideological foundation for urban redevelopment. They had provided a rationale for razing the run-down residential neighborhoods near the central business district even though many of them were not slums. They had also provided a rationale for building high- and middle-income housing on the cleared sites even though this housing would be far too expensive for the lower and working classes. But it was one thing to make a case for urban redevelopment and another to rebuild the inner city. And with the encouragement of the downtown business interests, planners, lawyers, economists, and other experts worked to identify the obstacles to urban redevelopment and to figure out how to overcome them. This was no mean task. But it was made somewhat easier because the advocates of slum clearance and low-cost housing had been wrestling with much the same issue since the late 1920s and early 1930s.

The experts identified three main obstacles to urban redevelopment. One was that it was very expensive to acquire land in the slums and blighted areas adjacent to the central business district. Property values there were extremely high, often, noted the Chicago plan commission, "out of [all] proportion to the future use value of the land." Developers had little interest in buying land in the slums and blighted areas "when they can buy land elsewhere in the city at much lower prices," said Charles B. Bennett, director of the Los Angeles City Planning Department. (By buying vacant land on the periphery instead, they could also avoid the additional expense of tearing down the existing structures.) Not even institutional investors who were inclined to back large-scale housing projects—and who, as a New York City banker remarked, "would be content with a modest return on their investment"—were willing to pay such inflated prices. It was the high price of real estate, more than anything else, that prevented urban redevelopment "on anything but the most piecemeal and sporadic basis," a congressional report concluded. To John Blanford, a federal housing administrator, the problem was more or less intractable. "There was once a theory," he said, "that time alone would solve this problem. It was argued that in time the competitive rebuilding of outlying areas would drain the value out of the slum areas, down to the point where they could be profitably rebuilt. But the theory has been shattered. . . . The only thing that has been drained has been the purse of those who, in the final analysis, pay for all the social and economic cost of slums."[77]

Another obstacle to urban redevelopment was that it was very hard to assemble the land. A typical city block might have twenty or even forty lots, many of which were owned by several persons, some of whom might be unable to sell because the title to the lots was clouded (or held by trusts with multiple beneficiaries, not all of whom could easily be found). Even if most of the owners were willing and able to sell, a handful of holdouts was all it took to stymie the process. For example, an attempt to stop the spread of blight in the vicinity of the University of Chicago failed because the developers were unable to assemble a single block of parcels. And to be effective, to create a wholesome and stable residential community in the inner city, required not a single block but ten or twenty blocks, declared Arthur W. Binns, an expert on the subject. Coleman Woodbury, another expert, agreed. Echoing the warnings of Edith Elmer Wood, Langdon Post, and other advocates of slum clearance, he argued that lot-by-lot or even block-by-block development was doomed. "For a reasonable chance of success, a redevelopment project, particularly a residential one, would have to be large enough to stand out against the surrounding blight and squalor"—which would otherwise envelop it.[78]

Yet another obstacle to urban redevelopment was that it was highly likely that the new housing would be too expensive for the old tenants. Once their homes were demolished, they would have nowhere to go except to other slums and blighted areas. Given the acute shortage of low-cost housing, they would be lucky to find apartments even there. The relocation of displaced families was "the real Achilles heel [of] urban redevelopment," said Ferd Kramer, president of the Metropolitan Housing and Planning Council of Chicago. It was so serious a problem that Charles Abrams, Catherine Bauer, and others argued that before the demolition of the existing buildings was even considered it was necessary to find or provide housing for the displaced tenants at rents they could afford—on the same sites, if possible, elsewhere if need be, in old buildings if available, in new ones if not. As Philip Klutznick, another member of Chicago's Metropolitan Housing and Planning Council, observed, "it would be inhuman and immoral to undertake a slum clearance and urban redevelopment program without a clearly defined method for the handling of displaced families." This did not mean the blighted areas now housing low-income groups should not be rebuilt for high- and middle-income groups, declared the ASPO Committee on Urban Redevelopment. What it meant was that any redevelopment program that replaced low-income housing with high- and middle-income housing without at the same time dealing with the relocation problem would not only impose a great hardship on the displaced families, but also move the slums and blighted areas from one spot to another.[79]

To all but a few advocates of urban redevelopment, it was evident that neither private enterprise nor public authority could overcome these obstacles on its own. Assuming that he had the capital, a private developer would have to negotiate with scores or even hundreds of property owners, a handful of whom could block his efforts. Most property owners would probably ask unreasonably high prices and, once the first few parcels were sold, the owners of the remaining ones would probably raise their prices. Forced to pay inflated prices, a developer would be lucky to earn even a modest return on his investment. He would also have to deal with what one observer called a host of "distasteful" problems, including protests from tenants, who opposed the demolition of their homes, pressures from housing reformers, who expected developers to help relocate the displaced families, and the bureaucratic red tape that was all but inevitable in a large-scale housing project near the center of the city.[80] Making matters worse was the uncertainty of the housing market. Walter Mattison and other advocates of urban redevelopment might believe that many middle- and upper-middle-class families were ready to move from the periphery to the center. But were they? No one knew, not even the developers.

What the developers did know was that by virtue of the standstill in residential construction in the 1930s and early 1940s there was a strong pent-up demand for high- and middle-income single-family homes on the periphery. Land there was relatively inexpensive. It cost one-fourth as much as land near the center, according to one estimate, one-fifth to one-tenth as much, according to another.[81] It was relatively easy to assemble, largely because ownership was highly concentrated. It was less difficult to develop vacant land on the periphery than to redevelop built-up land near the center; and it took less time. Bartholomew and other planners might bemoan the waste, inefficiency, and fiscal drawbacks of residential dispersal—or what would later be called urban sprawl. But for most developers, it was far more attractive to build single-family homes on the periphery for the many well-to-do Americans who wanted to move away from the center than to build apartment houses near the center for the few well-to-do Americans who might want to move back from the periphery.

Public officials could not overcome the obstacles to urban redevelopment either, at least not on their own. By exercising the power of eminent domain, they could acquire large parcels of land at fair market value. And with the help of the U.S. Housing Authority, they could build low-cost housing for the families that would be displaced by the redevelopment process. But to put up high- and middle-income housing would cost "untold millions of dollars," wrote the National Institute of Municipal Law Officers—far more than the hard-strapped cities could afford. Nor was money the only problem. An effort to demolish the slums and blighted areas would arouse fierce opposition from residents, many of whom were strongly attached to their homes and neighborhoods and few of whom could afford to live in high- and middle-income apartment houses. In the face of this opposition, advocates of urban redevelopment had to make a case that the area to be redeveloped was indeed blighted. But despite many attempts to define blight, the concept remained extremely vague. If, as one expert wrote, a blighted area "differs only in degree from one that is not blighted," how could anyone draw a distinction between a blighted area and an ordinary low-income neighborhood?[82]

There were also legal and moral issues. According to the courts, cities could "take" private property, provided they paid fair market value and used the property for a public purpose. Following this line of reasoning, the courts had recently allowed cities to clear slums and build low-income housing on the sites. But it was far from clear that they would uphold a program by which cities "took" private property in the blighted areas in order to build high- and middle-income housing. And it was far from clear that cities should press ahead even if the courts were inclined to go along. If cities had the money, advocates of public housing insisted, they should use it to build decent homes for the lower and working classes—not to subsidize housing for the upper middle and middle classes, which already had access to good housing on the outskirts of the city. Private real estate interests, especially the National Association of Real Estate Boards, had other objections. It was bad enough that many cities had already gone into the low-income housing business, they argued. It would be even worse if they now went into high- and middle-income housing. To do so would be to take a huge step toward the "socialization of real estate."[83]

If neither public authority nor private enterprise could overcome the obstacles to urban redevelopment on its own, perhaps they could overcome them by working together. Or so the downtown business interests and their allies hoped. The trouble was that public authority and private enterprise were not used to working together. Through the mid nineteenth century public authority had routinely joined forces with private enterprise to stimulate economic development. But later this practice gave way to what might be called, for lack of a better term, an adversarial arrangement. Under this arrangement, public authorities granted private companies a franchise to build and operate the street railways, gas systems, and other public utilities other than the waterworks. They also regulated these companies. Under the watchful eyes of the courts and state legislatures, public authorities regulated the building industry as well. They established fire zones, drafted building codes, imposed height limits, and formulated zoning regulations. They also granted building permits—and, at least in theory, inspected everything from elevators to fire escapes.

This adversarial arrangement was the subject of a nationwide debate in the early twentieth century. Some Americans attacked it as one of the principal sources of corruption in the cities. Others defended it as the most efficient way to promote private initiative and still protect the public interest. On one point, however, both sides agreed—this arrangement was only workable if private enterprise was eager to take on the project. But after World War I private enterprise had virtually no interest in building low-income housing, at least not under the existing building codes and other regulations that, in the eyes of the builders, made it all but impossible to earn even a modest return on capital. And by the late 1930s private enterprise had little or no interest in building anything, not even high- and middle-income housing, in blighted areas. What discouraged builders, Alfred Bettman told a Senate committee, was blight, a disease that is "something less visible, more subtle, deeper, than the mere age or structural obsolescence of the existing buildings," a disease so insidious that it does not respond to conventional remedies, a disease that is rapidly spreading all over the country.[84]

Given these circumstances, advocates of urban redevelopment concluded that the adversarial arrangement would have to be abandoned. What sense did it make to follow a regulatory approach if there was nothing to regulate? Instead of imposing regulations, local officials should offer inducements. One was to give urban redevelopment projects a long-term partial exemption from property taxes. Another was to use eminent domain to make it easier and less expensive to assemble large parcels of real estate. Both inducements were discussed in many cities; and in some they were made available. But with a few exceptions—the most conspicuous of which was Stuyvesant Town, a middle-income housing project built by the Metropolitan Life Insurance Company on eighteen square blocks of lower Manhattan—they did little to encourage private enterprise to rebuild the slums and blighted areas.[85]

What else could local officials do? How else could they induce private enterprise to engage in the highly risky business of rebuilding the slums and blighted areas, to bear with the bureaucratic red tape and long-drawn-out negotiations that were integral parts of the redevelopment process, and to endure the fierce attacks of the tenants and their supporters in labor unions and religious groups? By the early 1940s advocates of urban redevelopment had come up with an answer, at the heart of which was a radical, indeed unprecedented, proposal. Local officials would have to buy the property at fair market value and then sell it at a much lower price, a price so low that private developers could make a profit. As Hugh Potter, president of the Urban Land Institute, explained, they would have to bridge the gap between the market value of the blighted property, however inflated, and its "actual value for purposes of redevelopment."[86] To put it another way, in order to wipe out the slums and blighted areas adjacent to the central business district, local authorities would have to subsidize the construction of high- and middle-income housing.

In defense of this controversial proposal, its supporters made several points. They noted that some Americans opposed the idea of "writing down" property values on the ground that it would bail out the property owners in the slums and blighted areas. "Why," these Americans asked, "should the community buy up blighted property when the owners are demanding prices far in excess of its real value? Why [should] the public protect those owners from loss any more than other individuals or groups saddled with bad bargains?" If the issue were that simple, "Why indeed?" wrote economist Guy Greer, a consultant to the Federal Reserve Board and one of the principal advocates of urban redevelopment. But it was not that simple, he pointed out. The property owners could make a plausible case that if the authorities took their holdings they should pay fair market value, particularly in the case where the authorities assessed these holdings at fair market value. The property owners could also make a plausible case that since urban redevelopment was designed to benefit the community as a whole, the community as a whole should help pay for it. To these reasons George Herbert Gray, a consultant in architecture and city planning, added another. Through "lack of prudent foresight," the local authorities were partly to blame for the obsolescence of the physical infrastructure of the cities, which was one of the main causes of blight. If the public bore some of the responsibility for creating the blighted areas, it should bear some of the cost of eliminating them.[87]

Other Americans objected to the proposal to write down property values on the ground that it would cost too much. Given that the cities were so strapped for money, how, these Americans asked, could they afford to subsidize the rebuilding of slums and blighted areas? This was a fair question, advocates of urban redevelopment acknowledged. Indeed, wrote the Chicago Plan Commission, "At first glance, the redevelopment of blighted areas seems to be . . . too costly for most cities." But on close analysis, it makes good fiscal sense. A well-conceived redevelopment project would not only reduce municipal expenditures. It would also raise municipal revenues. One such project, wrote the Detroit Housing Commission, was designed for the Gratiot redevelopment area, a hundred-acre site located a few blocks northeast of Detroit's central business district. To acquire and clear the land would cost $3.75 million, the commission estimated. But even after a write-down of about 75 percent, the project would generate so much more in property taxes that the city would be able to amortize its investment in only fifteen years.[88] Redevelopment might increase property taxes in the short run, its sponsors conceded, but in the long run it would reduce them.

The cities could, of course, do nothing. They could "let nature take its course," wrote Homer Hoyt, the real estate economist, and Leonard C. Smith, a real estate appraiser. They could allow the slums and blighted areas to deteriorate, watch as their residents moved to the periphery, and wait until property values in the inner city sank so low that private developers were prepared to rebuild without a public subsidy. But the cities had followed that course for generations, Guy Greer pointed out, and the problem of blight had grown steadily worse. It made much more sense, he argued, for cities to "face up to the problem and buy the blighted areas as rapidly as possible, paying as little as possible but often paying more than can ever be recovered except indirectly through the enhancement of values throughout the whole community." Hoyt and Smith agreed. So did Alfred Bettman. Although it might be tempting to leave the owners of slum and blighted property to "stew in their own juice," it was not an option, he insisted, because "the rest of us," the ordinary citizens who "pay for the social and economic consequences" of blight, "stew in the same juice."[89]

As Bettman was well aware, the cities had no authority to "take" property and sell it, let alone to sell it at below fair market value. But the states—or, by constitutional amendment, the voters—could give the cities this authority. Early in the 1940s the downtown business interests launched a campaign to persuade the state legislatures to do so. They had some success in New York and a few other states before World War II forced them to put the campaign on hold. Toward the end of the war the advocates of urban redevelopment renewed their efforts. With the downtown business interests, and especially the Urban Land Institute, in the forefront, they managed to overcome the opposition of conservative real estate interests. Before long Maryland, Minnesota, and Pennsylvania gave their approval to urban redevelopment. By the end of the war about twenty states, and not only the heavily urbanized states of the northeast and midwest, had passed enabling acts, and several others, most of which would soon follow suit, were considering them.[90] (Following New York's lead, several states also abolished the regulations barring insurance companies and other fiduciary institutions from investing in redevelopment projects.)

The early enabling acts fell into two categories. Some entrusted urban redevelopment to private redevelopment corporations. They gave these corporations the power to "take" and raze land in the slums and blighted areas—or, in some states, to acquire land already "taken" by the municipality—and to build housing projects on the cleared sites. Tax abatements were common features of these acts, as were limits on dividends. Other enabling acts delegated urban redevelopment to public housing authorities. Under these acts, which had the strong support of organized labor and other members of the public housing lobby, the authorities were empowered to use public funds (or public credit) to build low-cost housing (and often required to rehouse the displaced tenants). The Urban Land Institute and other groups criticized both types of acts on the ground that they were housing, not redevelopment, acts. (The ULI also attacked the second type on the ground that it discouraged the participation of private enterprise.) As a result of this criticism, the later enabling acts (and before long the great majority of them) took a different approach. Under these acts, urban redevelopment was turned over to a public agency, an arm of the local government. It was empowered to "take" land, to clear it, and to sell (or lease) it, in whole or in part, to private firms or public bodies, which, in line with the city's master plan, would rebuild the cleared sites for their "best and highest use." Although some of these acts allowed tax abatements, few limited dividends. Although a few required that the agency certify that decent housing was available for displaced tenants at rents they could afford, this requirement, writes historian Marc A. Weiss, was honored "more in the breach than in the observance."[91]

In theory, the enabling acts gave local officials a good deal of control over urban redevelopment. Indeed, their approval was required at virtually every step in the process. In practice, however, they had relatively little say over which areas would be redeveloped. Given that the downtown business interests were the principal force behind urban redevelopment, local officials were under intense pressure to designate as slums and blighted areas the neighborhoods adjacent to the central business district—and, even if they were not the worst neighborhoods, to slate them for redevelopment first. Given that the rebuilding would have to be done by private enterprise, local officials were also under intense pressure to designate as slums and blighted areas those neighborhoods in which private capital was prepared to invest, which tended to be neighborhoods like the South End in Boston and Bunker Hill in Los Angeles, the chief virtue of which was proximity to the central business district. As Charles Bennett of the Los Angeles City Planning Department pointed out, "Community redevelopment is essentially a private undertaking, financed by private funds. If those funds are not forthcoming, there will be no redevelopment." Which neighborhoods will be redeveloped—and in what order—will therefore depend "largely upon the preferences of those who are ready and

willing to finance the respective projects." The National Institute of Municipal Law Officials agreed. "Private capital will dictate the area in which its
monies will be invested," it wrote. No city can "force the investor to put its
money into a particular area against its will."[92]

Most cities moved promptly to take advantage of the state enabling acts. Indianapolis set up a redevelopment agency in March 1945. Baltimore and St.
Louis followed a few months later. Philadelphia created one in 1946. And
Providence joined the fold a year later, as did Chicago. By the late 1940s all but
a handful of big cities had either established redevelopment agencies or
turned other bodies—such as the housing commission (in Detroit) or the city
planning commission (in Minneapolis)—into them. In charge of the typical
redevelopment agency was a five-man board, appointed by the mayor, on
which business and real estate interests were heavily represented. In Providence the board consisted of a banker, a builder, an architect, a manufacturer,
and a lawyer. In Philadelphia all but one of the five board members were realtors. And in Pittsburgh the board included a retired steel company executive,
a department store president, and, as chairman, Mayor David L. Lawrence,
Pennsylvania's most powerful Democratic politician. Funding came from
various sources. Business interests gave $150,000 in seed capital to the Pitts-
burgh Redevelopment Authority. The Indianapolis city council earmarked
ten cents per $100 of assessed value for urban redevelopment. The Milwau-
kee city council appropriated $1 million; and shortly after the voters approved
two bond issues—one for $2.5 million, the other for $3.5 million. The voters
also approved a $2 million bond issue in Providence, a $5 million bond issue
in Baltimore, and a $15 million bond issue in Chicago—to which the Illinois
state legislature added another $11 million.[93]

Most redevelopment agencies went about their business in the same way.
With the help of Harland Bartholomew and other city planners, they made
surveys of the slums and blighted areas. On the basis of the surveys, the staff
recommended that several of them, sometimes as many as fifteen or twenty,
be designated redevelopment areas. The board then reviewed them, accept-
ing some, though sometimes only after revising their boundaries, rejecting
others, and, on occasion, adding some that had not been on the list. The board
submitted its recommendations to the city council, which, after holding public hearings, officially designated the redevelopment sites and incorporated
them into the city's master plan. In the meantime, the redevelopment agencies urged the city council to provide the money to acquire and clear the
land—either by appropriating funds from general revenues, by levying a new
tax on private property, or by putting a bond issue on the ballot. They also ap-

pealed to private firms, the most responsive of which were life insurance companies, to rebuild the slums and blighted areas. After reaching agreement with a developer, the agency submitted the plan to the city council. If and when the council gave its approval, the agency acquired and cleared the land and then sold or leased it.[94]

This flurry of activity, which got under way in the early and mid 1940s and gathered momentum in the postwar years, produced a host of surveys and plans. And before long hundreds of slums and blighted areas, many of which were adjacent to the central business district, were slated for redevelopment. But by the end of the decade very little rebuilding had been done. Indianapolis, one of the first cities to set up a redevelopment agency, managed only to acquire most of the land for one of its two initial redevelopment projects. Detroit, which had mounted an ambitious redevelopment program, did little more than condemn the first ten blocks of the Gratiot redevelopment project and start condemnation proceedings on the remaining thirty-three. In Chicago the New York Life Insurance Company was making plans for Lake Meadows, a housing project on the near South Side, but it didn't break ground until the

Chicago's Lake Meadows (Architect and Building News, January 12, 1956)

*Pittsburgh's Gateway Center (*Equitable Builds a Gateway, *1964)*

early 1950s. And neither Michael Reese Hospital nor the Illinois Institute of Technology, two Chicago institutions that would later play an active part in urban redevelopment, had as yet built anything. In Pittsburgh the Equitable Life Assurance Society was negotiating with the redevelopment authority over the future of a twenty-three-acre blighted area in what had once been the core of downtown Pittsburgh. But the first phase of what would be called Gateway Center, three twenty-story office buildings, would not be built for several years. Only in New York—where the Metropolitan Life Insurance Company put up Stuyvesant Town (as well as Riverton, a small housing project in Harlem) and other developers erected a few housing projects in Manhattan and two of the outer boroughs—had any slums and blighted areas been rebuilt by 1950.[95]

One reason that few slums and blighted areas were rebuilt in the postwar years is that urban redevelopment was so new and complex a program that it took the redevelopment agencies a while to figure out how to implement it. A far more important reason was that these agencies operated under powerful legal, political, and fiscal constraints. By the early 1940s, it was clear that cities had the right to take private property in order to clear slums and build public housing. But it was not clear that they had the right to take private property and sell (or lease) it to developers. Nor was it clear that they had the right to sell (or lease) the land at less than fair market value. Shortly after the redevelopment agencies went into business, their opponents challenged the enabling acts on the grounds that taking land for urban redevelopment was not a public purpose and that selling it at less than fair market value was an illegal tax. With a few exceptions, the courts upheld the laws, ruling that the main objective of urban development was slum clearance, a public purpose to which the transfer of private property from one individual to another was "purely incidental." The courts also ruled that a write-down was not an illegal tax. The trouble was that in most cities it took so long for the lawsuits to work their way through the courts that the redevelopment process was delayed. A case in point is Detroit, where the housing commission began condemnation proceedings for the Gratiot redevelopment project in February 1947. A taxpayer's suit brought the proceedings to a halt eight months later. Although the Michigan Supreme Court ruled that the city had the right to sell land at less than fair market value in October 1948, it did not rule until December 1951 that the city had the right to take slum or blighted property for resale to private developers. In the end the housing commission spent almost five years just to acquire the Gratiot redevelopment area.[96]

Urban redevelopment also got bogged down in the city councils. As often as not, the councils were under strong pressure to reject the redevelopment agency's recommendations. This pressure came from residents who did not want to be displaced from their neighborhoods, even if planners labeled them slums or blighted areas, and businessmen who did not want to start anew in other locations. It also came from spokesmen for the lower and working classes, who stressed that the displaced tenants could not afford to rent apartments in the new housing projects and would be hard pressed to find decent apartments at reasonable rents elsewhere. To make matters worse, many slums and blighted areas were occupied largely by blacks and other minorities. Hence civil rights and liberal groups often objected to designation on the ground that it was a scheme to remove racial and ethnic minorities from neighborhoods in which they were not wanted. Pointing out that Metropolitan Life had excluded blacks from Stuyvesant Town, the nation's largest and best-known redevelopment project, these groups protested that the redevelopment laws had no specific provision against racial discrimination. And they pointed out that much of the private housing market, to which the displaced tenants would have to turn, was closed to blacks and other minorities.[97] These groups might have been less vociferous in their opposition if they could have counted on public housing to provide space for the displaced families. But public housing was on the defensive, its future in doubt. Little wonder the redevelopment agencies had as much trouble designating redevelopment areas as they had acquiring the land on which they stood.

Even if the courts rejected the legal challenges and the city councils withstood the political pressures, the redevelopment agencies faced another problem. They had to find the money to acquire and clear the redevelopment sites. The agencies appealed to the cities. But most cities were in dire financial straits, in no position to spare much for urban redevelopment. Not even the most prosperous of them could afford the large write-down required by private enterprise, observed a California planner. The agencies also appealed to the states, which were in better financial shape than the cities, but often dominated by rural interests unsympathetic to urban problems. The agencies appealed to the voters, too. But the voters could not be counted on. Although they approved bond issues in some cities, they rejected them in others— among them St. Louis, where a $10 million bond issue that was supported by scores of civic groups but opposed by the Negro Citizens' Committee, an organization sponsored by the local branch of the NAACP, failed to win a majority, much less the required two-thirds. In the end the redevelopment agencies got money from all three sources, but it was not enough. Urban redevelopment was much too expensive. For example, the Detroit Housing Commission spent more than $6 million to acquire a hundred-plus acres for the Gratiot redevelopment area, almost $50,000 per acre.[98] But according to experts, the slums and blighted areas covered not hundreds of acres but thousands—and, in a few cities, tens of thousands. Even before the end of World War II, it was plain that neither the cities nor the states could afford to acquire and clear the slums and blighted areas—and that if these run-down areas were to be rebuilt the federal government would have to provide most of the money.

Before the mid 1930s most Americans would have been dismayed at the idea that the federal government should help out. With few exceptions, they were deeply committed to the tradition of local self-government and extremely wary of federal intervention in urban affairs. They held that American cities were better off dealing with their problems on their own, that federal involvement would only make things worse. As a result of this attitude, historian Mark Gelfand has pointed out, the national government played a much less active role in urban affairs in the United States than in other countries. Aside from building harbors, improving rivers, and, among other things, housing defense workers during World War I, Washington ignored the nation's urban problems. This approach changed abruptly in the mid and late 1930s, a time when the country was reeling from the effects of the Great Depression. In an effort to reduce unemployment and provide relief, the Roo sevelt administration undertook a host of public works projects that deeply entangled the federal government in urban affairs. It also launched a public housing program that not only established the principle of federal aid for slum clearance, but also removed many of the political, legal, and organizational constraints on urban redevelopment. By the late 1930s and early 1940s many Americans, including many members of the National Association of Real Estate Boards and other conservative groups, had come to believe that the federal government had an obligation to help the cities rebuild the slums and blighted areas.[99]

The breakthrough came in 1941, shortly before the United States entered World War II, when three serious proposals were put forward spelling out how the federal government should meet this obligation. One was drafted by NAREB's Committee on Housing and Blighted Areas—and, with some changes, was adopted a year later by the Urban Land Institute. Another was written by Guy Greer and Alvin H. Hansen, a Harvard economist and strong advocate of Keynesian economics, after discussions with the National Resources Planning Board and the nation's major planning organizations. The third was prepared by the Federal Housing Administration, the agency that handled the government's housing programs. At the core of these proposals were the answers to several difficult questions. Which federal agency should oversee urban redevelopment? How much control should it exercise? Should the federal government provide the cities long-term or short-term subsidies? How much should urban redevelopment focus on building houses, how much on rebuilding cities? Should construction be done by private enterprise, public authority, or some combination thereof? Each proposal answered these questions in different ways. But on several vital points they all agreed—that federal subsidies were necessary for the acquisition and clearance of slums and blighted areas, that rebuilding had to be done on a large scale and in accord with the city's master plan, and that cooperation between public authority and private enterprise was essential.[100]

None of these proposals stood much of a chance once the country went to war. But in an effort to lay the groundwork for the postwar years, some of their sponsors pushed for congressional action. With the help of Alfred Bettman, a leading authority on planning and zoning law, Greer and Hansen drafted the Federal Urban Redevelopment Act, which was introduced by Senator Elbert Thomas, a Utah Democrat, in April 1943. At the request of the Urban Land Institute, Senator Robert F. Wagner, the New York Democrat who had led the fight for the Housing Act of 1937, submitted the Neighborhood Redevelopment Act two months later. Under both bills the federal government would lend cities money to acquire and clear slum and blighted properties that had been designated redevelopment areas and incorporated into the master plan—and which would subsequently be sold or leased to developers at below market value. But under the Thomas bill, by far the more radical, the federal government (or, to be precise, a new federal Urban Redevelopment Authority) would exercise a good deal of control over the process. Under the Wagner bill, which the senator called "an encouragement to enterprise bill," Washington would leave virtually all the decisions up to the cities, acting, in Gelfand's words, as "a benevolent banker," doing only what was necessary to safeguard its investment. Neither bill made it out of committee.[101] But along with several other bills that were introduced a few years later, the Thomas and Wagner bills provoked a vigorous debate over federal aid for urban redevelopment and triggered a political battle that would drag on until the end of the decade.

Supporters of federal aid for urban redevelopment argued that the cities were "an essential part of the nation," that they contained much of its population, produced much of its wealth, and paid much of its taxes. They are so vital to the nation's welfare that "the Federal Government cannot afford to sit by and let [them] deteriorate and decay," said Pittsburgh mayor David Lawrence. But to rebuild them would cost billions, even ten of billions, much more than the cities could afford. They could not count on much help from the states either. Short of a thorough overhaul of the nation's tax system, which, wrote Greer, was extremely unlikely, they had nowhere to turn to other than Washington. Without its help, nothing could be done "except in a few of the wealthier States," argued Thomas D'Allesandro, Jr., mayor of Baltimore and spokesman for the U.S. Conference of Mayors. Under ordinary circumstances, municipal funding would be preferable, conceded Charles T. Stewart. But circumstances were anything but ordinary. Decentralization was devastating the cities. "To propose that cities reeling under such a blow finance the operation that is necessary to effect a cure is to overlook the essential nature of the problem. It is like saying that each man should stand on his own two feet without recognizing the fact that a sick man needs some assistance."[102]

Opponents of federal aid for urban redevelopment countered that the rebuilding of slums and blighted areas was a purely local matter. It was one thing for the federal government to provide funds for low-income housing, Senator Taft told a strong supporter of urban redevelopment, but it was quite another for it to subsidize the rebuilding of run-down neighborhoods. "I cannot quite see what the Federal Government has got to do with how Cincinnati lets itself look, or how any other city lets itself look," he said. To arguments that redevelopment would stimulate business and generate employment, Taft replied: "If that justifies public works of a purely local character we would have Federal participation in building all the schools in the country, all the hospitals in the country, and everything else." Along the same line, another opponent asked, "Why should we bail out insolvent real estate . . . any more than we bail out insolvent shoe-shine parlors, grocery stores, manufacturing enterprises, or railroads?" And why, a Kansas congressman protested, should "the lowly taxpayers of southeastern Kansas . . . have to contribute to the re-building of the slums in New Jersey"? Some Americans also objected to fed-eral aid for urban redevelopment on the ground that the government had fiscal problems of its own. If Congress voted to subsidize the rebuilding of slums and blighted areas, it would increase the national deficit and create yet another huge and costly federal bureaucracy.[103]

By the end of World War II, the lines were drawn. In favor of federal aid for urban redevelopment were the downtown businessmen, big-city mayors, and city planners, the three groups that were in the forefront of the campaign to curb decentralization. The downtown businessmen saw it as a way to revital-ize the central business district, the big-city mayors as a way to alleviate the growing fiscal problem, and the city planners as a way to reorganize the me-tropolis along more efficient lines. Allied with these groups were several civic associations, which thought that urban redevelopment would wipe out the slums and blighted areas; labor unions, which hoped that it would generate employment in the postwar years; and business groups, which believed that it would give a boost to the building trades and related industries. Opposed to federal aid for urban redevelopment were a highly diverse group of rural con-gressmen who did not see how their constituents would benefit from the pro-gram, conservative realtors who felt that the federal government was already too deeply involved in the private sector, and housing reformers who believed that urban redevelopment was severely misguided. Among the most outspo-ken of them was Catherine Bauer. "In the sacred name of 'master plans,' 'Bold reconstruction,' 'saving cities,' and whatnot," she wrote, "it is proposed to bail out with Federal subsidy the owners of slum and blighted property—not in order to rehouse their present tenants properly, but to stimulate another wave of speculative overbuilding for well-to-do and thus, it is naively hoped, to turn the tide of decentralization and preserve downtown property values based on high densities and even higher hopes."[104]

The issue came to a head in August 1945, a couple of weeks before the end of World War II, when a subcommittee of the Special Senate Committee on Post-War Economic Policy and Planning recommended the establishment of a provisional program of federal aid for urban redevelopment. Since the subcommittee was chaired by Taft, who saw no reason the federal government should help rebuild the cities, it was not surprising that the program focused on clearing slums and improving housing—that, in Gelfand's words, housing was "the theme and urban redevelopment the variations." Federal aid would be provided only for areas that were "predominantly residential" or would be "redeveloped primarily for residential use." Most of the subcommittee's proposals were subsequently incorporated into a general housing bill that was sponsored by Taft, Wagner, and Allen J. Ellender, a Louisiana Democrat, and referred to the Committee on Banking and Currency, which was chaired by Wagner. If the Wagner-Ellender-Taft bill disappointed city planners, who felt it took a much too narrow approach to urban redevelopment, it outraged conservative businessmen, who feared it would lead to higher taxes. The bill also troubled downtown business interests, which protested that it gave the federal government far too much control over urban redevelopment. Despite these strong objections the Committee on Banking and Currency included federal aid for urban redevelopment in the General Housing Act of 1945, an omnibus bill that dealt with a wide range of federal housing programs, many of which were more controversial than urban redevelopment. In early April 1946 the committee sent the bill to the Senate, which passed it, with overwhelming bipartisan support, a week later.[105]

Things went much less smoothly in the House. Led by the U.S. Chamber of Commerce, the National Association of Home Builders, the U.S. Savings and Loan League, NAREB, and ULI, which denounced Wagner-Ellender-Taft as "one of the most dangerous bills introduced in years," the opposition rallied around a rival bill sponsored by Representative Jessie P. Wolcott of Michigan, ranking Republican on the House Committee on Banking and Currency. The Wolcott bill provided for federal aid for urban redevelopment—though it limited the federal government's contribution to one-half of net project cost, a measure that would have reduced the city's capacity to write down the value of slum and blighted property to a point where it could be redeveloped for low-income housing.* But on many other issues it differed greatly from the Senate bill. With the House sharply divided, both bills died in committee. In March 1948 Taft introduced another omnibus housing bill. The Senate passed it a year later—though only after adopting several amendments, one of which replaced short-term subsidies with long-term grants, a change that severely

---

* Net project cost was the difference between what the redevelopment agency spent to acquire and clear the site and what the developer paid for it.

weakened federal control over urban redevelopment. But this bill also died in committee in the House, which instead passed another bill sponsored by Wolcott that omitted federal aid for urban redevelopment and other even more controversial features of the Senate bill. After a few months of political wrangling, the lawmakers finally passed an omnibus housing bill from which federal aid for urban redevelopment and other major provisions of Taft-Ellender-Wagner had been removed. Although far from happy with the bill, President Harry S. Truman signed it.[106]

As the political battle dragged on, it became clear that there were two main stumbling blocks to federal aid for urban redevelopment. One was that its supporters were sharply divided over several major issues—for example, how the process should be managed, how the costs should be apportioned, and above all how the areas should be rebuilt. These issues not only pitted planners, reformers, and businessmen against one another; they also pitted planners against planners, reformers against reformers, and businessmen against businessmen. As Walter H. Blucher lamented in the mid 1940s, "there are several camps and each camp is more interested in cutting the throat of the other camp than in getting [a bill out of] Congress." As time passed, these camps were able to resolve many of their differences. But they still faced a larger stumbling block. From the outset federal aid for urban redevelopment was not considered by itself, only as part of omnibus housing bills, which dealt with a wide range of controversial programs. Among them were federal aid for public housing, federal loans for farm housing, and federal insurance for home mortgages. It was these programs (or proposed changes in these programs) that aroused the fierce opposition of realtors, bankers, and builders, blocking the omnibus housing bills and thereby stymieing federal aid for urban redevelopment.[107]

By far the most controversial of these programs was federal aid for public housing. On one side were NAREB, ULI, and several other trade associations that considered public housing a form of socialism. Many of these groups supported urban redevelopment, but not at the price of more public housing. As one of their spokesmen put it, "If I had to choose between seeing every old city in the country as an ash heap and seeing the government become a landlord to its own citizens, I should prefer to see the ash heaps." To these groups, no omnibus housing bill that provided federal aid for urban redevelopment was acceptable if it also provided federal aid for public housing. On the other side were the U.S. Conference of Mayors, the White House, organized labor, and a host of liberal groups, all of which believed that public housing was needed to solve America's housing problem. Many of these groups supported urban redevelopment, but not at the expense of public housing. They were willing to compromise on some points. They would go along with a proposal to replace short-term subsidies with long-term grants—though not with a proposal to lower the federal government's contribution from two-thirds to one-half of net project cost. But they would not support an omnibus housing bill that included federal aid for urban redevelopment if it left out federal aid for public housing.[108]

The stalemate was finally broken in 1949, thanks largely to the efforts of President Truman and the Democratic leaders in Congress. Fresh from his unexpected victory in the 1948 election, Truman urged the Eighty-first Congress, which was controlled by the Democrats, to enact the Wagner-Ellender-Taft bill. The Senate needed no urging. With a solid majority behind public housing, the bill sailed through in April. But it ran into strong opposition in the House, where a coalition of conservative Republicans and southern Democrats had kept public housing bottled up in committee for four years. The opposition was unable to prevent the House Committee on Banking and Currency from reporting out an omnibus housing bill that included federal aid for public housing and other provisions of the Senate bill. But it was able to prevail on the House Rules Committee to table the bill. Knowing that most of the members favored the bill, the House Democratic leadership threatened to resort to a new procedure by which a bill could be brought to the floor without the approval of the Rules Committee. In the face of this threat (and under strong pressure from the White House), the Rules Committee reversed itself. In the long and often acrimonious debate that followed, the opposition focused largely on public housing (and barely mentioned urban redevelopment). When the House voted, by a narrow margin, to retain federal aid for public housing, the battle was over. The House passed the bill in June. A conference committee worked out the differences between the Senate and House bills. And in mid July Truman signed the Housing Act of 1949, Title I of which provided for federal aid for urban redevelopment.[109]

Title I authorized the federal government to help the cities acquire and clear slum and blighted property in designated redevelopment areas and sell or lease it to private developers (or public agencies) at below market value. The help would be funneled through the Housing and Home Finance Agency, which was empowered to make $1 billion in long-term loans and $500 million in capital grants to local redevelopment agencies. The agencies would use the money to write down the value of the property to the point where it would attract the interest of developers. The federal grants could cover up to two-thirds of net project cost; the redevelopment agency would have to come up with one-third. To make things easier for the hard-strapped cities, this could be done not only by putting up cash but also by donating land, installing sewers, streets, and utilities, and building parks, playgrounds, and other facilities. In deference to Senator Taft, who took a very narrow view of urban redevelopment, Title I limited federal aid to slums and blighted areas that were "predominantly residential" or would be redeveloped for predominantly residential use. In either case, the areas would have to be rebuilt in line with the city's master plan. As a concession to the housing reformers, Title I also stipulated that the families displaced by urban redevelopment would have to be rehoused in "decent, safe, and sanitary dwellings" that were reasonably priced and conveniently located.[110]

Federal aid for urban redevelopment was adopted—and, as Mark Gelfand points out, adopted in a relatively short time—largely because it meant different things to different groups. Downtown business interests saw it as a way to lure the well-to-do from the periphery to the center, a development, they believed, that would slow down decentralization and shore up the central business district. To other business interests, especially the building trades, it was a way to stimulate private enterprise; and to organized labor, it was a way to generate employment. Big-city mayors viewed federal aid for urban redevelopment as an opportunity to replace low-income slums and blighted areas with middle- and high-income neighborhoods, a move, they thought, that would alleviate the growing fiscal problem. City planners viewed it as an opportunity to redesign the metropolis along more efficient lines—and, above all, to curb the haphazard residential dispersal that they believed was destroying the cities. Even many housing reformers, some of whom had once had reservations about federal aid for urban redevelopment, believed that in view of the postwar housing shortage it would be impossible to raze the slums and blighted areas without building additional public housing. "Seldom has such a variegated crew of would-be angels tried to sit on the same pin at the same time," wrote Catherine Bauer, one of the housing reformers who remained dubious about urban redevelopment.[111]

On the surface, federal aid for urban redevelopment seemed an extension of the Housing Act of 1937. The preamble to the Housing Act of 1949 stressed the nation's commitment "to remedy the serious housing shortage, to eliminate slums and blighted areas, and to realize as soon as feasible the goal of a decent home and a suitable living environment for every American family." This commitment was also emphasized in the report of the Senate Committee on Banking and Currency. It declared not only that "the primary purpose of federal aid . . . is to help remove the impact of slums on human lives rather than simply to assist in the redevelopment or rebuilding of cities," but also that "no slum-clearance program can successfully proceed without simultaneous provision for an adequate program of low-rent public housing for low-income families." Thus in addition to restricting federal aid for urban redevelopment to slums and blighted areas that were "predominantly residential" or would be redeveloped for predominantly residential use, the Housing Act of 1949 also authorized the federal government to subsidize the construction of an additional 810,000 low-income housing units and stipulated that the local authorities would have to find or build adequate housing for displaced families.[112]

But Title I of the Housing Act of 1949 was less noteworthy for what it did than for what it did not do. Despite the "predominantly residential" clause, it did not require the developers to build low-cost housing on the sites of the former slums and blighted areas. Provided the local redevelopment agency gave its approval, they could build high-priced apartment houses, office buildings, convention centers, and even parking lots. Nor did Title I require the cities to accept federal aid for public housing in return for federal aid for urban redevelopment. Although it did provide that displaced families should be relocated, the Housing and Home Finance Agency did not enforce this provision, and for the most part the local redevelopment agencies ignored it. Title I did not specify which slums and blighted areas should be designated redevelopment sites either. It left the decision up to the local redevelopment agencies, which tended to choose areas that were run down enough to justify demolition, but not so run down as to scare off developers. Hence most of the sites would be located near the central business district (or, in some cases, inside the central business district).[113] Indeed, Title I left virtually everything in the hands of the redevelopment agencies, which were extremely responsive to pressure from downtown businessmen and elected officials. With the subsidy coming in the form of long-term loans and capital grants, the government had little control over what these agencies did with the money.

Far from an extension of the Housing Act of 1937, Title I was a major departure in public policy. Its overriding objective was not to wipe out the slums in order to build decent housing and pleasant neighborhoods for low-income families. Rather it was to curb decentralization—to induce the well-to-do to move back to the center by turning the slums and blighted areas into attractive residential communities—and, by so doing, to revitalize the central business district and ease the cities' fiscal plight. Title I did little for the housing reformers, many of whom hoped that the redevelopment agencies would sell or lease the cleared sites at cut-rate prices to local housing authorities. But it did much for the downtown business interests, big-city mayors, and city planners who spearheaded the campaign against decentralization. It provided the money for urban redevelopment without which the state enabling acts were worthless. The redevelopment agencies could now undertake what one observer called the "drastic surgery" needed to clear the slums and blighted areas that ringed the central business district. And to clear them on a scale heretofore unheard of—not just parcels, not just blocks, but entire neighborhoods, some of which covered scores of acres.[114]

Even after Congress passed the Housing Act of 1949, it was not clear how long it would take the local redevelopment agencies to acquire and clear the slums and blighted areas—or, to put it another way, how long it would take them to overcome the opposition of the residents, many of whom had a strong attachment to their neighborhoods. If the designation process aroused enough opposition, it was not clear how long it would be before the housing reformers became disenchanted with the program—and, when they did, how long before the coalition that supported urban redevelopment fell apart. Even if the redevelopment agencies were able to acquire and clear some of the slums and blighted areas, it was not clear that private developers would be inclined to rebuild them—especially when they had so many other less risky and irksome ways to make a living. Even if private developers were inclined to buy (or lease) the cleared sites, it was not clear that many well-to-do Americans were prepared to move from their single-family homes on the periphery to apartment houses in the center. Finally, if many well-to-do Americans moved, it was not clear what would happen to the low-income families who were displaced to make room for them—whether, as some critics warned, the result would simply be to move the blight from one part of the city to another.[115]

But once Title I was on the books—once the local redevelopment agencies could apply for federal loans and grants to acquire and clear slum and blighted property and sell or lease the cleared sites to private developers at below market value—one thing was clear. And that is, in rebuilding the slums and blighted areas—in designating the redevelopment sites, in deciding on their future uses, and in negotiating with developers—these agencies were prepared to ride roughshod over their residents. In the interest of revitalizing the central business district, they would do whatever was necessary, even dispossess hundreds of thousands of low-income families (and thousands of small businessmen). That many of these people were members of racial and ethnic minorities, that most of them had no desire to move and no place to move to, and that some of their neighborhoods were not slums or blighted areas made no difference.[116] The redevelopment officials would show as little concern for the well-being of the people who lived in the redevelopment sites as the highway engineers showed for the well-being of the people who lived in the path of the freeways. From the perspective of these officials—and, even more important, from the perspective of the downtown business interests and their allies who had transformed slum clearance into urban redevelopment—these people were in the wrong place at the wrong time.

8

Just Another Business
District? Downtown in the
Mid Twentieth Century

In April 1950 the *St. Louis Post-Dispatch* published an article about downtown St. Louis, the eighth in a series about Greater St. Louis entitled "Progress or Decay? St. Louis Must Choose." Downtown St. Louis was ailing, wrote reporter Richard G. Baumhoff. Many office buildings were old and dingy. No new ones had been erected in a decade. And a few department stores were establishing branches in Clayton and other rapidly growing outlying business districts. Downtown's property values were on the rise, but its assessed value was lower than in 1930. Only 375,000 people, roughly one of every five, entered the central business district on weekdays, but as more than half of them came by car, traffic was congested and parking hard to find. While residential construction was booming on the periphery, the center was "encircled by a rotting ring of slums." But "downtown is not dying," Baumhoff declared. It is still "the center, the core, the heart that pumps the blood of commerce through the area's arteries." Efforts to revitalize it were under way. Downtown businessmen were renovating department stores and office buildings. Local officials were planning to build a system of expressways and provide additional off-street parking. And business and political leaders were mounting a campaign to redevelop the blighted areas adjacent to the central business district. What would come of these efforts was not clear. What was clear, wrote Baumhoff, was that the well-being of downtown and the well-being of the metropolitan area were synonymous. "Without a vigorous Downtown, St. Louis loses its chief economic reasons for existence; without a vigorous St. Louis, the whole metropolitan district falters and fails—economically, culturally, physically."[1]

As Baumhoff pointed out, St. Louis was not unique. Although the country was out of the depression, downtown was still in the doldrums. And there it would stay, the downtown business interests believed, unless the cities could slow down decentralization. But could they build the limited-access high-ways, off-street parking facilities, and rapid transit lines needed to enhance the accessibility of the central business district and make it competitive with the outlying business districts? Could they transform the slums and blighted areas into middle- and upper-middle-class neighborhoods and create new markets for downtown goods and services? To put it another way, was it possi-ble to reverse the long-term trends indicating that downtown's daytime popu-lation was increasing very little, if at all, that retail trade was growing much more slowly in the central business district than in the outlying business dis-tricts, and that property values were rising much less rapidly in the center than on the periphery? Downtown, most Americans realized, would never again be the business district, the place to which virtually everybody went every day to work, shop, do business, and amuse themselves. But whether it would retain its position as the central business district or, as a Los Angeles traffic engineer put it, turn into "just another" business district, and not nec-essarily the most attractive or most prosperous, remained to be seen.[2]

There were some signs that downtown was holding its own in the immedi-ate postwar years. Millions of Americans still poured into it on weekdays. "There are lots of people downtown," Business Week declared in 1951. After a decade and a half in which more office buildings had been torn down than put up, scores of new skyscrapers were erected in urban America, notably in mid-town Manhattan, downtown San Francisco, and the Chicago Loop. From 1945 to 1950 roughly thirty million square feet of new office space came on the market, an increase of about 14 percent, most of it in the central business dis-trict. And occupancy rates were over 95 percent. According to the National As-sociation of Building Owners and Managers, the central business districts were "maintaining, if not strengthening, their hold on [the] volume of office space." And in 1952 James C. Downs, a Chicago real estate analyst, assured the association's members that they need have no fear that the "downtown ar-eas" would one day become "ghost towns." Many of the leading department stores were undergoing costly renovations too. According to Business Week, Jordan Marsh (Boston) was putting $11 million into its downtown store. Gim-bel's (New York) was investing $5 million, Halle Bros. (Cleveland) $8 million, Neiman-Marcus (Dallas) $5 million, and Marshall Field (Chicago) $19 mil-lion. No "top drawer [department] store" had left the central business district, Richard C. Bond, president of Philadelphia's Wanamaker's, pointed out. De-spite the growing decentralization of retail trade, "it is still much too soon to count the urban center out of the picture," a Marshall Field executive insisted in 1952. "Our own experience over nearly a quarter-century indicates beyond any doubt that there remains now and for the predictable future a great retailing opportunity in the familiar downtown."³

In the meantime the campaign to curb decentralization was gathering momentum. Even before Congress created the interstate highway system in 1956, New York, Chicago, Los Angeles, and other cities were building huge limited-access highways running from the outlying residential sections to the central business district. These freeways, wrote journalist Hal Burton, "permit the motorist to skim above city streets or to whiz along below them" at speeds that would once have been inconceivable. Although some warned that the freeways would promote decentralization, many held that they might well be "the salvation of the central business district." To accommodate the heavy traffic generated by the freeways, Boston, Pittsburgh, Detroit, and other cities were also building large garages and parking lots. "The time is not likely to come when everybody who wants to park downtown can find a space, on or off the street," wrote Burton. "Yet, year by year, progress is being made." Moreover, even before Congress passed the Housing Act of 1949, several cities were moving ahead on plans to redevelop the slums and blighted areas adjacent to the central business district as well as the blighted commercial areas inside it. They ran into political obstacles, bureaucratic red tape, and legal challenges, but before long many projects were under way; and some, like Pittsburgh's Gateway Center and Chicago's Lake Meadows, were done— though whether these projects would lure the well-to-do from the periphery to the center was far from clear. "A firm start has been made to save the rotting core of America's biggest communities," wrote Chalmers M. Roberts, a *Washington Post* reporter, in 1952. "Downtown is coming back," said Sylvia Porter, a syndicated columnist, five years later.⁴

But there were other signs that downtown was not holding its own, much less coming back. Millions of Americans were moving to the suburbs, which grew more than four times as fast as the central cities, some of which lost population, in the 1940s. And many of them were no longer going downtown, even in the few cities with a fairly robust central business district. A case in point is Chicago, where between 1948 and 1952, a period of steady growth in the metropolitan area, the number of people entering the Loop fell by nearly 200,000, or about 20 percent. Fewer people went to the Loop in 1952 than in any year since 1926 (except 1935). Property values were rising more slowly in the central business districts, if they were rising at all, than in the outlying business districts. In the San Francisco Bay area, for example, values increased much more rapidly after the war in the San Mateo and Hayward business districts than in downtown San Francisco or downtown Oakland. Indeed, property values there were no higher in the early 1950s than in the late 1920s; adjusted for inflation, they were lower. After a brief respite during the war, the mass transit systems—the streetcars, els, and subways that had been so vital to the growth of downtown—resumed their long decline. The riding habit fell sharply in the few cities that had a rapid transit system. It fell even more sharply in the many cities that had only streetcars and motorbuses. In Detroit, for instance, the riding habit plunged from 238 in 1945 to 126 in 1951, a drop of nearly 50 percent in just six years, which was lower than it had been at any time since the depths of the depression.[5]

The proliferation of motels, nearly all of which were located outside the central business district, was another ominous sign. A relatively recent phenomenon, the motel—or, as it was originally known, the motor court or roadside inn—had first appeared in the 1920s, mostly in the South and West. But before the depression it had not posed much of a threat to downtown hotels. After World War II, however, the number of motels soared. Between 1948 and 1958, a decade during which the number of hotels, most of which were located inside the central business district, fell slightly, the number of motels rose by almost 60 percent. For every four hotels, there were now three motels. Another ominous sign was the seemingly inexorable decentralization of retail trade. Between 1948 and 1954 retail sales went down in many central business districts—by 10 percent in St. Louis, by 11 percent in Detroit, and by 16 percent in Pittsburgh, a city that had one of the country's most ambitious urban redevelopment programs. Where retail sales went up in the central business district, they went up more elsewhere in the metropolitan area—more than six times as much in New York, more than seven times as much in Cleveland, more than eight times as much in Seattle, and more than twenty times as much in Atlanta. Overall, the central business district's share of the metropolitan area's retail trade declined from 16 percent to 12 percent in the five largest cities and from 23 percent to 18 percent in the thirteen next largest ones.[6]

Even more ominous were two momentous developments, both of which got under way in the immediate postwar period. One was the emergence of the regional shopping center. For decades retailing had been moving away from downtown. Shopkeepers opened up hardware, clothing, and other stores in the outlying business districts. Developers built a few small shopping centers in the suburbs. Chains set up large stores in the outlying areas, proving that retail outlets offering standardized merchandise and ample parking could do a high volume even if they were located miles from the central business district. And department stores established branches in the suburbs. (They had no choice, wrote one journalist. They did not create the problems downtown. "They can and should help [solve them]; but in the meantime they had best roll with the punch and head for the suburbs.") But none of these developments had prepared Americans for the regional shopping centers that were built in the late 1940s and early 1950s. They were "quite unlike any other retail development in the nation," writes historian Richard Longstreth, referring to the first of them, the Crenshaw Center, which opened in southwest Los Angeles in late 1947."[7]

Among their many distinctive features, by far the most striking was size. They were immense. Some covered dozens of acres, housed fifty to a hundred stores, with half a million to a million square feet of floor space, and provided

Crenshaw Center, with downtown Los Angeles in the background, 1951 (Courtesy of the University of Southern California, on behalf of the USC Library Department of Special Collections)

parking for several thousand automobiles. Each regional shopping center was anchored by a large branch of a major department store—Detroit's Northland by J. L. Hudson, Seattle's Northgate by Bon Marché, and Boston's Shoppers' World by Jordan Marsh. New York's Cross County Center, which was located in Westchester County, a booming suburban area north of the city, was anchored by two, Wanamaker's and Gimbel's. Besides a department store, the regional shopping centers usually included chain stores, like Woolworth and W. T. Grant, apparel, hardware, drug, and furniture stores, a small bank, a supermarket, and perhaps a movie theater and one or more restaurants. "In effect," wrote Larry Smith, a Seattle real estate economist and shopping center consultant, "they are downtown business communities transferred to the residential areas."[8] Owned by real estate syndicates or major department stores, the regional shopping centers had strong competitive advantages. Located along one or more major highways, they were highly accessible to motorists. They provided ample parking, a wide selection of merchandise, and the much-touted "one-stop" shopping. Designed, developed, and managed as a unit, the regional shopping centers were also in a good position to respond swiftly to changes in the market.

Although a strong sign of the ongoing decentralization of retail trade, the regional shopping centers were not "a serious threat" to the central business district, Smith argued in 1952. Max S. Wehrly, executive director of the Urban Land Institute, agreed, pointing out that thus far these centers had not depressed business downtown (and might well have stimulated it). So did Philip M. Talbott, a vice president of Woodward & Lothrop, a Washington, D.C., department store, who held that regional shopping centers represented "additional business—not competition." Other Americans disagreed. There was only so much business to be done, insisted John Galbreath, a Columbus, Ohio, realtor; and as more was done in the regional shopping centers, less would be done in the central business district. Some observers also feared that as the shopping centers spread throughout the suburbs, the downtown stores would be forced to resort to "'bargain basement retailing' for whatever customers emerge from the encroaching slums." Whether things would get that bad was hard to say. But by the mid 1950s—by which time several well-known firms had closed their downtown department stores, something that had not happened even during the Great Depression—they were bad enough. The regional shopping centers had made "startling inroads" on downtown business, wrote the Buffalo City Planning Commission in 1956. If this trend continued, which seemed likely, the commission forecast the "economic collapse of the central business district."[9]

The other momentous development that got under way in the immediate postwar period was the incipient decentralization of office space—or, to be more precise, corporate office space. This development was even more unexpected than the emergence of the regional shopping center. For corporate offices had not followed the lead of the factories, wholesale houses, department stores, and other enterprises that had moved to the outlying business districts. Neither had most of the banks and investment banks, stock and commodity exchanges, insurance companies, law firms, accounting firms, and advertising agencies on which corporate America relied so heavily. Through World War II they had stayed in the central business district, and in the central business district they would remain, Americans believed. According to the conventional wisdom, they could not function anywhere but in a highly compact, extremely concentrated, and centrally located business district that brought together all the administrative, financial, legal, and technical expertise required to run the nation's economy.[10]

Starting in the late 1940s and early 1950s, however, a handful of small insurance companies moved their offices from Manhattan to Westchester County—one to White Plains, another to Port Chester, and yet another to Harrison. So did several large corporations, including General Foods and Standard Oil. A few others, among them General Electric and Union Carbide, were thinking about moving out of Manhattan, most to Westchester, some to New Jersey, Long Island, and southern Connecticut. And a few had already bought large tracts of land to build on. Offices were moving to the suburbs in other cities too. To give a couple of examples, MacManus, John & Adam, an advertising agency, left downtown Detroit for Bloomfield Hills, and Cargill, the country's largest grain trader, went from downtown Minneapolis to the shores of Lake Minnetonka. According to observers, many firms were moving because they needed more space and could not find it in the central business district except at exorbitant prices, often two and three times as much as they were paying. As one insurance company executive wrote, "Our prospective rent bill was staggering [if we remained in Manhattan]." Some firms were also fed up with downtown's noise and dirt, its traffic congestion and parking shortage. A bucolic setting, they believed, would make it easier to attract and retain qualified workers. Some firms might have moved in order to reduce the commuting time of their chief executives, many of whom lived in wealthy suburbs a short drive from their new offices. And though most executives were unwilling to admit it, a few firms might have moved out of fear that the central business district would be a prime target in the event of atomic war.[11]

Most observers downplayed the importance of this development. Only a tiny fraction of New York's many corporations had moved out of Manhattan, they pointed out. For every firm that left for the suburbs, noted the New York State Department of Commerce, "others have eagerly sought the space left behind." Despite a great surge of construction in the postwar period, the vacancy rate in New York's office buildings was only 2 percent. Many firms that had considered moving to the suburbs decided instead to stay put and modernize their quarters or erect new buildings. A few firms that had moved to the suburbs returned to the city. If there was not much of a trend to suburban offices in New York, wrote the *Wall Street Journal*, there was even less of one in other cities. There was no evidence that management was heading out of downtown in Boston, Chicago, Pittsburgh, and San Francisco.[12] But there was a trend, albeit a weak one. At least a few corporate executives no longer took it for granted that their firms had to be located in the central business district. And that was cause for alarm. For the central business district could survive the decentralization of industry and wholesaling. Some Americans held that it might even be better off without these messy and noisy activities. It might even survive the decentralization of retailing and entertainment. What it could not survive was the decentralization of office space, the loss of which would be disastrous not only for the downtown property owners but also for the downtown retailers and other businessmen whose well-being had come to depend more heavily than ever on the downtown workforce.

As downtown changed, so did the way Americans thought about it. Employing metaphors that were almost a century old, some still spoke of downtown as the "heart" and "hub" of the city and metropolitan area. As they saw it, there were some economic activities that could only be carried on in the central business district—which would always be home to the large department stores, tall office buildings, and grand hotels. There were other economic activities that could be carried on in the outlying business districts but had to be supervised from the central business district—which, said a department store executive, was the "nerve center" of the economy. Downtown, these Americans acknowledged, was no longer the only business district. But it was still the main one. And the main one it would always be. As two midwestern economists wrote in 1953, "There is nothing to indicate that the Loop—the world's greatest concentration of business establishments—will not continue as the economic mainspring of the Chicago metropolitan area." A Boston planner agreed. "No vision of the 'city of tomorrow[,]' no matter how decentralized or how dispersed, can conceive of no downtown," he declared two years later.[13]

Downtown, these Americans believed, was still as vital to the city as the heart was to the body and the hub to the wheel. "Like the human heart, it pumps life into the entire trading [area]," said a department store executive. Without it, wrote Baumhoff, the *St. Louis Post-Dispatch* reporter, the city is doomed. Downtown was a major source of revenue, too. Indeed, a Dayton realtor pointed out, the central business district generates so much more in taxes than it consumes in services that it subsidizes the residential property owners. Downtown was also the city's most striking feature, the feature, noted Walter S. Schmidt, "by [which] the city is judged and evaluated, not only by the visitors to it, who frequently see little else, but by the citizens themselves." Downtown was vital to the outlying sections as well, these Americans believed. The suburbs could not survive without the city, and the city could not survive without the central business district. "Even the largest, the most prosperous and best operated suburban communities in Greater Cleveland would dry up and blow away were it not for Cleveland in general and downtown Cleveland in particular," declared the *Lakewood Post,* a suburban Cleveland newspaper. "[What would] New York [be] without Fifth Avenue; Chicago without the Loop; or Philadelphia without Market, Chestnut and Walnut Streets?" asked a Philadelphia realtor. "Destroy these business areas, and you destroy the city." And if you destroy the city, "there would be no reasons for [its] sub-centers."[14]

But other Americans were less sanguine about the future of the central business district. Some doubted that it could hold its own against the outlying business districts. In time, wrote two Florida economists, downtown businesses will find it easier to move to their customers than to bring their customers to them. As that happens, the suburbs may well "absorb major portions of what used to be considered downtown commerce and industry, professional services, and commercialized recreation." It was too late to attempt to restore downtown to its "former unchallenged preeminence," a traffic expert pointed out shortly before the United States entered World War II. All that could be done was to try to create a balance between the central business district and the outlying business districts. Others thought that the central business district could hold its own—but only if the local authorities and downtown businessmen worked together to improve mass transit, build limited-access highways, provide off-street parking, and turn the inner-city slums and blighted areas into middle- and upper-middle-class neighborhoods. Even these measures might not be enough unless retailers stopped spending millions in the outlying areas and used the money to renovate their downtown stores. Downtown stores could compete with suburban stores, wrote Hal Burton, but not if they are "crippled by inertia, old-fashioned meth-ods, or plain bad merchandising."[15]

As revealing as what these Americans said was what they did. During the early and mid 1950s the Urban Land Institute, whose official position was that downtown was "the vital hub" of the metropolitan area, sent panels to a dozen cities to figure out how to revitalize their central business districts. At the same time periodicals convened roundtables at which merchants, realtors, planners, and engineers shared their thoughts about its plight, and trade and professional groups devoted parts of their annual meetings to a discussion of its problems. In one city after another downtown businessmen and property owners also established voluntary associations to promote the interests of the central business district—something they had been disinclined to do when downtown was in its heyday. By the mid 1950s virtually every city had at least one organization that was devoted exclusively to the well-being of the central business district. Los Angeles had two—the Downtown Businessmen's Asso-ciation and the Central Business District Association. There were so many of these associations that in 1954 delegates from thirty cities formed the Inter-national Downtown Executives' Association, a group of downtown associa-tions from the United States and Canada.[16] As much as anything, this prolif-eration revealed how deeply concerned downtown business interests were about the future.

The proliferation also revealed that many downtown businessmen and property owners no longer believed in spatial harmony. After more than two decades of rampant decentralization, during which time the central business district steadily lost ground to the outlying business districts, some still ad-hered to the traditional notion that rivalry between the center and the periph-ery was unnatural. But many now believed that rivalry within cities, especially between the central business district and the outlying business districts, was as natural as rivalry among cities. Some Americans went even further, argu-ing that the cities and the suburbs were locked in "mortal combat," to quote Edmond H. Hoben, assistant director of the National Association of Housing Officials. Perhaps no one made this point more forcefully than William Zeck-endorf, the flamboyant president of Webb & Knapp, a leading New York real estate firm, and one of the most outspoken supporters of urban redevelop-ment. "Satellite cities, which are the product of decentralization, are para-sites," he wrote in 1952. "Every satellite town saps off the buying power, the taxing power, and the vital factors that make for a cohesive, comprehensive, healthy city."[17]

Not everyone was concerned, let alone deeply concerned. Downtown, some believed, was no longer necessary. It was no longer true that "every city must have one large central business district," wrote E. E. East, chief engineer of the Automobile Club of Southern California. "We find in the metropolitan area of Los Angeles more than a hundred trading areas where every commodity and service essential to daily life may be obtained." East also pooh-poohed the idea that a business district "must be closely built-up to attract business." "This is a tradition handed down from the days of mass rail transportation," he explained. "It ignores the fact that an almost countless number of establishments are today doing a thriving business in locations far removed from closely built-up business centers."[18] Speaking at the national conference of planners in 1948, Hans Blumenfeld, a Philadelphia planner, took a similar position. Downtown, he insisted, was anachronistic. It was time for the advocates of urban redevelopment, "these modern King Canutes," to realize that decentralization was irreversible. "The densely crowded agglomeration of the 19th Century with its concomitant, the fantastic skyrocketing of urban land values, was a short-lived passing phenomenon." A product of an outdated transportation system, "it was bound to disappear forever; and I, for one say: good riddance!"

These Americans believed that a compact and highly congested central business district served only the interests of downtown businessmen and property owners. They agreed with Los Angeles planner Gordon Whitnall that the cities would be better off organized around a group of "well-balanced, self-contained community sub-centers" than around one central business district and many outlying residential sections. Decentralization, they conceded, had done severe damage. But it had in it "the seeds of a better urban existence for the mass of suffering humanity," said T. Ledyard Blakeman, executive director of the Detroit Metropolitan Area Regional Planning Commission. Provided it was "properly planned," decentralization would improve living and working conditions on the periphery and in the center. Novelist Louis Bromfield took this argument one step further. It was not just the central business district that was anachronistic; it was also the huge metropolitan area of which it was the most visible symbol. Bromfield, too, favored decentralization—but not so much the shift from the center to the periphery as the movement from big cities to small towns and rural areas and from the most developed regions to the least developed.[19]

The belief that the central business district had outlived its usefulness was heightened by the growing fear of atomic warfare. Less than a year after the United States obliterated Hiroshima and Nagasaki, some Americans were wondering whether the modern city was doomed. As early as 1948 Tracy B.

Augur, past president of the American Institute of Planners, declared that the only defense against atomic weapons was dispersal. "We cannot afford *not* to disperse our cities," he said. "If we delay too long," he warned, "we may wake up some morning and find that we haven't any country, that is, if we wake up at all that morning." Although some skeptics argued that dispersal would be impractical and ineffective, Augur and others made a strong impression on many Americans, even many who had a substantial stake in the well-being of the central business district. A good example is Albert D. Hutzler, president of Hutzler Brothers, Baltimore's leading department store. Asked at the 1948 Businessmen's Conference on Urban Problems, a conference sponsored by the U.S. Chamber of Commerce, "Isn't decentralization inevitable? Aren't we wasting money and energy in trying to delay it?" he replied:

> If you would have asked me that a few years ago, I would have been ex-
> tremely hot in saying it was not inevitable. I would have been tremen-
> dously strong in saying that our best course was redevelopment, spend-
> ing all the money necessary for it. However, I have wavered a little bit
> since the atomic bomb. I am quite serious. I wonder whether, from a
> military standpoint, it might be better to save this money to develop ad-
> ditional subsidiary sections and to let the central business district re-
> main fairly stationary.[20]

Hutzler had more to worry about than atomic warfare. For decades down-town Baltimore's department stores and other retailers had been losing ground, and there was no reason to think they would regain it. Between 1948 and 1954, during which time retail trade rose 25 percent in metropolitan Baltimore, it fell 2 percent in downtown Baltimore. And downtown's share of the metropolitan area's retail trade declined from over 20 percent to under 16 percent. Equally disquieting, the assessed value of the central business district dropped from $175 million in 1931 to $128 million in 1947—a decrease of 27 percent that occurred at the same time the assessed value of the city increased by 2 percent and the assessed value of the periphery by 26 percent. As late as the mid 1920s experts had predicted that downtown Baltimore would be so busy in 1950 that it would be necessary to double- and triple-deck the streets and to build subways and els to accommodate the hundreds of thousands of commuters. But when 1950 arrived, downtown was no busier than it had been in the mid 1920s. All this Hutzler knew. But one thing in particular puz-zled him. According to the conventional wisdom, a busy downtown was vital to the well-being of the city. But if things were slow in downtown Baltimore, they were even slower in downtown Los Angeles. Yet Los Angeles, Hutzler pointed out, was "the fastest growing city in the country" and by no means the "poorest."[21]

The growth of Los Angeles was phenomenal, as phenomenal as the growth of New York and Chicago. From a nondescript town of 11,000 in 1880, Los Angeles had grown by 1930 into the nation's fifth largest city, with more than 1.2 million people, and its fourth largest metropolitan area, with upward of 2.3 million. A major commercial entrepôt and industrial center, the ninth largest manufacturer in the country, it was already the metropolis of the Southwest and would in time replace San Francisco as the metropolis of the West Coast. The growth of Los Angeles slowed during the 1930s. But with the end of the Great Depression and the outbreak of World War II, it picked up again—and at a pace that astonished observers, one of whom called it "one of the most spectacular of all municipal growths." "People are swarming into Los Angeles at the rate of 3,000 per week," he wrote in 1949, "and they have not come to see [actor] Van Johnson's house. They have come to stay." By 1950 the city had nearly 2 million people, making it the fourth largest in the nation, and the metropolitan area had almost 4 million, making it the third largest after New York and Chicago. With a booming and highly diversified economy, an economy, reported Newsweek, "undergoing its greatest period of industrial expansion," Greater Los Angeles was also second among metropolitan areas in construction and auto production, third in employment, income, retail sales, wholesale trade, and banking, and fourth in manufacturing.[22]

Los Angeles was also the nation's—possibly, wrote Newsweek, the world's—most decentralized metropolis. The signs were visible everywhere, in the sprawling residential subdivisions, in the growing outlying business districts, and in the booming regional shopping centers. But nowhere were they more striking then in the sorry state of the central business district. From its heyday in the mid 1920s, downtown had gone steadily downhill. Things were very bad during the Great Depression and not much better afterward. Between the mid 1920s and early 1950s, during which time the population of Los Angeles County more than tripled, the number of people who went downtown rose less than 10 percent. On a typical weekday in 1953 only 15 percent of the population entered the central business district, down from 41 percent in 1926. Construction downtown, which had come to a halt in the 1930s and 1940s, was still dormant. The central business district's share of the metropolitan area's retail trade fell sharply too, from 30 percent in 1930 to 11 percent in 1948. And after the Crenshaw and other regional shopping centers opened, it plummeted to 6 percent in 1954. "It looks as though the fate of the downtown stores in that city has been sealed," wrote Business Week in 1951. "There hasn't been a lick of expansion in the downtown stores since the war. The trend is all outward."23

Los Angeles was not, as *Business Week* put it, "one of a kind," just the first of its kind—"the first modern, widely decentralized industrial city in America," journalist Carey McWilliams wrote.24 As such, it revealed that a city could grow and prosper without a vibrant downtown. It also revealed that the dispersal of residences might well be incompatible with the centralization of business, a possibility raised by John A. Miller in the early 1940s. In Los Angeles, as in other cities, it was no longer true that no matter where people lived, no matter how far from the center, they would travel downtown every day, that the more they went to the periphery to live, the more they would come to the center to work, shop, do business, and amuse themselves. Los Angeles also revealed that the efforts to curb decentralization might well be doomed. There was reason to think that people were not going to downtown L.A. because they did not want to. If so, more limited-access highways would not do much good. Nor would additional off-street parking, of which Los Angeles already had more than any other city. There was also reason to think that the well-to-do had no desire to move from the periphery to the center. If so, urban redevelopment would not do much good either. If the metropolis of the future was unfolding in Los Angeles, as many Americans believed, it did not bode well for Hutzler and other businessmen and property owners that downtown L.A. was or would soon be "just another" business district.

Epilogue

Late in 1951 *Urban Land,* the official publication of the Urban Land Institute, ran an editorial entitled "'Our Downtown'—Is It Growing or Dying?" a question that was on the minds of many of the institute's members. To help answer it, the editorial quoted at length from a leaflet written by Frank J. LaPin, a Portland, Oregon, realtor, whose words, it said, "apply in every American city." Downtown, wrote LaPin, has serious problems, among them run-down stores, narrow streets, and inadequate parking. But much was being done to solve them, especially by downtown merchants, who were spending millions to modernize their stores. Although much remained to be done, not the least of which was the construction of underground parking garages with connections to stores, hotels, theaters, and office buildings, downtown's prospects were bright. The central business district—"the heart of an active pulsating city," in LaPin's words—has more to offer than the outlying business districts. It has a greater variety of goods, a greater selection of amusements, and, above all, "more people, greater crowds." And more people and greater crowds it would always have, wrote LaPin. For "isn't it . . . a thrill for the average person to pass up and down the streets of 'Downtown,' see the countless window exhibits, ride the elevators and escalators, and rub elbows with the thousands who come and go?"[1]

LaPin was overly optimistic. For the average person it might have been a thrill to go downtown in the late nineteenth and early twentieth centuries. It might even have been a thrill in the 1920s, when the downtown hotels, department stores, office buildings, and movie theaters dazzled the senses—and, with their doormen, bellhops, elevator operators, shoeshine boys, salesgirls, floorwalkers, and ushers, offered a level of service that all but disappeared in the second half of the twentieth century. But by the mid twentieth century the thrill was largely gone—and not only in Los Angeles, but also in other cities where decentralization had not spread as fast. For many Americans—for many straphangers who were hard pressed to find a seat (and fed up with the run-down transit systems) and for many motorists who were hard pressed to find a parking space (and fed up with the chronic traffic jams)—a trip downtown was more an ordeal than a thrill. Before long things would get worse. As a result of the huge postwar migration from the rural South to the urban North, many blacks began to go downtown for the first time. With the streets full of young blacks, "always five or six at a time, loud and arrogant," his customers were afraid, said the owner of a downtown Baltimore jewelry store. He even had to escort some of them to the parking lot, he complained.[2] An integrated downtown was not the sort of thrill that most whites were looking for in the 1960s and 1970s.

During the nineteenth and early twentieth centuries it would not have mattered if it was not a thrill to go downtown. Most Americans would have gone downtown anyway. They had no choice. Not if they wanted to work in banks, insurance companies, and other components of the service sector. Not if they wanted to shop in department stores and do business with financial institutions. And not if they wanted to stay at hotels, eat at restaurants, and watch plays. But starting in the 1920s, Americans had a choice. As well as the central business district, they could go to the outlying business districts, many of which were only a short drive from their homes and had plenty of free parking—if little in the way of excitement. There they could patronize branch department stores, chain stores, branch banks, neighborhood movie theaters, and roadside motels and restaurants. The choice grew even wider in the postwar years, when developers built regional shopping centers and enclosed shopping malls. And by the 1960s and 1970s, or well before the coming of the "edge cities" that have so impressed contemporary observers, Americans could find and do most things on the periphery that they had once found and done only in the center.[3] They could still go downtown, but in most cases they no longer had to.

For the downtown business interests, the issue was clear. Either they had to write off their enormous investments in land, buildings, and businesses, which for some was not an option, or they had to try to find ways to make Americans want to go downtown. For most of them, it was an easy decision. And starting in the postwar years, they renewed their efforts to revitalize the central business district.[4] Often with the help of city officials and city planners, the other groups deeply concerned about decentralization, they attempted to make downtown more accessible by pushing for limited-access highways and off-street parking. They urged the federal government to subsidize urban mass transit too. They also attempted to create a new market for downtown goods and services by working to eliminate the slums and blighted areas adjacent to the central business district and replace them with middle- and upper-middle-class neighborhoods. Later on the downtown business interests encouraged the formation of a host of public-private partnerships to fill downtown with convention centers, malls, cultural centers, football stadiums, and baseball diamonds. They also exploited a host of other tools, ranging from zoning incentives to tax abatements and historic preservation, to attract people and capital to the central business district.

These efforts are an integral part of the history of downtown in the second half of the twentieth century—a subject that is beyond the scope of this book and that I am happy to leave to other historians. But based on what I have read and seen in recent years, I think it is safe to say that the results have been mixed. Leaving aside their often devastating impact on other parts of the city, the freeways have probably done more to spur decentralization than to curb it; and the urban redevelopment projects have probably done as much to weaken the central business district as to strengthen it. As for the downtown malls and other recent developments, it is too soon to say anything about their long-term impact. Downtown is doing better today than a decade ago in New York, Boston, and San Francisco, though not in Detroit, Tampa, and Los Angeles. But whether this is the result of the efforts of the downtown business interests and their allies is not clear. What is clear is that after all these efforts nowhere has the central business district regained the position it held in the 1910s and 1920s—or even in the 1940s and 1950s. Even after nearly a decade of unprecedented prosperity, nowhere, not even in New York, is downtown today anywhere as immense, as imposing, and as awesome as the downtown of the future depicted in the *New York World*'s "Pictorial Forecast of the City" one hundred years ago.

I have no idea what downtown will be like a hundred years from now—though I have doubts that the predictions made in the late twentieth century will be more accurate than those made in the late nineteenth. But I have a hunch that the future of downtown will be shaped less by how Americans respond to technological change than by how they define the good community. In my view, the decline of downtown was a result not so much of the deterioration of mass transit and the proliferation of private automobiles, of too much traffic and too little parking, as of the American vision of the "bourgeois utopia"—and of the local, state, and federal policies that helped Americans realize it. To put it another way, a nation of suburbs is not conducive to a vibrant downtown. Indeed, if the history of urban America is indicative, downtown will thrive only if Americans who have a choice prefer to live in or near the center—a preference that is taken for granted in Madrid, Paris, and other European cities. If there is reason today for optimism about the future of downtown, it can be found not in the many cities that have built downtown malls and convention centers, but in the few cities where many Americans have rejected the traditional concept of the good community and instead opted to live in apartments in or near the central business district.

Notes

Introduction

1. *Boston Globe*, February 11, 1988. See also Sam Bass Warner, Jr., *The Private City: Philadelphia in Three Periods of Its Growth* (Philadelphia, 1986), page 187.
2. Lincoln Steffens, *The Autobiography of Lincoln Steffens* (New York, 1931), volume 1, page 243; Shan Tabor to Robert M. Fogelson, February 14, 1991, author's files; *Charlotte Observer*, February 14, 1987.
3. These figures are for 1982, the last year for which the U.S. Census Bureau compiled them. In all likelihood, they would be even lower today. See U.S. Bureau of the Census, *1982 Census of Retail Trade: Major Retail Centers in Standard Metropolitan Statistical Areas* (Washington, D.C., 1984). See also *New York Times*, December 10, 1995.
4. Richard Russo, *The Risk Pool* (New York, 1989), pages 88–89; John Updike, *Rabbit at Rest* (New York, 1991), pages 183–184; William J. Coughlin, *Death Penalty* (New York, 1992), page 92.
5. Charles Abrams, *The Language of Cities* (New York, 1971), page 41; *St. Petersburg Times*, January 10, 1992; A. Q. Mowbray, *Road to Ruin* (Philadelphia, 1969), page 67; Joe T. Darden et al., *Detroit: Race and Uneven Development* (Philadelphia, 1987), page 258.
6. Joel Garreau, *Edge City: Life on the New Frontier* (New York, 1991), page 59. See also Bernard J. Frieden and Lynne B. Sagalyn, *Downtown, Inc.: How America Rebuilds Cities* (Cambridge, 1989), page 5; *CBS Evening News*, June 23, 1993; *Boston Globe*, February 1, 1994.
7. Eric Lax, *Woody Allen: A Biography* (New York, 1991), pages 20–21; *Baltimore Sun*, August 14, 1977; *Tampa Tribune*, January 20, 1992; *Transcript of the Tampa Architectural Review Commission Public Meeting on the Recommendation of the Tampa Gas Company Building and First National Bank Building for Landmark Designation*, October 12, 1992, page 54; William Kennedy, *O Albany!* (New York, 1983), pages 8–9.
8. Richard Moe and Carter Wilkie, *Changing Places: Rebuilding Community in the Age of Sprawl* (New York, 1997), page 177.

Chapter 1: The Business District

1. A. G. Gardiner, "Down Town," *New Republic*, August 18, 1920, pages 329–330.
2. Allan Nevins, ed., *The Diary of Philip Hone, 1828–1851* (New York, 1927), volume 1,

pages 41, 158, 196–197, 199, 202, 295–296, 336, 394, volume 2, page 872; Allan Nevins and Milton Halsley Thomas, eds., *The Diary of George Templeton Strong* (New York, 1952), volume 1, page 234, volume 2, pages 454–455; *Oxford English Dictionary*, 2d ed. (Oxford, 1989), volume 9, pages 1001–1002, volume 19, pages 320, 324.

3. *New York Times*, January 21, 1867; Nevins, ed., *Diary of Philip Hone*, volume 1, page 202; Charles Lockwood, *Manhattan Moves Uptown* (Boston, 1976), pages 94–96; Edward K. Spann, *The New Metropolis: New York City, 1840–1857* (New York, 1981), page 102; George William Curtis, *The Potiphar Papers* (New York, 1853), page 106.

4. *Oxford English Dictionary*, volume 19, page 1002; Henry P. Tappan, *The Growth of Cities: A Discourse* (New York, 1855), page 33; Nevins and Thomas, eds., *Diary of George Templeton Strong*, volume 1, page 135, volume 2, pages 70, 133–134, 137, 207, 233, 250, 276, 426; *Harper's New Monthly Magazine*, April 1852, page 413; Elaine Abelson, *When Ladies Go A-Thieving: Middle-Class Shoplifters in the Victorian Department Store* (New York, 1989), page 17; *Wood's Illustrated Hand-Book to New York and Environs* (New York, 1873), pages 6–7, 21, 23, 40, 43; George Makepeace Towle, *American Society* (London, 1870), volume 1, pages 281, 288.

5. *Boston Globe*, July 12, 1872, February 5, May 12, 1874; *[Chicago] Real Estate and Building Journal*, March 10, 1873, page 1; *Diary of Susan E. Parsons Brown Forbes (Mrs. Alexander Barclay Forbes), 1841–1907*, December 25, 1862, June 11, 1863, January 9, March 21, 1874, American Antiquarian Society, Worcester; Elias Colbert and Everett Chamberlin, *Chicago and the Great Conflagration* (Cincinnati, 1872), page 235; Linus M. Child, *Shall the Metropolis of New England Have an Elevated Railroad? Argument in Its Favor Before the Legislative Committee on Street Railways* (Boston, 1880), page 26; Charles Cist, *Sketches and Statistics of Cincinnati in 1851* (Cincinnati, 1851), pages 209–210; Elsie Martinez and Margaret LeCorgne, *Uptown/Downtown: Growing Up in New Orleans* (Lafayette, Louisiana, 1986), page 1; *San Francisco Examiner*, May 17, 1906; *Philadelphia Real Estate Record and Builders' Guide*, March 22, 1886, page 121.

6. *Webster's Imperial Dictionary of the English Language* (Chicago, 1904), pages 513, 1841; Sylva Clapin, *A New Dictionary of Americanisms* (New York, 1902), page 166; Noah Webster, *An American Dictionary of the English Language* (Springfield, Massachusetts, 1870), page 1454; Joseph E. Worcester, *A Dictionary of the English Language* (Boston, 1860), volume 2, page 1609; E. B. Lloyd, *Lights and Shades in San Francisco* (San Francisco, 1876), page 489; Lincoln Steffens, *The Autobiography of Lincoln Steffens* (New York, 1931), volume 1, page 243; Alan Raleigh, *The Real America* (London, 1913), page 38.

7. Montgomery Schuyler, "The Building of Pittsburgh: Part 1. The Terrain & the Rivers," *Architectural Record*, September 1911, page 207. See also U.S. Census Office, *Report on Vital and Social Statistics in the United States at the Eleventh Census: 1890. Part II. Vital Statistics* (Washington, D.C., 1896), pages 161–162, maps following pages 181 and 227.

8. U.S. Census Office, *Report on Transportation Business in the United States at the Eleventh Census: Part I. Transportation by Land* (Washington, D.C., 1895), page 688, and *Part II. Transportation by Water* (Washington, D.C., 1894), page 43; *[Chicago] Real Estate and Building Journal*, April 25, 1891, page 577, September 19, 1891, page 1355; William Leach, *Land of Desire: Merchants, Power, and the Rise of a New American Culture* (New York, 1993), pages 30–31, 137–138; David Nasaw, "Cities of Light, Land-

scapes of Pleasure," in David Ward and Olivier Zunz, eds., *The Landscape of Modernity: Essays on New York City* (New York, 1992), pages 274–277; Harold L. Platt, *City Building in the New South: The Growth of Public Services in Houston, Texas, 1830–1910* (Philadelphia, 1983), page 94; William Archer, *America To-Day: Observations & Reflections* (London, 1900), pages 38–39.

9. *Argument of Mayor Matthews Before the Committee on Transit of the Massachusetts Legislature. April 4, 1894* (Boston, 1894), pages 7–8; *Report of the Rapid Transit Commission to the Massachusetts Legislature. April 5, 1892* (Boston, 1892), page 10; E. K. Morse, "Pittsburgh Subways," *Proceedings of the Engineers' Society of Western Pennsylvania* (March 1907), page 50; *Electric Railway Journal*, August 7, 1909, page 212; Julian Ralph, *Our Great West* (New York, 1893), page 7; *Chicago Tribune*, December 30, 1891.

10. *[Chicago] Real Estate and Building Journal*, February 20, 1897, page 149; *Chicago Tribune*, December 16, 1891. See also David Ward, *Cities and Immigrants: A Geography of Change in Nineteenth Century America* (New York, 1971), page 87.

11. Christine Stansell, *City of Women: Sex and Class in New York, 1789–1860* (New York, 1986), page 69; John F. Kasson, *Rudeness and Civility: Manners in Nineteenth Century Urban America* (New York, 1990), page 117; David Thomason, "The Men's Quarter of Down Town Nashville," *Tennessee Historical Society Quarterly*, Spring 1982, pages 48–66; John C. Schneider, "Skid Row as an Urban Neighborhood, 1880–1960," in Jon Erickson and Charles Wilhelm, eds., *Housing the Homeless* (New Brunswick, 1986), pages 169–172; Kathy Piess, *Cheap Amusements: Working Women and Leisure in Turn-of-the-Century New York* (Philadelphia, 1986), pages 38–41; Abelson, *When Ladies Go A-Thieving*, pages 20–22; Julian Ralph, "The City of Brooklyn," *Harper's New Monthly Magazine*, April 1893, pages 659–660; Lillie Hamilton French, "Shopping in New York," *Century Magazine*, March 1901, pages 651–652.

12. *A Visit to the States: A Reprint of Letters from the Special Correspondent of The Times* (London, 1887), page 46; Bayrd Still, ed., *Mirror for Gotham: New York as Seen by Contemporaries from Dutch Days to the Present* (New York, 1956), page 187; W. G. Marshall, *Through America; or, Nine Months in the United States* (London, 1881), page 23; James Dabney McCabe, *New York by Sunlight and Gaslight* (New York, 1882), pages 54, 187; U.S. Census Office, *Report on Transportation Business at the Eleventh Census: Part I. Transportation by Land*, pages 684–685.

13. McCabe, *New York by Sunlight*, page 143. See also *American Architect and Building News*, July 4, 1885, page 10, August 20, 1892, page 109; Anna A. Rogers, "Why Marriages Fail," *Atlantic Monthly*, September 1907, page 294; Abelson, *When Ladies Go A-Thieving*, page 127.

14. Junius Henri Browne, *The Great Metropolis: A Mirror of New York* (Hartford, 1869), page 262. See also Ralph, *Our Great West*, pages 2–3; Marshall, *Through America*, page 231; *American Architect and Building News*, July 10, 1886, pages 13–14, July 11, 1903, page 16; L. Schick, *Chicago and Its Environs* (Chicago, 1891), page 100.

15. J. B. Lippincott & Co., *Philadelphia and Its Environs* (Philadelphia, 1873), page 2; *American Architect and Building News*, November 30, 1889, page 253; Schick, *Chicago*, page 91; Howard L. Preston, *Automobile Age Atlanta: The Making of a Southern Metropolis, 1900–1935* (Athens, Georgia, 1979), pages 76–77; Don H. Doyle, *Nashville in the New South, 1880–1930* (Knoxville, 1985), pages 69–78; Christopher Silver, *Twentieth-Century Richmond: Planning, Politics, and Race* (Knoxville, 1984), pages 27–29.

16. *Philadelphia Real Estate Record and Builders' Guide*, February 8, 1886, page 49. See

also Francis A. Walker, *The Statistics of the Population of the United States [Compiled] from the Original Returns of the Ninth Census* (Washington, D.C., 1872), pages 212, 244–245; U.S. Census Office, *Report on the Social Statistics of Cities in the United States at the Eleventh Census: 1890* (Washington, D.C., 1895), pages 9–12.

17. Nevins, ed., *The Diary of Philip Hone*, volume 1, page 202; *[New York] Real Estate Record and Builders' Guide*, March 24, 1877, pages 219–220, April 20, 1889, page 543, March 10, 1900, page 403; Henry C. Binford, *The First Suburbs: Residential Communities on the Boston Periphery, 1815–1860* (Chicago, 1988), page 179; Curtis, *The Potiphar Papers*, pages 104–106; Robert M. Fishman, *Bourgeois Utopias: The Rise and Fall of Suburbia* (New York, 1987), pages 128–129; Massachusetts General Court, Joint Special Committee on Transit, "Hearing on Subways in Boston," March 13, 1894, volume 4, page 59, Massachusetts State Library, Boston.

18. Sam Bass Warner, Jr., *Streetcar Suburbs: The Process of Growth in Boston, 1870–1900* (Cambridge, 1962), page 153; Howard Gillette, Jr., "The Emergence of the Modern Metropolis: Philadelphia in the Age of Its Consolidation," in William W. Cutler III and Howard Gillette, Jr., eds., *The Divided Metropolis: Social and Spatial Dimensions of Philadelphia, 1800–1974* (Westport, Connecticut, 1980), page 15; *Chicago Tribune*, February 25, 1893; *Boston Globe*, May 6, 1873; *[New York] Real Estate Record and Builders' Guide*, April 12, 1890, page 414; Gwendolyn Wright, *Building the Dream: A Social History of Housing in America* (New York, 1981), pages 108–109; James Fullarton Muirhead, *America the Land of Contrasts* (Boston, 1898), page 207.

19. *American Architect and Building News*, June 30, 1877, page 203, July 27, 1878, pages 27–28; *Report and Testimony of the Special Committee of the [New York State] Assembly to Investigate the Desirability of Municipal Ownership of the Street and Elevated Railroads of the Various Cities of the State* (Albany, 1896), volume 2, pages 1105–1106.

20. Olmsted, Vaux & Co., "Report Accompanying Plan for Laying Out the South Park," in S. B. Sutton, ed., *Civilizing American Cities: A Selection of Frederick Law Olmsted's Writings on City Landscapes* (Cambridge, 1971), pages 157–158; Frederick Law Olmsted, *Public Parks and the Enlargement of Towns* (Cambridge, 1870), page 15; Frederick Law Olmsted et al., "Report to the Staten Island Improvement Commission of a Preliminary Scheme of Improvements," in Albert Fein, ed., *Landscape into Cityscape: Frederick Law Olmsted's Plans for a Greater New York City* (Ithaca, 1967), pages 182–183; *New York Daily Tribune*, December 28, 1879.

21. Olmsted et al., "Report to the Staten Island Improvement Association," pages 182–183; Richard M. Hurd, "The Structure and Growth of Cities," *Municipal Affairs*, Spring 1902, page 38; *American Architect and Building News*, July 27, 1878, page 28; *[New York] Real Estate Record and Builders' Guide*, October 1, 1881, page 921.

22. *Remarks of Henry W. Muzzey, Esq. on the "Act to Permit Joe V. Meigs and Associates to Build an Elevated Railway, with the Consent of the Cities and Towns in Which It May Be Located," to the Massachusetts House of Representatives, March 7, 1882* (Boston, 1882), page 6; *California Architect and Building News*, May 15, 1888, page 58; *Chicago Tribune*, June 7, 1885; *Arguments of Henry R. Whitney and Prentiss Cummings, in Opposition to Allowing Cities and Towns to Impose Taxes for the Use of Streets by Private Corporations, Made Before the Committee on Cities and the Committee on Taxation, of the Massachusetts Legislature, Sitting Jointly* (Boston, 1891), page 40; *Philadelphia Real Estate Record and Builders' Guide*, February 27, 1888, page 85.

23. *St. Louis Post-Dispatch*, January 19, 1896. See also Olmsted et al., "Report to the

Staten Island Improvement Association," page 175; Richard M. Hurd, *Principles of City Land Values* (New York, 1903), pages 82–83.

24. Adna Ferrin Weber, *The Growth of Cities in the Nineteenth Century: A Study of Statistics* (Ithaca, 1965), page 467. See also Hurd, *Principles of City Land Values*, page 77; Homer Hoyt, *One Hundred Years of Land Values in Chicago* (Chicago, 1933), page 140.

25. *[New York] Real Estate Record and Builders' Guide*, June 15, 1878, page 515; *Philadelphia Real Estate Record and Builders' Guide*, May 10, 1886, page 205.

26. Nicholas B. Wainwright, ed., *A Philadelphia Perspective: The Diary of Sidney George Fisher Covering the Years 1834–1871* (Philadelphia, 1967), page 316; Joel Arthur Tarr, "From City to Suburb: The 'Moral' Influence of Transportation Technology," in Alexander B. Callow, ed., *American Urban History* (New York, 1973), pages 202–212; *[New York] Real Estate Record and Builders' Guide*, June 1, 1872, page 251, April 29, 1876, page 321, October 4, 1879, page 780, February 15, 1881, page 113, February 4, 1882, page 95.

27. Edward Dana Durand, "Street and Electric Railways," in U.S. Bureau of the Census, *Street and Electric Railways, 1902: Special Reports of the Census Office* (Washington, D.C., 1905), pages 26–29; *Arguments of Henry R. Whitney and Prentiss Cummings*, page 40; Hurd, *Principles of City Land Values*, pages 94–96; Hurd, "The Structure and Growth of Cities," pages 41–42.

28. *Detroit Free Press*, November 21, 1869; Tappan, *The Growth of Cities*, pages 31–32; *Tenth Annual Report of the Board of Commissioners of the Central Park: 1866*, pages 143–144; Michael Holleran, *Boston's "Changeful Times": Origins of Preservation and Planning in America* (Baltimore, 1998), pages 25–27, 143–144.

29. Ronald Sanders, *The Downtown Jews: Portrait of an Immigrant Generation* (New York, 1969), page 43; David Schuyler, *The New Urban Landscape: The Redefinition of City Form in Nineteenth-Century America* (Baltimore, 1986), page 26; Holleran, *Boston's "Changeful Times,"* pages 25–27; *Philadelphia Real Estate Record and Builders' Guide*, February 8, 1886, page 49.

30. *St. Louis Dispatch*, January 19, 1896.

31. *Chicago Tribune*, June 10, 1883; *[New York] Real Estate Record and Builders' Guide*, October 29, 1881, page 1009, March 17, 1894, page 407, December 14, 1901, page 820; *American Architect and Building News*, May 30, 1896, page 87.

32. *Chicago Tribune*, October 15, 1891; Joint Special Committee on Transit, "Hearings on Subways in Boston," March 8, 1894, volume 19, pages 6–7, 14–15, 23; *Chicago Real Estate and Building Journal*, February 20, 1897, page 149; *Report of the Rapid Transit Commission to the Massachusetts Legislature*, page 68.

33. *Chicago Tribune*, November 11, 1891; *American Architect and Building News*, April 9, 1898, page 121; Roger Lotchin, "San Francisco: The Patterns and Chaos of Growth," in Kenneth T. Jackson and Stanley K. Schultz, eds., *Cities in American History* (New York, 1972), page 153; *[Chicago] Real Estate and Building Journal*, April 25, 1891, page 577.

34. Child, *Shall the Metropolis of New England Have an Elevated Railroad?* pages 29–30. See also Joint Special Committee on Transit, "Hearing on Subways in Boston," February 27, 1894, volume 3, page 75; *St. Louis Post-Dispatch*, January 19, 1896; *[New York] Real Estate Record and Builders' Guide*, April 12, 1890, page 414.

35. Amory H. Bradford, "The Suburbs and the Cities," *Open Church*, October 1898, pages 351–353; David R. Goldfield and Blaine A. Brownell, *Urban America: A History*

(Boston, 1990), page 127; William R. Martin, "The Financial Resources of New York," *North American Review*, November–December 1878, page 438; *[New York] Real Estate and Record Builders' Guide*, September 21, 1872, page 99, July 29, 1878, pages 556–557; Clifton K. Yearley, *The Money Machines: The Breakdown and Reform of Governmental and Party Finance in the North, 1860–1920* (Albany, 1972), chapters 1 and 2.

36. David Ward, *Poverty, Ethnicity, and the American City, 1840–1925* (Cambridge, England, 1989), page 47; Bradford, "The Suburbs and the Cities," pages 351–353; *[New York] Real Estate and Builders' Guide*, October 4, 1879, page 779; Robert M. Fogelson, *America's Armories: Architecture, Society, and Public Order* (Cambridge, 1989), pages 23–29.

37. *Detroit Free Press*, February 10, 1866. See also A. F. Weber, "Suburban Annexations," *North American Review*, May 1898, page 616; Fishman, *Bourgeois Utopias*, page 127; Towle, *American Society*, volume 2, pages 34–35, 37–38; *New York Times*, February 23, 1894.

38. *[New York] Real Estate Record and Builders' Guide*, April 29, 1876, page 321, May 19, 1877, page 395, October 4, 1879, page 779; *[Chicago] Real Estate and Building Journal*, November 24, 1888, page 602; Kenneth T. Jackson, "Metropolitan Government Versus Suburban Autonomy," in Jackson and Schultz, eds., *Cities in American History*, pages 447–452; Jon C. Teaford, *City and Suburb: The Political Fragmentation of Metropolitan America, 1850–1970* (Baltimore, 1979), chapters 2 and 3.

39. O. B. Bunce, "The City of the Future," *Appletons' Journal*, February 10, 1872, pages 157–158; O. B. Bunce, "The 'City of the Future' Once More," ibid., November 2, 1872, pages 495–496.

40. Ralph, *Our Great West*, page 32; *American Architect and Building News*, June 30, 1877, page 203, July 27, 1878, page 27, July 16, 1904, page 17.

41. Charles Mulford Robinson, "Cities of the Present," *Architectural Record*, December 1910, page 459; Hurd, "The Structure and Growth of Cities," page 39; *American Architect and Building News*, June 30, 1877, page 203; Frederick Law Olmsted and James R. Croes, "Preliminary Report of the Landscape Architect and the Civil and Topographical Engineer, Upon the Laying Out of the Twenty-third and Twenty-fourth Wards," in Fein, ed., *Landscape into Cityscape*, page 352; Adna F. Weber, "Rapid Transit," *Municipal Affairs*, Fall 1902, page 412.

42. Everett Chamberlin, *Chicago and Its Suburbs* (Chicago, 1874), page 188; *Philadelphia Real Estate Record and Builders' Guide*, July 27, 1887, page 289; "Parisian 'Flats,'" *Appletons' Journal*, November 18, 1871, page 561; Wright, *Building the Dream*, pages 141–151.

43. *American City*, July 1910, page 3; *[New York] Real Estate Record and Builders' Guide*, April 20, 1889, page 542; Patricia Mooney Melvin, *The Organic City: Urban Definition and Community Organization, 1880–1920* (Louisville, 1987), page 15; *Baltimore Sun*, February 9, 1904; Spann, *The New Metropolis*, page 186.

44. *[New York] Real Estate Record and Builders' Guide*, July 5, 1873, page 311, April 29, 1876, page 321, May 19, 1877, pages 395–396, March 11, 1882, page 213, March 18, 1882, page 242, January 4, 1908, pages 3–4; *[Chicago] Real Estate and Building Journal*, November 24, 1888, page 602.

45. Olmsted, Vaux & Co., "Preliminary Report upon the Proposed Suburban Village at Riverside, near Chicago," in Sutton, ed., *Civilizing American Cities*, page 295; Binford, *The First Suburbs*, page 171–178; Robert M. Fogelson, *The Fragmented Metropolis: Los Angeles, 1850–1930* (Cambridge, 1967), pages 144–146.

46. J. F. Harder, "The City's Plan," *Municipal Affairs*, March 1898, page 33. See also Thomas Curtis Clarke, "Rapid Transit in Cities, II: The Solution," *Scribners' Magazine*, June 1892, page 745; "The Triangle's 'Thru' Traffic," *Better Traffic*, October 1931, page 1.

47. A South Carolinian, *Glimpses of New-York City* (Charleston, 1852), page 12. See also Hurd, *Principles of City Land Values*, page 17; *Architecture and Building*, October 23, 1897, page 145; *Congressional Globe*, January 16, 1872, page 408; Colbert and Chamberlin, *Chicago*, pages 137–138; *Chicago Tribune*, December 16, 1891.

48. Joseph L. Arnold, "The Neighborhood and City Hall: The Origins of Neighborhood Associations in Baltimore, 1880–1911," *Journal of Urban History*, November 1979, pages 22–23; Seattle City Planning Commission, Rapid Transit Committee, "Seattle Rapid Transit Report to the City Planning Commission" (1924), page 94, Graduate School of Design Library, Harvard University.

49. *[New York] Real Estate Record and Builders' Guide*, May 9, 1868, page 1; Ann Durkin Keating, *Building Chicago: Suburban Development and the Creation of a Divided Metropolis* (Columbus, Ohio, 1988), pages 59–60; Arnold, "The Neighborhood and City Hall," pages 10–21; Zane Miller, *Boss Cox's Cincinnati: Urban Politics in the Progressive Era* (New York, 1968), pages 116–117; Terence J. McDonald, *The Parameters of Urban Fiscal Policy: Socioeconomic Change and Political Culture in San Francisco, 1860–1906* (Berkeley, 1986), pages 177–178.

50. *[New York] Real Estate Record and Builders' Guide*, February 9, 1901, pages 228–229; *Report of the Subway Advisory Commission Appointed by Sub-Committee on Subways Local Transportation Committee Chicago City Council* (Chicago, 1926), pages 60–61; *Chicago Commerce*, March 31, 1911, page 19.

51. McDonald, *The Parameters of Urban Fiscal Policy*, page 188; *Report of the Subway Advisory Commission*, page 61; *San Francisco Examiner*, May 11/12/17/29, 1906; Judd Kahn, *Imperial San Francisco: Politics and Planning in an American City, 1897–1906* (Lincoln, Nebraska, 1978), page 178–183.

52. Seymour J. Mandelbaum, *Boss Tweed's New York* (New York, 1965), pages 114–118; *Not Wanted: Elevated Railways in the City of Boston. Report of the Committee on Street-Railways of the Legislature of Massachusetts of 1879. Stenographic Notes of the Testimony and Arguments* (Boston, 1879), pages 84–85; Joel A. Tarr, "Infrastructure and City Building in the Nineteenth and Twentieth Centuries," in Samuel P. Hays, ed., *City at the Point: Essays in the Social History of Pittsburgh* (Pittsburgh, 1989), page 125; Mark Goldman, "Buffalo's Black Rock: A Neighborhood and the City," *Journal of Urban History*, August 1979, pages 458–460; *[New York] Real Estate Record and Builders' Guide*, April 29, 1876, page 321, March 11, 1882, page 213; *[Chicago] Real Estate and Building Journal*, September 1, 1888, page 422, February 2, 1889, page 66, February 20, 1897, page 149.

53. Howard W. Gillette, Jr., "Philadelphia's City Hall: Monument to a New Political Machine," *Pennsylvania Magazine of History and Biography*, April 1973, pages 234–237; *Omaha Bee*, March 29, 1903; Martyn John Bowden, "The Dynamics of City Growth: An Historical Geography of the San Francisco Central District, 1850–1931" (Ph.D. diss., University of California at Berkeley, 1967), pages 277–280, 295–302.

54. Oscar and Lilian Handlin, *Liberty in Expansion, 1760–1850* (New York, 1989), page 35; Charles N. Glaab, "Historical Perspective on Urban Development Schemes," in Leo F. Schnore, ed., *Social Science and the City* (New York, 1969), pages 197–219.

55. "New York as It Will Be in 1999: Pictorial Forecast of the City," supplement to the *New York World*, December 30, 1900.

56. Spann, *The New Metropolis*, pages 101–102; *[New York] Real Estate Record and Builders' Guide*, June 4, 1881, page 572; George E. Waring, "Greater New York a Century Hence," *Municipal Affairs*, December 1897, page 713.

57. Wainwright, ed., *A Philadelphia Perspective*, page 316; James Parton, "Pittsburgh," *Atlantic Monthly*, January 1868, page 22; D. J. Kenny, *Illustrated Cincinnati: A Pictorial Hand-book of the Queen City* (Cincinnati, 1874), page 12; *California Architect and Building News*, May 15, 1888, page 58.

58. *Philadelphia Real Estate Record and Builders' Guide*, June 27, 1887, page 289; Durand, "Street and Electric Railways," page 32; Royal Commission on London Traffic, *Appendices to the Report of the Royal Commission on London Traffic with Index* (London, 1906), pages 73–74; *[New York] Real Estate Record and Builders' Guide*, May 19, 1877, page 395, June 22, 1889, page 871, June 8, 1901, page 1011, March 15, 1902, page 460.

59. *New York World*, December 30, 1900; *[New York] Real Estate Record and Builders' Guide*, September 7, 1889, page 1206, June 8, 1901, pages 1010–1011; *American Architect and Building News*, October 21, 1901, page 9; H. G. Wells, "Anticipations: An Experiment in Prophecy.—I.," *North American Review*, June 1901, pages 812–815; H. G. Wells, *Anticipations of the Reaction of Mechanical and Scientific Progress Upon Human Life and Thought* (New York, 1902), pages 62–67.

60. *[New York] Real Estate Record and Builders' Guide*, April 29, 1876, page 321, October 4, 1879, page 779, March 11, 1882, page 213; *[Chicago] Real Estate and Building Journal*, November 24, 1888, page 602; *Not Wanted: Elevated Railways in the City of Boston*, page 213; W. W. Wheatly, "Transporting New York's Millions," *World's Work*, May 1903, page 3434; *Report of the Rapid Transit Commission to the Massachusetts Legislature*, page 1087.

Chapter 2: Derailing the Subways

1. *Report of the Rapid Transit Commission to the Massachusetts Legislature. April 5, 1892* (Boston, 1892), pages 10–11; *Boston Evening Transcript*, February 27, 1894; *Argument of Mayor Matthews Before the Committee on Transit of the Massachusetts Legislature, April 4, 1894* (Boston, 1894), pages 7–8; *Hearing in the Matter of the Elevated Railroad. Opening Argument and Evidence on the Petition of Joe V. Meigs et als.* (Boston, 1881), page 73; *[New York] Real Estate Record and Builders' Guide*, January 13, 1883, page 15; Glenn Yago, *The Decline of Transit: Urban Transportation in German and U.S. Cities, 1900–1970* (Cambridge, England, 1984), page 135.

2. U.S. Census Office, *Report on Transportation Business in the United States at the Eleventh Census: 1890. Part I. Transportation by Land* (Washington, D.C., 1895), pages 682, 683, 793, and *Part II. Transportation by Water* (Washington, D.C., 1894), page 43; U.S. Census Office, *Report on the Social Statistics of Cities in the United States at the Eleventh Census: 1890* (Washington, D.C., 1895), page 50; Edward Dana Durand, "Street and Electric Railways," in U.S. Bureau of the Census, *Street and Electric Railways, 1902: Special Reports of the Census Office* (Washington, D.C., 1905), pages 8, 29.

3. Glen E. Holt, "The Changing Perception of Urban Pathology: An Essay on the Development of Mass Transit in the United States," in Kenneth T. Jackson and Stanley K. Schultz, eds., *Cities in American History* (New York, 1972), pages 324–331; U.S. Cen-

sus Office, *Report on Transportation Business at the Eleventh Census: Part I. Transportation by Land*, pages 681–685, 694; Durand, "Street and Electric Railways," pages 6–26, 149–156.

4. Holt, "The Changing Perception of Urban Pathology," pages 327–331; *Rapid Transit Assured: A Feast of Thanksgiving* (1877), pages 11, 15, 20; *Chicago Tribune*, December 2, 1891; *New York Times*, March 23, 1866, January 21, 1867; *Argument of Mayor Matthews Before the Committee on Transit*, page 9; *Remarks of Henry W. Muzzey, Esq., on the "Act to Permit Joe V. Meigs and Associates to Build an Elevated Railway, with the Consent of the Cities or Towns in Which It May Be Located," to the Massachusetts House of Representatives, March 7, 1882* (Boston, 1882), page 2; *California Outlook*, August 26, 1911, pages 3–4.

5. *New York Times*, January 21, 1866, March 27, 1867; *Exposé of the Facts Concerning the Proposed Elevated Patent Railway Enterprise in the City of New-York. 1866* (New York, 1866), page 47; Linus M. Child, *Shall the Metropolis of New England Have an Elevated Railroad? Argument in Its Favor Before the Legislative Committee on Street Railways* (Boston, 1880), page 24; *Philadelphia Real Estate Record and Builders' Guide*, June 20, 1888; A. P. Robinson, *Report Upon the Contemplated Metropolitan Railroad, of the City of New York* (New York, 1865), pages 8–9; *[New York] Real Estate Record and Builders' Guide*, April 11, 1868, page 1; "The Future of New York," *Galaxy*, April 1870, pages 550–553.

6. Durand, "Street and Electric Railways," pages 35–36; Charles W. Cheape, *Moving the Masses: Urban Public Transit in New York, Boston, and Philadelphia, 1880–1912* (Cambridge, 1980), parts 1–3; Holt, "The Changing Perception of Urban Pathology," pages 331–332; E. R. Kinsey and C. E. Smith, *Report on Rapid Transit in St. Louis* (St. Louis, 1926), pages 244–264.

7. Robert B. Reed, *The New York Elevated* (South Brunswick, New Jersey, 1978), chapter 2; James Blaine Walker, *Fifty Years of Rapid Transit 1864–1917* (New York, 1918), chapter 6; *Report of a Special Commission Designated by the [New York State] Assembly to Ascertain the Best Means for the Transportation of Passengers in the City of New York* (1867), pages 41–110; American Society of Civil Engineers, *Rapid Transit and Terminal Freight Facilities* (1875), pages 10–15; *New York Times*, January 21, 1866; *[New York] Real Estate Record and Builders' Guide*, April 11, 1868, page 1.

8. Walker, *Fifty Years of Rapid Transit*, chapters 2–5, 7; *New York Times*, March 23, 1866; Cheape, *Moving the Masses*, pages 28–29.

9. Walker, *Fifty Years of Rapid Transit*, chapter 8; James B. Swain, *Suggestions in Advocacy of the Route, Plans, Construction, and Operation of the Metropolitan Transit Railroads* (Albany, 1972); *To the Friends of Rapid Transit* (1871), pages 6–9; Cheape, *Moving the Masses*, page 29; American Society of Civil Engineers, *Rapid Transit*, pages 3, 10–12; *[New York] Real Estate Record and Builders' Guide*, January 18, 1873, page 24, May 21, 1881, page 519; "Rapid Transit in New York," *Appletons' Journal*, May 1878, page 399.

10. U.S. Census Office, *Report on the Social Statistics of Cities, Compiled by George E. Waring: Part I. The New England and Middle States* (Washington, D.C., 1886), page 557. See also Walker, *Fifty Years of Rapid Transit*, chapter 3.

11. Walker, *Fifty Years of Rapid Transit*, chapters 7 and 9; Reed, *The New York Elevated*, chapters 4 and 5; Cheape, *Moving the Masses*, pages 32–39; *Report of a Meeting Held at Chickering Hall, June 21st 1877, to Protest Against the Destruction of Property by Elevated Railroads, Without Compensation to Owners* (New York 1877), pages 10–15, 35–65;

Rapid Transit Assured, pages 7–16, 19–25; American Society of Civil Engineers, *Rapid Transit,* pages 12–15; *[New York] Real Estate Record and Builders' Guide,* June 17, 1876, page 471.

12. Walker, *Fifty Years of Rapid Transit,* pages 112–113; Reed, *The New York Elevated,* pages 117–126; *Not Wanted: Elevated Railways in the City of Boston. Report of the Committee on Street-Railways of the Legislature of Massachusetts of 1879. Stenographic Notes of the Testimony and Arguments* (Boston, 1879), pages 30–105; W. G. Marshall, *Through America; or, Nine Months in the United States* (London, 1881), pages 24–28; *[New York] Real Estate Record and Builders' Guide,* April 10, 1880, pages 335–336, October 2, 1880, pages 848–849, April 30, 1881, page 420, November 26, 1892, page 683; *American Architect and Building News,* July 13, 1878, pages 15–16, October 12, 1878, page 121; Bayrd Still, *Mirror for Gotham: New York as Seen by Contemporaries from Dutch Days to the Present* (New York, 1956), pages 219–220.

13. *Not Wanted: Elevated Railways in the City of Boston,* pages 183–211; Child, *Shall the Metropolis of New England Have an Elevated Railroad?;* Charles E. Powers, *Shall the Metropolis of New England Have an Elevated Railroad? Opening Argument in Its Favor Before the Legislative Committee on Street Railways* (Boston, 1880); *Opening Argument and Evidence on the Petition of Joe V. Meigs et als.; Philadelphia Real Estate Record and Builders' Guide,* March 22, 1886, page 121, May 25, 1886, page 229, September 6, 1886, pages 410–411, November 1, 1886, page 526, December 13, 1886, pages 508–509.

14. Reed, *The New York Elevated,* page 145; Cheape, *Moving the Masses,* pages 122–124, 175–176; Robert David Weber, "Rationalizers and Reformers: Chicago Local Transportation in the Nineteenth Century" (Ph.D. diss., University of Wisconsin, 1971), pages 34–35; Kinsey and Smith, *Rapid Transit for St. Louis,* page 1; *Not Wanted: Elevated Railways in the City of Boston,* pages 15, 30–105, 111–118, 143–164, 170–171; *Elevated Railways. Opening Argument for the Remonstrants by Hon. Moody Merrill, Before the Street Railway Committee of the Legislature of Massachusetts Wednesday, February 25, 1880* (Boston, 1880), pages 10–19; *American Architect and Building News,* March 20, 1880, page 114; *Philadelphia Real Estate Record and Builders' Guide,* January 3, 1887, page 637; *[Chicago] Real Estate and Building Journal,* September 1, 1888, page 422, February 2, 1889, page 66; Brian J. Cudahy, *Cash, Tokens, and Transfers: A History of Mass Transit in North America* (New York, 1990), page 19.

15. *Philadelphia Real Estate Record and Builders' Guide,* May 24, 1886, page 229; *[New York] Real Estate Record and Builders' Guide,* October 2, 1880, pages 848–849; Reed, *The New York Elevated,* pages 145–148; Cudahy, *Cash, Tokens, and Transfers,* pages 67–71; *Chicago Tribune,* December 2, 1891; Weber, "Rationalizers and Reformers," pages 35–36, 181–182, 194–198; Cheape, *Moving the Masses,* pages 120–136, 175–176; Kinsey and Smith, *Rapid Transit for St. Louis,* page 1; Durand, "Street and Electric Railways," page 36.

16. *Electric Railway Journal,* February 11, 1911, page 249, August 9, 1913, pages 222–224; *Engineering News-Record,* July 19, 1923, page 87; Reed, *The New York Elevated,* pages 151–157; *Engineering News,* March 5, 1905, pages 183–185; *Report of the Transit Commissioner to the Honorable Mayor and City Council of the City of Pittsburgh* (Pittsburgh, 1917), page 128; Ernest C. Moses, "The Elevated Railway and Civic Beauty," *The World To-Day,* February 1907, pages 161–169; William A. McGarry, "The Noiseless Elevated," *Scientific American,* January 1922, pages 6–7; *Chicago Herald,* October 27, 1883.

17. *[New York] Real Estate Record and Builders' Guide*, January 4, 1890, page 2, June 18, 1892, pages 951–952, December 10, 1892, page 760, June 29, 1895, page 1084; *Philadelphia Real Estate Record and Builders' Guide*, January 3, 1887, page 637; *[Chicago] Real Estate and Building Journal*, May 4, 1889, page 276; *Chicago Herald*, October 27, 1883; *Pittsburgh Sun*, July 1, 1919; *Los Angeles Times*, April 14–26, 1926; Building Owners and Managers Association of St. Louis, *The St. Louis Traffic Problem* (St. Louis, 1925), page 18.

18. *[New York] Real Estate Record and Builders' Guide*, June 18, 1892, pages 951–952, June 30, 1906, page 1237; *Engineering News*, September 15, 1898, page 68; Royal Commission on London Traffic, *Appendices to the Report of the Royal Commission on London Traffic with Index* (London, 1906), page 129; Cheape, *Moving the Masses*, pages 147–150; Kinsey and Smith, *Rapid Transit for St. Louis*, pages 296, 300–306; Scott Bottles, *Los Angeles and the Automobile: The Making of the Modern City* (Berkeley, 1987), chapter 5; *Report of the Boston Transit Commission Relative to the Removal of the Elevated Railway Structure on Washington and Main Streets in Boston and the Construction of a Tunnel and Subway in Place Thereof* (Boston, 1914), pages 8–18; Reed, *The New York Elevated*, chapter 17.

19. *[New York] Real Estate Record and Builders' Guide*, May 21, 1881, page 519, April 28, 1883, pages 170–172, December 24, 1887, pages 1611–1612, January 31, 1891, page 155, November 19, 1892, pages 650–651; Cheape, *Moving the Masses*, page 73; *American Architect and Building News*, June 25, 1881, pages 301–302, February 18, 1882, page 74; *Chicago Tribune*, October 11, November 7/29, December 1/12, 1891; *Philadelphia Real Estate Record and Builders' Guide*, November 15, 1886, page 550.

20. *Report of a Special Commission Designated by the Senate to Ascertain the Best Means for the Transportation of Passengers*, pages 38–43, 47–51, 56–59; *First Annual Report of the Boston Rapid Transit Commission for the Year Ending August 15, 1895* (Boston, 1895), pages 10–12; Cheape, *Moving the Masses*, pages 137–140; Kinsey and Smith, *Rapid Transit for St. Louis*, pages 266–269.

21. *New York Times*, March 31, 1871; *American Architect and Building News*, October 1, 1881, page 153; Cheape, *Moving the Masses*, pages 73, 140–142; Massachusetts General Court, Joint Special Committee on Transit, "Hearing on Subways in Boston," March 26, 1894, volume 10, page 43, March 29, 1894, volume 13, pages 68–69, Massachusetts State Library, Boston; *Boston Evening Transcript*, April 11/13, 1894.

22. American Society of Civil Engineers, *Rapid Transit*, page 11; William S. Twining, "The Investigation of Traffic Possibilities on Proposed Subway Lines," *Annals of the American Academy of Political and Social Science*, January 1911, page 65; George Duncan Snyder, *City Passenger Transportation in the United States* (London, 1913), page 108; *Electric Railway Journal*, December 27, 1913, page 1349, October 9, 1915, page 776; *Rapid Transit Assured*, page 14; *[New York] Real Estate Record and Builders' Guide*, December 8, 1888, page 1443; *Report and Testimony of the Special Committee of the Assembly to Investigate the Desirability of Municipal Ownership*, volume 2, pages 1189, 1264; Walker, *Fifty Years of Rapid Transit*, page 133.

23. *Chicago Tribune*, October 15, 1891; Cheape, *Moving the Masses*, pages 129–130, 140; Joint Committee on Transit, "Hearing on Subways in Boston," March 6, 1894, volume 7, page 22, March 29, 1894, volume 13, pages 54–55, 64; *[New York] Real Estate Record and Builders' Guide*, May 21, 1881, page 519, June 4, 1881, page 572, March 30, 1889, page 412, February 4, 1893, page 174; Wm. Barclay Parsons, "Rapid Transit in

New York," *Scribners' Magazine*, May 1900, page 554; *Report of the Rapid Transit Commission to the Massachusetts Legislature*, pages 6, 155, 162; John P. Fox, "The Transit Situation in Pittsburgh," *Charities and the Commons*, February 6, 1909, pages 847–848; James Dabney McCabe, *New York by Sunlight and Gaslight* (1882), pages 187–190.

24. Cheape, *Moving the Masses*, pages 73–74; Joint Committee on Transit, "Hearing on Subways in Boston," March 6, 1894, volume 7, pages 20, 31; *Report of the Rapid Transit Commission to the Massachusetts Legislature*, page 162; *Report and Testimony of the Special Committee of the Assembly to Investigate the Desirability of Municipal Ownership*, volume 2, pages 1108, 1342–1348; *[New York] Real Estate Record and Builders' Guide*, November 19, 1892, pages 650–651; Royal Commission on London Traffic, *Appendices to the Report*, page 129.

25. Parsons, "Rapid Transit in New York," pages 554. See also Clay McShane, *Down the Asphalt Path: The Automobile and the American City* (New York, 1994), pages 12–13, 88, 114; *Report and Testimony of the Special Committee of the Assembly to Investigate the Desirability of Municipal Ownership*, volume 2, pages 1344–1348; Joint Committee on Transit, "Hearing on Subways in Boston," March 6, 1894, volume 7, pages 22–23, 31; Cheape, *Moving the Masses*, pages 139–140.

26. Cheape, *Moving the Masses*, chapters 3 and 5.

27. Mark S. Foster, *From Streetcar to Superhighway: American City Planners and Urban Transportation* (Philadelphia, 1981), page 39; U.S. Bureau of the Census, *Fifteenth Census of the United States: 1930. Volume 1: Population* (Washington, D.C., 1931), page 18; U.S. Census Office, *Report on Transportation Business at the Eleventh Census: Part I. Transportation by Land*, pages 684–685.

28. Bion Joseph Arnold, *Report on the Engineering and Operating Features of the Chicago Transportation Problem*, (New York, 1905), pages 83–99; Homer Hoyt, *One Hundred Years of Land Values in Chicago* (Chicago, 1933), page 388; Bion J. Arnold, *Report on the Pittsburgh Transportation Problem* (Pittsburgh, 1910), page 75; Barclay Parsons & Klapp, *Report on a Rapid Transit System for the City of Detroit* (1918), pages 17, 110–112; Barclay Parsons & Klapp, *Report on a Rapid Transit System for the City of Cleveland* (1919), page 13; Kinsey and Smith, *Rapid Transit for St. Louis*, pages 29–31.

29. *[New York] Real Estate Record and Builders' Guide*, November 26, 1892, page 683, August 10, 1893, page 221, October 31, 1903, page 774; W. W. Wheatly, "Transporting New York's Millions," *World's Work*, May 1902, page 3423; Durand, "Street and Electric Railways," page 24; *Electric Railway Journal*, May 4, 1910, pages 857–860, January 5, 1929, page 1; *Report of the Public Service Commission for the First District of the State of New York: 1910*, volume 3, pages 22–49; F. W. Doolittle, *Studies in the Cost of Urban Transportation* (New York, 1916), pages 322–324; Barclay Parsons & Klapp, *Rapid Transit for Cleveland*, page 2; Barclay Parsons & Klapp, *Rapid Transit for Detroit*, pages 21–24.

30. Durand, "Street and Electric Railways," page 35; *Electric Railway Journal*, November 2, 1912, pages 967–968; *American Architect and Building News*, April 16, 1881, page 181; Arnold, *Pittsburgh Transportation Problem*, pages 73–74; *Report of the Public Service Commission for the First District*, volume 3, pages 27, 32; *Philadelphia Real Estate Record and Builders' Guide*, November 15, 1886, page 550; *[New York] Real Estate Record and Builders' Guide*, August 10, 1893, page 221, September 30, 1893, page 369.

31. *Providence Board of Trade Journal*, March 1914, page 224; Boston Transit Commission, *Removal of the Elevated Railway Structure*, pages 8–9; *Boston City Record*, April

10, 1920, page 403; Chamber of Commerce of the State of New York, *Rapid Transit in New York and Other Great Cities* (New York, 1905), pages 162–163; Doolittle, *Cost of Urban Transportation,* page 333; John P. Fox, "Rapid Travel of the Future," *World's Work,* September 1906, pages 8000–8006; Kinsey and Smith, *Rapid Transit for St. Louis,* pages 265–272.

32. Holt, "The Changing Perception of Urban Pathology," page 332; Foster, *From Streetcar to Superhighway,* pages 78–90; Kinsey and Smith, *Rapid Transit for St. Louis,* pages 251–255, 262–264; Bion J. Arnold, *Report on the Traction Improvement and Development Within the Providence District to the Joint Committee on Railroad Franchises Providence City Council* (Providence, 1911), page 13; *Providence Board of Trade Journal,* September 1913, page 347, December 1913, page 521, January 1914, pages 33–34, March 1914, pages 221–224; *Report of the Joint Special Committee on Subways and Report of Engineer William W. Lewis Together with Resolution and Draft Act to Provide Rapid Transit in Providence* (Providence, 1914), pages 5–38.

33. Paul Barrett, *The Automobile and Urban Transit: The Formation of Public Policy in Chicago, 1900–1930* (Philadelphia, 1983), pages 6–7, 183–190; Donald Finley Davis, *Conspicuous Production: Automobiles and Elites in Detroit, 1899–1933* (Philadelphia, 1988), pages 172–173; Evan W. Thomas, "An Analysis of Proposals to Provide Adequate and Rapid Mass Transportation for the Los Angeles Area" (Master's thesis, UCLA, 1939), pages 101–103; Barclay Parsons & Klapp, *Rapid Transit for Detroit,* page 6; *American City,* September 1928, page 158; Henry Brinckerhoff, *The Problem of Street Traffic in Modern Cities* (1924), pages 6, 13; *Proceedings of the Twenty-first Annual Convention of the National Association of Building Owners and Managers: 1928,* page 95.

34. *Report of the [Cincinnati] Board of Rapid Transit Commissioners: 1928,* pages 7–10; *Seattle Magazine,* April 1965, pages 8–9; Barrett, *The Automobile and Urban Transit,* pages 188–189; Davis, *Conspicuous Production,* pages 172–173; *Cleveland Plain Dealer,* April 15, 1920; *Electric Railway Journal,* April 9, 1927, page 668.

35. Bottles, *Los Angeles and the Automobile,* pages 34–41, 133; Davis, *Conspicuous Production,* pages 172–173; *Cleveland Plain Dealer,* April 16/20, 1920; Barrett, *The Automobile and Urban Transit,* pages 9–21; Holt, "The Changing Perception of Urban Pathology," pages 332–337; *Providence Board of Trade Journal,* March 1914, page 224.

36. Neil M. Clark, "The Story of a Great Engineer," *American Magazine,* August 1921, pages 16–17, 82–88; Arthur Goodrich, "William Barclay Parsons," *World's Work,* May 1903, pages 3467–3471; Barclay Parsons & Klapp, *Report on Detroit Street Railway Traffic and Proposed Subway Made to the Board of Street Railway Commissioners City of Detroit* (Detroit, 1915), pages 19–21, 52; Barclay Parsons & Klapp, *Rapid Transit for Cleveland,* page 6; Detroit Rapid Transit Commission, *Rapid Transit System for the City of Detroit* (Detroit, 1926), pages 19–20; George Duncan Snyder, *City Passenger-Transportation in the United States* (London, 1912), pages 3–6.

37. Arnold, *Chicago Transportation Problem,* page 17; Arnold, *Pittsburgh Transportation Problem,* page 11; Barclay Parsons & Klapp, *Rapid Transit in Cleveland,* pages 7–8; *Chicago Daily Journal,* January 31, 1924; *Cleveland Plain Dealer,* April 13, 1920; *Los Angeles Times,* June 3, 1920; Seattle City Planning Commission Rapid Transit Committee, "Seattle Rapid Transit Report to the City Planning Commission" (1924), page 4; D. L. Turner, "Rapid Transit Progress in Detroit, Pittsburgh, and Northern New Jersey," *Electric Railway Journal,* December 1925, pages 191–192.

38. *Report of the [Detroit] Rapid Transit Commission to the Mayor's Finance Committee*

(Detroit, 1926), pages 15–17; Brinckerhoff, *The Problem of Street Traffic*, page 13; Henry M. Brinckerhoff, "Rapid Transit: A Vital Element in Metropolitan Transportation," *Electric Railway Journal*, September 26, 1925, pages 500–502; *Proceedings of the Engineers' Society of Western Pennsylvania*, November 1920, page 488; *Pittsburgh Post*, July 3, 1919; *Boston Evening Transcript*, February 27, 1894; *Report of the Transportation Survey Commission of the City of St. Louis* (1930), page 109; John A. Miller, "The Chariots That Rage in the Streets," *American City*, July 1928, pages 111–114.

39. Roy Lubove, *The Progressives and the Slums: Tenement House Reform in New York City, 1890–1917* (Pittsburgh, 1962), chapters 1–3; Howard Gillette, Jr., "The Emergence of the Modern Metropolis: Philadelphia in the Age of Its Consolidation," in William W. Cutler III and Howard Gillette, Jr., eds., *The Divided Metropolis: Social and Spatial Dimensions of Philadelphia, 1800–1974* (Westport, Connecticut, 1980), page 19; *New York Times*, January 21, 1866; Joel Arthur Tarr, "From City to Suburb: The 'Moral' Influence of Transportation Technology," in Alexander B. Callow, Jr., ed., *American Urban History* (New York, 1973), pages 202–212; E. B. Lloyd, *Lights and Shades in San Francisco* (San Francisco, 1876), page 175; Durand, "Street and Electric Railways," pages 27–28.

40. *New York Times*, January 21, 1866; Adna F. Weber, *The Growth of Cities* (New York, 1899), page 471; Adna F. Weber, "Rapid Transit," *Municipal Affairs*, Fall 1902, pages 409–414; Charles H. Cooley, "The Social Significance of Street Railways," *Proceedings of the American Economic Association at the Fourth Annual Meeting: 1890*, pages 71–72; Detroit Rapid Transit Commission, *Proposed Financial Plan for a Rapid Transit System for the City of Detroit* (Detroit, 1923), page 38; *Rapid Transit Assured*, page 15; *Pittsburgh Gazette-Times*, July 13, 1911; *Cincinnati Enquirer*, April 13, 1916; *Cleveland Plain Dealer*, April 13, 1920.

41. Doolittle, *Cost of Urban Transportation*, page 333; *Cincinnati Enquirer*, April 13, 1916; *Pittsburgh Post*, July 2/4, 1919; *American Architect and Building News*, March 19, 1881, page 133; Kinsey and Smith, *Rapid Transit for St. Louis*, page 309; Detroit Rapid Transit Commission, *Report of the [Detroit] Rapid Transit Commission to the Mayor's Finance Committee*, page 9.

42. Ernest Poole, "A City's Dream of a City," *Everybody's Magazine*, July 1910, page 3; *Report to the Mayor of Baltimore by the Committee on Mass Transportation* (1955); *Baltimore News American*, November 21, 1983; *Electric Railway Journal*, January 28, 1911, page 178; *Seattle Post-Intelligencer*, September 7, 1919; Kinsey and Smith, *Rapid Transit for St. Louis*, pages 309, 318.

43. American Society of Civil Engineers, *Rapid Transit*, page 30. See also Weber, "Rationalizers and Reformers," pages 45–46, 114–115; *Report of a Special Commission Designated by the Senate to Ascertain the Best Means for the Transportation of Passengers*, page 58; Kinsey and Smith, *Rapid Transit for St. Louis*, pages 266–270; *[New York] Real Estate Record and Builders' Guide*, October 7, 1893, page 398; Walker, *Fifty Years of Rapid Transit*, pages 126–130.

44. Cheape, *Moving the Masses*, pages 36, 87–88; *Report of the Rapid Transit Commission to the Massachusetts Legislature*, pages 86–94; Kelker, De Leuw & Co., *Report and Recommendations on a Comprehensive Transit Plan for the City and County of Los Angeles* (1925), pages 82–86. On the decline of the electric railway industry, see Stanley Mallach, "The Origins of the Decline of Urban Mass Transportation in the United States, 1890–1930," *Urbanism Past and Present*, Summer 1989, pages 1–15.

45. Cheape, *Moving the Masses*, pages 73–82; *[New York] Real Estate Record and Builders' Guide*, June 10, 1893, page 902, August 19, 1893, page 219, August 26, 1893, page 246.

46. Fox, "Transit Situation," page 847; *Report of Transit Commissioner City of Philadelphia July, 1913* (Philadelphia, 1913), page 11; Twining, "Traffic Possibilities," pages 61–63; *Electric Railway Journal*, April 4, 1914, page 755, February 2, 1929, page 239; *Report of the Rapid Transit Commission to the Massachusetts Legislature*, page 6; E. K. Morse, "The Transit Commission," *Proceedings of the Engineers' Society of Western Pennsylvania* (February 1918–January 1919), page 459; Paul R. Leach, *Chicago's Traction Problem* (Chicago, 1925), page 27; Cleveland Association of Building Owners and Managers, *Cleveland's Traffic Problem* (Cleveland, 1924), page 7; *Los Angeles City Club Bulletin*, January 30, 1926, page 3.

47. *Seattle Post-Intelligencer*, December 2, 1908, January 20/23, February 3/4, 1909; *Los Angeles Times*, April 21, 1923; *Electric Railway Journal*, June 30, 1928, pages 1083–1084; James Judson Gillespie, "Going Nowhere: Pittsburgh's Attempt to Build a Subway, 1910–1935" (Bachelor's thesis, Massachusetts Institute of Technology, 1990), pages 21–25; Kinsey and Smith, *Rapid Transit for St. Louis*, pages 273, 321.

48. Kinsey and Smith, *Rapid Transit for St. Louis*, page 273; Cheape, *Moving the Masses*, page 79; *[New York] Real Estate Record and Builders' Guide*, November 19, 1892, page 651, December 3, 1892, page 716, January 7, 1893, page 5, August 10, 1893, page 221.

49. *Report of the Rapid Transit Commission to the Massachusetts Legislature*, pages 98–99; *Report and Testimony of the Special Committee of the Assembly to Investigate the Desirability of Municipal Ownership*, volume 1, pages 8–18; Robert M. Fogelson, *The Fragmented Metropolis: Los Angeles, 1850–1930* (Cambridge, 1967), chapter 11.

50. Fogelson, *The Fragmented Metropolis*, page 240. See also *[New York] Real Estate Record and Builders' Guide*, May 24, 1890, page 774, November 19, 1892, page 651, January 7, 1893, page 6; *Report and Testimony of the Special Committee of the Assembly to Investigate the Desirability of Municipal Ownership*, volume 1, page 14; *Report of the Rapid Transit Commission to the Massachusetts Legislature*, pages 98–99; Barrett, *The Automobile and Urban Transit*, page 33; Delos F. Wilcox, *Analysis of the Electric Railway Problem* (New York, 1921), chapter 24.

51. *[New York] Real Estate Record and Builders' Guide*, June 10, 1893, pages 903–904; *Report and Testimony of the Special Committee of the Assembly to Investigate the Desirability of Municipal Ownership*, volume 1, page 18, volume 2, pages 1, 195, 1271–1272; Fogelson, *The Fragmented Metropolis*, page 240; *Proceedings of the American Street and Interurban Railway Association: 1906*, pages 346–370.

52. Barrett, *The Automobile and Urban Transit*, pages 33–36; Wilcox, *Electric Railway Problem*, chapter 24; Fogelson, *The Fragmented Metropolis*, pages 232–233; *[New York] Real Estate Record and Builders' Guide*, May 24, 1890, page 773; Cheape, *Moving the Masses*, pages 78–79, 131–133; *Proceedings of the Engineers' Society of Western Pennsylvania*, May 1913, pages 206–207; *Report and Testimony of the Special Committee of the Assembly to Investigate the Desirability of Municipal Ownership*, volume 1, pages 534–543, volume 2, pages 1, 580–1598.

53. *[New York] Real Estate Record and Builders' Guide*, August 30, 1892, pages 235–236, June 10, 1893, page 902; Fogelson, *The Fragmented Metropolis*, page 233; Wilcox, *Electric Railway Problem* (New York, 1921), pages 147–148; *Report of the Rapid Transit Commission to the Massachusetts Legislature*, pages 99–100; Twining, "Traffic Possi-

bilities," pages 62–63; *Proceedings of the Engineers' Society of Western Pennsylvania,* November 1909, page 468; *Cleveland Plain Dealer,* April 23, 1920.

54. *[New York] Real Estate Record and Builders' Guide,* December 3, 1892, page 716, December 10, 1892, page 760, January 7, 1893, page 5; Cheape, *Moving the Masses,* pages 79–81; Barrett, *The Automobile and Urban Transit,* pages 202–204; *Detroit News,* February 4, 1929.

55. Melvin G. Holli, *Reform in Detroit: Hazen Pingree and Urban Politics* (New York, 1969), page 116; Barclay Parsons & Klapp, *Rapid Transit for Detroit,* page 32; Kinsey and Smith, *Rapid Transit for St. Louis,* pages 283–285.

56. Gillespie, "Going Nowhere," pages 6–20. See also E. K. Morse, "Pittsburgh Subways," *Proceedings of the Engineers' Society of Western Pennsylvania,* March 1907, pages 49–62; "Rapid Transit for Pittsburgh," ibid., November 1909, pages 459–490; Arnold, *Pittsburgh Transportation Problem,* pages 11–13, 78–85.

57. Gillespie, "Going Nowhere," pages 21–28; *Pittsburgh Dispatch,* January 22, August 3, September 5, 1913, December 29, 1915, March 21, 1916; *Electric Railway Journal,* February 22, 1913, pages 340–341, October 19, 1914, page 787, December 5, 1914, page 1238, March 27, 1915, page 644.

58. Gillespie, "Going Nowhere," pages 29–30; *Pittsburgh Dispatch,* April 9, May 7, 1919; *Pittsburgh Post,* March 11, May 27, 1919.

59. Gillespie, "Going Nowhere," pages 31–40. See also *Pittsburgh Dispatch,* June 22/25/26, July 1–10, 1919; *Pittsburgh Post,* July 1–10, 1919.

60. Gillespie, "Going Nowhere," pages 41–50; *Electric Railway Journal,* July 12, 1919, page 84, December 8, 1928, page 1102; Water Street District and Lower Downtown Improvement (Triangle I) Association, "A Subway-Elevated Loop Plan" (1926), page 23; *Greater Pittsburgh,* May 1932, pages 1–2.

61. *Cleveland Press,* September 20, 1905, July 7–8, 1917; *Municipal Journal,* July 5, 1917, pages 15–16; Barclay Parsons & Klapp, *Rapid Transit for Cleveland,* pages 1–10; Greater Cleveland Transportation Committee, *Report on Passenger Transportation in the Cleveland Metropolitan Area* (Cleveland, 1925), page 42.

62. *Cleveland Plain Dealer,* April 6/11/13/15/17/23/24/28, 1920; *Cleveland Press,* April 6/24, 1920.

63. *Cleveland Plain Dealer,* April 23, 1920; *Cleveland Press,* April 19/24/26/27, 1920.

64. *Cleveland Press,* March 24/28/31, April 19/24, 1920; *Cleveland Plain Dealer,* April 7–9/13, 1920.

65. *Cleveland Press,* April 28–29, 1920; *Cleveland Plain Dealer,* April 23/28, 1920; *Electric Railway Journal,* June 20, 1928, pages 1083–1084, August 4, 1928, page 198, September 15, 1928, pages 476–477, December 29, 1928, page 1129; William E. Pease, "Shaker Heights Develops Interurban Railroad," *Civil Engineering,* November 1930, pages 88–90.

66. Beeler Organization, *Report to the City of Cincinnati on a Rapid Transit Railway* (New York, 1927), pages 16–17, 23–27, 135–136; *Report of the [Cincinnati] Board of Rapid Transit Commissioners: 1928,* pages 5–23; Carl W. Condit, *The Railroad and the City: A Technological and Urbanistic History of Cincinnati* (Columbus, 1977), pages 164–176; Detroit Rapid Transit Commission, "Rapid Transit System and Plan Recommended for Detroit and the Metropolitan Area" (1958), pages 17–22; Davis, *Conspicuous Production,* pages 159–169.

67. *Cincinnati Enquirer,* October 4, 1916, March 23/28, April 4/13/15, 1917, March 6–29,

1919; *Electric Railway Journal*, June 16, 1928, page 1005; *Report of the Chicago Traction and Subway Commission* (Chicago, 1916), pages 251, 409–411; Daniel L. Turner and Winters Haydock, *Report on a Recommended Subway in the First and Second Wards of Pittsburgh, or Proposed First Step in a Rapid Transit Program* (Pittsburgh, 1925), pages 24–25; Milo R. Maltbie, "Transportation and City Planning," *Proceedings of the Fifth National Conference on City Planning: 1913*, page 113.

68. Philadelphia Department of City Transit, *A Study and Review of the Problem of Passenger Transportation in Philadelphia by a Unified System of Lines* (Philadelphia, 1916), pages 12–13; Detroit Rapid Transit Commission, *Rapid Transit for Detroit*, page 23.

69. Ralph E. Heilman, "The Chicago Subway Problem," *Journal of Political Economy*, December 1914, pages 992–995; Barrett, *The Automobile and Urban Transit*, chapter 1, pages 93–94.

70. Heilman, "Chicago Subway Problem," pages 995–996; *Synopsis of an Address to the Irish Fellowship Club, March 2nd, 1912, by Mr. John Ericson, Chairman of the Harbor and Subway Commission, Chicago* (1912), pages 3–16; *Joint Report on Comprehensive System of Passenger Subways for the City of Chicago by the Harbor and Subway Commission and Sub-Committee of the Council Committee on Local Transportation* (1912), pages 1–8; *Chicago Commerce*, December 6, 1912, page 7.

71. Heilman, "Chicago Subway Problem," pages 996–999; Cook County Real Estate Board Transportation Committee, *The Transportation Problem of Chicago* (1912), pages 3–15; *Supplemental Report on Comprehensive System of Passenger Subways for the City of Chicago by the Harbor and Subway Commission* (1912), pages 1–24; Barrett, *The Automobile and Urban Transit*, pages 93–94.

72. Heilman, "Chicago Subway Problem," pages 998–1002; *Chicago Tribune*, March 3, 1914; *Chicago Commerce*, March 13, 1914, pages 4–5, March 20, 1914, pages 16–21, 27, 41.

73. Heilman, "Chicago Subway Problem," pages 999–1003; *Chicago Tribune*, March 19, April 5, 1914; *Chicago Commerce*, March 13, 1914, pages 4–5, March 20, 1914, pages 22–26.

74. Donald F. Davis, "The City Remodelled: The Limits of Automotive Industry Leadership in Detroit, 1910–1929," *Histoire Sociale/Social History*, November 1980, pages 467–469.

75. Detroit Rapid Transit Commission, *Rapid Transit for Detroit*, pages 23, 26–29; *Report of the [Detroit] Rapid Transit Commission to the Mayor's Finance Committee*, pages 18–20; *Electric Railway Journal*, February 18, 1922, page 293; *St. Louis Post-Dispatch*, October 10, 1926; *Detroit News*, February 14/15, 1925, August 17, 1926; Davis, "The City Remodelled," page 469.

76. Detroit Rapid Transit Commission, *Rapid Transit for Detroit*, pages 19–22, 29; *Report of the [Detroit] Transit Commission to the Mayor's Finance Committee*, pages 7–9, 18; Davis, *Conspicuous Production*, pages 172–173; Davis, "The City Remodelled," page 469.

77. Davis, "The City Remodelled," pages 469–474; Rightor, "The Progress of Rapid Transit in Detroit," *National Municipal Review*, May 1927, pages 310–313.

78. Davis, "The City Remodelled," pages 473–481; *Detroit News*, January 27/29, February 4/9/14, March 10/17, April 2, 1929; Howard P. Jones, "Barber Shop Opinion and Rapid Transit in Detroit," *National Municipal Review*, June 1929, pages 359–363.

79. Arnold, *Pittsburgh Transportation Problem*, pages 82–83; Kinsey and Smith, *Rapid Transit for St. Louis*, pages 273–274; Cheape, *Moving the Masses*, pages 90–91, 145.

80. *[New York] Real Estate Record and Builders' Guide,* May 28, 1892, pages 845–846; Barrett, *The Automobile and Urban Transit,* pages 4, 67; Kinsey and Smith, *Rapid Transit for St. Louis,* pages 274–275.

81. Detroit Rapid Transit Commission, *Proposed Financial Plan,* pages 34–36; Kelker, De Leuw, *Rapid Transit for Los Angeles,* pages 173–174; Mallach, "Origins and Decline of Urban Mass Transportation," pages 3–5; *Cincinnati Enquirer,* April 13, 1916; *Cleveland Plain Dealer,* April 13, 1920; Foster, *From Streetcar to Superhighway,* page 38; *Report of the Subway Advisory Commission Appointed by the Sub-Committee on Subways Local Transportation Committee Chicago City Council* (Chicago, 1926), pages 68–70.

82. Kelker, De Leuw, *Rapid Transit for Los Angeles,* pages 178–180; Kinsey and Smith, *Rapid Transit for St. Louis,* page 280; Detroit Rapid Transit Commission, *Proposed Financial Plan,* pages 37–39; Barrett, *The Automobile and Urban Transit,* pages 193–205.

83. Kelker, De Leuw, *Rapid Transit for Los Angeles,* pages 192–195; Kinsey and Smith, *Rapid Transit for St. Louis,* pages 276–277; *Report of the [Detroit] Rapid Transit Commission to the Mayor's Finance Committee,* pages 11–13; *Report of the New Jersey Transit Commission to the General Assembly of the State of New Jersey* (1927), pages 56–59.

84. *Report of the New Jersey Transit Commission,* pages 56–59; *Proceedings of the Fifth National Conference on City Planning: 1913,* pages 133–134; Kinsey and Smith, *Rapid Transit for St. Louis,* pages 274–275; *Report of the [Chicago] Subway Advisory Commission,* pages 72–73.

85. Barclay Parsons & Klapp, *Report on Detroit Street Railway Traffic,* pages 25–26; *Report of the New Jersey Transit Commission,* pages 64–66; American Electric Railway Association, *Economics of Rapid Transit* (ca. 1930), page 41; Detroit Rapid Transit Commission, *Proposed Financial Plan,* pages 16–22, 30–54.

86. Kelker, De Leuw, *Rapid Transit for Los Angeles,* pages 172–181; American Electric Railway Association, *Economics of Rapid Transit,* pages 39–53; Kinsey and Smith, *Rapid Transit for St. Louis,* pages 273–281; *Report of the [Chicago] Subway Advisory Commission,* pages 65–95; *Electric Railway Journal,* September 4, 1926, pages 369–370, January 19, 1929, pages 136–137; Beeler Organization, *Report to the City of Cincinnati,* pages 137–138.

87. Detroit Rapid Transit Commission, *Proposed Financial Plan,* pages 40–42, 53–54; Kelker, De Leuw, *Rapid Transit for Los Angeles,* pages 174–175, 192–195; Kinsey and Smith, *Rapid Transit for St. Louis,* pages 275–277; *Report of the [Chicago] Subway Advisory Commission,* pages 78–79; American Electric Railway Association, *Economics of Rapid Transit,* pages 39–53.

88. *Seattle Municipal News,* April 13, 1929; "[Second] Conference on the Rapid Transit Question Called by the [Los Angeles] Board of City Planning Commissioners" (1930), pages 16–17; *Detroit News,* February 4/14, 1929; Davis, "The City Remodelled," pages 475–477.

89. Gillespie, "Going Nowhere," pages 48–49; *[Pittsburgh] Progress,* January 1929, pages 8–9; *Electric Railway Journal,* April 9, 1927, page 668; Davis, "The City Remodelled," pages 475–477; *Detroit News,* February 4, April 2, 1929.

90. *Report of the New Jersey Transit Commission,* pages 63–64.

91. Henry Curran, "The Economic Height of Building as Illustrated by the Office Building," in U.S. Chamber of Commerce, *Economic Height of Buildings: The Skyscraper Attacked and Defended* (1927), pages 19–20. See also *Proceedings of the Fifth National Conference on City Planning: 1913,* pages 134–135.

92. *Opening Argument for the Remonstrants by Hon. Moody Merrill*, page 46.

93. *[New York] Real Estate Record and Builders' Guide*, April 29, 1876, page 321, March 11, 1882, page 213; *[Chicago] Real Estate and Building Journal*, September 1, 1888, page 422, February 2, 1889, page 66, March 4, 1893, page 267, February 20, 1897, page 149.

94. *[New York] Real Estate Record and Builders' Guide*, June 1, 1912, page 1157, June 13, 1914, page 1050, March 20, 1915, page 458; *Statement of A. Merritt Taylor, Director of the Department of City Transit, City of Philadelphia, Submitted to the Public Service Commission of the Commonwealth of Pennsylvania at Harrisburg, July 26, 1915*, pages 6–7; *[First] Conference on the Rapid Transit Question Called by the [Los Angeles] Board of City Planning Commissioners* (1930), pages 42–49; *Detroit News*, January 27, February 4, 1929; Jones, "Barber Shop Opinion," page 360; Davis, "The City Remodelled," pages 478–479; "[Second] Conference on the Rapid Transit Question," page 16; Bottles, *Los Angeles and the Automobile*, page 168.

95. *[Chicago] Real Estate and Building Journal*, February 20, 1897, page 149; Hoyt, *One Hundred Years of Land Values*, pages 91–92, 225–227, 249–255; Malcolm J. Proudfoot, "The Outlying Business Centers of Chicago," *Journal of Land and Public Utility Economics*, February 1937, pages 57–70; Heilman, "Chicago Subway Problem," page 1002.

96. *Chicago Tribune*, March 20, June 3–6/10–11, 1909. See also *[Chicago] Real Estate and Building Journal*, February 20, 1897, page 149; Heilman, "Chicago Subway Problem," page 995.

97. Heilman, "Chicago Subway Problem," pages 995–1003; Tomaz F. Deuther, *Local Transportation* (Chicago, 1924), pages 23–25; *Report of the Chicago Traction and Subway Commission*, pages 409–412; Barrett, *The Automobile and Urban Transit*, pages 93–94, 100–103, 185–190, 195–205; *Chicago Tribune*, April 1–8, 1925.

98. *Chicago Tribune*, June 4, 1909, November 1, 1918; *Synopsis of an Address by Mr. John Ericson*, page 16; Deuther, *Local Transportation*, page 78; *Chicago Commerce*, March 31, 1911, pages 19–26, September 26, 1918, page 9, October 10, 1918, page 22; *Joint Report on Comprehensive System of Passenger Subways*, page 16; *Supplemental Report on Comprehensive System of Passenger Subways*, page 20; *Report of the [Chicago] Subway Advisory Commission*, pages 59–61.

99. *Report of the [Chicago] Subway Advisory Commission*, pages 61–63. See also Deuther, *Local Transportation*, page 78; Heilman, "Chicago Subway Problem," page 998; *Chicago Commerce*, March 31, 1911, pages 24–25.

100. *Chicago Commerce*, January 17, 1913, page 11; Deuther, *Local Transportation*, pages 77–80; Cook County Real Estate Board, *Transportation Problem of Chicago*, pages 3–15; Barrett, *The Automobile and Urban Transit*, pages 99–103.

101. Deuther, *Local Transportation*, pages 77–80; Cook County Real Estate Board, *Transportation Problem of Chicago*, pages 3–15.

102. "Rapid Transit for Chicago," *Buildings and Building Management*, October 11, 1926, page 52; *Electric Railway Journal*, September 4, 1926, pages 369–370; Barrett, *The Automobile and Urban Transit*, page 101; Hoyt, *One Hundred Years of Land Values*, page 192, 322–323.

103. Foster, *From Streetcar to Superhighway*, pages 74–76.

104. Deuther, *Local Transportation*, page 74; Foster, *From Streetcar to Superhighway*, pages 38–41, 75–76; Daniel L. Turner, "Is There a Vicious Circle of Transit Development

and City Congestion?" *National Municipal Review,* June 1926, pages 321–325; *New Republic,* November 28, 1928, pages 29–30; Curran, "Economic Height of Building," page 17; Harold S. Buttenheim, "The Problem of the Standing Vehicle," *Annals of the American Academy of Political and Social Science,* September 1927, pages 144, 154–155; *American City,* August 1928, page 148; *National Municipal Review,* May 1927, page 290; *Proceedings of the Sixtieth Annual Convention of the American Institute of Architects: 1927,* page 156.

105. Turner, "Transit Development and City Congestion," pages 321–325; Curran, "Economic Height of Building," pages 16–21; *American City,* September 1926, page 318.

106. *Proceedings of the Fifth National Conference on City Planning: 1913,* pages 114–116, 129. See also Arnold, *Pittsburgh Transportation Problem,* page 81; *Proceedings of the Second National Conference on City Planning: 1910,* pages 126–129; *[New York] Real Estate Record and Builders' Guide,* March 21, 1914, pages 499–500; *Report of the Transportation Survey Commission of the City of St. Louis* (1930), pages 98–99.

107. *[New York] Real Estate Record and Builders' Guide,* March 21, 1914, pages 499–500; *Report of the Transportation Survey Commission of St. Louis,* pages 98–99; *Electric Railway Journal,* August 9, 1913, page 221.

108. Turner, "Transit Development and City Congestion," page 325; Henry A. Brinckerhoff, "Rapid Transit: A Vital Element in Metropolitan Transportation," *Electric Railway Journal,* September 26, 1925, page 503; William J. Wilgus, "Transportation in the New Region," *Papers and Discussions at the International City and Regional Planning Conference: 1925,* page 246; *American City,* August 1928, page 148, July 1929, page 135.

109. Mark Stewart Foster, "The Decentralization of Los Angeles During the 1920s" (Ph.D. diss., University of Southern California, 1971), pages 112–113; Bion J. Arnold, "The Transportation Problem of Los Angeles," *California Outlook Supplement,* November 4, 1911, page 17; Fogelson, *The Fragmented Metropolis,* pages 78–79, 151–153, 175–176.

110. Bottles, *Los Angeles and the Automobile,* pages 101–102, 127–132; *Los Angeles Times,* February 14, 1922; Foster, "The Decentralization of Los Angeles," pages 117–121; *Electric Railway Journal,* May 9, 1925, pages 731–735.

111. *Los Angeles Times,* November 27, December 17, 1925, January 29, 1926; Bottles, *Los Angeles and the Automobile,* pages 132–134, 141–142, 147–148; Foster, "The Decentralization of Los Angeles," pages 124–125; *[First] Conference on the Rapid Transit Question,* pages 42–49, 57–58; "[Second] Conference on the Rapid Transit Question," pages 8–9, 11–19.

112. S. A. Jubb et al., "Report on Rapid Transit," *Los Angeles City Club Bulletin Supplement,* January 30, 1926, pages 3–9. See also *[First] Conference on the Rapid Transit Question,* pages 42–44.

113. C. A. Dykstra, "Congestion De Luxe—Do We Want It?" *National Municipal Review,* July 1926, pages 394–398. See also Gordon Whitnall, "Relation of Downtown Commercial Districts to Outlying Business Districts," *Pacific Municipalities,* April 1928, pages 127–132; J. O. Marsh, "Rapid Transit," *California Conference on City Planning: Bulletin No. 15* (1929), pages 1–2; Foster, "The Decentralization of Los Angeles," pages 126–129; Bottles, *Los Angeles and the Automobile,* pages 163–164.

114. *[First] Conference on the Rapid Transit Question,* pages 40–49, 57–64; "[Second] Conference on the Rapid Transit Question," pages 5–7, 15–19; Fogelson, *The Fragmented*

Metropolis, chapter 7; Foster, "The Decentralization of Los Angeles," pages 133–135; Bottles, *Los Angeles and the Automobile,* pages 166–168, 173–174.

115. *Electric Railway Journal,* January 1930, page 19; U.S. Bureau of the Census, *Census of Electrical Industries, 1937: Street Railways and Trolley-Bus and Motorbus Operations* (Washington, D.C., 1939), pages 22–23; U.S. Census Bureau, *Special Reports: Street and Electrical Railways 1907* (Washington, D.C., 1910), pages 53–54, 62.

116. U.S. Census Bureau, *Census of Electrical Industries 1937,* page 22; Charles H. Stevens, "Philadelphia City Transit Improvements," *Engineers and Engineering,* August 1930, pages 217–221. A few isolated rapid transit lines were built in other cities—one in Rochester, for example, and another in Cleveland.

117. *Report of the Transportation Survey Commission of St. Louis,* pages 88–97; Massachusetts General Court, *Final Report of the Joint Special Committee on the Finances and Control of the Boston Elevated Railway Company* (Boston, 1925), pages 4–7; Massachusetts General Court, *Report of the Joint Special Committee on Boston Elevated and Metropolitan Transportation District* (Boston, 1926), page 40; Curran, "Economic Height of Building," page 21; *American City,* August 19–26, pages 316–318; J. B. Atkins, "America After Thirty Years," *Living Age,* July 1928, pages 1043–1044.

118. Durand, "Street and Electric Railways," page 24; F. W. Hild, "The Effect of Rate of Fare on Riding Habit," *Electric Railway Journal,* January 13, 1914, pages 230–231; "Factors Affecting Riding Habit in Large Cities," ibid., December 22, 1928, pages 1070–1072, January 5, 1929, pages 9–14; John A. Beeler, "What Price Fares?" *Transit Journal,* June 1932, pages 263–266.

119. *Report of the [Chicago] Subway Advisory Commission,* pages 60–61.

Chapter 3: The Sacred Skyline

1. *[New York] Real Estate Record and Builders' Guide,* June 4, 1881, page 572.

2. Earle Shultz, *The Effect of Obsolescence on the Useful and Profitable Life of Office Buildings* (1922), pages 210–216; John C. Rupertus, "History of the Commercial Development of Franklin Street" (Master's thesis, University of South Florida, 1980), chapters 9–10; J. B. Lippincott & Co., *Philadelphia and Its Environs* (Philadelphia, 1873), page 3; M. M. Yeakle, *The City of St. Louis To-Day: Its Progress and Prospects* (St. Louis, 1889), pages 108–109, 257–258; *Omaha Daily Bee,* March 29, 1903; Martyn John Bowden, "The Dynamics of City Growth: An Historical Geography of the San Francisco Central District, 1850–1931" (Ph.D. diss., University of California at Berkeley, 1967), volume 1, pages 275–277; Wm. H Babcock & Sons, *Report on the Economic and Engineering Feasibility of Regrading the Bunker Hill Area Los Angeles* (1931), pages 50–51.

3. Bowden, "Dynamics of City Growth," volume 1, pages 292–295; *Boston Globe,* March 28, 1872. See also Richard M. Hurd, *Principles of City Land Values* (New York, 1903), chapter 6.

4. Homer Hoyt, *One Hundred Years of Land Values in Chicago* (Chicago, 1933), pages 89–90; Bowden, "Dynamics of City Growth," volume 1, pages 295–302; A. C. David, "The New Fifth Avenue," *Architectural Record,* July 1907, pages 2–3; Yeakle, *St. Louis,* pages 108–109; *Chicago Tribune,* December 2, 1910; *[New York] Real Estate Record and Builders' Guide,* November 10, 1906, page 761; George A. Hurd, "Real Estate Bonds as an Investment Security," *Real Estate Magazine,* July 1912, pages 7–8.

5. *Architecture and Building*, January 23, 1897, page 37; Edgar Allen Forbes, "The Sky-scraper," *World's Work*, May 1911, page 14398; Hoyt, *One Hundred Years of Land Values*, pages 149–153; Hurd, *Principles of City Land Values*, pages 99–100.

6. For a useful summary of attitudes toward the skyscraper, see Stanley Peter Andersen, "American Ikon: Response to the Skyscraper, 1875–1934" (Ph.D. diss., University of Minnesota, 1960), chapters 2–4.

7. William H. Jordy and Ralph Coe, eds., *American Architecture and Other Writings by Montgomery Schuyler* (Cambridge, 1961), volume 2, page 442. See also Bessie Louise Pierce, ed., *As Others See Chicago: Impressions of Visitors, 1673–1933* (Chicago, 1933), page 396; Winston Weisman, "New York and the Problem of the First Skyscraper," *Journal of the Society of Architectural Historians*, March 1953, pages 15–18; Hoyt, *One Hundred Years of Land Values*, pages 149–150; Paul Goldberger, *The Skyscraper* (New York, 1981), page 4.

8. Weisman, "The Problem of the First Skyscraper," pages 15–18; Jordy and Coe, eds., *American Architecture*, page 427; Christopher Tunnard and Henry Hope Reed, *American Skyline* (New York, 1956), page 102; Dana F. White, *The Urbanists, 1865–1915* (New York, 1989), page 51; *[New York] Real Estate Record and Builders' Guide*, December 16, 1882, page 124; Julian Ralph, *Our Great West* (New York, 1893), page 3; *Philadelphia Real Estate Record and Builders' Guide*, February 27, 1888, page 85.

9. *American Architect and Building News*, March 21, 1891, page 189. See also Weisman, "The Problem of the First Skyscraper," pages 18–19; Hoyt, *One Hundred Years of Land Values*, page 150; Michael Holleran and Robert Fogelson, "'The Sacred Skyline': Boston's Opposition to the Skyscraper, 1891–1928," MIT Center for Real Estate Development Working Paper Number 9 (1982), page 8.

10. Jordy and Coe, eds., *American Architecture*, pages 429–433, 443–444; Hoyt, *One Hundred Years of Land Values*, page 150; Holleran and Fogelson, "'The Sacred Skyline,'" pages 17–18; *American Architect and Building News*, December 12, 1891, page 170; *[New York] Real Estate Record and Builders' Guide*, June 23, 1900, pages 1087–1088.

11. *American Architect and Building News*, February 9, 1901, page 48; William Archer, *America To-Day: Observations and Reflections* (London, 1900), pages 18–19; Goldberger, *The Skyscraper*, pages 4–15; Paul Bourget, *Outre-Mer: Impressions of America* (New York, 1895), page 115; Henry Ericsson and Lewis E. Myers, *Sixty Years a Builder* (Chicago, 1942), page 370; Andersen, "American Ikon," page 155; J. M. Neil, "Paris or New York? The Shaping of Downtown Seattle," *Pacific Northwest Quarterly*, January 1914, pages 22–23; *[New York] Real Estate Record and Builders' Guide*, June 5, 1897, page 961, August 29, 1903, page 374, June 25, 1911, page 1186.

12. Hoyt, *One Hundred Years of Land Values*, page 157; *Engineering Record*, January 18, 1896, page 109; *[New York] Real Estate Record and Builders' Guide*, March 17, 1894, page 405, June 14, 1894, page 969; *American Architect and Building News*, September 21, 1907, page 89; *Chicago Tribune*, February 9, 1896; Goldberger, *The Skyscraper*, page 8; *Scientific American*, July 25, 1908, page 59; Forbes, "The Skyscraper," page 14391; Montgomery Schuyler, "'The Towers of Manhattan' and Notes on the Woolworth Building," *Architectural Record*, February 1913, pages 98–103.

13. Barr Ferree, "The Modern Office Building," *Inland Architect and News Record*, February 1896, page 4; *[New York] Real Estate Record and Builders' Guide*, June 11, 1892, page 916; Bayrd Still, *Mirror for Gotham: New York as Seen by Contemporaries from Dutch Days to the Present* (New York, 1956), pages 257–260; Pierce, ed., *As Others See*

Chicago, page 352; Philip Burne-Jones, *Dollars and Democracy* (New York, 1904), pages 60–61; Archer, *America To-Day*, page 18; *American Architect and Building News*, June 24, 1908, page 209.

14. *[New York] Real Estate Record and Builders' Guide*, July 14, 1877, page 555; *American Architect and Building News*, February 23, 1878, page 70, March 11, 1883, page 62, February 27, 1892, page 72, November 20, 1900, page 17; Norma Evenson, *Paris: A Century of Change, 1878–1978* (New Haven, 1979), pages 150–152; *Report of the [New York City] Heights of Building Commission* (New York, 1913), pages 23, 120–134.

15. *[New York] Real Estate Record and Builders' Guide*, January 20, 1883, pages 28–29, March 3, 1883, page 80, April 12, 1884, page 370, April 19, 1884, page 402, February 4, 1888, pages 141–142, February 18, 1888, page 208, March 17, 1894, pages 406–407; *American Architect and Building News*, March 15, 1884, page 121, April 18, 1885, page 181, November 20, 1886, page 237; *New York Times*, March 30, 1884.

16. *[New York] Real Estate Record and Builders' Guide*, April 19, 1884, page 402, February 4, 1888, pages 141–142, March 17, 1904, page 407; *New York Times*, March 30, 1884; *American Architect and Building News*, February 1, 1896, page 49; *San Francisco Examiner*, September 25, 1895; *St. Louis Post-Dispatch*, December 12, 1895; *Denver Post*, December 16, 1908; *Seattle Post-Intelligencer*, March 6, 1910.

17. *American Architect and Building News*, February 15, 1890, page 42, February 20, 1897, page 58; *[New York] Real Estate Record and Builders' Guide*, April 21, 1894, page 615, June 23, 1894, pages 1009–1010, September 6, 1902, pages 317–318, January 4, 1908, page 17; Robert Henderson Robertson, "Faults and Virtues of Our High Buildings," *Independent*, May 31, 1900, pages 1316–1318; Burton J. Hendrick, "Limitations to the Production of Skyscrapers," *Atlantic Monthly*, October 1902, pages 486–492.

18. *[New York] Real Estate Record and Builders' Guide*, March 17, 1894, page 405; Schuyler, "'The Towers of Manhattan,'" pages 98–103.

19. *American Architect and Building News*, August 28, 1880, pages 104–105, April 11, 1891, page 17, January 2, 1892, page 2, December 10, 1898, pages 864–865, April 8, 1899, page 15; *American Architect*, November 11, 1908, pages 17–18; *[New York] Real Estate Record and Builders' Guide*, January 20, 1893, page 28, June 16, 1894, page 969; *[Chicago] Real Estate and Building Journal*, October 24, 1891, page 1534; *St. Louis Post-Dispatch*, December 12, 1895; *Chicago Tribune*, October 13, November 15, December 18, 1891.

20. *Transactions of the American Society of Civil Engineers: 1900*, page 417; *American Architect and Building News*, November 7, 1888, page 226, December 19, 1896, page 94, February 20, 1897, page 64; *Chicago Tribune*, October 13, 1891, April 10, 1898; Andersen, "American Ikon," pages 72–73; *[New York] Real Estate Record and Builders' Guide*, June 23, 1894, pages 1009–1010, August 11, 1894, pages 194–195; *Architecture and Building*, January 18, 1896, pages 32–33.

21. *[New York] Real Estate Record and Builders' Guide*, January 20, 1883, page 28, March 17, 1894, page 407, August 15, 1908, page 335; *Engineering Record*, January 18, 1896, pages 109–110; Henderson, "Faults and Virtues," page 1317; Forbes, "The Skyscraper," page 14397; *American Architect and Building News*, May 30, 1896, page 86, September 2, 1900, page 89; Minneapolis Civic and Commerce Association, *Report of the Municipal Committee on Limitation of Heights of Buildings*, page 11; Charles H. Alden, "Regulations for the Height of Buildings," *Pacific Builder and Engineer*, February 10, 1912, page 116; *Chicago Tribune*, October 15, 1891.

22. *[New York] Real Estate Record and Builders' Guide*, March 17, 1894, pages 406–407; *Chicago Tribune*, October 13/15, 1891, January 5, 1911; *American Architect and Building News*, November 21, 1891, pages 117–118, June 20, 1893, page 100; Holleran and Fogelson, "'The Sacred Skyline,'" page 9.

23. *[New York] Real Estate Record and Builders' Guide*, March 16, 1907, page 532, November 14, 1908, page 920; *[Chicago] Real Estate and Building Journal*, October 24, 1891, page 1534; *Chicago Tribune*, October 13/15, November 15, 1891, February 24, 1896; *St. Louis Post-Dispatch*, December 12, 1895; *Hearings Before [the Boston] Commission on Height of Buildings* (Boston, 1916), page 66; August Gatzert, *Limitation of Building Heights in the City of Chicago* (1913), page 7.

24. *[Chicago] Real Estate and Building Journal*, December 17, 1892, page 161; *American Architect and Building News*, May 30, 1896, page 87, October 3, 1896, page 2; *Chicago Tribune*, October 15, November 11, 1891; *[New York] Real Estate Record and Builders' Guide*, October 29, 1881, page 1009, December 14, 1891, page 820; *Boston Evening Transcript*, October 27, 1893; Gatzert, *Limitation of Building Heights*, page 10.

25. *[Chicago] Real Estate and Building Journal*, October 24, 1891, page 1534, February 20, 1897, page 149; *St. Louis Post-Dispatch*, December 12, 1895; *[New York] Real Estate Record and Builders' Guide*, March 17, 1894, page 405, June 5, 1897, page 961, December 14, 1901, page 820; *Architecture and Building*, December 10, 1892, page 164, January 13, 1897, page 37, April 9, 1898, page 121; Ralph, *Our Great West*, page 8; *Chicago Tribune*, October 15, 1891; *American Architect and Building News*, May 30, 1896, page 86.

26. *Report of the [New York City] Heights of Buildings Commission*, pages 19–21; *[Chicago] Real Estate and Building Journal*, August 8, 1891, page 1134; *American Architect and Building News*, May 12, 1894, page 58, May 30, 1896, page 86, February 20, 1897, page 59, February 27, 1904, page 65; *[New York] Real Estate Record and Builders' Guide*, March 17, 1894, page 405, June 5, 1897, page 961, June 12, 1897, page 1006; A. H. Robertson, "Height Limits of Fireproof Buildings," *Seattle Municipal News*, July 20, 1912, page 1; *Architecture and Building*, May 16, 1896, pages 32–33; Gatzert, *Limitation of Building Heights*, pages 4–6.

27. *Chicago Tribune*, October 13, 1891; *St. Louis Post-Dispatch*, December 12, 1895; Henderson, "Faults and Virtues," page 1317; *American Architect and Building News*, May 30, 1896, page 86; Jordy and Coe, eds., *American Architecture*, page 445; *American Architect*, January 18, 1908, page 24; *[New York] Real Estate Record and Builders' Guide*, June 11, 1892, page 916; April 21, 1894, page 616.

28. Jordy and Coe, eds., *American Architecture*, pages 445–446. See also White, *The Urbanists*, page 51; Forbes, "The Skyscraper," page 14397; Merrill Schleier, *The Skyscraper in American Art, 1890–1931* (Ann Arbor, 1986), pages 9–10; Ernest Flagg, "The Limitation of Height and Area of Buildings in New York," *American Architect*, March 25, 1908, page 125; Holleran and Fogelson, "'The Sacred Skyline,'" pages 14–15; Andersen, "American Ikon," pages 87–88; Montgomery Schuyler, "To Curb the Skyscraper," *Architectural Record*, October 1908, pages 300–302.

29. Andersen, "American Ikon," pages 122–124; *[New York] Real Estate Record and Builders' Guide*, March 16, 1907, page 533; Jordy and Coe, eds., *American Architecture*, page 446; Schleier, *The Skyscraper in American Art*, pages 11–12; Maxim Gorky, "The City of Mammon: My Impressions of America," *Appletons' Magazine*, August 1906, page 178.

30. *American Architect*, May 1909, page 148; Schleier, *The Skyscraper in American Art*, page 10; Henry James, *The American Scene Together with Three Essays from "Portraits of Places"* (New York, 1946), pages 78, 232; Burne-Jones, *Dollars and Democracy*, page 61; *Architecture and Building*, January 18, 1896, pages 32–33; *American Architect and Building News*, November 19, 1904, page 64.

31. F. W. Fitzpatrick, "Lessons of the Baltimore Fire," *Inland Architect and News Record*, March 1904, pages 10–13. See also *American Architect and Building News*, May 29, 1897, pages 70–71, May 14, 1898, page 53, December 10, 1898, page 85; Fitzpatrick, "Tall Buildings the Safest," *American Architect*, November 2, 1907, pages 139–140; *American Architect*, May 13, 1908, page 162; *[New York] Real Estate Record and Builders' Guide*, May 22, 1896, page 298, September 21, 1907, page 434; *St. Louis Post-Dispatch*, February 9, 1906; *California Architect and Building News*, October 1895, page 110; C. H. Blackall, "High Buildings," *Brickbuilder*, February 1896, page 28.

32. *American Architect and Building News*, December 1, 1888, page 258, April 20, 1898, page 149, October 10, 1903, page 10; *American Architect*, February 20, 1904, page 57, November 9, 1907, page 147; *San Francisco Examiner*, May 11/15, 1906; *Chicago Tribune*, October 13, 1891; Blackall, "High Buildings," pages 28–29; *Inland Architect and News Record*, October 1892, pages 24–25; *[New York] Real Estate Record and Builders' Guide*, August 1, 1894, pages 194–195, July 11, 1908, page 73; Andersen, "American Ikon," page 73.

33. *Chicago Tribune*, October 13/15, 1891; *[Chicago] Real Estate and Building Journal*, September 19, 1891, page 1355; *St. Louis Post-Dispatch*, December 19, 1895; Ferree, "The Modern Office Building," page 4; *California Architect and Building News*, October 1895, page 111; *[New York] Real Estate Record and Builders' Guide*, March 17, 1894, page 406; Calvin Tomkins, "The Tall Buildings of New York," ibid., November 5, 1907, page 516.

34. *American Architect and Building News*, December 4, 1891, page 141; *Inland Architect and News Record*, June 1891, page 58, October 1892, pages 24–25, February 1902, page 1; *Chicago Tribune*, November 11, 1891; Ferree, "The Modern Office Building," page 4; *St. Louis Post-Dispatch*, December 12/19, 1895; *Architecture and Building*, April 9, 1898, page 121; *[New York] Real Estate Record and Builders' Guide*, February 22, 1896, page 298.

35. *[Chicago] Real Estate and Building Journal*, April 25, 1891, page 577, October 17, 1891, page 1498, October 24, 1891, page 1534; *Chicago Tribune*, October 13, November 12, 1891, December 10, 1912; Neil, "Paris or New York?" page 23; Tomkins, "The Tall Buildings of New York," page 516; *New York Times*, September 18, 1908.

36. *St. Louis Post-Dispatch*, December 11/19, 1895, January 19, 1896; *American Architect and Building News*, July 14, 1891, page 12; Hurd, *Principles of City Land Values*, page 102; Blackall, "High Buildings," page 29; *Chicago Tribune*, November 11, 1891; *Architecture and Building*, April 9, 1898, page 121; *California Architect and Building News*, May 15, 1888, page 58; *[Chicago] Real Estate and Building Journal*, April 24, 1891, page 577; *Chicago Commerce*, December 26, 1913, page 20.

37. *[Chicago] Real Estate and Building Journal*, October 24, 1891, page 1534; *[New York] Real Estate Record and Builders' Guide*, March 17, 1894, pages 406–407; Blackall, "High Buildings," page 29; *California Architect and Building News*, October 1895, page 110; *Chicago Tribune*, April 9, 1898; *Transactions of the American Society of Civil Engineers: 1900*, pages 468–469; *American Architect and Building News*, May 18,

1901, page 49, March 22, 1902, page 90; *American Architect*, May 20, 1908, page 163.

38. *[New York] Real Estate Record and Builders' Guide*, January 4, 1908, page 17. See also ibid., June 5, 1897, page 961, June 12, 1897, page 1006, December 14, 1901, page 815, October 18, 1902, pages 561–562; *[Chicago] Real Estate and Building Journal*, September 19, 1897, page 1355; *Transactions of the American Society of Civil Engineers: 1900*, page 455; *American Architect and Building News*, February 20, 1897, page 58, May 1, 1897, page 33, February 15, 1902, page 49; Ferree, "The Modern Office Building," page 4; *California Architect and Building News*, October 1895, page 111.

39. *[New York] Real Estate Record and Builders' Guide*, June 11, 1892, page 916, March 17, 1894, page 406; *St. Louis Post-Dispatch*, December 12/19, 1895; Blackall, "High Buildings," page 29; Flagg, "Limitation of Height and Area of Buildings," pages 125–126; *American Architect*, September 30, 1908, page 112, October 6, 1909, page 139, March 26, 1913, pages 171–172; *San Francisco Examiner*, June 24, 1906; Schleier, *The Skyscraper in American Art*, pages 14, 53.

40. Schleier, *The Skyscraper in American Art*, pages 17, 29, 33–35; John Corbin, "The Twentieth Century City," *Scribner's Magazine*, March 1903, pages 210–211; Andersen, "American Ikon," pages 138–141; Holleran and Fogelson, "'The Sacred Skyline,'" pages 30–32, 39–40.

41. *Seattle Post-Intelligencer*, April 4, 1910; Andersen, "American Ikon," pages 127–130, 142–145; *Chicago Tribune*, November 5, 1891; *San Francisco Examiner*, September 28/30, 1895; *St. Louis Post-Dispatch*, December 12, 1895; Archer, *America To-Day*, page 89; Schleier, *The Skyscraper in American Art*, pages 14–15.

42. *American Architect and Building News*, April 8, 1889, page 15; *[New York] Real Estate Record and Builders' Guide*, March 17, 1894, pages 406–407, April 21, 1894, page 616; Dankmar Adler, "Municipal Building Laws," *Inland Architect and News Record*, May 1895, pages 36–38; *Chicago Tribune*, October 23, November 7, 1891; *[Chicago] Real Estate and Building Journal*, June 8, 1889, page 347.

43. *[Chicago] Real Estate and Building Journal*, October, 24, 1891, page 1534.

44. Holleran and Fogelson, "'The Sacred Skyline,'" pages 16–20. See also Mona Domosh, "Shaping the Commercial City: Retail Districts in Nineteenth-Century New York and Boston," *Annals of the American Association of Geographers*, June 1990, pages 268–284.

45. Holleran and Fogelson, "'The Sacred Skyline,'" pages 16–19. See also *Boston Evening Transcript*, October 27, 1893; *American Architect and Building News*, October 14, 1899, pages 545–546.

46. Holleran and Fogelson, "'The Sacred Skyline,'" pages 17, 20, 23–28. See also Blackall, "High Buildings," pages 28–29; *American Architect and Building News*, February 1, 1896, page 49, April 8, 1899, page 15.

47. Holleran and Fogelson, "'The Sacred Skyline,'" page 24; *American Architect and Building News*, July 16, 1904, pages 17–18; *Hearings Before [the Boston] Commission on Height of Buildings*, pages 54–55; *Report of the Commission on Height of Buildings in the City of Boston: 1904*, pages 5–6, 9–10; *Report of the Commission on Height of Buildings in the City of Boston: 1905*, pages 1–2. On streets between sixty-four and eighty feet wide, a building could be erected no higher than one and a quarter times the width of the street on which it stood.

48. *Hearings Before [the Boston] Commission on Height of Buildings*, passim. See also

Holleran and Fogelson, "'The Sacred Skyline,'" pages 40–42; *[New York] Real Estate Record and Builders' Guide*, October 11, 1913, page 661.

49. *Chicago Tribune*, December 15, 1901. See also William Cronon, *Nature's Metropolis: Chicago and the Great West* (New York, 1991).

50. *Chicago Tribune*, October 7/13/15/23, November 5/15/18, December 18/23, 1891; *[Chicago] Real Estate and Building Journal*, October 17, 1891, page 1498, October 24, 1891, page 1534, November 21, 1891, page 1679; *American Architect and Building News*, November 21, 1891, page 117; Adler, "Municipal Building Laws," pages 36–38; Hoyt, *One Hundred Years of Land Values*, page 153.

51. *Chicago Tribune*, October 7/13/15/17, November 5/11/24, 1891, January 16/17, February 20, 1892, January 25, 1893; *American Architect and Building News*, November 21, 1891, page 117, December 5, 1891, page 141; *Inland Architect and News Record*, June 1891, pages 58–59, October 1892, pages 24–25, March 1893, page 20; *[Chicago] Real Estate and Building Journal*, June 8, 1889, page 346, November 28, 1891, page 1713; Adler, "Municipal Building Laws," pages 36–38.

52. Earle Shultz and Walter Simmons, *Offices in the Sky* (Indianapolis, 1959), page 285; *American Architect and Building News*, January 18, 1896, page 33, February 29, 1896, page 99, February 15, 1902, page 29; *Architecture and Building*, January 4, 1896, page 2, April 9, 1898, pages 121–122; *Chicago Tribune*, March 17/23/24/29, 1898; *American Architect and Building News*, May 14, 1898, page 53.

53. Hoyt, *One Hundred Years of Land Values*, pages 210–211, 224; *Chicago Tribune*, December 28, 1901, January 5/23, February 4, 1902, December 6/12/20, 1910, December 18/20, 1913; Chicago Real Estate Board Zoning Committee, *Studies on Building Height Limitations in Large Cities* (Chicago, 1923), pages 14, 65–66; *American Architect and Building News*, July 13, 1901, page 13, February 8, 1902, page 48; *Chicago Commerce*, December 26, 1913, page 20.

54. Holleran and Fogelson, "'The Sacred Skyline,'" pages 35–36; *Chicago Tribune*, December 19/21, 1913; Ericsson and Myers, *Sixty Years a Builder*, page 328; Peter B. Wright, "Additions to Chicago's Skyline," *Architectural Record*, July 1910, pages 15–16.

55. *Baltimore Sun*, February 8/9/14/15/17/18/23, March 1/8/11, 1904; Fitzpatrick, "Lessons of the Baltimore Fire," pages 10–13. See also Garrett Power, "High Society: The Building Height Limitation on Baltimore's Mount Vernon Place," *Maryland Historical Magazine*, Fall 1984, page 197–219.

56. *St. Louis Post-Dispatch*, December 11/12/19/22, 1895, January 19, 1896; *Architecture and Building*, January 4, 1896, pages 1–2.

57. *St. Louis Post-Dispatch*, December 11/12/19/22/29, 1895, January 5/19, 1896.

58. Ibid., January 26, February 2/9, 1896, April 2, 1897; *Inland Architect and News Record*, February 1896, page 2; *Brickbuilder*, May 1897, pages 107–108.

59. *Denver Post*, December 1–2, 1908; John R. Pickering, "Blueprint of Power: The Public Career of Robert Speer in Denver, 1878–1918" (Ph.D. diss., University of Denver, 1978), pages 134–135.

60. *Denver Post*, December 3–6/11, 1908.

61. Ibid., December 6–23, 1908; Pickering, "Blueprint of Power," page 135.

62. *Seattle Post-Intelligencer*, February 26, March 6, April 17, 1910; Neil, "Paris or New York?" pages 22–24.

63. *Seattle Post-Intelligencer*, February 18/26, March 6, April 24, 1910; Neil, "Paris or New York?" page 22–24.

64. *Seattle Post-Intelligencer,* July 9, 1911, January 7, 1912; Alden, "Regulations for the Height of Buildings," pages 116–117; *Seattle Municipal News,* July 20, 1912, pages 1–2, September 28, 1912, page 3; Neil, "Paris or New York?" pages 24–33.

65. *Report of the [New York City] Heights of Buildings Commission,* pages 22–23; Arthur C. Comey, "Maximum Building Height Regulation," *Landscape Architecture,* October 1912, pages 19–24; Albertson, "Height Limits of Fireproof Buildings," page 2; Alden, "Regulations for the Height of Buildings," page 116.

66. *Report of the [New York City] Heights of Buildings Commission,* pages 22–23; Comey, "Maximum Building Height Regulation," page 22.

67. *Report of the [New York City] Heights of Buildings Commission,* pages 15–17, 79–86; *Chicago Tribune,* December 19, 1913; Pierce, ed., *As Others See Chicago,* page 396; Still, ed., *Mirror for Gotham,* pages 257–260, 279–284.

68. *[New York] Real Estate Record and Builders' Guide,* March 17, 1894, pages 405–407. See also ibid., January 20, 1883, pages 28–29, April 12, 1884, page 370, April 19, 1884, page 402; *Engineering Record,* December 26, 1896, pages 67–68; *American Architect and Building News,* March 5, 1884, page 121, April 18, 1885, page 181, November 20, 1886, page 237.

69. *[New York] Real Estate Record and Builders' Guide,* April 21, 1894, page 615, February 1, 1896, page 173; *New York Times,* July 14, 1895, January 3/28, February 13, March 6, 1896; *American Architect and Building News,* May 30, 1896, pages 86–87. In the case of properties that stood on a public square, on a street more than 100 feet wide, or opposite the end of a street more than 60 feet wide, the owners could build above 150 feet—but only if a committee consisting of the president of the Health Department, the Superintendent of Buildings, and a member of the Council of the Fine Arts Federation certified that the proposed building was "neither detrimental to the health or comfort of the citizens, nor injurious to the beauty of the city."

70. *American Architect and Building News,* May 30, 1896, pages 86–87; *[New York] Real Estate Record and Builders' Guide,* February 1, 1896, page 173, February 22, 1896, page 298; *New York Times,* February 16/27, March 10/12, 1896; White, *The Urbanists,* page 197.

71. *New York Times,* February 27, March 12, 1896; *American Architect and Building News,* May 30, 1896, pages 86–87; *[New York] Real Estate Record and Builders' Guide,* February 1, 1896, page 173.

72. *[New York] Real Estate Record and Builders' Guide,* March 17, 1894, page 406, June 23, 1894, pages 1009–1010, March 28, 1896, page 619, December 19, 1896, page 918, March 17, 1897, page 414, March 26, 1898, page 546, January 7, 1899, page 2; *New York Times,* May 9, 1899; *Transactions of the American Society of Civil Engineers: 1900,* pages 456, 472; Henderson, "Faults and Virtues," pages 1316–1318; *American Architect and Building News,* May 18, 1901, page 49, March 22, 1902, page 90.

73. *[New York] Real Estate Record and Builders' Guide,* December 14, 1901, page 815, September 6, 1902, pages 317–318, October 18, 1902, pages 561–562, March 3, 1906, page 363, August 18, 1906, page 294; *New York Times,* October 6, December 29, 1907.

74. *[New York] Real Estate Record and Builders' Guide,* May 16, 1903, page 975, August 18, 1906, page 294, March 16, 1907, pages 532–533, August 17, 1907, page 249, September 14, 1907, pages 394–395, September 21, 1907, page 434; *New York Times,* December 29, 1907, January 31, 1908.

75. *New York Times,* May 7, 1906, March 11, 1908; *[New York] Real Estate Record and*

Builders' Guide, September 28, 1907, pages 472, 475, March 14, 1908, pages 441–442, March 28, 1908, page 544, June 13, 1908, page 1122, August 15, 1908, pages 332, 335, August 22, 1908, page 376; *American Architect*, March 25, 1908, page 106; Flagg, "Limitation of Height and Area of Buildings," pages 125–126.

76. *[New York] Real Estate Record and Builders' Guide*, March 14, 1908, page 439, July 18, 1908, page 127, July 25, 1908, page 173, October 24, 1908, page 773, November 14, 1908, page 919; *American Architect*, September 16, 1908, pages 91–92, November 11, 1908, page 15.

77. *[New York] Real Estate Record and Builders' Guide*, October 10, 1908, pages 688, 691, October 24, 1908, page 773, November 7, 1908, page 875, November 14, 1908, pages 919–921, November 21, 1908, pages 971–972; *American Architect*, November 18, 1908, page 161, November 18, 1908, pages 15–17.

78. *[New York] Real Estate Record and Builders' Guide*, August 18, 1906. See also *New York Times*, February 27, 1909; *American Architect*, March 3, 1909, page 80.

79. *[New York] Real Estate Record and Builders' Guide*, June 12, 1909, pages 1188–1189, March 29, 1913, page 657, November 15, 1913, page 893; Schuyler, "'The Towers of Manhattan,'" pages 98–103; *American Architect and Building News*, September 21, 1907, page 89; *American Architect*, May 13, 1908, page 162, October 6, 1909, page 139, March 26, 1913, pages 171–172; *Chicago Commerce*, July 6, 1917, page 13; Holleran and Fogelson, "'The Sacred Skyline,'" pages 39–40.

80. *Final Report [of the New York City] Commission on Building Districts and Restrictions* (New York, 1916), chapters 3–6; Robert H. Whitten, "The Building Zone Plan of New York City," *[New York] Real Estate Record and Builders' Guide*, February 3, 1917, pages 21–22; *American Architect*, August 9, 1916, page 83; Seymour I. Toll, *Zoned American* (New York, 1969), pages 180–181.

81. Toll, *Zoned American*, chapters 3–6. See also *Report of the [New York City] Heights of Buildings Commission; Final Report [of the New York City] Commission on Building Districts and Restrictions;* Stanislaw J. Makielski, Jr., *The Politics of Zoning: The New York Experience* (New York, 1966), chapter 1; and Marc A. Weiss, "Skyscraper Zoning: New York's Pioneering Role," *Journal of the American Planning Association*, Spring 1992, pages 201–212.

82. *Final Report [of the New York City] Commission on Building Districts and Restrictions*, pages 73–76, 213–226; *[New York] Real Estate Record and Builders' Guide*, December 20, 1913, page 1117, January 23, 1915, page 128, February 6, 1915, page 206, February 20, 1915, page 292, April 8, 1916, page 543, July 22, 1916, page 107; *American Architect*, May 10, 1916, page 306; Keith D. Revell, "Regulating the Landscape: Real Estate Values, City Planning, and the 1916 Zoning Ordinance," in David Ward and Olivier Zunz, eds., *The Landscape of Modernity: Essays on New York City, 1900–1940* (New York, 1992), page 40.

83. *[New York] Real Estate Record and Builders' Guide*, March 8, 1913, page 495, March 15, 1913, page 562, April 19, 1913, page 823, October 3, 1914, page 543, December 26, 1914, page 1036. See also Revell, "Regulating the Landscape," page 40; Weiss, "Skyscraper Zoning," page 208.

84. *[New York] Real Estate Record and Builders' Guide*, February 22, 1913, page 387, July 1, 1916, page 5, July 29, 1916, page 143; *American Architect*, June 10, 1914, page 300; *Final Report [of the New York City] Commission on Building Districts and Restrictions*, pages 13, 112–113, 166–171; Revell, "Regulating the Landscape," page 35.

85. *Proceedings [of the] Eighth Annual Convention of the National Association of Building Owners and Managers: 1915*, page 172; *[New York] Real Estate Record and Builders' Guide*, December 7, 1912, page 1064, March 8, 1913, page 505, April 8, 1916, page 543, August 5, 1916, page 183, August 19, 1916, pages 254–255; *Moody's Magazine*, June 1914, page 288; Revell, "Regulating the Landscape," pages 32–33; Toll, *Zoned American*, pages 68–71.

86. *Proceedings [of the] Eighth Annual Convention of the National Association of Building Owners and Managers: 1915*, pages 168–173; *[New York] Real Estate Record and Builders' Guide*, April 8, 1916, pages 543–544, July 22, 1916, pages 107–109, August 5, 1916, pages 183, 188; *Final Report [of the New York City] Commission on Building Districts and Restrictions*, page 137–138, 148–150.

87. Toll, *Zoned American*, pages 149–150; Revell, "Regulating the Landscape," page 32; *Proceedings [of the] Eighth Annual Convention of the National Association of Building Owners and Managers: 1915*, pages 172–173; *[New York] Real Estate Record and Builders' Guide*, July 1, 1916, pages 5–6, July 22, 1916, pages 107–109; *Final Report [of the New York City] Commission on Building Districts and Restrictions*, pages 4–5, 13–14, 166–171; *Report of the [New York City] Heights of Buildings Commission*, page 56–57.

88. Whitten, "The Building Zone Plan of New York City," page 45; *Final Report [of the New York City] Commission on Building Districts and Restrictions*, pages 32–37; *American Architect*, November 11, 1908, pages 15–17, April 9, 1916, page 83.

89. *Final Report [of the New York City] Commission on Building Districts and Restrictions*, pages 3, 32–37, 236–237; Frank Lord, "Zoning Resolution Is Logical Solution of Present Chaotic Conditions," *[New York] Real Estate Record and Builders' Guide*, August 19, 1916, page 254.

90. *American Architect*, May 10, 1916, page 305–306.

91. Marc A. Weiss, "Density and Intervention: New York's Planning Traditions," in Ward and Zunz, eds., *The Landscape of Modernity*, page 47; *American Architect*, December 19, 1917, pages 460–461, January 29, 1919, pages 178–179, September 3, 1919, page 311, January 28, 1920, page 122, February 18, 1920, pages 216–221; Toll, *Zoned American*, pages 194–195; *Chicago Commerce*, October 18, 1917, pages 9, 20, 22–23, November 25, 1922, pages 34–36; John Ihlder, "City Zoning Is Sound Business," *Nation's Business*, November 1922, pages 19–20; Charles M. Fisher, "An Outline of City Zoning," *National Real Estate Journal*, May 21, 1923, pages 15–19.

92. *American Architect*, September 10, 1913, page 107.

93. St. Louis City Plan Commission, *The Zone Plan* (St. Louis, 1919), pages 17–43; St. Louis City Plan Commission, *Ten Years' Progress on the City Plan of St. Louis, 1916–1926* (St. Louis, 1927), pages 47–50; Gustav J. Requardt, "How to Pass a Zoning Ordinance," *Proceedings of the American Society for Municipal Improvements: 1923*, pages 137–144; Chicago Real Estate Board Zoning Committee, *Studies on Building Height Limitations*, pages 199–201.

94. Holleran and Fogelson, "'The Sacred Skyline,'" pages 33–34, 42–45.

95. *Proceedings of the Seventeenth Annual Convention of the National Association of Building Owners and Managers: 1924*, pages 31–32, 39–43; Horace Groskin et al., *How Zoning Restrictions Will Reduce Present and Future Real Estate Values* (Philadelphia, 1922), pages 3–11, 13–23, 27–29; *Philadelphia Evening Bulletin*, January 10, 1922.

96. Milwaukee Board of Public Land Commissioners, *Restricted Heights of Buildings* (Milwaukee, 1920); *Proceedings of the American Society for Municipal Improvements Con-*

vention: 1920, pages 64–69; Akron City Planning Commission, *Limitation of Heights of Buildings* (1922), page 3; Marc A. Weiss, "The Real Estate Industry and the Politics of Zoning in San Francisco, 1914–1928," *Planning Perspectives*, September 1988, pages 314–315; Roy Lubove, *Twentieth-Century Pittsburgh: Government, Business, and Environmental Change* (New York, 1969), pages 94–95; Theodora Kimball Hubbard and Henry Vincent Hubbard, *Our Cities To-Day and Tomorrow: A Survey of Planning and Zoning Progress in the United States* (Cambridge, 1929), pages 162–163.

97. *Annual Report of the Zoning Commission of the City of Philadelphia: 1920*, pages 3–9, *1921*, pages 25–26; James W. Follin, "City Planning and Zoning in Philadelphia," *Journal of the Engineers' Club of Philadelphia*, August 1920, page 323; Joseph G. Wagner and George R. Mackenzie, "Proposed Zoning Ordinance for Philadelphia," *Engineers and Engineering*, February 1922, pages 33–48, 64.

98. *Annual Report of the Zoning Commission of the City of Philadelphia: 1922*, pages 4–5; Groskin et al., *Zoning Restrictions*, pages 11–12, 19–21; *Philadelphia Evening Bulletin*, January 26, 1922.

99. Groskin et al., *Zoning Restrictions*, pages 11–12, 19–21; *Philadelphia Evening Bulletin*, January 10/26, 1922.

100. *Annual Report of the Zoning Commission of the City of Philadelphia: 1922*, pages 4–6; Edward M. Bassett, "Address on Zoning," *Engineers and Engineering*, February 1922, pages 49–51, 64; Lawson Purdy, "Zoning and Its Relation to City Development," ibid., October 1922, pages 352–355; *Philadelphia Evening Bulletin*, January 19/26, February 2/16, 1922; William P. Gest, *The Principles of Zoning* (1923), page 50.

101. Weiss, "Skyscraper Zoning," pages 207–208; Weiss, "The Politics of Zoning in San Francisco," pages 314–315; Andrew J. King, *Law and Land Use in Chicago: A Prehistory of Modern Zoning* (New York, 1986), chapter 8; Chicago Real Estate Board Zoning Committee, *Studies in Building Height Limitations*, passim; Paul Barrett, *The Automobile and Urban Transit: The Formation of Public Policy in Chicago, 1900–1930* (Philadelphia, 1983), pages 187–188.

102. Herbert B. Dorau and Albert G. Hinman, *Urban Land Economics* (New York, 1928), pages 332–335; *Proceedings of the Twentieth Annual Convention of the National Association of Building Owners and Managers: 1927*, page 230; Chicago Real Estate Board Zoning Committee, *Studies on Building Height Limitations*, page 59; *Los Angeles Times*, March 2, 1924.

103. Weiss, "Skyscraper Zoning," page 207; *Proceedings of the Nineteenth Annual Convention of the National Association of Building Owners and Managers: 1926*, pages 266–280; *Proceedings of the Twentieth Annual Convention of the National Association of Building Owners and Managers: 1927*, pages 281–344; *Proceedings of the Twenty-First Annual Convention of the National Association of Building Owners and Managers: 1928*, pages 121–143.

104. Hubbard and Hubbard, *Our Cities*, pages 179–180; Weiss, "Skyscraper Zoning," pages 207–208; Weiss, "Density and Intervention," pages 63–66; *Architectural Record*, July 1925, pages 88–90; *American City*, August 1929, page 150, November 1929, page 5.

105. "The Skyscraper: Babel or Boon?" *New York Times Magazine*, December 5, 1926, pages 1–2; Harvey Wiley Corbett, "Up With the Skyscraper," *National Municipal Review*, February 1927, pages 95–101; Henry H. Curran, "The Skyscraper Does Cause Congestion," ibid., April 1927, pages 229–234; U.S. Chamber of Commerce, *The*

Economic Height of Buildings: The Skyscraper Attacked and Defended (Washington, D.C., 1927), pages 9–21; Frederic A. Delano, "Skyscrapers," *American City,* January 1926, pages 1–9; "Skyscrapers—The Arguments For and Against Them," *Buildings and Building Management,* February 1, 1926, pages 37–41.

106. Jacob A. Crane, Jr., "Height Limitations in Zoning," *Proceedings of the American Society of Civil Engineers,* February 1925, pages 194–206; *Proceedings of the Nineteenth Annual Convention of the National Association of Building Owners and Managers: 1926,* pages 266–271, 273–277; *Proceedings of the Twentieth Annual Convention of the National Association of Building Owners and Managers: 1927,* pages 217–226, 232–238; *Proceedings of the Twenty-First Annual Convention of the National Association of Building Owners and Managers: 1928,* pages 123–126, 136–143; Delano, "Skyscrapers," pages 7–8; Henry Curran, "The Economic Height of Building as Illustrated by the Office Building," in U.S. Chamber of Commerce, *The Economic Height of Buildings: The Skyscraper Attacked and Defended,* pages 16–17; Andersen, "American Ikon," chapter 4; W. C. Clark, "Determining the Economic Height of Modern Office Buildings," *Annals of Real Estate Practice: 1929,* pages 826–851.

107. Henry James, "Is the Skyscraper a Public Nuisance?" *World's Work,* May 1927, pages 70–71; "The Skyscraper: Babel or Boon?" page 2; Curran, "The Skyscraper Does Cause Congestion," pages 231–232; Curran, "Economic Height of Building," pages 17–21; *American City,* September 1926, pages 316–317; Delano, "Skyscrapers," page 2; *New York Times,* October 31, 1926.

108. Henry H. Curran, "What Height Limitations Can Do for New York Realty," *Building Investment and Maintenance,* November 1926, page 21; "The Skyscraper: Babel or Boon?" page 2; Curran, "Economic Height of Building," page 20; *American City,* July 1929, page 135; Ernest K. Lindley, "Feedpipes for Skyscrapers," *American Review of Reviews,* August 1928, page 177; Daniel L. Turner, Jr., "Is There a Vicious Circle of Transit Development and City Congestion?" *National Municipal Review,* June 1926, page 324; Henry M. Brinckerhoff, "Rapid Transit: A Vital Element in Metropolitan Transportation," *Electric Railway Journal,* September 26, 1925, page 503.

109. *Proceedings of the Nineteenth Annual Convention of the National Association of Building Owners and Managers: 1926,* pages 271–273; *Proceedings of the Twentieth Annual Convention of the National Association of Building Owners and Managers: 1927,* pages 194–197; *Proceedings of the Twenty-First Annual Convention of the National Association of Building Owners and Managers: 1928,* pages 198–217; *Proceedings of the Twenty-Second Annual Convention of the National Association of Building Owners and Managers: 1929,* pages 74–75; Corbett, "Up With the Skyscraper," pages 97–98; Harvey Wiley Corbett, "The Economic Height of Buildings as Illustrated by the Office Building," in U.S. Chamber of Commerce, *The Skyscraper,* pages 12–13; "The Skyscraper: Babel or Boon?" pages 1–2; Robins Fleming, "For and Against the Skyscraper," *Civil Engineering,* June 1935, pages 50–51.

110. "The Skyscraper: Babel or Boon?" pages 1–2; Corbett, "Up With the Skyscraper," page 98; Corbett, "Economic Height of Buildings," pages 12–13; *Proceedings of the Twenty-Second Annual Convention of the National Association of Building Owners and Managers: 1929,* pages 74–75; M. McCants, "Tall Buildings and Traffic Congestion," *Architect and Engineer,* December 1924, pages 103–108; E. J. McIlraith, "Traffic and Transportation Problems," *Annals of Real Estate Practice: 1928,* page 1114; Brinckerhoff, "Rapid Transit," page 503.

111. *Literary Digest*, December 11, 1926, pages 12–13; "The Skyscraper: Babel or Boon?" page 2; Curran, "Economic Height of Building," pages 18, 21; Curran, "What Height Limitations Can Do for New York Realty," pages 54, 56, 58; *New York Times*, October 31, 1926, November 17, 1930; Lewis Mumford, "Is the Skyscraper Tolerable?" *Architecture*, February 1927, pages 67–69; Andersen, "American Ikon," pages 205–220; Harland Bartholomew, "Discussion of the Urban Auto Problem," *National Municipal Review*, July 1920, pages 444–447.

112. Corbett, "Economic Height of Buildings," pages 10–12; "The Skyscraper: Babel or Boon?" pages 1–2; Corbett, "Up With the Skyscraper," pages 100–101; *Proceedings of the Twentieth Annual Convention of the National Association of Building Owners and Managers: 1927*, pages 182, 196; *Proceedings of the Twenty-First Annual Convention of the National Association of Building Owners and Managers: 1928*, pages 121–125; McIlraith, "Traffic and Transportation Problems," pages 1109–1111, 1118.

113. Clark, "Determining the Economic Height of Modern Office Buildings," pages 826–827. See also Thomas Adams, "Skyscrapers and Spaciousness," *American City*, March 1930, pages 89–91; Thomas Adams, "Limiting the Size of Buildings," *Civil Engineering*, October 1932, pages 642–646; R. L. Duffus, "The Vertical City," *New Republic*, July 3, 1929, pages 168–172.

114. *Literary Digest*, December 11, 1926, page 13; *[New York] Real Estate Record and Builders' Guide*, December 25, 1927, page 7, August 4, 1928, page 5; Raymond M. Hood, "A City Under a Single Roof," *Nation's Business*, November 1929, page 206.

115. Weiss, "Density and Intervention," page 68; *American City*, September 1929, page 130; *Literary Digest*, September 28, 1929, page 29; *Report of the [New York City] Heights of Buildings Commission*, pages 15–16; *National Real Estate Journal*, September 16, 1929, page 65; *Engineering News-Record*, August 1, 1929, page 170; Weiss, "Skyscraper Zoning," page 208; "The Skyscraper: Babel or Boon?" page 1; Corbett, "Up With the Skyscraper," page 97; *Housing*, March 1931, pages 47–51.

116. Weiss, "Density and Intervention," pages 59–61, 68; *Literary Digest*, September 28, 1929, page 29; *American City*, August 1929, page 130, November 1929, page 5.

117. St. Louis City Plan Commission, *Problems of St. Louis* (St. Louis, 1917), page 20; "Subsurface Terminal for Los Angeles," *Electric Railway Journal*, January 31, 1925, pages 179–180; *Proceedings of the Seventeenth Annual Convention of the National Association of Building Owners and Managers: 1924*, pages 45–46, 641–642; *Proceedings of the Twenty-First Annual Convention of the National Association of Building Owners and Managers: 1928*, pages 88–100; George R. LeBaron, "Specializing in Central Business Property," *National Real Estate Journal*, November 19, 1923, pages 21–22; W. C. Clark, "Causes of Obsolescence," ibid., July 1925, pages 26–27.

118. Earle Shultz, "The Office Building and the City," *Architectural Forum*, September 1924, page 141; *Proceedings of the Seventeenth Annual Convention of the National Association of Building Owners and Managers: 1924*, pages 45–56; *Proceedings of the Twenty-First Annual Convention of the National Association of Building Owners and Managers: 1928*, pages 88–100; Clark, "Causes of Obsolescence," pages 26–29; N. C. Soule, "What Causes Shifting Values in Business Districts?" *National Real Estate Journal*, October 14, 1929, pages 34–38.

119. *Proceedings of the Twenty-First Annual Convention of the National Association of Building Owners and Managers: 1928*, page 93; *American Architect and Building News*, July 13, 1901, page 13; *National Real Estate Journal*, September 16, 1929, page 65.

Chapter 4: The Central Business District

1. Ernest W. Burgess, "The Growth of the City: An Introduction to a Research Project," in Robert E. Park, Ernest W. Burgess, and Roderick D. McKenzie, *The City* (Chicago, 1966), pages 47–62. See also Howard J. Nelson, "The Form and Structure of Cities: Urban Growth Patterns," in Larry S. Bourne, ed., *Internal Structure of the City: Reading on Space and Environment* (New York, 1971), page 78.

2. *Baltimore Sun*, February 8, 1904; Newark City Plan Commission, *City Planning for Newark* (Newark, 1913), plan facing page 1; *Report of the Chicago Traction and Subway Commission* (Chicago, 1916), page 64; Kelker, De Leuw, *Report and Recommendations on a Comprehensive Rapid Transit Plan for the City and County of Los Angeles* (Chicago, 1925), page 35; McClellan & Junkersfeld, *Report on Transportation in the Milwaukee Metropolitan District to the Transportation Survey Committee of Milwaukee* (1928), volume 1, page 26; Miller McClintock, *A Report on the Street Traffic Control Problem of the City of Boston* (Boston, 1928), page 154; H. Morton Bodfish, "Changes in the Central Business District of a Growing City," *National Real Estate Journal*, October 28, 1926, pages 17–19.

3. Bion J. Arnold, *Report on the Pittsburgh Transportation Problem* (Pittsburgh, 1910), page 49; *Proceedings of the Tenth National Conference on City Planning: 1918*, page 26; *Electric Railway Journal*, November 14, 1908, page 1375; McClellan & Junkersfeld, *Transportation in the Milwaukee Metropolitan District*, volume 1, pages 25–27.

4. Bodfish, "Changes in the Central Business District," page 17. See also Edgar M. Horwood and Ronald R. Boyce, *Studies of the Central Business District and Urban Freeway Development* (Seattle, 1959), pages 9–14.

5. *Electric Railway Journal*, August 7, 1909, page 212; *Report of the Rapid Transit Commission to the Massachusetts Legislature. April 5, 1892* (Boston, 1892), page 11; *Boston Evening Transcript*, January 8, 1915; *Chicago Commerce*, September 1, 1923, page 28; Mason Case, "Development of the Outlying Business District and Its Effect on Downtown Realty Values," *Annals of Real Estate Practice: 1930*, pages 65–67; Burgess, "The Growth of the City," page 52.

6. Burgess, "The Growth of the City," page 52.

7. Homer Hoyt, *One Hundred Years of Land Values in Chicago* (Chicago, 1933), page 336; U.S. Bureau of the Census, *Fifteenth Census of the United States: 1930. Metropolitan Districts: Population and Area* (Washington, D.C., 1932), page 10–13; Donald M. Baker, *A Rapid Transit System for Los Angeles, California* (1933), page 37-e; Donald H. Davenport, *The Retail Shopping and Financial Districts of New York and Its Environs* (New York, 1927), pages 18–19.

8. Miller McClintock, "Street Traffic and Rental Values," *Proceedings of the Nineteenth Annual Convention of the National Association of Building Owners and Managers: 1926*, page 238; *Proceedings of the Twentieth Annual Convention of the National Association of Building Owners and Managers: 1927*, page 185; William Leach, *Land of Desire: Merchants, Power, and the Rise of a New American Culture* (New York, 1993), pages 22–23, 114–115, 280–281; Paul Gleye, *The Architecture of Los Angeles* (Los Angeles, 1981), page 218; Thomas Adams, "Foreword," in Robert Murray Haig, *Major Economic Factors in Metropolitan Growth and Arrangement* (New York, 1928), page 4.

9. Edward H. Bennett, *The Chicago Business District and the Subway Question* (1926), page 10; Burgess, "The Growth of the City," page 52; Robert H. Whitten, "Compari-

son of the New York and Paris Subway Systems," *Electric Railway Journal*, December 11, 1909, pages 1178–1184; Haig, *Major Economic Factors*, pages 33–36; Leach, *Land of Desire*, page 19; Harvey Warren Zorbaugh, *The Gold Coast and the Slum: A Sociological Study of Chicago's Near North Side* (Chicago, 1929), page 2.

10. McClintock, *Street Traffic Control Problem of the City of Boston*, page 76; E. R. Kinsey and C. S. Smith, *Rapid Transit for St. Louis* (St. Louis, 1926), page 141; *Proceedings of the American Society of Civil Engineers*, September 1926, page 1464; McClellan & Junkersfeld, *Transportation in the Milwaukee Metropolitan District*, volume 2, page 48; Kelker, De Leuw, *Rapid Transit for Los Angeles*, pages 36–37; Miller McClintock, *A Report on the Street Traffic Control Problem in San Francisco* (San Francisco, 1927), page 17; Miller McClintock, *Report and Recommendations on the Metropolitan [Chicago] Street Traffic Survey* (Chicago, 1926), page 15; R. D. McKenzie, *The Metropolitan Community* (New York, 1933), pages 283–284; Harold M. Lewis, *Transit and Transportation* (New York, 1928), page 39; Baker, *Rapid Transit System for Los Angeles*, page 45.

11. Emil Swensson, *Report [to the] Pennsylvania State Railroad Commission in the Matter of the Complaint of the City of Pittsburgh Against Pittsburgh Railways Company* (Pittsburgh, 1910), page 5; I. K. Rolph, *The Location Structure of Retail Trade Based Upon a Study of Baltimore* (Washington, D.C., 1933), page 6; Christopher Silver, *Twentieth Century Richmond: Planning, Politics, and Race* (Knoxville, 1984), pages 27–29; Blaine A. Brownell, *The Urban Ethos of the South, 1920–1930* (Baton Rouge, 1975), pages 33–34; John C. Schneider, "Skid Row as an Urban Neighborhood, 1880–1960," in Jon Erickson and Charles Wilhelm, eds., *Housing the Homeless* (New Brunswick, 1986), pages 169–170; Paul Groth, *Living Downtown: The History of Residential Hotels in the United States* (Berkeley, 1994), chapters 2–5; Mark Jefferson, "A Hopeful View of the Urban Problem," *Atlantic Monthly*, August 1913, page 358.

12. *[New York] Real Estate Record and Builders' Guide*, September 18, 1915, page 476; Mark Jefferson, "The Real New York," *Bulletin of the American Geographical Society*, October 1911, pages 737–740; *Baltimore Sun*, December 17, 1928. See also Amos H. Hawley, *The Changing Shape of Metropolitan America: Deconcentration Since 1920* (Glencoe, Illinois, 1956), chapter 2, and Kenneth A. Jackson, *The Crabgrass Frontier: The Suburbanization of the United States* (New York, 1985), chapter 10.

13. Diomede Carito, *In the Land of Washington: My Impressions of the North-American Psyche* (Naples, 1913), pages 97–98; Alan Raleigh, *The Real America* (London, 1913), page 95; Paul H. B. D'Estournelles De Constant, *America and Her Problems* (New York, 1915), page 238; Geo. A. Birmingham, *Connaught to Chicago* (London, 1914), pages 54–55.

14. Leach, *Land of Desire*, pages 46–49, 333–334, 338–344; Rupert Brooke, *Letters from America* (New York, 1916), pages 29–34; Raleigh, *The Real America*, pages 46–47; Bayrd Still, *Mirror for Gotham: New York as Seen by Contemporaries from Dutch Days to the Present* (New York, 1956), page 260.

15. *Final Report [of the New York City] Commission on Building Districts and Restrictions* (New York, 1916), pages 86–88, 111–112, 123–127, 190–194; Scott Bottles, *Los Angeles and the Automobile: The Making of the Modern City* (Berkeley, 1987), pages 55–56, 71–74; J. B. Atkins, "America After Thirty Years," *Living Age*, July 1928, page 1044; R. F. Kelker, Jr., *Report and Recommendations on a Physical Plan for a Unified Transportation System for the City of Chicago* (1923), page 41. See also Clay McShane, *Down the Asphalt Path: The Automobile and the American City* (New York, 1994), pages 193–194.

16. Henry M. Brinckerhoff, "Functions of Rapid Transit Lines in Cities," *Engineering News-Record*, December 23, 1920, page 1235; U.S. Works Progress Administration, *Traffic Survey Data on the City of St. Louis* (ca. 1938); McShane, *Down the Asphalt Path*, page 122.

17. Hoyt, *One Hundred Years of Land Values*, pages 297–298, 336–337; J. Rowland Bibbins, "The Economic Spiral: The Problem of Concentrated Cubage in Our Cities," *City Planning*, July 1927, page 207; Kinsey and Smith, *Rapid Transit for St. Louis*, page 129; Baker, *Rapid Transit System for Los Angeles*, page 41; *Cincinnati Enquirer*, March 22, 1919; Geo. F. Washburn to Patrick O'Hearn, May 10, 1916, in *Hearings Before [the Boston] Commission on Height of Buildings* (Boston, 1916), following page 233.

18. Hoyt, *One Hundred Years of Land Values*, pages 345–346; "Increase in Los Angeles Down-Town Land Values 1907–1926," *Eberle & Riggleman Economic Service Weekly Letter*, November 22, 1926, pages 265–268; *[New York] Real Estate Record and Builders' Guide*, January 13, 1883, pages 14–15; Paul H. Nystrom, *The Economics of Retailing* (New York, 1915), pages 138–139; Burgess, "The Growth of the City," page 52.

19. Edward Ewing Pratt, *Industrial Causes of Congestion of Population in New York City* (New York), page 42; Allen R. Pred, "The Intrametropolitan Location of American Manufacturing," in Bourne, ed., *Internal Structure*, pages 384–385; Charles C. Colby, "Centrifugal and Centripetal Forces in Urban Geography," *Annals of the Association of American Geographers*, March 1933, pages 5–6; Graham Romeyn Taylor, *Satellite Cities: A Study of Industrial Suburbs* (New York, 1915), pages 1–6, 92–94; *Survey*, March 4, 1911, pages 898–899; Donald F. Davis, "The City Remodelled: The Limits of Automotive Industry Leadership in Detroit, 1910–1929," *Histoire Sociale/Social History*, November 1980, pages 455–456; Walter C. K. Baumgarten, "The Location and Planning of Industrial Areas," *City Planning*, April 1933, pages 63–71; Haig, *Major Economic Factors*, pages 33–34.

20. Pred, "American Manufacturing," pages 384–386; Hoyt, *One Hundred Years of Land Values*, pages 317–320; Taylor, *Satellite Cities*, pages 6, 129–134; Colby, "Centrifugal and Centripetal Forces," pages 4–11; *Survey*, March 4, 1911, pages 898–899; *[New York] Real Estate Record and Builders' Guide*, April 22, 1911, page 773; *Report of the New York City Commission on Congestion of Population* (New York, 1911), pages 122–126; John D. Fairfield, *The Mysteries of the Great City: The Politics of Urban Design, 1877–1937* (Columbus, Ohio, 1993), page 58.

21. *[New York] Real Estate Record and Builders' Guide*, April 28, 1883, page 169, March 9, 1907, page 482, July 20, 1907, page 92; Charles K. Mohler, *Report on Passenger Subway and Elevated Railroad Development in Chicago* (Chicago, 1912), page 44; Fairfield, *Mysteries of the Great City*, pages 150–152; *Proceedings of the Fifteenth National Conference on City Planning: 1923*, pages 60–61, 109–110; *Architectural Forum*, February 1920, page 94.

22. Moses King, *King's Handbook of New York City* (Boston, 1892), pages 273–274, 276–277, 289; Walter Muir Whitehill, *Museum of Fine Arts Boston: A Centennial History* (Cambridge, 1970), volume 1, pages 1–15; Walter Muir Whitehill, *Boston Public Library: A Centennial History* (Cambridge, 1956), chapters 4 and 7; *Museum News*, July 1, 1926, page 1, November 1, 1927, page 1, February 1, 1928, page 1; M. A. DeWolfe Howe, *The Boston Symphony Orchestra 1881–1931* (Boston, 1931), pages 94–115; Daniel L. Bluestone, "Detroit's City Beautiful and the Problem of Commerce," *Journal of the Society of Architectural Historians*, September 1988, page 246; Montgomery

Schuyler, "The Building of Pittsburgh: Part III. A Real Civic Center," *Architectural Record*, September 1911, pages 229–243; Helen Lefkowitz Horowitz, *Culture and the City: Cultural Philanthropy in Chicago from the 1880s to 1917* (Lexington, Kentucky, 1976), pages 116–117.

23. *Museum News*, November 1, 1927, page 1, February 1, 1928, page 1; Bluestone, "Detroit's City Beautiful," pages 245–262; Whitehill, *Museum of Fine Arts*, volume 1, pages 97–99; Horowitz, *Culture and the City*, page 113; *Hartford Daily Times*, April 20, 1905; *Plan of Seattle: Report of the Municipal Plans Commission Submitting Report of Virgil G. Bogue, Engineer* (Seattle, 1911), page 46; *American Architect and Building News*, November 19, 1904, page 64; Lawrence W. Levine, *Highbrow/Lowbrow: The Emergence of Cultural Hierarchy in America* (Cambridge, 1988), pages 172–173.

24. Horowitz, *Culture and the City*, page 117; Bluestone, "Detroit's City Beautiful," page 262.

25. I. K. Rolph, *Vehicular Traffic Congestion and Retail Trade* (Washington, D.C., 1926), page 19. See also *Proceedings of the American Society of Civil Engineers*, September 1926, page 1454; Miller McClintock, "Street Traffic Problems in Central Business Districts," *Proceedings of the Twenty-Second Annual Convention of the National Association of Building Owners and Managers: 1929*, page 73; McClintock, *Street Traffic Control Problem in San Francisco*, page 84; Kinsey and Smith, *Rapid Transit for St. Louis*, page 126; Howard L. Preston, *Automobile Age Atlanta: The Making of a Southern Metropolis 1900–1935* (Athens, Georgia, 1979), page 133.

26. Davenport, *The Retail Shopping and Financial Districts*, pages 34–54; Haig, *Major Economic Factors*, page 37; Cuthbert E. Reeves, *The Valuation of Business Lots in Downtown Los Angeles* (Los Angeles, 1932), page 19; McClintock, *Street Traffic Control Problem in San Francisco*, page 86; Morton Bodfish and Ralph J. Lueders, "Forces of Decentralization in Chicago," *Savings and Homeownership*, July 1953.

27. William K. Bowden and Ralph Cassady, Jr., "Decentralization of Retail Trade in the Metropolitan Market Area," *Journal of Marketing*, January 1941, pages 270–275; Haig, *Major Economic Factors*, page 103; John A. Miller, Jr., "Increasing the Efficiency of Passenger Traffic in City Streets," *Proceedings of the American Society of Civil Engineers*, May 1926, pages 830–831; Rolph, *The Location Structure of Retail Trade*, pages 4–6; Leach, *Land of Desire*, pages 272–275; Hoyt, *One Hundred Years of Land Values*, pages 225–226; Warren Thompson, "The Future of the Large City," *American Mercury*, July 1930, pages 332–333.

28. P. A. O'Connell, "Relation of Retail Distribution to Real Estate Values," *Bulletin of the National Retail Dry Goods Association*, January 1932, pages 15–16; Edwin R. Dibrell, "The Effects of Branch Store Expansion," ibid., October 1946, page 54; Leach, *Land of Desire*, pages 279–280; Richard Longstreth, *City Center to Regional Mall: Architecture, the Automobile, and Retailing in Los Angeles, 1920–1950* (Cambridge, 1997), pages 84–85; *Proceedings of the Twelfth Annual Convention [of the] Retail Delivery Association of the National Retail Dry Goods Association: 1928*, page 213.

29. Robert A. M. Stern, Gregory Gilmartin, and Thomas Mellins, *New York, 1930: Architecture and Urbanism Between the Two World Wars* (New York, 1987), pages 244–264; Douglas Gommery, *Shared Pleasure: A History of Movie Presentation in the United States* (Madison, 1992), pages 18–46; Reeves, *Valuation of Business Lots*, page 19; McClintock, *Street Traffic Control Problem in San Francisco*, page 86; William M. Tanney, "Depreciation and Obsolescence in Theatres," *Appraisal Journal*, April 1939, pages

152–153; McClellan & Junkersfeld, *Transportation in the Milwaukee Metropolitan District*, volume 2, page 21.

30. Leach, *Land of Desire*, pages 273–274, 280–281; Baker, *Rapid Transit System for Los Angeles*, page 37-d; Hoyt, *One Hundred Years of Land Values*, pages 225–227, 249–255, 261, 336–337.

31. Frederick Law Olmsted, Harland Bartholomew, and Charles H. Cheney, *A Major Traffic Street Plan for Los Angeles* (Los Angeles, 1924), page 18; Bibbins, "The Economic Spiral," page 100; *Proceedings of the Tenth Annual Convention [of the] National Association of Building Owners and Managers: 1917*, page 112; McClellan & Junkersfeld, *Transportation in the Milwaukee Metropolitan District*, volume 1, pages 25–26; *Proceedings of the Federal Electric Railways Commission* (Washington, D.C., 1920), volume 2, pages 1180–1185; McClintock, *Street Traffic Control Problem in San Francisco*, page 83; McClintock, *Street Traffic Control Problem of the City of Boston*, page 125; *Los Angeles Times*, November 1, 1924; Miller, "Passenger Traffic in City Streets," pages 831–832.

32. *[First] Conference on the Rapid Transit Question Called by the [Los Angeles] Board of City Planning Commissioners* (1930), page 43; McClintock, *Street Traffic Control Problem in San Francisco*, page 84; Gordon Whitnall, "Relation of Downtown Commercial Districts to Outlying Business Districts," *Pacific Municipalities*, April 1928, page 131; *New York Times*, November 17, 1930; Rolph, *Vehicular Traffic Congestion*, page 3.

33. "Ultimate Remedies for the Traffic Problem," *American City*, July 1929, page 135; Edward T. Hartman, "To Prevent the Hardening of Street Arteries," ibid., July 1925, page 10; "Congested Traffic," *New Republic*, November 28, 1928, pages 30–31; Mark Stewart Foster, "The Decentralization of Los Angeles During the 1920's" (Ph.D. diss., University of Southern California, 1971), pages 149–150; Mark S. Foster, *From Streetcar to Superhighway: American City Planners and Urban Transportation* (Philadelphia, 1981), pages 70–73; Harold S. Buttenheim, "The Problem of the Standing Vehicle," *Annals of the American Academy of Political and Social Science*, September 1927, pages 154–155; Harland Bartholomew, "Discussion of the Urban Auto Problem," *National Municipal Review*, July 1920, pages 445–446.

34. Tomaz F. Deuther, *Local Transportation* (Chicago, 1924), pages 77–80. See also Paul Barrett, *The Automobile and Urban Transit: The Formation of Public Policy in Chicago, 1900–1930* (Philadelphia, 1983), pages 101–102.

35. *Proceedings of the American Electric Railway Association: 1930*, pages 131–135; McClintock, "Street Traffic Problems in Central Business Districts," pages 72–73; Chicago Real Estate Board Zoning Committee, *Studies on Building Height Limitations in Large Cities* (Chicago, 1922), page 188; D. Wendell Beggs, "How Community Shopping Centers Affect Central Business Property," *National Real Estate Journal*, December 8, 1930, pages 29–30; *Literary Digest*, December 11, 1926, page 13.

36. Chicago Real Estate Board Zoning Committee, *Studies on Building Height Limitations*, pages 184–187; *[First] Conference on the Rapid Transit Question*, page 40; *Proceedings of the American Electric Railway Association: 1930*, pages 133–134; McClintock, "Street Traffic and Rental Values," page 236; Beggs, "Community Shopping Centers," page 30; McClintock, "Street Traffic Problems in Central Business Districts," page 72; Harvey Wiley Corbett, "The Economic Height of Buildings as Illustrated by the Office Building," in U.S. Chamber of Commerce, *Economic Height of Buildings: The Skyscraper Attacked and Defended* (Washington, D.C., 1927), page 10.

37. E. J. McIlraith, "Traffic and Transportation Problems," *Annals of Real Estate Practice: 1928*, pages 1110–1111; Olmsted, Bartholomew, and Cheney, *A Major Traffic Street Plan for Los Angeles*, page 18; *Proceedings of the American Electric Railway Association: 1930*, pages 131–132; Corbett, "Economic Height of Buildings," page 10; Chicago Real Estate Board Zoning Committee, *Studies on Building Height Limitations*, pages 185–186; McClintock, "Street Traffic and Rental Values," pages 259–260.

38. *Report of the Transportation Survey Commission of the City of St. Louis* (1930), page 108; McIlraith, "Traffic and Transportation Problems," pages 1109–1110; *Report of the New York City Commission on Congestion of Population*, page 149; Chicago Real Estate Board Zoning Committee, *Studies on Building Height Limitations*, page 187; Kinsey and Smith, *Rapid Transit for St. Louis*, page 127; *Literary Digest*, December 11, 1926, page 13.

39. *Proceedings of the American Electric Railway Association: 1930*, pages 131–135; Case, "Development of the Outlying Business District," page 75; George R. LeBaron, "Specializing in Central Business Property," *National Real Estate Journal*, November 19, 1923, pages 21–22.

40. Olmsted, Bartholomew, and Cheney, *A Major Traffic Street Plan for Los Angeles*, page 18; Haig, *Major Economic Factors*, pages 42–43; McKenzie, *The Metropolitan Community*, page 71; Charles Mulford Robinson, *The Width and Arrangement of Streets: A Study in Town Planning* (New York, 1911), page 20.

41. *[First] Conference on the Rapid Transit Question*, pages 40–41; *Chicago Commerce*, March 31, 1911, pages 24–25; J. C. Nichols, "The Planning and Control of Outlying Shopping Centers," *Journal of Land and Public Utility Economics*, January 1926, pages 17–22.

42. Foster, *From Streetcar to Superhighway*, pages 69–73.

43. Ralph E. Heilman, "The Chicago Subway Problem," *Journal of Political Economy*, December 1914, page 998; *Report of the [Chicago] Subway Advisory Commission*, pages 61–63; C. D. Pollock, *Report of the Seattle Traffic Research Commission* (1928), pages 634D10–634D11.

44. *Architectural Forum*, July 1910, pages 71–72; Foster, "The Decentralization of Los Angeles," page 246; George E. Kessler, "Cincinnati's Problem of Centralization and Decentralization," *Proceedings of the Twelfth National Conference on City Planning: 1920*, page 33; Chicago Real Estate Board Zoning Committee, *Studies on Building Height Limitations*, page 173; *[New York] Real Estate Record and Builders' Guide*, March 23, 1912, pages 6–7; Brinckerhoff, "Functions of Rapid Transit Lines in Cities," page 1236; McClintock, "Street Traffic and Rental Values," page 237; Whitnall, "Relation of Downtown Commercial Districts to Outlying Business Districts," page 131; Herbert B. Dorau and Albert G. Hinman, *Urban Land Economics* (New York, 1928), page 62.

45. *For the Good of San Francisco: 20 Years of Civic Service by the Down Town Association* (1927), pages 9–17; *Skyscraper Management*, May 1939, page 6; Los Angeles Central Business District Association, *A Quarter Century of Activities, 1924–1949* (1949), page 6; *Report of the [Chicago] Subway Advisory Commission*, pages 60–61; *Chicago Commerce*, March 31, 1911, page 25.

46. *For the Good of San Francisco*, pages 12–13; *Skyscraper Management*, May 1939, page 16; *New York Times*, February 17, 1918; *Chicago Commerce*, April 7, 1911, pages 4–5, June 30, 1911, pages 19–20, September 29, 1911, pages 8–10, May 9, 1913, pages 16–18, September 5, 1913, page 30, July 24, 1914, pages 40–41; Barrett, *The Automobile and Urban Transit*, pages 101–102, 187–190.

47. *Hearings Before the [Boston] Commission on Height of Buildings*, pages 42–45, 159–163, 221–223.

48. Marc A. Weiss, *The Rise of the Community Builders: The American Real Estate Industry and Urban Land Planning* (New York, 1987), pages 86–96. See also *Los Angeles Times*, August 6, 1920.

49. *Los Angeles Examiner*, March 28, 1909; William May Garland, "Strong Stand Urged on Wilshire Boulevard," *Los Angeles Realtor*, July 1923, page 12; *Los Angeles Times*, October 30, November 1/7, 1924; Weiss, *The Rise of the Community Builders*, page 100; Foster, "The Decentralization of Los Angeles," pages 248–249; Robert M. Fogelson, *The Fragmented Metropolis: Los Angeles, 1850–1930* (Cambridge, 1967), page 261.

50. *Los Angeles Times*, April 6/8/11/26/28/29, 1926; J. F. Sartori to Edward A. Dickson, ca. 1925; James R. Martin to Edward A. Dickson, March 23, 1926, Edward A. Dickson papers, Special Collections Division, University of California Library, Los Angeles; Weiss, *The Rise of the Community Builders*, page 100; Foster, "Decentralization of Los Angeles," pages 249–250; Fogelson, *The Fragmented Metropolis*, pages 261–262.

51. *Los Angeles Times*, February 19, March 9, April 13/17/25, June 27, 1919, June 1/3/6/7, 1923; Fogelson, *The Fragmented Metropolis*, pages 262–264; Robert Gottlieb and Irene Wolt, *Thinking Big: The Story of the* Los Angeles Times, *Its Publishers, and Their Influence on Southern California* (New York, 1977), pages 152–153. See also *Chicago Tribune*, October 13, 1891.

52. *Cincinnati Enquirer*, February 4, March 6/8/15, 1919.

53. Ibid., March 15/16/18/19/20/21/22/27, 1919.

54. Ibid., March 19/20/21/22/26/27/28/29, 1919.

55. *Baltimore Sun*, June 14, 1925.

56. *[New York] Real Estate Record and Builders' Guide*, February 11, 1905, page 297, December 18, 1909, page 1087, March 20, 1915, page 460, September 8, 1917, page 300, March 23, 1918, page 7, August 3, 1918, page 124, April 16, 1921, pages 485–486, July 28, 1923, pages 101–102.

57. *[New York] Real Estate Record and Builders' Guide*, January 26, 1907, page 174; Burgess, "The Growth of the City," page 52; George A. Damon, "Relation of the Motor Bus to Other Methods of Transportation," *Proceedings of the Sixteenth National Conference on City Planning: 1924*, pages 87–88; *[First] Conference on the Rapid Transit Question*, page 50; Brownell, *Urban Ethos in the South*, pages 66–69.

58. Carol Willis, "Forgotten Episodes in American Architecture: The Titan City," *Skyline*, October 1982, page 26. See also Raymond M. Hood, "A City Under a Single Roof," *Nation's Business*, November 1929, pages 19–20, 206; George W. Gray, "The Future of the Skyscraper," *New York Times Magazine*, September 13, 1931, pages 1–2, 12.

59. Lewis Mumford, "The Sacred City," *New Republic*, January 27, 1926, pages 270–271. See also Whitnall, "Relation of Downtown Commercial Districts to Outlying Business Districts," pages 127–132; Fogelson, *The Fragmented Metropolis*, pages 161–163.

60. *Baltimore Sun*, June 14, 1925; Charles K. Mohler, "Public Utility Regulation by Los Angeles," *Annals of the American Academy of Political and Social Science*, May 1914, pages 116–117; Francis Lee Stuart, "Solving Manhattan's Transportation Problem," *Civil Engineer*, October 1930, page 9; Zorbaugh, *The Gold Coast and the Slum*, page 40; California Railroad Commission, *Application 1424: Reporter's Transcript* (1915), volume 2, pages 1163–1165, California Public Utilities Commission files, Sacramento.

Chapter 5: The Specter of Decentralization

1. Walter H. Blucher, "The Economics of the Parking Lot," *Planners' Journal*, September–October 1936, pages 113–119; L. V. Echols, "Industry Retains Gains in Office Occupancy," *Skyscraper Management*, June 1938, page 7; Walter R. Kuehnle, "Central Business District Paradox," *Appraisal Journal*, January 1935, pages 138–143; Nathan L. Smith, "Baltimore's Parking Problem and How It Can Be Solved," *Proceedings [of the] Seventeenth Annual Meeting [of the] Institute of Traffic Engineers: 1946*, page 9.

2. Everett B. Murray, "Future Control of Office Building Production," *Proceedings of the Twenty-Seventh Annual Convention of the National Association of Building Owners and Managers: 1934*, pages 173–180; *National Real Estate Journal*, December 9, 1929, page 38; Geo. W. Klein and Leo G. Varty, "January Survey Shows 27.57% Average Office Vacancy," *Skyscraper Management*, February 1934, pages 8–9; Homer Hoyt, *One Hundred Years of Land Values in Chicago* (Chicago, 1933), pages 345–347.

3. Malcolm P. McNair, "Department Store Operating Problems," *Bulletin of the National Dry Goods Association*, February 1933, pages 25–27, 88; Malcolm P. McNair, "1932 Department Store Expense Rise to a New Peak," ibid., June 1933, pages 30–33, 107–108; Edward C. Romine, "Are We Justified in Being Optimistic Regarding Business in 1932?" ibid., January 1932, pages 11–15; William Leach, *Land of Desire: Merchants, Power, and the Rise of a New American Culture* (New York, 1993), pages 273–274; Horwath & Horwath, *Hotel Operations in 1929*, pages 12, 22–23; *Hotel Management*, March 1934, page 198.

4. George W. Gray, "The Future of the Skyscraper," *New York Times Magazine*, September 13, 1931, pages 1–2.

5. Hoyt, *One Hundred Years of Land Values*, pages 265–276, 344–347, 399; Morton Bodfish and Ralph J. Lueders, "Forces of Decentralization in Chicago," *Savings and Homeownership*, July 1953.

6. Earle Shultz and Walter Simmons, *Offices in the Sky* (Indianapolis, 1959), pages 153–163; *Buildings and Building Management*, February 23, 1931, page 68; Murray, "Office Building Production," page 175; Leach, *Land of Desire*, pages 273–274, 279–281; Robert A. M. Stern, Gregory Gilmartin, and Thomas Mellins, *New York, 1930: Architecture and Urbanism Between the Two World Wars* (New York, 1987), pages 201–223.

7. U.S. Department of Commerce, *Historical Statistics of the United States: Colonial Times to 1970* (Washington, D.C., 1975), part 1, pages 135, 224, part 2, pages 667, 844, 850; Roy J. Johnson, "Commercial Occupancy Hits All-Time High," *Skyscraper Management*, June 1945, pages 6–9; *Horwath Hotel Accountant*, February 1944, pages 6–7, December 1944, page 2; Horwath & Horwath, *Hotel Operations in 1943*, page 4.

8. New York Regional Plan Association, *Information Bulletin No. 74* (October 1949), pages 2–3; D. Grant Mickle, "Effect of Urban Decentralization upon Traffic Problems," *Proceedings [of the] Twelfth Annual Meeting [of the] Institute of Traffic Engineers: 1941*, page 66; Chicago Department of Streets and Electricity, Bureau of Street Traffic, "Cordon Count Data on the Central Business District" (1949), page 2; Park Martin, *Redevelopment of Pittsburgh's Golden Triangle* (1954); San Francisco Department of City Planning, "Daily Trips in San Francisco" (1955), table 6; Harland Bartholomew and Associates, *A Report on Off-Street Parking and Traffic Control in the [Oakland] Central Business District and Three Outlying Centers* (St. Louis, 1947), page 60.

9. Coverdale & Colpitts, *Report to the Los Angeles Metropolitan Transit Authority on a Monorail Rapid Transit Line for Los Angeles* (1954), page 62.

10. Coverdale & Colpitts, *Report to the Los Angeles Metropolitan Transit Authority*, page 59; Murray D. Dessel, "Central Business Districts and Their Metropolitan Areas: A Summary of Geographic Shifts in Retail Sales Growth, 1948–1954," U.S. Department of Commerce, *Area Trend Series, No. 1*, November 1957, page 11; Richard P. Doherty, "Decentralization of Retail Trade in Boston," *Journal of Marketing*, January 1942, pages 281–286; Regional Plan Association, *The Economic Status of the New York Metropolitan Region in 1944* (New York, 1944), pages 50–55; Samuel C. McMillan, "Decentralization of Retail Trade," *Traffic Quarterly*, April 1954, pages 215–216.

11. Ralph Cassady, Jr., and W. K. Bowden, "Shifting Retail Trade Within the Los Angeles Metropolitan Market," *Journal of Marketing*, April 1944, pages 401–403; McNair, "Department Store Operating Problems," pages 26–27; Carl N. Schmalz, "Department Store Problems the Next Five Years and the Next Twenty-Five," *Proceedings [of the] 20th Annual Convention [of the] Controllers' Congress of the National Retail Dry Goods Association: 1939*, pages 11–12; Edwin R. Dibrell, "The Effects of Branch Store Expansion," *Bulletin of the National Retail Dry Goods Association*, April 1946, pages 16–17, 54–56; New York Regional Plan Association, *Regional Plan Bulletin Number 78*, December 1951, pages 4–5; U.S. Census Bureau, *Geographic Distribution of Retail Trade in Chicago, Illinois* (Washington, D.C., 1937), page 27.

12. *Architectural Forum*, January 1938, page 14; Homer Hoyt, "Downtown Needs Stabilizing Factors," *Real Estate*, July 26, 1941, page 11; "Traffic Jams Business Out," *Architectural Forum*, January 1940, pages 64–65; Huber Earle Smutz, "Street and Off-Street Parking" (1941), page 6.

13. Blucher, "The Economics of the Parking Lot," page 119; "Traffic Jams Business Out," pages 64–65; "Rebuilding the Cities," *Business Week*, July 6, 1940, page 36.

14. Louis C. Wagner, "Economic Relationships of Parking to Business in Seattle Metropolitan Area," in *Highway Research Board: Special Report 11: Parking as a Factor in Business* (Washington, D.C., 1953), page 65; U.S. Chamber of Commerce, *Your City Is Your Business: A Complete Report on the Businessmen's Conference on Urban Problems* (Washington, D.C., 1947), pages 192–193; Eugene Whitmore, "Why Downtown Shopping Declines," *American Business*, August 1940, page 19; Gordon Whitnall, "Urban Disintegration and the Future of Land Investments," *Journal of Land and Public Utility Economics*, November 1941, pages 440–442.

15. Hoyt, *One Hundred Years of Land Values*, pages 345–346; *Final Report [of the New York City] Commission on Building Districts and Restrictions* (New York, 1916), pages 112–113.

16. Whitmore, "Why Downtown Shopping Declines," pages 18–21; American Automobile Association, Safety and Traffic Engineering Department, "Parking and Terminal Facilities: Summary of Questionnaire" (1940), pages 37–38; *National Real Estate Journal*, February 1940, page 13.

17. Mason Case, "Development of the Outlying Business District and Its Effect on Downtown Realty Values," *Annals of Real Estate Practice: 1930*, page 75.

18. R. F. Hewitt, "Decentralization and the Future of Central Business Districts," *Proceedings of the Twenty-Ninth Annual Convention of the National Association of Building Owners and Managers: 1936*, page 37; Whitmore, "Why Downtown Shopping Declines," pages 18–21, 41; John A. Miller, Jr., "Is the Downtown Shopping Area Doomed?" *Bulletin of the National Retail Dry Goods Association*, July 1935, page 24.

19. Shultz and Simmons, *Offices in the Sky,* page 225; Hewitt, "Decentralization and the Future of Central Business Districts," page 35; R. F. Hewitt, "Changing Condition," and John R. Fugard, "The Office Building of Today and Tomorrow," *Proceedings of the Thirty-First Annual Convention of the National Association of Building Owners and Managers: 1938,* pages 131–146; Leo J. Sheridan, "Future of Central Business Districts," George Richardson, "The Future of Central Business Districts," T. T. McCrosky, "Decentralization and Recentralization," and Philip W. Kniskern, "Offsetting the Ravages of Decentralization," *Proceedings of the Thirty-Fourth Annual Convention of the National Association of Building Owners and Managers: 1941,* pages 81–115.

20. *National Real Estate Journal,* February 1940, pages 13–17, June 1941, page 42.

21. Hewitt, "Changing Conditions," pages 132–133; A. A. Oles, "Let's Take a Look at Suburban Business Areas," *Skyscraper Management,* January 1935, page 12; Hewitt, "Decentralization of Central Business Districts," page 35; *Buildings and Building Management,* March 1940, page 21, September 1941, pages 59–60; Sheridan, "Future of Central Business Districts," pages 95–96.

22. Hewitt, "Changing Conditions," page 133; Hewitt, "Decentralization and the Future of Central Business Districts," page 35; Richardson, "Future of Central Business Districts," page 97; *Proceedings of the Thirty-First Annual Convention of the National Association of Building Owners and Managers: 1938,* page 142; Sheridan, "Future of Central Business Districts," pages 82–83, 88–89; Fugard, "The Office Building of Today and Tomorrow," page 144.

23. A. F. Schnell, "Business Property Obsolescence," *Skyscraper Management,* January 1935, page 9; Kniskern, "Offsetting the Ravages of Decentralization," page 114; *Proceedings of the Thirty-First Annual Convention of the National Association of Building Owners and Managers: 1938,* page 142; *Buildings and Building Management,* March 1940, page 21; Richardson, "Future of Central Business Districts," page 100; Hewitt, "Changing Conditions," pages 132–133.

24. Hewitt, "Decentralization and the Future of Central Business Districts," pages 37–39; Charles F. Palmer, "Centralization of Business," *Skyscraper Management,* February 1940, page 3; Shultz and Simmons, *Offices in the Sky,* page 229; *Proceedings of the Thirty-First Annual Convention of the National Association of Building Owners and Managers: 1938,* page 139; Oles, "Let's Take a Look at Suburban Business Areas," page 13; Kniskern, "Offsetting the Ravages of Decentralization," page 114.

25. Miller McClintock, "Street Traffic Problems in Central Business Districts," *Proceedings of the Twenty-Second Annual Convention of the National Association of Building Owners and Managers: 1929,* pages 72–73; *National Municipal Review,* January 1925, page 51; I. K. Rolph, *Vehicular Traffic Congestion and Retail Business* (Washington, D.C., 1926), pages 1–23; Hewitt, "Decentralization and the Future of Central Business Districts," pages 37–38; *Proceedings of the Thirty-First Annual Convention of the National Association of Building Owners and Managers: 1938,* pages 138–140; E. A. Tyler, "Reviving the Downtown District," *Skyscraper Management,* May 1943, page 10.

26. John A. Miller, "Cities on the Toboggan," *Transit Journal,* February 1941, pages 44–47. See also Homer Hoyt, "Effect of Decentralization upon the Office Building," *Proceedings of the Thirtieth Annual Convention of the National Association of Building Owners and Managers: 1937,* pages 113–115; *Proceedings of the Thirtieth Annual Convention of the National Association of Building Owners and Managers: 1937,* page 123; Miles

Colean, "The Public Moves Away," *Skyscraper Management*, August 1940, pages 3-4; Kniskern, "Offsetting the Ravages of Decentralization," page 110.

27. Joseph Laronge, "Are We Decentralizing?" *Buildings and Building Management*, December 1938, pages 20-21, 57-60.

28. Alan F. Schnell, "Is Decentralization the Word for It?" *Skyscraper Management*, March 1939, pages 10-11, 38; George J. Eberle, "The Business District," in George W. Robbins and L. Deming Tilton, eds., *Los Angeles: Preface to a Master Plan* (Los Angeles, 1941), pages 127-141.

29. Richardson, "Future of Central Business Districts," pages 101-102; *Proceedings of the Twenty-Ninth Annual Convention of the National Association of Building Owners and Managers: 1936*, page 42; Alan F. Schnell, "Downtown Development in the '40s," *Skyscraper Management*, May 1940, pages 7, 30; Kniskern, "Offsetting the Ravages of Decentralization," page 114; Hewitt, "Decentralization and the Future of Central Business Districts," pages 38-39; T. T. McCrosky, "Decentralization and Recentralization," *Proceedings of the Thirty-Fourth Annual Convention of the National Association of Building Owners and Managers: 1941*, pages 108-110; Palmer, "Centralization of Business," page 4; Colean, "The Public Moves Away," pages 30-31.

30. Carlton Schultz, "Factors in Decentralization," *Buildings and Building Management*, April 1940, page 31; McCrosky, "Decentralization and Recentralization," page 107; *Buildings and Building Management*, September 1941, pages 59-60; Carlton Schultz, "A Property Manager's View of Decentralization," *National Real Estate Journal*, July 1940, page 12.

31. *Downtown Merchantman*, March 15, 1943, pages 1, 4.

32. Earle Burke, "Holding Downtown Tenants," *Buildings and Building Management*, March 1940, pages 23-24, 61-62; Richardson, "Future of Central Business Districts," pages 96-103; *Skyscraper Management*, May 1939, page 16, June 1939, page 31; *American Society of Planning Officials Newsletter*, March 1938, page 25.

33. *Baltimore Sun*, April 21, 1941; *Skyscraper Management*, September 1941, pages 20-21; Tyler, "Reviving the Downtown District," pages 10-11, 32; *Urban Land Institute Bulletin*, May 1943, page 4; Roy Lubove, *Twentieth-Century Pittsburgh: Government, Business, and Environmental Change* (New York, 1969), pages 106-109.

34. *Downtown Merchantman*, June 1943, pages 1, 4; Tyler, "Reviving the Downtown District," page 11. See also Richardson, "Future of Central Business Districts," pages 98-100.

35. *Downtown Association of Milwaukee: 1944*, pages 15-17; *Downtown Merchantman*, April 1945, pages 1-3; Burke, "Holding Downtown Tenants," pages 23-24; *Baltimore Sun*, September 6, 1948; *Skyscraper Management*, June 1939, page 31; William S. Walker, "Fighting Property Depreciation in Downtown Pittsburgh," *Civil Engineering*, September 1940, page 592.

36. Schnell, "Downtown Development in the '40s," page 7; Burke, "Holding Downtown Tenants," page 24.

37. Garnett Laidlaw Eskew, *Of Land and Men: The Birth and Growth of an Idea* (Washington, D.C., 1956), chapters 2-5; "Urban Decentralization," *Buildings and Building Management*, December 1939, pages 28, 58; "Protecting Downtown Districts," *National Real Estate Journal*, February 1940, pages 16-17.

38. Eskew, *Of Land and Men*, pages 49-51, 57-61; "New Institute Will Study Urban Decentralization," *Buildings and Building Management*, June 1940, pages 25, 66.

39. Urban Land Institute, *Decentralization: What Is It Doing to Our Cities?* (Chicago, 1940), pages 1-5; Harland Bartholomew, *The Present and Ultimate Effect of Decentralization upon American Cities* (Chicago, 1940), page 4-11.

40. Eskew, *Of Land and Men*, pages 52, 57-58, 62-75; Herbert U. Nelson to Members and Trustees of the Urban Land Institute, December 30, 1940, in William H. Ballard, *A Survey in Respect to the Decentralization of the Boston Central Business District* (1940); "What Can Be Done to Conserve and Revitalize Our Downtown Business Areas?" *Urban Land*, October 1945, pages 2-5.

41. Eskew, *Of Land and Men*, pages 58-60, 65-66, 75-76.

42. Ibid., pages 82-91, 97-145.

43. Hugh E. Young, ed., "Traffic and City Planning as They Affect Business Districts," *Journal of the Western Society of Engineers*, October 1940, pages 257, 237. See also Lubove, *Twentieth-Century Pittsburgh*, pages 110-111.

44. Hoyt, *One Hundred Years of Land Values*, page 347; K. Lee Hyder and Howard J. Tobin, *Proposals for Downtown Milwaukee* (Chicago, 1941), pages 33, 44-46; Wagner, "Economic Relationships of Parking to Business," page 65; Richard J. Seltzer, *Proposals for Downtown Philadelphia* (Chicago, 1942), pages 23-24; A. J. Stewart, *Proposals for Downtown Louisville* (Washington, D.C., 1942), pages 20-21; Ballard, *Decentralization of the Boston Central Business District*, pages 49-50; Cuthbert E. Reeves, *The Valuation of Business Lots in Downtown Los Angeles* (Los Angeles, 1932), page 23.

45. Urban Land Institute, *Technical Bulletin No. 18*, May 1952, page 16; "Rebuilding Our Cities," pages 36-37; Young, ed., "Traffic and City Planning," pages 234-235; U.S. Chamber of Commerce, *Your City Is Your Business*, page 193.

46. Robert H. Armstrong and Homer Hoyt, *Decentralization in New York* (Chicago, 1941), pages 10-11. See also Winlock Miller, "Business Property Tax Assessments," *Proceedings of the Thirty-First Annual Convention of the National Association of Building Owners and Managers: 1938*, pages 84-96.

47. Fred K. Vigman, *Crisis of the Cities* (Washington, D.C., 1955), pages 14-20; Carl H. Chatters, "Municipal Finance," in Clarence E. Ridley and Orin F. Nolting, eds., *What the Depression Has Done to Cities* (Chicago, 1935), pages 1-6; Young, ed., "Traffic and City Planning," page 251.

48. Vigman, *Crisis of the Cities*, pages 20-25; A. Miller Hillhouse, *Tax Limits Appraised* (Chicago, 1937), pages 1-7, 38-39; Edward Blythen, "Dangers of Metropolitan Decentralization," *Greater Cleveland*, April 23, 1942, pages 135-138.

49. Mark S. Foster, *From Streetcar to Superhighway: American City Planners and Urban Transportation, 1900-1940* (Philadelphia, 1981), pages 28-29, 70-72, 101-105; David Ward, *Poverty, Ethnicity, and the American City, 1840-1925* (Cambridge, England, 1989), pages 135-138; Harold S. Buttenheim, "The Problem of the Standing Vehicle," *Annals of the American Academy of Political and Social Science* (September 1927), page 155; Gordon Whitnall, "Relation of Downtown Commercial Districts to Outlying Business Districts," *Pacific Municipalities*, April 1928, pages 127-132.

50. Foster, *From Streetcar to Superhighway*, pages 146-147; Norman J. Johnston, "Harland Bartholomew: Precedent for the Profession," *Journal of the American Institute of Planners*, March 1975, pages 115-124; Harland Bartholomew, "Is City Planning Effectively Controlling City Growth in the United States?" *Planning Problems of Town, City and Region: Papers and Discussions at the Twenty-Third National Conference on City Planning: 1931*, pages 6-7; Bartholomew, *Effect of Decentralization upon American Cities*, page 8.

51. C. A. Dykstra, "Congestion De Luxe—Do We Want It?" *National Municipal Review,* July 1926, pages 394–398; C. A. Dykstra, "A City Works at Planning," *Planning Problems of City, Region, State, and Nation Presented at the Twenty-Sixth National Conference on City Planning: 1934,* pages 9–10; Mark Stewart Foster, "The Decentralization of Los Angeles During the 1920's" (Ph.D. diss., University of Southern California, 1971), pages 200–202; *National Real Estate Journal,* June 1941, page 42; Whitnall, "Urban Disintegration," pages 440–451.

52. Bartholomew, *Effect of Decentralization upon American Cities,* pages 8–11; Harland Bartholomew, "Preventing Disintegration of Cities," *Civil Engineering,* May 1933, pages 259–262; Harland Bartholomew, "Decentralization: A Nationwide City Problem," *Planning and Civic Comment,* January 1948, pages 57–58; Dykstra, "A City Works at Planning," page 9; Foster, *From Streetcar to Superhighway,* pages 147–148.

53. Homer Hoyt, "Urban Decentralization," *Journal of Land and Public Utility Economics,* August 1940, page 73. See also Foster, *From Streetcar to Superhighway,* pages 148–149; Scott Bottles, *Los Angeles and the Automobile: The Making of the Modern City* (Berkeley, 1987), page 195; Bartholomew, "Decentralization: A Nationwide Problem," page 61; Bartholomew, *Effect of Decentralization upon American Cities,* page 8.

54. Harland Bartholomew, "Planning Considerations in the Location of Housing Projects: I. The Case for Downtown Locations," *Planners' Journal,* March–June 1939, page 33; Bartholomew, *Effect of Decentralization upon American Cities,* page 7; Bartholomew, "Preventing Disintegration of Cities," page 260; Whitnall, "Urban Disintegration," page 442; Foster, *From Streetcar to Superhighway,* pages 147–149.

55. Bartholomew, *Effect of Decentralization upon American Cities,* pages 8–9.

56. *Proceedings [of the Thirty-Second] National Conference on City Planning: 1940,* pages 112–113.

57. Charles L. Kendrick, "Decentralization in Detroit," *Freehold,* April 1, 1940, page 237. See also Young, ed., "Traffic and City Planning," page 236.

58. Ellsworth Huntington, "Climate and City Growth," *Survey,* October 1, 1932, page 447; Ernest M. Fisher, "Economics of Decentralization," *Appraisal Journal,* April 1942, page 141; E. E. East, "Los Angeles' Street Traffic Problem," *Civil Engineering,* August 1942, pages 436–437; Carol Aronovici, "Let the Cities Perish," *Survey,* October 1, 1932, page 439.

Chapter 6: Wishful Thinking

1. *Baltimore Sun,* April 21, May 20/21, June 12/25, 1941. See also California Railroad Commission, *Application 1602: Reporter's Transcript* (1921), page 134, California Public Utilities Commission files, Sacramento.

2. San Francisco Department of City Planning, "Daily Trips in San Francisco" (1955), table 6; Roger W. Toll, "Traffic Investigation in Denver," *Electric Railway Journal,* August 21, 1915, page 311; R. F. Kelker, Jr., *Report and Recommendations on a Physical Plan for a Unified Transportation System for the City of Chicago* (1923), pages 39–40; Ross D. Eckert and George W. Hilton, "The Jitneys," *Journal of Law and Economics* (October 1972), pages 293–325.

3. John A. Beeler, "What Price Fares?" *Transit Journal,* June 1932, pages 263–266; American Transit Association, *Transit Fact Book: 1945,* pages 15–19; American Transit Association, *Transit Fact Book: 1951,* pages 7–8. By at any time since the turn of the

century, I mean at any time other than the mid 1930s, the worst years of the Great Depression, when the riding habit was even lower.

4. Kelker, *Unified Transportation System*, page 40; Chicago Department of Streets and Electricity, Bureau of Street Traffic, "Cordon Count Data on the Central Business District" (1949), page 2; U.S. Works Progress Administration, *Traffic Survey Data on the City of St. Louis* (1937); Donald M. Baker, *A Rapid Transit System for Los Angeles California* (1933), page 37-e; Coverdale & Colpitts, *Report to the Los Angeles Metropolitan Transit Authority on a Monorail Rapid Transit Line for Los Angeles* (1954), page 62; *Automobile Facts*, January 1941, page 2.

5. Paul Barrett, *The Automobile and Urban Transit: The Formation of Public Policy in Chicago, 1900–1930* (Philadelphia, 1983), pages 104–120; *Los Angeles Times*, July 25, 1909; Robert M. Fogelson, *The Fragmented Metropolis: Los Angeles, 1850–1930* (Cambridge, 1967), chapter 7; Stanley Mallach, "The Origins of the Decline of Urban Mass Transportation in the United States," *Urbanism Past and Present*, Summer 1979, pages 1–15; U.S. Department of Commerce, *Historical Statistics of the United States: Colonial Times to 1970* (Washington, D.C., 1975), part 2, page 716; Baker, *Rapid Transit System for Los Angeles*, page 37-e; Clay McShane, *Down the Asphalt Path: The Automobile and the American City* (New York, 1994), pages 126–127.

6. *Baltimore Sun*, May 21, 1941. See also David Whitcomb, "Maintaining Values in Central Business Districts," *Proceedings of the Twenty-Second Annual Convention of the National Association of Building Owners and Managers: 1929*, page 95.

7. *[New York] Real Estate Record and Builders' Guide*, March 8, 1873, page 107, October 8, 1881, page 940; *American Architect and Building News*, July 27, 1878, pages 27–28, August 20, 1892, page 109; *Scientific American*, April 25, 1903, page 310; Clay McShane, "Urban Pathways: The Street and the Highway, 1900–1940," in Joel A. Tarr and Gabriel Dupuy, eds., *Technology and the Rise of the Networked City in Europe and America* (Philadelphia, 1988), page 68; *Los Angeles Times*, July 25, 1909.

8. McShane, *Down the Asphalt Path*, pages 122, 193–194; Mark S. Foster, *From Streetcar to Superhighway: American City Planners and Urban Transportation, 1900–1940* (Philadelphia, 1981), pages 43–44; Amos Stote, "The Ideal American City," *McBride's Magazine*, April 1916, page 89; Scott Bottles, *Los Angeles and the Automobile: The Making of the Modern City* (Berkeley, 1987), pages 59–60; *[New York] Real Estate Record and Builders' Guide*, February 17, 1917, page 220; Howard L. Preston, *Automobile Age Atlanta: The Making of a Southern Metropolis, 1900–1935* (Athens, Georgia, 1979), pages 116–117; Raymond Unwin, "America Revisited—A City Planner's Impressions," *American City*, April 1923, page 334.

9. John A. Miller, Jr., "The Chariots That Rage in the Streets," *American City*, July 1928, pages 113–114; Stephen Child, "Restricted Traffic District Proposed," ibid., April 1927, pages 507–510; V. R. Stirling and Rensselaer H. Toll, "How to Eliminate Traffic from Downtown Sections," *National Municipal Review*, June 1929, pages 369–371; Robert H. Whitten, "Unchoking Our Congested Streets," *American City*, October 1920, pages 351–354; *Proceedings of the American Society of Civil Engineers*, September 1926, pages 1453–1454; *Boston City Record*, January 23, 1926, pages 100–101.

10. Miller, "The Chariots That Rage in the Streets," page 113; St. Louis Building Owners and Managers Association, *The St. Louis Traffic Problem* (St. Louis, 1925), pages 4, 16; Blaine A. Brownell, "A Symbol of Modernity: Attitudes Toward the Automobile in Southern Cities in the 1920s," *American Quarterly*, March 1972, pages 24–25; E. R.

Kinsey and C. E. Smith, *Report on Rapid Transit for St. Louis* (St. Louis, 1926), page 147; *Engineering Magazine*, August 1906, page 738; *Baltimore Sun*, June 14, 1925; Stote, "The Ideal American City," page 89.

11. Julius F. Harder, "The City's Plan," *Municipal Affairs*, March 1898, page 34; *Proceedings of the American Society of Civil Engineers*, September 1926, pages 1459–1460; Louis G. Simmons, "The Solution of Big Cities Traffic Problems," *Illustrated World*, October 1917, page 267; *[Pittsburgh] Progress*, April 1922, page 2; Frederick Law Olmsted, Harland Bartholomew, and Charles Henry Cheney, *A Major Traffic Street Plan for Los Angeles* (Los Angeles, 1924), pages 12–14.

12. Cleveland Building Owners and Managers Association, *Cleveland's Traffic Problem* (Cleveland, 1924), pages 6–7; Harland Bartholomew, "Basic Factors in the Solution of Metropolitan Traffic Problems," *American City*, July 1925, pages 38–39; *Cassier's Magazine*, August 1907, pages 374–375; Morris Knowles, "City Planning as a Permanent Solution of the Traffic Problem," *Planning Problems of Town, City, and Region: Papers and Discussions at the International City and Regional Planning Conference: 1925*, page 60; "The Triangle's 'Thru' Traffic," *Better Traffic*, October 1931, page 6; Ernest P. Goodrich, "The Urban Auto Problem," *Proceedings of the Twelfth National Conference on City Planning: 1920*, page 84; Miller McClintock, *Street Traffic Control* (New York, 1926), pages 70–85.

13. Miller McClintock, *Report and Recommendations of the Metropolitan Street Traffic Survey* (Chicago, 1926), page 48; *[New York] Real Estate Record and Builders' Guide*, September 26, 1908, page 591, May 28, 1910, page 1137; *American Architect*, June 1, 1910, page 15; *Proceedings of the Engineers' Society of Western Pennsylvania*, November 1919, page 488; Sidney Clarke, "Special Report on Traffic Relief," in *Report of the Transportation Survey Commission of the City of St. Louis* (1930), page 117; McShane, "Urban Pathways," page 77; McShane, *Down the Asphalt Path*, pages 213–216; Theodora Kimball Hubbard and Henry Vincent Hubbard, *Our Cities To-Day and Tomorrow* (Cambridge, 1929), chapter 12.

14. Raymond S. Tompkins, "Are We Solving the Traffic Problem?" *American Mercury*, February 1929, page 155; Cleveland Building Owners and Managers Association, *Cleveland's Traffic Problem*, page 6; Barrett, *The Automobile and Urban Transit*, pages 155–161; McShane, *Down the Asphalt Path*, chapter 9; McShane, "Urban Pathways," page 77; *Baltimore Sun*, May 15, 1932; J. Rowland Bibbins, "The Growing Transport Problem of the Masses," *National Municipal Review*, August 1920, pages 517–522. See also McClintock, *Street Traffic Control*, chapters 7–8, 11–12, 14.

15. John Ihlder, "The Automobile and Community Planning," *Annals of the American Academy of Political and Social Science*, November 1924, page 204; E. S. Taylor, "The Plan of Chicago in 1924," ibid., pages 225–229; Arthur A. Shurtleff, "The Circumferential Thoroughfares of the Metropolitan District of Boston," *City Planning*, April 1926, pages 76–84; Hubbard and Hubbard, *Our Cities*, pages 196, 204–205; "By-Pass Highways for Traffic Relief," *American City*, April 1928, page 89; Olmsted, Bartholomew, and Cheney, *A Major Traffic Street Plan for Los Angeles*, page 28.

16. Preston, *Automobile Age Atlanta*, pages 118–125; *American Architect*, May 28, 1919, pages 756–758; McShane, *Down the Asphalt Path*, pages 31–40, 220–223; McShane, "Urban Pathways," pages 71–74, 79–82.

17. Paul Barrett, "Public Policy and Private Choice: Mass Transit and the Automobile in Chicago Between the Wars," *Business History Review*, Winter 1975, pages 482–483;

Current Affairs in New England, July 12, 1926, pages 3–4; "The Triangle's 'Thru' Traffic," page 1; Oscar Handlin, ed., *This Was America* (Cambridge, 1949), page 491; "Congested Traffic," *New Republic,* November 28, 1928, pages 29–31; *Report of the Committee on Traffic to His Honor Howard W. Jackson, Mayor of Baltimore, Maryland* (1923), page 5; Clarke, "Special Report on Traffic Relief," page 117; Bottles, *Los Angeles and the Automobile,* pages 101–102, 118–119.

18. "Traffic Problems and Suggested Remedies," *Public Works,* June 1924, pages 177– 180; Carol Aronovici, "Down-Town Parking," *Community Builder,* December 1927, pages 28–34; Olmsted, Bartholomew, and Cheney, *A Major Traffic Street Plan for Los Angeles,* page 18; George A. Damon, "Relation of the Motor Bus to Other Methods of Transportation," *Planning Problems of Town, City, and Region: Papers and Discussions at the International City and Regional Planning Conference: 1925,* page 270.

19. McShane, *Down the Asphalt Path,* pages 50, 204; *[New York] Real Estate Record and Builders' Guide,* October 8, 1881, page 940, October 15, 1881, page 964, May 10, 1882, page 500; *American Architect and Building News,* August 20, 1892, page 109, December 24, 1892, page 189; *Scientific American,* April 25, 1903, page 310. See also Howard P. Segal, *Technological Utopianism in American Culture* (Chicago, 1985), pages 25–26.

20. *Cassier's Magazine,* August 1907, pages 374–375; Goodrich, "The Urban Auto Problem," page 82; Greater Cleveland Transportation Committee, *Report on Passenger Transportation in the Cleveland Metropolitan Area* (1925), page 21; *Proceedings of the American Society of Civil Engineers,* September 1926, pages 1444–1446, December 1926, pages 2003–2004; Miller McClintock, *A Report on the Street Traffic Control Problem of the City of Boston* (Boston, 1928), page 245; Olmsted, Bartholomew, and Cheney, *A Major Traffic Street Plan for Los Angeles,* page 15; Unwin, "America Revisited," page 334.

21. McClintock, *Street Traffic Control,* chapters 8, 10; McClintock, *Street Traffic Control Problem in the City of Boston,* chapters 9, 11; Goodrich, "The Urban Auto Problem," pages 82–83; *Proceedings of the American Society of Civil Engineers,* December 1926, pages 2003–2004; McShane, *Down the Asphalt Path,* pages 187–188, 199; Olmsted, Bartholomew, and Cheney, *A Major Traffic Street Plan for Los Angeles,* page 16; McShane, "Urban Pathways," page 79.

22. Goodrich, "The Urban Auto Problem," pages 81–82; McClintock, *Street Traffic Control,* pages 75–81; *Scientific American,* August 1923, page 86; Alvan Macauley, *City Planning and Automobile Traffic Problems* (Detroit, 1925), page 20; *[New York] Real Estate Record and Builders' Guide,* March 5, 1904, page 482, October 16, 1909, page 677, December 22, 1917, page 804; *Engineering Magazine,* August 1906, pages 737–738; McShane, *Down the Asphalt Path,* page 205.

23. McClintock, *Street Traffic Control,* pages 55–56; Ernest Flagg, "The City of the Future," *Scientific American,* September 1927, pages 238–242; Merchants' Association of New York, *Control of Street Traffic* (1924), page 24; Goodrich, "The Urban Auto Problem," pages 81–82; *[New York] Real Estate Record and Builders' Guide,* March 26, 1921, page 393; *Chicago Tribune,* December 3, 1927; Harvey D. Dunn, "Solving Boston's Traffic Problems," *Boston Business,* November 1929, page 5; *Report of the Transportation Survey Commission of the City of St. Louis,* page ix; *Detroit News,* January 27, 1929.

24. "Prize-Winning Plans for Super-Highway," *American City,* July 1927, pages 19–22; Wyatt B. Brummitt, "The Superhighway," ibid., January 1929, pages 85–88; Mc-

Shane, *Down the Asphalt Path*, pages 214, 221–222; Detroit Rapid Transit Commission, *Proposed Super-Highway Plan for Greater Detroit* (Detroit, 1924), pages 16–21; Sidney D. Waldon, "Superhighways and Regional Planning," *Planning Problems of Town, City, and Region: Papers and Discussions at the Nineteenth Annual Conference on City Planning: 1927*, pages 162–164; Eugene S. Taylor, "Chicago's Superhighway Plan," *National Municipal Review*, June 1929, pages 371–376.

25. Foster, *From Streetcar to Superhighway*, pages 94–95; "The City of the Future," *Popular Mechanics*, August 1924, page 228; Harvey Wiley Corbett, "Up With the Skyscraper," *National Municipal Review*, February 1927, page 99; Henry Harrison Suplee, "A Five-Storied Street," *Cassier's Monthly*, June 1923, pages 57–60; "And This? Dr. John A. Harriss Proposes Six-Deck Street," *American City*, June 1927, pages 803–805; Ernest Flagg, "The Plan of New York, and How to Improve It," *Scribner's Magazine*, August 1904, pages 253–256; *New York Times*, January 7, 1923.

26. Harold M. Mayer and Richard C. Wade, *Chicago: Growth of a Metropolis* (Chicago, 1969), pages 310–311; *Chicago Commerce*, May 31, 1924, pages 11–12, June 14, 1924, page 1, August 14, 1926, pages 9–10; E. J. Brehaut, "How Other Cities Are Trying to Solve the Traffic Problem," *Our Boston*, October 1926, pages 7–8; *New York Times*, January 21, April 25, June 15, August 8, 1926; Donald F. Davis, *Conspicuous Production: Automobiles and Elites in Detroit, 1899–1933* (Philadelphia, 1988), page 171; Edward N. Hines, "Progress in Superhighway Planning and Construction, Detroit Region," *Engineering News-Record*, June 5, 1930, pages 40–43.

27. Olmsted, Bartholomew, and Cheney, *A Major Traffic Street Plan for Los Angeles*, pages 15, 51–53; *New York Times*, August 8, 1926; *Chicago Commerce*, June 14, 1924, page 1; Detroit Rapid Transit Commission, *Vehicular Traffic in the Business District of Detroit* (Detroit, 1924), page 19; "Ultimate Remedies for the Traffic Problem," *American City*, July 1929, page 135; Preston, *Automobile Age Atlanta*, pages 134–136; *Pacific Outlook*, January 1920, page 20; McShane, "Urban Pathways," page 76.

28. Olmsted, Bartholomew, and Cheney, *A Major Traffic Street Plan for Los Angeles*, page 15; Whitten, "Unchoking Our Congested Streets," page 351; E. J. McIlraith, "Do High Buildings Cause Traffic Congestion?" *Electric Railway Journal*, June 1929, page 636; *Proceedings of the American Society of Civil Engineers*, September 1926, page 1454; Russell Van Nest Black, "The Spectacular in City Building," *Annals of the American Academy of Political and Social Science*, September 1927, pages 50–56; Henry Brinckerhoff, *The Problem of Street Traffic in a Modern City* (1924), page 13; Aronovici, "Down-Town Parking," page 35.

29. Lester S. Ready, J. O. Marsh, and Richard Sachse, *Joint Report on Street Railway Survey, City of Los Angeles* (Los Angeles, 1926), pages 97–98. See also Greater Cleveland Transportation Committee, *Report on Passenger Transportation*, page 22; John A. Dewhurst, "The Automotive Vehicle and Its Effect on Transportation," *Electric Railway Journal*, September 26, 1925, page 481; Miller, "The Chariots That Rage in the Streets," page 114; John P. Hallihan, "Capacity and Economy of Various Forms of Transit in Cities," *American City*, February 1931, pages 137–138.

30. Harland Bartholomew, "Discussion of the Urban Auto Problem," *National Municipal Review*, July 1920, pages 445–446; *Proceedings of the Twelfth National Conference on City Planning: 1920*, page 99; John A. Beeler, "Planning Transportation for the City of the Future," *Electric Railway Journal*, September 26, 1925, page 528; B. F. Fitch, "The Place of the Motor Truck in the Modern City Plan," *Annals of the American Academy of*

Political and Social Science, September 1927, pages 201–202; McClintock, "Street Traffic Problems in Central Business Districts," pages 74–78; *Chicago Tribune,* March 2, 1929.

31. Whitcomb, "Maintaining Values in Central Business Districts," page 95; Miller Mc-Clintock, "Street Traffic and Rental Values," *Proceedings of the Nineteenth Annual Convention of the National Association of Building Owners and Managers: 1926,* pages 236–243; Brinckerhoff, *The Problem of Street Traffic,* page 6; Milwaukee Board of Public Land Commissioners to Downtown Association of Milwaukee, April 20, 1940, page 4, Graduate School of Design Library, Harvard University.

32. Knowles, "City Planning as a Permanent Solution of the Traffic Problem," page 57; Clarke, "Special Report on Traffic Relief," pages 118–119; Harland Bartholomew, "Street Replanning in Downtown Districts of Large Cities," *Planning Problems of Town, City, and Region: Papers and Discussions at the Twenty-First National Conference on City Planning: 1929,* pages 205–209; U.S. House of Representatives Committee on Roads, *Hearings [on] Federal Aid for Post-War Highway Construction* (Washington, D.C., 1944), volume 2, page 782; *New York Times,* January 7, 1923; "The Best Remedies for Traffic Congestion Are the Common Sense Ones," *Mass Transportation,* December 1937, pages 389–390.

33. Miller McClintock, "Efficient Movement of Traffic a Vital Community Problem," *Proceedings of the American Transit Association and Its Affiliated Associations: 1935,* page 98; David J. St. Clair, *The Motorization of American Cities* (New York, 1986), pages 136–138; House Committee on Roads, *Hearings [on] Federal Aid for Post-War Highway Construction,* volume 2, pages 761–766.

34. Clarke, "Special Report on Traffic Relief," pages 118–119; Cincinnati City Planning Commission, *Motorways* (1947), pages 152–153; Hawley S. Simpson, "The Economic Justification of Traffic Improvements in Cities," *Engineers and Engineering,* March 1931, pages 64–66.

35. Bottles, *Los Angeles and the Automobile,* pages 216–220; David A. Brodsly, *L.A. Freeway: An Appreciative Essay* (Berkeley, 1981), pages 98–103; Thomas Sugrue, "Miller McClintock," *Scribner's Magazine,* December 1937, pages 9–10, 12–13, 99; *Time,* August 3, 1936, pages 41–43.

36. Foster, *From Streetcar to Superhighway,* page 110; Los Angeles Transportation Engineering Board, *A Transit Program for the Los Angeles Metropolitan Area* (1939), page 4; Christopher Tunnard and Boris Pushkarev, *Man-Made America: Chaos or Control* (New York, 1963), pages 160–166; Edward M. Bassett, "The Freeway—A New Kind of Thoroughfare," *American City,* February 1930, page 95; Miller McClintock, "The Place of Transit in the World of Tomorrow," *Transit Journal,* June 1939, page 223; L. S. Robbins, "The Need for a Comprehensive System of Arterial Highways in Metropolitan Cleveland" (1940), page 131; Arthur W. Dean, "Bypass Roads and City Access," *Engineering News-Record,* June 24, 1937, page 946; McShane, "Urban Pathways," pages 79–84; Norman Bel Geddes, *Magic Motorways* (New York, 1940), page 6; Hugh E. Young, ed., "Traffic and City Planning as They Affect Business Districts," *Journal of the Western Society of Engineers,* October 1940, page 241.

37. "Intensive Street-Traffic Studies in Chicago," *Engineering News-Record,* November 24, 1932, page 613; Chicago City Council Committee on Traffic and Public Safety, *A Limited Way Plan for the Greater Chicago Traffic Area* (Chicago, 1933), volume 2, page 48; Bartholomew, "Street Replanning," page 208; Dunn, "Solving Boston's Traffic Prob-

lems," page 5; Dean, "Bypass Roads," page 947; House Committee on Roads, *Hearings [on] Federal Aid for Post-War Highway Construction*, volume 1, page 74, volume 2, page 758; Geddes, *Magic Motorways*, page 211; Joseph Barnett, "Express Highway Planning in Metropolitan Areas," *Proceedings of the American Society of Civil Engineers*, March 1946, page 293; U.S. Bureau of Public Roads, *Toll Roads and Free Roads* (Washington, D.C., 1939), page 92.

38. A. E. Nemetz, "Combating Decentralization with Fast Highways," *Buildings and Building Management*, September 1940, page 46. See also Fred Grumm, "Freeways Relieve Traffic Congestion and Conserve Property Values," *California Highways and Public Works*, May–June 1944, page 6; Leonard A. Bergman, "New York State to Build Highways Through Cities as Check on Decentralization," *Civil Engineering*, November 1946, page 477; Joseph Laronge, "Are We Decentralizing?" *Buildings and Building Management*, December 1938, page 58; Cleveland Regional Plan Association, "Express Highway Plan for the Cleveland Metropolitan Area," *Publication No. 18*, November 1944, page 1; Bottles, *Los Angeles and the Automobile*, pages 138–140.

39. John A. Miller, "Cities on the Toboggan," *Transit Journal*, February 1941, pages 46–47; *Transit Journal*, November 1939, pages 446–447; Alan A. Altshuler, *The City Planning Process: A Political Analysis* (Ithaca, 1965), pages 40–43; Walter Prichard Eaton, "The 'Good Roads' Delusion," *New York Herald Tribune Magazine*, March 27, 1932, page 5; Curtis G. Bradfield, "The Relation of Urban Expressways to Mass Transportation Facilities," *Proceedings of the American Society of Civil Engineers*, December 1948, pages 1597–1604.

40. Bradfield, "Urban Expressways," pages 1600, 1604; Theodore Caplow, "Express Transit Streets to Speed All Traffic," *American City*, May 1948, page 123; Charles Gordon, "Getting Around in the City of the Future," *Electrical Engineering*, April 1940, page 149; "Highways and Transportation in Relation to Each Other and to Other Planned Development," *Proceedings [of the] National Conference on Planning: 1940*, page 35; Walter H. Blucher, "Transportation Facilities in the Future American City," *Proceedings [of the] Fourteenth Annual Meeting [of the] Institute of Traffic Engineers: 1943*, page 11.

41. Foster, *From Streetcar to Superhighway*, page 163; Lloyd Aldrich, "Los Angeles Plans Parkway System," *Traffic Engineering*, August 1947, pages 472–481; Bradfield, "Urban Expressways," page 1587; *Proceedings of the American Society of Civil Engineers*, September 1946, page 1254; *Boston Business*, February 1941, page 22; Robert Moses, "New Highways for a Better New York," *New York Times Magazine*, November 11, 1945, page 11; Robert A. Caro, *The Power Broker: Robert Moses and the Fall of New York* (New York, 1974), pages 769–770.

42. Citizens' Council on City Planning, *Express Highways in Philadelphia* (1947), pages 5–6; Donald M. Baker, "Financing Express Highways in Metropolitan Areas," *American City*, October 1946, page 93; Barrett, *The Automobile and Urban Transit*, pages 150–151; Bottles, *Los Angeles and the Automobile*, pages 230–234; St. Clair, *The Motorization of American Cities*, chapter 6; Mark S. Rose, *Interstate: Express Highway Politics, 1941–1956* (Lawrence, Kansas, 1979).

43. *American City*, November 1944, page 17; "Report of Committee on Elevated Highways," *Proceedings [of the] Thirty-Sixth Annual Convention [of the] American Road Builders' Association: 1939*, pages 288–295; Caro, *The Power Broker*, page 1152; "Fully-Depressed Expressway Planned for Downtown Detroit," *Engineering News-Record*,

January 11, 1945, pages 111–115; William A. Proctor, "Problems Involved in the Planning and Development of Through-Traffic Highways" (Master's thesis, Stanford University, 1939), volume 1, pages 339–341, 467–471, 476–481, 487–491, volume 2, pages 614–615, 662–663, 901–907.

44. *Los Angeles Times,* April 14/16/18/21/23/25/26, 1926; St. Louis Building Owners and Managers Association, *The St. Louis Traffic Problem,* page 18; Edward A. Dana, "What Lies Ahead for Rapid Transit?" *Transit Journal,* September 14, 1935, page 331; *San Francisco Examiner,* October 8/28, 1937.

45. John P. Fox, "Rapid Transit of the Future," *World's Work,* September 1906, page 8000; *Special Report of the Boston Transit Commission Relative to the Removal of the Elevated Railway Structure on Washington and Main Streets in Boston and the Construction of a Tunnel and Subway in Place Thereof* (Boston, 1914), pages 3–5; *New York Times,* November 15, 1922, January 7, May 29, November 12/19, December 11/18, 1923, February 19, October 12/26, November 13, 1924, November 7, 1925, April 4, 1926, January 16, 1927, June 4, 1929; Massachusetts Division of Metropolitan Planning, *Report on Improving Transportation Facilities in the Boston Metropolitan District* (Boston, 1926), page 40; Flagg, "The City of the Future," pages 240–241.

46. *New York Times,* May 25, December 11/18, 1923, October 26, 1924, January 16, February 15/20, 1927, August 24, 1929, February 6/7, March 30, May 18, September 24, 1930, November 15, 1938, February 22, 1940; Robert C. Reed, *The New York Elevated* (South Brunswick, New Jersey, 1978), chapter 17; S. H. Bingham, "Report to the New York Transit Authority [on the] Demolition of the Third Avenue Elevated Line South of 149th Street" (1954), pages 1–4; *Engineering News-Record,* October 13, 1938, page 455, June 27, 1940, page 8; Commonwealth of Massachusetts, *Report of the Legislative Commission on Rapid Transit* (Boston, 1945), pages 97–98; Detroit Rapid Transit Commission, *Rapid Transit Plan for Metropolitan Detroit* (1949), pages 33–34.

47. *Transit Journal,* November 1935, page 407. See also ibid., May 1934, page 148, May 1938, pages 154–155; *Mass Transportation,* January 1941, page 2; Caro, *The Power Broker,* pages 520–525.

48. McClintock, *Street Traffic Control,* page 54; "Congested Traffic," page 30; "Fully-Depressed Expressway Planned for Downtown Detroit," page 111; Simpson, "Economic Justification of Traffic Improvements," page 67; Hallihan, "Capacity and Economy of Various Forms of Transit in Cities," pages 137–138; Philip Harrington, *A Comprehensive Superhighway Plan for the City of Chicago* (Chicago, 1939), pages 32–33; Caro, *The Power Broker,* pages 522–523; Proctor, "Through-Traffic Highways," volume 2, pages 901–907; Barnett, "Express Highway Planning in Metropolitan Areas," page 297; *Civil Engineering,* January 1954, page 52; Ralph R. Leffler, "Two Deck Elevated Highways," *Illinois Automobile Magazine,* Spring 1945, page 14.

49. *New York Times,* April 25, 1926; "New York to Have $13,500,000 Elevated Express Highway," *American City,* July 1926, pages 8–10; *Chicago Commerce,* May 31, 1924, pages 11–12, June 14, 1924, page 1; *Proceedings of the American Society of Civil Engineers,* September 1946, pages 1259–1260; Lewis R. Watson, Jr., and R. A. Boucher, "Washington's Limited Access Highways," *Public Works,* May 1948, pages 28–29; Caro, *The Power Broker,* page 520.

50. *Engineering News-Record,* October 14, 1937, page 625; Mason D. Pratt, "Closing an Open Letter to San Francisco," *Bus Transportation,* February 1937, page 88; "Report of Committee on Elevated Highways," *Proceedings of the Thirty-Sixth Annual Convention*

[of the] American Road Builders' Association: 1939, pages 281–297; Clyde G. Conley, *A Remedy for Traffic Congestion* (1937), pages 3–4, 7; V. G. Iden, "Elevated Highway Design for Speed, Safety, and Beauty," *American City*, May 1938, pages 46–48; "Report of Committee on Elevated Highways," *Proceedings [of the] Thirty-Fifth Annual Convention [of the] American Road Builders' Association: 1938*, pages 492–500; "Report of Committee on Elevated Highways," *Proceedings [of the] Thirty-Seventh Annual Convention [of the] American Road Builders' Association: 1940*, pages 475–489.

51. Leffler, "Two Deck Elevated Highways," pages 10, 13–14; "Traffic Jams Business Out," *Architectural Forum*, January 1940, pages 64–65; Conley, *A Remedy for Traffic Congestion*, page 12; Pratt, "Closing an Open Letter," page 88; Robert Moses, "A Report by Mr. Moses on New York Traffic," *New York Times Magazine*, November 4, 1945, pages 45–46; Flagg, "The City of the Future," pages 239–240; Miller McClintock, *Report on San Francisco Traffic Survey* (San Francisco, 1937), pages 253–254; "Report of Committee on Elevated Highways" (1939), page 288; "Report of Committee on Elevated Highways," *Proceedings [of the] Thirty-Eighth Annual Convention [of the] American Road Builders' Association: 1941*, pages 227–228.

52. John. S. Crandall, "The Express Road and the Highway System," *Civil Engineering*, October 1937, page 691. See also "Elevated Highways Only Solution to Traffic Congestion," *Architect and Engineer*, April 1939, page 52; "Report of Committee on Elevated Highways" (1938), page 497, (1939), page 295, (1940), page 488; *New York Times*, January 7, 1923.

53. Miller McClintock, "The Place of Transit in the World of Tomorrow," *Transit Journal*, June 1939, page 223; Clarke, "Special Report on Traffic Relief," page 109; Bureau of Public Roads, *Toll Roads and Free Roads*, page 93; *Civil Engineering*, January 1954, pages 50–53; Harrington, *A Comprehensive Superhighway Plan*, pages 22–23; "Report of Committee on Elevated Highways" (1940), page 485, (1941), pages 236–239; McClintock, *San Francisco Traffic Survey*, page 246; Robbins, *Arterial Highways in Metropolitan Cleveland*, page 31.

54. "Report of Committee on Elevated Highways" (1941), page 229; Norman Bel Geddes, "Traffic and Transit in the World of Tomorrow," *Transit Journal*, August 1939, page 272; "Report of Committee on Elevated Highways" (1939), page 285; Foster, *From Streetcar to Superhighway*, page 163; "Highways and Transportation in Relation to Each Other and to Other Planned Development," pages 50–52, 58–59; Simpson, "Traffic Improvements in Cities," pages 66–67; Harrington, *A Comprehensive Superhighway Plan*, pages 22–23.

55. McClintock, "Street Traffic and Rental Values," page 247; John Ihlder, "Coordination of Traffic Facilities," *Annals of the American Academy of Political and Social Science*, September 1927, page 5; Bottles, *Los Angeles and the Automobile*, page 64; Blaine A. Brownell, *The Urban Ethos in the South, 1920–1930* (Baton Rouge, 1975), page 119; *Philadelphia Evening Bulletin*, December 30, 1926; J. Borton Weeks, "Philadelphia's Traffic Problems and Their Solution," *Annals of the American Academy of Political and Social Science*, November 1924, page 240.

56. Ready, Marsh, and Sachse, *Joint Report on Street Railway Survey*, page 15; "Traffic Problems and Suggested Remedies," pages 177–180; W. W. Arnheim, "Business Must Tackle Parking," *Nation's Traffic*, January 1929, page 10; *National Municipal Review*, April 1923, page 205; John Ihlder, *Automobile Parking in Business Districts* (Washington, D.C., 1928), page 119.

57. McClintock, *Metropolitan [Chicago] Street Traffic Survey*, pages 115–116; Barrett, *The Automobile and Urban Transit*, pages 54–55; *American Architect and Building News*, August 20, 1892, page 109, May 18, 1895, pages 61–62.

58. Kelker, De Leuw & Company, "Traffic Regulation and Control," in *Report of the Transportation Survey Commission of the City of St. Louis*, page 84; Charles Mulford Robinson, *City Planning* (New York, 1916), page 121; *Municipal Journal*, March 2, 1916, page 305; Barrett, *The Automobile and Urban Transit*, pages 61–63; Miller McClintock, *A Report on the Street Traffic Control Problem of San Francisco* (San Francisco, 1927), pages 155–157; *Engineering News-Record*, October 14, 1926, page 618; Preston, *Automobile Age Atlanta*, pages 125–126.

59. Chicago City Council Committee on Local Transportation, *The Anti-Parking Ordinance* (1920); Bottles, *Los Angeles and the Automobile*, pages 64–67; Lucius Storrs, "The Place of the Street Car in the Modern City Plan," *Annals of the American Academy of Political and Social Science*, September 1927, page 189; *Chicago Commerce*, November 29, 1912, page 6, July 20, 1917, page 4; Barrett, *The Automobile and Urban Transit*, pages 61–63, 134–135; Cleveland Building Owners and Managers Association, *Cleveland's Traffic Problem*, pages 4–5.

60. Herbert S. Swan, "Our City Thoroughfares—Shall They Be Highways or Garages?" *National Real Estate Journal*, July 3, 1922, page 9; Hugh E. Young, "Day and Night Storage and Parking of Motor Vehicles," *Proceedings of the Fifteenth National Conference on City Planning: 1923*, pages 181–182, 208–209; Harold S. Buttenheim, "The Problem of the Standing Vehicle," *Annals of the American Academy of Political and Social Science*, September 1927, pages 144–155; McClintock, "Street Traffic and Rental Values," pages 247–248; McClintock, *Street Traffic Control*, pages 138–139.

61. Young, "Storage and Parking of Motor Vehicles," pages 182–183; "St. Louis Attacks the Problem of Municipal Parking," *American City*, November 1928, page 165; Henry P. Maybury, "Traffic Problems in Great Cities," *Municipal Journal and Public Works Engineer*, October 30, 1925, page 1592; Committee on Local Transportation, *The Anti-Parking Ordinance*; Aronovici, "Downtown Parking," page 32.

62. *Proceedings of the American Society of Civil Engineers*, September 1926, page 1466, December 1926, page 2003; Kinsey and Smith, *Rapid Transit for St. Louis*, pages 151–152; *Chicago Commerce*, November 29, 1912, page 6; Barrett, *The Automobile and Urban Transit*, pages 134–135; Preston, *Automobile Age Atlanta*, pages 127–128; Cleveland Association of Building Owners and Managers, *Cleveland's Traffic Problem*, pages 4–5.

63. McShane, *Down the Asphalt Path*, page 197; Harry C. Koch, "The Control of Curb Parking," *Traffic Engineering*, February 1945, pages 176–177; Cleveland Heath, "Down-town Traffic Regulation," *American City*, September 1924, page 200; McClintock, *Metropolitan [Chicago] Street Traffic Survey*, pages 146–148; "'Where Shall They Park?'" *American City*, March 1928, page 130; "Parking Regulations," ibid., February 1929, pages 139–140; American Electric Railway Association, *Bulletin No. 402* (1932), page 95.

64. *Chicago Commerce*, July 20, 1917, page 4, August 17, 1917, page 12; *Engineering News-Record*, October 3, 1925, page 563; McClintock, *Street Traffic Control*, pages 149–150; "Parking Restrictions and Reactions in Several Large Cities," *American City*, March 1930, pages 122–123; McShane, *Down the Asphalt Path*, page 197; Barrett, *The Automobile and Urban Transit*, pages 62–63; Miller McClintock, "Parking—When,

Where, and Why?" *American City*, April 1924, page 369; *Philadelphia Evening Bulletin*, March 16, 1927; *[New York] Real Estate Record and Builders' Guide*, July 28, 1917, page 107.

65. McClintock, *Street Traffic Control*, pages 149-150; McClintock, "Parking—When, Where, and Why?" page 360; Koch, "Control of Curb Parking," pages 176-177; Barrett, *The Automobile and Urban Transit*, pages 62-63; McShane, *Down the Asphalt Path*, page 197; William B. Powell, "City Traffic Problems," *Engineers and Engineering*, March 1927, page 59; McClintock, *Street Traffic Control Problem in San Francisco*, pages 148-149; *Philadelphia Evening Bulletin*, February 18, March 10, 1927.

66. Arnheim, "Business Must Tackle Parking," pages 11-12; Preston, *Automobile Age Atlanta*, page 127; McClintock, *Street Traffic Control*, page 150; McClintock, "Parking—When, Where, and Why?" page 360; *Philadelphia Evening Bulletin*, January 14, 1927.

67. *Engineering News-Record*, October 14, 1926, page 618; McClintock, "Parking—When, Where, and Why?" page 360; *Current Affairs in New England*, June 15, 1925, page 6; J. Haslett Bell, "Traffic Relief Through Parking Regulation," *American City*, August 1924, page 141; Powell, "City Traffic Problems," page 59; Leslie J. Sorenson, "Parking and Loading," *Engineers and Engineering*, January 1931, page 5; Raymond S. Tompkins, "Are We Solving the Traffic Problem?" *American Mercury*, February 1929, pages 158-159.

68. *Philadelphia Evening Bulletin*, December 23, 1926-January 14, 1927; *Philadelphia Inquirer*, January 14, 1927.

69. *Philadelphia Evening Bulletin*, February 10-March 18, 1927; *Philadelphia Inquirer*, February 13, 1927.

70. Bottles, *Los Angeles and the Automobile*, pages 64-89. See also William F. Peters, "Parking Regulations and Their Effect on Central Districts," *Annals of Real Estate Practice: 1927*, pages 223-224.

71. Preston, *Automobile Age Atlanta*, pages 125-130. See also Atlanta *Constitution*, December 5/7/8, 1922, April 4/6, 1926.

72. McClintock, *Metropolitan [Chicago] Street Traffic Survey*, chapter 9; Sorenson, "Loading and Unloading," pages 65-66; *Chicago Tribune*, January 18, December 15, 1927, January 10-28, February 2/3, 1928; *Baltimore Sun*, February 10, 1929; J. W. Baskin, "Chicago Succeeds with 'No Parking' Experiment," *Retailing*, October 11, 1937, page 13; Barrett, *The Automobile and Urban Transit*, pages 158-160, 266; "The Loop Has Adequate Parking Spaces," *Chicago Commerce*, September 24, 1927, pages 11, 24-25; "'No Parking,' Says Chicago," *Dry Goods Economist*, July 7, 1928, pages 12-13, 90; Charles Gordon, "Elimination of Parking Proves Successful in Chicago Loop District," *Electric Railway Journal*, February 23, 1929, pages 312-318.

73. McClintock, "Street Traffic and Rental Values," page 248; *Philadelphia Evening Bulletin*, January 13, March 4/7/16, 1927; Miller, "The Chariots That Rage in the Streets," page 113; Powell, "City Traffic Problems," page 59; Barrett, *The Automobile and Urban Transit*, pages 134-135, 158-160; Bottles, *Los Angeles and the Automobile*, pages 67-68, 83-84; *[Boston] City Record*, November 15, 1926, pages 4-5, 9, 12-13; *Current Affairs in New England*, September 7, 1925, page 8.

74. *Philadelphia Evening Bulletin*, March 3/4/7/8, 1927; Bottles, *Los Angeles and the Automobile*, pages 67-68, 81-85; *Transactions of the National Safety Council: 1931*, page 96; *Chicago Tribune*, January 21, 1928.

75. Sorenson, "Loading and Unloading," page 5; Leon R. Brown, "A Plan to Relieve Park-

ing Problem," *Nation's Traffic*, October 1929, page 40; *Philadelphia Evening Bulletin*, February 17, March 8, 1927; Bottles, *Los Angeles and the Automobile*, pages 84–87.

76. *Current Affairs in New England*, June 15, 1924, pages 5–6; *Philadelphia Evening Bulletin*, December 31, 1926, January 10, 1927; *Philadelphia Inquirer*, February 13, 1927; *Chicago Tribune*, January 18, 1927; Bottles, *Los Angeles and the Automobile*, pages 68–69, 86–87.

77. *Philadelphia Evening Bulletin*, February 12/17, March 7/8, 1927; Bottles, *Los Angeles and the Automobile*, pages 87–88; Preston, *Automobile Age Atlanta*, page 127; McClintock, *Metropolitan [Chicago] Street Traffic Survey*, pages 152–154; Ihlder, *Automobile Parking in Business Districts*, page 10; McClintock, "Parking—Where, When, and Why?" page 361; Buttenheim, "The Problem of the Standing Vehicle," pages 151–152; *Current Affairs in New England*, January 10, 1927, page 4; Barrett, *The Automobile and Urban Transit*, page 135.

78. *Engineers and Engineering*, March 1929, page 84; Michigan State Highway Department, *Street Traffic City of Detroit, 1936–1937* (Lansing, Michigan, 1937), page 76.

79. "Loop Has Adequate Parking Spaces," pages 11, 24–25; Lee J. Eastman, "The Parking Garage Merits Encouragement as an Important Factor in Traffic Relief," *American City*, January 1929, pages 156–157; *American City*, January 1930, page 155; I. K. Rolph, *Vehicular Traffic Congestion and Retail Trade* (Washington, D.C., 1926), pages 33–44; Kelker, De Leuw, "Traffic Regulation and Traffic Control," page 85; Louis Rothschild, "Where Shall the Shopper Park?" *Nation's Business*, November 1925, page 23; American Electric Railway Association, *Bulletin No. 402*, page 97.

80. "A Report on a Survey of Traffic and Arterial Streets and Trunk Highways [in Minneapolis]" (1940), pages 81–82; Orin F. Nolting and Paul Oppermann, *The Parking Problem in Central Business Districts* (Chicago, 1938), pages 2–3, 8–11; Thomas H. MacDonald, "The Problem of Parking Facilities," *Public Roads*, July 1941, page 106; Huber Earle Smutz, "Street and Off-Street Parking" (1941), page 6; Walter H. Blucher, "The Economics of the Parking Lot," *Planners' Journal*, September–October 1936, pages 113–119; Arthur Pound, "No Parking," *Atlantic Monthly*, March 1938, page 389; *American City*, February 1934, page 68.

81. *Cleveland Plain Dealer*, October 20, 1933; Chicago Department of Streets and Electricity, Bureau of Street Traffic, *Cordon Count Data on the Central Business District* (1949), page 1; MacDonald, "The Problem of Parking Facilities," page 103; Young, ed., "Traffic and City Planning," page 243; Los Angeles Seeks Solution to the Parking Problem," *Skyscraper Management*, December 1945, page 14–15, 31; *Boston Business*, June 1946, page 227; J. Edw. Tufft, "Forestalling Decentralization," *Buildings and Building Management*, March 1942, pages 30–31.

82. Harry C. Koch, "Parking Facilities for the Detroit Central Business District," *Proceedings [of the] Tenth Annual Meeting [of the] Institute of Traffic Engineers: 1939*, pages 73–74; MacDonald, "The Problem of Parking Facilities," page 106; Pound, "No Parking," page 389; Milton C. Mumford, "A Review of the Parking Problem," *Urban Land*, June 1947, page 3.

83. "Automobile Parking and Traffic Congestion Go Hand-in Hand," *Mass Transportation*, January 1938, pages 11–15; *Cleveland Plain Dealer*, October 19/20, 1933; *San Francisco Examiner*, October 7/12/14/26, 1937; Pound, "No Parking," page 389; L. I. Hewes, "Metropolitan Freeways and Mass Transportation," *Transactions of the Commonwealth Club of California*, August 5, 1946, pages 107–108.

84. "Is the Park-O-Meter the Answer?" *Skyscraper Management,* February 1936, pages 14, 35; Leon R. Brown, "Effective Control by Parking Meters," *American City,* August 1937, pages 53–54; "Parking Meters . . . *Cure or Curse?" Transit Journal,* August 1937, page 277; J. Seburn, "Experience with Parking Meters," *Public Works Engineers' Yearbook: 1941,* pages 220–221; *Baltimore Sun,* May 31, 1938; "Survey Proves Popularity of Parking Meters," *Skyscraper Management,* January 1939, page 26; "Value of Metered Parking," ibid., April 1938, page 10; "Traffic Snarl," *Architectural Forum,* January 1938, page 16; "The Parking Meter Makes Good," *American City,* March 1937, pages 89–91.

85. "The Parking Meter Makes Good," page 89. See also "Is the Park-O-Meter the Answer?" page 14; "A Promising Solution of the Parking Problem," *American City,* August 1936, page 60; "Street Parking Meters Recommended," *Greater Cleveland,* November 12, 1936, pages 49–50; Paul S. Robinette, "Eliminating Business-District Congestion in Toledo," *American City,* March 1938, page 79; Brown, "Effective Control by Parking Meters," page 54; "Value of Metered Parking," page 30.

86. "Street Parking Meters Recommended," page 59; "The Parking Meter Makes Good," page 89; "Is the Park-O-Meter the Answer?" pages 14, 35; "Parking Meters . . . *Cure or Curse?"* page 278; "Value of Metered Parking," pages 10, 30; "A Promising Solution of the Parking Problem," *American City,* August 1936, page 60; Brown, "Effective Control by Parking Meters," page 54.

87. *Baltimore Sun,* July 12/13/14/20/23/27, August 6/7, 1937.

88. Ibid., July 1/14/20, August 6/7, December 6, 1937.

89. Ibid., May 28, June 14/16/21/25/28, 1938.

90. Ravy Mitten, "Sorry, You Can't Park There," *Nation's Business,* November 1947, page 62; Seward H. Mott and Max S. Wehrly, eds., "Automobile Parking in Central Business Districts," *Urban Land Institute Technical Bulletin No. 6,* July 1946, page 5; Robert A. Mitchell, "Relieving Traffic Congestion," *Traffic Engineering,* December 1946, page 461; Edward J. Seltzer, "Where Shall I Park?" *Appraisal Journal,* January 1949, page 116; C. T. McGavin, "The Parking Problem," ibid., April 1941, pages 156–157.

91. John A. Miller, "They're All Afraid to *Mention* It . . . ," *Transit Journal,* August 1938, page 275; Harold S. Buttenheim, "City Highways and City Parking—An American Crisis," *American City,* November 1946, page 117; McClintock, *Street Traffic Control,* pages 147–149; Aronovici, "Down-Town Parking," page 34; *Current Affairs in New England,* January 20, 1927, page 4; *Good Roads,* September 1928, page 518; *Baltimore Sun,* June 12/25, July 1, October 4, 1941.

92. Walter H. Blucher, "More About the Parking Problem," *Public Works Engineers' Yearbook: 1942,* pages 91–94; Nolting and Oppermann, *The Parking Problem in Central Business Districts,* pages 2–11; Burton W. Marsh, "Solving the Automobile Parking Problem," *Public Management,* January 1941, page 12; American Automobile Association, Safety and Traffic Engineering Department, "Parking and Terminal Facilities: Summary of Questionnaire Data" (1940), pages 2–4; "Downtown Oakland Fights Decentralization," *National Real Estate Journal,* January 1941, pages 20–21.

93. F. W. Lovejoy, "What Can Be Done About Traffic Congestion?" *Civil Engineering,* May 1946, page 204; Gordon Whitnall, "Urban Disintegration and Land Values," *Journal of Land and Public Utility Economics,* November 1941, page 446; MacDonald, "The Problem of Parking Facilities," pages 106–108; Alan F. Schnell, "Downtown Development in the '40s," *Skyscraper Management,* June 1940, page 14.

94. Aronovici, "Down-Town Parking," page 139; Harvey D. Dunn, "The Traffic Solution—Day Garaging of Cars," *Boston Business*, April 1930, page 45; Bartholomew, "Discussion of the Urban Auto Problem," page 447; Buttenheim, "The Problem of the Standing Vehicle," pages 151–152; "Parking Regulations," *American City*, February 1928, page 140; Nolting and Oppermann, *The Parking Problem in Central Business Districts*, pages 3–8.

95. Marston Campbell, Jr., "Private Business Should Do the Job," *Transactions of the Commonwealth Club of California*, July 3, 1950, pages 318–321. See also *Wall Street Journal*, September 29, 1952; George W. Keith, "Traffic Crisis—Is Subsidized Parking the Answer?" *Public Utilities Fortnightly*, April 29, 1954, pages 533–541; David D. Bohannon, "Public Ownership of Off-Street Parking Facilities," *Transactions of the Commonwealth Club of California*, July 3, 1950, pages 313–314; B. M. Stanton, "Private Versus Public Ownership of Off-Street Parking," in U.S. Chamber of Commerce, *Business Action for Better Cities: A Complete Report on the Businessmen's Conference on Urban Problems* (Washington, D.C., 1952), pages 13–20.

96. *Baltimore Sun*, July 27, 1937; Robert Moses to F. H. La Guardia, a memo dated July 10, 1944, Graduate School of Design Library, Harvard University; Moses, "A Report by Mr. Moses on New York Traffic," page 46; Caro, *The Power Broker*, pages 769, 900, 918; Mitten, "Sorry, You Can't Park There," page 87; Stanton, "Private Versus Public Ownership of Off-Street Parking," pages 113–120; Bohannon, "Public Ownership of Off-Street Parking Facilities," pages 313–314.

97. Miller, "Cities on the Toboggan," page 47; H. H. Allen, "Everyone Can't Ride in Automobiles," *American Transit Association Convention-in-Print* (1944), 2d Session, Number 3, page 16; *Transactions of the Commonwealth Club of California*, July 3, 1950, page 326; R. Gilman Smith, "Downtown Parking vs. Public Transit," *Traffic Engineering*, July 1950, page 387.

98. MacDonald, "The Problem of Parking Facilities," page 104; Mitten, "Sorry, You Can't Park There," page 62; Bohannon, "Public Ownership of Off-Street Parking Facilities," pages 308–311, 312–313; Vining T. Fisher, "In Favor of City-Sponsored Parking Facilities," *Transactions of the Commonwealth Club of California*, July 3, 1950, pages 315–317; Jay D. Runkle, "A Downtown Merchant Looks at the Future of Downtown Shopping," *Stores*, November 1947, page 68.

99. "Boston Should Provide Off-Street Parking and Tunnels Says Staves," *Boston Business*, June 1946, page 227; Dayton City Commission and City Plan Board, "Off-Street Parking" (1949), pages 2–3; Chicago Association of Commerce and Industry Parking Committee, *Parking Plan for the Central Area of Chicago* (1949), pages 13–14, 31.

100. "Off-Street Parking News Round-up," *Traffic Engineering*, August 1948, pages 553–557, 582–583; LaVerne Johnson, "Off-Street Parking News Round-up," ibid., January 1950, pages 163–165, February 1950, pages 201–204; "Off-Street Parking," ibid., February 1946, pages 207–209; Wehrly and Mott, eds., "Automobile Parking in Central Business Districts," pages 5–15.

101. Thirty Fourth Street–Midtown Association, *What Are the Nation's Cities Doing About Traffic and Parking?* (New York, 1948), pages 8–17; Wehrly and Mott, eds., "Automobile Parking in Central Business Districts," pages 8–10; "Off-Street Parking News Round-up," pages 553–554, 582; Johnson, "Off-Street Parking News Round-up," page 164; American Municipal Parking Association Parking Committee, *Parking Space* (Washington, D.C., 1956), pages 31–37.

102. Foster, *From Streetcar to Superhighway*, page 158.

103. Ibid., pages 116–126, 156–157; American Transit Association, *Moving People in Modern Cities* (New York, ca. 1944), page 23; Detroit Rapid Transit Commission, *Rapid Transit Plan for Metropolitan Detroit* (Detroit, 1949), pages 34–37; Mallach, "The Origins of the Decline of Urban Mass Transportation," page 14.

104. John P. Hallihan, "Transit Facilities of Cities," *Annals of the American Academy of Political and Social Science*, September 1927, pages 61–62; American Transit Association, *Moving People*, pages 20–25; *Mass Transportation*, January 1948, page 82; Detroit Rapid Transit Commission, *Rapid Transit Plan for Metropolitan Detroit*, pages 34–37.

105. Arthur M. Schlesinger, Jr., *The Age of Roosevelt: The Coming of the New Deal* (Cambridge, 1958), pages 282–288.

106. *Detroit News*, October 2–November 9, 1933. See also Foster, *From Streetcar to Superhighway*, pages 154–156; Bottles, *Los Angeles and the Automobile*, pages 168–169; *Ninth Annual Report of the [Chicago] Department of Subways and Superhighways: 1947*, pages 22–35.

107. Bottles, *Los Angeles and the Automobile*, page 283; *Detroit News*, October 28, 1933; *Cleveland Plain Dealer*, June 16/17/21/22, October 10/16/18, 1933; *San Francisco Examiner*, October 16/21/29, November 1/3, 1937; Foster, *From Streetcar to Superhighway*, pages 165–167; Harry C. Koch, "Financing Transit!" *American City*, March 1939, pages 101–103.

108. Foster, *From Streetcar to Superhighway*, pages 165–166; *Cleveland Plain Dealer*, June 16, 1933; *San Francisco Examiner*, November 3, 1937; Bottles, *Los Angeles and the Automobile*, pages 168–169; *Detroit News*, November 8, 1933; Detroit Rapid Transit Commission, "Rapid Transit System and Plan Recommended for Detroit and the Metropolitan Area" (1958), page 30; *Ninth Annual Report of the [Chicago] Department of Subways and Superhighways: 1947*, pages 23–35; *Engineering News-Record*, April 1943, pages 1, 12.

109. *Planning Problems of Town, City, and Region*, page 266; Detroit Rapid Transit Commission, *Proposed Superhighway Plan*, pages 16–18; Foster, *From Streetcar to Superhighway*, page 154; "Will the Riding Public Stand for a Decaying Transit Business?" *American City*, December 1947, pages 97–98; Los Angeles Central Business District Association, *Los Angeles Parkway and Transit System* (Los Angeles, 1946), pages 4, 8; Detroit Rapid Transit Commission, *Rapid Transit Plan for Metropolitan Detroit*, (pages 5, 11, 45; American Institute of Planners Committee on Urban Transportation, *Urban Freeways* (New York, 1947), pages 16–25.

110. Arthur F. Ager, "Report on Engineering Survey of Operations and Facilities of the Pacific Electric Railway Company" (1947), page 147. See also DeLeuw, Cather & Company, Harold M. Lewis, and Joe R. Ong, *City of Los Angeles Recommended Program for Improvement of Transportation and Traffic Facilities* (1945), page 24; *American City*, October 1951, page 145; William R. Pollard, "Expediting Traffic by Transit," *Proceedings of the Annual Meeting [of the National Conference on City Planning]: 1946*, pages 36–37; Charles E. DeLeuw, "Mass Transportation at the Local Level," *Proceedings of the Annual National Conference [on Planning]: 1949*, page 137.

111. DeLeuw, Cather & Company, Lewis, and Ong, *Program for Improvement of Transportation and Traffic Facilities*, page 24; Hugh H. Winter, "Development of a Freeway System in the Los Angeles Metropolitan Area," *Traffic Quarterly*, April 1949, page 115; S.

Adler, "The Dynamics of Transit Innovation in the Los Angeles Metropolitan Area," *Society and Space,* 1986, pages 321–335; *Public Works Engineers' Yearbook: 1941,* page 205.

112. Charles D. Forsythe, "Development of Rapid Transit and Superhighways in Chicago" (1953), pages 6–7; "Chicago Plans Eight-lane Expressway," *Engineering News-Record,* April 19, 1945, pages 78–80; Carl D. Condit, *Chicago, 1940–1970: Building, Planning, and Urban Technology* (Chicago, 1974), pages 236–237; Detroit Rapid Transit Commission, *Rapid Transit Plan for Metropolitan Detroit,* pages 13–14; Adler, "Transit Innovation in Los Angeles," pages 324–326.

113. Murray D. Dessel, "Central Business Districts and Their Metropolitan Areas: A Summary of Geographical Shifts in Retail Sales Growth," U.S. Department of Commerce, Office of Area Development, *Area Trend Series, No. 1,* November 1957, page 11.

114. *Coordinated Transportation for Hartford: A Report of the Department of Engineering to the Commission on the City Plan* (1947), page 6; Charles M. Nelson, "Expressways and the Planning of Tomorrow's City," *Proceedings of the Annual National Planning Conference: 1950,* pages 119–120; Ernest M. Fisher, "Economics of Decentralization," *Appraisal Journal,* April 1942, page 138; Dessel, "Central Business Districts and Their Metropolitan Areas," page 11.

115. "Automobile Is Accelerating Urban Decentralization," *National Real Estate Journal,* October 1939, page 33.

116. Moses, "New Highways for a Better New York," page 11; V. E. Gunlock, "Chicago Builds $230,000,000 Superhighway System," *Civil Engineering,* February 1951, pages 38–39; St. Clair, *The Motorization of American Cities,* page 152; "Address of Lewis Mumford," page 5, in "The New Highways: Challenge to the Metropolitan Region," a symposium sponsored by the Connecticut General Life Insurance Company in September 1957, Graduate School of Design Library, Harvard University.

Chapter 7: Inventing Blight

1. U.S. House Committee on Roads, *Hearings [on] Federal Aid for Post-war Highway Construction* (Washington, D.C., 1944), volume 2, pages 764–780.

2. Homer Hoyt and Leonard C. Smith, "The Valuation of Land in Business Areas," *Appraisal Journal,* July 1943, page 201. See also Miles Colean, *American Housing: Problems and Prospects* (New York, 1944), page 16.

3. See chapter 5 above.

4. T. T. McCrosky, "Decentralization and Recentralization," *Proceedings of the Thirty-Fourth Annual Convention of the National Association of Building Owners and Managers: 1941,* page 108; J. Frederic Dewhurst and Associates, *America's Needs and Resources* (New York, 1947), page 421; Ernest M. Fisher, "Economics of Decentralization," *Appraisal Journal,* April 1942, page 138; Walter J. Mattison, "Blight and Mass Transportation in Metropolitan Communities," *Virginia Law Review,* November 1950, page 868; U.S. House Committee on Public Buildings and Grounds, *Hearings [on] Postwar Planning* (Washington, D.C., 1944), page 423.

5. *Proceedings of the National Conference on Postwar Housing: 1944,* pages 11–13; Philip W. Kniskern, "Blighting the Blight," *Real Estate,* July 5, 1941, page 18; Hoyt and Smith, "The Valuation of Land," page 199; H. M. Propper, "Saving Our Blighted Downtown Areas," *Nation's Business,* May 1940, page 20; Charles T. Stewart, "Protecting the Cen-

tral Districts," *Skyscraper Management*, July 1943, page 26; John R. Fugard, "The Office Building of Today and Tomorrow," *Proceedings of the Thirty-First Annual Convention of the National Association of Building Owners and Managers: 1938*, page 144.

6. House Committee on Public Buildings and Grounds, *Hearing [on] Post-war Planning*, page 423; Robert J. Howitz and Deil S. Wright, *Profile of a Metropolis: A Case Book* (Detroit, 1962), pages 15–16; Marc A. Weiss, "The Origins and Legacy of Urban Renewal," in J. Paul Mitchell, ed., *Federal Housing Policy and Programs: Past and Present* (New Brunswick, 1985), pages 254–255; Catherine Bauer, "Redevelopment: A Misfit in the Fifties," in Coleman Woodbury, ed., *The Future of Cities and Urban Redevelopment* (Chicago, 1953), page 9; John F. Bauman, *Public Housing, Race, and Renewal: Urban Planning in Philadelphia, 1920–1974* (Philadelphia, 1974), page 131.

7. Roy Lubove, *The Progressives and the Slums: Tenement House Reform in New York City, 1890–1917* (Pittsburgh, 1962), chapters 1–4; David Ward, *Poverty, Ethnicity, and the American City, 1840–1925* (Cambridge, England, 1989), chapters 2–3; Robert M. Fogelson, *America's Armories: Architecture, Society, and Public Order* (Cambridge, 1989), chapter 1; *New York Times*, June 6, 1880.

8. Lubove, *The Progressives and the Slums*, chapters 1–4; Christine Cousineau, "Tenement Reform in Boston, 1870–1920: Philanthropy, Regulation, and Government Assisted Housing," a paper delivered at the Third National Conference on American Planning History (1989), pages 14–15; E. R. L. Gould, "The Housing of City Masses," *International Quarterly*, January 1905, page 361; Thomas Lee Philpott, *The Slum and the Ghetto: Neighborhood Deterioration and Middle-Class Reform, Chicago, 1880–1930* (New York, 1978), pages 15–16, 22–26, 37.

9. Lubove, *The Progressives and the Slums*, chapters 1–4; Philpott, *The Slum and the Ghetto*, pages 15–16, 37–39; Alizina Parsons Stevens, "The Tenement House Curse: II. Some Chicago Tenement Houses," *Arena*, April 1894, pages 664–665; B. O. Flower, "The Tenement House Curse: Some Side Lights on the Tenement House Evil, by the Editor of the Arena," ibid., page 674; Lawrence M. Friedman, *Government and Slum Housing: A Century of Frustration* (Chicago, 1968), page 28.

10. Flower, "Some Side Lights on the Tenement House Evil," page 674; *American Architect and Building News*, December 10, 1892, page 165; E. R. L. Gould, "The Housing Problem," *Municipal Affairs*, March 1899, page 109; Friedman, *Government and Slum Housing*, pages 27–28; Walter J. Swaffield, "The Tenement House Curse: III. Tenement-House Life in Boston," *Arena*, April 1894, page 672; Stevens, "Some Chicago Tenement Houses," pages 666–667; *New York Times*, February 23, 1894.

11. Robert M. Fogelson, "The Parsimony of 'the large-hearted rich': An Essay on the Waning of the City and Suburban Homes Company," in Gina Luria Walker & Associates, ed., *The City and Suburban Homes Company's York Avenue Estate: A Social and Architectural History* (New York, 1990), part 1, pages 19–20; William Howe Tolman, "The Tenement House Curse: I. Evils of the System," *Arena*, April 1894, page 662; *New York Times*, July 16, 1877, February 18, 1900.

12. *New York Times*, February 23, 1894, November 14, 1896; Tolman, "Evils of the System," pages 660–661; Ward, *Poverty, Ethnicity, and the American City*, page 66; E. R. L. Gould, "The Only Cure for the Slums," *Forum*, June 1895, page 500; Fogelson, "The Parsimony of 'the large-hearted rich,'" page 19; Tenement House Department of the City of New York and Tenement House Committee of the Charity Organization Society, *For You* (New York, 1917).

13. Lubove, *The Progressives and the Slums*, pages 82–84; Gould, "The Only Cure for the Slums," page 500; Ward, *Poverty, Ethnicity, and the American City*, pages 43–44; Ernest Poole, *The Plague in Its Stronghold* (1903), page 24; Gwendolyn Wright, *Building the Dream: A Social History of Housing in America* (New York, 1981), page 119–120.

14. Tolman, "Evils of the System," page 660; "What to Do for the Slums," *Gunton's Magazine*, May 1898, page 318; Ward, *Poverty, Ethnicity, and the American City*, page 111; Fogelson, "The Parsimony of 'the large-hearted rich,'" page 20; Gould, "The Only Cure for the Slums," page 500.

15. Ward, *Poverty, Ethnicity, and the American City*, pages 73–75; Lubove, *The Progressives and the Slums*, pages 132–136, 140–144; Friedman, *Government and Slum Housing*, pages 33–39; Cousineau, "Tenement Reform in Boston," pages 13–23; Philpott, *The Slum and the Ghetto*, pages 102–103.

16. Fogelson, "The Parsimony of 'the large-hearted rich,'" pages 9–36; Lubove, *The Progressives and the Slums*, pages 8–9, 33–39, 100–113; Friedman, *Government and Slum Housing*, pages 75–87; Eugenie Ladner Birch and Deborah S. Gardner, "The Seven Percent Solution: A Review of Philanthropic Housing, 1870–1910," *Journal of Urban History*, August 1981, pages 403–438.

17. Ward, *Poverty, Ethnicity, and the American City*, pages 76–77; Fogelson, "The Parsimony of 'the large-hearted rich,'" pages 20–21; Lubove, *The Progressives and the Slums*, pages 110–111. See also Joel Arthur Tarr, "From City to Suburb: The 'Moral' Influence of Transportation Technology," in Alexander B. Callow, Jr., *American Urban History* (New York, 1973), pages 206–208.

18. "What to Do for the Slums," page 320; *[New York] Real Estate Record and Builders' Guide*, September 6, 1884, page 905; Ward, *Poverty, Ethnicity, and the American City*, pages 111–113; Robert W. De Forest and Lawrence Veiller, eds., *The Tenement House Problem* (New York, 1903), volume 1, pages 385–417; Jenna Weissman Joselit, "The Landlord as Czar: Pre–World War I Tenant Activity," in Ronald Lawson, ed., *The Tenant Movement in New York City, 1904–1984* (New Brunswick, 1986), pages 19–20.

19. *Report of the [New York City] Mayor's Committee on Housing* (New York, 1924), pages 5–9; Robert M. Fogelson, "An Essay on the Ethnic Make-up of the York Avenue Estate," in Gina Luria Walker & Associates, ed., *The City and Suburban Homes Company*, part 3, pages 18–21; Lubove, *The Progressives and the Slums*, pages 165–166; Friedman, *Government and Slum Housing*, pages 47–48; Mary Kingsbury Simkovitch, *The City Worker's World in America* (New York, 1917), page 35; Mabel L. Walker, *Urban Blight and Slums: Economic and Legal Factors in Their Origin, Reclamation, and Prevention* (Cambridge, 1938), page 13.

20. Lawrence Veiller, "Slumless America," *Proceedings of the Twelfth National Conference on City Planning: 1921*, page 154; Lawrence Veiller, "The Abolition of Slums in the United States," *Housing*, June 1931, page 81; Ralph Adams Cram, "Scrapping the Slum," *Proceeding of the Seventh National Conference on Housing: 1918*, pages 242–243; Edith Elmer Wood, *Slums and Blighted Areas in the United States* (Washington, D.C., 1935), pages 17–18, 26–27, 55–56; Philpott, *The Slum and the Ghetto*, pages 107–108; Fogelson, "The Parsimony of 'the large-hearted rich,'" pages 36–37; *Report of the Housing Committee of the Reconstruction Commission of the State of New York* (Albany, 1920), page 33.

21. Friedman, *Government and Slum Housing*, pages 44–48. See also Lawrence M. Friedman and Michael J. Spector, "Tenement House Legislation in Wisconsin: Reform

and Reaction," *American Journal of Legal History,* January 1965, pages 41–63; Lubove, *The Progressives and the Slums,* pages 151–158, 166–174; Philpott, *The Slum and the Ghetto,* pages 101–108; Cousineau, "Tenement Reform in Boston," pages 15–16, 18–21; *Report of the [New York] State Board of Housing: 1930,* pages 71–76; Wright, *Building the Dream,* page 129; Carol Aronovici, "Housing the Poor: Mirage or Reality?" *Law and Contemporary Problems,* March 1934, pages 148–157.

22. Philpott, *The Slum and the Ghetto,* pages 93–94; Cousineau, "Tenement Reform in Boston," pages 5–11; Friedman, *Government and Slum Housing,* pages 81–86; Fogelson, "The Parsimony of 'the large-hearted rich,'" pages 3–4, 36–53; *[New York] Real Estate Record and Builders' Guide,* October 23, 1926, page 5, November 6, 1926, page 5, December 11, 1926, page 5.

23. Fogelson, "An Essay on the Ethnic Make-up of the York Avenue Estate," pages 6–9, 15–18.

24. Lubove, *The Progressives and the Slums,* page 93; James Ford, *Slums and Housing* (Cambridge, 1936), volume 2, chapter 27; Edith Elmer Wood, "A Century of the Housing Problem," *Law and Contemporary Problems,* March 1934, pages 142–146.

25. Max Page, "The Creative Destruction of New York City: Landscape, Memory, and the Politics of Place, 1900–1930" (Ph.D. diss., University of Pennsylvania, 1995), pages 114–118, 128–132; *New York Times,* November 22, 1896; I. N. Phelps Stokes, "A Plan for Tenements in Connection with a Municipal Park," in De Forest and Veiller, eds., *The Tenement House Problem,* volume 2, page 59.

26. Page, "The Creative Destruction of New York," pages 114–118, 126–128; Jacob A. Riis, "The Clearing of Mulberry Bend," *Review of Reviews,* August 1895, pages 172–178; *[New York] Real Estate Record and Builders' Guide,* June 22, 1889, page 867; Lubove, *The Progressives and the Slums,* page 79; Philpott, *The Slum and the Ghetto,* pages 94–96; Cousineau, "Tenement Reform in Boston," pages 19–20; Veiller, "The Abolition of Slums in the United States," page 35; Boston City Planning Board, *The North End: A Survey and Comprehensive Plan* (Boston, 1919), pages 40–42.

27. Riis, "The Clearing of Mulberry Bend," pages 175–176; Jacob A. Riis, *A Ten Years' War: An Account of the Battle with the Slums in New York* (New York, 1900), pages 176–179; Murray Seasongood, Lawrence Veiller, and Newman F. Baker, "Some Legal Aspects of the Problem of Blighted Areas and Slums," *American City,* February 1932, page 94; Page, "The Creative Destruction of New York," pages 133–138.

28. Report of the Mayor's Committee on Housing," page 15. See also Gould, "The Housing of City Masses," pages 355–356; "The Perils of Slum Clearance," *Housing,* May 1933, pages 42–43; Lawrence Veiller, "Slumless America," page 158; Veiller, "The Abolition of Slums," page 86; Joseph Platzker, "Community Facts and Statistics as a Basis for a Slum Clearance Program," *Proceedings of the National Conference on Slum Clearance: 1933,* page 34.

29. *[New York] Real Estate Record and Builders' Guide,* June 22, 1889, page 867; Thomas Adams, "Scrapping the Slum," *Proceedings of the Seventh National Conference on Housing: 1918,* page 314; Philpott, *The Slum and the Ghetto,* pages 94–95; Page, "The Creative Destruction of New York," page 110; Fogelson, "The Parsimony of 'the large-hearted rich,'" page 23; Royal Commission on London Traffic, *Appendices to the Report of the Royal Commission on London Traffic with Index* (London, 1906), page 75; Veiller, "The Abolition of Slums," pages 86–87; Gould, "The Housing of City Masses," page 362.

30. Jacob A. Riis, *How the Other Half Lives* (New York, 1989), page 216; Page, "The Creative Destruction of New York," pages 128, 138–139; *Report of the Housing Committee of the Reconstruction Commission*, page 34; *Report of the Mayor's Committee on Housing*, page 15.

31. Walker, *Urban Blight and Slums*, pages 110–123; Anthony Jackson, *A Place Called Home: A History of Low-Cost Housing in Manhattan* (Cambridge, 1976), pages 189–192; *Report of the New York State Board of Housing: 1930*, page 60; Peter Marcuse, "The Beginning of Public Housing in New York," *Journal of Urban History*, August 1986, pages 356–362; Catherine Bauer, " Slum Clearance or Housing," *Nation*, December 27, 1933, page 730; Aronovici, "Housing the Poor," page 150.

32. Adams, "Scrapping the Slum," page 316; Veiller, "Slumless America," pages 158–159.

33. Eugenie Ladner Birch, "Woman-Made America: The Case of Early Public Housing Policy," *Journal of the American Institute of Planners*, April 1978, pages 130–144; Wood, "A Century of the Housing Problem," pages 137–147; Catherine Bauer, "Slums Aren't Necessary," *American Mercury*, March 1934, pages 296–305; Marcuse, "Beginnings of Public Housing," pages 354–355; U.S. Senate Committee on Education and Labor, *Hearings [on] Slum and Low-Rent Public Housing* (Washington, D.C., 1935), pages 5, 84, 110–111; U.S. Senate Committee on Education and Labor, *Hearings [on the] United States Housing Act of 1936* (Washington, D.C., 1936), pages 52, 159–160; *Report of the Housing Committee of the Reconstruction Commission*, page 39.

34. Roy Lubove, "At War with Itself: The City and Suburban Homes Company and the Model Tenement Movement: Part II. A New Generation, a New Era in Housing," in Gina Luria Walker and Associates, ed., *The City and Suburban Homes Company*, part I, pages 11–12, 25–29.

35. Walker, *Urban Blight and Slums*, page 311. See also Grosvenor Atterbury, "How to Get Low Cost Houses," *Proceedings of the Fifth National Conference on Housing: 1916*, pages 91–101; *Report of the Housing Committee of the Reconstruction Commission*, pages 41, 47–52; Roy Lubove, "At War with Itself," pages 19–25; Roy Lubove, "New Cities for Old: The Urban Reconstruction of the 1930s," *Social Studies*, November 1962, pages 203–213; John M. Gries and James Ford, eds., *Slums, Large-Scale Housing, and Decentralization* (Washington, D.C., 1932), chapter 2.

36. Arthur C. Holden, "Facing Realities in Slum Clearance," *Architectural Record*, February 1932, page 75; Edith Elmer Wood, "Slum Clearance—What? Why? How?" *Proceedings of the National Conference of Slum Clearance: 1933*, page 21; Marcuse, "Beginnings of Public Housing," page 361; Walker, *Urban Blight and Slums*, page 112.

37. Lubove, "At War with Itself," pages 27–29, 36–40; Jackson, *A Place Called Home*, pages 188–196; James S. Ford, *Slums and Housing* (Cambridge, 1936), volume 2, pages 518–519; Earl Thomas Hanson, *Urban Redevelopment in the United States* (Urbana, Illinois, 1952), pages 4–5.

38. Jackson, *A Place Called Home*, pages 202–205; *Survey*, July 15, 1931, page 395; Timothy L. McConnell, *The Wagner Housing Act: A Case Study of the Legislative Process* (Chicago, 1957), chapter 3; Senate Committee on Education and Labor, *Hearings on the United States Housing Act of 1936*, page 52; Wood, "A Century of the Housing Problem," page 146; Lubove, "At War with Itself," page 47; Wood, *Slums and Blighted Areas*, page 121.

39. Friedman, *Government and Slum Housing*, pages 104–105; J. Joseph Huthmacher,

Senator Robert F. Wagner and the Rise of Urban Liberalism (New York, 1968), pages 210–212; McConnell, *The Wagner Housing Act,* chapter 3; Senate Committee on Education and Labor, *Hearings [on the] United States Housing Act of 1936,* pages 330–331, 338–343; Aronovici, "Housing the Poor," pages 150–151; Marcuse, "Beginnings of Public Housing," pages 361–363; Henry Wright, "New Homes for a New Deal, II: Abolishing Slums Forever," *New Republic,* February 21, 1934, pages 41–44; Lewis Mumford, "New Homes for a New Deal, III: The Shortage of Dwellings and Direction," ibid., February 28, 1934, pages 69–72.

40. Joel Schwartz, *The New York Approach: Robert Moses, Urban Liberals, and the Redevelopment of the Inner City* (Columbus, Ohio, 1993), pages 32–34; Ford, *Slums and Housing,* volume 2, pages 704–706.

41. Friedman, *Government and Slum Housing,* pages 101–103; Gilbert A. Cam, "Government Activity in Low-Cost Housing," *Journal of Political Economy,* July 1939, pages 359–363; Mark A. Gelfand, *A Nation of Cities: The Federal Government and Urban America, 1933–1965* (New York, 1975), pages 60–61.

42. Friedman, *Government and Slum Housing,* pages 104–113; Cam, "Government Activity in Low-Cost Housing," pages 373–376. See also Huthmacher, *Wagner,* pages 206–208; McDonnell, *The Wagner Housing Act,* chapters 3–15.

43. Raymond A. Mohl, "Trouble in Paradise: Race and Housing in Miami During the New Deal Era," *Prologue,* Spring 1987, pages 7–14.

44. Schwartz, *The New York Approach,* pages 34–37.

45. Senate Committee on Education and Labor, *Hearings [on the] United States Housing Act of 1936,* pages 329–330. See also Garnett Laidlaw Eskew, *Of Land and Men: The Birth and Growth of an Idea* (Washington, D.C., 1959), chapters 1–5.

46. U.S. Congress, Joint Committee on Housing, *Hearings [on a] Study and Investigation of Housing* (Washington, D.C., 1948), part 3, page 2, 879; McCrosky, "Decentralization and Recentralization," page 106; Urban Land Institute, *Decentralization: What It Is Doing to Our Cities* (Washington, D.C., 1940), pages 1–4; R. F. Hewitt, "Changing Conditions," *Proceedings of the Thirty-First Annual Convention of the National Association of Building Owners and Managers: 1938,* page 133; Senate Committee on Education and Labor, *Hearings [on the] United States Housing Act of 1936,* pages 203–204.

47. Hoyt and Smith, "The Valuation of Land," pages 201; Richmond City Planning Commission, *A Master Plan for the Physical Development of the City of Richmond* (Richmond, 1946), page 90; Charles T. Stewart, "Our Disease—Disintegration: For Healthy Land Values the Remedy Is Reintegration," *Real Estate,* April 12, 1941, page 7.

48. Kniskern, "Blighting the Blight," page 18; Alexander L. Trout, "Is Downtown Detroit Becoming a 'Desert in a Housing Swamp'?" *Real Estate and Building,* August 1939, page 5; Stewart, "Protecting Our Central Districts," page 26; "Slum Surgery in St. Louis," *Architectural Forum,* April 1951, page 129; Propper, "Savings Our Blighted Downtown Areas," page 22; Charles F. Edgecomb, "Urban Redevelopment Is Under Way: I. Detroit," *Proceedings of the Annual Meeting [of the] American Society of Planning Officials: 1947,* page 153; Carl S. Wells, *Proposals for Downtown Detroit,* (Washington, D.C., 1942), page 24.

49. Merlo J. Pusey, "Reclaiming Our Slums," *Yale Review,* Summer 1939, pages 728, 732; Robert F. Marshall, "Slum Clearance: A Flight from Reality," in M. B. Schnapper, compiler, *Public Housing in America* (New York, 1939), page 278; U.S. House Committee on Banking and Currency, *Hearings [on a Bill] to Create a United States Housing*

Authority (Washington, D.C., 1937), page 151; Robert Moore Fisher, *Twenty Years of Public Housing* (New York, 1959), page 11; Schwartz, *The New York Approach*, chapter 2; Rosalie Genevro, "Site Selection and the New York City Housing Authority, 1934–1939," *Journal of Urban History*, August 1986, pages 334–352.

50. Fisher, *Twenty Years of Public Housing*, page 11; Pusey, "Reclaiming Our Slums," page 739; Harold L. Ickes, "The Federal Housing Program, *New Republic*, December 19, 1934, page 144; Joint Committee on Housing, *Hearing [on a] Study and Investigation of Housing*, part 1, page 903; Senate Committee on Education and Labor, *Hearings [on] Slum and Low-Rent Public Housing*, page 104; Florence Fleming Corley, "Atlanta's Techwood and University Homes Projects: The Nation's Laboratory for Public Housing," *Atlanta History*, Winter 1987–1988, pages 17–35; Schwartz, *The New York Approach*, chapter 2.

51. Edgecomb, "Urban Redevelopment Is Under Way," page 153.

52. Weiss, "Urban Renewal," pages 253–274. See also Joint Committee on Housing, *Hearings [on a] Study and Investigation of Housing*, part 3, pages 3512–3513; U.S. Senate Committee on Banking and Currency, *Hearings [on the] General Housing Act of 1945* (Washington, D.C., 1946), part 2, page 773; Catherine Bauer, "Housing in the United States: Problems and Policy," a reprint from the *International Labour Review*, July 1945, page 18.

53. Weiss, "Urban Renewal," page 264.

54. *Proceedings of the Fourth National Conference on City Planning: 1912*; pages 100–115.

55. Veiller, "The Abolition of Slums," page 82; C. Earl Morrow and Charles Herrick, "Blighted Districts: Their Cause and Cure," *City Planning*, October 1925, page 160; Harland Bartholomew, "Can Blighted Areas Be Rehabilitated?" *Annals of Real Estate Practice: 1930*, page 480; Gries and Ford, eds., *Slums, Large-Scale Housing, and Decentralization*, page 1–2; William A. Stanton, "Blighted Districts in Philadelphia," *Proceedings of the Tenth National Conference on City Planning: 1918*, page 76.

56. U.S. House Committee on Public Buildings and Grounds, *Hearings [on] Post-War Planning* (Washington, D.C., 1944), pages 660–661. See also Harland Bartholomew, "The Neighborhood—Key to Urban Redemption," *Proceedings of the [National] Conference on Planning: 1941*, page 217; Hugh E. Young, "The Story of Chicago's Physical Development," *Real Estate*, April 13, 1940, page 20; Walter J. Mattison, "Creating Jobs by Elimination of Blighted Areas in Cities," *Municipalities and the Law in Action* (1945), page 246; J. Frederic Dewhurst and Associates, *America's Needs and Resources* (New York, 1947), pages 413–414.

57. Lubove, *The Progressives and the Slums*, chapters 1–3; Ward, *Poverty, Ethnicity, and the American City*, chapters 2–3.

58. Harland Bartholomew, "Technical Problems in Slum Clearance: The City Planner's Viewpoint," *Planning and National Recovery: Planning Problems Presented at the Twenty-Fifth National Conference on City Planning: 1933*, page 121; Henry Wright, "Housing—Where, When, and How?" *Architecture*, July 1933, page 2; Walter J. Mattison, "Blighted Areas—They Must Go," *Downtown Merchantman*, April 15, 1944, page 1; Edward S. Burrell, "The Social Problem Involved in Securing the Benefits of Slum Elimination," *Planning and National Recovery*, page 134.

59. "Urban Redevelopment," *Tomorrow's Town*, November 1944, page 1; James T. Paterson, *The Dread Disease: Cancer in the Modern American Culture* (Cambridge, 1987), pages 28–29; E. R. L. Gould, "The Housing Problem in Great Cities," *Quarterly Jour-*

nal of Economics, May 1900, page 388; Veiller, "Slumless America," page 158; Wood, "Slum Clearance," page 19; Thomas C. Desmond, "Blighted Areas Get a New Chance," *National Municipal Review,* November 1941, pages 629, 641; Homer Hoyt, "Rebuilding American Cities After the War," *Journal of Land and Public Utility Economics,* August 1943, page 366.

60. *[Boston] City Record,* February 12, 1949, page 163; Senate Committee on Education and Labor, *Hearings [on the] Housing Act of 1936,* page 30; Raymond S. Short, "Redevelopment in Philadelphia: An Approach to Survival," *Economic and Business Bulletin,* September 1950, page 3; Stewart, "Our Disease—Disintegration," page 8; Morrow and Herrick, "Blighted Areas," page 166; Hoyt, "Rebuilding American Cities," page 364.

61. Senate Committee on Education and Labor, *Hearings [on] Slum and Low-Rent Public Housing,* pages 29–30, 67–69, 161; Wood, *Slums and Blighted Areas,* page 19.

62. Wood, *Slums and Blighted Areas,* pages 20–21; Senate Committee on Education and Labor, *Hearings on Slum and Low-Rent Public Housing,* pages 29–30; F. J. C. Dresser, "The Slum: Its Cost and Challenge," *Public Works Engineers' Yearbook: 1947,* pages 153–160; *Report of the Urban Redevelopment Commission to the Members of the General Assembly of the State of Ohio* (1946), page 14; U.S. Senate Special Committee on Post-War Economic Policy and Planning, Subcommittee on Housing and Urban Development, *Hearings on Post-War Economic Policy and Planning* (Washington, D.C., 1945), pages 1233–1234.

63. Walker, *Urban Blight and Slums,* chapter 5.

64. House Committee on Public Buildings and Grounds, *Hearings [on] Post-War Planning,* pages 662–663; Woods, *Slums and Blighted Areas,* page 18; James Sweinhart, *What Detroit's Slums Cost Its Taxpayers* (1946), page 12.

65. Senate Special Committee on Post-War Economic Policy and Planning, *Hearings [on] Post-War Economic Policy and Planning,* part 9, page 1614.

66. Senate Committee on Education and Labor, *Hearings [on] Slum and Low-Rent Public Housing,* page 161; Aronovici, "Housing the Poor," page 151; Genevro, "Site Selection and the New York City Housing Authority," page 341; House Committee on Banking and Currency, *Hearings [on a Bill] to Create a United States Housing Authority,* pages 230–231; Senate Special Committee on Post-War Economic Policy and Planning, *Hearings [on] Post-War Economic Policy and Planning,* part 13, page 1971; Ickes, "The Federal Housing Program," page 155; Wood, "Slum Clearance," page 19.

67. Senate Special Committee on Post-War Economic Policy and Planning, *Hearings [on] Post-War Economic Policy and Planning,* part 13, page 1971. See also House Committee on Banking and Currency, *Hearings [on a Bill] to Create a United States Housing Authority,* page 132; Genevro, "Site Selection and the New York City Housing Authority," page 336; Walker, *Urban Blight and Slums,* pages 114–117, 122–123, 129.

68. Walker, *Urban Blight and Slums,* pages 116–117, Genevro, "Site Selection and the New York City Housing Authority," pages 348–349; Charles W. Killam, "City Planning and Blighted Areas," *Weekly Bulletin [of the] Michigan Society of Architects,* December 7, 1942, page 6; Schwartz, *The New York Approach,* pages 26–32; Jackson, *A Place Called Home,* page 192; Senate Committee on Banking and Currency, *Hearings [on the] General Housing Act of 1945,* part 1, page 549.

69. Frederic Dewhurst and Associates, *America's Needs and Resources,* page 418; Edgecomb, "Urban Redevelopment Is Under Way," page 153; Mattison, "Blight and Mass

Transportation," pages 862–865; Boston City Planning Board, *Report on the Income and Cost Survey of the City of Boston* (1935), pages 6–7.

70. Boston City Planning Board, *Report on the Income and Cost Survey*, pages 1, 6–7.

71. Mattison, "Blight and Mass Transportation," page 862; Senate Committee on Banking and Currency, *Hearings [on the] General Housing Act of 1945*, part 1, page 500; House Committee on Public Buildings and Grounds, *Hearings [on] Post-War Planning*, pages 421–422.

72. Alfred Bettman, "Urban Redevelopment Legislation," in Harlean James, ed., *American Planning and Civic Annual* (Washington, D.C., 1944), page 54. See also Walter H. Blucher, "Rehabilitation of the Blighted District—A Cooperative Enterprise," in Harlean James, ed., *American Planning and Civic Annual* (Washington, D.C., 1935), page 274; Propper, "Saving Our Blighted Downtown Areas," page 92; Ford, *Slums and Housing*, volume 2, page 611; *Planning and National Recovery*, page 145.

73. Bettman, "Urban Redevelopment Legislation," page 54; "Report of the Committee on Urban Redevelopment," *Proceedings [of the] National Conference on Planning: 1941*, page 254; Senate Special Committee on Post-War Economic Policy and Planning, *Hearings [on] Post-War Economic Policy and Planning*, part 11, pages 1738–1739.

74. House Committee on Public Buildings and Grounds, *Hearings [on] Post-War Planning*, pages 508–510. See also Bettman, "Urban Redevelopment Legislation," page 54.

75. Elizabeth Wood, "Realities of Urban Redevelopment," in National Association of Housing Officials, compiler, *Urban Redevelopment* (1948). See also U.S. House Committee on Banking and Currency, *Hearings [on] Amendments to the United States Housing Act of 1937* (Washington, D.C., 1938), page 96; Senate Committee on Education and Labor, *Hearings [on] Slum and Low-Rent Public Housing*, page 104; Charles Abrams, "Slum Clearance or Vacant Land Development?" in Schnapper, compiler, *Public Housing in America*, pages 90–91; Philip V. I. Darling, "Some Notes on Blighted Areas," *Planners' Journal*, January–March 1943, pages 11–14.

76. Senate Special Committee on Post-War Economic Policy and Planning, *Hearings [on] Post-War Economic Policy and Planning*, part 9, pages 1619–1620; *Proceedings [of the] National Conference on Planning: 1941*, page 261.

77. Senate Committee on Banking and Currency, *Hearings [on the] General Housing Act of 1945*, part 1, page 111. See also Chicago Plan Commission, *Housing Goals for Chicago* (1946), page 135; Joint Committee on Housing, *Hearings [on a] Study and Investigation of Housing*, part 4, page 3728; Senate Special Committee on Post-War Economic Policy and Planning, *Hearings [on] Post-War Economic Policy and Planning*, part 12, page 1974; Paul A. Pfretzschner, "Urban Redevelopment: A New Approach to Urban Reconstruction," *Social Research*, Winter 1953, page 422.

78. Coleman Woodbury, "Housing in the Redevelopment of Cities," *Land Economics*, November 1949, page 402. See also Trout, "Is Downtown Detroit Becoming a 'Desert in a Housing Swamp'?" page 7; Chicago Plan Commission, *Housing Goals for Chicago*, page 135; Pfretzschner, "Urban Redevelopment," page 419; National Association of Municipal Law Officials, *American Cities After the War—A Plan for the Elimination of Blighted Areas* (1943), page 4; Arthur W. Binns, "Housing and Blighted Areas," *National Real Estate Journal*, November 1941, page 15.

79. Ferd Kramer, "The Role of Private Enterprise," *Proceedings of the Annual National Planning Conference: 1950*, page 33; Abrams, "Slum Clearance or Vacant Land Devel-

opment?" pages 90–91; Bauer, "Housing in the United States," page 19; Arnold R. Hirsch, *Making the Second Ghetto: Race and Housing in Chicago, 1940–1960* (Cambridge, England, 1983), pages 102–103; "Report of the Committee on Urban Redevelopment," *Proceedings [of the] National Conference on Planning: 1941*, page 261.

80. Kramer, "The Role of Private Enterprise," page 32. See also Senate Committee on Banking and Currency, *Hearings [on the] General Housing Act of 1945*, part 1, page 111.

81. Kramer, "The Role of Private Enterprise," page 32; Chicago Plan Commission, *Housing Goals for Chicago*, page 135. See also Mel Scott, "What's Stopping Urban Redevelopment?" *American City*, April 1948, page 99.

82. National Institute of Municipal Law Officers, Committee on Post-War Planning, *American Cities After the War* (1943), page 4; Robert C. Klove, "A Technique for Delimiting Chicago's Blighted Areas," *Journal of Land and Public Utility Economics*, November 1941, pages 483–484; Asher Achinstein, "Some Economic Characteristics of Blighted Areas," ibid., February 1935, page 38.

83. "Report of the Committee on Urban Redevelopment," *Proceedings of the Annual Meeting [of the American Society of Planning Officials]: 1943*, page 102; "Blighted Areas in California Cities," *Landscape Architecture*, April 1946, page 112; Bauman, *Public Housing, Race, and Renewal*, page 92; Coleman Woodbury and Frederick S. Gutheim, *Rethinking Urban Redevelopment* (Chicago, 1949), page 15.

84. Senate Special Committee on Post-War Economic Policy and Planning, *Hearings [on] Post-War Economic Policy and Planning*, part 9, page 1605.

85. Schwartz, *The New York Approach*, chapters 3–4; Woodbury, "Housing in the Redevelopment of Cities," pages 103–104; Weiss, "Urban Renewal," page 256.

86. Schwartz, *The New York Approach*, pages 94–95; Hirsch, *Making the Second Ghetto*, pages 103–104; Woodbury, "Housing in the Redevelopment of Cities," pages 402–403; Hugh Potter, "Assembly and Redevelopment of Lands in Substandard Urban Areas Discussed," *Urban Land*, March 1944, page 1.

87. Guy Greer, "A New Start for the Cities," *Fortune*, September 1944, pages 186, 189; George Herbert Gray, *Housing and Citizenship: A Study of Low-Cost Housing* (New York, 1946), pages 162–163.

88. Chicago Plan Commission, *Housing Goals for Chicago*, page 134; San Francisco Planning and Housing Association, *Blight and Taxes* (1947), pages 13–14; Joint Committee on Housing, *Hearings [on a] Study and Investigation of Housing*, part 1, page 589; Detroit Housing Commission, *The Detroit Plan: A Program for Blight Elimination* (1946), pages 6–7.

89. Hoyt and Smith, "The Valuation of Land," pages 204–205; *Proceedings [of the] National Conference on Planning: 1941*, page 233; Greer, "A New Start for the Cities," page 189; Bettman, "Urban Redevelopment," page 58.

90. Jon C. Teaford, *The Rough Road to Renaissance: Urban Revitalization in America, 1940–1985* (Baltimore, 1990), pages 34–35, 106; Eskew, *Of Land and Men*, chapter 10; Della Richman, "State Urban Redevelopment Legislation," in Clarence Ridley and Orin F. Nolting, eds., *The Municipal Year Book, 1946* (Chicago, 1946), pages 311–315.

91. Weiss, "Urban Renewal," pages 260–262. See also Seward H. Mott, "Urban Redevelopment Legislation Analyzed," *American City*, August 1945, pages 83–84; Teaford, *Rough Road to Renaissance*, page 106.

92. Otto K. Jensen, "Indianapolis Finds Its Answer to Urban Blight," *Federal Home Loan*

Bank Review, August 1946, pages 329–331; *[Boston] City Record*, February 12, 1949, page 163; U.S. Housing and Home Finance Agency, "Summary of Local Redevelopment Programs" (1950); "Criteria Used in Delimiting Redevelopment Areas: A Symposium," *Journal of the American Institute of Planners*, Summer 1950, page 116; National Institute of Municipal Law Officials, *American Cities After the War*, page 5.

93. "Urban Redevelopment Progress in Indianapolis," *Urban Land*, September 1946, page 1; Robert S. Alexander and Drayton S. Bryant, *Rebuilding a City: A Study of Redevelopment Problems in Los Angeles* (Los Angeles, 1951), pages 24–35; *Planning and Civic Comment*, July 1945, page 29; Louis B. Wetmore, "The Redevelopment Program of Providence, Rhode Island," *Journal of the American Institute of Planning*, Spring 1949, pages 11–15; Hirsch, *Making the Second Ghetto*, pages 109–110; Teaford, *Rough Road to Renaissance*, page 106; Bauman, *Public Housing, Race, and Renewal*, pages 98–99; Jeanne R. Lowe, *Cities in a Race with Time* (New York, 1968), page 140.

94. *Planning and Civic Comment*, July 1945, page 29; Wetmore, "The Redevelopment Program of Providence," pages 11–16; "Criteria Used in Delimiting Redevelopment Areas," pages 109–121.

95. Alexander and Bryant, *Rebuilding a City*, chapter 6; Mowitz and Wright, *Profile of a Metropolis*, pages 17–19; Hirsch, *Making the Second Ghetto*, chapter 4; Lowe, *Cities in a Race with Time*, pages 140–143; Schwartz, *The New York Approach*, chapter 4, 6–9.

96. Mowitz and Wright, *Profile of a Metropolis*, pages 17–20. See also "Report of the Committee on Urban Redevelopment," *Proceedings of the Annual Meeting [of the American Society of Planning Officials]: 1943*, page 102; Hanson, *Urban Redevelopment Legislation*, pages 16–18; Alexander and Bryant, *Rebuilding a City*, page 25; Short, "Redevelopment in Philadelphia," pages 5–6; American Society of Planning Officials, *Urban Redevelopment Decisions* (1950), pages 1–3.

97. Louis B. Wetmore and Edward J. Milne, "Rebuilding Our Cities—Is There Any Progress?" *American City*, March 1948, page 76; Richard J. Steiner, "Urban Redevelopment—Baltimore Initiates the Job By Designating Redevelopment Areas," in National Association of Housing Officials, compiler, *Urban Redevelopment*; Hirsch, *Making the Second Ghetto*, chapter 4; Bauman, *Public Housing, Race, and Renewal*, page 94; "Urban Rebuilding Plans Face Many Hurdles," *American City*, August 1948, page 95; Alexander and Bryant, *Rebuilding a City*, pages 31–34.

98. Scott, "What's Stopping Urban Redevelopment?" page 100; Alexander and Bryant, *Rebuilding a City*, pages 24–35; Short, "Redevelopment in Philadelphia," page 11; *Journal of Housing*, December 1948, pages 304–305; Mowitz and Wright, *Profile of a Metropolis*, page 20.

99. Gelfand, *A Nation of Cities*, chapters 1–3; Weiss, "Urban Renewal," pages 263–264.

100. Gelfand, *A Nation of Cities*, chapter 4; Weiss, "Urban Renewal," pages 200–261.

101. Gelfand, *A Nation of Cities*, chapter 4. See also Ashley A. Foard and Hilbert Fefferman, "Federal Urban Renewal Legislation," in James Q. Wilson, ed., *Urban Renewal: The Record and the Controversy* (Cambridge, 1967), pages 75–79.

102. Charles T. Stewart, "Preparation for Postwar Building in Cities," *Proceedings of the 30th Business Meeting and Conference on Postwar Planning of the Mortgage Bankers Association of America: 1943*, page 130. See also Joint Committee on Housing, *Hearings [on a] Study and Investigation of Housing*, part 1, pages 174, 191; Senate Special Committee on Post-War Economic Policy and Planning, *Hearings [on] Post-War Economic Policy and Planning*, part 9, pages 1620–1621; Guy Greer, "City Planning and Re-

building," *Journal of Land and Public Utility Economics*, August 1942, pages 288–289; U.S. Senate Committee on Banking Currency, *Hearings [on the] Housing Act of 1949* (Washington, D.C. 1949), page 536.

103. Walter J. Mattison, "Rehabilitation of Blighted Areas as a Post-War Measure for Cities," *Municipalities and the Law in Action* (1944), page 398; Senate Special Committee on Post-War Economic Policy and Planning, *Hearing [on] Post-War Economic Policy and Planning*, part 9, pages 1614–1616; Friedman, *Government and Slum Housing*, page 149; House Committee on Public Buildings and Grounds, *Hearing [on] Post-War Planning*, pages 518–525; U.S. Senate Committee on Banking and Currency, *Hearings [on] Bills Pertaining to National Housing* (Washington, D.C., 1947), pages 301–303; Arthur Binns, "Is the Wagner Bill for Rebuilding Our Cities Desirable? No!" *National Real Estate Journal*, October 1943, pages 16, 18–20.

104. Weiss, "Urban Renewal," page 270. See also Friedman, *Government and Slum Housing*, pages 149–150; U.S. House Committee on Banking and Currency, *Hearings [on the] Housing Act of 1949* (Washington, D.C., 1949), pages 538–546; Senate Committee on Banking and Currency, *Hearings [on the] General Housing Act of 1945*, part 1, page 428; Huthmacher, *Wagner*, pages 322–323; Joint Committee on Housing, *Hearings [on a] Study and Investigation of Housing*, part 4, pages 4112–4113; Senate Committee on Banking and Currency, *Hearings [on] Bills Pertaining to National Housing*, pages 301–303.

105. Gelfand, *A Nation of Cities*, pages 136–147; Foard and Fefferman, "Federal Urban Renewal Legislation," pages 76–82.

106. Foard and Fefferman, "Federal Urban Renewal Legislation," pages 82–87; *Urban Land*, September 1943, pages 1–4; Gelfand, *A Nation of Cities*, pages 144–147.

107. Philip J. Funigiello, *The Challenge to Urban Liberalism: Federal–City Relations During World War II* (Knoxville, 1978), pages 228–230. See also Gelfand, *A Nation of Cities*, pages 130–131, 147–148; Foard and Fefferman, "Federal Urban Renewal Legislation," pages 79–87.

108. Gelfand, *A Nation of Cities*, pages 136–147. See also *Urban Land*, September 1943, pages 1–4; Senate Committee on Banking and Currency, *Hearings [on the] General Housing Act of 1945*, part 1, page 427; Friedman, *Government and Slum Housing*, page 149.

109. Gelfand, *A Nation of Cities*, page 151; Foard and Fefferman, "Federal Urban Renewal Legislation," pages 88–91.

110. Gelfand, *A Nation of Cities*, pages 151–152; Foard and Fefferman, "Federal Urban Renewal Legislation," pages 93–95, 104–106; Weiss, "Urban Renewal," pages 262–263, 271.

111. Gelfand, *A Nation of Cities*, pages 152–156; Friedman, *Government and Slum Housing*, pages 149–150; Weiss, "Urban Renewal," pages 270–271.

112. Gelfand, *A Nation of Cities*, page 152; Mowitz and Wright, *Profile of a Metropolis*, pages 22–23.

113. Weiss, "Urban Renewal," pages 263, 271; Gelfand, *A Nation of Cities*, pages 154–156; Friedman, *Government and Slum Housing*, pages 150–154; Bernard J. Frieden and Lynne B. Sagalyn, *Downtown, Inc.: How America Rebuilds Cities* (Cambridge, 1989), pages 22–25; Joe T. Darden et al., *Detroit: Race and Uneven Development* (Philadelphia, 1987), page 159; Carl Abbott, *The New Urban America: Growth and Politics in Sunbelt Cities* (Chapel Hill, 1981), pages 162–163.

114. Friedman, *Government and Slum Housing*, pages 150–154; Weiss, "Urban Renewal," pages 270–272; "Chicago Redevelops," *Architectural Forum*, August 1950, page 99; Frieden and Sagalyn, *Downtown, Inc.*, page 27.

115. Darling, "Some Notes on Blighted Areas," pages 14–15. See also William Alonso, "The Historic and Structural Theories of Urban Form: Their Implications for Urban Renewal," *Land Economics*, May 1964, pages 227–231.

116. Frieden and Sagalyn, *Downtown, Inc.*, pages 27–37. See also Herbert J. Gans, *The Urban Villagers: Group and Class in the Life of Italian-Americans* (New York, 1962), chapters 13–14.

Chapter 8: Just Another Business District?

1. *St. Louis Post-Dispatch*, April 23, 1950.

2. Scott L. Bottles, *Los Angeles and the Automobile: The Making of the Modern City* (Berkeley, 1987), page 195.

3. *Business Week*, October 6, 1951, page 138; *Reduction of Urban Vulnerability: Part V of the Report on Project East River* (New York, 1952), page 60b; *Architectural Forum*, June 1952, page 59; Richard C. Bond, "Apropos—Any City," *Urban Land*, October 1953, page 4; *Proceedings of the Annual National Planning Conference: 1952*, pages 42–43.

4. Bernard J. Frieden and Lynne B. Sagalyn, *Downtown, Inc.: How America Rebuilds Cities* (Cambridge, 1989), pages 20–25; Hal Burton, *The City Fights Back* (New York, 1954), chapters 5, 6, 11; Jon C. Teaford, *The Rough Road to Renaissance: Urban Revitalization in America, 1940–1985* (Baltimore, 1990), pages 93–99, 107–113; *Architectural Forum*, June 1953, pages 46–47; Chalmers M. Roberts, "How Other Cities Fight 'Downtown Blight,'" in Washington Post Company, *Progress or Decay? 'Downtown Blight' in the Nation's Capital* (1952), page 4; Cleveland Rapid Transit System, *The Future of Metropolitan Cleveland Depends on the Subway* (1957), page 36.

5. W. L. C. Wheaton, "Is Economic Disaster Ahead for Our Cities?" *National Real Estate and Building Journal*, May 1953, page 39; "How to Rebuild Cities Downtown," *Architectural Forum*, June 1955, page 123; Chicago Department of Streets and Electricity, Bureau of Street Traffic, "Cordon Count Data on the Central Business District" (1949), page 2; Paul F. Wendt, "Urban Land Value Trends," *Appraisal Journal*, April 1958, pages 260–262; Teaford, *Rough Road to Renaissance*, pages 104–105; William J. Watkins, *Parking as a Factor in Business: Part 3. Relationship Between Downtown-Automobile Parking Conditions and Retail-Business Decentralization* (Washington, D.C., 1953), page 103.

6. Warren James Belasco, *Americans on the Road: From Autocamp to Motel, 1910–1945* (Cambridge, 1979), chapter 6; Harris, Kerr, Forster & Company, *Trends in the Hotel-Motel Business: Twenty-seventh Annual Review* (1962), pages 2–3; U.S. Bureau of the Census, *1954 Census of Business: Central Business District Statistics Summary Report* (Washington, D.C., 1958), pages 10–11; Murray D. Dessel, "Central Business Districts and Their Metropolitan Areas: A Summary of Geographic Shifts in Retail Sales Growth, 1948–1954," U.S. Department of Commerce, Office of Area Development, *Area Trend Series, No. 1* (Washington, D.C., 1957), pages 10–11.

7. Meredith L. Clausen, "Northgate Regional Shopper Center—Paradigm from the Provinces," *Journal of the Society of Architectural Historians*, May 1984, page 146; *City Planning*, January 1931, page 40; "Suburban Shopping Centers," *National Real Estate*

Journal, December 1938, pages 30–32; *Architectural Record*, September 1940, pages 32–42; Dero A. Saunders, "Department Stores: Race for the Suburbs," *Fortune*, December 1951, pages 99, 173; Richard Longstreth, *City Center to Regional Mall: Architecture, the Automobile, and Retailing in Los Angeles, 1920–1950* (Cambridge, 1997), page 230.

8. Larry Smith, "The Economic Base of the Community," in U.S. Chamber of Commerce, *Business Action for Better Cities: A Complete Report of the Businessmen's Conference on Urban Problems* (Washington, D.C., 1952), page 45. See also "Suburban Retail Districts," *Architectural Forum*, August 1950, pages 106–109; Clausen, "Northgate Regional Shopping Center," pages 150–156; "Regional Shopping Centers," *American City*, May 1954, pages 126–127; "Shoppers' World," *Architectural Forum*, December 1951, pages 186–187; C. D. Palmer, "The Shopping Center Goes to the Shopper," *New York Times Magazine*, November 29, 1952, page 37.

9. Smith, "Economic Base," pages 45–48; "Will Today's Shopping Centers Succeed?" *National Real Estate and Building Journal*, February 1953, pages 23–24; J. Gordon Dawkins, "Solving the Downtown Problem," *Stores*, August 1955, page 6; Arthur Rubloff, "Regional Shopping Centers and Their Effect on the Future of Our Cities," in Harlean James, ed., *American Planning and Civic Annual* (Washington, D.C., 1953), page 49; "Marshall Field's New Shopping Center," *Architectural Forum*, December 1954, pages 186–187; Mabel Walker, "The Impact of Outlying Shopping Centers on Central Business Districts," *Public Management*, August 1957, page 173; Buffalo City Planning Commission, "A Proposed Shopping and Transportation Concourse for Downtown Buffalo" (1956), page 2.

10. Larry Smith, "Maintaining the Health of Our Central Business Districts," *Traffic Quarterly*, April 1954, pages 116–117; H. W. Lochner & Co. and DeLeuw, Cather & Co., *Highway and Transportation Plan [for] Knoxville, Tennessee* (Chicago, 1948), page 4.

11. "Offices Move to Suburbs," *Business Week*, March 17, 1951, pages 79–83; "Big Business Going Rural," ibid., June 28, 1952, pages 88–90; *Architectural Forum*, June 1953, page 43; "Should Management Move to the Country?" *Fortune*, December 1952, pages 142–143, 164–170; "Office Decentralization," *Urban Land*, October 1950, page 3.

12. "Should Management Move to the Country?" page 143; *Architectural Forum*, January 1953, pages 43–45; Cleveland Rapid Transit System, *The Future of Metropolitan Cleveland*, page 36; *American Society of Planning Officials Newsletter*, December 1955, page 98; George J. Eberle, "Metropolitan Decentralization and the Retailer," *Journal of Retailing*, December 1946, page 93.

13. Richard J. Seltzer, "Where Shall I Shop?" *Appraisal Journal*, January 1949, pages 118–119; *Detroit News*, February 25, 1955; Burton, *The City Fights Back*, pages 10, 24–25; Philip M. Talbott, "Rescuing 'Downtown' and Its Transit," *Public Utilities Fortnightly*, December 8, 1955, page 942; Eberle, "Metropolitan Decentralization," page 93; Smith, "Our Central Business Districts," page 117; *Urban Land*, March 1950, page 4; Morton Bodfish and Ralph J. Lueders, "Forces of Decentralization in Chicago," *Savings and Homeownership*, July 1953; William H. P. Smith, "Greater Boston's Big Headache," *Greater Boston Business*, August 1955, pages 7–8.

14. Talbott, "Rescuing 'Downtown,'" page 942; *St. Louis Post-Dispatch*, April 23, 1950; Cleveland Rapid Transit System, *The Future of Metropolitan Cleveland*, pages 37–38; "How to Rebuild Cities Downtown," page 236; J. Ross McKeever, "A View of the

Year," *Urban Land*, January 1955, page 4; L. P. Cookingham, "Introductory Remarks," in Harlean James, ed., *American Planning and Civic Annual* (Washington, D.C., 1954), page 12; Seltzer, "Where Shall I Shop?" page 119.

15. Reinhold P. Wolff and Frederich H. Bair, Jr., "Are We Reaching City Limits?" *Dun's Review*, April 1951, page 78; Theodore T. McCrosky, "Decentralization and Parking," *Proceedings [of the] Annual Meeting [of the] Institute of Traffic Engineers: 1941*, page 63; McKeever, "A View of the Year," page 4; Jay D. Runkle, "A Downtown Merchant Looks at the Future of Downtown Shopping Areas," *Stores*, November 1947, pages 68–70; Henry A. Barnes, "Downtown Baltimore: Prosperity or Doom?" *Baltimore*, June 1956, page 21; Burton, *The City Fights Back*, page 155.

16. *Detroit News*, February 25, 1955; Burton, *The City Fights Back*, pages 11–15; 223–224, 260; "How to Rebuild Cities Downtown," page 122; Alan A. Altshuler, *The City Planning Process: A Political Analysis* (Ithaca, 1965), page 202; Teaford, *Rough Road to Renaissance*, pages 49–50; Longstreth, *City Center to Regional Mall*, chapter 8; Donald C. Hyde, "Transit Isn't *That* Sick," *Public Utilities Fortnightly*, September 29, 1955, page 460.

17. William Zeckendorf, "Cities Versus Suburbs," *Atlantic Monthly*, July 1952, page 24. See also *Urban Land*, March 1950, page 3; U.S. Chamber of Commerce, *Better Cities . . . Better Business: A Complete Report on the Businessmen's Conference on Urban Problems* (Washington, D.C., 1948), page 155; Sy Adler, "Why BART and No LART? The Political Economy of Rail Rapid Transit Planning in the Los Angeles and San Francisco Metropolitan Areas, 1945–1957," *Planning Perspectives*, May 1957, pages 149–157; *Proceedings [of the] National Conference on Planning: 1941*, page 231.

18. E. E. East, "Los Angeles' Street Traffic Problem," *Civil Engineering*, August 1942, page 436. See also Hans Blumenfeld, "Alternative Solutions for Metropolitan Development," *Proceedings of the Annual National Planning Conference: 1948*, page 20.

19. T. Ledyard Blakeman, "Regional Planning and Decentralization," in U.S. Chamber of Commerce, *Better Cities . . . Better Business*, pages 162–163; Louis Bromfield, "The Flight from the Cities," *Town and Country Planning*, Summer 1949, pages 110–111.

20. U.S. Chamber of Commerce, *Your City Is Your Business: A Complete Report on the Businessmen's Conference on Urban Problems* (Washington, D.C., 1947), pages 222–223. See also Louis Wirth, "Does the Atomic Bomb Doom the Modern City?" *New Jersey Municipalities*, April 1946, pages 25–29; Tracy B. Augur, "Decentralization Can't Wait," *Proceedings of the Annual National Planning Conference: 1948*, pages 27–35; Charles B. Merriam, "Problems of Reorganizing Our Great Cities," ibid., pages 35–42; Paul Boyer, *By the Bomb's Early Light* (New York, 1954), pages 148–152, 175–176, 320–321, 327–328.

21. U.S. Chamber of Commerce, *Your City Is Your Business*, page 223. See also Dessel, "Central Business Districts and Their Metropolitan Areas," page 11; Albert D. Hutzler, "Decentralization and the Central District," in U.S. Chamber of Commerce, *Your City Is Your Business*, pages 192–193; *Baltimore Sun*, June 14, 1925.

22. Robert M. Fogelson, *The Fragmented Metropolis: Los Angeles, 1850–1930* (Cambridge, 1967), chapters 4 and 6; Sam Boal, "Los Angeles Has It, But What Is It?" *New York Times Magazine*, September 14, 1949, page 37; "City of the Angels: It's Still an Age of Miracles," *Newsweek*, August 3, 1953, pages 64–66.

23. "City of the Angels," page 66; Coverdale and Colpitts, *Report of the Los Angeles Metropolitan Transit Authority on a Monorail Rapid Transit Line for Los Angeles* (1954), page

62; Longstreth, *City Center to Regional Mall*, pages 199–201, 221–226; Dessel, "Central Business Districts and Their Metropolitan Areas," page 11; "There Are Lots of People Downtown," *Business Week*, October 6, 1951, page 140.

24. Carey McWilliams, "Look What's Happened to California," *Harper's*, October 1949, page 28. See also "There Are Lots of People Downtown," page 140; John A. Miller, "Cities on the Toboggan," *Transit Journal*, February 1941, page 46; James W. Rouse, "Will Downtown Face Up to Its Future?" *Urban Land*, February 1957, pages 3–4.

Epilogue

1. "'Our Downtown'—Is It Growing or Dying?" *Urban Land*, December 1951, pages 2, 5.
2. *Baltimore Sun*, March 7, 1972.
3. Joel Garreau, *Edge City: Life on the New Frontier* (New York, 1991).
4. See Jon A. Teaford, *The Rough Road to Renaissance: Urban Revitalization in America, 1940–1985* (Baltimore, 1990), and Bernard J. Frieden and Lynne B. Sagalyn, *Downtown, Inc.: How America Rebuilds Cities* (Cambridge, 1989).

Acknowledgments

It would be hard to name all the people who helped with *Downtown*. Even if I tried, I would probably leave some out. Still, a partial list is better than none.

The MIT Provost's Fund in Humanities, Arts, and Social Sciences gave me a grant that covered most of the costs. My thanks to Dean Philip Khoury and former dean John De Monchaux. MIT's Department of Urban Studies and Planning lent additional support, for which I would like to thank Professor Bish Sanyal, head of the department. The Urban Studies Department and the MIT Undergraduate Research Opportunities Program funded several research assistants, for whom Paul Dans, Joanna Stone, Terry Wade, and Kelly Davenport will have to stand. These youngsters have all gone on to other things, I am happy to report.

Downtown could have been written without a grant and research assistants—though it would have taken much longer. But it could not have been written without libraries—the Boston, New York, and other great public libraries and the wonderful MIT and Harvard libraries, especially MIT's Rotch and Humanities libraries and Harvard's Loeb, Baker, and Widener libraries. We may live in an age of cyberspace, but I find these institutions as indispensable today as I did a generation ago. My thanks to Margaret de Popolo, head of Rotch, Teresa Tobin, head of Humanities, and their colleagues—as well as to Ann Whiteside of the Loeb.

Robert Fishman, Bernard Frieden, David Handlin, Clay McShane, and Pauline Maier read all or parts of an earlier version of *Downtown* and suggested ways to improve it. I probably should have followed their advice more closely. Nancy Kirk and Phillip King, my manuscript editors, did a fine job, as did Brenda Blais, who typed much of the manuscript, John Cook, who made most of the illustrations, and Nancy Ovedovitz, who designed the book. Thanks also to Ike Williams (and his associate Hope Benekamp) of the

Palmer & Dodge Agency, Patricia Fidler of Yale University Press and, Bea, Sue, and the late John Whiting, in whose farmhouse I wrote much of the book.

Family and friends provided much needed moral support. Besides Maria Fuente, none have been more steadfast than Donald and Dorothy Gonson, to whom *Downtown* is dedicated.

Index

This book was typeset in Scala, a recently designed typeface characterized by nearly-horizontal serifs. The typesetting was done by The Composing Room of Michigan, Inc. The book was designed by Nancy Ovedovitz, and the production was handled by Maureen Noonan. It was printed by R.R. Donnelley & Sons, Harrisonburg, Virginia.